The Grover E. Murray Studies in the American Southwest

Also in the series

Texas, New Mexico,
and the Compromise of 1850

Texas, New Mexico and the Compromise of 1850

Boundary Dispute and Sectional Crisis

Mark J. Stegmaier

Texas Tech University Press

First cloth edition © 1996 by The Kent State University Press

This book is typeset in Minion Pro. The paper used in this book meets the minimum requirements of ANSI/NISO Z39.48-1992 (R1997). ∞

Library of Congress Cataloging-in-Publication Data
Stegmaier, Mark Joseph, 1945-
    Texas, New Mexico, and the Compromise of 1850 : boundary dispute and sectional crisis / Mark J. Stegmaier.
        p. cm. — (The Grover E. Murray Studies in the American Southwest)
    Originally published: Kent, Ohio : Kent State Press, c1996. With new pref.
    Includes bibliographical references and index.
    Summary: "A comprehensive analysis of the Texas-New Mexico boundary dispute and resulting Compromise of 1850"--Provided by publisher.
    ISBN 978-0-89672-697-0 (pbk. : alk. paper) 1. New Mexico—Boundaries—Texas. 2. Texas—Boundaries—New Mexico. 3. Compromise of 1850. I. Title.
    F801.S75 2011
    973.6'4—dc23   2011033889

Printed in the United States of America
12 13 14 15 16 17 18 19 20 / 9 8 7 6 5 4 3 2 1

Texas Tech University Press
Box 41037 | Lubbock, Texas 79409-1037 USA
800.832.4042 | ttup@ttu.edu | www.ttupress.org

Preface

THE REVISIONS IN THIS NEW EDITION OF *TEXAS, NEW MEXICO, AND THE COM-PROMISE of 1850* make no substantial changes to the account of the crisis and compromise of 1850, which I related in the original 1996 edition of the book. The principal alterations involve corrections of minor errors and misspellings that appeared in the first edition. Luckily there were not too many of these, but I am happy to have a chance to correct them now.

When the book was first published by Kent State University Press, the work received very favorable reviews in historical journals from critics. It has been cited by various scholars in works concerning the 1850 crisis and listed among suggested readings in several U.S. history textbooks. I was proud to receive prizes from the Texas State Historical Association—the Coral Tullis Prize—and from the New Mexico Historical Society—the Gaspar Perez de Villagra Award. Now, thanks to Texas Tech University Press, this work is made available in a new edition for those interested in the sectional conflict and in one of the most important boundary disputes in United States history.

MARK J. STEGMAIER
Cameron University
2012

In memory of my father,
Harry Ignatius Stegmaier, Sr.,
and my mother,
Frances Veronica Birmingham Stegmaier

✣

❧

Contents

꧁

List of Maps

Acknowledgments

MANY INDIVIDUALS AND INSTITUTIONS HAVE BEEN VERY HELPFUL IN THE PREPA-
ration of this book. First and foremost, my wife, Diane DeBell Stegmaier, provided constant encouragement, constructive criticism, and excellent assistance
as the manuscript typist. Diane and our sons, Jim and Joe, deserve special gratitude for their patience in allowing me to somehow engineer every family trip
for several years to allow me to be in proximity to research facilities.

A generous grant of sabbatical leave by President Don Davis and the administration of Cameron University and funding from the university's research committee proved indispensable to the completion of my book. The reduction of
my teaching load provided by the Department of History and Humanities at
the university was extremely beneficial.

John T. Hubbell of The Kent State University Press maintained unflagging
interest in and support for the project since I first contacted him about it several years ago. He and his staff at the Press have been a pleasure to work with in
the publication of the work. Craig Simpson of the University of Western Ontario
evaluated an earlier version of the entire manuscript and the final product has
enormously benefited from his extensive commentary.

William W. Freehling of SUNY-Buffalo, Michael Holt of the University of
Virginia, and Donald A. Ritchie of the U.S. Senate Historical Office have kindly
corresponded with me and discussed particular points relative to the Compromise of 1850. Robert Craig of Cameron University's printing office produced
all of the non-contemporary maps in the book.

Numerous colleagues, students, and acquaintances have contributed mate-rially to the preparation of the book. They include: Steve Beckman, Cathie Berg, Mary Margaret Birmingham, Linda Bozard, Susan Brinson, Jeffrey P. Brown, Max Burson, Nancy Chandler, Susie Cooke, John E. Crawford, James Dirkse, Amalia Gensman, Mark Gibson, Jay Grigg, Dana Hardacker, Kent Keeth, Margaret Kerchief, Gary and Elizabeth Lankford, Teresa Lubrano, Leandrea Lucas, Donna Manca, Sean McGivern, David H. Miller, John Molleston, Rob-ert Nay, Kenneth Neighbours, Sandra Quayle-Gilbert, Paula Raney, Larry Shanahan, Laura Smith, Sally Soelle, Philip Supina, Michael Welsh, Mervin Whealey, and Sue Wilson.

Among the many institutions at which I have used research materials, the Periodicals and Manuscripts Divisions of the Library of Congress and the Mili-tary Records Branch of the National Archives proved especially invaluable. Ralph Elder and his staff of the Barker Texas History Center at the University of Texas and Michael Green and his staff at the Texas State Archives were always helpful in guiding me through their numerous collections. Other depositories and li-braries that contributed most significantly to the research include: American Antiquarian Society, Worcester, Massachusetts; Collections Deposit Library and Perry-Castaneda Library, University of Texas; State Records Center and Archives, Santa Fe, New Mexico; Beinecke Library and Sterling Library, Yale University; Perkins Library, Duke University; Clements Library and Bentley Historical Li-brary, University of Michigan; New York Public Library and New York Histori-cal Society; New York State Library, Albany; Rhees Library, University of Roch-ester; St. Louis Public Library; Cincinnati Public Library and Cincinnati Historical Society; Carnegie Library, Pittsburgh; Ohio Historical Society, Co-lumbus; University of Georgia Library, Athens; Southern Historical Collection, University of North Carolina, Chapel Hill; Massachusetts Historical Society, Boston Public Library, Boston Atheneum; Enoch Pratt Free Library, Baltimore; Huntington Library, San Marino, California; Pennsylvania Historical Society, Philadelphia; Hayden Library, Arizona State University, Tempe; and University of Texas Library, El Paso.

Introduction

THE SECTIONAL CRISIS LEADING UP TO THE AMERICAN CIVIL WAR HAS BEEN examined over the decades by many historians from many different angles. Some have constructed their histories to emphasize some particular theme of Civil War causation. Others have examined in detail certain events, the critical decisions of individual leaders, and the dramatic fluctuations in the political party system as pieces in the fabric of sectional conflict. Certainly one of the major occurrences of the antebellum period that has received much attention from historians and biographers is the crisis and Compromise of 1850.

Traditionally this subject has been treated primarily as a function of three major issues: California statehood, the status of slavery in national territories, and the fugitive slave law. The following work, however, departs from traditional scholarship by stressing the role of the Texas–New Mexico boundary dispute, an issue hitherto vastly underrated in significance.[1] I have attempted to relate the story of the boundary dispute as fully as possible and to write a new account of the 1850 crisis from the vantage point of the Texas–New Mexico issue.

Most accounts place undue emphasis on the early stages of the 1850 crisis in Congress, particularly on the famous speeches of February and March 1850 by Senators Clay, Calhoun, Webster, and Seward. Without denying the significance of these famous orations and their widely different interpretations of the overall sectional conflict, it must also be noted that these addresses had little to do with the actual dynamics of Congress's attempts to resolve the issues. The boundary dispute was present from the beginning of the 31st Congress, and, even in the early months of the first session, the numerous and varied proposals to settle that particular issue indicated the immense difficulty that this problem posed for pro-compromise forces attempting to forge a working majority. As will become clear in the subsequent chapters, the boundary dispute gradually assumed the foremost importance of any issue in the proceedings, especially during June 1850 and thereafter. It soon emerged as the issue on which not only the fate of compromise in general depended but also the very survival of the Union. No other topic of debate included elements that, if not settled, could have directly led to military action, bloodshed, and civil war. Political leaders in Washington and the public at large slowly awakened to the realization that if the boundary dispute could not be peacefully settled neither could any other issue. Conversely, people understood that, once the boundary question was resolved, the settlement of all the other pending issues would easily follow.

The dynamics of the contest were complex, and the suspense was at times nerve-racking, as political leaders grappled with the crisis in Washington. But this is not simply an account of the first session of the 31st Congress. The story also involves significant political developments in Texas and New Mexico, developments that exerted powerful influence on the proceedings in Congress and the actions of presidents Taylor and Fillmore. The role of the U.S. Army in the crisis, hitherto generally neglected, proved to be quite dramatic and, to some extent, tragic. So if at times the following narrative seems to stray a bit from the boundary dispute itself into collateral matters, this device simply reflects my desire to fit the main topic into the larger mainstream of events in state, territory, and nation.

The Texas–New Mexico issue did not suddenly spring forth out of nowhere in 1850. The dispute had a long period of gestation, and the first few chapters of this study deal with the pre-1850 development of what turned out to be the only boundary dispute in U.S. history that seriously threatened to disrupt the Union itself.

In marshaling the evidence to prove the significance of the Texas–New Mexico boundary dispute, I employed both traditional and nontraditional research methods. I utilized manuscript collections, official documents, and printed primary and secondary sources extensively. Contemporary newspapers, a vast storehouse of information often underused by historians, proved invaluable to this study. In particular, the many columns written to a diverse array of local presses by Washington correspondents provided new information on this part of the sectional conflict.

Also involved were certain techniques of roll call voting analysis, the Rice Index of Cohesion and the Rice Index of Likeness, both first developed by Professor Stuart A. Rice in the 1920s. These are easily understood measures of the degree of cohesiveness within a legislative voting bloc and of the relationship between any two legislative voting blocs, respectively. The Index of Cohesion is the percent majority within a bloc minus the percent minority within the same bloc. The index will range from 1.000 for unanimity in bloc voting down to .000 for a perfect split within the bloc vote. The Index of Likeness is the complement of the difference between the percent of "yes" votes of any two blocs. The index will range from 1.000 for complete voting agreement between two blocs down to .000 for completely opposite voting by two blocs. These techniques are applied to both the U.S. Congress and to the Texas Legislature.[2]

Chapter One

ॐ

The Boundary Dispute
from Its Origins to the Mexican War

THE TEXAS–NEW MEXICO BOUNDARY DISPUTE ACTUALLY ORIGINATED IN THE contest between Spain and France for imperial domain in the New World during the seventeenth and eighteenth centuries. Based on Robert de La Salle's landing on the Texas coast in 1685, the French manufactured a paper claim to all lands east of the Rio Grande. The Spanish had been present in New Mexico since Juan de Oñate's founding of the province in 1598 and in Texas since the establishment of missions and outposts there in the 1690s. But during the eighteenth century the French persisted to claim that their Louisiana extended to the Rio Grande.

When Napoleon sold the huge and undefined Louisiana to the United States in 1803, President Thomas Jefferson seized on the earlier French claim to the Rio Grande. The Spanish feared this claim and held that any U.S. pretension to the Rio Grande as a southwestern boundary of the Louisiana Purchase was devoid of legitimate foundation and a threat to Santa Fe. As the Spanish defined boundaries for the northern provinces of their New World empire in 1805, the limits of Texas did not even approach the Rio Grande, much less New Mexico. The Medina River was considered the boundary between Texas and the province of Coahuila, while the Nueces River separated Texas from the province of Nuevo Santander (Tamaulipas).[1]

In 1819 President Monroe's secretary of state, John Quincy Adams, reluctantly retreated from the U.S. claim to the Rio Grande, as he and Spanish minister Luis de Onís defined the boundary between U.S. and Spanish possessions, leaving Texas under Spanish rule. The treaty of 1819 angered some Americans who believed that Adams had jettisoned a just U.S. claim stretching to the Rio Grande. Texas, firmly excluded from the United States by the treaty, became a province of Mexico in 1821, following Mexico's successful revolt against Spain.[2]

In the 1820s, Mexico combined Texas and Coahuila into a single province and also embarked on what ultimately proved to be a disastrous policy for Mexico when it established a liberal colonization policy that soon brought an influx of large numbers of Americans into Texas. Whatever the Mexicans may have declared the boundaries of the province to be, the American immigrants arrived there imbued with their own preconception that the Rio Grande was the southwestern boundary of Texas. Mexico also opened New Mexico and Santa Fe to American influence in the 1820s by permitting trade with Missouri over the Santa Fe Trail. American merchants and fur traders soon developed a presence in Taos and Santa Fe, and some of them married into prominent Mexican families. Leaders in Texas proper, such as Stephen Austin, quickly began developing plans to directly connect Texas to Santa Fe and hopefully divert trade away from the Santa Fe Trail toward Texas ports on the Gulf Coast.[3]

President John Quincy Adams's administration launched some diplomatic efforts in the mid-1820s to acquire Texas, but to no avail, and in 1828 signed a convention with Mexico reaffirming the 1819 treaty line. The Mexican government's realization of the dangerous situation developing in Texas coincided with renewed diplomatic efforts by expansion-minded President Andrew Jackson to acquire Texas. Jackson certainly wanted Texas; he believed that Adams had wrongly bargained it away in 1819 and wished to further U.S. expansion toward the Pacific. Jackson's diplomatic efforts proved abortive, however, and in 1832 the U.S. Senate ratified the treaty reaffirming the Adams-Onís line.[4]

The Texas Revolution finally came in 1835–36. Tensions and disagreements had been mounting gradually. Sam Houston wrote to his old friend President Jackson in February 1833 that Texas would probably soon declare independence from Mexico for the whole region east of the Rio Grande and that nearly all Texans desired U.S. annexation. Houston's predictions proved to be only slightly premature. The assumption of dictatorial power by Gen. Antonio Lopez de Santa Anna in Mexico provided the last straw. By late 1835 Texas was in revolt, the revolutionary council decreeing in October their commitment "to drive every Mexican soldier beyond the Rio Grande." The Mexican general who surrendered San Antonio to Texas in December 1835 agreed to retreat beyond the Rio Grande with his troops. Stephen Austin counseled Sam Houston that Texas should not declare a specific boundary in any declaration of independence in order to leave open the possibility for an advance into Chihuahua and New Mexico. Others, such as William Wharton, urged that Texas limit itself to the Rio Grande. Texas leaders refrained from proclaiming a boundary until they won their contest with Mexico, but their conviction that the boundary should be on the Rio Grande remained unaltered, as the president of the provisional government, David Burnet, declared in March 1836.[5]

Following several defeats, stunning and decisive victory came to the Texas army under Gen. Sam Houston in April 1836 at San Jacinto, where General Santa Anna himself was captured. Houston advised Gen. Thomas Jefferson Rusk, secretary of war under the provisional government, that among the terms to be forced on Santa Anna should be a boundary extending the entire length of the Rio Grande and then north to the 1819 Adams-Onís line. The subsequent Treaty of Velasco on May 14, 1836, part public and part secret, was, however, less definite than Houston had hoped for. Part of the public agreement simply required the Mexicans to evacuate all their forces across the Rio Grande, for General Santa Anna had insisted that Mexico would more likely honor his agreements if a boundary were not yet specifically delineated. Therefore Article 4 of the secret agreement simply stated that in the final treaty the limits of Texas would not extend beyond the Rio Grande. As it was, the Mexican government soon repudiated Santa Anna's treaties anyway, and the treaties did nothing to solve the boundary problem. They did not even end the war.[6]

Most Americans fondly welcomed the news of Texas's great victory, although they were not certain yet that the new republic would be able to sustain its independence against Mexico. Jackson was disappointed when his agent in Texas, Henry M. Morfit, reported that the Texans had shied away from extending a boundary claim to the Pacific and had instead chosen to confine their limits to the Rio Grande. Jackson, through Secretary of State John Forsyth, had urged U.S. minister Anthony Butler in 1835 to purchase such a Pacific boundary from Mexico. Jackson had since hoped that Texas might assert this boundary and, through U.S. annexation of Texas, fulfill his grand design of spreading American sovereignty to Pacific shores. Jackson did at least want to extend diplomatic recognition to the Texas Republic, if not annex it, and the Texas population overwhelmingly favored annexation. But annexation, and even U.S. recognition, encountered roadblocks in 1836 due to the first major intrusion of the slavery controversy into the Texas question.[7]

Congress passed a resolution in early July 1836 leaving the matter of Texas recognition to the president's discretion when he deemed its government capable of maintaining independence. But Jackson delayed. He was not sure if the fledgling republic could maintain its independence from Mexico for long, and he dreaded the impact on public opinion of charges by abolitionists and Massachusetts representative John Quincy Adams that the proposal for recognition of Texas was a maneuver by Southerners and Northern Democrats to pave the way for a new slave empire in the Southwest. In addition, Jackson wished to downplay the Texas issue so that it would not undermine Democrat Martin Van Buren's appeal in Northern states during the presidential election campaign in 1836.[8]

Following Van Buren's election, Jackson continued to exhibit a cautious frame of mind on the Texas issue. On December 21 he sent to the new session of Congress a short message in which he advised further delay in U.S. recognition of Texas until Mexico or other major powers had recognized the new republic. Jackson may have hoped that such a moderate approach might influence Mexico to allow the United States to peaceably annex Texas.

The Texans themselves pursued their own course of action. Sam Houston was inaugurated as the first president of Texas in October 1836, and he chose Thomas J. Rusk as his secretary of war and Stephen Austin as secretary of state. The Texas leadership still hoped to achieve recognition, if not annexation, by the U.S. before Jackson left office. Austin adopted a flexible approach on the boundary question; on November 18 he authorized William Wharton, Texas's emissary to the United States, to propose, if the U.S. seriously objected to the inclusion of the established Mexican settlements of the upper Rio Grande Valley within Texas, a line running between the Nueces and Rio Grande up to the Pecos, or Puerco, River and thence running north between the Pecos and the Rio Grande up to the Adams-Onís line of 1819.[9]

While Austin's instructions indicated that the boundary was negotiable, the Texas Congress was less flexible. On November 3, 1836, Rep. Thomas Jefferson Green of Bexar County (San Antonio) introduced a bill defining the Texas boundary's southwest limit as the entire length of the Rio Grande. If any controversy attended the measure during its course through the legislature, no evidence of it has survived, and on December 19 it became law. The Texas boundary law appears to have originated primarily with reference to the embryonic republic's relations with Mexico. As Sen. Richard Ellis of Red River County, then president pro tem of the Texas Senate, later disclosed, the boundaries were thus fixed "solely and professedly with a view of having a large margin in the negotiation with Mexico, and not with the expectation of retaining them as they now exist." In other words, Texas spread an expansive claim in 1836 as an advanced bargaining position in future peace negotiations with Mexico.[10]

In Washington in the first months of 1837, Jackson still cast his eyes toward the Pacific Coast. After Sam Houston released General Santa Anna, the Mexican leader traveled to Washington for a cordial interview with President Jackson on January 19 before returning to Mexico. Jackson declared that Mexico must recognize Texas's independence, and only then could the United States, as part of the process of annexing Texas, work out a boundary arrangement with Mexico involving a U.S. purchase of the Rio Grande line up to 38° north latitude (well north of Santa Fe) and then to the Pacific Coast. Santa Anna replied that the Mexican Congress must decide the matter. In February Jackson reiterated the Pacific Coast theme in a talk with Texas emissary William Wharton, impressing upon Wharton that Texas should lay claim to part of California and that opposition to Texas on the slavery issue would dissolve with New England fishing interests' desire for access to San Francisco Bay. Jackson was still reticent about asking Congress to recognize the Texas Republic. He now leaned toward recognition but wanted Congress to initiate the action. Under the urging of Wharton and others, Congress did just that. Near the end of the short session, both houses passed a recognition resolution, and Jackson, in the last official act of his administration, endorsed it on March 3, 1837.[11]

Sam Houston, realizing that Texas could not afford large military expenditures, determined to follow a policy of nonaggression in relation to Mexico while diplomatically continuing to pursue annexation to the United States. He instructed the new minister in Washington, Memucan Hunt, to press the Rio Grande claim; but, if the U.S. objected, Texas would accept annexation at the Nueces River boundary and even territorial status rather than statehood. Hunt energetically promoted the Texas cause, but President Martin Van Buren had never liked the extravagant Texas boundary claim; he feared that annexation might disrupt the Democratic party on the slavery issue and did not wish to provoke Mexico into a military confrontation. Administration officials encouraged Hunt not to cease his efforts, but Congress, under the anti-Texas vigilance of John Quincy Adams and with concerns over the economic panic of 1837, also ignored Texas annexation. Texas finally withdrew its offer of annexation in October 1838, and both governments, frustrated by the connection between annexation and the slavery issue, lost interest in the project for several years thereafter.[12]

In December 1838, Mirabeau Buonaparte Lamar succeeded Sam Houston as president of Texas. Lamar dreamed of a domain extending from the Sabine to the Pacific and as far to the southwest as might be required to protect the young republic against Mexico. But Lamar understood that financial realities would prevent extensive Texas military operations. The republic had incurred a public debt of only a few hundred thousand dollars during the revolution itself, but the debt had mounted steadily once Texas was forced to set up and pay for a civil government establishment. Various bond and treasury note issues amounted to nearly two million dollars by November 1838, increasing to over seven million dollars by November 1841. Lamar hoped instead to solve Texas's difficulties with Mexico on the diplomatic front. In the spring of 1839, the Lamar administration attempted to secure U.S. mediation between Mexico and Texas and, simultaneously, to purchase recognition of Texan independence and the Rio Grande boundary from Mexico itself. But the United States refused to mediate unless Mexico also requested it, and Mexico would receive none of Lamar's diplomats.[13]

During these early years of Texas's efforts to achieve recognition of its Rio Grande boundary claim, New Mexico's leaders remained unconcerned with the new republic. Native New Mexican leaders were aware and wary of growing American influence in the province during the 1830s, but these few hundred Americans were not numerous enough to dominate politics and society there as the Americans in Texas had done. Although New Mexico remained loyal to Mexico when Santa Anna became dictator in the mid-1830s, New Mexicans strongly resented centralist control and in an 1837 revolt overthrew centralist governor Albino Perez. Eventually Manuel Armijo assumed power in 1838 to begin a regime of nearly a decade, during which he dispensed large land grants to both native citizens and American merchants.[14]

Whatever lack of concern New Mexicans had demonstrated, President Lamar forced them to change their attitude in 1841. Frustrated in his diplomatic maneuvers and also in the failure of Texas to replenish its finances through negotiation of a loan in Europe, Lamar looked to Santa Fe for a solution to all of Texas's troubles. Lamar's basic interests lay in diverting the lucrative Santa Fe trade from Missouri to Texas and in gaining control over New Mexico's reported wealth of untapped gold and other mining resources. Reports from several people in Santa Fe boasting of the desire of New Mexicans to become part of Texas only added to President Lamar's self-delusion about the receptiveness of New Mexico to Texas's overtures. The Texas Congress displayed little interest in Lamar's project, however, because Texas could not afford the expense of an expedition and because many members seriously doubted the reported eagerness of New Mexicans to unite with Texas. The impetuous President Lamar thereupon drew funds from the treasury on his own authority and organized an expeditionary force of several hundred men under Gen. Hugh McLeod to march to Santa Fe. Sam Houston and his followers condemned the enterprise as foolhardy and unauthorized by the legislative branch, but the expedition went forward nonetheless.[15]

The whole project was poorly conceived and organized. McLeod's men were told that their mission was peaceful and that the people of New Mexico would welcome them. Lamar's letter of April 14 and his address of June 5, 1841, both directed to the people of Santa Fe, presumed the readiness of his intended subjects to accept Texan jurisdiction and citizenship, but at the same time he referred so often to the inevitability of the process and to Texan military power that the peaceful invitation sounded like a veiled threat.[16]

Mexican military officials quickly learned of the expedition and warned Governor Armijo, who in turn requested instructions from Mexico City. General Santa Anna informed Armijo that he should stop the Texans before they reached Santa Fe for fear that many New Mexicans might actually support the Texans. Armijo, whose absolute rule had alienated many citizens, feared this too, but he was able to rally his people against the expedition by warning that the Texans were coming to burn, plunder, and kill. Armijo's task was made easier by the ineptitude of the poorly outfitted expedition itself. Having departed their camp near Austin on June 18, McLeod's men lost their way in the wastelands, ran out of food supplies, and were in such miserable condition by the time they arrived in New Mexico that they had no choice but to ignominiously surrender to Armijo's troops. Brutal treatment by New Mexican authorities and several years of prison in Mexico City became the sad lot of McLeod's expedition. The only serious attempt by the Republic of Texas to directly extend its jurisdiction to the upper Rio Grande had come to a dismal end.[17]

By the time the bad news of the expedition's capture reached Texas in January 1842, Sam Houston had taken office for another term as president. The Texas Congress reacted to the disaster in New Mexico by censuring Lamar for his role in it and furiously denouncing Mexican cruelty to the expedition prisoners. The legislators demanded retribution and passed—overriding President Houston's veto—a ridiculously bombastic and practically meaningless measure extending the area claimed by the Republic of Texas to include the Californias and much of northern Mexico.[18]

President Houston fully understood that the republic's dire financial straits would not permit large-scale military operations against Santa Fe. But he also firmly believed in the justice of Texas's claimed boundaries and felt humiliated that the prosperous Missouri–Santa Fe trade continued to cross the republic's claimed lands without Texas deriving any revenues or other economic benefit from it. He undoubtedly also wished to quench somewhat Texas extremists' thirst for action. Therefore Houston authorized two small raids against the New Mexicans. First, in May 1843, Col. Charles A. Warfield and a few dozen men descended on the unsuspecting town of Mora, east of Santa Fe, looting stores, stealing horses, and murdering a few local inhabitants before leaving the terrified community and soon after disbanding. A larger raiding party, about two hundred Texans under Maj. Jacob Snively, attempted during that summer to intercept and loot a traders' caravan on the Santa Fe Trail. Snively's group fought one engagement against an advanced detachment of Governor Armijo's militia and killed twenty-three men. However, U.S. dragoons caught up with the Texans at the end of June, disarmed them, and sent them marching back to Texas. The raids of 1843 only served to further embitter New Mexicans against Texans. The Mexican government, wary of growing American influence in New Mexico and offended by the Texans' raids, placed excessively high tariff duties on the Missouri-Santa Fe trade and closed Taos as a port of entry. Consequently, commercial traffic on the Santa Fe Trail dwindled greatly in the early 1840s.[19]

It was also in 1843 that the U.S. government renewed its interest in Texas annexation. President John Tyler, the Virginia Whig who assumed the office on the death of William Henry Harrison in 1841, had vetoed Whig-sponsored banking bills, inducing the Whigs to read him out of the party. Therefore, by 1843 Texas annexation appeared to Tyler a good issue on which to reinvigorate his administration's popularity. John Quincy Adams had been suspicious of President Tyler on Texas even before this time and had accused the administration in an 1842 speech of direct involvement in the "incursion of banditti from Texas against Santa Fe" in the 1841 expedition.[20] Actually, Tyler did not begin to concentrate on Texas until he became convinced that the British were attempting to manipulate the Texans into making peace with Mexico, remaining independent, and possibly even abolishing slavery.

Sam Houston, desirous of U.S. annexation but frustrated by U.S. inaction, did what he could to lead Tyler into believing that he was seriously considering British offers to mediate the conflict with Mexico. He correctly estimated that rampant U.S. anglophobia would hasten the annexation process. Secretary of State Abel Upshur of Virginia and his successor, John Calhoun of South Carolina, conducted negotiations with Texas emissaries James Pinckney Henderson and Isaac Van Zandt in Washington, agreeing on a treaty of annexation on April 12, 1844.

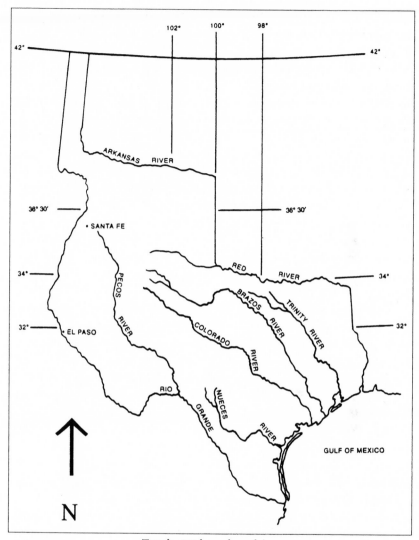

Texas's 1836 boundary claim.

Under the terms of the proposed treaty, Texas would become a U.S. territory, and the United States would assume the public debt of Texas up to ten million dollars. The treaty did not specify a southwestern boundary for Texas on the supposition that this would now become a matter for the U.S. and Mexican governments to negotiate. Opposition to Senate ratification of the annexation treaty developed immediately, especially among antislavery Northerners. But also occupying a central role among opponents during the Senate's ratification debate was Democrat Thomas Hart Benton of Missouri. Benton denounced the treaty during his three-day speech of May 16, 18, and 20 as an outrage to Mexico designed to precipitate war, a measure to reelect John Tyler as president on a Southern-oriented independent ticket, and a disunion conspiracy directed by Calhoun.[21]

Although he did not emphasize the theme in his speech, Benton also opposed the Texas treaty in order to protect Missouri's trade with Santa Fe. Mexican hostility since the Texas Revolution had already prompted that country to reduce trade with the U.S., and a war resulting from the proposed Texas annexation treaty would disrupt the once-lucrative trade entirely. Benton referred to this situation in his speech and to the necessity of protecting trade caravans from such "banditti" as Snively's marauders. These considerations led Senator Benton to suggest an alternative plan of annexation. His plan was to leave the Rio Grande Valley, with its strictly Mexican settlements, including the Santa Fe region, under Mexican rule. He would annex the "old" Texas as it had existed under Spain and Mexico, bounded on the south and west by the Nueces River Valley. Never before in his career had he questioned the legitimacy of the Rio Grande boundary; in fact, on several occasions he had cited it as the U.S. boundary relinquished in 1819. But now Benton argued that the United States could acquire the "old" Texas honorably and peaceably, without dismembering Mexico's several provinces that lay on both sides of the Rio Grande. Without directly pointing out the obvious in his speech, Benton's plan would also move the western boundary of Texas a safe distance from New Mexico and from Missouri's oft-threatened trade route to Santa Fe and Taos.[22]

When the treaty came to a final vote on ratification in the Senate on June 8, it received only sixteen yeas to thirty-five nays. On June 10 Benton offered a bill that would authorize the president to begin tripartite U.S.-Mexico-Texas negotiations to adjust boundaries and to annex Texas. The western boundary of the annexed territory would extend from the prairie west of the Nueces River along various highlands northward to 42° north latitude. Texas itself was to be admitted as a state, with limits established by its legislature so that it did not exceed in size the largest existing state. The remainder of the annexed region would be designated "Southwest Territory," which would ultimately be divided equally into free and slave states. On June 11 Benton proposed to modify his own bill to stipulate the line of 100° west longitude as the western limit of slavery. The Senate tabled Benton's bill on June 15, two days before the session adjourned, but this plan would become the model for similar boundary proposals by Benton in later years.[23]

The Texas question became the central campaign issue in the election of 1844. Democratic candidate James K. Polk of Tennessee and the party platform unequivocally supported Texas annexation, while Whig nominee Henry Clay of Kentucky waffled and hedged on the issue. Polk won the contest in November by a slim margin, and both the outgoing President Tyler and he interpreted the election as a popular mandate for Texas annexation. The election result figured largely in Tyler's annual message of December 3, 1844, as a rationale for his recommendation to Congress that it should act to annex Texas.[24]

During the short second session of the Twenty-eighth Congress prior to Polk's accession, many proposals were introduced in the two houses relating to Texas annexation. Senator Benton of Missouri reintroduced his bill from the previous session on December 11, 1844, but he subsequently withdrew the measure on February 5, 1845, and substituted in its place a plan that urged that Texas be annexed as a state with unspecified boundaries as soon as a new U.S. treaty with the republic could be negotiated. Benton had come under intense pressure from his constituents and the legislature in Missouri and from his friend Andrew Jackson to support annexation. Other than Benton's initial bill, none of the bills and resolutions for annexation suggested a specific southwestern boundary. Several proposed that Texas itself be no larger than the largest then-existing state and that remaining lands be granted territorial status. Nearly all the proposals stipulated that all boundary questions were to be adjusted by negotiation between the U.S. and Mexico after annexation. On very few occasions during the session did a speaker even mention New Mexico, except for a few annexation opponents who reminded their colleagues that the 1836 metes and bounds established by Texas law included the Santa Fe region, which they said was clearly governed by Mexico as part of its territory.[25]

In an effort to attract Southern Whig votes, annexationist Democrats in the House ultimately supported the joint resolution offered by Tennessee Whig Milton Brown on January 13, 1845. Brown's resolution included: the annexation of Texas as a state; the retention by Texas of both its public lands and its debt; the annexation of all lands rightfully and properly included within Texas, with the boundary to be worked out by the U.S. and Mexico; the potential later subdivision of Texas into no more than four additional states of "convenient" size; and the prohibition of slavery above 36°30' north latitude and admission of states below that line with or without slavery. This last provision extended to Texas the line earlier used in the Missouri Compromise of 1820 to ban slavery north of 36°30' north latitude while permitting it south of that line in the territory of the Louisiana Purchase. The House passed Brown's resolution on January 25 by a vote of 120 to 98. On February 27 the Senate adopted an amendment by Robert J. Walker of Mississippi, in league with Benton, to permit the president the choice of annexing Texas via the joint resolution or of offering to conduct negotiations for a new treaty of annexation. The Senate approved the Walker version by a 27 to 25 vote, and the House concurred 132 to 75 on February 28. President Tyler signed the joint resolution on March 1. Anxious to garner as much credit as possible for completing the annexation, Tyler and his cabinet quickly agreed to send the joint resolution to Texas rather than leave incoming President Polk the choice of annexation method after his inauguration the next day. Neither Benton nor Polk was pleased by Tyler's action, but Polk and his new cabinet quickly endorsed the result.[26]

As news of the annexation resolution spread through Texas, overwhelming public enthusiasm for it rolled over the opposition. The Mexican government desperately agreed to recognize Texas independence in a move to block annexation, with boundaries to be determined later, but Texan popular opinion paid no heed to the diplomatic offer. A special session of the Texas Congress, called by Houston's successor, Anson Jones, rejected Mexico's overtures and endorsed annexation in June 1845. Despite some public dissent at the lack of confirmation in the annexation resolution for Texas's claimed limits, the legislators did not attach any conditions that might embarrass the process, such as an explicit reassertion of the 1836 claim to the Santa Fe region.

A special convention at Austin on July 4, presided over by Thomas Jefferson Rusk, immediately ratified annexation and proceeded during July and August to write a state constitution. In accordance with the annexation resolution leaving the boundary to be settled by the U.S. and Mexico, the Texas convention placed no boundary definition clause in its constitution, although a committee report on August 27 at the meeting did reaffirm Texans' conviction in the right to the 1836 boundary claim. On July 11 the convention also established a select committee to consider empowering the legislature to cede Texas's public domain to the U.S. in exchange for assumption of the new state's debt, but nothing further was done about the proposal. It was an idea, however, that would receive intermittent attention from Texas officials and legislators in subsequent years. On August 12 another committee suggested apportioning state legislative seats for the Santa Fe region, but this proposal was not included in the final constitution. Patterned on those of other slave states, the constitution was ratified, as was annexation itself, by a huge margin in a public referendum on October 13.[27]

While Texas completed its part in the annexation process, the aggressively expansionist President James K. Polk remained absolutely convinced of the righteousness of the Rio Grande boundary claim. He desired not only to secure Mexican acceptance of Texas's absorption into the U.S. but also to purchase New Mexico and California. He hoped to induce Mexico to agree to annexation in satisfaction of unpaid U.S. claims against Mexico, claims that Mexico simply could not afford to pay in money. Besides making diplomatic overtures to the Mexican government on this matter, Polk, fearful of rumors that Mexico planned to invade Texas, ordered Gen. Zachary Taylor and his army into Texas in the summer of 1845. Mexican authorities, however, were impressed by neither U.S. diplomacy nor the show of force. Polk's most ambitious diplomatic effort involved the dispatch of John Slidell of Louisiana to Mexico City in November 1845 with an offer for Texas and the Southwest. Secretary of State James Buchanan, in his (and the administration's) instructions to Slidell, firmly expressed a desire to purchase New Mexico but admitted that the region lying north of 32° north latitude had never been under actual Texan jurisdiction. None of this really affected Slidell's mission, for the new Mexican government of Gen. Mariano Paredes y Arrillaga refused to receive or discuss a settlement with Slidell. The Paredes government could never have acceded to Polk's demands without being immediately overthrown. Slidell finally gave up in March 1846 and returned to the United States.[28]

Meanwhile Texas had officially been admitted to the Union as a state. In his December 2, 1845, message at the opening of the Twenty-ninth Congress, President Polk declared that Congress should quickly admit the new state and proclaimed that the whole process represented a "bloodless" extension of U.S. boundaries to the Rio Grande. Both houses of Congress quickly acceded to the president's wishes, despite some Northern Whig objections over slavery extension. President Polk signed the joint resolution of admission on December 29.[29]

With the United States counting Texas as a state and Mexico still insisting that Texas was one of its provinces, events quickly escalated toward war. Taylor's army was ordered to the Rio Grande in March 1846 and Mexican forces also advanced northward. By April Polk and most of his advisers had decided that the United States must declare war—even without a precipitating event. On April 25, however, a skirmish did take place when Mexican forces crossed the river, and U.S. troops suffered casualties. Polk now possessed a more solid pretext on which to base his demand for war. In his war message of May 11, the president defended his policies and declared that Mexico had invaded the United States and shed American blood on American soil and that therefore a state of war already existed by Mexico's own action. Polk harbored no doubts that any land north of the Rio Grande lay within the United States. Despite dissenting opinions against the war, principally by some Northern Whigs, both houses of Congress enacted the war bill, and President Polk signed it on May 13. The brief debates in Congress on the bill had primarily concerned whether the Nueces (as most Whigs held) or the Rio Grande (the Democratic view) was the correct boundary. A few Whig opponents, especially Rep. Joshua Giddings of Ohio, specifically cited the fact that Santa Fe and other settled parts of New Mexico east of the Rio Grande had clearly been under Mexican jurisdiction and never under that of Texas, despite its 1836 law.[30]

One of the first military operations that President Polk intended to undertake was the occupation of New Mexico, thus removing any question over which country possessed jurisdiction in the region. With Texan forces naturally drawn into Taylor's operations in Texas and then northern Mexico, the conquest of Santa Fe assumed a definite Missouri orientation. On May 13 Polk ordered Col. Stephen Watts Kearny at Fort Leavenworth to call on the governor of Missouri for volunteers and, with these and his regular forces, to set out for Santa Fe, ostensibly to protect American traders. Missouri volunteers eagerly flocked to the popular Kearny's standard, and his Army of the West grew to nearly 1,700 men. He was to seize control of both New Mexico and California and to establish temporary civil governments therein. Sen. Thomas Hart Benton worked vigorously in Washington to ensure that Kearny's army would march to New Mexico on behalf of Missouri's interests, not those of Texas. Benton helped plan the expedition and enlisted the services of James Magoffin, a long-time resident of Chihuahua and the husband of a cousin of Governor Armijo, to smooth the way for Kearny's entry into New Mexico. Colonel Kearny and his army left Fort Leavenworth on June 30, heading west on the Santa Fe Trail.[31]

After the New Mexican officials and populace became cognizant of the state of war existing between the two countries, Governor Armijo worked to organize a local defense force. This force ultimately numbered considerably more men than Kearny could muster, but the New Mexicans were poorly armed and organized. After Kearny reached Bent's Fort in July, he began issuing vague proclamations of peaceful intent to the people of New Mexico. Kearny was more specific about the rationale for the U.S. takeover in a personal note that he sent to Governor Armijo on August 1, which cited the annexation of Texas, with Texas's claim to the entire length of the Rio Grande, as the basis for U.S. possession of

New Mexico. He referred to the same grounds two weeks later in a speech at Las Vegas. Meanwhile, Kearny sent a small party of men into Santa Fe under a flag of truce to confer with Armijo. These emissaries, consistent with Kearny's pronouncement, attempted to mollify Col. Diego Archuleta and those New Mexicans counseling Armijo in favor of armed resistance by arguing that Kearny and the United States would not extend their claim or possession to include territory west of the Rio Grande, implying that the area west of the river might retain a government loyal to Mexico. Texans apparently never learned of the way in which their 1836 claim was utilized in the conquest of New Mexico, for they would certainly in later years have employed its usage by Kearny as a principal defense of the Texas claim to jurisdiction over the Santa Fe region.[32]

Kearny's use of the Texas claim was obviously planned carefully in advance, probably by Benton and by Polk's advisers in Washington. The stratagem worked in further dissolving any New Mexican desire to resist the American advance. Governor Armijo did march his troops out to meet the U.S. forces, but the demoralized force soon dwindled away, and Armijo himself fled southward. On August 18 Kearny, now a brigadier general, entered unmolested into Santa Fe with his Army of the West and declared the area annexed to the United States. The fiction of U.S. occupation being limited to the eastern side of the Rio Grande vanished a few days later on August 22 when Kearny, as military governor, issued a new proclamation declaring that he intended all of New Mexico on both sides of the Rio Grande for the United States. Disgruntled New Mexicans such as Archuleta felt cheated and humiliated by this but could do nothing for the time being except seethe with resentment.[33]

General Kearny quickly ordered Col. Alexander Doniphan and several other legally trained soldiers to devise a law code for the civil governance of the new U.S. possession. The code designated the region as "the territory of New Mexico," established various offices, guaranteed civil liberties, and contained other provisions. It stipulated no particular boundaries for New Mexico. Kearny proclaimed the code in September and appointed Charles Bent as governor, Donaciano Vigil as territorial secretary, and Joab Houghton, Carlos Beaubien, and Antonio José Otero as territorial justices. Bent was a popular Taos merchant who had married into a New Mexican family. The intelligent and liberal-minded Vigil had long served as secretary to Governor Armijo and thus provided needed continuity with the previous regime. Houghton, a politically ambitious Santa Fe merchant from New York, had been living in New Mexico since 1843 and had served as assistant to U.S. consul Manuel Alvarez since 1845. Otero and Beaubien were both prominent merchants.[34]

Kearny departed from Santa Fe on September 25 to take part in the conquest of California, leaving Colonel Doniphan and the civil appointees in charge of organizing the government in the new territory. These officials paid no heed whatsoever to the Texas claim east of the Rio Grande, which General Kearny had initially invoked in establishing the U.S. right of possession over New Mexico. But Texans, as they soon made clear, had no intention of forgetting or relinquishing the Lone Star's 1836 claim to the Santa Fe region. Thus began the dispute between Texas and the U.S. government over jurisdiction in that part of New Mexico east of the Rio Grande. The contest was destined to endure for several years and, when it became intermingled with the rapidly intensifying sectional crisis between North and South over the slavery expansion issue, would pose a serious threat to the continuation of the Union itself.

Chapter Two

ༀ

Santa Fe County, Texas,
or New Mexico Territory, U.S.A.?
1846–1850

THE SECOND SESSION OF THE TWENTY-NINTH CONGRESS OPENED IN WASHINGTON in December 1846 before President Polk understood the outlines of the occupation government established by General Kearny. His annual message of December 8 opened with a lengthy defense of his decision for war against Mexico. In his defense of the Rio Grande as the legitimate boundary between the two countries, Polk cited the 1836 Texas law defining that river as its boundary. Otherwise the president did not seem concerned with the relationship of Texas's claim to the area of New Mexico on the eastern side of the Rio Grande. In discussing the erection of "temporary governments" in California and New Mexico, Polk spoke of New Mexico as a distinctly separate entity from Texas; he made reference to the conquest of "the province of New Mexico, with Santa Fe, its capital."[1]

The Whig attack on Polk's message stressed the apparent contradiction of establishing a government over a region already within the limits of one of the states. Whig speakers exploited the sensitive issue of Texas's claimed jurisdiction over an area where it obviously had never exercised—and still did not exercise—any possession or authority. On December 22 Polk transmitted the Kearny Code to Congress. Polk acknowledged that the Kearny Code, while claiming to establish only a "temporary" government, in some ways appeared to set up a permanent territorial government over New Mexico and had extended the political rights of U.S. citizens to the inhabitants before the region was officially annexed to the United States. The president declared that these sections of the code would not receive his sanction, but he also excused the excesses by attributing them to a patriotic desire to extend rights to the newly conquered people. He did not address the boundary question.[2]

When news of Kearny's government in New Mexico reached Texas, Governor J. P. Henderson was alarmed at its very existence. Kearny's action clearly implied to Henderson that the federal government was setting up an adverse claim to that of Texas east of the Rio Grande. Henderson protested any such claim in a letter to Secretary of State Buchanan on January 4, 1847, but the governor also admitted that Texas could not exercise its jurisdiction and would not object to the new government at Santa Fe, provided that the federal government expressly recognize Texas's claims. Buchanan answered on February 12, citing President Polk's reference to the temporary, wartime necessity of Kearny's new government, which would cease with the conclusion of a peace treaty. Buchanan declared that this government could not "injuriously affect" the rights that the president believed Texas justly possessed over the whole area east of the Rio Grande, once the Mexican claim to it was extinguished by the treaty. The secretary of state's letter mollified Henderson for the time being, but the administration was inconsistent in its statements on the boundary issue, and this inconsistency would continue. Polk would sometimes tilt toward the Texas claim, sometimes lean toward Santa Fe as part of a separate territory. Whichever side he favored on this touchy subject, he was sure to offend someone. By appearing to support each side at different times, Polk safely confused everyone as to his position.[3]

In the Senate and House debates during the session, the Santa Fe question came into the discussion on only a few occasions. The debates of both houses primarily focused on the lower Rio Grande, whether the Nueces or the Rio Grande was the true boundary of Texas, and which nation had invaded the other's territory to start the war. The Wilmot Proviso controversy—begun at the end of the previous session when Rep. David Wilmot, a Pennsylvania Democrat, had unsuccessfully attempted to attach an amendment to a war appropriation bill for the purpose of banning the introduction of slavery from any lands acquired by the United States from Mexico in the war—also became a dominant issue in the second session of the Twenty-ninth Congress.[4]

During House debates in January and February, various minor occasions arose that permitted Democrats Andrew Johnson of Tennessee and Timothy Pilsbury and David Kaufman of Texas to defend the Texas claim to New Mexico and Whigs Caleb Smith of Indiana and Luther Severance of Maine to attack it. By far the most controversy in the session was generated by debates over the three-million-dollar war appropriation bill. The Northern majority in the House, both Whigs and Democrats, attempted to attach the Wilmot Proviso to the bill, and in several instances speakers directed their remarks to the Santa Fe question. On February 8 Wilmot himself argued that slavery was banned in both California and New Mexico by previous Mexican law. He voiced dark suspicions that the Kearny Code's limitation of voting to free male citizens implied that slavery might have already entered New Mexico. Whigs Alexander Harper of Ohio and Charles Hudson of Massachusetts both assailed the Texas claim to New Mexico in speeches on February 13. Harper stressed the anomaly of the U.S. forces marching in to seize an area supposedly part of an existing state of the Union, while Hudson emphasized that the United States had always recognized New Mexico's attachment to Mexico and had maintained a consul at Santa Fe. In the Senate, Whig John Davis of Massachusetts employed arguments similar to Hudson's. On the last day of the session, March 3, the House finally receded from its Wilmot Proviso rider and the three-million-dollar war appropriation passed Congress.[5]

The occasional references to New Mexico and Santa Fe during the second session of the Twenty-ninth Congress did indicate an awareness of the issue on the part of members and began the development of arguments that would be used in subsequent sessions. Certainly Horace Greeley of the *New York Tribune* had no intention of letting the matter rest. In editorials following the close of the second session, Greeley reminded his readers of the Texas claim to New Mexico and how "intensely" Mexican the area had always been. In subsequent years Greeley would elaborate on a theme that Wilmot had touched on in one of his speeches in the session: the extension of Texas law over New Mexico was the only likely way for any real slavery expansion to practicably take place. The subject of the Texas debt had arisen during the session, thanks to petitions from Texas bondholders for federal government payment of the debt, given that the U.S. had taken over Texas's customs houses and other revenue sources pledged for the debt when Texas was annexed. During the session Congress had paid little heed to the petitions, but even Greeley grudgingly admitted that the bondholders had a case for federal relief.[6]

In New Mexico itself, the indigenous population and the American occupiers seemed unconcerned about the Texas claim or the slavery issue. With the war still in progress, many people seemed unsure whether the conquerors would even keep New Mexico when a peace was finally made. After the departure of Kearny and Doniphan from Santa Fe, Col. Sterling Price of the Missouri Volunteers found himself in charge of the New Mexico theater, or what the War Department in November 1846 designated as the Ninth Military Department.

Price's regime became notable for its near-total loss of discipline among the volunteer regiments, as bored soldiers succumbed to the gambling halls and brothels of Santa Fe, and for the Taos Rebellion in January 1847, in which Gov. Charles Bent was killed. Price's troops quickly put down the revolt and a number of participants were tried and executed. Two of the suspected organizers, Fr. José Antonio Martinez and Diego Archuleta, were not brought to trial. Army discipline improved somewhat as regulars replaced the homeward-bound volunteers, but rumors of revolt by resentful citizens still loyal to Mexico continued to plague Price.[7]

The political situation in New Mexico was extremely confusing in 1847. New Mexican leaders did not even think in terms of the Texas claim, which they considered spurious at best, but rather of being able to establish their own government as General Kearny had promised. Former U.S. consul Manuel Alvarez even talked of running for a delegate's seat in Congress. The high hopes engendered by Kearny soon vanished. After Governor Bent's death, the territorial secretary, Donaciano Vigil, became acting governor, but he lacked any real power under the U.S. military command, especially after President Polk made it clear that New Mexicans were not U.S. citizens yet. Nonetheless, Vigil and the other Kearny appointees quietly made progress in establishing the basic machinery for civil government. The three Kearny judges, often working without pay when the government payroll did not arrive as scheduled, built the foundations of a legal system and a civil bureaucracy.[8]

Acting Governor Vigil issued a circular on July 1 for elections to organize the New Mexico legislature called for under the Kearny Code. The *Santa Fe Republican* began weekly publication in September and constantly advocated the organization of some form of civil government to supplant the military despotism. Several military officers themselves were among the speakers at an October 24 rally arguing that having no civil government was better than having one whose acts could be nullified by the military commander. One of the principal speakers was Capt. William Z. Angney, a Missourian destined to take a very active part in New Mexican politics over the next several years.[9]

Price, now promoted to brigadier general, issued an order in November appointing Donaciano Vigil as governor. When the legislature assembled on December 6, Governor Vigil urged the passage of laws modeled after the legal codes of the various states. Aside from matters of local New Mexican concern, the chief issue addressed by the legislature was annexation to the United States. In the New Mexico House of Representatives, D. Rafael Armijo introduced an annexation bill, but several members opposed it on the ground that this was a subject properly belonging to higher government and not to a local legislature. Ultimately a bill was passed to hold elections, fifteen days after the legislature adjourned, for delegates to a convention specifically to address the annexation issue.[10]

The legislative meeting of December 1847 may have appeared rather insignificant, but Texans reacted to the news of the New Mexico legislature as anything but insignificant. After the exchange of correspondence between Governor Henderson and Secretary Buchanan early in the year, Texans had paid little attention to the New Mexico question for the remainder of 1847. They assumed that, with war's end, their 1836 boundary claim would be recognized by the Polk administration. During the gubernatorial race in the late summer and fall, George Wood, the ultimate victor over several other candidates, proposed to renew the earlier Texan idea of selling the public lands of the state, though not political sovereignty over them, to the federal government for enough money to retire the Texas debt. Wood also favored the division of Texas into slave states.[11]

Outgoing Governor Henderson opened the Second Legislature of Texas on December 15 with a message in which he cited Buchanan's letter as evidence that the Polk administration fully recognized the 1836 Texas boundary claim. He also opposed any ban against slavery in newly acquired territories. Governor Wood, in his inaugural speech on December 21, also promised to sustain the 1836 limits set by Texas. On December 29, Wood sent his first message to the legislature urging the members to support his plan to sell the public lands to the federal government. He made no reference to Santa Fe, and Texas as yet had apparently received no information that New Mexico had even planned to hold its own legislature.[12]

During the early stages of the session in January and February, Santa Fe appeared to be of only mild concern to Texas's political leaders. The legislature considered Governor Wood's plan to simply sell the public lands to the federal government and also passed a measure to organize the militia of the Santa Fe area. On February 21 the Democrats conducted their state convention in the House chamber of the Capitol and approved resolutions urging the Polk administration to maintain the 1836 "true boundaries" of Texas and pledging support only to candidates for president and vice president who promised to do the same. Within the next few days, news arrived in Austin that New Mexico's own legislature had met and was planning a convention.[13]

The first legislative reaction to this thunderbolt came on February 25 when the House's State Affairs Committee recommended passage of a joint resolution

Inset from Cordova-Creuzbaur map, from J. DeCordova's Map of the State of Texas . . . , 1849.
Courtesy of Dolph Briscoe Center for American History, University of Texas at Austin.

protesting the organization of a separate government by U.S. authorities within
the limits of Texas. Three days later the Senate's State Affairs Committee issued
a report defending the 1836 boundary and Texas's claim to New Mexico,
recommending that a Texas county and judicial district be organized in that
region and submitting two bills for those purposes. The theme of the committee's
report was that any delay in taking such action would only invite further attempts
to reduce Texas's limits; not "one inch" of the state's soil should be yielded, the
report said. Governor Wood chimed in with a message to the legislature on
March 2 arguing that the federal government was now engaged in a dismemberment plot against the state. He demanded action; any silence would be in-

terpreted as submission. The state's congressional delegation must oppose anything that did not recognize the Texas title, and the state legislature must enforce Texan jurisdiction at Santa Fe.[14]

Within the next few weeks various pieces of legislation made their way through both houses. One was a bill to organize Santa Fe County, which designated the entire area west of the Puerco, or Pecos, River and north to 42° north latitude as within that one county. Companion to this measure was a bill creating the Eleventh Judicial District of Texas in that new county. On March 6 the Senate's select committee on Santa Fe strongly supported the appointment of a judge to organize the county and a dispatch of Texas militia to New Mexico by Governor Wood if any resistance developed. In a report on both bills on March 9, the House's Federal Relations Committee declared its conviction that the two laws, when enforced by Texas, would convince the president to finally order federal forces in New Mexico to cooperate with Texas authorities. Reiterating the view expressed by other political leaders in Texas, the committee held that inaction by the state now would be taken as a "waiver" of Texas's rights. Both bills were finally enacted on March 11.

On March 16, Governor Wood appointed Spruce M. Baird, a red-haired Nacogdoches lawyer in his early thirties who had fought in Wood's company earlier in the Mexican War, as judge of the Eleventh Judicial District, and James W. Webb, well-known and long-experienced Texas lawyer, jurist, and politician, as district attorney. The legislature also approved a resolution to require the governor to issue a proclamation to Santa Fe to organize a county government and to request the president, if necessary, to order the U.S. military in New Mexico to assist Texas officials to quell resistance to Texan jurisdiction. A high degree of unanimity was reported to have characterized these deliberations, although no records of speeches or debates for this legislature now exist. On March 23, Governor Wood wrote to President Polk informing him of these measures.[15]

News of the Texan reaction to New Mexico's government did not reach Washington until the Senate and House were advanced into the first session of the Thirtieth Congress. The Mexican War's military action was effectively over before the politicians had taken their seats in December. Gen. Winfield Scott's army had captured Mexico City on September 13, 1847. All that remained was negotiation of a peace treaty with Mexican commissioners by U.S. envoy Nicholas Trist. In his annual message of December 7, Polk discussed the instructions given to Trist relating to boundaries and mentioned the contiguity of New Mexico to the U.S. He did not explain whether he considered New Mexico as lying on both sides of

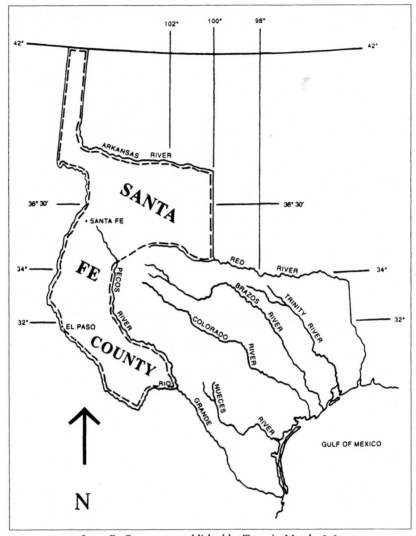

Santa Fe County as established by Texas in March 1848.

the Rio Grande or, according to the Texan viewpoint, simply on the western side
of the river. The president argued that both Upper California and New Mexico
were already U.S. possessions and that U.S. laws should be extended over the
conquered area without waiting for a treaty. He requested Congress to provide
for the early establishment of territorial governments over the region.[16]

On the matter of those territorial governments, Congress proved dilatory. Much of the session, as had been the case in the previous one, was devoted to partisan speeches on the cause of the war, Nueces vs. Rio Grande, and slavery in the new territories. One problem that was destined to plague the senators and representatives was that, amidst a welter of often conflicting and inaccurate maps, many members of Congress were woefully confused about geography in the regions where Congress would probably have to establish boundaries for territories. The Senate received a reminder of the Texas debt issue at the beginning of the session when Leslie Combs, a prominent Kentucky holder of Texas bonds, petitioned for federal payment, but the Senate paid the matter scant attention.[17]

During the first months of the session, Whigs would occasionally pounce on the Santa Fe issue, denying that New Mexico had ever been anything but Mexican. The 1836 Texas boundary law was repugnant to the 1845 Texas annexation resolutions, which Whigs claimed had left the boundary an open question; and Whigs dismissed the boundary provisions of the 1836 treaty with Santa Anna as an invalid instrument forced on the dictator while he was a prisoner. Democrats, especially the Texans, defended the whole 1836 boundary, which Texas argued had been the boundary of the state at its admission into the Union and which they believed Congress had tacitly recognized in the annexation resolutions.[18]

On February 22, 1848, Polk laid the Treaty of Guadalupe Hidalgo before the Senate for ratification. Attached to the treaty was a map with the new boundary marked on it; the map itself, a very inaccurate commercial map by John Disturnell, placed the El Paso area half a degree too far north and nearly two degrees too far east. Article 5 of the treaty ran the U.S.-Mexico boundary up the Rio Grande to an unspecified "southern boundary of New Mexico" before turning west. As the Senate deliberated over the treaty, the Whigs struggled, consistent with their view of the war, to diminish the amount of territory that Mexico would be forced to cede. On March 9, Whig senator John Davis of Massachusetts delivered a vehement denunciation of Texas's pretensions to Santa Fe. The whole Whig effort was to no avail, however, as the Senate ratified the treaty. Mexico also approved the settlement, and on July 6 President Polk presented the final treaty to the Senate.[19]

In his July 6 message, the president stressed that, now that peace had been concluded, Congress should immediately establish territorial governments. His plea inaugurated a month of frenzied activity in Congress. The first response to the message originated in the House on July 10, when Southern Whig leader Alexander Stephens of Georgia introduced a resolution requesting President

Polk for information on the boundaries of California and New Mexico and the character of the civil governments established therein by U.S. military commanders. Stephens's main thrust was to continue the Whig exploitation of the unclear Texas–New Mexico boundary situation. When Stephens badgered Timothy Pilsbury of Texas about the boundary and the existence of the Kearny government, Pilsbury refused to debate the matter with him and answered that Texas knew its boundary and that it was not the business of Congress. When Stephens pressed on, Democrat Robert McLane of Maryland delivered an elaborate reply to Stephens in defense of the Texan claim to the whole region covered in its 1836 law. The House passed the Stephens resolution that same day after the debate on it.[20]

On July 12, Whig John M. Clayton of Delaware launched in the Senate the first serious attempt to form territorial governments in the post–Mexican War West by proposing that the sensitive topic should be given to a select committee to formulate a compromise. The Senate agreed and a committee of eight went to work. Senator Clayton reported a bill from this committee on July 18, and it became known as the Clayton Compromise. It proposed organizing territorial governments in Oregon, California, and New Mexico, with Oregon allowed to retain the antislavery laws already passed by its provisional government and the other two territories prohibited from legislating in reference to slavery. Any question of slavery arising in the territorial courts could be appealed to the U.S. Supreme Court. The bill was silent as to boundaries. Most Democrats and some Southern Whigs supported the Clayton Compromise formula, but Northern Whigs and a few others refused to do this for fear that the bill, by not explicitly banning slavery, would promote further extension of it. The New Mexico boundary was also a concern voiced by Northern Whigs; they wanted the boundary determined before a territorial government was established and feared that, if Congress recognized the validity of the Texan claim, New Mexico would become no more than a sparsely populated region west of the Rio Grande. Slavery would thus be extended over Santa Fe via Texas law. Despite Northern Whig dissent, the Clayton Compromise passed the Senate on July 27, only to be tabled in the House on the next day without even a reading.

The House majority preferred to enact a separate Oregon Territory bill, with a clause extending the 1787 Northwest Ordinance's ban on slavery to the new territory. During the debate on the Oregon bill on August 1, David Kaufman of Texas surprised the House with an amendment to divide the entire Mexican cession from the Rio Grande to the Pacific at the Missouri Compromise line (36°30' north latitude) into two territories—California on the north and New

Mexico on the south. The scheme, of course, would leave Texas's 1836 claim intact. The House refused even to allow the introduction of Kaufman's amendment as ungermane to the bill. The House passed its antislavery version of the Oregon bill, and, on August 12, to the outraged astonishment of many Southern leaders, the Senate finally accepted that version.[21]

While the Senate was engrossed in Clayton Compromise debate on July 24, President Polk sent to the House a message and documents in answer to Stephens's resolution. As lately as April 22, he had personally assured Representative Kaufman of Texas that he favored Texas keeping control of the entire area east of the Rio Grande. But the July 24 message represented a definite shift by Polk away from support of Texas's position. Polk still admitted that Texas did possess a claim east of the Rio Grande, but he also stated that New Mexico's ancient boundaries had lain on both sides of that river, that Texas had never had actual possession of it, and that the population of the Santa Fe region gave its allegiance wholly to Mexico prior to the U.S. conquest. The president's leaning toward New Mexico on the boundary question was probably based on his desire for the Clayton Compromise to pass Congress in order to settle the nagging territorial slavery issue. Polk realized that giving New Mexico a territorial government would be meaningless unless New Mexico included Santa Fe, Taos, and the other settled communities east of the Rio Grande. Between the two sides of the boundary argument, Polk was beginning to advocate the more tangibly realistic, and pro–New Mexico, viewpoint. Polk's message immediately set off another Texas–New Mexico boundary debate in the House, with Kaufman and Pilsbury parrying Whig attacks on the Texas claim. Whigs criticized the mere "paper title" of Texas to Santa Fe, while Kaufman and Pilsbury of Texas ardently defended the legitimacy of their state's title. The first session of the Thirtieth Congress ended without Congress providing territorial governments for California or New Mexico.[22]

One political leader who was frustrated by the session's failure to establish Western governments was Sen. Thomas Hart Benton, the Missouri Democrat. After Congress adjourned, Benton decided to take matters into his own hands. On August 28 he addressed a letter to the peoples of California and New Mexico, advising them, in the absence of congressional action, to assemble in conventions and set up their own governments. Benton also advised them to totally abstain from any agitation of the slavery issue until after they had achieved statehood. President Polk, distrusting Benton's motives, decided with his cabinet to send a counterletter to California, informing them that the administration considered Benton's plan illegal and that they should continue to obey the military government. But Polk dispatched no such letter to New Mexico, and Benton's proposal accorded well with sentiments already developing rapidly among elements at Santa Fe, who were becoming weary of the U.S. military government in 1848. Even before they knew of Benton's letter, Santa Fe leaders were busily hatching their own schemes of government.[23]

In early 1848 New Mexicans realized that the military action of the war was virtually over. Governor Vigil and the three Kearny judges, especially Vigil's good friend Joab Houghton, worked with what limited official authority they possessed to build the foundations of civil government structure in New Mexico, even though their exclusive exercise of power ultimately began to alienate some elements in the territory and provided the seeds for dissent and factionalism in New Mexican politics.[24]

The convention to consider annexation to the U.S. met at Santa Fe in February. The *Santa Fe Republican* boosted the annexation cause in its editorials both leading up to and following the convention. In one editorial the *Republican* even stated that it was New Mexicans' duty to decide the slavery question there themselves. On February 8 General Price informed the delegates that New Mexico was permanently part of the U.S. already and really left the delegates no choice on the matter. The convention, understandably, did nothing and adjourned very shortly after it began. General Price, as the military governor, was the only power that counted.[25]

No further political developments of significance took place in New Mexico until July. During the second week of that month, news reached Santa Fe of Governor Wood's and the Texas Legislature's determination to enforce the Lone Star's claim east of the Rio Grande. A *Santa Fe Republican* editorial on July 16 chided the Texans that, if they did send officials to New Mexico, those agents would receive less attention than "a passing gust of our dusty winds." The editorial argued that Texas itself was impotent to enforce the claim, that the people of New Mexico would never consent to it, and that the U.S. government, which had had a consul at Santa Fe, would never recognize it. Three days later, on July 19, Santa Fe learned from arriving soldiers that the Treaty of Guadalupe Hidalgo had finally been ratified. New Mexico was now officially part of the United States, although just what lands constituted New Mexico remained in doubt.[26]

The various shreds of news set off much political excitement in New Mexico. The *Republican* continued its sarcastic editorial fusillade against the Texans for several months. *Republican* articles described the claim as contemptible and designed by Texas simply to extort money from the federal government by selling this "paper" claim to the United States. One editorial promised "tar and feathers" for any Texan officials who showed up in New Mexico. The Santa Fe paper urged Texas to "show some little sense and drop this question."[27]

Publicly considering the Texas claim a joke, New Mexican leaders did not intend to remain passive about the issue. During July and August public interest in politics increased and planning to establish a territorial government began. Public meetings were held during the first week in August at Santa Fe to protest the Texas claim. New Mexico's residents were beginning to assert themselves and resentment against continued military government became commonplace among both the Anglo- and Mexican-American groups.[28]

General Price and his forces departed from Santa Fe on August 26. Price left Maj. Benjamin Beall in charge ad interim until the new department commander and military governor, Bvt. Lt. Col. John M. Washington, could reach New Mexico. Washington's arrival was not expected until late September. Beall did not resist and may even have encouraged popular efforts then afoot under Governor Vigil and his friend Judge Houghton to organize an effective civil government. The movement was an indigenous one; it was not inspired, as earlier historians have suggested, by Benton's notorious letter nor by Benton's friend W. Z. Angney. Benton's letter, dated August 28, could not have even been known in New Mexico until sometime in October, and Angney was absent in Missouri and in Washington for several months, not returning to Santa Fe until the end of October. New Mexican politicians wanted to take some action before the new military governor, who might possibly frown on it, arrived and in time for their petition to be presented when Congress met in December 1848. Texans might enjoy thinking that the incipient government movement at Santa Fe was organized by a mere rabble of "gamblers and monte dealers," but the New Mexicans demonstrated a considerable amount of political savvy in their efforts.[29]

Governor Vigil issued a call for election of delegates to assemble in convention at Santa Fe on October 10, 1848. The only existing information about the process involved in this election is derived from the later biased reports of the Texas agent Spruce Baird. According to Baird the whole operation was rigged by the Kearny government officials to ensure that associates of their clique would control the convention. Baird stated that an anti-Texas "secret conclave" of officeholders and office-seekers devised the scheme in such a way as to allow as little time as possible for an opposing slate of candidates to develop. The proclamation, Baird said, was issued only five days before the elections were to be held, and poll-books were made out and distributed to precincts headed by the names of those candidates supported by the "conclave." According to Baird at least, the Vigil-Houghton faction lost all but one race anyway, given popular discontent over the method by which the elections were set up.[30]

When the convention met on October 10, some disruption of unknown origin occurred that led to the withdrawal of about a third of the delegates, all Mexican-Americans but one. The majority of the delegates who remained were also Mexican-American, and the convention proceeded to choose Father Martinez, the Taos priest, as president. The main order of business was initially to form a constitution and apply to Congress for either a territorial or state government. At one meeting delegates denounced the Texas claim as an attempt to defraud the New Mexican people and declared that it possessed no shadow of validity "except in the wicked imagination of grasping demagogues." On October 14 the delegates ultimately adopted a petition asking Congress to grant New Mexico a territorial government, with appointed territorial officials and a delegate in Congress. The convention defined no boundary, but protested against any dismemberment of New Mexico in favor of Texas, and prayed Congress to exclude slavery during the territorial stage. Lawyer James H. Quinn moved, and the delegates agreed, that the petition should be sent to Senators Benton and Clayton to offer at the upcoming second session of the Thirtieth Congress. Judge Houghton transmitted the petition to Clayton on October 16 with an accompanying letter in which he strongly condemned the Texas claim and labeled slavery as impracticable in competition with the cheap labor already present in New Mexico.[31]

On the day the convention had begun, Bvt. Lt. Col. John M. Washington entered Santa Fe at the head of four dragoon companies badly needed to reinforce the meager military contingent holding New Mexico. The War Department had finally specified some boundaries for Colonel Washington's Ninth Military Department in General Order 49, dated August 31, 1848. The line dividing the New Mexico department from the Eighth, which covered Texas, was to begin at the intersection of 32° north latitude with the Rio Grande near El Paso and extend in a straight line northeastward to the intersection of Choctaw Creek with the Red River. The latter point lay about halfway between 100° west longitude and the northeast corner of Texas, at about the dividing line between Grayson and Fannin counties. Colonel Washington and his troops received a warm welcome from the people in their new jurisdiction.[32]

After about a month in Santa Fe, Colonel Washington acutely experienced the need for official guidance on the Texas claim issue. Spruce Baird, the Texas judge, arrived on the evening of November 10. Neither Colonel Washington nor anyone else in New Mexico realized it, but Judge Baird had already gravely sabotaged his own mission at its very inception through his own double-crossing treachery. James W. Webb had been appointed district attorney for Santa Fe County and had arranged with Baird to act together in the effort. They originally planned to first go to Washington and persuade the Polk administration to issue orders to the military governor at Santa Fe, which would permit Baird and Webb to begin their duties when they reached their destination. Such official instructions were deemed crucial—apparently by both men at the beginning—to their cause. Whether they could have succeeded in securing those instructions is at least highly doubtful, given the political storm it would raise in Washington. Anyway, neither man came close to Washington, and Webb never came close to Santa Fe.

Baird and Webb agreed to meet in New Orleans in late April 1848 and travel together from that point. They never did. James Webb left Austin so that he could be in New Orleans by April 25. He apparently expected to find Baird waiting there for him, but he could not locate the judge. Webb waited for two days and then departed for Macon, Georgia, after leaving a letter at New Orleans for Baird. Webb undoubtedly thought that Baird had somehow been delayed or detained, and they had already prearranged that Webb would wait at Macon for Baird if they did not meet in New Orleans. Webb had probably chosen Macon for the rendezvous since that is the area where he had spent his youth. James Webb cooled his heels in Macon until early October before receiving any word from Baird. Webb had by this time decided to proceed directly to Santa Fe alone and had already sent his books ahead to Independence, Missouri, hoping he could still connect up with Baird. Baird's letter to Webb, dated September 27 at Lexington, Missouri, informed Webb that Baird was just then setting out for Santa Fe and that District Attorney Webb need not come out until the following spring.

Spruce Baird, without telling Webb, had traveled with his wife to New Orleans and then by steamer had proceeded up the Mississippi to St. Louis and thence up the Missouri to his father-in-law's plantation at Lexington, a town just east of Independence. Settling his wife with her parents, Baird wrote the letter to Webb and headed west to Independence and the Santa Fe Trail. Why Baird treated Webb in so humiliating a fashion is not entirely clear, but Spruce Baird's actions appear to have been carefully calculated and timed to prevent Webb's journeying to Santa Fe prior to the ensuing spring. Baird kept his own whereabouts secret from Webb until October, knowing that he could still make it to New Mexico before winter set in but that Webb almost certainly could not arrange his affairs and venture out on the trail before the threat of winter snows stopped him. For some reason

Baird did not want James Webb to accompany him. That reason was probably Baird's desire to operate as independently as possible. He may have been jealous of the far more experienced Webb and fearful that Webb would become the dominant figure on the mission. Spruce Baird was always looking out for his own best economic interests, too, and may have believed that he would be freer to pursue those interests at Santa Fe without Webb's prying eyes. Given these considerations, Baird convinced himself that he could manage Texas's interests, and/or his own, without Webb and without first getting orders from the Polk administration directing the Santa Fe commander to aid the Texan attempt to organize a county. Off Baird went to New Mexico, most likely tagging along with a caravan of traders on the Santa Fe Trail.

Back in Macon the flabbergasted James Webb discussed the situation with some members of Congress from Georgia and decided that the Texan cause at Santa Fe would be nugatory in the absence of positive pro-Texas instructions from the federal government to the U.S. military in New Mexico. Webb resigned himself, therefore, to delay his journey until spring and exerted his efforts for several months, though to no avail, to persuade the Polk administration to issue the desired orders. Ultimately Webb himself prepared to leave for Santa Fe and set out in March 1849 from Macon. He traveled as far as New Orleans, where he fell victim to the great Asiatic cholera epidemic of 1849. He survived the attack, but only after spending three weeks in bed in a debilitated condition. Believing himself incapable of proceeding any further on the mission, Webb resigned as district attorney and returned home to Texas.[33]

Meanwhile Judge Baird had begun work in Santa Fe on his own hook. He was not the only accession to the political scene there. W. Z. Angney, having resigned his military commission, reached Santa Fe from Missouri at the end of October, as did the Kearny government's attorney general, Hugh N. Smith, who had been on a business trip to Missouri. A former army paymaster who would soon make his presence felt in New Mexican politics, Richard H. Weightman, was already on hand, having taken up permanent residence at the end of August. Baird himself was reported to have appointed a sheriff and clerks to assist him, but the identities of these men remain unknown. Baird, after arriving on November 10, spent nearly two weeks learning what situation he faced before presenting himself to Colonel Washington; he encountered few people who could speak English and many who seemed altogether ignorant of the Texas claim. He also became familiar with the *Republican*'s anti-Texas propaganda, which told Mexican-Americans in particular that Texas would destroy their religion, confiscate their property, hang former "rebels" against Texas, and enslave their women and children. Some viewed "Judicial Envoy" Baird and his "entourage" as a "monstrosity," while others saw him as "harmless and inoffensive." Most local inhabitants believed that only a very few of the Anglo-Americans and none of the Mexican-Americans would give aid and comfort to the Texan judge.[34]

Baird first sought to dispel some of the anti-Texas bitterness by holding a public meeting on November 20 to explain his mission and the Texas claim. The meeting, before a sizable audience, began with addresses by Baird in defense of the Texas claim east of the Rio Grande and by Angney against it. According to one eyewitness, Judge Baird defended Texas's rights with some degree of "ingenuity." The same writer, however, stated that Angney and another lawyer who spoke that evening completely "floored" the Texan. Angney pressed for one resolution condemning the Texas claim and another attacking the continued existence of the Kearny government. The officials and adherents of that government naturally disdained Angney's move against them and their power. Angney's faction became known as the "No Government" party. The meeting adjourned until another evening, when a vote was taken on the resolutions. Only a small group attended this meeting, and it passed the anti-Texas resolution by an 8 to 1 vote, Baird himself the lone dissenter. When opposition developed to Angney's resolution against the Kearny government, the organizers adjourned it to yet another evening but never held that meeting.[35]

Judge Baird finally presented himself to Colonel Washington on November 22. Baird delivered his credentials and, by way of justifying his demands, extracts from the earlier Henderson-Buchanan correspondence on the temporariness of the military government. The Texan also complained about the anti-Texas propaganda in the newspaper published on the government-controlled printing press. In a written statement to Colonel Washington, Baird proclaimed Texas's determination not to surrender the claim and informed the commander that Texan authority now superseded that of the Kearny government.[36]

Colonel Washington wasted no time in responding to the Texan judge. He sent a note, also on November 22, telling Baird quite bluntly that he considered the Kearny government legitimate and still in effect, that its integrity would be maintained "at every peril," and that he would turn over the jurisdiction only when ordered to do so by the president or Congress. Why Baird had thought he could induce the new military governor to immediately turn over New Mexico east of the Rio Grande to him without a specific directive from Colonel Washington's own higher authority to that effect is a mystery, especially since that had been a major consideration for both Baird and James W. Webb initially. No commander would have given in to Baird under those circumstances.

That first confrontation actually played into Colonel Washington's hands and provided him with an opportunity to enhance his image with the local populace. By not acceding to Baird's demands, the military governor at least showed that he was not an advocate of the Texan position so abhorrent to the great majority of New Mexicans. The military government might not be popular, but any stand against the Texas claim was bound to win praise from New Mexicans for Colonel Washington.[37]

Having encountered almost nothing but hostility in Santa Fe, at public meetings, in the *Republican,* and from Colonel Washington himself, Spruce Baird finally resigned himself to the fact that his further efforts on Texas's behalf would be useless until orders emanated from the Polk administration instructing Colonel Washington to give up his civil jurisdiction east of the Rio Grande to the Texan judge. Judge Baird wrote back to Governor Wood and Secretary of State Washington D. Miller in December informing them of his decision to delay further organizational activity. He requested that the governor send him new instructions and various documents and, extolling the great untapped mineral wealth of New Mexico, inquired about gaining rights to saline deposits for himself and other parties. But Baird also misled the Texan officials by claiming that the Texas cause was increasing in popularity among both Anglo- and Mexican-Americans and that he would have no difficulty organizing the county once the U.S. government sanctioned the Texas claim. His portrayal of a rosier picture than actually existed for Texas probably reflected his desire to remain in New Mexico to further his own personal interests; the Texas government would have recalled him if he had acknowledged his mission a failure. So Baird settled down to practice law in Santa Fe and to invest in various business enterprises.[38]

Although Baird did not learn of it, the administration did transmit a policy statement to Colonel Washington, dated October 12, which, though it could be interpreted in various ways, appeared to side with Texas. The letter from Secretary of War William Marcy informed the military governor that any civil authority that Texas might establish east of the Rio Grande was to be respected and in no way interfered with by the military except to help sustain that Texan authority "on proper occasions." Marcy stated that, until Congress acted to give New Mexico a territorial government, things were to remain as they were. The letter could have only confused Colonel Washington; things were to stay the same until Congress acted, but he was to respect any civil authority the Texans might set up. Marcy's ambiguous order soon became irrelevant in any case, for a new administration was about to assume the reins of power in Washington.[39]

The Texas–New Mexico boundary question was hardly even noticeable during the national election of 1848. What to do about slavery in the new territories became the predominant issue. The Democrats nominated Sen. Lewis Cass of Michigan for president, and he advocated settling the territorial slavery problem by allowing the people of the territories to decide the issue for themselves (i.e., popular sovereignty). The Whigs nominated Gen. Zachary Taylor of Louisiana, a career officer with no political experience. Taylor, though a slaveholder, did not believe that slavery could ever spread to the territories, did not feel that the South should demand the right to spread it, and at times did not appear averse to a congressionally mandated ban against slavery extension. A third party, the Free-Soilers, chose former Democratic president Martin Van Buren of New York on a platform promoting the Wilmot Proviso in the territories. A major issue with Texans during the campaign was General Taylor's condemnation of Texas atrocities against Mexicans during the war.

Zachary Taylor won the presidential election in November over his two opponents, but Taylor lost badly in Texas. Texas gave Cass 11,644 votes (68.9 percent), Taylor 5,281 votes (31.0 percent), and Van Buren 2 votes. The only counties that Taylor carried in Texas were extreme southern counties near the border with Mexico. Texas was a heavily Democratic state, but Taylor's dislike of Texan soldiers in the Mexican War undoubtedly added to Cass's sweep of the state. The news of General Taylor's election was brought to Santa Fe by traders from Chihuahua on January 25, 1849.[40]

James K. Polk hoped that he and the short second session of the Thirtieth Congress would be able to resolve the question of slavery in the territories and organize governments in the West before Zachary Taylor and the Whigs took office. On the boundary question, Polk once again leaned toward the Texan viewpoint, and Secretary Marcy's generally pro-Texas orders of October 12 reflected Polk's attitude. Governor Wood reinforced his state's argument in a long letter to Polk, dated October 6. The letter declared that after annexation the federal government had become Texas's "agent and trustee" in adjusting the boundary with Mexico but had acquired no right to take territory that the United States recognized as Texas. Wood did extend a flicker of possibility that a land-for-money swap could be worked out but added that he was not authorized to say that such a deal could be consummated. The governor also informed President Polk of the appointments of Baird and Webb to organize the Texas county of Santa Fe. The president neither responded to Governor Wood nor acted decisively in favor of Texas. Polk had already seen how disruptive that issue could be in previous legislative sessions. He now sought a comprehensive settlement of this and other territorial subjects.[41]

On December 5 President Polk opened the new session of Congress with his last annual message. Therein he referred to New Mexico as "an intermediate and connecting territory" between Texas and the Pacific Coast and called for the organization of territorial governments in California and "that part of New Mexico lying west of the Rio Grande and without the limits of Texas." His own preferred method for quieting the territorial slavery issue, Polk said, was via an extension of the Missouri Compromise line to the Pacific. He did not specify what he meant by "New Mexico"; he requested a government only in the area west of the Rio Grande but implied that some of New Mexico lay on the eastern side of the river. Polk may have concluded that establishment of government west of the Rio Grande was at least possible, without raising the nagging boundary question. He expressed strong opposition to any ban on slavery in the territories. Northern Whigs and Free-Soilers would undoubtedly press the Wilmot Proviso's application to the West, and Southerners of both parties, Texans included, would be certain to fight it. The Texans could also be counted on to defend their complete boundary claim.[42]

During the short session, Congress considered a wide array of plans to provide governments for the Western territories. Sen. Stephen Douglas of Illinois, chairman of the Senate Committee on Territories, produced a bill to admit the whole region between the Rio Grande and the Pacific Coast as a single state of California, with a provision to allow Congress to subdivide it into new states east of the Sierra Nevada range. However, Southerners who dominated the Judiciary Committee, to which the bill was referred, rejected Douglas's proposal and suggested instead that two territories be established and that New Mexico lie entirely west of the Rio Grande. Rep. William B. Preston, a Virginia Whig, introduced a similar single-state bill in the House, with the boundary between Texas and the new state adjudicated by the Supreme Court. Preston later altered it into a two-state bill and finally reverted to the one-state formula, but Preston's choice of arbiter on the boundary question remained the Supreme Court. The House did not enact any of Preston's versions. A Senate select committee devised a bill for the admission of both California and New Mexico as states, with New Mexico's eastern boundary only vaguely defined as that between itself and Texas. The Senate never seriously considered the bill. Whig representative Henry Hilliard of Alabama offered a plan that would have bounded California on the south at 34°30' north latitude and given Texas the remainder of the Mexican cession below 36°30' north latitude, including the region below California, which would stretch Texas to the Pacific. Hilliard's measure engendered no interest in the House.[43]

Certain proposals in Congress's short session specifically concerned New Mexico. On December 13 Senators Benton and Clayton introduced the petition of New Mexico's October convention for territorial government on both sides of the Rio Grande. John C. Calhoun immediately charged that New Mexico's petition for a free territory was "a most insolent one" designed to exclude Southerners from the region they had helped conquer. Despite Southern opposition, New Mexico's petition was printed and referred to committee by a 33 to 14 vote; it was not resurrected, but it had elicited a very favorable response from Northern antislavery groups. Later in January, John A. Dix, a New York Free-Soil senator, would introduce resolutions passed by the New York State Legislature bidding Congress to establish a government for New Mexico and to protect its area east of the Rio Grande from the Texas claim. Despite a furious rebuttal by Senator Rusk, the Senate agreed to print these resolutions.[44]

The House Committee on Territories did concoct a bill to establish a territorial government for New Mexico, with slavery excluded, and thus preserve the region from Texas. Indiana Whig Caleb Smith reported the bill from committee on January 3, 1849. The measure designated that the territory would lie on both sides of the Rio Grande and that its boundary on the east would extend southward from the intersection of 100° west longitude and the Arkansas River to the intersection of the same meridian with the Red River and from that point diagonally in a southwesterly direction to the intersection of the southern line of New Mexico (unspecified) and the Rio Grande. The inveterate champion of New Mexico, Horace Greeley, was filling out a vacancy in the New York delegation during this short session, and he described this measure as "the great bill" of the session. But he also expressed his conviction that Texas would "resist it to the death" and that its prospect in the Senate would be "gloomily doubtful." While the Whig majority on the Territories Committee made no report in support of the bill, Representative Pilsbury of Texas filed a minority report containing one of the most complete litanies of documentary evidence in support of Texas's 1836 boundary claim.[45]

Smith's New Mexico Territory bill made no progress after its emergence from the Committee on Territories. The vehemence of Southern and Texan sentiments appeared to frighten some Northern Whigs into caution and delay. Near the end of the short session in late February, however, Horace Greeley proposed an amendment to another measure to create a state of New Mexico with the boundaries delineated in Smith's bill. Kaufman of Texas immediately rose to ask Greeley if he was stealing enough land from Texas for "his Fourierite bill," a reference to Greeley's previous advocacy of utopian socialist communes. Greeley chided Kaufman for discussing land-stealing when, without federal protection for New Mexico's territorial integrity, Texas would steal all of New Mexico east of the Rio Grande. Greeley's amendment was rejected.

A bit later the House acceded to one of Caleb Smith's moves to take up his New Mexico Territory bill. Whig Samuel Vinton of Ohio moved to amend the bill to state that nothing in the bill would impair the boundary claim of Texas and would allow Texas to bring suit in the U.S. Supreme Court to settle the dispute. Vinton's aim may have been to gain some Southern support, but he only succeeded in rousing Greeley's formidable temper and another lengthy debate on the boundary. Greeley preferred a decision by Congress, where the North predominated, to one by a Supreme Court dominated by presumably pro-Texas slaveholders. Southern members also objected to Vinton's move because it even called the Texas claim into question. The House did not seriously consider the bill again.[46]

The boundary dispute also played a role in the notable episode known as the Southern Caucus during the short session. In response to congressional moves to impose the Wilmot Proviso and to outlaw the District of Columbia's slave trade, Senator Calhoun attempted to unite the Southern delegations of both parties into a common front against Northern policies and possibly into a Southern political party. But Calhoun found the Southern response to his call at best lukewarm. Moderates, especially the Whigs, abhorred Calhoun's sectional party ideas and suspected him of disunion intent. President Polk was openly hostile to the caucus, as were both of the Texas senators. Thomas Jefferson Rusk in particular, to Calhoun's chagrin, assumed a leading role in the caucus meetings in suggesting more moderate, Unionist language than the version of the caucus's "Southern Address," which Calhoun had written. Calhoun's wording breathed defiance at Northern aggression and promised Southern resistance rather than allow emancipation and race war to destroy the South.

At a caucus session on January 13, Calhoun expressed astonishment at Rusk's plea and reminded him that the other Southern states had courageously supported Texas so far and also, in a veiled threat, "that Texas had vitally important questions yet unsettled" (i.e., the boundary). Rusk politely refused to back off, and he undoubtedly assumed that Calhoun's veiled threat was a bluff; he could not imagine any Southern radical acting under any circumstances prejudicial to the Texas boundary claim. But Calhoun was not bluffing, as he would prove a few days later.[47]

On January 16, Senator Calhoun went to visit President Polk at the White House to try to persuade Polk to support the Southern movement. Polk reiterated his strong Unionism and then switched the conversation to the need for governments in California and New Mexico without the Wilmot Proviso being attached to them. The president had been working with Senator Douglas on a new plan that Douglas offered up later that day in the Senate. But Stephen Douglas's new bill was limited to organizing a state government for California, which was to be bounded on the east by the Sierra Mountains. Douglas and President Polk also wanted to solve the Texas–New Mexico problem, but they desired to gain Texan and Southern "ultra" acquiescence in a specific plan before venturing it in Congress. Polk relayed to Calhoun Douglas's suggestion that in return for ceding the barren areas north of 36°30′ north latitude within its claim, Texas might be granted jurisdiction over all of New Mexico south of that line on both sides of the Rio Grande. This extraordinary proposition, if it could have ever been enacted, would have added immensely to Texas's area of control. But Calhoun at this point was intransigently venomous toward the Texans, excitedly telling Polk that they had betrayed the South. Calhoun would agree to nothing, thus giving himself a small measure of vengeance on Rusk and Houston. It is extremely doubtful that the Northern-dominated House would have ever passed such a proposition anyway, but without Calhoun's earnest support, it stood no chance in the Senate either.[48]

On January 22, after further attempts by Rusk to water down the sentiments of Calhoun's "Southern Address," the caucus approved the extremist version by a 36 to 19 vote. In the Texan delegation, Houston and Rusk both voted against the address, Pilsbury voted for it, and Kaufman abstained. Only 48 of 121 Southerners in Congress signed the manifesto, all but two of them Democrats. Houston sloughed it all off as a second nullification attempt. Rep. Horace Greeley wrote to his *New York Tribune* on January 15 that the Wilmot Proviso and other matters discussed in Calhoun's "Southern Address" were irrelevant to the immediately vital issue anyhow. That issue was New Mexico, Greeley said, and whether or not this area, formerly free under Mexican law, was to be swallowed up by slave Texas. Slavery, he wrote, could not cross the Rio Grande, but it might, under the pretense of Texan county organization, grasp hold of three-quarters of New Mexico, a parcel the size of New England.[49]

A desperation effort to grant some semblance of civil government to the territories and to avoid the boundary question engaged both houses of Congress in the final few days of the session and led frayed and frustrated tempers to threaten each other with personal violence. On February 20 Isaac Walker, a young Democratic senator from Wisconsin, offered an amendment to the civil and diplomatic appropriation bill to extend the U.S. Constitution and laws to the whole region from the Rio Grande to the Pacific Coast and to authorize the president virtually dictatorial power to make rules for governance in the area and to appoint civil officials. The Senate adopted the Walker Amendment by a close vote on February 26 and passed the appropriation bill itself on February 28. The House, however, amended Walker's proposal to make it applicable on both sides of the Rio Grande and to apply the Mexican antislavery laws to the region. The Senate, ultimately realizing that the impasse with the House could not be overcome, receded from the Walker amendment altogether. The appropriation bill then passed and Congress adjourned. The issues of California, New Mexico, and the boundary remained for the Thirty-first Congress, having totally stalemated congressional efforts in the short session in their attempt to solve the territorial crisis.[50]

Zachary Taylor took the oath of office as twelfth president of the United States on Monday, March 5, 1849. His inaugural address was general and uninspiring, giving no solid indication of his plans to handle the nation's problems. The new president was sixty-four years old, of medium height and muscular build, with a long nose, prominent cheekbones, and deep lines in his face. Excellent qualities of mind might have eased the transition, but no one considered Zachary Taylor to possess high intellect. He was hampered in conversation by an unsettling speech impediment, which caused him to pause several times before completing a sentence. He could be quite charming to the ladies at White House soirees, but, in personal confrontation with political leaders who did not agree with him, Taylor could easily lose his temper. As for Texas, Taylor had been contemptuous of atrocities against Mexicans committed by Texas militiamen in the war. Taylor certainly did not believe that slavery would spread farther west, and he therefore considered the Wilmot Proviso needlessly inflammatory. Nor did he believe that Santa Fe had ever been or ever would be part of Texas.[51]

Having seen Congress deadlocked on what to do about government in the Mexican cession, Taylor and his advisers devised a plan that they hoped would avoid the touchy issue of slavery in territories. They decided to send emissaries to both California and New Mexico to encourage the people to assemble constitutional conventions and apply to Congress for immediate statehood at the beginning of the next session in December. The administration anticipated that both California and New Mexico would form free states. The question of slavery in national territories could thus safely be bypassed. The administration took for granted that no one would object to a statehood convention deciding to ban slavery. The plan was simple and straightforward and would present Congress with a virtual fait accompli in December. Chosen in April for the mission to California was Thomas Butler King of Georgia; he reached his destination in early June. Subsequently, California held its convention and petitioned Congress to be admitted as a free state. The person selected to advocate statehood in New Mexico was the newly appointed Indian agent for that area, James S. Calhoun of Georgia. It is not known exactly what instructions he received from the administration. Calhoun did not arrive at Santa Fe until July.[52]

While awaiting developments in New Mexico, Taylor did not drastically alter the policies of the Polk administration. Taylor administration officials were already aware from newspaper reports that the Texan judge, Spruce Baird, was in Santa Fe. President Taylor's secretary of war, George Crawford of Georgia, issued new instructions to Colonel Washington on March 26. The new orders repeated portions of Marcy's earlier ones but added a slight change that must have greatly pleased the Ninth Department's commander. Rather than imply, as Marcy had, that Colonel Washington should aid Texan officials, Crawford implied that the commander should assume a position of neutrality. The March 26 order informed Colonel Washington that he was to arrange his command so as not to conflict with any Texan authorities who might show up. On April 3 the army issued a new general order that completed the separation of the Eighth and Ninth departments by leaving the two department commanders responsible (as with other departments) directly to the adjutant general and secretary of war. The order eliminated the single overall commander previously in charge of these two departments.[53]

Texans were considerably wary of the new administration's views on the Texas boundary claim. Sam Houston certainly entertained no illusions that Zachary Taylor would help Texas, writing on May 7 that Taylor would slap Texas whenever he got the chance. Houston knew whereof he wrote.[54]

Since Colonel Washington's initial confrontation with Judge Baird of Texas, Baird caused the commander no more concern until March 1849. Continuing anti-Texas propaganda in the *Santa Fe Republican* finally roused the Texan official from his low profile. Spruce Baird responded with some newspaper articles of his own, which the editor obligingly published. On March 9 the *Republican* even printed the Texas Legislature's Santa Fe County law and portions of the Texas state constitution, all with a short introduction by Baird. But the judge then learned that the *Republican* intended to follow this with the publication of an anti-Texas article by one of the U.S. officers. Baird promptly protested to Colonel Washington on March 21 that, if the agitation did not cease, he would feel absolved from his former promise to suspend Texas's formal claim of jurisdiction. Colonel Washington answered the same day, admonishing Baird not to consider adverse newspaper articles as influencing the Texas claim issue in the slightest. Washington also expressed his desire to put the issue to rest and to work with Baird to settle the problem in a mutually satisfactory manner, and Washington seems to have suppressed the officer's article. This action and the colonel's moderate response helped to convince Baird to await the daily expected news of what the recent session of Congress might have done about New Mexico and the boundary. If word arrived that Congress had done nothing, Baird informed Governor Wood on March 30, he planned to issue copies of his official proclamation—already printed up—of jurisdiction and call for county elections. In the same letter Baird also exaggerated the positive impact he was having on New Mexican opinion and again asserted that he could easily organize the county if the right news arrived from Congress.[55]

The congressional news that reached Santa Fe by the end of March, however, provided an account of the session only to the end of January. Even that partial report was sufficient to incense the New Mexicans, for they learned how little regard Congress had shown their recent petition for government. On April 7 the *Santa Fe Republican* printed several angry editorials condemning the congressional "neglect" of New Mexico. Judge Baird took Congress's inaction on the petition to mean that jurisdiction over the Santa Fe region was probably going to be relinquished to Texas by the federal government. The Texan judge informed Colonel Washington that he would consider all further court proceedings under the Kearny judges as null and void. Colonel Washington seized on the fact that New Mexico had so far received only an incomplete report on the congressional session and responded that the judge should delay any action until the next mail, and a more complete report on Congress, arrived in a few days. The unaggressive Baird desisted until mid-June, when he had another batch of his proclamations printed. Meanwhile, the *Santa Fe Republican* continued to express indignation at the Texas claim.[56]

Back in Austin, Governor Wood and Secretary Miller were very impressed by Baird's view of Texan prospects in New Mexico. W. D. Miller replied on

April 14, encouraging Baird on the governor's behalf to be conciliatory toward the people. On April 17 Governor Wood sent to Baird his proclamation for the general election to be held in Santa Fe County. The new county was listed in Senate District 20, along with Bexar, Medina, Guadalupe, Gillespie, and Comal counties; the district was entitled to one member in the Texas Senate. Santa Fe County was also listed in House District 41 with Bexar, Medina, and Gillespie counties; this district was to elect two members to the Texas House of Representatives. Baird's March 30 letter did not come to Austin until June. Despite Baird's positive attitude in the letter, Governor Wood discerned that Baird was not making substantial progress and that the U.S. military governor was blocking the judge from performing his duties. Therefore, on June 30 George Wood wrote a letter to the new president, Zachary Taylor, requesting to know why the federal government had, unexpectedly and unjustly, laid an adverse claim to the Santa Fe region. The governor again emphasized Texas's need of its public lands to pay its debt and requested that the president issue orders to the U.S. military in New Mexico to aid Texan authorities. Wood had received no reply to his earlier letter to President Polk and he asked President Taylor to reply to this one before the Texas Legislature met in November.[57]

Judge Baird received Governor Wood's election proclamation on or about July 1. Baird met with Colonel Washington on July 3 to request his aid in organizing the county and to discuss continued newspaper hostility to Texas and plans afoot for another New Mexico convention. Colonel Washington attempted to calm Judge Baird's concerns by posing as a believer in the validity of the Texan claim while reiterating that the military governor could do nothing for Texas until the federal government ordered him to. And, of course, he now possessed orders from Crawford that were more neutral than Marcy's earlier pro-Texas ones. Spruce Baird felt comforted by Colonel Washington's solicitude and convinced himself that he would not be able to hold elections and make returns to Austin in time for the next state legislative session. He was also eager to visit his family in Lexington, Missouri. In exchange for Baird's promise not to issue his election proclamation, Colonel Washington promised to keep the press from agitating against Texas, to allow no new convention under his authority or sanction, and to reform the court proceedings of the Kearny judges. Washington also informed Baird that he was soon slated for replacement as the military governor. Baird designated his fellow lawyer and former Texan Palmer J. Pillans to act as Baird's agent during his absence.[58]

Spruce Baird departed from Santa Fe a few days later. Predictably, his mission had failed. The Texas mission might have been impossible anyway, but

Baird had further assured its ruination by his treachery toward James W. Webb, and the accumulation of so many of his own business interests in New Mexico further compromised his devotion to the cause of Texas. Colonel Washington had proven to be very adroit at handling Baird and his demands.

Able as he may have been, however, Colonel Washington never enjoyed popularity in Santa Fe. Partly this represented general resentment against the military government, but also the civil government advocates may have resented the colonel's promises to Baird not to support a new convention. The earlier petition had failed to impress Congress, but the friends of civil government were anxious to try again before the first session of the Thirty-first Congress began in December. The previous convention had met while Major Beall was temporarily in command. Beall, now promoted to lieutenant colonel, appears to have been closely associated with the promoters of civil government in Santa Fe. On July 15, William S. Messervy, W. Z. Angney, Francis X. Aubry, and many others of this group wrote a letter to Secretary of War Crawford requesting that Crawford place Beall in command of the department.[59]

At about the time this letter was dispatched, Indian Agent James S. Calhoun, his family, and an escort of six companies of badly needed reinforcements reached Santa Fe. Whatever his secret instructions were from President Taylor's administration to encourage a statehood movement in New Mexico, Calhoun quickly discovered that this would be a slow process amidst the keenly developing political factions in Santa Fe. Dissent against the three Kearny judges, particularly Joab Houghton, had been gradually building among elements resentful of their power. The most dynamic leader of the opposing faction was Richard H. Weightman, now a Santa Fe lawyer and a rough-and-tumble politician prone to physical violence. On July 24 Weightman and seven other members of the Santa Fe bar charged the three judges with abuse of their power and petitioned them to resign in the "public interest." The judges naturally refused to comply. Judge Houghton replied on July 27 that the lawyers had no right to dictate to him and that the whole affair had been gotten up by its "instigator" Weightman for selfish purposes. The bitterness between the two factions would continue to intensify in ensuing months.[60]

Texas did not dispatch any more agents to Santa Fe in 1849 but did significantly pave the way for its ultimate jurisdictional control over the El Paso area by the establishment of communications to that region from San Antonio. This resulted from two expeditions searching for practicable wagon routes. One was a private expedition financed by Austin's citizens and led by Dr. John S. "Rip"

Ford and U.S. Indian Agent Robert S. Neighbors. Early in 1849 they pioneered a route from San Antonio across the Pecos River to El Paso, the so-called "upper road." The other was a military expedition by Lieutenants W. H. C. Whiting and William F. Smith of the U.S. Topographical Engineers in early 1849. They went out to El Paso roughly along the Neighbors-Ford route but pioneered a more southerly and better-watered route, the "lower road," on their return trip. Many Texans hoped that the roads to El Paso would provide the foundation for the building of a transcontinental railroad through Texas to El Paso and then through the Gila River Valley to California.[61]

Senators Houston and Rusk returned to Texas after Congress adjourned to defend their performance during the previous sessions, particularly their opposition to Calhoun's "Southern Address." Calhounite radical leader Louis T. Wigfall and the *Marshall Texas Republican* in Harrison County, the slaveholding and Southern extremist heart of Texas, roundly condemned the two senators and regularly expounded on the dangers of abolition and race war during the Texas political campaign of 1849.[62]

While Rusk, Houston, and Wigfall hardly touched the Santa Fe question in their addresses, the outcomes of the Texas gubernatorial race and the Second Congressional District seat contest hinged largely on the boundary issue. Governor Wood and Representative Pilsbury were both candidates for reelection to their respective offices. Wood's main challenger was Peter H. Bell, a native Virginian of cultivated bearing who had served as an officer in the Texas Rangers and had fought at San Jacinto in 1836 and at Buena Vista in 1847. Pilsbury's main opponent was Volney Howard, a lawyer and formerly a fiercely partisan Democratic newspaper editor in Mississippi.[63]

Both Wood and Pilsbury appear to have anticipated easy reelection victories. They were both incumbents and their principal opponents had not yet taken active roles in Texas politics; Bell's career had been in the military and Howard had been in the state for only a few years. But Bell and Howard each had a trump card to play, and each played it well—the boundary dispute. Pilsbury had recently assumed a Southern extremist stance in Congress but had appeared indifferent about the Santa Fe issue in 1847 and 1848. Wood had nothing substantial to show for his efforts on New Mexico: his emissary, Spruce Baird, had made no significant progress for Texas; he had written letters to two presidents and neither had responded; and his close association with Sam Houston garnered him the hostility of Houston's bitter enemies. Another factor was personal attractiveness: Bell was more extroverted than the stolid, portly Wood and, at age thirty-seven, was more than fifteen years younger than the incumbent.[64]

Every candidate in the campaigns felt compelled to speak his views on the boundary question. Governor Wood's position was that Texas should sell the area north of 36°30' north latitude to the federal government to satisfy the debt. The two candidates who adopted the toughest, most uncompromising stands on New Mexico were Volney Howard and Peter Bell. Howard proclaimed the Texas title perfect and argued that the Lone Star should send its militia to take armed occupation of Santa Fe County if necessary. He opposed the sale of any of the area, unless it was the portion above where slavery could exist and until after Texas had taken actual possession of all it claimed. Howard pounced on Pilsbury's 1847–48 record of softness in defending the state's title. Peter H. Bell also rang out the call to arms in his public utterances and did not discuss selling any of Texas's claim. Bell declared that he did not believe that the American public would support federal interposition of U.S. forces against the armed force that Texas might send to Santa Fe to protect the civil officials of Texas there. He was willing, Bell said, to make the experiment even if the United States did intervene.[65]

Howard quickly pulled in front of the lackluster Pilsbury in the congressional race. Wood continued to believe, on into mid-July at least, that he would win an easy victory over his opposition. One of Wood's advisers, Col. F. L. Hatch, warned him in June that he had to take a forceful stand on the boundary question, writing to the governor that "this is the charm now to catch the people, particularly the western people." When the election was held in August, however, it was apparent that Bell was the one who had seized the talisman. Both Bell and Howard won their races rather easily.[66]

The boundary dispute was an issue not only in the Texas political campaigns of 1849 but also in New York campaigns. Horace Greeley considered the elections in New York in November to be crucial in determining the fate of New Mexico. Greeley's basic theme in his October and early November editorials was that a victory by Whigs for House seats from New York was essential in order to save New Mexico from Texas and slavery. Greeley's crusade for a New Mexico independent of Texas had much to do with keeping the issue alive in the Northern consciousness as they prepared to send delegations to the Thirty-first Congress.[67]

The movement for another New Mexico convention, which had begun in May, continued to develop after Baird's departure for Missouri in July. The object this time was not only to petition Congress for civil government organization but to dispatch an agent to Washington to plead New Mexico's cause. Colonel

Washington's pledge to Baird not to sanction the planned convention presented only a temporary obstacle to those desirous of a meeting. The colonel's absence on a military expedition left Lieutenant Colonel Beall, an ally of the convention organizers, again in temporary command. Beall either knew nothing of Washington's pledge or, if he did know, considered it nonbinding in the absence of express orders from Colonel Washington in relation to it.[68]

Both of the emerging political factions in New Mexico participated in the move for a convention. One faction, the smaller one, became known as the "state party" since they argued that New Mexico should ask for immediate admission to the Union, as California was in the process of doing. James Calhoun undoubtedly let it be known that statehood for New Mexico was President Taylor's preference. Richard Weightman, Manuel Alvarez, Palmer Pillans, W. Z. Angney, William Messervy, and Calhoun—mainly ambitious politicians outside the existing civil-military power structure—led this bloc. The opposing majority faction favored a territorial form of government. Leadership of this group consisted primarily of Kearny government officials, of whom Judge Joab Houghton was the most prominent. Other leaders included his fellow judges Carlos Beaubien and Antonio José Otero, Donaciano Vigil (who seems to have resigned his nominal governorship by this time), District Attorney Hugh N. Smith, Taos trader Ceran St. Vrain, Dr. Henry Connelly, and other important personages. The great majority of Mexican-American leaders became affiliated with this "territory" faction.[69]

The center of convention planning was Santa Fe. Resolutions passed at public meetings in August requested that Lieutenant Colonel Beall call for mass meetings at designated sites in each county on September 10 to elect delegates to a convention that would meet in Santa Fe on September 24. Beall duly issued the proclamation called for in the resolutions. The veneer of decorum and political civility, however, was rather thin in a frontier town like Santa Fe. The bitter personal rivalry of Weightman and Houghton finally compelled these two into fighting an inconclusive duel, with no one injured, on September 9 outside Santa Fe.[70]

On the day following the duel, September 10, New Mexicans gathered in their public meetings to elect delegates. The campaign, which lasted more than two weeks, had been quite intense. The "state party" of Weightman and Angney (a bit later to be dubbed the "Alvarez faction") and the "territory party" of Houghton and Smith sent their emissaries into every county in their attempt to secure a majority of delegates at the convention. Angney and the minority utilized every political device they could to win friends for their side, but the

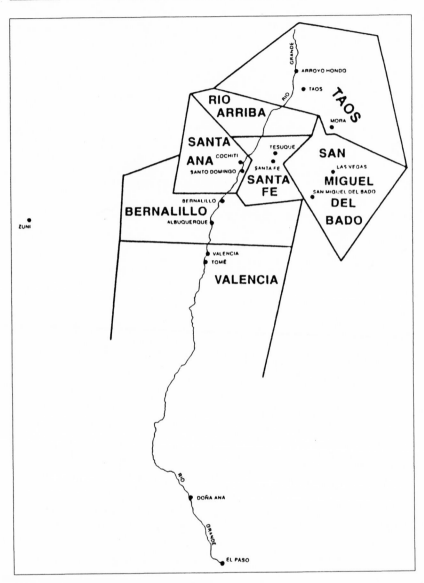

Counties as established by New Mexico, 1840–50.

long-time influence of Houghton and his cohorts proved almost impregnable. Hugh N. Smith literally ran for the job of lobbying for New Mexico's cause in Washington, distributing a circular letter in his own behalf throughout the counties. When the meetings had ended on September 10, the "territory party" had won an overwhelming majority—16 of 21 delegates.[71]

Excitement in New Mexico grew as the convention neared, and on September 24 the delegates assembled at Santa Fe. Fr. José Antonio Martinez, one of the delegates from Taos County, was unanimously elected president of the convention, a position he had occupied in the 1848 convention. Lawyer James Quinn, a nondelegate and close Houghton ally, was chosen secretary over Palmer Pillans. The election of a delegate to Congress was conducted at this first day's assembly. William C. Skinner of Valencia County nominated Hugh N. Smith for the office, and he received 15 votes as opposed to 3 for Weightman and 1 for Houghton. None of the vote-getters was a delegate. Houghton's faction had demonstrated its nearly complete dominance in this first test of voting strength. Father Martinez next appointed a committee of five to work out a constitution for the territory.

The last day of the session, September 26, was another triumph for the "territory party." In fact Judge Houghton, Donaciano Vigil, and Colonel Washington were invited to take honorary seats at the last session. Colonel Washington, just returned from his military expedition, let it be clearly known that he did not approve of this convention called in his absence. But the commander nonetheless accepted the convention's invitation and thereby adorned the meeting with official sanction. W. C. Skinner then offered a majority report of the five-man committee in favor of a territorial form of government, while Dr. Joseph Naugle of Rio Arriba County presented a minority report that, in part, instructed Hugh Smith to seek statehood if territorial government proved unfeasible. The majority report was approved 16 to 3. The instructions given to Smith by the convention avoided the slavery question but did limit the suffrage to free white males, thus excluding blacks from citizenship, and demanded retention of the peonage system, or debtor's servitude, so long a tradition in New Mexico. The convention attempted to avoid the boundary dispute with Texas by proposing, in its very general recommendation on limits, that New Mexico would be bounded on the "east by the state of Texas." Their work completed, the convention adjourned, and Hugh Smith headed east for the nation's capital to press his and New Mexico's cause.[72]

During the months prior to the opening of the Texas legislative session in November, Judge Baird deluged the outgoing Wood administration with a flood of reports on New Mexico. The New Mexicans most fearful of Texas, Baird wrote, were grantees of large tracts of land under the pre-1846 Armijo government, for whom the judge showed no sympathy, given that the grants were made in open defiance of the 1836 Texas law defining the boundary. In several of his reports Baird warned against any division of Texas, proclaimed the certainty that the region was suited to slavery, and urged Texas to construct a Pacific railroad to bind the entire Southwest to Texas. A decided change developed in Baird's letters after he received news of the September 24 convention at Santa Fe. His optimism for the future of Texas's cause in New Mexico waned, replaced in his October 20 letter by a compromise proposal to let New Mexico establish a territorial government over the settled region, as long as Texas retained rights to public land proceeds, mines, and the like. He suggested a boundary beginning north of El Paso and running northeast; Baird felt that such a line would secure the Chihuahua trade for Texas through El Paso and would ensure Texan possession of the Pecos Valley. All that Texas stood to lose would be a "troublesome and worthless" population that could cause only great mischief for the state.[73]

Naturally Baird argued that he had performed his duties for Texas in Santa Fe as well as could be expected under adverse circumstances, but many frustrated Texans disagreed and accused Baird of looking after his own interests in New Mexico rather than those of Texas. Some even demanded that he be tried for treason. The Texas Senate voted 16 to 2 on January 5, 1850, to withhold Baird's $1,750 salary, but the Texas House of Representatives did nothing more than appoint a committee to investigate the judge's conduct. Baird attempted to parry the attacks by writing personally to Governor Bell and sending another letter, which was published in the newspapers. He admitted to the governor that he had purchased land with a flour mill on it but saw nothing wrong with such business activity. The published letter gave a more general and lengthy account of his service, without mention of his personal business interests. Apparently Baird's explanations deflected a good deal of the anger against him, for the matter then died out.[74]

While the pro-Texas presses all agreed on the significance of New Mexico, they differed widely on how Texas might best accomplish its goals. A fiery writer in the *St. Louis Republican* demanded that Texas militarily crush the rebellion, even if it entailed laying waste to New Mexico and leveling every dwelling place therein. Numerous Texans shared that opinion, as evidenced by the letters to incoming Governor Bell from those offering their own or others' military services for such an expedition. However, the predominant attitude of the editorialists was one of moderation. While adhering to the pro forma Southern line

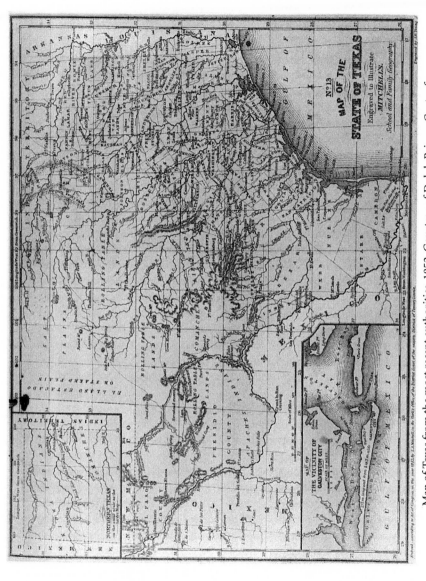

Map of Texas from the most recent authorities, 1852. Courtesy of Dolph Briscoe Center for American History, University of Texas at Austin.

that total devastation of New Mexico and Texas would be preferable to abject surrender of an inch of territory, the Whig *New Orleans Picayune* cautioned the Texans to act in a calm and conciliatory manner before plunging the nation into the chaos of civil war by precipitate military action. The *Bonham* (Tex.) *Advertiser* also supported the exhaustion of peaceful means before any resort to arms; Texas, it said, should reassure New Mexicans of Texan protection for their rights and send more persuasive officials than Baird to Santa Fe.[75]

Houston's leading paper, the *Democratic Telegraph*, reflected all the Texan fears, determination, and, simultaneously, desire for a moderate solution if attainable. Earlier in May, the newspaper had suspected federal hostility toward the Texas claim in the army's decision to divide Texas and New Mexico into separate U.S. military departments. In September it reported that Gen. George M. Brooke, the U.S. commander of the Eighth Military Department (Texas), opposed the 1836 claim. Even the question of location for the Texas capital became entangled in the New Mexican web; the *Telegraph* argued that removal of the capital from Austin to some site further east would stimulate the move to dismember Texas and establish a separate free-soil polity in New Mexico. Despite its sensitivity on the Santa Fe issue, the Houston paper decried a military solution and believed that Texas should once more request federal help in enforcing the Texan claim. One of its editorials in November 1849 again suggested the possibility of relinquishing the Texan claim in exchange for Federal assumption of the Texas debt. If Federal recalcitrance proved incorrigible or if Congress chose to admit Hugh Smith as New Mexican delegate, the *Telegraph* declared, then would be the time for Texas to withdraw its delegation from Congress and to consider reverting to its former status as an independent republic.[76]

The November assembly of the Texas Legislature was given especial urgency with the arrival at Austin in late October of the first definite information relative to the September convention in Santa Fe, although this report mistakenly indicated that immediate statehood was to be the aim of the convention. At the beginning of the session, outgoing Governor Wood, in his final annual message, recommended the adoption of unspecified "energetic" measures that would provide the governor with ample power and means to enforce Texan jurisdiction east of the Rio Grande. He proposed sending commissioners to Washington to convince the federal authorities of Texan determination, urged the construction of a good road from Austin to Santa Fe, and recommended a suitable disposal of the public domain to retire the public debt. He also broached the subject of the federal purchase of the remote northwestern portion of Texas for use as an Indian refuge. The overall tone of the New Mexico segment of the message was belligerent, as Wood spoke of defending Texas honor with power.[77]

For Wood's proposed "energetic" measures to be enacted, he needed the endorsement of a fairly unisonous legislature anxious to take radical action. Most of the legislators were men in their thirties and forties, and nearly all hailed originally from slaveholding states; the great majority consisted of farmers and lawyers, and about 40 percent were slaveholders themselves.[78] They also reflected the divided feelings of the Texas populace; all agreed they were being cheated and robbed by the federal government, but many did not wish to send Texas troops to conquer Santa Fe, an action that almost certainly would result in a bloody collision with U.S. forces.

Differing views on the proper means for resolving the crisis were evident in the House debate on the Santa Fe question on November 29 and December 3. On the 29th, following the arrival the previous evening of Baird's report on the New Mexican convention, Rep. James S. Gillett from Lamar County on the Red River introduced a joint resolution that would instruct the Texas delegation in Congress to withdraw if Congress admitted Hugh Smith as a delegate from New Mexico. Representatives from widely separated counties—William Stewart of Gonzales in the southwest and Joshua Johnson from Titus in the northeast corner—attacked Gillett's plan. James C. Wilson, from the counties on Matagorda Bay, and William Fields, from Liberty and Polk counties in the southeast corner, defended the proposal vigorously and, in Fields's case, even threatened secession. On December 3 Wilson offered a substitute resolution instructing the Texas delegation to protest any congressional recognition of New Mexico as a dismemberment of Texas and authorizing the governor to use military force to suppress what Wilson later termed the "greasers" revolt. Neither Gillett's nor Wilson's proposal was extreme enough for Benjamin Tarver of Washington County north of Austin or Jeremiah Clough of Harrison County in the northeast (the two counties with the most slaves in Texas); they believed any protest cast a shadow on a clear title and favored the immediate use of Texas's military forces to protect their civil officials. With no prospect of unity behind these or other suggested proposals, the House on December 3 referred all of them to the special joint committee on the Santa Fe issue.[79]

While the joint committee appointed in late November tackled the maze of diverse proposals on New Mexico, the legislature began the process of passing related acts on which the lawmakers attained general consensus. Two of these

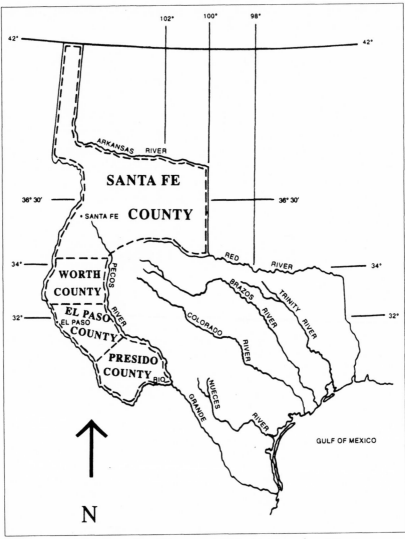

Western counties of Texas as established in December 1849.

acts subdivided the once-huge Santa Fe County into four counties; one limited Santa Fe County to the far northwest segment of the Texan claim, while another created the counties of Worth, El Paso, and Presidio to the south. The four together were to form one Texas senate district, but Santa Fe County would have its own representative in the lower house as opposed to a single representative for the other three counties combined. Another law adjusted the Eleventh Judicial District to encompass the new arrangement of counties. A further law provided that a single commissioner be appointed to organize each county.[80]

On December 21 the legislators took a brief respite from their labors to attend the inauguration of Peter H. Bell as the new governor. George Wood, in his valedictory address, reiterated the theme that Texas must defend its title to Santa Fe to the last extremity and surrender it only when the state had no soldiers left to fight. By contrast, Governor Bell's inaugural speech was extremely moderate, full of generalities and platitudes, and proclaimed the need for Texas both to defend her own rights and to stand by the Union.[81]

Governor Bell made his plans more explicit in his first message to the legislature a few days later on December 26. By this stage of the legislative session, Bell, even with his lack of political experience, could discern that Wood's proposal for blatant military resolution of the Santa Fe issue was a dead letter. Bell's more cautious program called for a conditional use of state military forces. The new governor did propose that a "sufficient" military force be sent to assist Texan civil officials in extending jurisdiction over the four counties and said that he anticipated no interference with this move by the federal authorities on the scene. Bell felt that Texas should dispatch a commissioner to Washington to demand firmly, but without threats, a termination of civil government functions by the U.S. military east of the Rio Grande. Only if the federal government continued its resistance to Texan demands should Texas utilize the whole power of the state to subdue New Mexico. As to the payment of what by that time amounted to a ten-million-dollar debt, Governor Bell favored the use of land certificates and also the sale of the several hundred miles of Texas territory above 36°30' north latitude—the Missouri Compromise line—to the federal government. More remarkable was Bell's suggestion that the legislature should even permit the governor to entertain any federal proposal for the purchase of the area between 34° and 36°30' north latitude—an area that included Santa Fe. The governor cited Texan financial liabilities, heavy interest on the debt, and the remoteness of the region from Texas proper as reasons for considering such a federal purchase, although he also declared that Texas would sell only the soil, not its sovereignty over the area. Texas, he said, owed it to the South and to the protection of slavery to maintain its political sovereignty over New Mexico east of the Rio Grande.[82]

Before dealing with Bell's proposals, the two houses did pass the four bills relative to Santa Fe and the other counties in the first few days of January 1850.

As soon as the bill authorizing the appointment of a commissioner was approved on January 4, Governor Bell selected the ruggedly handsome, thirty-six-year-old former U.S. Indian agent Robert Simpson Neighbors for the position. Neighbors requested on January 8 that he be allowed to draw his $550 salary in advance to avoid financial embarrassment. The House easily approved the request two days later, but the Senate delayed approval of this seemingly uncontroversial measure until February 8, just prior to the session's end. By that time Neighbors was long departed on his journey. The Senate delay in sanctioning the commissioner's salary advance reflected that body's indecision over general policy in reference to Santa Fe. On the last day of the session, February 11, the legislature quietly passed a joint resolution reasserting the 1836 Texan boundary claim. Concerning the related matter of slavery itself, the legislature in late January adopted a joint resolution defending constitutional rights to slave property in the territories and promising Southern states' resistance to any federal interference with those rights or with the right to hold slaves in the District of Columbia. The legislators followed with a joint resolution providing for the election of eight Texas delegates to the proposed Southern-rights convention at Nashville.[83]

The major proposals in Bell's message, however, were simply too extreme to make headway in a badly divided legislature. On January 24 the Senate State Affairs Committee reported that under ordinary circumstances a cession by Texas to the federal government of land north of the Missouri Compromise line would be correct policy. But, given the utterly disrespectful attitude of high U.S. officials toward Texas and its claim, such a cession would be "impolitic and unwise" and would demonstrate a lack of self-respect on the part of Texas. An attempt on February 1 in the House to amend a public debt bill to embrace Santa Fe in any land sold to the United States was quickly rejected.[84]

The proposals more seriously considered dealt with potential Texan action to enforce its jurisdiction over Santa Fe. Having digested a menagerie of ideas and plans, the special joint committee on Santa Fe reported on January 25 and 26 that the Taylor administration had proven unalterably hostile toward Texas and that Texas must either take positive action to maintain its claim or submit to arbitrary federal power. The committee recommended that if the U.S. government proceeded to establish a territorial government for New Mexico, then the governor should employ the total military and financial resources of Texas to extend and enforce the state's rightful jurisdiction. A joint resolution embodying these provisions passed the Senate on January 30 by a very slim margin after several hotly contested and evenly divided roll calls. However, the

House refused to take up the resolution until February 9 and then killed the measure by failing to pass it to a third reading.[85]

The Senate voting on this joint resolution covered six roll-call votes and demonstrated the very clear-cut division of Senate blocs on the issue. These roll calls covered procedure, amendments, and, the final one, the third reading and passage. A "moderate" bloc opposed the measure while a "radical" bloc favored it (see Appendix A). On the six roll calls, only one member of the moderate bloc cast a stray vote, out of sixty votes cast, while only five stray votes were cast out of sixty-nine by the radical bloc. The Rice Index of Cohesion for the "moderate" bloc measures .967 out of a possible 1.000. The cohesion value for the radical bloc is .855. Each bloc was not only highly cohesive but also remarkably consistent in voting against the opponent bloc. The Rice Index of Likeness on these roll calls is .089 out of a possible 1.000, a very low value indicative of almost diametrically opposite voting by the two blocs. The voting pattern was somewhat sectional. Eight of the radical bloc represented more westerly counties of Texas; only one of the moderate bloc represented such a county. Nine of the ten moderate members hailed from east Texas, as compared to only four of the twelve radical members.[86]

When it became clear, as the session neared its adjournment, that the committee's "force" resolution was hopelessly stalled in the House, the special joint committee brought forth a series of specific proposals. One measure was a bill to establish a "court of organization" of three judges for Santa Fe County. A second bill stipulated that the governor should raise a company of fifty-six men to escort the judges and enforce their decrees. Accompanying the two bills was a joint resolution instructing the Texas delegation in Congress to demand that the president order U.S. authorities in Santa Fe to support and assist the Texas officials. These three measures constituted a virtual admission by the joint committee that they had lost faith in the ability of Commissioner Neighbors to accomplish these goals. The Texas House took up the committee proposals on February 5 and passed them on February 9. The Senate considered only the "court of organization" bill but voted 15 to 1 to postpone it indefinitely. The session closed and Robert Neighbors was left to do the best he could.[87]

A few weeks before the legislature adjourned, Sen. Benjamin Rush Wallace of San Augustine County described the quandary of that session in a letter to his friend Senator Rusk in Washington. He pointed out that, even though "incendiary resolutions" had been introduced, Texas would adopt no strong measures until U.S. policy on Santa Fe became definite. Wallace's letter indicated, then, that the division in the Texas Legislature was between those anxious for immediate forceful action and those who opposed such steps as long as a glimmer of doubt existed about the federal government's attitude toward the Texas claim. The state "will be willing to gambol as the lamb or roar as the Lion according to circumstances," Wallace wrote. A hostile federal policy would explode the disunion "volcano" in Texas. Texans would not allow anyone else to pluck Santa Fe from them, he said, even if the area were worthless, like a man's beard.[88]

Chapter Three

❧

Neighbors, Munroe, and McCall
Three Men & the Fate of New Mexico

COMMISSIONER ROBERT NEIGHBORS WAS ABOUT TO PLUNGE HEADLONG INTO
A situation over which he had little control. While the issue was one of national
importance in the sectional crisis, Neighbors was primarily concerned with the
completion of his immediate mission of organizing Texas counties where Texas
had never before exercised de facto jurisdiction. The mission coincided conveniently with a hiatus in Neighbors's career as an Indian agent. When Whig
Zachary Taylor assumed the presidency, Democrat Neighbors had been "ro-
tated" out of his agency. Neighbors was certainly popular in the El Paso region,
where people fondly remembered how Neighbors and Rip Ford had pioneered
a wagon road in 1849 from San Antonio to El Paso, and he could be expected to
organize that county with relative ease. However, Robert Neighbors was a novice in political affairs and would be on totally unfamiliar ground once he traveled north from El Paso into the maelstrom of competing factions in Santa Fe.[1]

The Texas commissioner was not the only newcomer destined to play a role
in the fate of New Mexico in 1850. Bvt. Col. John Munroe had already arrived at
Santa Fe, replacing Colonel Washington as department commander in October 1849, and Lt. Col. George McCall was on his way from Washington as a
special emissary of the Taylor administration and would reach Santa Fe a few
weeks before Neighbors.

John Munroe, a tall Scots immigrant, was possessed of a remarkably ugly
bulldog countenance, a precise and stubborn intellect, and a bad temper in the
morning before he relaxed with strong drink around noon. But what he lacked

in personality and looks, Munroe made up for in a long career of efficient service in the artillery. He had served under Taylor in Florida and at Buena Vista and most recently had been stationed in Georgia. Munroe proceeded from Savannah to New York, whence he and another officer led recruits for two dragoon companies to Fort Leavenworth, where they were joined by two companies of infantry also destined for New Mexico. The whole group, numbering some 250, traversed the nine hundred weary miles of the Santa Fe Trail during the late summer of 1849 and finally arrived at their destination in October.[2]

Munroe's no-nonsense temperament would be amply tested by the multi-faceted situation over which he was now the supreme military and civil authority. His fewer than one thousand scattered troops, mainly infantry of limited usefulness against mobile Indian raiders on horseback, reportedly faced tens of thousands of "hostiles." Munroe's first order relative to this situation was very popular and reassuring to the citizenry; he commanded that all officers of the department remain within the confines of that department. Munroe was also responsible for maintaining law and order among the settlers. Santa Fe, with its gambling halls and other houses of vice, took on near-biblical proportions of degeneracy for the more religious California-bound emigrants who sojourned there. Newspaper accounts of murder and other violence were still all too commonplace, despite the military's good efforts to maintain order.[3]

Munroe also had to contend with the unabated competition between the "state" and "territory" factions. Following the September convention and the departure of "delegate" Hugh Smith for Washington, the "state" party (Weightman, Calhoun, Alvarez, Pillans, et al.) continued its assault against Houghton, his fellow judges, and virtually everyone in the "territory" faction. In early October, this group organized a meeting in Santa Fe at which William S. Messervy blamed federal authorities in Washington for abandoning New Mexico to the abuses inherent in military government. In December and January Weightman and his faction organized a petition drive and letter-writing campaign in an attempt to induce either Colonel Munroe or the Taylor administration to throw out Judge Houghton, but the federal authorities in Santa Fe and Washington did not choose to do so. The "state" faction believed that the great majority of New Mexicans deeply resented the Kearny government appointees but were so numbed by oppression and fearful of the arbitrary power that they succumbed to it. Despite some popular resentment, though, the "territory" group retained the loyalty of most New Mexicans.[4]

Well-founded rumors of the War Department's more neutral stance toward Texan officials in New Mexico and information about Texan activities in the El

Paso area spurred the "state" bloc into action. Beginning on November 24, the group issued a newspaper called the *New Mexican*, the first issue of which argued that Congress was unlikely to establish a territorial government for New Mexico since the slavery issue was so intertwined with territories. California had formed a state government; the Utah Mormons were reportedly doing the same. New Mexico's peculiar situation, the paper claimed, made statehood an imperative. Col. John C. Frémont had estimated that the California–New Mexico boundary lay roughly not over fifty miles west of the Rio Grande, and Texas claimed everything east of the Rio Grande; if Taylor remained neutral, New Mexico might be reduced to a thin strip of territory west of the Rio Grande unless New Mexicans boldly established a state constitution. Two weeks later, on December 8, the statehood faction published its manifesto in the *New Mexican*, reiterating many of the same points stressed in the earlier editorial. They argued that a territorial government would merely exchange the military for another ruling group of outsiders chosen by Washington. Only as a state could New Mexico protect its own interests. The address played on New Mexican fears of being swallowed up by Texas on the east and south and cited reports of individual Texan land claims east of El Paso and as far north as Doña Ana. Texas "is quietly, day after day, approaching your capital."[5]

The "territory" party responded a few days later with their own broadside manifesto against the views of the "Alvarez group," as they referred to it. Houghton and his compatriots maintained that Congress would indeed grant them a territorial government quite capable of satisfying New Mexico's needs. The "territory" party refuted the argument for state government by asserting that New Mexico's people fiscally could not then shoulder the extra burden of taxation caused by the establishment and maintenance of a state government. Under territorial government, the federal government would assume many administrative costs. Regarding the slavery issue, the territorial broadside insisted that Congress would be dominated by realistic moderates who would understand the impossibility—due chiefly to climatic and geographic factors—of forcing slavery into New Mexico; therefore, Congress would grant the territorial government that New Mexico's convention and delegate requested. The "territory" party declared that statehood was an impossibility for New Mexico until Congress set a definitive boundary between New Mexico and Texas and until a joint U.S.-Mexican commission delineated the boundary between the two countries.[6]

The two documents showed clearly that the "state" party aggressively utilized the boundary dispute with Texas to promote New Mexico statehood, while the "territory" party obviously downplayed the issue to avoid conflict with Texas.

Certainly great majorities of both factions and the populace in New Mexico dreaded a Texan takeover and opposed the introduction of African slavery into the region, preferring instead to continue debtor's servitude or peonage as a system of forced labor. An army officer at Santa Fe, Bvt. Maj. Henry L. Kendrick, said there were but three subjects that excited New Mexicans: "Taxation, which they dislike; slavery, which they hate, and Texas, which they most cordially abhor." The supreme irony of the two political manifestos was that the "state" party, which so heavily emphasized the Texas issue in its address, was the faction least opposed to Texas. Richard Weightman, the unscrupulous former Missourian, was not a Texas agent, despite charges to the contrary; he simply pursued political opportunism depending on events in Austin or Washington. One actual Texas agent can be identified among the signers of the "state" manifesto—Palmer J. Pillans, the former Texan who then worked for the army quartermaster at Santa Fe and also practiced law. Pillans had worked with Baird and also corresponded with Texas officials. Given the way in which the "state" party presented evidence apparently supporting the Texas claim, someone like Pillans could as easily assent to and sign the address as one genuinely fearful of Texas. As for James Calhoun, he may have been President Taylor's agent, but he was also a Southerner from Georgia and apparently kept Senator Rusk of Texas informed of New Mexican developments. The main interest of most members in the "state" group was the struggle for power against the entrenched politicians who comprised the bulk of the "territory" faction, no matter what methods or allegiances were necessary.[7]

Colonel Munroe undoubtedly gained valuable knowledge about the competing factions and political issues of New Mexico from the manifestos. His first practical experience with the boundary problem, however, arose from understandable confusion over it on the part of Munroe's subordinate commander at El Paso, Maj. Jefferson Van Horne. El Paso del Norte (now Ciudad Juarez) was originally the name of the settlement on the western, or Mexican, bank of the Rio Grande. A handful of American settlements and trading posts were set up on the American side in the late 1840s, among them Frontera, Coon's Ranch (or Franklin), and Magoffinsville. In September 1849 Van Horne and six companies of the 3d U.S. Infantry Regiment established the American military presence at what they termed the "Post Opposite El Paso." The principal encampment was at Coon's Ranch; another post was occupied at San Elizario, about twenty-two miles south on the "island" that also held the settlements of Ysleta and Socorro. The San Elizario position was held by two companies under command of Bvt. Maj. William S. Henry, who had brought his wife and family along on the Van Horne expedition.[8]

Almost as soon as Van Horne arrived in the area, he found himself besieged by complaining citizens. Richard Howard of San Antonio, who had escorted the Whiting-Smith expedition and who also professed to be an authorized Texas surveyor, represented a group of Texans claiming exclusive rights to the salt deposits east of El Paso, while the prefect of the New Mexican government, T. Frank White of Frontera, asserted that he had exclusive rights to collect taxes for the Kearny government in the lands staked out by Howard and his friends. Van Horne pointed out that an earlier general order of 1848 had defined the line between the Eighth (Texas) and Ninth (New Mexico) military departments as 32° north latitude, which was said to be south of El Paso. But, as Van Horne noted, the 32° north latitude line was actually fifteen miles north of El Paso, and even before the war New Mexico had not exercised jurisdiction south of that line. Van Horne did not know which side to take and, therefore, on September 23 wrote to his commander at Santa Fe for clarification of the matter. This letter's details of the jurisdictional conflict at El Paso somehow leaked out in Santa Fe and provided at least some of the impetus for the "state" party's newspaper alarms.[9]

Munroe referred the jurisdiction issue to the Adjutant General's Office for an authoritative determination. While awaiting a reply from Washington, Munroe instructed Van Horne on December 28 that, in the absence of any acting civil authority, he should enforce the laws of the Kearny government at Santa Fe in order to provide citizens with civil protection until such time as Texas assumed those duties or until Congress settled the Texas-New Mexico boundary question. Munroe's order to Van Horne did not violate the War Department's neutrality mandate, which had arrived at Santa Fe by that time; he simply instructed Van Horne to exercise governmental authority where there was none in place until Texas set up the civil jurisdiction it claimed. Munroe meant Van Horne's extension of jurisdiction to be conditional and temporary, "a matter of necessity not of right."[10]

By the time the War Department received word of what was going on at El Paso, the department had already issued General Order 58 in December. The new order redefined the boundary between the Eighth and Ninth departments and clearly placed the settlements from San Elizario northward in the Ninth Military Department. When the War Department received Van Horne's September letter, the adjutant general responded in February 1850 that the department could not settle the Texas–New Mexico jurisdiction question and that Munroe should follow previous orders. When Munroe's December instructions to Van Horne reached Washington, however, Secretary of War Crawford misinterpreted Munroe's order as an attempt to settle the boundary dispute adverse to Texas. He directed the adjutant general to reiterate to Munroe that the executive branch had no right to decide the issue and that the only laws in force were those of New Mexico at the time of conquest, or ones that Texas might impose. This reprimand led Munroe to apologize to the adjutant general in his letter of May 23, 1850, stating that he should have continued the jurisdiction originated by Colonel Washington over the "island" of San Elizario but not extended it further. War Department involvement in the El Paso question was superfluous anyway, for, by the time the adjutant general's missives reached New Mexico, events had rendered them obsolete.[11]

El Paso was the first major target of the Texas commissioner, Maj. Robert Neighbors, who readied himself for his departure from Austin in the first week of January 1850. His instructions from Texas secretary of state James Webb, dated January 8, outlined the process Neighbors was to follow in conducting county elections and what offices should be established. Webb provided the commissioner with numerous copies, in English and Spanish, of the Texas constitution and laws to facilitate his task and admonished him to combine "firmness and decision" with "mildness and courtesy of manner" in dealing with the people of the new Texas counties. Neighbors himself left Austin on January 10 or 11.[12]

Another agent besides Neighbors, Bvt. Lt. Col. George A. McCall, was preparing for his journey to New Mexico. Before Neighbors received his instructions from Texas authorities, McCall had received his orders from Secretary of War Crawford to aid the statehood movement in New Mexico. As an officer in the 3d U.S. Infantry, McCall was due to rejoin his regiment in New Mexico after convalescing from an illness incurred during the Mexican War. A few days after being ordered to Santa Fe, McCall received a letter from Secretary Crawford requesting McCall, then in Philadelphia, to stop in Washington for an interview with him before leaving for New Mexico. Crawford provided McCall with a letter of instructions, dated November 19, 1849, which pointed out that, since Congress had failed to provide a civil government to the people of New Mexico, they themselves might decide to remedy the situation and ask for admission as a state. The key passage declared, "Should the people of New Mexico wish to take any steps towards this object, . . . it will be your duty, and the duty of others with whom you are associated not to thwart but to advance their wishes." This carefully worded order was obviously constructed to raise as little controversy as possible when it would later be made public during the clamorous congressional debates of 1850.[13]

Meanwhile, in Texas, Commissioner Neighbors first journeyed to San Antonio, where Francis X. Aubry, the famous trapper and trader, provided Neighbors with information about the political attitudes in New Mexico. While at San Antonio, Neighbors met and talked with Colonel McCall, who had arrived there on December 31, but McCall did not reveal to Neighbors his mission for the Taylor administration. Neighbors was accompanied by eight other persons when he left San Antonio in mid-January. Colonel McCall remained behind, gathering enough mules and food for his dragoon recruits and learning what he could about the route from topographical engineers and other officers. McCall's detachment left San Antonio on February 2.[14]

One of the eight who accompanied the Texas commissioner who can be identified with certainty was William Cockburn, a thirty-seven-year-old Scots immigrant who had been in Texas since the 1830s and resided in Austin with his wife and four children. He had served as doorkeeper and general handyman for the Texas House of Representatives, beginning in 1841, and for the Texas Constitutional Convention of 1845. Most recently he had identified himself as a trader, but of what it is not clear. Neighbors brought Cockburn along to assist in the organization of El Paso County. Had Neighbors realized what other interests Cockburn planned to pursue, he surely would have left him behind.[15]

Others involved in the expedition included two young black men—one the slave of Cockburn, the other the slave of Dr. Joseph Rowe of Travis County. Whether Rowe was also accompanying Neighbors is uncertain, since he may have simply hired out a slave to Neighbors to help in the journey with such tasks as caring for the pack animals. Another possible member of the commissioner's entourage was John James of San Antonio, and later of Socorro, New Mexico. He would later help Neighbors, as Cockburn did, in organizing the El Paso County elections (but it is possible that James had already moved to Socorro before Neighbors's arrival). Evidence on the possible identities of the others who journeyed with Neighbors has not turned up.[16]

The Neighbors party did not follow the Neighbors-Ford "upper road"; instead they traveled on the Whiting-Smith "lower road," which the Van Horne expedition with the 3d U.S. Infantry had recently used. Such winter trips as Neighbors undertook were always susceptible to hazardous weather conditions, and the Neighbors party encountered snowstorms, the worst of which dumped four or five inches of snow on the ground. Under these conditions, the party's mules broke down, and the commissioner had to abandon his multiple copies of Texas laws and other documents. At some point on the journey, the two slaves apparently took horses and bolted from camp in a bid for freedom, only to be attacked on February 20 on the western side of the Pecos River by four lawless ruffians from Leaton's Fort, a private trading establishment well to the southwest on the Rio Grande. One victim was discovered still alive the next day by Colonel McCall's men, but the young man succumbed three days later. (The Neighbors party itself did manage to rescue a Mexican boy from Indian captors on January 24 at Devil's River, and Neighbors later returned the boy to his mother near Laredo.)[17]

The commissioner and his party passed through the farming communities of the "island" and reached the cluster of trading posts in the El Paso vicinity, probably on February 16 or 17, after a thirty-two-day trip from San Antonio. The largely Mexican and Pueblo Indian population of the region particularly feared that Texans and other whites would steal their lands, as exemplified most obviously by the maneuvering of Richard Howard and friends to control the "salines" in total disregard of the long-standing claims of those holding Mexican titles. The Mexicans and Pueblos were well aware of the cultural superiority assumed by the aggressive Anglos, such as Howard or a former mayor of Mobile who was now a trader in the El Paso area, Charles A. Hoppin. Major Neighbors was aware of native fears, as Judge Baird had also been, and the commissioner believed that Texas must pledge security for the old land titles in order to win the adherence of the Mexican-Indian majority to the organization of El Paso as a county of Texas.[18]

Actually, Neighbors found his task of organizing El Paso County an easy one. He tried to calm the fears of older settlers over land titles by personally pledging that the General Land Office of Texas would honor no more claims in the area until the existing titles were investigated, even though he had no assurance that the Texas government would validate this move. Even if the natives were not fully convinced, they offered no opposition to Texas organization. The Anglo settlers were exuberant at the prospect of civil organization under Texan auspices, something that Hoppin had been pleading with Governor Bell to institute. Major Van Horne, following Munroe's order of December 28, placed no barriers in Neighbors's way. Even the New Mexican prefect, T. Frank White of Frontera, relinquished his jurisdiction over the area from Doña Ana south to San Elizario to the Texas commissioner. Neighbors, with Cockburn and other assistants, busily posted election notices and circulated Governor Bell's proclamation extolling the virtues of finally receiving county jurisdiction in the area Texas had long claimed.[19]

The elections took place on March 4 and were accompanied by the traditional Mexican fandangos to celebrate the event. The American newcomers dominated politics from the start. The strongly pro-Southern Charles A. Hoppin won the election for chief justice of the county, while Samuel W. Barker became county clerk and LeRoy Vining sheriff. San Elizario was chosen as the county seat. Voters also cast ballots, as other Texans were doing that year, to decide the site of the state capital, and El Paso County gave 760 votes for Austin as against three for Huntsville and one for San Antonio. On March 23, in a letter from Doña Ana, Neighbors joyously reported to Governor Bell that El Paso County was fully organized. He recommended several people as possible choices for notaries public and particularly lauded the assistance of John James and William Cockburn. Neighbors dispatched this letter and the election results back with Cockburn, who, in a party with thirteen others, conducted a remarkably fast return trip to Austin in twenty-one days.[20]

Had Neighbors known of Cockburn's plans prior to his Austin journey, the commissioner would have been less ebullient about his success. While at Doña Ana, Cockburn had successfully enlisted the post commander, Bvt. Maj. Enoch Steen, in the Texan cause by selling him a Texas headright for a 640-acre parcel of land—a parcel including the town of Doña Ana and surrounding lands, all of which were presumably owned under earlier Mexican titles by the wealthy Guadalupe Miranda and others. Cockburn's actions directly contradicted Neighbors's pledges and confirmed indigenous settlers' worst fears of the Texans. Neighbors appears to have been totally ignorant of this arrangement before he departed for Santa Fe in the last week of March. What authority Cockburn had, if any, for making such a grant is not recorded, and the document involved in the transaction seems not to have been recorded locally or with the Texas General Land Office. In fact it is likely that Cockburn simply swindled Major Steen with a bogus headright and escaped back to Austin with whatever Steen paid him. All that Neighbors appeared cognizant of was Steen's effusive adherence to the Texas cause. As the commissioner declared to Governor Bell in his March 23 letter, "The Majr. is a gallant officer, and a perfect Gentleman. He is a perfect *Texan* in principle, and the strongest *advocate* of our claims, I have yet found in this Territory. He declares openly, that he would resign his Commission and take up arms to defend the Texas Claim to this Territory."[21]

The offended citizens of Mexican descent no longer trusted Neighbors enough even to protest to him; instead, they quietly drafted a petition, dated March 12 and signed by Guadalupe Miranda, Rafael Ruelas, and more than forty others, and sent it directly to Colonel Munroe at Santa Fe. They protested that the Steen headright violated their natural rights, promises made to them by General Kearny, and guarantees under the Treaty of Guadalupe Hidalgo. This incident may have been the immediate cause for the founding of the town of Mesilla on the western bank of the Rio Grande by Rafael Ruelas and others in 1850 beyond any possible Texan claim and on what they believed would be the Mexican side of the international boundary when the line was finally determined; they founded Mesilla to avoid just such American land-grab schemes as the Steen headright. The protest did not specify which Texan sold the headright to Steen, leaving the impression in Santa Fe that Neighbors himself was responsible for it. The petitioners may have entrusted their document into the hands of Colonel McCall, for he and his men were passing through Doña Ana at about the time the petition was dated. If this was so, the Doña Ana protest reached Colonel Munroe on the night of March 20, when McCall arrived at Santa Fe.[22]

Major Steen, fifty years old at the time, was a career dragoon officer who had served on numerous expeditions on the Great Plains before serving bravely in the Mexican War. He had come to Doña Ana in 1849 to establish the dragoon post and, because of his aggressive and effective campaigns against the Apaches, had become quite popular among the local citizens. The reason why this otherwise commendable military leader allowed himself to be seduced into a land scheme by Cockburn is easily discernible. While Neighbors was at Doña Ana, Steen showed him and Sheriff Vining various ore samples, including one with traces of gold from the Gila River area. Deposits of copper and silver were also known to be in the hills near Doña Ana, and many people were hoping that the region might provide a bonanza of mineral wealth. Steen, it seems, sought to put himself in a position peculiarly advantageous for reaping profits from the anticipated rush by gaining ownership of the town that would be in the center of the mining boom (Las Cruces, of which Doña Ana is now a small appendage, did not yet exist).[23]

Before receiving the protest against the Steen headright, Munroe had received a February 23 letter from Neighbors about his mission. Munroe responded on March 12 with a short, blunt order to Steen and six other post commanders that they and their commands observe a "rigid non-interference" with Neighbors or Texan judicial authorities. This directive was quite consistent with War Department orders to maintain neutrality and not really inconsistent with Munroe's own earlier order to Van Horne, although the order to Van Horne could be, and was, interpreted by free-soil advocates back east as too pro-Texas.[24]

Neighbors was still at Doña Ana when the noninterference order arrived, and he saw Steen's copy. The commissioner certainly interpreted the letter to mean that Munroe himself would at least not oppose Neighbors's organizational efforts once he reached Santa Fe. He had also received communications from pro-Texas citizens—Pillans doubtless among them—to come to Santa Fe as soon as possible. Commissioner Neighbors had long since concluded that Santa Fe should be his next goal; remote Worth County, immediately to the north, depended entirely on the situation at Santa Fe, while Presidio County to the south was so dominated by hostile Indians and Ben Leaton's ruffians that Neighbors dared not attempt organization there without a substantial military escort. The road to Santa Fe was so dangerous that one did not venture out alone on it, and Neighbors awaited a suitable opportunity to join up with some sizable group of traders or soldiers heading north. Bvt. Maj. William S. Henry provided that opportunity.[25]

Henry was another career officer, a West Pointer who had served valorously in the Mexican War and then commanded the 3d U.S. Infantry post at San Elizario. When Henry's family wished to return East and Henry's request for permission to conduct them to San Antonio was denied as being counter to Colonel Munroe's stated policy that all officers remain in the Ninth Military Department, Henry took his family to Santa Fe, whence they could accompany Colonel Washington's wagon train heading east on the Santa Fe Trail. He detailed a lieutenant and fifteen men from his post to serve as a military escort. The Henry party left San Elizario about March 23 and reached Doña Ana probably two days later. While stopped there, Major Steen gave Henry ore samples from the surrounding hills to be analyzed in Santa Fe for their precious mineral content. Commissioner Neighbors of Texas also joined the expedition when it left Doña Ana for Santa Fe on March 28. Even if Major Henry had not yet received his copy of Munroe's "rigid non-interference" order, he surely saw Steen's copy at Doña Ana and should have realized that his travel arrangements with Neighbors might be easily frowned on in Santa Fe. But Henry agreed with the Texan viewpoint, and orders to the contrary were no obstacle to him. As he later stated, he considered it his duty "to help Neighbors and to further his political mission out of respect to Texas & in a firm belief that her claim to the country to which he was sent to effect a political organization was undoubted." The whole situation presented a nice irony: a Texas official was provided with a U.S. Army escort to proceed to Santa Fe to demand that the U.S. Army commander in New Mexico relinquish to Texas all his civil jurisdiction east of the Rio Grande.[26]

The journey from Doña Ana to Santa Fe required eleven days and covered nearly three hundred miles of the most desolate terrain. The worst part began about twelve miles north of Doña Ana and was appropriately known as the "Jornada del Muerto," the journey of death. This was a ninety-mile stretch of tableland devoid of water. The Henry-Neighbors party was constantly on the look-out for signs of hostile Indians, but no confrontations occurred. They arrived at Santa Fe safely on April 8.[27]

Robert Neighbors could not have imagined how heavily the odds were weighted against him in Santa Fe even before he left Doña Ana. Before sending Neighbors's February 23 letter on to the adjutant general, Colonel Munroe had shared the contents of it with the leader of the territorial faction, Judge Houghton. The irrepressible Houghton had wasted no time in issuing a stirring call to action. His proclamation, issued in Spanish on March 13 (the day after Munroe sent his non-interference order), warned the populace of the Texas commissioner's intrusion into New Mexico, urged them to resist "the unjust usurpation" by Texas, and encouraged the citizens both to boycott any elections Neighbors might hold and to respect none of his actions. Houghton demanded that protest meetings be organized throughout the territory and that their resolutions be forwarded to Santa Fe for publication. These actions, Houghton stated, should help render Neighbors's mission as useless as that of Judge Baird the previous year.

The resolutions adopted a few days later by one of the several Santa Fe meetings cited numerous maps and documents as authority for denying that Texas had any legitimate claim over the area, that Texas had ever successfully exercised any jurisdiction in New Mexico, or that the United States had ever treated New Mexico as part of Texas. The resolutions challenged Governor Munroe to prohibit Texas county organization; if he did not, they stated, he would be abandoning his duties as governor. "We shall then by all means and at all hazards vindicate the integrity of our Soil & just rights and bring to punishment those seditious persons if any there be who may be found aiding and supporting the Texan authorities." The resolutions were then transmitted to Munroe in the hope that they would influence him to be anything but neutral. By all accounts, these mid-March days in Santa Fe were filled with suspense and excitement, especially among the American leaders of the "territory" faction and the intensely anti-Texas Mexican majority. Factional leaders circulated rumors in the Mexican community, including one that Texas planned to impose exorbitant taxes on the New Mexican people.[28]

The anti-Texas forces were bolstered in their fervor on the evening of March 20 by the advent of Taylor's own emissary, Col. George McCall. Delaying not a moment in his mission, McCall on that very evening communicated to several leading citizens, and undoubtedly Munroe also, the nature of the cause he was "to advance" and enlisted them in it. From his arrival, Colonel McCall occupied the leading position in concerting the movement for statehood. Any assumption that this Taylor administration agent was doing no more than carrying out his November 19, 1849, instructions from Secretary Crawford would be incorrect, for what McCall did was actually quite different from what he was officially ordered to do. The Crawford letter had only mandated that McCall and the rest of the military were to advance rather than thwart popular wishes. This order implied that the initiative in the movement was to originate with the local inhabitants; the army's role was to be a relatively passive one. McCall, however, seized the initiative in directing the movement on his arrival. One could surely argue that his action merely reflected an overly enthusiastic interpretation of his orders, rather than an implementation of additional unwritten instructions.[29]

But there is evidence that lends credence to the proposition that McCall was indeed carrying out a secret agenda quite aside from Crawford's instructions. The collection of McCall's letters in the Library of Congress Manuscripts Division consists almost entirely of several long drafts of letters and parts thereof to a single addressee—Col. William W. S. Bliss in Washington. Colonel Bliss was no ordinary army officer; he was President Zachary Taylor's son-in-law, private secretary, and one of his very closest advisers. This means that Col. George McCall was reporting in his lengthy epistles directly to President Taylor himself. Under ordinary circumstances, McCall would have conveyed such reports to the adjutant general or the secretary of war; but McCall's reports bypassed these ordinary channels and went directly to the White House. An army officer such as McCall would never have undertaken to do this without prior arrangement with Bliss, Taylor, and possibly other close advisers. Bliss certainly would have been one of them, but Senator William Seward, then at home in New York, had not been present to advise McCall. The very establishment of extraordinary and secret communication procedures implies that McCall was ordered to play much more than a passive or secondary role in New Mexico. That he did embark precipitously on the statehood task indicates that he understood quite clearly that he was to assume the initiative himself under secret, additional instructions from the Taylor administration.[30]

Colonel Bliss and President Taylor almost certainly originated this intrigue involving McCall. Taylor must have felt uncomfortable sometimes amidst the swirl of Washington politics, but he had an abiding faith in his fellow military officers and in their ability to implement his wishes on policy in New Mexico.

Indian Agent Calhoun had not acted decisively enough in fostering a statehood movement; Taylor wanted the New Mexicans to apply quickly for immediate statehood and thus force Congress to focus attention on his program rather than on their own plans, which he vehemently disliked. Therefore it was quite natural for President Taylor to send an army officer to New Mexico with orders to hasten its statehood movement. The instructions to Colonel McCall, aside from Crawford's official ones, were apparently given to him only in unwritten form.

Secretary of War George Crawford was probably unaware of Colonel McCall's true role. Of all the cabinet members, he was the one most opposed to New Mexico statehood and most closely in touch with Southern radicals of like mind. Two of Crawford's closest associates were his fellow Georgians, Representatives Robert Toombs and Alexander Stephens. If Crawford had known McCall's true intentions, he would have certainly given this information to his friends. That Crawford never caught on is a tribute to the planning and execution of Taylor's inner circle. Apparently Crawford was told to provide McCall with a set of instructions that—it could be argued by administration supporters when their publication was demanded—demonstrated that the Taylor administration had not improperly intervened in New Mexican affairs or engaged in "executive usurpation." At the scene of action in Santa Fe, however, it would be quite a different story. Just how positive a role McCall and Munroe were actually playing would, it was apparently hoped, remain murky and clouded enough that the anti–New Mexico bloc would be rendered ineffective until New Mexico statehood was accomplished. A bold scheme it was, and McCall and Munroe did their best to make it work.[31]

McCall quickly learned the facts of political life in Santa Fe from Munroe and others. He realized that the key to the success of his statehood mission lay, strangely enough, with the "territory" faction. The original "state" party appeared to be a hopeless minority whose influence was very limited in Santa Fe itself and almost nonexistent outside the city. The only newspaper, the *New Mexican,* had now become an organ of the Houghton faction; it had been sold in early February to an army sutler-contractor and was being edited by Judge Houghton and the quartermaster's chief clerk, Thomas S. J. Johnson. The Mexican population was almost entirely in their camp. McCall's goal, therefore, was to convert the "territory" party to the cause of statehood and possibly even arrange a coalition between the two factions in order to present a united front. He outlined his program to the leaders of the "territory" party as the desire of

President Taylor's administration. Judge Houghton and his allies agreed at a "secret conclave," according to one source, to yield their position and even compromise with their enemies of the "state" faction to establish a state government. But when a committee of the two factions met to iron out differences, the Weightman faction proved too arrogant, imperious, and unconciliatory. Thereupon the "territory" group transformed itself into the new "state" party and decided to establish the state government themselves and exclude their bitter rivals from any participation in the offices of the new regime. Judge Houghton and the new "state" party held organizational meetings, decided on a ticket they would sponsor, and issued an address in Spanish to the people. Appreciating that earlier they had badly overplayed their hand, the Weightman-Alvarez group now expressed renewed interest in coalition on the condition that Richard Weightman run as candidate for the U.S. Senate. The Houghton faction absolutely rejected this demand. It was at this juncture that Commissioner Neighbors reached Santa Fe, on April 8.[32]

Up to this point, Robert Neighbors assumed that his task at Santa Fe would prove difficult, but not insurmountable. The obstacles were in fact impossible for him to have overcome, and he began to understand the severe disadvantage he was operating under when he dutifully called on the military governor. Colonel Munroe received the Texan courteously but coolly. Neighbors quickly understood that Munroe would not assist the Texas cause and that he had no authority to abolish the Kearny government without an express order from the War Department. Munroe bluntly informed Neighbors that the military government would remain in force until an act of Congress instituted another in its place. When Neighbors pointedly asked him if he would acknowledge Texas jurisdiction once civil officers had been elected under Neighbors's authority, Munroe replied that he could not answer that, but he refused to remove Kearny government officials from office unless ordered to do so by the U.S. government. That being the case, Neighbors explained that Governor Bell of Texas would probably resort to military force in order to extend the state's jurisdiction over Santa Fe. As Neighbors related it, Munroe answered: "That would be the proper course for Texas to pursue; there will in that case be no opposition."[33]

Munroe was evasive, and his last response to Neighbors was simply patronizing, although the Texas commissioner took him at his word. Munroe had toyed with Neighbors. At no time in the interview did he allude to McCall's orders from the administration to promote a state government, and at no time in that conversation, nor during the remainder of Neighbors's stay in Santa Fe, did Munroe raise the issue of the Doña Ana protest. Colonel Munroe undoubtedly presumed that Neighbors himself had instigated the land grant to Major Steen as part of a more far-reaching Texan subterfuge to despoil Mexicans of their lands. Given his notions—however mistaken—about Neighbors, it is obvious that Munroe, beneath the veneer of official cordiality, held Neighbors in utter contempt. This would explain Munroe's insincerity in discussing the basic issues with the Texan.

Neighbors then visited with Judge Joab Houghton, the archenemy of Texas. Houghton exercised great influence and power over the civil officials of New Mexico, the Mexican population, the new "state" party, and the only press in the territory. No subtlety or evasion colored Houghton's meeting with Neighbors. He unceremoniously informed the Texas commissioner that he would maintain the present government and order the arrest and imprisonment of anyone who should attempt to enforce the laws of Texas there.[34]

Neighbors received a considerably friendlier reception from members of the original "state" party, especially Pillans, Weightman, and Angney. As Pillans admitted, their primary interest in Neighbors was the assistance he might contribute to their cause of overthrowing Houghton and his minions. While they apparently expressed themselves not unfavorably toward Texas jurisdiction and county organization, they were sadly disappointed that Neighbors came there "clothed with no power" against the power of the entrenched government. Not even a district judge accompanied him to conduct court. When Neighbors met with the old "state" faction, probably on the evening of April 12, he was informed of the hopelessness of the Texas cause in Santa Fe unless Texas sent troops to enforce its jurisdiction. A leader in the Houghton faction, J. L. Collins, later declared that, at Weightman's urging, this meeting approved an ambiguous resolution rejecting Texas jurisdiction as having no foundation in law or justice but expressing willingness to submit to it as a matter of expediency. Under these circumstances, Commissioner Neighbors decided to delay issuing a call for elections, saying he would do so on a future occasion.[35]

The Houghton-Munroe-McCall cabal sprang into action. Only two days after the Texas commissioner entered the town, an "Extra" edition of the *New Mexican* was published on April 10, and in an editorial letter from "One of Your Party," dated April 7, referred to two major pieces of distressing news from Washington: that extremists and the Taylor administration opposed New Mexico's request for territorial status and rendered that cause useless; and that the slavery issue had not only ruined the New Mexican territory plans but also gravely threatened the Union itself. Therefore, the writer urged, New Mexico must abandon its earlier proposal, form a state constitution in accord with the president's wishes with an unequivocal declaration on slavery, and thus help save the Union by removing the volatile territorial slavery question altogether. Also included in the special edition were Spanish translations of President Taylor's January 21 message recommending statehood for California and New Mexico, of Crawford's orders to McCall, and of U.S. Senate debates of February 20 demonstrating the strong Southern opposition to Senator Clay's compromise proposals as well as an editorial, in Spanish, stressing the same basic themes as the editorial letter and encouraging people to petition Governor Munroe to call a constitutional convention.[36]

These events occurred amidst a public atmosphere of great apprehension and excitement in Santa Fe. Public gatherings to discuss the issues sometimes degenerated into riotous commotion and near bloodshed. At one evening session, resolutions introduced by the Weightman group did not accord with the desires of most Anglo-Americans in attendance. The resolutions were therefore referred to a committee, which was instructed to revise them and make its report the following evening. When the committee reported its revisions, obviously opposed to Texas and the Neighbors mission, trouble brewed. Palmer Pillans, Texas agent and member of Weightman's clique, had anticipated that the new resolution would be strongly adverse to Texas's interests and had come to the meeting prepared to block its passage. Pillans brought reinforcements with him, gathered from the teamsters and other employees who worked with Pillans in the quartermaster's department. These rowdies created such a disturbance that the meeting was forced to adjourn without action. Another attempt the next evening to resume the meeting produced the same result; Pillans and his bullies intimidated the others into another adjournment. But the Houghton faction had majority support among the Anglo-Americans in town, and they organized their turnout better for the fourth session of the meeting. They conducted this one in the daytime in the town plaza, and the Houghton faction possessed clear numerical superiority. Weightman, Pillans, and their armed ruffians disrupted the proceedings and prevented Facundo Pino, a young leader of the Houghton group, from speaking. Then they started a brawl, which quickly escalated into a riot in the public plaza. Colonel Munroe finally quelled the tumult by sending in the troops of the Santa Fe garrison. The military presence prevented the two factions from killing each other. Tensions and "bad blood" in the community, however, remained very high for several days thereafter.[37]

On April 13 the Houghton faction published and posted notices, in both Spanish and English, that requested citizens to attend a public meeting at the courthouse in Santa Fe on the following Saturday, April 20. The stated purpose of the assembly would be to pass resolutions in favor of state government and to petition Colonel Munroe to issue a call for a constitutional convention. Judge Houghton simultaneously ordered the prefects in other towns to convene similar meetings.[38]

Given the potential explosiveness of the situation, Neighbors wisely did nothing more than lodge an official letter of protest with Munroe on April 15. Neighbors deemed such a convention to violate the provision of the U.S. Constitution that determined that no state should be formed within another state's boundaries without the consent of that state's legislature. He also cited the Texas annexation resolutions, the preamble of the Texas Constitution, and the joint resolution of December 29, 1845, admitting Texas into the Union as documents guaranteeing the Texas boundary as *Texas* defined it. Colonel Munroe obligingly sent the commissioner's protest on to the adjutant general (with Colonel Washington's wagon train on April 16) for the consideration of the secretary of war.[39]

Neighbors informed Governor Bell that his mission in Santa Fe had become untenable. He strongly recommended that Texas, without delay, should march four hundred to eight hundred men into New Mexico to secure the state's jurisdiction. He firmly believed that the influence of the Weightman clique was more widespread than it actually was and that the addition of Texan military forces would rally pro-Texas elements to overthrow the Houghton faction. Neighbors was putting as positive and hopeful a gloss as he could on Texas's dismal chances, even assuming that the group that had befriended him there was more pro-Texas than simply anti-Houghton. In anticipation that Texas would provide troops quickly, Neighbors promised to check on forage and supplies in New Mexico. He decided to remain in Santa Fe a few days longer to see if he could accomplish any delay in the plans for a statehood convention. But Neighbors's cause was hopeless.[40]

The meeting at the courthouse assembled as scheduled on Saturday, April 20, with the Houghton-Munroe-McCall forces fully in charge. Army paymaster Maj. Francis A. Cunningham presided, and Governor Munroe's private secretary, Samuel Ellison, served as secretary. Judge Houghton acted as the principal spokesman to the crowd of one or two hundred, which was, as described by Neighbors, largely made up of government employees in the quartermaster's and other departments. The meeting adopted a petition stating that seven-eighths of the people of New Mexico preferred statehood and asking that Governor Munroe call a convention, which Munroe did three days later, on April 23. His proclamation ordered elections for twenty-one convention delegates from the various counties to be conducted on May 6, with the convention itself to assemble at Santa Fe on May 15. Richard Weightman's enemy, J. L. Collins, later claimed that Weightman pleaded in vain with Munroe to limit his proclamation to the sparsely settled area west of the Rio Grande and, even after the proclamation's issuance, encouraged the people on the western side of the river to establish an independent state government. If Weightman ever resorted to this level of chicanery, no corroborative evidence of it is now available. Such a move by Weightman could have been intended only to give his minority faction some political power in the more remote trans-Rio Grande region.[41]

Once Colonel Munroe had issued his proclamation, Robert Neighbors wasted no more time at Santa Fe. He departed the town on April 24, once again in the company of Major Henry and his contingent of soldiers. Henry had traveled as far as Las Vegas with the wagon train, which included his family, and had then returned to Santa Fe. He seems to have taken for granted that Munroe would not object to his allowing Neighbors to join him on the return from Santa Fe, although Henry could not have been blind to the "rigid non-interference" order nor to the antagonistic stance taken by Munroe toward Neighbors and his cause. After arriving at Doña Ana on May 3, Neighbors inquired about purchasing corn to feed his animals, but Henry informed him that "Uncle Sam" would foot the bill and then signed a doctored return for forage that included the commissioner's horses with those of the army.[42]

Major Steen had already received a report at Doña Ana on the ore samples he had given Henry. While there was no chemist or assayist at Santa Fe, Maj. Henry Kendrick examined the samples and pronounced the lead specimen to contain a fair amount of silver and the copper specimen to be very rich. Steen also received from Santa Fe information that startled and angered Commissioner Neighbors greatly. While Colonel Munroe had never broached the subject of the Doña Ana protest to Neighbors during his sojourn at the capital, the military governor had indeed called Steen to task for his purchase of a Texas headright. In a letter dated April 15, Munroe demanded that his subordinate explain his laying claim to property already possessed and occupied by Doña Ana citizens and lectured Steen on the potential impact of his deed on those citizens: "From your official position the assumption of this claim has created more alarm and anxiety amongst the Mexican population throughout the Territory than acts of private individuals would have done and is likely to lead to their committing serious sacrifices both personal & of property." Munroe realized immediately that any U.S. validation or even toleration of the Steen headright would lead to the dispossession of the Mexican people of Doña Ana holding their titles under the previous regime, an eventuality that Munroe considered patently unjust. And, by implication, if Texas could get away with U.S. acquiescence in the Cockburn-Steen transaction, then the old land titles in New Mexico anywhere east of the Rio Grande would automatically be endangered. Therefore Major Steen's land-grab was of much more than just local significance.[43]

Enoch Steen boldly defended his actions in his reply to Munroe on April 29. He stated that he knew little about the petitioners, except that several were aliens and citizens of Mexico, and others were peons who were probably induced to sign the petition without knowing or caring about its contents. Steen dismissed the application of the Treaty of Guadalupe Hidalgo guarantees to this situation since, as Steen declared, the region east of the Rio Grande had been part of Texas since 1836; the validity of his claim, he defiantly asserted, could be properly adjudicated only by Texas authorities. Cognizant of no prohibition against army officers purchasing lands, he had purchased the headright from Cockburn, he admitted. Major Steen registered no objection to Munroe's plan to send all of the relevant documents in the case to the War Department, but he suggested that Munroe might more appropriately dispatch the documents to the Texas governor or legislature. Without elaboration, Steen promised that his action would not cause property or personal sacrifice on anyone's part. For consistency's sake, Steen listed his post in the letter as "Doña Ana, Texas"; before this his correspondence had always designated his post as "Doña Ana, New Mexico."[44]

On May 20, Colonel Munroe mailed the protest and correspondence on the matter to Adjutant General Roger Jones. In his cover letter Munroe pointed out the military and economic importance of Doña Ana as the principal settlement between El Paso and Santa Fe and also reiterated his view on the Steen headright: "Within the new Jurisdiction of Texas extended to include Doña Ana the most unfounded claim will be set up which if they do not actually lead to despoiling the people of their Property by direct action will in reality tend to the same end by inducing them through their fears to sacrifice it and remove elsewhere."[45]

Robert Neighbors did not learn of the Steen headright or the protest against it until he returned to Doña Ana and Steen showed him the protest. Neighbors urgently wrote that day, May 3, from "Doña Ana, Texas" to Colonel Munroe, vehemently denying that he had any connection with the Steen headright or that he had owned or sold any such certificates. Neighbors indignantly inquired why the governor had not revealed the charges to him while he had been in

Santa Fe and closed with a demand that Munroe transmit his denial to the War Department, with which request Munroe complied. One can only guess at Neighbors's reaction when he learned what had been going on behind his back. He must have been utterly dumbfounded at Cockburn's treachery and Steen's greed. He also undoubtedly realized that whatever leg he might have had to stand on in dealing with the U.S. authorities at Santa Fe had been kicked out from under him. William Cockburn, in his attempt to secure the loyalty of Major Steen to the Texan cause, had inadvertently labeled the entire Neighbors mission as a treacherous land robbery in the eyes of U.S. officials.

Neighbors returned from Doña Ana through El Paso to Austin, arriving at the Texas capital on June 3. In his report to Governor Bell the next day, he seems to have been so embarrassed by the Steen headright that he chose to narrate the story of his mission and its partial failure for Bell without any mention of the Cockburn-Steen transaction. Robert Neighbors could at least take credit for the successful organization of El Paso County, which surely influenced the inclusion of most of that particular area within the limits of Texas when the Texas–New Mexico boundary was finally determined.[46]

At some point on his return journey, Neighbors almost certainly crossed paths with Judge Spruce M. Baird, who was headed back to Santa Fe. The protean, peripatetic Mr. Baird had undergone changes in attitude toward his position since returning to Austin from Missouri. On February 20 he had tendered his resignation as judge of the Eleventh Judicial District, saying that it had become a "sinecure." He declared his belief that Congress would finally confirm the Texas title to New Mexico but stated that the Texas Legislature had left its appointed officers there without the strength to enforce Texas jurisdiction at present. In April, however, with the arrival of the news of Neighbors's success in El Paso, Baird began to look more positively on Texan prospects at Santa Fe. At the suggestion of Governor Bell and Secretary of State James Webb, Baird withdrew his resignation on April 18 and left for New Mexico two days later in a party of traders and emigrants. No matter how hopeless Neighbors may have informed him that the Texas cause had become above Doña Ana, the determined judge was not dissuaded from reaching his destination of Santa Fe.[47]

Meanwhile, the Thirty-first Congress of the United States was wrestling with the boundary dispute and the numerous other threatening issues of the 1850 sectional crisis. No one in Congress yet understood how vigorously the executive branch had already maneuvered on its own to promote New Mexican statehood or how, through the efficient agency of Colonels McCall and Munroe, the struggle to save most of New Mexico from the clutches of Texas was rapidly progressing toward victory. At least it so appeared to the New Mexicans, now that the Taylor administration had clearly thrown the considerable weight of its influence into the balance in favor of a New Mexican polity on both sides of the Rio Grande independent of Texas.

Chapter Four

❧

The Momentous Thirty-First
Congress Begins

IN LATE 1849 MOST AMERICANS, NORTH AND SOUTH, TOILED THROUGH THEIR daily tasks, convinced that the political process would finally resolve the sectional issues in a compromise reminiscent of the 1820–21 and 1832–33 measures that had saved the Union. There were other Americans, however, who were not so certain about the security of the Union. Sectional controversies, particularly in relation to those issues connected with the Mexican War, indeed appeared dangerous to some, especially the political moderates among Whigs and Democrats. Free-Soilers and most Northern Whigs desired the Wilmot Proviso as the means to prevent slavery from extending into the West and also favored the immediate admission of California to full statehood. Southerners, on the other hand, viewed the Wilmot Proviso as a grievous insult to them and their property and considered California's tipping of the U.S. Senate balance in favor of the North a harbinger of further Northern legislative aggression against Southern slavery. Southern leaders had defended the positive righteousness of African slavery for a long time; they could not tolerate the Wilmot Proviso's stigmatization of slavery itself as evil, whether or not slavery possessed an iota of potentiality for practical employment in Western territories. So as the Thirty-first Congress began, the Texas–New Mexico boundary dispute constituted nothing more than a minor distraction amidst such major issues as the Proviso and California statehood.[1]

Moderate Whigs who retained confidence in the ability of Taylor and his advisers saw merit in the simplicity of the administration's plan to admit

California to statehood, to leave the remainder of the Mexican cession without civil governments until they were prepared to enter the Union as states, and to solve the other issues one by one. The president's plan avoided the Wilmot Proviso in territories altogether. Northern Whigs were mostly willing to support Taylor's plan if Congress failed to enact the Proviso and were certain that Gen. Zachary Taylor's Jackson-like nationalism would quell any Southern disunionism.

Other moderate Whigs, such as Henry Clay of Kentucky, viewed the president's plan as unacceptable in the South, with disunion and consequent bloodshed very real possibilities. The plan's very simplicity seemed inadequate. Most Southerners definitely opposed California's addition to free-state political power in the U.S. Senate. If Southerners had realized just how quickly Taylor planned to follow up California with New Mexico's admission as a state, they would have been doubly horrified. Even if only California were admitted, Southern Democrats and Whigs both feared that the North in Congress would then block any bills favorable to the South. If any Southern states reacted to this situation by attempting disunion, many moderate Whigs were not convinced that Taylor would be able to prevent a wholesale disruption of the Union. An angry public meeting in October 1849 in Jackson, Mississippi, had called for an assembly of delegates from all the Southern states to meet at Nashville in early June. Disunionists looked hopefully to the Nashville Convention's potential to fulfill their designs, while moderate Southerners dreaded the possibility that, by June, the national situation would have so worsened that a majority of Southerners would be converted to secessionism.[2]

By late 1849 Southern Whigs had grown increasingly distrustful of Zachary Taylor's willingness to protect the South's interests, particularly those interests related to slavery. Taylor, a Louisiana Whig and slaveholder, had become increasingly dependent on policy advice from Northern antislavery Whigs such as William Seward of New York and Southern Whigs in his cabinet, Secretary of State John Clayton of Delaware and Navy Secretary William B. Preston of Virginia, who seemed at best indifferent to Southern rights in the West. Taylor's plan was similar to Clayton's proposed compromise of 1848 and to Preston's bill early in 1849. President Taylor's remarks in speeches given in the North in the summer of 1849, that slavery was a moral and political evil and that the North need entertain no fear of slavery extension, angered Southern Whig politicians constantly besieged by fire-eating Democrats who charged that the Whigs as a whole could not be trusted on the slavery issue. Whig losses to Democrats in the South in late 1849 underscored the need for Southern Whigs to convince the administration to adopt policies that could appeal to Southerners.[3]

Southern moderates in both parties retained an abiding faith that a settlement of sectional issues could be reached and that the South could remain safely in the Union with the free states. The prospect of additional free states in the West did not necessarily mean disunion for these moderates, as long as such statehood was not accomplished through an express prohibition barring slaveowners' human property from Western territories. Southern moderates' hopes depended, of course, on Northern willingness to end antislavery agitation, and that very dependence placed Southern moderates in a terribly vulnerable position within the Southern political arena—against their Southern extremist enemies.

A major part of the problem for the Southern moderates, especially Whigs, was Zachary Taylor himself. The politically inexperienced general-as-president was a misanthrope in Washington politics, and his cabinet was dull and mediocre, from the indolent Secretary Clayton on down. The only representative of the Deep South in the cabinet was Secretary of War George Crawford of Georgia, who had little impact on policy matters. The patronage policies of the cabinet members had been so favorable to antislavery Northern Whigs that aggrieved Whigs of other factions by the end of 1849 were clamoring for Taylor to replace his cabinet with a more equitable one. President Taylor could never bring himself to do that, even as his cabinet continued to grow increasingly unpopular in early 1850. For one thing, he was loyal to his subordinates; for another, he was such a neophyte in national politics that he could not readily decide on replacements.[4]

Positively alarming to Southerners was the extraordinary amount of influence that New York's new antislavery Whig senator William H. Seward seemed to exercise over Taylor, his cabinet, and New York's federal patronage. Ingratiating his way into Taylor's circle even before the inauguration in March 1849, the suave Seward had soon begun attending cabinet meetings and had become one of President Taylor's most confidential advisers. Seward had managed to wholly eliminate Vice President Millard Fillmore's influence over patronage. It would have been wise of Zachary Taylor to have kept such a politically polarizing entity as Seward and his scheming New York mentor Thurlow Weed at arm's length; that he did not do so destroyed much of his credibility with his fellow Southerners.[5]

Rather than attempt to unite the Whig party or even to enlist the help of its foremost old leaders, Daniel Webster and Henry Clay, President Taylor adopted an adversarial stance toward Webster and Clay. Taylor was convinced that the Whig stalwarts were solely interested in stealing his job from him in 1852. Moreover, his inability to utilize the extraordinary experience and talents of Webster and Clay seriously hamstrung his ability to deal with Congress. Without leading spokesmen for the administration in Congress able to splice together a working coalition, the Taylor administration's simplistic policy was doomed to failure even before the new Congress began its session.[6] Southern Whigs incensed at being ignored by the administration, Southern Democrats convinced that Taylor's policy was strictly to the North's advantage, Free-Soilers still committed to the Wilmot Proviso, and Northern Democrats promoting their own alternative solution—popular sovereignty—as an answer to the sectional dilemma in the territories would all certainly oppose the president's plan in Congress, at least without some substantial alterations.

The probability that Congress might change, reject, or substitute a different plan for Taylor's pointed up another glaring inadequacy in the president as a political leader. Zachary Taylor was unalterably wedded to the administration plan; any disagreement with it, especially by politicians against whom he held grudges, was quickly interpreted by him as an enemy assault. His "mulish" inflexibility when confronted may have been an admirable trait on a battlefield, but it became worse than useless in the crisis of 1850.[7]

Under these circumstances, with both national parties in disarray and an executive branch unable to effectively influence Congress, those who looked with foreboding on the approach of the Thirty-first Congress had reason to fear. Several possibilities for disaster presented themselves, most hinging on the potential for disunion at June's Nashville Convention if Congress by that time had passed legislation inimical to the South. But a much more immediate danger was already becoming apparent to many leaders at the end of 1849. By that time news was reaching Washington of the belligerent attitude that the governor and legislature of Texas were again voicing toward the reluctance of the Santa Fe region to agree to Texas's claimed jurisdiction. Of all the issues presenting themselves in 1850, this one alone—the boundary dispute—offered the immediate potential for bloodshed and subsequent evils if Texas should send a militia force into New Mexico. President Taylor's already-strong distaste for Texans and his belief that the Texan claim to New Mexico east of the Rio Grande was invalid, combined with his stalwart inflexibility, only added to the volatility of this situation.[8]

The Congress that would attempt to resolve the crisis over Texas–New Mexico and all the other issues, with or without executive guidance, was divided into numerous sectional and party groupings. Several famous statesmen of the previous political generation would mix the twilight of their careers with the hopes and aspirations of newer, younger members. Whig Henry Clay returned after an absence of several years in Kentucky. Quite conscious of his "Great Pacificator" status from the Missouri and nullification crises, Clay was nearly seventy-three years old, gaunt, and suffering from a tubercular cough, but he was confident that he could still inspire people and again save the Union. Daniel Webster of Massachusetts, he of the "Godlike" voice, intimidating stare, and Whig nationalist convictions, was also present. The third member of the "triumvirate," John Calhoun of South Carolina, was dying of tuberculosis and possessed only a shadow of his former strength, yet he remained the leading symbol of the South's and slavery's interests. Only a bit less famous than these three was Missouri Democrat Thomas Hart Benton, who, after nearly three decades in the Senate, was still proud of his great size and booming voice and still feared as a gladiator of Senate debate. Benton could be counted on to support what he viewed as his state's best interests and those of Santa Fe and believed that the South should simply acknowledge that slavery could find no safe haven in the West.

Among the emerging Senate leaders were Stephen A. Douglas, Illinois Democrat, and William Seward, New York Whig. Douglas, a short, stumpy, thirty-six year old, already had gained a reputation for energetic leadership and, as chair of the important Committee on Territories, had in previous sessions attempted to play a significant role in the formulation of territorial policy. Douglas championed an idea earlier put forward by aged and jowly Senator Lewis Cass of Michigan. Under this plan, known as "popular sovereignty," the issue of slavery in the territories would be left to the decision of the territorial inhabitants themselves as a means of getting the issue away from congressional agitators. Seward, thin and hawk-nosed, with an unimpressive speaking voice and a very gracious manner, was new to the Senate but already well known for his antislavery views and his close ties to President Taylor. Southerners loathed Seward, both for his antislavery fervor and his penchant for political intrigue.

Among other extremists on the Northern side of the slavery issue were two Free-Soilers, the stern Salmon Chase of Ohio and the fat, jolly, lazy John P. Hale of New Hampshire. Aside from Calhoun, the most prominent Southern Democratic radicals in the Senate were his South Carolina colleague, white-haired Andrew P. Butler; Louisiana's French Creole Pierre Soulé; both of Virginia's senators, James M. Mason and Robert M. T. Hunter; and President Taylor's former son-in-law and Mexican War hero, Jefferson Davis of Mississippi.

While nearly all the Southern Whig senators were moderates and Unionists anxious for compromise, several Southern Democratic moderates were noteworthy. One of these was Henry Foote, Davis's Mississippi colleague. Small in physique and nearly bald, Foote was probably the most eccentric of all the Senate's characters. At times given to fierce invective, Foote could also be the soul of good fellowship with the most ardent antislavery men. Full of nervous energy during Senate debates, Foote could never sit still nor remain quiet for long. Politically he supported the fortunes of Lewis Cass and his doctrine of popular sovereignty; since that was not a popular notion in Mississippi, Foote could be counted on to balance the ledger in debate by attacking both Seward and Benton whenever he got the chance in order to boost his popularity back home.[9]

The Texas senators were both Democratic moderates, and they occupied an extremely delicate position in this Congress. Both Houston and Rusk strongly desired compromise of the sectional issues, but both were also, publicly at least, forced to defend the 1836 Texas claim to all territory east of the Rio Grande. Both were still immensely popular in Texas for their roles in the Texas Revolution. But both had also come under increasing criticism from Southern radical elements in Texas, especially for opposing Calhoun's "Southern Address." So sensitive were Rusk's supporters in the Texas Legislature about his pending re-election that they postponed the vote on it until a later session in hopes that Rusk's performance at the current congressional session would reassure doubters of Rusk's loyalty to Texan and Southern interests. Rusk and Houston both wanted to find a way to cede the Santa Fe region in exchange for the U.S. assumption of Texas's outstanding debt without appearing to betray Texas's interests. The Texas bondholder lobby in Washington, headed by James Hamilton of South Carolina, earnestly sought the same sort of bargain.[10]

The House of Representatives was the much larger and less distinguished body. Free-Soilers Joseph M. Root and Joshua R. Giddings of Ohio, David Wilmot of Pennsylvania, Horace Mann of Massachusetts, and the others of their persuasion bitterly opposed anything less than the imposition of the Proviso to exclude slavery from the territories. Many of the Northern Whigs sympathized with that goal but also wished to be loyal to their Whig president's plan. On the opposite side were Southern fire-eaters such as Armistead Burt of South Carolina, Samuel W. Inge of Alabama, Richard K. Meade and James A. Seddon of Virginia, and Albert Gallatin Brown of Mississippi. One of Texas's two representatives, Volney Howard, was firmly within this Southern "ultra" bloc and wished no compromise whatever on the Texas claim to Santa Fe.

House moderates from the North were primarily Democrats in favor of popular sovereignty. One of these, John A. McClernand of Illinois, chaired the House Committee on Foreign Relations and worked very closely with Douglas on the passage of bills. A large majority of Southern Whig representatives were moderates. Two of their principal leaders were the Georgia "twins," Alexander H. Stephens and Robert Toombs. They were anything but "twins" in physical appearance: Stephens was diminutive and frail-looking—"like the shadow of a pigmy that has died of the jaundice," wrote one enemy journalist—while his close friend Toombs was a very large man with a large face and long black hair. Both were Unionists who felt embarrassed by the Northern drift of the president whom they had promoted for that office; both hoped they could convince Taylor to give the South a program that would allow the Whigs to survive in Southern politics; both could match any fire-eater in vehemence in order to press their cause. On the Democratic side, three of the Southern moderates were among the House's foremost leaders: Howell Cobb of Georgia, a short, rotund, clear-voiced Unionist, who, not yet forty years old, was soon to be the speaker of the House; Cobb's close associate, Linn Boyd of Kentucky, a red-faced, white-haired man of sixty years and a very experienced chairman of the Committee on Territories; and Thomas H. Bayly of Virginia, the dignified-looking, bespectacled, auburn-haired chairman of the Ways and Means Committee. David Kaufman of Texas, a lesser-known Southern Democratic moderate, was also destined to play a significant role in this session.[11]

A preview of how chaotic the session might become occurred during the first three weeks of December 1849 when the House of Representatives attempted to elect a speaker. Southern Whigs deserted Robert C. Winthrop of Massachusetts, the Whig candidate, for refusing to renounce antislavery measures, and Free-Soilers rejected him as a "doughface" in the service of the South. The end result after a ferocious struggle was the election of Southern Democrat Howell Cobb of Georgia on December 22 and the prompt installation of Democrats in charge of the significant House committees. Many interpreted the Whigs' failure to organize the House as another sign of the administration's weakness.[12]

The Senate had begun its work less uproariously, but the slavery issue had nevertheless managed to creep into the debate over whether to welcome a famous Irish temperance crusader, Fr. Theobald Mathew, into the Senate chamber. The black-haired, red-faced Democratic senator from Alabama, Jere Clemens, an uncouth, young tobacco-spitter, challenged the priest's admission because the cleric was also tainted with antislavery sentiments. William Seward ventured to defend Father Mathew, and Seward received his first vicious verbal assault from Foote of Mississippi. The Senate voted on December 20 to admit Mathew.[13]

On December 24, once the House had elected Cobb as speaker, President Taylor sent his annual message to Congress. He favorably endorsed California's decision to form a state constitution but ignored New Mexico, except to say that he expected that region "at no very distant period" to follow California's example. He urged Congress to avoid "exciting" sectional topics while awaiting the action of California and New Mexico. Of course Taylor had recently sent Colonel McCall to make sure that New Mexico acted sooner rather than later. In the *New York Tribune* Horace Greeley chastised the president for his "nonaction" on New Mexico, for Greeley was convinced that an indigenous statehood movement would take so long to develop that Texas would probably stop the move altogether by sending a military force to occupy the territory. Southerners did not like Taylor's plan on the West at all, and Texans were mortified that the president would speak of the Santa Fe area as a separate entity from Texas. Given that Taylor did not mention the boundary question, observers expected Congress to quickly pass a resolution demanding that the president provide information on the administration's handling of the boundary dispute.[14]

The anticipated resolutions were introduced in the Senate on December 27. One of these, by Clemens of Alabama, requested information on the circumstances of California's government organization process and on the president's attitude toward New Mexico and any steps taken to organize a state convention there. The other resolution, by Sam Houston, demanded that President Taylor submit to the Senate all recent government correspondence in reference to the New Mexico issue and a statement of reasons why the U.S. military in New Mexico had refused to recognize the Texan judicial authority of Judge Baird. The Senate adopted Houston's resolution on January 7, 1850, without a roll call and, after some debate, passed Clemens's resolution on January 17 by a vote of 48 to 3.[15]

As the year turned, Washington was further reminded of the boundary dispute. Hugh N. Smith of New Mexico arrived at the capital at the end of December claiming a seat as "delegate." Smith's instructions from the September convention at Santa Fe were quickly printed in the newspapers. The fact that those instructions did not specify a boundary line led many to conclude, along with Smith's own statements, that the Santa Fe group were willing to compromise on the boundary. Others appreciated the fact that the instructions said nothing about slavery. The *Union,* Washington's Democratic press, asked why the administration should demand statehood for people who clearly expressed a desire for territorial government. The Texas papers condemned the whole movement in Santa Fe, and the *Houston Telegraph* promised that the Texas delegation would not remain in Congress if Smith, elected by the "designing demagogues, and gambling loafers" of Santa Fe, was permitted a seat. This Texan viewpoint was echoed in Washington by Rep. Volney Howard, who printed a letter in the *Union* on January 3 in which he proclaimed that Texas would defend its claim to the last rifle if the United States attempted to recognize a separate territorial government within Texas. Howard did express his hope that such a collision could be avoided, but that, he said, depended on whether Texas was treated justly.[16]

While the House of Representatives busied itself with the election of minor officials of that chamber, the Senate began its initial consideration of various proposals related to the territories and the District of Columbia. Senator Foote of Mississippi had been working on a solution to the territories problem since November at least and gave notice in late December that he would soon introduce his bill. As a prelude to his bill, Foote submitted a resolution on January 15 stating that it was the duty of Congress to give territorial governments to California, Deseret (the Mormon name for Utah), and New Mexico. Nothing came of Foote's resolution.[17]

Thomas Hart Benton upstaged Foote, however, by submitting his own proposal first on January 16. Benton's bill, similar to his 1844 proposal, was designed to protect Missouri's long-standing trade relationship with New Mexico by eliminating the Texas claim to Santa Fe. Benton argued that Texas was simply too large and that it should cede to the U.S. all its claim west of 102° west longitude and north of the Red River in exchange for fifteen million dollars, which would more than retire Texas's debt. Within the area retained by Texas, Benton stipulated that when the population west of a line formed by the 98° west longitude line and the Colorado River should reach 100,000, that region should form a separate state. In his remarks on the bill, Benton emphasized as a reason "of new and pressing urgency" for his bill the threatened military collision of Texas and New Mexico, to which, he declared, the United States would necessarily become a party. The Senate referred the bill to the Judiciary Committee rather than to Douglas's Committee on Territories; all realized that the Judiciary Committee, with a majority of Southerners, would never report Benton's bill back to the Senate floor. Texans certainly would never support a bill that would force them to relinquish the El Paso area and its potential importance as a center for trade and migration routes to California's gold fields.[18]

Foote then introduced his more comprehensive bill. Notice and some details of it had been in the press for weeks and it had already been printed in the Senate. Foote, embarrassed by Benton's maneuver, accused the Missourian of stealing the basic idea from his bill and of being in league with the unholy purposes of

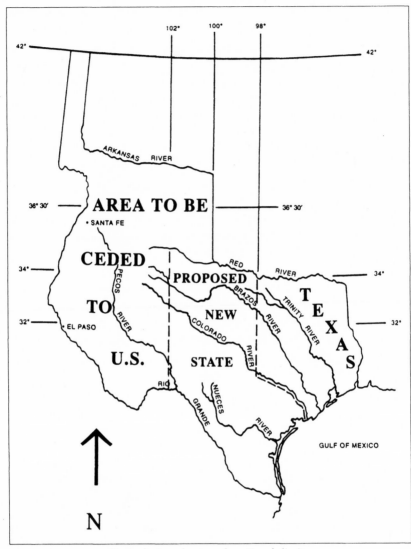

Benton's 1850 plan to reduce Texas's limits.

Northern free-soil proponents. After long endurance of Foote's verbal tirade, Benton stalked out of the chamber. Foote confessed in his address that originally he had planned to propose a compromise boundary line between New Mexico and Texas running from El Paso northeast to the headwaters of the Red River.

However, he said, Northern hostility had convinced him that Texas and the South must stand firm and not compromise on Texas's 1836 claim.[19]

Foote's bill would organize four territorial governments. One would be California, with the boundaries it claimed but with a provision for further subdivision if Congress so desired. Deseret and New Mexico would also become territories, but New Mexico Territory would lie entirely west of the Rio Grande. Within Texas, Foote would, with the state's consent, establish a new territory named Jacinto east of the Brazos River. (His geography was a bit askew here, since he thought the Brazos extended all the way to the northern boundary of Texas.) Texas proper would encompass the entire remainder of Texas's 1836 claim. That way the South would not have to fear the formation of a new free state out of Texas's domain in the region north of 36°30', since the northern region would remain part of Texas. Foote believed that Texas would continue as a slave state and that Jacinto would give the South two slave state senators to balance California when it was finally admitted. Foote's bill made no proposal on the Texas debt, the District of Columbia, or fugitive slaves, but Andrew P. Butler of South Carolina brought forth a new and much stricter fugitive slave bill from his Judiciary Committee on January 16.[20]

To which committee Foote's bill was to be referred was not decided until January 22. Foote desired reference to Butler's Judiciary Committee, since he felt the Southerners on it would give it the most favorable hearing; Butler put the case for his committee on the ground that the bill involved the subdivision of an existing state. However, Northern senators plus Spruance and Wales of Delaware voted 25 to 22 on January 22 to dispatch Foote's proposal and a government memorial from Deseret to Douglas's Committee on Territories. That committee was as unlikely to adopt Foote's scheme as Butler's was to adopt Benton's. Antislavery Northerners considered Foote's bill merely another attempt to manufacture a new slave state, and Greeley's *Tribune* especially condemned it for placing 75 percent of New Mexico's land and 95 percent of its population within Texas. Some Texans derived some satisfaction from the fact that both the Benton and Foote bills appeared to recognize the validity of Texas's Rio Grande boundary. Whether or not Foote's plan was practical, the Mississippi senator deserved credit for devising the first program that sought to resolve several territorial issues together; it thus paved the way for subsequent plans with a similar basis.[21]

On January 21, the day before Foote's bill was referred to committee, Taylor responded to Clemens's resolution with a brief special message on California and New Mexico. His policy, it stated, was to encourage statehood for those two areas

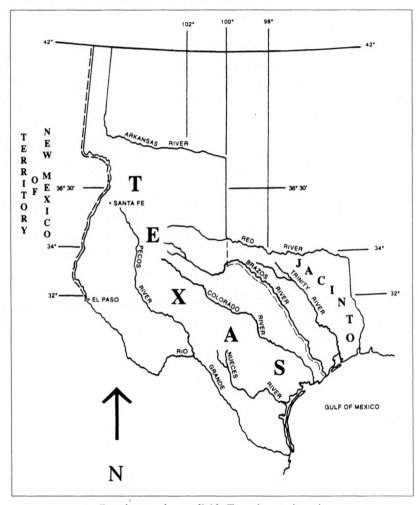

Foote's 1850 plan to divide Texas (approximate).

in order to avoid the excitement and agitation caused by the question of slavery in territories. Then, once New Mexico had been admitted to statehood, the Supreme Court could resolve the boundary dispute as one between two states. In the meantime, New Mexico retained legal protection through its former Mexican laws and U.S. Army protection from Indian attacks. Taylor again stated that he expected New Mexico to apply for statehood "at no very distant period." Members of Congress had no inkling of the steps taken by Taylor to ensure that this prediction would come true much more quickly than they could imagine.[22]

Taylor's January 21 message did not clarify the situation. It seemed designed to answer the Clemens resolution without enlightening Congress as to the administration's exact program. Representative Kaufman urged Governor Bell to draw no particular inferences from the message and informed him that Representative Toombs, supposedly still in Taylor's confidence, insisted that the administration would place no impediment in the way of Texas's jurisdiction at Santa Fe. Kaufman also told the governor in his letters that several Northern Whigs had privately uttered sentiments most emphatically defending the Texas claim, although these Whigs also wished for the Supreme Court to decide the boundary. The *Washington Union* editorialized that Texas would not wait for the arbitration of the Supreme Court before taking New Mexico by force.[23]

Henry Clay had so far bided his time, but on the evening of January 21 he began to involve himself in the crisis. He paid an unannounced visit on that rainy night to the lodgings of Daniel Webster. Webster listened attentively as Clay poured out his fears of imminent disunion if the older party leaders could not develop a plan that would alleviate the tensions. Webster, even though he was not yet convinced that the Union was in danger of dissolution, was impressed by Clay's plea and promised his general support for a compromise, without any agreement on details.[24]

Clay knew that he could command little support in Congress and none in the executive branch. He had had brief and polite visits with Taylor and Clayton in December in an atmosphere described by one correspondent as "armed neutrality." Despite the mutual dislike between Clay and Taylor and Clay's undoubted desire to play a leading role in party and Congress once again, Clay's interest in devising his own compromise plan was fueled by his fear of disunion. Clay found as little favor with most Southerners as he did with Taylor. He was entirely out of step with the Calhounite demand for the right to take slave property into the territories, and his endorsement of gradual emancipation in Kentucky and of the colonization movement, along with his remarks concerning natural barriers to slavery in the Western territories, predisposed most Southerners of both parties to oppose any program he might sponsor.[25]

Nonetheless, Clay did devise a plan of compromise, and on January 29 he offered it as a set of eight resolutions in the Senate. His was a comprehensive plan to solve all the outstanding difficulties of the sectional crisis. Clay favored

California's admission under its constitution and with its claimed boundaries. Congress should establish territorial governments in the remainder of the Mexican cession, with no mention of slavery, since Clay believed that slavery could not exist there by reason of nature and the earlier Mexican abolition law. Other resolutions opposed interference with slavery in the District of Columbia without the consent of the people of the District and Maryland or without compensation, favored prohibition of the slave trade in the District, and advocated the enactment of a more effective fugitive slave law.[26]

Clay's third and fourth resolutions proposed that the Texas–New Mexico boundary be defined and that the U.S. government pay an as-yet-unspecified amount of money to Texas to satisfy its creditors. The third resolution suggested that the boundary run up the Rio Grande "to the southern line of New Mexico" and then eastward to the 1819 treaty line between Spain and the United States. However, Clay never specified where "the southern line of New Mexico" lay. Many believed that the proper southern boundary for New Mexico lay as far north as 34° north latitude, which, if used as a dividing line, would have left Texas with all its slaveholding areas of Northeast Texas intact. Others—and this had been the prevailing understanding at the time of the Guadalupe Hidalgo treaty—assumed that 32° north latitude, near El Paso, was the southern limit of New Mexico; if extended eastward to the eastern boundary of Texas, this line would have barred slavery in North Texas under Clay's suggested plan. Clay, in devising his compromise, certainly did not intend to promote the latter view, which Texans and all other Southerners at the time would have deemed absurd. The Southern extremists in Harrison County, Texas—which lay above 32°— were about as likely to accede peacefully to such a proposal as those in Charleston, South Carolina, would have been! Clay's knowledge of Southwestern geography was just as imprecise as that of most other Washington politicians, and the lack of clarity led to Clay's misleading phraseology. His proposal for a Texas–New Mexico boundary was an indefinite, general model designed to serve as a basis from which Congress, in its deliberations, could demarcate a compromise boundary. Clay eschewed discussion of where the "true boundary" lay because, he said, it was such a complex and difficult subject. He did, however, deny the validity of the 1836 Texas claim to those parts of New Mexico east of the Rio Grande; Texas, Clay admitted, possessed a "plausible" claim but not a good title. He was willing to pay Texas for relinquishment of that claim.[27]

In the conclusion of this, his initial address on compromise, Clay asked the North to magnanimously make concessions to a South threatened by destruction, his indirect way of referring to the possible servile war depicted more colorfully and specifically by radical Southern Democrats. Rusk of Texas, in a remark made immediately after Clay finished, vaguely alluded to the Kentuckian's plan as a proposition to take away half of his state's territory. Clay replied by stating that Rusk misunderstood his suggested boundary, and he still did not give an opinion as to where the southern line of New Mexico lay. A few weeks later, on February 19, Sen. Solomon Downs, a Louisiana Democrat, repeated Rusk's criticism. Aside from these initial reactions, however, no one else at the time seems to have interpreted Clay's third resolution in this way, although the notion has been revived in a few modern works of scholarship. Only Southerners chose to respond to Clay's resolutions on January 29 itself, all of them objecting to one part of his plan or another in brief speeches. Besides Rusk, Foote and Davis of Mississippi and William R. King of Alabama all defended the entirety of the Texan claim. Several dissented from Clay's view that the Mexican law abolishing slavery remained in effect in the new territories. Northern antislavery elements found Clay's plan equally objectionable; they wished no compromise on slavery in territories and no stricter fugitive slave law.[28]

On the next day, January 30, Taylor teased the Senate in regard to his New Mexico policy by revealing a bit more of it in a short message and in documents transmitted in response to the Senate's resolution of January 7. The president stated that he had received no information on any interference by the U.S. military at Santa Fe with Texan judicial authority and no letters from the Texas governor and asserted that the boundary was more properly a legislative than an executive matter. Among the documents delivered to the Senate was Crawford's November 19 order to McCall; this was the Senate's first view of the order, but President Taylor did not discuss it in his message. As for Taylor's statement that he had received no communication from the Texas governor (George Wood), this was probably an evasion designed to safeguard the chief executive from having to answer the governor of Texas in a policy statement that he did not wish to make then. Crawford's order to McCall, however, was sufficient to convince Senator Rusk and Representative Kaufman of the administration's hostility to Texas on the New Mexico issue.[29]

House speechmaking during the latter part of January had been dominated by Southern fire-eaters. They charged that California's admission would destroy the Senate balance and thus pave the way for the North to employ its congressional strength to abolish slavery in the South. They predicted that the South might soon face the horrors of Santo Domingo's slave uprising. Several observers gave special notice to a suggestion by Thomas Clingman, North Carolina Whig, that the South could resort to the tactic of demanding repeated, time-consuming roll-call votes in the House to stop appropriations bills, and thus government functions, if no settlement satisfactory to the South was enacted. While none of the fire-eaters mentioned the boundary dispute, Volney Howard vigorously defended his state's position on that subject.

On February 4, the House proceedings became significant for the defeat of the Wilmot Proviso on two separate votes and for that chamber's first move regarding Hugh N. Smith, the New Mexico convention's choice for territorial delegate in Congress. Free-Soilers Joseph Root and Joshua Giddings of Ohio initiated the Proviso moves that failed. Many Northern Whigs, now committed to following President Taylor's policy of avoiding the Proviso, dodged these votes; Robert Winthrop, Massachusetts Whig, left his seat on both occasions and retreated behind the screen at the back of the chamber while his name was being called. The unwillingness of the House to vote for the Wilmot Proviso at least left the door open for compromise. Also on February 4, Illinois Whig Edwin Baker presented Smith's credentials as a delegate from New Mexico, which the House eventually referred to the Committee on Elections.[30]

During the next two days, February 5 and 6, Henry Clay opened the Senate debate on his resolutions in an eloquent address before packed galleries. He promoted his plea for concessions by both North and South, chiding the North that natural barriers and prevailing Mexican law rendered the Wilmot Proviso superfluous in the territories and warning the South that disunion would bring on a war that would destroy slavery. As he proceeded through the issues, he proclaimed that none was "so difficult and troublesome" as the boundary dispute as it related to the slavery question. At some length Clay argued that the western boundary of Texas had never been fixed and was still an open question to be properly settled by the U.S. government, an argument contrary to the opinion of most Southerners. The Kentuckian phrased his own concept of the boundary in the same vague terms he had used on January 29, without further definition of "the southern limits of New Mexico." He believed that U.S. payment of the Texas debt should be adequate compensation to the state for whatever part of its land claim it would be required to cede.[31]

Despite criticism by extremists from both North and South, Clay's speech of February 5 and 6 began to raise public morale. Here at last, presented with Clay's oratorical persuasiveness, was a program that envisioned a comprehensive settlement. Citizens began organizing public rallies in many cities and towns in support of compromise in general. Moderate Whigs now possessed a distinct alternative to Taylor's plan. Speaker of the House Howell Cobb and other moderate Southerners regained confidence that an overall settlement could be forged. Even a few who held Southern "ultra" opinions began to think that a reasonable solution might be developed from Clay's basic ideas. Clay's valiant promotion of compromise even helped effect a reconciliation between him and his long-time Democratic political enemy Thomas Ritchie, editor of the *Washington Union*. In a meeting at the Kentuckian's quarters in the National Hotel on February 10, both cordially agreed on the need for compromise, and Ritchie's *Union* took up the cause in its editorials and maintained its pressure in favor of compromise throughout the struggle.[32]

Those with the greatest vested interest in the settlement of the boundary dispute and other issues met at the National Hotel on the day after the Clay-Ritchie rapprochement, February 11: James Hamilton and the Texas bondholder lobbyists. What course of action the meeting decided on is not known, but the Texas bond lobby exerted pressure for compromise throughout the crisis. On February 13 Henry Clay introduced in the Senate a petition from Hamilton and financier William S. Wetmore requesting payment of the Texas debt; the petition was referred to the Judiciary Committee. The bondholders feared two circumstances that might prevent their being fully paid. One was that Texas itself would partially repudiate the debt by scaling it down to the extent of the actual specie funds that Texas had received for its bonds, according to the value of Texas Republic money at the dates of the different bond issues. Under a Texas law of 1848, the comptroller's office of that state had issued par-value certificates amounting to only about half the amount of claims filed at the office.[33]

The other circumstance dreaded by the bondholders was disunion, an event that could wipe out their whole financial interest in the Texas debt if Texas should join the secessionists. During February several Southern states began selecting delegates to attend the Nashville Convention. In Washington itself disunion talk had become so commonplace that one correspondent characterized it as having "the pertinacity of Egyptian frogs" in every congressional dish. The single most frightful possibility to the bondholders was that Texas might provoke the disunion movement by invading New Mexico. By mid-February Washington's press had relayed to the public the alarming news of the appointment of Major Neighbors by Texas, his departure for El Paso and Santa Fe, and New Mexico's determination to resist the Texas claim.[34]

In the days following Clay's speech, other senators had begun to speak on the sectional issues. On February 8 Sam Houston briefly defended the Texas title east of the Rio Grande in a pro-Union address promoting extension of the Missouri Compromise line to the Pacific as the best solution to the territories crisis. Unfortunately for the compromise forces, Houston left Washington after the speech to return home to Texas to attend to family matters. He would not return to Washington until April 19. Henry Foote followed Houston's speech on the 8th with notice of intent to offer a series of amendments as a substitute for Clay's plan. The major ingredients of Foote's alternative were a proposal to divide California at 36°30' north latitude and a proposal for Texas to sell its territory north of 34° north latitude to the United States for unspecified millions of dollars.[35]

But with the arrival from California of its constitution and of most of its proposed congressional delegation, interest by Congress in Texas–New Mexico quickly took a back seat to the California statehood issue. Southerners were immediately on guard lest the Northern majority employ its overwhelming numerical superiority in the House to pass a California admission bill. The great test of strength came on February 18 as James Doty, Wisconsin Free-Soil Democrat, pressed for his resolution to instruct the Committee on Territories to report a bill for California's admission to statehood unencumbered by any package of solutions to the remaining issues. True to Representative Clingman's earlier recommendation on parliamentary tactics, Southerners in the House, led by Toombs and Stephens of Georgia and also advised by Calhoun, called for the yeas and nays on various motions some thirty times that day. It required only one-fifth of the body—and Southerners easily mustered the requisite number—to demand a roll-call vote. Each such vote took fifteen to eighteen minutes to accomplish. The Southerners continued this tactic until after midnight, when Speaker Cobb adjourned the day's session, with Doty's resolution not in the order of business for the following day.[36]

These events of February 18 proved to be of extreme significance in the crisis. The success of Southern tactics that day utterly doomed Taylor's plan. Neither the president nor the Northerners could have done a thing to push California statehood alone through the House against a Southern minority determined to stop it by demanding constant procedural roll calls. As far as progress in solving the issues of the crisis was concerned, the Southern victory immobilized the House for months. Not until April would the boundary question again enter into the House deliberations. Volney Howard did, however, send out another of his fiery public letters, this time to the *Galveston News* on February 21, advocating the Nashville Convention, warning that the Wilmot Proviso could still present a threat to slavery in West Texas, and urging Texas to capture Santa Fe by force "at all hazards" before agreeing to any compromise on the region.[37]

Given the stalemate in the House, attention naturally shifted back to the Senate as the only possible avenue of settlement. On February 13 Henry Foote moved reference of the California constitution to a special committee of fifteen to work out a "definitive settlement" of this and the other sectional issues. As the debate on this matter of reference continued on February 14, 15, 20, and 25, it was clear that Benton, Clay, and Douglas opposed connecting the resolution of the California problem with other issues. Benton, although a Democrat, was developing into the most effective Senate spokesman for President Taylor's plan. Clay and Douglas both desired an overall compromise but believed that handling each issue separately was the most efficient path to follow.[38]

Foote and most Southern compromisers favored California statehood only if combined with measures acceptable to the South on other issues. Southern supporters of compromise feared that, if a California statehood bill was enacted by itself, the North would then either block any further action on the remaining territories, according to Taylor's plan, or seek to impose the Wilmot Proviso on any new national territories established. On February 14, subsequent to a statement by Clay that he opposed combining the various subjects in one bill, Foote accused Clay of falling into the grasp of Benton and even Seward, first proposing an overall settlement and then reneging on it by proposing to settle the issues one by one. The Mississippian even questioned how Clay could still claim to be a Southern man representing a slave state. Clay responded with an eloquent defense, but he was clearly wounded by Foote's attack and began to retreat somewhat. He stated that he had wished the Senate to pass its judgment on each of his resolutions in succession, but that, once they had been referred to committee, a committee might see fit to write the territorial governments and the Texas boundary and debt into a single bill. It was Clay's first step—taken in frustration and exasperation—toward what he termed Foote's "omnibus" idea.[39]

Taylor, meanwhile, did not possess an effective administration floor leader in the Senate and was unable to effectively influence Congress; therefore, Taylor resorted to threatening what he knew best—military force. Around the middle of February the president promised some Southern visitors that, if secession were attempted, he would maintain the Union by blockading all the Southern ports to ensure tariff collections and that he himself would lead volunteers from Northern and Western states to put down any rebellion. But he also expressed his belief that the people of the South would put down disunion themselves and replace secessionist members of Congress. According to one account of the meeting, he calmly threatened to hang the first person who attempted disunion. Later that same month, at a February 28 dinner for some antislavery

congressmen, Taylor stressed to Horace Mann of Massachusetts that a block-
ade would halt secession without bloodshed.[40]

Some observers worried, however, that the violence that would begin disunion might erupt in Congress itself. On the surface, social exchanges were
pleasant enough, and even the most ardent antagonists would readily agree to
pair off with each other so that one or another or both might avoid voting on
roll calls. But not all was good fellowship. Jefferson Davis of Mississippi came
close to fighting a duel with William Bissell, an Illinois Democrat, over whose
troops had done what in the Mexican War. Several reporters remarked at the
frequency with which congressmen carried concealed pistols in the Senate and
House. More frightening to one observer were the numerous sharp penknives
he saw displayed on members' desks. One rumor circulated that a general me-
lee was to be staged in Congress, coordinated with plans to blow up the Capitol and White House. Given the guns and knives in abundance, such rumors
should have surprised no one.[41]

Anxious to keep the nation's peace, several leaders in Congress believed that
compromise was achievable but not via the formulas suggested so far. One of
these was Illinois senator Stephen Douglas. This dynamic, pragmatic politician
had been working within his Committee on Territories to construct a plan to
resolve at least the Western issues. Newspapers in early February had reported
the "Douglas Compromise" as involving California statehood, territorial governments for Deseret and New Mexico, inclusion of land east of the Rio Grande
in New Mexico and compensation to Texas for it, and a new slave state to be
carved from Texas to balance off California. On February 19, after the House's
chaotic marathon session on Doty's resolution, Douglas and his allies, Reps.
John McClernand and William A. Richardson of Illinois, organized a meeting
between Northern and Southern moderates of the House at Speaker Cobb's
residence in order to devise a program mutually satisfying to both sections.
Joining McClernand, Richardson, and Cobb were Ohio Democrat John K.
Miller, Kentucky Democrat Linn Boyd, and Georgia Whigs Alexander Stephens
and Robert Toombs.

The seven assembled on the evening of February 19 and agreed on a series of
proposals that would be developed into bills for both houses through the coordinated actions of the respective committees on territories: California's admission as a free state; two territorial governments in the remaining Mexican cession, with popular sovereignty to determine the slavery question therein; cession
of some of Texas's land in exchange for money to pay its debt; and opposition
to abolition in the District of Columbia. The final bills would be the work of

the committees themselves. Stephens and Toombs seemed especially enthusiastic about popular sovereignty, rather than the silence of Clay's plan regarding slavery in the territories. Stephens believed that this would free the territorial legislatures to protect Southerners' claimed rights. On the other hand, moderate Democrats from the North liked popular sovereignty for a very different reason; they, believing that the West was unfit for slavery by climate and geography, were willing to take a chance on popular sovereignty because they were firmly convinced that territorial legislatures would never accord legal protection for slave property.[42]

Douglas and his friends were not the only ones attempting to formulate new plans at this stage. Daniel Webster forged another one in February. He had continued to believe for several weeks after his meeting with Clay that the Union itself was not really endangered. Not all of Clay's scheme was workable; Webster decidedly disliked the idea of combining measures, and he saw some merit in Taylor's "nonaction" plan. However, by late February, Webster's fear of disunion had become heightened, possibly by preparations for the Nashville Convention, possibly by the vehemence of Southern congressional sentiment. Positive public response to Clay's proposals in New York and Philadelphia may have influenced Webster to consider that the Northern public would react favorably to a different compromise scheme. It would have been very gratifying to Webster personally to frame a program that might supplant and supersede that of his old intraparty rival. Webster also seems to have concluded that the only practicable plan would be one distinctly to the South's advantage and offered by a Northerner.[43]

According to one report, Senator Webster had begun piecing his ideas together around February 10. On Saturday evening, February 23, he consulted with several Southerners about the issues and how best to resolve them. Others who may have had a role in these deliberations were Sen. Daniel Dickinson of New York and Rep. David Kaufman of Texas, both Democrats. On February 24 the *New York Herald* first mentioned the plan's expected provisions, which included: a free state of California north of 36°30' north latitude; territorial governments for Deseret and New Mexico with no mention of slavery; the subdivision of Texas into three states; and financial compensation of Texas for lands east of the Rio Grande that it would cede to the U.S. About the same time, Philadelphia's *North American* divulged the boundaries that Webster had in mind: Texas would be reduced to the area between the Sabine and Trinity rivers; a second state would extend from the Trinity to the Colorado River, and a third state would stretch from there to the Rio Grande; the land north of 34° north latitude would be

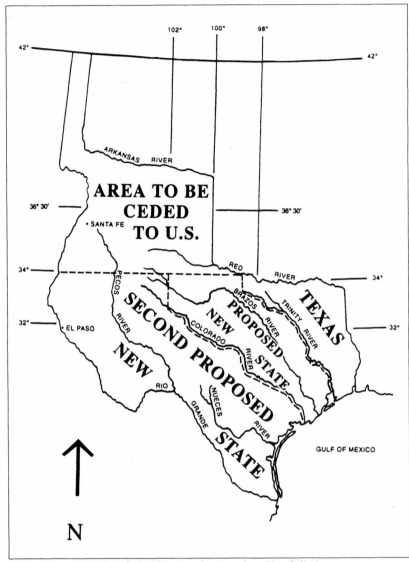

Webster's (Bell's) 1850 plan to reduce Texas's limits.

included in New Mexico Territory. The second and third proposed states would be slave states to balance California and a future free state. One version of the scheme was also reported to include a new fugitive slave law.[44]

Webster never presented his program. Several of his Northern Whig confreres were aghast when they first saw the details of his plan in the newspapers. Sen. John Davis and Rep. George Ashmun of Massachusetts, Sen. Truman Smith of Connecticut, and others severely counseled Webster that his provisions would be considered so pro-Southern in New England that it would destroy him politically. The use of the Missouri Compromise line in California and the subdivision of Texas into more slave states would be extremely unpopular in the North. The harsh reaction of his Whig colleagues finally convinced Senator Webster to delay offering his proposals and finally to divorce himself officially from them. Sen. John Bell of Tennessee, another Whig friend, further removed the burden from Webster's shoulders by offering to introduce an altered version of the scheme himself, which he did on February 28. To historians and biographers, it has always been labeled as "Bell's Plan," a tribute to how successfully Webster's involvement in its organization was covered up by Bell's move. As he began to introduce the plan on the 28th, Bell admitted that the resolutions he offered were not his own; he claimed to be only a "compiler" of ideas that had been considered by a dozen or more senators. He declared that he believed that only a compromise offered from the North, since the North was politically the more powerful section, would be likely to settle this issue—a veiled reference to Webster's authorship. After explaining his set of resolutions, Bell, one of the most moderate of all Southern leaders, warned the North that they were gravely mistaken to believe that the South was not in earnest regarding its demands.[45]

Bell's resolutions contained one major change from the program reportedly devised by Webster; he dropped the Missouri Compromise line and stipulated that California should be admitted to statehood with the boundaries it claimed. The propositions for the subdivision of Texas were exactly the same as those reported as part of Webster's plan in the press. For conceding its land claims beyond the Colorado River and above 34° north latitude, Texas would receive unspecified millions of dollars to pay its creditors. The boundaries for his suggested Territory of New Mexico were vague, except on the Texas side, and the boundaries for an unnamed territory for the Mormon settlements were even vaguer. These territories would be formed "without any restriction as to slavery." Neither fugitive slaves nor the District of Columbia were subjects of Bell's proposals.[46]

Bell's resolutions initially received some supportive comments, but they would fail as a basis for compromise, just as all other schemes focused on the subdivision of Texas did. Not only would the great majority of Northern legislators not countenance a subdivision, but the Texans did not desire it either. Texans could appreciate the need for more slave states and the intent of the 1845 annexation resolutions to permit Texas to subdivide into as many as four additional states, but, when it came to the practical accomplishment of this, Texans were at best reticent and mostly hostile to the idea in 1850. Many were fearful of the economic and trade implications of dividing the old imperial republic into states of middling size. More worrisome was the slavery question in west Texas. That frontier region beyond the Colorado was still sparsely populated, and the whites there possessed only a few slaves. The reality was that any state in that area would probably become a free state if detached from eastern, slaveholding parts of Texas. Texans' dread of a free-soil territory or state on their northern and western border in New Mexico was only compounded when they considered that a state carved out of the frontier even closer to the settled parts of Texas would likely also become a free state.[47]

Further hardening Texan resistance to subdivision at the time was their concern over demands by some residents of the lower Rio Grande Valley for separate government from Texas. The "Brownsville separatists" dispatched two petitions to Congress, one introduced by Seward on February 27 and the other introduced by Clay on March 11. The roots of the movement lay in the traditional resentment of this isolated frontier region against a Texas state government seemingly indifferent to its concerns and in the fears of many persons in the region, particularly those of Mexican descent, that Texas would not recognize their land titles as valid. Texans tended to view the whole affair as a seditious operation probably connected to the similar Northern abolitionist plot to dismember the Santa Fe region from Texas. Congress did little with the petitions except refer them to committee in March. Senator Rusk put in some brief words of protest when Clay introduced the second petition. The Texas Legislature and Governor Bell responded to the Brownsville movement with promises of security for property titles in the area, and by June 1850 the movement had mostly died out. However, demands for separate government by citizens of the lower Rio Grande Valley stiffened Texan determination to oppose subdivision of the state.[48]

But amidst the constant speechmaking that took place from early February through the first several days of April, the Rio Grande petitions were little more than a minor annoyance to most senators. A few of the senators, however, did discuss the Texas–New Mexico boundary dispute. On February 27 Rusk delivered an elaborate, document-laden defense of his state's claim, citing material from the early eighteenth century to President Polk's messages. On March 27

Ohio Free-Soiler Salmon P. Chase argued that much of the land claimed by Texas was yet in dispute and not among the territory "properly" and "rightfully" included within Texas under the vague annexation resolutions of 1845. On the next day, antislavery Whig Roger S. Baldwin of Connecticut questioned the constitutionality of the Texas annexation resolutions, and on April 5 Illinois Democrat James Shields argued that the New Mexico area had never been under Texas's actual possession or authority.[49]

The most famous speeches of the whole session were Calhoun's on March 4, Webster's on March 7, and Seward's on March 11. Calhoun, in his last major speech (delivered for the dying South Carolinian by Sen. James M. Mason of Virginia), all but despaired for continuity of the Union. Webster, heedless of anticipated outrage by New England abolitionists against him, courageously delivered his famous plea for compromise, although not for any specific plan. He agreed with Clay and the Northern Democrats that nature had effectively barred slavery from the West and also included in his address a vehement espousal of Texas's right to subdivide into more states under the annexation resolutions of 1845—the only remnant of his recent plan. Seward made only a brief reference to the Texas issue, but his address became famous for proclaiming continued Northern hostility to slavery extension based on a "higher law" than the Constitution. What this implied to Southerners was that Seward and those who acted with him would never cease their congressional agitation of the slavery question. President Taylor's immediate reaction to Seward's speech was anger, but within a week or so Seward had smoothed over the rift with the president.[50]

On March 12 the Senate resumed consideration of Foote's resolution for a select committee, now to consist of thirteen members. Foote had altered it to a motion to refer Senator Bell's proposals to such a committee, even though he intended and assumed that this committee would consider a settlement covering the whole gamut of sectional issues. During discussions on March 12 to 14, the Senate made no progress on Foote's move. But on March 12 Henry Clay for the first time publicly agreed to accede to the formation of Foote's proposed committee as an avenue of potential compromise, even though Clay declared his doubt that the "experiment," as he termed it, would succeed in its mission.[51]

Douglas, meanwhile, in his Committee on Territories, was formulating two bills for the organization of Western governments. One provided simply for California statehood, with the boundaries it claimed. The second combined the other territorial matters and included: territorial governments for Utah and New Mexico with no restriction as to the legislatures' authority over the slavery

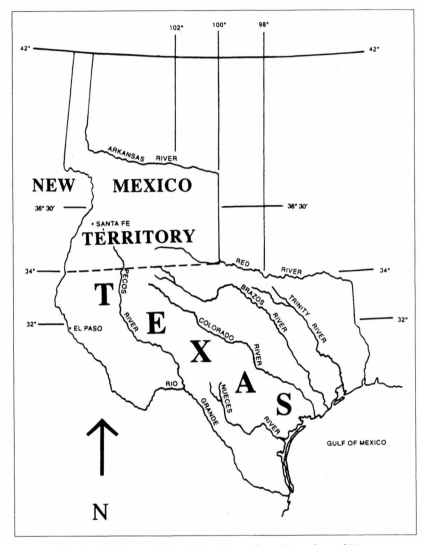

Douglas-McClernand plan of 1850 for northwest boundary of Texas.

issue in the territories; and Texas's cession of its land claims east of the Rio Grande and northwest of a line beginning at the intersection of that river with 34° north latitude and running northeastward to the intersection of the Red

River with 100° west longitude, in exchange for which Texas would receive ten million dollars. Both Cass and Clay had advised Douglas to retain California statehood in a separate bill, but the second bill did indicate Douglas's amenability to the concept of combining several diverse subjects in one measure. Unfortunately this did not obviate the Southerners' fear that, once the California bill passed, the North would drop consideration of the territories.

This consideration may have affected the mode by which Douglas's scheme was introduced into the House of Representatives on April 3 by John McClernand. Though not a member of the House Committee on Territories, he introduced the bill in conjunction with committee member William A. Richardson. What precise impact the House committee may have had in shaping the bill is not clear. The provisions were the same as in the Senate bills, but McClernand offered the whole package in a single bill, California included. Overall, the Douglas-McClernand plan received some positive comments in the press, but one political leader who was unimpressed by it was Volney Howard of Texas. In remarks at the bill's introduction and in a letter to the *Houston Telegraph,* Howard argued that McClernand's bill not only decided the boundary adverse to Texas's title but that New Mexico would abolish slavery on lands claimed as part of Texas east of the Rio Grande and that the bill would do nothing to remove the various Indian tribes from the Texas frontier.[52]

On March 26 Henry Foote moved for the Senate to take up Douglas's bills for consideration. Foote's nemesis, Benton of Missouri, immediately launched into a quick plea for California alone, which set off a two-day exchange of invective between the two men.[53] A few days later, on March 31, the Southern extremists suffered a grievous loss to their ranks when their illustrious leader for the previous two decades, John C. Calhoun, died. His death removed the most formidable Southern opponent of compromise, and during the months to follow no other Southern radical leader in Washington proved able to assume his mantle as the embodiment of Southern and proslavery thought.

During the week prior to Calhoun's death, the Taylor administration encountered a new contingent of Texans promoting their interests in Washington. Former Texas governor George Wood, Texan Whig leader William Ochiltree, and Texas state senator Adolphus Sterne arrived on about March 23 to lobby on the state's behalf and to gauge the administration's attitude toward the Lone Star. One specific item on their agenda was the procurement of money from the federal government to pay Texas volunteers who had been called to service to assist in frontier defense against Indians. Wood also wanted to gain insight into the boundary views of President Taylor and his advisers, who portrayed themselves to Wood as willing to accommodate Texas and quite prepared to support the arrangement of boundary and debt in the Douglas-McClernand proposal. Taylor and friends said nothing to Wood about their plan in progress for New Mexico's statehood.[54]

The administration, especially certain cabinet members, were much more concerned with their own political survival than they were with Wood or the Texas issue. Beleaguered throughout the session by accusations of weakness and incompetence, Taylor's cabinet lost whatever shred of public confidence it had still retained when the Galphin scandal broke in late March. Secretary of War George Crawford pocketed over $100,000 as agent for the heirs of this complex Georgia claim arising from debts owed by Indians to a fur trader during the American Revolutionary era. Secretary of the Treasury William Meredith and Attorney General Reverdy Johnson approved the legality of the payment. However legal it may have been, Crawford's profiteering while a member of the cabinet, with the connivance of two fellow cabinet members, struck the public as gross corruption. Loyal to his subordinates as always and believing Crawford innocent of wrongdoing, President Taylor could not even bring himself to change his unpopular cabinet at this most opportune moment. Aghast Whig leaders friendly to Taylor begged him to replace the "Galphins," as hostile editors dubbed them. Taylor considered suggestions for possible substitutes but never took the final step of forcing his original cabinet, or several members thereof, to resign.[55]

Thurlow Weed visited Washington in mid-April to engineer a cabinet transition, if he could. He discovered that Taylor was under enormous pressure, not only from the Galphin scandal but also from Southern demands to veto any separate bill for California statehood. Alexander Stephens and Robert Toombs badgered Taylor with this demand in an interview, possibly on April 12 or 13, when the Senate discussion of whether to establish a select committee had once again returned to center stage. When the stubborn president informed his two visitors that he would sign any bill he deemed constitutional and that he would execute the laws, the Georgians answered that such a course of action would bring disunion. Taylor angrily, and characteristically, responded that he himself would lead the army in putting down the rebellion and would without reluctance hang the traitors. After the dejected Stephens and Toombs exited, Sen. Hannibal Hamlin, a Free-Soil Democrat from Maine, went in to find President Taylor furiously pacing back and forth. He then emphatically urged Hamlin to stand firmly against any "Omnibus" bill that the compromisers might devise, for an "Omnibus" would mean disunion. With an oath, the president then reiterated his intent to execute anyone attempting treason. The next visitor, Thurlow Weed, found Taylor still excitedly pacing to and fro, and the president detailed for him what had transpired.[56]

The Senate, meanwhile, wrestled with Senator Foote's resolution to submit Bell's resolutions and (as altered by Foote on April 11) Clay's more comprehensive resolutions to a select committee of thirteen members. Foote once again made clear that his main concern in seeking to combine other measures with California was to guard against the Wilmot Proviso being added to territorial bills. Foote's preference for a single bill on these topics was also predicated on the need for the measure to pass the House of Representatives, without Southerners there resorting again to their effective blocking tactics.[57]

Thomas Hart Benton passionately opposed the connection of California with any other subject. Benton introduced a whole series of resolutions to instruct the prospective committee against such a combination and opposed the whole idea of a select committee doing "hugger-mugger" work behind closed doors. Douglas also saw little value in the select committee plan but resigned himself to its formation after several attempts to block it (including a move by himself to table Foote's resolution) failed to pass. Henry Clay and Lewis Cass buttressed Foote's position during the debates, while Hale of New Hampshire and Hamlin of Maine reinforced Benton's views. Voting followed rather consistent patterns during these days; most Northerners plus Benton and the Delaware senators voted against reference to the committee, while Southerners and several Northern Democrats favored the Foote resolution. Webster and Douglas voted sometimes one way, sometimes the other. The boundary dispute and its dangers arose only once in the debate, on April 8. After Benton had posited that combining California statehood with a boundary-debt proposal to Texas would give Texas a virtual veto over California, Henry Clay responded in defense of solving issues together. He stressed that above all other issues Congress must resolve the twin problems of New Mexico and the boundary dispute before a civil war erupted between Texas and New Mexico.[58]

It was in connection with debate on April 17 that the most notorious incident of the session occurred. Following several hours of discussion, Benton claimed that Clay was attempting to cut off discussion of Benton's proposals to disconnect California from any other subject. The old Missouri Unionist declared that his resolutions were designed to strike directly at what he interpreted as the root cause of all the sectional trouble—Calhoun's "Southern Address" and its disunionism. Foote, suddenly exchanging his compromiser's cloak for Southern extremist garb to go after Benton, labeled the statement as an insult to the late, lamented Calhoun, Foote himself, and every other Southerner involved in the "Southern Address." When Foote chose to denounce Benton in a biting, personal fashion, Benton started after him from his seat about twenty feet away. The diminutive Foote began backing down the nearest aisle toward the space in front of the secretary's table. Several senators had intercepted Benton and convinced him to return to his seat when Benton suddenly noticed that Foote had pulled a loaded, five-chambered revolver from his pocket. Benton again advanced down an aisle toward Foote, asking all to take notice that Foote had brought a gun there to assassinate him with. While various members wrestled Benton to a halt, Foote surrendered his pistol to another senator. It had all happened very quickly, too quickly for the hard-of-hearing vice president to be able to react effectively. An investigating committee later issued a report on the affair but recommended no punitive action against Foote. The confrontation injured nothing more than Senate dignity.[59]

Whether this incident occurred spontaneously or may have been deliberately provoked by Foote to galvanize the Senate into action on his resolution is not certain. Whether planned or not, the shock effect may have had some influence on senators, for the next day, April 18, the Senate voted down all of Benton's amendments to Foote's committee proposal by varying majorities and then voted 30 to 22 in favor of referring Bell's and Clay's resolutions to a select committee of thirteen. The committee quickly went to work under Henry Clay's leadership to devise a comprehensive compromise program. New Mexico's citizenry, in the meantime, acted on the advice of Colonel McCall, President Taylor's emissary, to develop an initiative of their own that was quite at odds with the aims of the Committee of Thirteen.[60]

Chapter Five

⁊ʮ

New Mexico Seeks Statehood

WHILE POLITICIANS IN WASHINGTON GROPED FOR SOLUTIONS TO THE SEC-
tional issues, politicians in New Mexico, encouraged by Colonels McCall and
Munroe, organized their drive to establish a state government. Neighbors's failed
mission on behalf of Texas may have contributed an added urgency to their
efforts. Neighbors had come alone this time and in peace; it seemed probable
that the next Texas commissioner, be it Neighbors or someone else, would
arrive at Santa Fe in the company of an armed force of Texas volunteers to
enforce his decrees. New Mexicans, aside from a very few, did not wish Texan
jurisdiction. The Taylor administration, through McCall and Munroe, had recently assured New Mexicans that the federal government would support the
formation of a government in New Mexico separate from that of Texas. It was
clear that the president wished New Mexico to form a state government rather
than the territory that the indigenous politicians had originally proposed, and,
given the alternatives of Texan jurisdiction or continued military government,
most New Mexicans eagerly embraced their opportunity to curry favor with
Taylor in framing the type of government he desired.

Munroe's proclamation of April 23 had designated Monday, May 6, for the
election of delegates, who were to convene on May 15 to begin drafting a state
constitution. The Houghton faction, which had converted into the "new" pro-
statehood party, enjoyed a nearly total domination over New Mexican politics
at that stage. The opposing Weightman-Alvarez faction exercised little influence among the populace; its solicitude for Neighbors and its new theme that
New Mexico should not form a state government without Texas's consent did

not add to its popularity. Adding to the Houghton faction's overwhelming influence were its control of the only newspaper in New Mexico, its enjoyment of undivided support from the U.S. military establishment, and its control of the civil patronage of the military government. The Houghton faction literally controlled the election of delegates, since Munroe's proclamation specified that the county prefects, all of whom owed their appointments to Houghton and his clique, would oversee the establishment of precincts and appoint the three-member returning boards to judge the elections in each county. Prefects themselves ran for election as delegates in all but two counties, with their election virtually assured.

Colonel Munroe's subordinate officers wielded their considerable power in the statehood cause. Capt. A. W. Reynolds, the quartermaster, was a Houghton zealot angling to become one of the new state's first senators. Probably not by coincidence, Reynolds paid off the employees of his department for the first time in several months on May 4, only two days before the election for delegates. Other officers were reported by a member of the "old" state party to be actively engaged in the campaign, hoping for promotions in a new regiment to be organized at the behest of the new state's senators.[1]

The only known attempt to exert leverage by a member of the "old" state party during the election consisted of a notice sent to the Pueblo Indian settlements by Indian Agent Calhoun on May 2 warning them not to take part in the election of delegates. He stated that their participation might undermine the tribe's status as a separate people under the direct authority of the federal government and possibly force them to become subject to state laws under New Mexico's proposed government. Calhoun did seem genuinely concerned for the welfare of the Indians in this and in his other pronouncements.[2]

The Houghton faction's lopsided victory on May 6 was no surprise. McCall related that they enjoyed a majority of 17 to 3 in delegates when the convention assembled at Santa Fe on May 15. Among the faction leaders in attendance as delegates were Judge Houghton himself; his colleague, Judge Antonio José Otero; Attorney General Murray F. Tuley; Taos trader Ceran St. Vrain; and Taos attorney James H. Quinn, who served as president of the convention. One member who leaned toward the "old" state faction was Padre José Manuel Gallegos, a very influential priest from Albuquerque. Serving as secretaries of the convention were Robert Cary, former Taos prefect, and Donaciano Vigil, the territorial secretary.[3]

Framing the constitution itself was relatively easy; Joab Houghton and Murray Tuley had already drafted the document before the convention began.

With their vast numerical superiority over the opposition, Houghton and friends probably anticipated a short convention. But trouble arrived on the second day of the convention in the person of Diego Archuleta. Highly suspected of having instigated the Taos Rebellion and the murder of Governor Bent but never prosecuted for his alleged complicity, Archuleta remained a heroic figure to many Mexican-Americans and had won a seat in the convention. Realizing that the friends of the deceased Bent at the convention would contest his seat, Archuleta had decided not to attend. But he was a member of the Weightman-Alvarez group, and for his party's sake Archuleta agreed to become an "element of discord," as McCall termed it, in hopes of preventing the convention from approving a constitution.

Archuleta's opponents, despite their lingering anger over Governor Bent's death, should have allowed Archuleta to take his seat without demur. But several of them who had already voiced their determination not to sit in the same convention with him immediately challenged the legality of his election. After two days of rancorous debate, the convention voted 11 to 7 to exclude Archuleta (those not voting included a delegate not yet arrived and two who absented themselves just before the vote). But the dissension desired by the Weightman-Alvarez faction had been created. Several of the Mexican-American delegates threatened to withdraw as Saturday's session ended. By Monday, May 20, these delegates were angry enough to question in committee certain parts of the draft constitution to which they had earlier raised no objections. Unable to report the document as ready on the 20th, the convention adjourned to May 21. Leaders of the "old" state party continued to foment Mexican-American resentment against Archuleta's ouster. By ten o'clock on the evening of the 20th, the minority faction believed they had commitments to leave the convention from enough delegates to deny the convention a quorum. Aware of the plan to break up the convention the next day, the Houghton faction countered the move by convincing some of the most ardent devotees of Bent to permit a reconsideration of the Archuleta expulsion vote, to then admit him, and to finally pass the constitution with no further delays. These measures were taken on the next morning, and quiet was once again restored to the convention.[4]

On May 21, the day Archuleta's seat was restored, the draft constitution was read to the delegates in both English and Spanish, and voting then began on each section of the document. The work was completed by May 24, and the convention approved the constitution that day, having made only slight amendments to the Houghton-Tuley draft. Attached to the constitution was a cédula, or schedule, part of which requested that Colonel Munroe order elections for

June 20, both for the purpose of conducting a popular referendum on the document and for electing state officials and legislators. Even a Texan enemy of the New Mexico proceedings, Charles Hoppin in Doña Ana, credited the convention managers for good strategy in setting both elections on the same day. In order to support a favorite candidate for a particular office, the voter would of necessity have to vote for the constitution under which that office was to be established. The convention also issued a supporting memorial to the U.S. Congress urging New Mexico's admission and issued a short address to their constituents defending the product of their labors.[5]

The convention closed on Saturday, May 25, with the signing of the constitution, the memorial to Congress, the short address, and a separate memorial to President Taylor on Indian affairs. Seventeen convention members signed the first three documents. Diego Archuleta and a few others did not. Twelve of the signers also added their names to the memorial on Indian affairs, itself a fascinating exercise in self-promotion by members of the convention. This memorial not only recommended that the president utilize more mounted riflemen or light cavalry in New Mexico for defense against Indian attacks, but it went so far as to recommend the appointment of a specific slate of officers for the first regiment of these troops. The convention recommended Ceran St. Vrain for colonel, Thomas S. J. Johnson for one of the two majors, and several other convention delegates among the ten recommended captains and four recommended lieutenants. Understandably, the convention delegates among the recommended appointees refused to endorse the memorial. The memorial certainly confirmed the prior suspicions of the Weightman-Alvarez faction about the vested self-interest of military officers who promoted the convention.[6]

In most respects the constitution resembled those of other states. It established three branches of government, a bicameral legislature, and the usual state offices from governor on down. Of particular interest in relation to the boundary dispute and the sectional crisis were the sections on the new state's claimed limits and on slavery. The boundary section followed immediately after the preamble and prescribed a line beginning at the dam in the Rio Grande near El Paso running due east to 100° west longitude and due north on that meridian to its intersection with the Arkansas River; then up that river to its source and then in a direct line to the intersection of 111° west longitude with the Colorado River; then due south on that meridian to the Gila River and up that river to some point yet to be determined as the international boundary by a U.S.-Mexican commission; then east along this international boundary line to the Rio Grande and, finally, down the Rio Grande to the place of beginning.

Just as Texas had laid claim to the settled parts of New Mexico, so did the New Mexico convention audaciously lay claim to an area that included at least two longitudinal degrees of territory within the settled area of Texas.[7]

Immediately following the boundary statement came a section on slavery that outlawed such servitude for any male after he reached the age of twenty-one and for any female after she reached the age of eighteen, "unless they be bound by their own consent after they arrive at such age [i.e., peonage], or are bound by law for punishment of crime." However qualified that section may have sounded, the delegates more forcefully expressed their antislavery feelings in their brief address "to the people of New Mexico." This address, and the antislavery clause in the constitution, were probably authored by antislavery New York native Joab Houghton. The address termed African slavery "naturally impracticable" in New Mexico and condemned it as "a curse and a blight . . . a moral, social, and political evil" wherever it had existed. The observant Charles Hoppin in Doña Ana interpreted the double standard of the antislavery clause to be on the one hand designed to secure Northern free-soil sympathizers in Congress behind New Mexico statehood and on the other hand designed to attract the votes of Mexican-Americans for the constitution on election day by not interfering with the peonage system to which the Mexican-American population was so attached.[8]

Three days after the convention concluded, Colonel Munroe issued the desired proclamation for the June 20 elections. Two ballots—one on acceptance of the constitution and one for the state officers and legislators—would be cast. Munroe also directed the new legislature to convene on July 1 for the limited purposes of organizing the state government and petitioning Congress to accept New Mexico's constitution. However, wisely displaying his need to set strict parameters on the new government's authority until Congress saw fit to extend its blessing to New Mexico's statehood, Munroe cautioned that action of the new government's officers and legislature would "remain inoperative" until Congress should admit New Mexico as a state. He declared that the existing military government that he headed would continue in force until Congress should choose to substitute a different one.[9]

Twenty-four days of arduous political campaigning ensued. The "new" state party entered the fray fully anticipating another easy victory at the polls for their constitution and their slate of executive and legislative candidates. McCall initially believed that their party would run the very wealthy Judge Otero for governor or, if he did not want to run, the trader Ceran St. Vrain. For whatever reason, the Houghton faction instead nominated for governor Dr. Henry

Connelly, another prominent trader. Connelly, who had married into the prominent Chavez family and lived in Bernalillo, had resided in New Mexico for many years and was very popular. During the campaign, however, he was absent back East on a trading expedition. Ceran St. Vrain was nominated for lieutenant governor. Hugh Smith, still in Washington, became the "new" state party's candidate for the U.S. House of Representatives, and Houghton and Capt. A. W. Reynolds, the army quartermaster, hoped to have enough members of their party elected to the legislature to ensure their selection as New Mexico's first two U.S. senators. Others in their party hoped for appointments to state positions under the new governor.[10]

The Houghton faction's overwhelming confidence led to a disastrous underestimation of their opponents. That two of the three major candidates of the "new" state party were not even present in New Mexico for the campaign added some incentive to the "old" state party, and the Weightman-Alvarez faction fielded a full slate of non-absentee candidates for state offices and the legislature. Capitalizing on their resurgent appeal among Mexican-Americans, fostered during the Archuleta affair, the "old" state party nominated Tomás Cabeza de Baca for governor and Manuel Alvarez for lieutenant governor. For the U.S. House of Representatives the party ran William S. Messervy, a Massachusetts native. Richard H. Weightman, the faction's most vigorous leader, exerted mighty efforts in the campaign in his desire to gain enough supporters in the forthcoming legislature to defeat his archenemy Houghton in the contest for a U.S. Senate seat.[11]

Weightman utilized every bit of his influence with the Mexican-American community. He defended the Roman Catholic faith and the authority of its clergy. Weightman, Alvarez, and company also negated any advantage that the Houghton faction figured to derive from having framed the state constitution. The "old" state party fully supported the constitution, reminding voters that they had been the original statehood advocates. The Weightman-Alvarez group also struck a responsive chord in the electorate by running a patently antiestablishment campaign. They stressed all the accumulated popular resentments against the continued military government and the civilian officials who served it—Houghton and his confreres of the "new" state party. Styling themselves "friends of the people," the "old" state party hammered away at the reputed corruption and maladministration of the Kearny government appointees.[12]

Both sides canvassed the Pueblo Indian settlements for votes, considering their approximately two thousand votes the key to victory if the Mexican-American voters split rather evenly. Propaganda, promises, and threats confused the Indians. Agent Calhoun had warned them away from the convention delegate

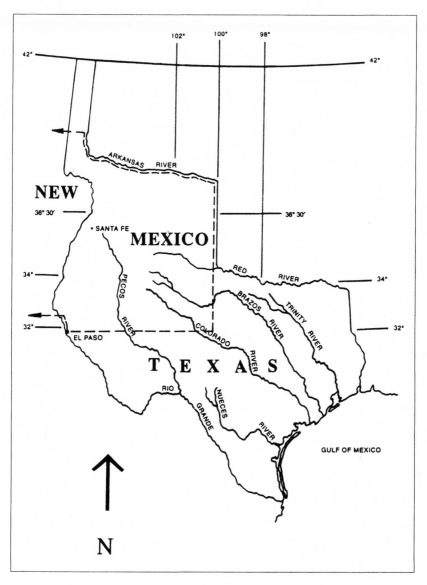

New Mexico's boundary east of the Rio Grande
according to its proposed state constitution of 1850.

elections, and now candidates were pleading for their votes. On June 6 Colonel Munroe informed the various pueblos that Indians were entitled to vote in the election but need not do so, as they chose, and that no government official had a right to interfere with their free exercise of the suffrage. Richard Weightman had much support among the Pueblo Indians, for he had been appointed by Indian Agent Calhoun as an attorney to defend the Tesuque Pueblo in a lawsuit brought against it by some of the Houghton faction's alcaldes.

Nevertheless, the "old" state party's gubernatorial candidate, Cabeza de Baca, confused the Indians of the Cochiti Pueblo by his overly aggressive pitch. After Cabeza de Baca told Indian leaders that the Houghton faction candidate for governor, if elected, would take away the Pueblos' possessions and reduce them to the status of Navajos and Apaches, the bewildered Cochiti leaders promptly paid a personal visit to Colonel Munroe on June 10. The chief of the delegation and his people were unused to this sort of election campaign and needed firm advice from Colonel Munroe on how to proceed. The chief also told Munroe that they wished to be governed by Americans rather than by the Mexican officials who had oftentimes oppressed them. Munroe's immediate response to the chief's plea for guidance was not recorded, but it undoubtedly resembled the proclamation that Agent Calhoun and he addressed to the Pueblo towns two weeks later on June 25, which was meant to reassure the Pueblos that their persons and property would be as secure as before the election and that the internal government and customs of the Pueblo towns would be enforced until other laws, or the president of the United States, might direct otherwise.[13]

Two commentaries stressed that the campaign was quite "violent." Certainly the campaign could not have been devoid of the unruliness characteristic of frontier electioneering. It was assuredly the most intensely exciting political campaign that the indigenous population had ever experienced. The Mexican-American populace entered into it with the utmost enthusiasm. The "new" state party, caught somewhat off guard by the vigor of the opposition's campaign and appeal, brought the whole apparatus of the Kearny government to bear to assist the Houghton faction. The 150 or so civil officials spread throughout New Mexico were, except for five or six individuals, committed to the Houghton candidates and employed what influence they could for them. A leader of the Santo Domingo Pueblo on the Rio Grande, Juan Estevan Aragon, favored the Houghton faction and paid visits to all the other pueblos at the behest of Territorial Secretary Donaciano Vigil. The quartermaster's department employees, with a few exceptions, wielded their power over corn and forage contracts to garner votes for the "new" state party. The publishers of the *New Mexican* gave their editorial support to the Houghton faction and refused to print ballots for the Weightman-Alvarez candidates. This forced the "old" state party to mobilize their supporters to write out fifteen to twenty thousand ballots by hand. In reference to Alvarez's Spanish origins, Houghton's men ridiculed Manuel Alvarez as a *gachupín*, a derisive term for Spanish loyalists during Mexico's war for independence. Kearny government officials on occasion resorted to intimidation. Word circulated that an army officer had orders to arrest Juan Baptiste Le Conte, a leader of the "old" state party, to prevent his presence at Arroyo Hondo, just north of Taos, on election day. The Houghton faction also attempted to frighten voters at Mora, an "old" state party stronghold southeast of Taos.[14]

By the time June 20 arrived and voters went to the polls, indications favored a victory for the Weightman-Alvarez party, despite the enormous efforts of the Kearny government and its supporters to control the election. Due to Dr. Connelly's tremendous popularity or to the political ineptitude of his opponent, or possibly to both factors, only the governorship appeared certain for the "new" state party candidate. In Southern New Mexico Connelly had the support of both parties. On election day the scale of victory by the Weightman-Alvarez faction in the other races finally became apparent. Despite reputed vote suppression and vote stealing by Houghton's officials in several counties and from the Zuni Pueblo, the "old" state party carried every county but one, Santa Fe probably being the exception. The constitution received nearly unanimous endorsement by a vote of 8,371 to 39. Henry Connelly defeated Tomás Cabeza de Baca 5,768 to 2,724 for the governorship. Manuel Alvarez became lieutenant governor over Ceran St. Vrain by a margin of 4,586 to 3,870. William Messervy was chosen as U.S. representative 4,934 to 4,374 over Hugh Smith. Judging from the number of votes cast, popular interest in the Messervy-Smith contest was greater than in the others; while fewer than 8,500 votes were cast in reference to the constitution, the governorship, or lieutenant governorship, just over 9,300 votes were cast for Messervy and Smith together. More significantly, the "old" state party won a large majority of seats in both houses of the new legislature. What had begun as an uphill battle for the Weightman-Alvarez faction only a matter of weeks before had become an overwhelming triumph on June 20.[15]

With their solid legislative majority, the delirious Weightman-Alvarez forces relished the opportunity to make the most of their electoral mandate when the legislature convened on July 1. Governor-elect Connelly was still back East, which meant that Lieutenant Governor-elect Alvarez would actually lead the new government; thus, the Houghton faction's only major victor proved useless to his party by his absence. Nonetheless, Houghton and friends laid plans to disrupt the legislature's proceedings, just as the "old" state party had created trouble at the constitutional convention with the Archuleta affair.

On Monday, July 1, the senators and representatives attempted to organize a legislative body. Miguel Montoya, a Houghton faction stalwart and most recently a signatory to the Doña Ana petition against the Steen headright, presented himself as a duly elected state representative. His credentials were initially accepted, but information arrived soon thereafter that his opponent had received a clear majority of votes and was entitled to the seat. Montoya's credentials were then repudiated by the majority that represented the Weightman-Alvarez faction. Six representatives, apparently the only "new" state men among those present, immediately drafted and signed an insultingly worded protest against the exclusion of Montoya. The decisive "old" state party majority promptly reacted by securing the two-thirds vote necessary to expel the six protesters for "disorderly conduct," as provided in Article 3, section 10 of the new constitution. Two men who had been challenging the credentials of two Santa Fe representatives who were expelled were then admitted to those seats. The Houghton group had seemingly concocted the Montoya scheme, albeit in vain, as a means of denying the proper number of representatives to constitute a quorum for doing business. In a related maneuver, Judge Houghton issued a warrant for the arrest of one representative as an accomplice to a murder committed nearly four years previously and had him imprisoned. The move was so blatantly partisan, however, that when the accused was brought before two justices of the peace on a writ of habeas corpus, the prosecutor refused to press the case, even though he was a member of Houghton's faction. Houghton's tactics failed to disrupt the new legislature, and Lieutenant Governor Alvarez issued a proclamation for new elections to be held on August 20 to fill those seats that had been vacated.[16]

The most important task for the new legislature, and the one that Houghton sought to prevent, was the selection of two U.S. senators to press the cause of New Mexico statehood in Congress. The New Mexico Senate, with Joseph Naugle serving as president, and the House, with W. Z. Angney as speaker, conducted the selection process. Joab Houghton and Capt. A. W. Reynolds, the candidates of the "new" state party, were quickly dropped from serious consideration. For several days, however, the legislature discussed the merits of Weightman, Calhoun, Angney, and Dr. James D. Robinson. Robinson, anxious for any patronage position, according to Colonel McCall, was apparently bought off by the promise of appointment as state auditor. What convinced Calhoun and Angney to drop from contention is not clear, but after a few days the legislature chose Maj. Francis A. Cunningham, a well-respected military paymaster, to join Weightman, a former paymaster, as U.S. senator. The choice of Cunningham was unsolicited, and he was out of town on escort duty with a mail party at the time. Cunningham had also not been involved in politics; he may have been a compromise choice satisfactory to those who favored other contenders. Weightman seems to have had no competition. Voting took place on July 11, and the results were a good indication of the "old" state party's supremacy in the legislature. The votes received were: Weightman 19; Cunningham 17; Reynolds 3; and Houghton 1. Richard Weightman, his credentials and other documents in hand, departed Santa Fe for Washington on July 15.[17]

But electing two U.S. senators was not all that Acting Governor Alvarez and friends had in mind. They contemplated further action, the purpose of which was to immediately put the new government fully into operation and control over New Mexico, even though Congress had not admitted the region to statehood or settled the boundary dispute. This move represented not only the belief of New Mexico's new leaders that they were, through the democratic process, now entitled to exercise the functions of a political sovereign, but also that this was meant to complete the overthrow of the Kearny government, military rule, and the Houghton faction. Manuel Alvarez eloquently enunciated these themes in his inaugural address of, appropriately, July 4. As Alvarez saw it, the popular will, which he called "our only and our sovereign guide," had been fairly manifested and a constitution in accord with that will adopted. Alvarez admitted that the power of Congress was supreme over their own but also expressed his belief that, since it appeared "highly improbable" at that time that Congress would grant them a territorial organization, in all likelihood New Mexico's choice to adopt a state constitution would not be interfered with. The acting governor told the legislators: "If your organization is good for any one act, it is good for all; if it be good to elect senators to Congress, it is sufficient to make all constitutional reforms in our system and our laws necessary for our peace, honor, or security."[18]

Col. John Munroe was not blind to what was happening. He had already stipulated in his proclamation of May 28 the extremely limited nature of the powers of the new government until Congress should recognize its validity. He also realized that the political party that had assumed control of the new government bitterly resented Munroe's and McCall's undisguised support of the Houghton faction and its Kearny government functionaries. Munroe understood that the Alvarez government would extend its authority as far and as quickly as it could no matter how forcefully he might admonish against it. But

Colonel Munroe also did not wish to initiate confrontation by immediately assuming a hostile attitude before the legislature actually dared to pass laws he felt
were outside its proper sphere of jurisdiction. Therefore, on July 4 Munroe sent
both houses of the legislature a short message simply reminding the lawmakers
of their limitations as outlined in his May 28 proclamation.

If Alvarez's inaugural sentiments of July 4 were not a clear enough indication that the acting governor had no intention of abiding by Munroe's proclamation, his message of Monday, July 8, to the legislature left no doubt. In this
address Alvarez outlined various problems and then suggested the passage of
numerous laws covering such diverse subjects as vagrancy, peonage, prefects
and alcaldes, the status of the Pueblo Indians, public schools, taxation and
loans, criminal justice, and elections. He also recommended that the legislature
send a memorial to Congress on the need for a more efficient system of frontier defense. While the legislators took these matters under consideration, an
alarmed Colonel Munroe called Manuel Alvarez to his office for a conference
on July 10. The military governor told Alvarez that he would disregard any actions of the legislature that overstepped the bounds of his May 28 proclamation,
that he would continue to sustain the Kearny government authorities, and that
he considered the newly elected government's course "unwarranted and revolutionary" in its organization of departments and assumption of broad legislative powers. On the next day, Thursday, July 11, Munroe sent Alvarez an 1849
opinion of Gen. Bennett Riley relative to political authority in California. Riley,
basing his views on an earlier U.S. Supreme Court decision, had held that the
Guadalupe Hidalgo Treaty conferred on the inhabitants of California the rights
of U.S. citizens but entitled them to no political power nor share in the government until California should be admitted to statehood.[19]

Alvarez and the legislature defied Munroe when on Friday, July 12, the acting governor sent his nominations for secretary of state, auditor, treasurer, and
four supreme court judges to the legislature for confirmation. And the legislature passed a law providing for the election of alcaldes, sheriffs, and other local
officials on August 12. Both maneuvers were designed to supplant the Kearny
government officials under Munroe, especially Judge Houghton, with officials
of the new regime. Munroe responded immediately in protest to Alvarez's note
announcing his recommended appointments, informing Alvarez that this action was clearly beyond the scope of the newly elected officials' powers, subver-
sive of government, illegal, and injurious to New Mexico. He declared that the
attempt of Alvarez's nominees to exercise official functions would constitute a
direct violation of their duties as U.S. citizens. Munroe reaffirmed his intention

to support with all means at his disposal the Kearny government officeholders. Alvarez answered with his own letter that day, condemning Munroe's interposition of his authority against the civil power erected by the people themselves. While deprecating any collision between the new government and Munroe's forces, Alvarez defiantly expressed the determination of the new government to peacefully organize itself and to continue its work of reform in replacing the old government's personnel. Alvarez followed this up on July 13 with a much longer discourse in defense of his government. In it he cogently argued that the people of New Mexico, under direct guidance from the president and in the absence of any government organization by Congress, had written a state constitution and were establishing the government for which it called. He cited previous documents emphasizing the temporariness of military government and demanded that, as had happened in California on the completion of its constitution, the military governor relinquish all civil authority to the government recently elected under New Mexico's own constitution.[20]

Rather than continue debate, Munroe and McCall sought to take advantage of some dissension in the legislature over Alvarez's appointments. The dissent originated among prominent Mexican-American legislators aligned with the "old" state party who believed that Alvarez and friends were pressing their party's agenda too far and too fast. These Mexican-Americans protested Alvarez's nominations and desired the replacement of only a handful of obnoxious alcaldes and prefects rather than the wholesale sweep contemplated by the new election law. When the law passed despite their objections, these angry legislators hinted that they might just leave and go home to await whatever action the U.S. Congress might take. McCall attempted to convince the dissenters to take their case directly to Colonel Munroe, who would then act on their protest. But the "old" state party leaders knew what was up, and they worked assiduously on the Sabbath to persuade the disgruntled legislators to toe the party line and not succumb to the machinations of military officers who seemed determined to protect Kearny officials from removal from office.[21]

When the legislature reassembled on Monday, July 15, McCall saw his hopes dashed. All the former Mexican-American dissenters pledged to support the new government under New Mexico's constitution. Both Colonels Munroe and McCall were stunned and frustrated by this turnabout. Munroe portrayed Mexican-Americans as ignorant people of unstable character, while McCall described them as easily excitable men totally controlled by Anglo leaders. Neither officer could credit the Mexican-Americans of the Weightman-Alvarez faction with the capacity to act independently.[22]

Adding to the humiliation of Munroe and McCall, the legislature endorsed
on May 15 the stand taken by Alvarez in his exchange with the military governor. The preamble condemned Munroe's determination to employ his power
to block the overwhelming popular will for the new state government to go
into immediate operation. The military regime of previous years was termed
"sinking, ineffective and abhorrent." The resolutions declared the people's right
to organize a civil government and stated that it superseded the Munroe government. Munroe's restrictions on the new government were called illegal and
unauthorized by higher authority and also directly contrary to the principles
of government proclaimed by President Taylor. The legislature's memorial to
Congress, which may have also been approved on July 15, reiterated some of
the same ideas on government. Going well beyond Alvarez's original recommendation of a memorial on frontier defense, the document recited a litany of
wrongs suffered by the people at the hands of the military government. The
legislators defended the legitimacy of their own new government as necessi-
tated by congressional inaction, encouraged by the president, and consistent
with the U.S. Constitution.[23]

The legislature kept one of its moves on July 15 from Colonel Munroe, for it
was not included on a list of the legislature's actions that he sent to Washington. Having taken such an uncompromising position vis-à-vis Munroe, it is
easy to understand why the lawmakers kept a more compromising resolution
under wraps until they needed to announce it. The members resolved on the
15th that any officials elected on August 12 would not exercise any jurisdiction
under the authority of the state government until after November 1. Such a
delay might allow Alvarez and his party to work out a modus operandi with
Munroe. For the time being, however, the legislature apparently did not inform the military governor about this particular resolution.[24]

The legislature continued its defiance of Colonel Munroe during its last session on Tuesday, July 16, by ratifying all of Acting Governor Alvarez's nominations for offices. Among those confirmed were Palmer Pillans as chief justice of
the state supreme court and Diego Archuleta as third associate judge of that
court. The bitterly vindictive Col. George McCall described the appointees as
dissipated, untalented, ignorant, treacherous, or combinations thereof. The legislature—having confirmed these nominations, passed the election law and a
few lesser acts, memorialized Congress and protested to Munroe, and elected
U.S. senators—adjourned on the 16th with plans to reassemble on December 1.[25]

McCall believed that the newly elected government officials and lawmakers
had all agreed among themselves that, despite their actions in the legislature,

they would not attempt to enforce those measures until they had received word from Washington of congressional or executive action there regarding New Mexico's status. McCall ascribed this decision on their part to Colonel Munroe's firm determination to interpose his forces against them if they did attempt to overthrow the military government. Munroe himself did not seem to share Colonel McCall's confidence that the "old" state party would now hibernate for a while. In his letter to Adjutant General Jones on July 16, Munroe called the situation "grave," accused the new state government of trying to "supersede" his own, and desperately requested instructions for his guidance from Washington. He defended his resistance to Alvarez's demands in part because the boundary with Texas remained yet unadjusted and because he believed Congress would eventually grant New Mexico only a territorial government. Ironically, an Albuquerque correspondent to the *New Mexican,* also writing on July 16, declared that the main object of the Alvarez government that Munroe so opposed was to counter the Texan attempt to annex New Mexico.[26]

To ensure that Alvarez and his officials caused no disruption, Colonel Munroe began dispatching troops to various towns when rumors of insurrectionary movements reached Santa Fe, and he also began recalling soldiers from outlying posts and concentrating his forces at key points. The threatened revolt proved imaginary, and the rumors of such may have been manufactured by Houghton's officials for the purpose of maintaining a strong military presence to overawe the populace. According to Richard Weightman, Munroe's government manufactured scares and called out the soldiers in order to discredit the contention that New Mexico was civilized enough for state government, at least under Alvarez. The "new" state party that had organized the statehood convention was now trying to halt the statehood movement. Munroe's tactics did achieve the results he desired; his show of force severely diminished the ardor of the new state government's advocates for continued political action.[27]

But Manuel Alvarez was too proud and too certain of the moral and political righteousness of his position to submit to Munroe without a struggle. On July 20, only a few days after the legislators had departed Santa Fe, Alvarez issued his proclamation for elections of alcaldes and sheriffs to be held on the second Monday in August, the 12th. As if one controversy was not enough, the recently returned Judge Spruce Baird further muddied the political waters on July 20 by issuing from Albuquerque a proclamation for Texas state elections to be held in Santa Fe County's six districts on August 5. Baird pleaded for people to declare themselves citizens of Texas by participating in these elections. No one in New Mexico listened to Baird. The *New Mexican* simply ridiculed him as an "imposter" and warned the populace not to give credence to the Texas claim by voting on August 5. The Weightman-Alvarez faction, which only a few months previous had somewhat favored Texan commissioner Robert Neighbors, now shunned Baird. Circumstances had now changed, the "old" state party was now ascendant in New Mexico's politics, and any association with Texas or its claims had become anathema to the Weightman-Alvarez faction. Lacking local support, Baird never held his elections.[28]

Munroe ignored Baird just as everyone else in New Mexico did. But the military governor took the Alvarez proclamation seriously. In a circular addressed to the county prefects on July 23, Territorial Secretary Vigil, by order of Munroe, instructed these officials that the new state government had "no legal existence" until Congress should admit New Mexico to statehood and that the Kearny government would be sustained. Vigil told them to disregard Alvarez's proclamations. The columns of the *New Mexican* did service in Munroe's cause, calling Acting Governor Alvarez a "usurper" and attacking his proclamation and his assumption of power to appoint subordinate state officers. In its July 30 issue, the paper even went so far in its attempt to discredit the Alvarez regime as to print false reports that the latest mail had brought news that Congress had already enacted the bill organizing New Mexico and Utah as territories and admitting California as a state.[29]

No actual electioneering activity appears to have taken place as the August 12 elections approached. Colonel Munroe's show of force had squelched any enthusiasm for the Alvarez government's elections, as letters to Alvarez testified. A few days before the voters were supposed to cast ballots, both Alvarez and Munroe moderated their positions somewhat. On August 8 Acting Governor Alvarez issued a proclamation reminding the New Mexican populace of the theretofore secret July 15 resolution that elected officials would not enter on the performance of their official duties until after November 1. The next day, August 9, Colonel Munroe had Secretary Vigil distribute an order to the county prefects not to oppose the scheduled elections but also not to participate in them nor to recognize the voting results as conferring any authority on those elected. There is no evidence that elections were actually conducted in any of the counties. Neither were any elections held on August 20 to fill vacant seats in the legislature.[30]

In addition to the task of keeping the local populace in line, Munroe also had to deal with two of his own officers whose loyalty might be suspect if the Texans invaded New Mexico. Given their recent performances in relation to the mission of Robert Neighbors, Munroe strongly desired to have both Maj. William S. Henry and Maj. Enoch Steen quietly removed from the territory before any potential conflict with Texans began. Since both were military officers, the command structure was efficiently utilized to solve the problem without raising any public controversy. But the authorities in Santa Fe were also anxious to impress on the other officers in the department the difficulty they could find themselves in if they gave aid and comfort to the Texans. Major Henry was chosen to be the scapegoat and subjected to court martial proceedings.

Major Henry was certainly the more convenient choice for this object lesson than Major Steen would have been. The documents concerning Steen had been forwarded to Washington and would be acted on from there in due course. Steen's headright was also a very sticky question, directly raising the controversial boundary question. A court martial of Steen was out of the question, at least until higher authorities back East had a chance to examine the case and decide on a course of action. Even then, it is doubtful if Colonel Munroe would have wanted to put Steen on trial; it probably could not have been done without causing an outcry among Texan political leaders in Austin and in Washington, and this is exactly what Colonel Munroe and the Taylor administration would have wished to avoid.

Ordering Major Henry to leave New Mexico was no problem. He had wanted to return to the East and was chosen by Colonel McCall in late May to report for recruiting duty in New York on September 1. Henry was initially informed that he could leave San Elizario on July 1, but on June 12 Munroe's adjutant suspended Henry's order to report for recruiting service and ordered him to remain in the department to answer charges. The charges were rather petty by themselves— which is what made them so convenient, for no one outside of military circles was likely to pay any attention to them. Feeding Robert Neighbors's horses at public expense constituted the substance for the principal charge against Henry. But in order to deemphasize this charge as the real reason to try Major Henry, others were dredged up, some dating from previous years. These charges were that Major Henry had utilized public property to transport his family and their personal belongings and that Henry had recently detailed several of his soldiers, without Colonel Munroe's knowledge, to accompany his family to Fort Leavenworth. And finally Henry was charged with feeding Neighbors's animals from public stores and signing a false forage return that lumped the Texas commissioner's horses in with the U.S. military's animals.[31]

On July 2, Munroe's headquarters at Santa Fe ordered a court martial convened at Doña Ana on July 15. The court consisted of nine officers, with Bvt. Col. Charles A. May as presiding officer and Majors Van Horne, Cunningham, and Steen among the other members of the court, with 1st Lt. James H. Simpson of the Topographical Engineers acting as judge advocate (i.e., the prosecutor). Henry conducted his own defense and pleaded not guilty to all charges. During three days of testimony, Major Henry vigorously cross-examined each of the prosecution's witnesses and at the end of the trial issued a statement defending his own conduct.

On July 18 the court found Henry not guilty of employing army property for his family's personal use but guilty of detailing soldiers to escort his family. On the charge that involved his dealing with Neighbors, the court found Henry guilty on all specifications, but not guilty of fraud. Sentence was passed the next day, and Major Henry was ordered to repay the quartermaster's department ten dollars as the value of the forage provided to Commissioner Neighbors's animals. The court also ordered that a public reprimand of Henry's actions be posted in each military department headquarters in the nation and that Henry be suspended from rank, command, and pay for six months. The members of the court petitioned for remission of the sentence relating to suspension of rank and pay, however, due to Henry's prior record of good service and because they felt that Henry had taken his action in regard to Neighbors due to "generous but false notions of his position and duties." Munroe granted the petition and his adjutant issued an order on August 4 for Major Henry to be released and sent on his way to New York on recruiting service. The trial had served its purpose; an example had been made.[32]

Enoch Steen was dealt with less harshly, although the issues raised by his actions were far more serious and sensitive. When the documents concerning the Steen headright and the Doña Ana petition reached Washington, Taylor administration officials realized immediately that this type of action must be promptly disavowed. On July 3 Secretary of War Crawford ordered the Adjutant General's Office to have Major Steen replaced and ordered to Fort Leavenworth. Two days later, on July 5, Asst. Adj. Gen. Lorenzo Thomas sent the order to Colonel Munroe directing that, when a subaltern of Steen's company arrived in the Ninth Military Department, Steen was to turn over his command to that officer and remove to Fort Leavenworth to await further orders. Thomas added that the secretary of war expected military officers to protect citizens and quiet their fears regarding security of property but that Major Steen's course had had the contrary effect. This order did not reach Santa Fe until the beginning of September, when Munroe's department headquarters transmitted it to Steen. In mid-October Bvt. Capt. Abraham Buford arrived with a contingent of recruits and took over for Major Steen.[33]

In December Captain Buford discovered that Steen, just after receiving his marching orders from headquarters, had deeded a piece of his claimed headright to the post sutlers at Doña Ana. Part of the property that Steen claimed was a three-hundred-foot building that housed the 1st Dragoons Regiment and the store of sutlers Charles M. Ogden and Charles A. Hoppin. Major Steen sold the store section of the building to Ogden and Hoppin on September 10 for fifty dollars and recorded the deed at Franklin, Texas, on October 18. Upon discovering the transaction, Captain Buford sent the deed to Colonel Munroe's headquarters and told Ogden and Hoppin to be prepared to give up possession of the building to Guadalupe Miranda, who had owned it before the Steen headright, if the sutlers could not make a satisfactory arrangement with Miranda to retain it as their store. Whether Ogden and Hoppin ever retrieved their fifty dollars from Major Steen is not known.[34]

Colonels Munroe and McCall had some interesting times during the statehood movement in New Mexico. But, having helped to sponsor it, they soon found themselves unable to easily control it once the Weightman-Alvarez faction had won the elections. They had effectively handled the removal of Majors Henry and Steen and made an example of Henry to warn off other officers who might befriend the Texans. The question of what would happen to New Mexico's statehood or to the military government remained to be decided by the politicians in Washington. Meanwhile, everything remained on hold in New Mexico.

Chapter Six

༄

Texas–New Mexico
and the Omnibus Bill Debate,
May 8–July 9, 1850

NEWS OF THE DEVELOPING SITUATION IN NEW MEXICO SLOWLY WENDED ITS way to Washington via St. Louis. Not until May 4 did a telegraphic report from St. Louis communicate the news of Robert Neighbors's arrival at Santa Fe. Henry Clay's Committee of Thirteen had nearly completed their work by that date. Daniel Webster reported that at its first meeting on April 20 the committee voted against combining disparate subjects into a single bill. Confident that the committee therefore would propose separate bills, Webster left Washington for a trip to Boston. Three other members departed the capital as part of the official escort that would accompany the body of the deceased John C. Calhoun back to South Carolina.[1]

The remaining nine members of the committee assembled again on Thursday, April 25. Committee majorities adopted California statehood with the state's boundaries as then defined in its proposed constitution and proposed that Utah and New Mexico be given territorial governments without a prohibition against slavery and with the territorial legislatures forbidden to legislate in reference to the delicate subject. The committee then voted by a decided majority to repudiate its previous commitment to separate bills and to unite the California and territory measures in one bill.

The Texas–New Mexico boundary proved a major sticking point, as members could not agree on its location. Proposals on the "southern line of New Mexico" varied from 32° to 34° north latitude; Henry Clay suggested a line from El Paso to the northernmost source of the Red River and from there to 42°

north latitude. Neither could the committee agree on how much monetary compensation to grant Texas for land claims it would cede. The committee rejected Senator Bell's resolution to subdivide Texas, something that neither Texans nor other Southerners really desired for fear that states carved from west Texas would become free states. Senator Clay retreated the next day, April 26, to Riversdale, the estate of National Hotel proprietor Charles Calvert near Bladensburg, Maryland, to write bills and a report.[2]

Clay returned to Washington several days later, as did most of the absentee members of the committee. Webster was still absent and would not have approved uniting the measures. At a final committee meeting on Sunday, May 5, the majority confirmed the decisions reached previously, but John Berrien of Georgia dissented, as most other Southerners would, from the restriction that would prevent territorial legislatures from passing any laws in reference to slavery, even ones that might protect Southerners' rights to slave property during the territorial stage of government.[3]

And the committee remained at an impasse over the boundary. A *Washington Union* editorial on May 2 pointed out that this issue involved not only the peace of Texas and New Mexico but also, to some extent, the "tranquillity of the Union." Berrien remained desirous of a line at or near 34° north latitude, while the uncompromising Senator Mason of Virginia wanted the committee to eliminate from the bill everything relating to Texas.

With the committee facing the dismal and embarrassing prospect of reporting to the Senate without a solution to this most volatile issue, Sen. Thomas J. Rusk of Texas came to the rescue. Both Houston and Rusk would have preferred the 34° north latitude line, but the terrain between that line and El Paso to the south was quite desolate and seemingly of little use to anyone. The Texans wished at the very least to retain El Paso, which they envisioned as one day being a major point on a transcontinental railroad. Therefore the committee had discussed a line beginning on the Rio Grande about twenty to thirty miles north of El Paso. Southerners felt that such a line would also retain settlements below the Jornada del Muerto desert within the bounds of Texas and conveniently separate the hostile Texans and New Mexicans from each other. But the committee was stymied as to where the line should run from there. On the evening of May 6, Rusk conversed with Berrien and then wrote out various suggestions. One suggestion provided for Texan acceptance of the bill's propositions before New Mexico's government went into effect. Rusk's other suggestion was that the boundary should run from the Rio Grande northeastward "to the point where the 100th degree of west Longitude crosses the Red River"; this was the eastern terminus of the line suggested earlier in the Douglas-McClernand plan and, previous to that, in the House's New Mexico Territory bill of January 1849. Rusk averred that he had originally planned to offer this line as an amendment to the bill and that he had had it ready even prior to the appointment of the Committee of Thirteen. The process by which a majority of the committee quickly approved of Rusk's line is unknown; nonetheless, it became part of the committee's plan for a line from El Paso northward on the Rio Grande for twenty miles and from that point northeast to the intersection of the Red River and 100° west longitude.[4]

Stephen Douglas later claimed that the Committee of Thirteen had simply tied his California and territories bills together with a "wafer," only making minor changes. While granting that Clay may have thanked Douglas for the use of his bills, it is obvious that the committee and Senator Rusk adopted a boundary that included within the limits of Texas substantially less territory than would have been the case under Douglas's bill. The decision to place the different measures in a single bill appears to have been designed to maximize the chances for passage of the entire package, particularly in the House of Representatives.[5]

On Wednesday, May 8, Henry Clay delivered the committee's report and proposals to the Senate. The report began with a discussion of the committee's decision against forming any new states within Texas itself. The committee majority, Clay said, had decided to combine several measures in one bill and he discussed the individual provisions. Clay's report emphasized the political rationale for uniting the subjects (i.e., forcing members to vote for certain items they did not like in order to pass the ones they wanted). The report then stated that the committee had eliminated the Wilmot Proviso as an unnecessary abstraction and a "fruitful source of distraction and agitation." Clay declared his expectation that both Utah and New Mexico would follow California's example and eventually become free states. The bill, as it was then worded, would prevent the territorial legislatures from passing any laws "in respect to African slavery." By implication, the decision on slavery would be made by the people of Utah and New Mexico when they convened to write state constitutions.

When Clay reached the boundary-debt segment of the report, he minimized the differences between the committee's bill and that of the Douglas-McClernand plan. Douglas's 34° north latitude line was considerably farther north than Clay's, but the Kentucky senator's understatement of the difference between the proposals reflected his desire to secure Douglas's help in passing the Omnibus bill. The report made clear that in exchange for Texas's surrender of a portion of its claim east of the Rio Grande, Texas would be reimbursed sufficiently to pay off its

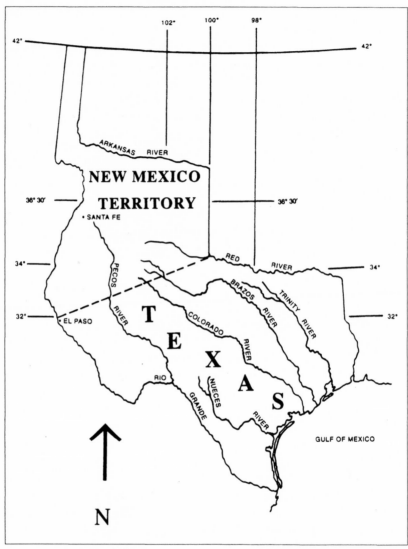

Committee of Thirteen proposal for Texas–New Mexico boundary.

creditors. However, the committee had been unable to fix a specific dollar figure and Clay well knew that some border state Whigs such as Joseph Underwood of Kentucky and James A. Pearce of Maryland would object to anything framed as a trade-off, since they held on principle that Texas had no legitimate claim to the region given up. Clay hoped that the Senate would work out a figure that Underwood and Pearce could accept for the sake of compromise.[6]

Clay concluded his report with a discussion of the new fugitive slave bill and the bill to restrict the slave trade in the District of Columbia. While no minority report was filed, dissenting members of the committee voiced some of their objections in general terms. Southern extremists still worried primarily about California's disruption of the Senate balance and the possible imposition of the Wilmot Proviso in Utah and New Mexico, in addition to the two issues directly relating to slavery. They certainly could not favor Clay's plan and certainly did not want to support any congressional scheme until they had a chance to formulate their own program at the Nashville Convention in June. No more fond of the Committee of Thirteen's bills were Northern Free-Soilers, most Northern Whigs, and some of the Northern Democrats. They wanted California and the Proviso; anything less smacked of slavery extension. Naturally, the Northern Whigs in this bloc felt comfortable with President Taylor's plans for California and New Mexico statehood and did not believe he would veto the Wilmot Proviso if Congress passed it. Most Southern Whigs and many Northern Democrats favored an overall compromise settlement, whether through the Omnibus plan of the committee or through the separate bills favored by Senator Douglas.[7]

The comments in Congress immediately following Clay's report did not yet indicate that the boundary dispute loomed very large in political considerations. But awareness of that nagging problem was present even as Clay presented his bills. Since May 4, when the *National Intelligencer* had reprinted W. C. Skinner's report from the *St. Louis Republican,* Washingtonians had realized that Texas agent Robert Neighbors was on his way to Santa Fe and that Colonel Munroe had issued an order for his forces not to interfere with the commissioner. For several weeks thereafter the Free-Soilers—revealing how little they really knew of President Taylor's actual plans—pilloried Munroe's noninterference order as proof that the administration was positively abetting the Texas plot to dismember New Mexico and spread slavery to the banks of the Rio Grande. Horace Greeley attacked the administration's seeming "nonaction" as incompetent and demanded a forthright policy by Taylor of protecting New Mexico from Texas. Thurlow Weed was in Washington in mid-May, again to discuss possible cabinet changes, and talked rather cavalierly about the need to coerce the South, even if it led to "fighting" and "blood-letting." A few presses began to take up the theme that there existed a serious danger of collision, with untold consequences, between Texas and New Mexico.[8]

The Senate debate on the Omnibus bill formally opened with Clay's speech on Monday, May 13. This elder statesman would exert every energy during the grueling months ahead to achieve a workable compromise and would constantly work, sometimes showing an imperious temper, to marshal a coalition strong enough to pass the bill. Whatever twinges of resentment Clay still held against President Taylor, his motives for pressing compromise were sincere and patriotic. In his address on May 13, Clay clearly expressed his view that the president's plan was not comprehensive enough to resolve the crisis. When he discussed the need for Congress to provide governments for the people of Utah and New Mexico, Clay specifically referred to the Neighbors mission and the likelihood of imminent "civil commotion" and even bloodshed as grounds for prompt congressional action on the matter of territorial governments.[9]

The administration wasted no time in attacking the committee's plan. When the administration newspaper, the *Republic,* printed an editorial attempting to minimize the differences between the committee's and the president's plans, the editors were immediately replaced by Allan Hall, who was more attuned to administration wishes. Many Southern Whig papers and a few in the North, torn between Clay and a Whig president, continued to editorialize that the two plans were similar rather than hostile to each other and that either one was acceptable.[10]

Clay next spoke in the Senate on May 15. After Stephen Douglas unsuccessfully attempted to table the Omnibus in order to proceed to solve the crisis through separate bills, Jefferson Davis proposed an amendment that would have prevented territorial legislatures from interfering with property rights in slaves. Clay, while discussing the various viewpoints on the status of slavery in areas claimed by Texas east of the Rio Grande, disclosed his opinion that the *lex loci,* the prior Mexican law excluding slavery, continued to prevail there. He also declared that he did not support the introduction of slaves into territory already free. After Thomas Rusk again defended Texas's title and Jefferson Davis declared his belief that the war had obliterated Mexican law in the region, Clay responded that the committee's bill would solve the problem by purchasing the Texas claim and thus buying "our peace with Texas." On May 16, Jere Clemens of Alabama gave notice that he intended to introduce an amendment to strike out section 39 of the bill—the boundary-debt portion—and substitute a clause confirming the Texas claim of 1836 and providing that Indian tribes in the area would be removed to the region north of 34° north latitude.[11]

After maintaining a fairly neutral position since his takeover of the *Republic,* Allan Hall finally published on May 20 an editorial strongly attacking the Omnibus plan. On May 21 Clay retaliated by denouncing Taylor's plan as totally unsatisfactory. The Union could not survive if the pending issues—"five bleeding wounds"—remained unresolved. He accused the administration of leaving New Mexico at the mercy of Texas, given that Taylor's military governor had issued an order to his forces not to interfere with Neighbors. If the boundary remained unsettled, Clay said, the New Mexican people, with their "insuperable antipathy" toward Texas, would resist Texan jurisdiction "to the last extremity." In the Kentuckian's opinion, only compromise could bring peace and solve the problems. Pierre Soulé of Louisiana answered Clay with a typical Southern Democratic "ultra" attack on Clay's view of the continuing validity of Mexican law in the territories and on Clay's compromise as just another method of despoiling the South of its constitutional rights.[12]

Henry Clay's "five bleeding wounds" speech represented his final break with the Taylor administration. A few days later on May 27, Allan Hall responded for the administration in the *Republic* with a lengthy defense of Taylor's program. A major theme emphasized in this and later editorials was that, by waiting until New Mexico sought statehood, the boundary question could be submitted to the adjudication of the U.S. Supreme Court after New Mexico was admitted, for the boundary would then amount to a controversy between two states. The *Republic* also ridiculed Clay's plan in a comical parable "Five Bleeding Wounds and Thirteen Doctors," in which a reliable old family doctor attempting to set a broken arm was superseded by a committee of thirteen learned physicians who nearly killed the patient by their insistence on treating several unrelated ailments at the same time.[13]

The House, meanwhile, temporarily bound up one "wound," the potentially troublesome issue of whether Hugh Smith should be recognized as a delegate from New Mexico. The Committee on Elections had devised its majority and minority reports in April, a few days after the Senate had voted to form the Committee of Thirteen. The House considered these on May 22 and a majority—five Democrats and one Southern Whig—decided that it would be "inexpedient" for the House to recognize Smith. The minority—three Northern Whigs—argued that Smith should be granted delegate status as the representative of an organized community and that a denial of such status by the House would be tantamount to recognition of the Texas claim to the region east of the Rio Grande. William Strong, the pro-compromise Pennsylvania Democrat who chaired the committee, defended the majority report at length in his remarks to the House on May 22. Strong cited two major bases for the majority's decision: that there existed, as yet, no territorial government for Smith to represent and that any recognition of Smith as delegate would implicitly deny any validity for the Texas claim. Though Strong himself dissented from the Texas claim, he said, a dispute nevertheless existed and must be settled before any delegate from the area should be accorded recognition as delegate by the House. Since a prolonged debate on this issue threatened to disrupt the California debate then progressing in that chamber, the congressmen, on a voice vote, chose to postpone further consideration of Smith's seating until July.[14]

Simultaneously with this discussion of Smith's credentials in the House, Smith released for publication a stirring letter he had sent to his New Mexican constituents after learning of the committee's decision. Smith declared that his mission in Washington had failed, was sabotaged by the "slave interest" of the South and the "selfish, venal, and ambitious" bond speculators and power brokers of the North. The root of this, according to Smith, was the demand of a declining South for an equal voice in the U.S. Senate. To further this goal, the South aimed to set aside New Mexico's antislavery policy, to dismember the region in favor of Texas, and to introduce slave labor up to the Rio Grande. Smith portrayed the federal government as now abandoning New Mexico to the mercy of Texas, and therefore Smith urged "FOR THE PRESENT RELY UPON YOURSELVES: assert your rights by the establishment of a State government interdicting slavery; gird yourselves up to resist its introduction into your territory as a whole, or into any part by means of dismemberment; and the time will come, when the masses of the Union will rally around your cause, and enable you to defy and defeat all the machinations of your enemies." Hugh Smith did not appear to have realized that President Taylor had already set in motion the statehood process in New Mexico.[15]

Once the House chose to defer a decision on Smith, the debates and speeches in both chambers of Congress for the remainder of May concerned matters other than the boundary dispute—California, territorial slavery, and nonsectional issues. In the Senate Thomas Hart Benton, who disliked Clay, opposed the Texas claim to New Mexico, and saw no future for slavery in the West, cooperated fully with the administration. Taylor Whigs wanted to defeat the bill to pave the way for the president's own plan and the admission of two new free states. Working from an entirely different agenda, but also opposed to the bill, were radical Southern Democrats, for whom the destruction of the U.S. Senate's free state–slave state balance presaged the march of abolitionism on the Southern states themselves. Feeling besieged from the North and betrayed by Southerners such as Clay and Foote, radical Southern Democrats hoped to stop this bill and forge Southern unity behind a Southern program.

To defeat the Omnibus, they would have to form a temporary alliance with their Free-Soil–Northern Whig enemies. On what issue the two groups could ally was not yet clear, and some Northern extremists still believed the Southern "ultras" would finally vote for Clay's program. But the two factions began consulting on a plan to defeat the mutually abhorred Omnibus.[16]

With the Taylor administration and the extremists of both sections bitterly arrayed against the bill, the task for those factions supporting the Omnibus seemed almost insurmountable. The public at large appeared to favor the Omnibus or any other overall settlement, and public rallies and resolutions encouraged the efforts of the compromise bloc in Congress. The forces opposed to the bill were at least unified on a simple goal—developing a combined strategy for killing the Omnibus. Those who desired a compromise settlement differed widely on means of achieving it and what it should entail. Foote and some others wanted an Omnibus bill, and Clay had now completely converted to its support. Douglas and his friends promoted the separate bills as the only workable solution and were ambivalent about the Omnibus; they might support it as long as it survived, but they anticipated its quick demise. Most Southern Whigs supported the bill and would also back the separate bills if the Omnibus failed. However, only two Northern Whigs were considered likely to vote for the compromise package—Webster of Massachusetts, despite his dislike of an Omnibus, and Cooper of Pennsylvania, who supported the compromise as part of his contest for power in Pennsylvania against Governor William F. Johnston and Johnston's "lackey" in Taylor's cabinet, Treasury Secretary William Meredith.[17]

The competing coalitions vied for the votes of a rather large group of undecided or not-quite-decided senators. Among Northerners, many Democrats who wanted to support the bill were constricted by state legislative instructions not to support any measure without the Wilmot Proviso, although Michigan soon removed its incubus from Cass and Felch. Northern senators most often mentioned as doubtful included Bradbury of Maine, Norris of New Hampshire, Felch of Michigan, Walker of Wisconsin, and Shields of Illinois—all Democrats. A larger group of Southern senators were usually listed as doubtful. Among Southern Whigs, these included Spruance and Wales of Delaware, considered unlikely to support the bill because of their close ties to Secretary of State Clayton; Pearce of Maryland, Underwood of Kentucky, and Bell of Tennessee, who did not wish to desert a Whig president's plan and who still believed that Texas legitimately did not extend beyond the Nueces; and Berrien of Georgia, desirous of amendments to make the bill more acceptable to the South. Berrien's position was shared by Southern Democrats King and Clemens of Alabama and Sebastian of Arkansas. The votes of Rusk and Houston of Texas were said to depend on the final shape of the bill in relation to the boundary and debt; both men publicly defended the 1836 Texas claim while sincerely working to achieve a compromise.

In correspondents' reports, no senator was accorded the position of principal intriguer as often as William Seward. Seward did indeed appear the most active organizer of opposition to the bill. He quite freely conversed with Southern "ultras" on ways to defeat the bill and personally ingratiated himself with slaveholders who considered his ideas absolutely anathema to the continued existence of their "peculiar institution."

Seward seemed most determined to convert Sen. Thomas J. Rusk to the anti-Omnibus bloc, and his dealings with the Texan provide an enlightening glimpse at Seward's methods. The New Yorker assumed, as most other Northern extremists did, that Texas's only interest in maintaining what to the North was a spurious claim to New Mexico was Texas's desire to sell the claim for enough money to pay off the bondholders. Working from this assumption, Seward believed that he could seduce Rusk into opposing the committee's bill. Possibly Seward felt that Rusk was amenable to his cajolery because Rusk had proved supportive of federal appointments for friends of Seward and Weed. Anyway, Seward called on Thomas Rusk and told him that he believed Texas to be in "bad company"—the compromise bloc—and that he wished to treat Texas fairly. He admitted to Rusk that he did not believe that Texas possessed a valid title to New Mexico but did believe that the federal government should pay the Texas debt. Seward promised that he and his friends would vote for that at any time, as long as Texas agreed to relinquish its claim to New Mexico. He therefore requested Rusk to draw up a bill to that effect and promised that he, Seward, would see that it was introduced in the House of Representatives. Seward told Rusk that he was a better friend of Texas than those supporting the Omnibus and that Rusk had best separate himself from the bill's advocates. The bill he proposed, Seward insisted, could pass, whereas the Omnibus could not. Rusk was understandably suspicious of the proposal and did not draw up the bill, despite Seward's entreaties on several subsequent occasions. Seward never made clear just what limits he felt Texas should have, and he never understood that the money, while extremely important to Texas, was not the state's only consideration. Seward did not give up on this matter, and Rusk would eventually turn these machinations against him. Seward overestimated his own and underestimated Thomas J. Rusk's political astuteness.[18]

A new note of urgency in regard to the New Mexico situation came to Washington on June 1 or 2 with the arrival of Col. John M. Washington from Santa Fe via St. Louis. Washington not only reported to President Taylor but also related to reporters the story of the Santa Fe riot, which Weightman and Pillans had fomented prior to his departure. These correspondents reported the riot, its suppression by Munroe's forces, and New Mexican determination to resist the Texan claim. Washington's information may have convinced some congressmen of the necessity for a quick compromise settlement, but it undoubtedly added to the desire of Taylor Whigs and Benton to implement the president's plan as quickly as possible. The news from Santa Fe certainly convinced Hugh N. Smith to remain in Washington until July, hoping that the recent news might cause the House to recognize him as a delegate. What Colonel Washington told Taylor and other administrative and military officials about the political situation in New Mexico was never recorded, but he did bring with him a report to Colonel Bliss from Colonel McCall.[19]

On June 3 the Nashville Convention assembled; but Calhoun's hoped-for Southern unity was nonexistent, and lack of Southern interest in the meeting at Nashville proved it. Most Southern people desired a peaceful settlement of the issues, and as long as hope for a viable congressional compromise existed, more radical solutions such as those contemplated at Nashville would enjoy a very limited influence. Only nine states sent delegates, and the greater portion were from Tennessee, leading to charges that the convention was unrepresentative. The meeting's proponents naturally disavowed any disunionist intent, but the gathering smacked of disloyalty to most people, even many Southerners, given the presence of such "ultras" as Robert Barnwell Rhett of South Carolina, Nathaniel Beverly Tucker of Virginia, and William L. Yancey of Alabama among the delegates.

Texas was one of the states that had shown a minimum of interest in the meeting. Between the legislature's approval of sending delegates and the March elections for them in Texas, there had been only a month's time for preparations. Texas was to select four delegates from each of its two congressional districts. Many people in outlying areas were not even aware of the election by the day of the poll; most of the Texas newspapers were opposed to the state's participation at Nashville, and many Texans considered it unseemly for the newest state of the Union to attend a convention associated in the public mind with disunionist schemes. Nevertheless, at the March canvass several candidates were elected delegates, but the turnout was so embarrassingly small that only one of those elected decided to attend the convention. That one was former Governor J. P. Henderson, Senator Rusk's law partner and close friend.[20]

Once he reached Nashville, Henderson made it clear that, in addition to his interest in Southern rights generally, he wished to secure from the convention a commitment on Texas's claims east of the Rio Grande. On the fifth day of the convention, Friday, June 7, Henderson offered two resolutions. One asserted the boundary claimed under the Texas law of 1836, while the other declared it the duty of other slave states to stand by Texas against the takeover of any Texas land "without her consent, freely given." Henderson's proposal left open the possibility that his state might agree to a suitable deal with the federal government. After delegate William O. Goode of Virginia presented a longer series of resolutions relative to the Texas boundary and debt, Virginia secessionist N. B. Tucker added two more resolutions in relation to the boundary dispute. The first would pledge the whole South to oppose federal attempts to seize Texas territory for the purpose of preventing Texans and other Southerners from employing slaves in the region. Tucker's second resolution, in exchange for Southern support, would require that Texas not betray the interests of the Southern states by accepting federal money "for admitting an enemy within her gates, and establishing there a stronghold of abolition and a harbor for fugitive slaves."[21]

After the resolutions committee considered these and many other proposals, the Nashville Convention adopted a set of twenty-eight resolutions, five of which concerned Texas. These resolutions defined the Texas boundary as under its 1836 law; declared that no portion of it should be transferred to the federal government without an express declaration that it would be slave territory; obligated the federal government to admit four new slave states from Texas, even in the region ceded by Texas; and included the two resolutions proposed by Tucker. The convention's resolutions were, as a whole, moderate in content, demanding equal rights for slavery in the territories and showing a willingness to settle for an extension of the Missouri Compromise line to the Pacific. The address of the convention, authored by South Carolina secessionist Robert Barnwell Rhett, was more extremist in tone. Part of Rhett's address attacked the Omnibus bill on the same ground as Tucker's resolution—that any territorial claim surrendered by Texas would become a stepping-stone for abolition and totally hem slavery in on the West. The convention adjourned on June 13 with provisions made for a second session in the fall.[22]

Nearly everyone considered the convention a failure. Southern extremists tried to console each other with statements that some Southerners had at least decided on some Southern-rights planks, but most were sorely disappointed.

J. P. Henderson was generally satisfied with the pledges given to Texas at the convention and informed Rusk that he considered the Texan pledge required by Tucker's resolution only fair to the South. As many other delegates did, Henderson returned home and spoke at public meetings in favor of the Nashville resolutions. William Yancey in Montgomery, Alabama, and William O. Goode in Petersburg, Virginia, roused audiences about the need to defend Texas. The opinions expressed at the time, either praising the meeting's significance or condemning its uselessness, meant nothing while the compromise proposals were pending in Washington. Only if no settlement emerged from the first session of the Thirty-first Congress could the second session of the Nashville Convention assume any significance.[23]

Most Senate discussion in the first week of June concerned proposals to deal with slavery's status in territories. These labors resulted in Senate passage on June 5 of an amendment by John Berrien of Georgia to prevent territorial legislatures from prohibiting or establishing slavery rather than passing any laws in respect to the institution, as the Omnibus originally proposed. This reflected the Southern desire that a territorial legislature should not be stopped from passing laws to protect slave property already in a territory. A nearly solid Southern phalanx provided most votes for its passage. Douglas of Illinois was unhappy with it, since he and his friends desired territorial legislatures to be unrestricted on the slavery question, but his attempt to erase the Berrien amendment was defeated on June 5. Also, four different versions of territorial slavery exclusion all went down to defeat at the hands of Southerners and pro-compromise Northerners.[24]

The Senate's growing awareness of the boundary dispute's seriousness, enhanced by Washington's information, briefly emerged in these debates on June 5 and 6. In remarks on June 5, Democratic "ultra" Hopkins Turney of Tennessee attacked the committee bill for excising enough land from Texas below 36°30' north latitude to form two new slave states; Turney was certain that, as a territory separated from Texas, the region would become a free state. The suitability of New Mexico for territorial government came up in a discussion of peonage in New Mexico on June 6. A more significant reference to the boundary dispute that day was made by Sen. Roger S. Baldwin of Connecticut in defense of his proposal that would confirm the Mexican laws against slavery as still in force in the territories. Baldwin made clear that his amendment was designed as an answer to Berrien's regarding territory to be ceded by Texas to New Mexico east of the Rio Grande under the Omnibus provisions.[25]

On Friday, June 7, the first full Senate debate over the boundary dispute took place, occasioned by the amendment of Sen. Jere Clemens of Alabama to confirm the 1836 boundary claimed by Texas, with a provision for removal of all the Indian tribes north of 34° north latitude. Rusk and the radical Southern Democrats vigorously supported the amendment. Even the pro-compromise Foote postured with the "ultras" on a proposal he knew could not pass. All other Senate blocs either favored some land cession by Texas or rejected the state's claims as altogether illegitimate. The day ended with Clemens's amendment overwhelmingly defeated 37 to 17. The struggle over Clemens's amendment on June 7 marked the real beginning of the titanic congressional fight over the boundary issue. Once they had addressed this subject, senators would discover that they could not free themselves from it.[26]

In the House in early June, however, representatives continued making speeches about California and slavery in the territories with no discussion of the boundary dispute. On two occasions, congressmen briefly stated new boundary plans. Volney Howard of Texas suggested that Texas might be willing to trade its claims north of 34° north latitude in exchange for a federal grant to Texas of a large parcel of land stretching westward from the Rio Grande to the Colorado River. Richard Meade of Virginia advocated a vaguely defined line heading due east from the Rio Grande and thence north to 36°30' north latitude. The boundary dispute finally entered the House debate on June 10 when Democrat John McClernand of Illinois, defending his earlier bill, cited Texan organization of a military force to capture Santa Fe as the reason "the peace of the whole country is suspended by a hair liable to be snapped by the slightest accident or indiscretion." That same day Texas Democrat David Kaufman, after defending slavery in general, defended the Texas boundary claim of 1836 in detail and argued that Texas would not settle for any compromise line below 34° north latitude. His more radically "ultra" colleague, Volney Howard, speaking on June 11, now abandoned even his impracticable boundary suggestion of a week earlier and opposed any cession by Texas that would provide an opportunity for west Texas slaves to escape to free territory. Howard believed the land purchase for "hush" money proposed in the Omnibus would lead to two free states in New Mexico and a further loss of Southern political equilibrium.[27]

A contest developed on June 11 as Northern members sought to push Free-Soil Democrat James Doty's unmixed California statehood bill through the House. The whole Southern bloc opposed this and during the next several days effectively invoked the five-minute rule in the House. A member would offer an amendment, deliver a five-minute speech on it, and withdraw the amendment only to have another member immediately renew the amendment and advocate it for another five minutes. Northern members saw no way to break the Southern delaying strategy and reluctantly gave up on June 17. The House shifted to nonsectional measures. This Southern parliamentary victory again demonstrated the political impossibility of President Taylor's plan.[28]

House failure to pass the Doty bill allowed the Senate to concentrate on its own measure. From June 8 through June 14, the Senate struggled over Texas–New Mexico amendments. Most of the speeches were short, but Benton of Missouri, Cass of Michigan, and Dayton of New Jersey provided longer, prepared addresses. On June 10 Benton attacked the Omnibus plan for holding California hostage to the settlement of unrelated issues, considered the granting of any territory west of 102° west longitude to Texas as an extension of slavery into an area that was properly New Mexico and free, and warned that the United States would defend New Mexico against any Texan invasion. Cass spoke the next day, June 11, for compromise and described the potential violence in New Mexico as a threat to the whole fabric of American society, for such violence would inevitably involve other states. William Dayton, New Jersey Whig, on June 11 and 12 defended the interference of U.S. military officers at Santa Fe with the schemes of the Texas commissioner and discounted the possibility that Texas would really launch its forces into New Mexico.[29]

Much of the discussion during these few days concerned where the boundary should touch the Rio Grande. Suggestions included: El Paso itself; a point some twenty miles to the north; the southern end of the Jornada, which would place Doña Ana in Texas; and 34° north latitude. Stephen Douglas offered an amendment for a line from the southern end of the Jornada eastward to the mountain range and north along that range to the Red River. Few senators, nearly all of them Southerners, voted for it. The most significant amendment was that offered on June 12 by Tennessee extremist Hopkins Turney to simply strike out section 39—the Texas boundary-debt provisions—from the bill. Given the inability of compromisers to agree on a particular line, Turney and other enemies of the bill saw an opportunity to destroy not only these particular sections but, with them, the bill itself and possibly the whole concept of compromise. Northern and Southern extremists had needed a vehicle on which they could combine their votes, and the boundary-debt arrangement in the Omnibus was that vehicle. It was the sole issue on which antislavery and proslavery forces could unite, at least for the purpose of ridding that part from the bill. Without that part, which had recently assumed greater significance, the Omnibus would fall and leave every issue in the same unsettled state in which Congress had begun the session.[30]

Striking at the boundary-debt bargain represented more than a target of convenience. This had become the single most explosive issue of the package, the one issue that could precipitate bloodshed, which in turn could polarize national public opinion and possibly begin a civil war. Secession-minded Southerners may have actually been hoping for bloodshed on the Texas–New Mexico border in order to rally Southern whites to their cause. Northern "ultras," equally eschewing compromise, either believed that Texas was merely bluffing or believed that U.S. forces would easily put down any invasion attempt. To Southern radicals, compromise on Texas–New Mexico represented a surrender of slave soil to free soil, while to Northern radicals it represented a capitulation of free soil to the "Slave Power." To either group a compromise on Texas–New Mexico was inconceivable.

As soon as Turney had introduced his amendment on June 12, Henry Foote immediately castigated it as an attempt to leave the boundary dispute unadjusted so that a "bloody conflict" was certain to result. The following day, June 13, Seward declared his support for the Turney amendment because he opposed the entire bill as stealing land from New Mexico and delaying California's admission. He labeled the Neighbors mission to Santa Fe as proof of Texan aggression and demanded that the federal government use its authority and power to protect New Mexico. Clay briefly replied to Seward, but his criticism paled in contrast to Foote's verbal tirade. It was the most personally insulting attack on a fellow member of Congress delivered in either chamber during the entire session. Despite numerous calls to order by Vice President Fillmore, Foote accused Seward of desiring to foment war by leaving the boundary unadjusted and called him "a counselor to bloodshed and violence." He charged Seward with encouraging the Taylor administration to resort to military force and predicted a civil war in which the whole South and many in the North would come to the aid of Texas. In a final piece of character assassination, Foote portrayed Seward as one who planned to further his own political career by such fratricidal war, possibly even becoming president if his side were victorious. Seward chose to ignore Foote's personal remarks in a brief response, and after further debate Kentucky senator Joseph Underwood moved to adjourn. His motion passed 30 to 23.[31]

The roll-call vote on Underwood's motion was significant as being the first of many on which the coalition of Northern and Southern radicals voted together, in this case for the adjournment (see Appendix B, vote A). On June 14 two senators whose votes were considered "swing" votes—King of Alabama and Berrien of Georgia—both expressed opposition to Turney's amendment; both saw the inclusion of the Texas sections as crucial to any compromise.

After a long debate involving many participants, the Senate voted down Turney's attempt to strike out section 39 by a vote of 27 to 24. Several observers at the time referred to it as a test vote on the bill. Stephen Douglas had become ill and paired with Jere Clemens; they were among several members who did not vote on this roll call (see Appendix B, vote B). Having dispensed with the first severe threat to the bill, the Senate turned its attention once again to California and slavery in the territories.[32]

The president and his cabinet kept close watch on congressional proceedings, but it is doubtful that Taylor was overly concerned as long as the Senate bill did not pass. Taylor's faith remained fixed on his own plan, already worked out in California and then in the process of being worked out by his military agents in New Mexico. He intended that the military establishment there be strengthened to repel any Texan invasion. On June 17 Congress passed a bill to increase the army units serving on the frontiers to control hostile Indians; but Taylor understood clearly how those additional troops could also be used to fight Texans if need be. Having been handed the ability to substantially reinforce the army in the Ninth Military Department, Taylor took an opportunity to answer a Senate resolution of June 11 requesting any presidential orders adverse to Texas and any military correspondence relevant to New Mexico.[33]

Taylor's message of June 17 stated that no orders adverse to Texan authority had been issued and that Robert Neighbors, "styling himself commissioner" of Texas, had traveled to Santa Fe to organize counties under Texan jurisdiction. The president declared that he himself had no power to decide the boundary question and no desire to interfere with it, but he also asserted that the region to which Neighbors had gone had actually been captured from Mexico by U.S. forces and occupied by them since the conquest. U.S. possession should be maintained until the boundary could be decided by competent authority. There existed "no reason for seriously apprehending" that Texas would attempt to practically interfere with U.S. possession of New Mexico. The message overall seemed unexceptional, but it was the first time Taylor publicly declared his position that the Santa Fe region was a possession of the United States and that such possession would be continued. Free-Soilers now backed off from their earlier accusations that the president was acting as a Texas agent. Southern extremists, on the other hand, now saw the president obviously opposed to Texan jurisdiction at Santa Fe.[34]

In late June congressional intensity on the sectional issues slackened. The Doty bill remained sidetracked in the House, and a Southern attempt to divide California failed in the Senate. Henry Clay gallantly and impatiently fought on, despite illness, exhaustion, frustration at delay, and despondency. Most estimates of the probable Senate vote on the compromise indicated that the bill would fail. The most positive estimates were that the vote at best stood even, with several members still in doubt. Clay and Sen. David Atchison of Missouri both wrote letters to Willie Mangum, at his wife's sickbed in North Carolina, to return as soon as possible to bolster their beleaguered forces in Washington.[35]

Taylor meanwhile was haunted by the Galphin claim, which lessened public faith in the integrity of his cabinet. Taylor was still considering the removal and replacement of Crawford, Meredith, and Johnson at the end of June, and some House members were even prepared to implicate the president himself in the scandal.[36]

All these matters quickly became of secondary importance in comparison with the momentous tidings from New Mexico. Rumors that New Mexico was calling a statehood convention circulated in Washington as early as June 18. Three days later the capital received a telegraphic dispatch from New Orleans with information derived from the *Galveston Civilian* about Colonel Munroe's proclamation. While some in Washington, including "delegate" Hugh N. Smith of New Mexico, initially greeted the report with skepticism, most believed in the veracity of the dispatch. Shocked pro-compromisers tried to content themselves with thoughts that the threatened action of New Mexico might trigger a congressional stampede to the Omnibus bill, and the bill's enemies and president's friends interpreted the news as damning to the bill's chances.

Washington hardly had time to digest this report from New Orleans when another, much more significant, dispatch arrived via telegraph from St. Louis on the morning of June 26. Based on letters from New Mexico, this report related that the Santa Fe convention had already drafted its free-state constitution with boundaries stretching well east of the Rio Grande. The swiftness of the convention's action astounded Washington. The president's men and the Free-Soilers exulted. Horace Mann of Massachusetts could hardly contain his elation in a letter to his friend Charles Sumner as he contemplated what he believed was the imminent death of slavery expansion: "I think we have got the hydra down now, & will cut off the last of its heads, & burn the wound with a hot iron, according to the classical recipe." The New Mexico news set off a tremendous debate in the nation's press over the merits of the case, its prospective impact on the sectional crisis, and the question of whether or not President Taylor had unduly interfered in New Mexico to bring about its constitution. Taylor's enemies proclaimed that he had ordered Munroe to call the convention (although they seemed unaware of anything tangible except Crawford's official order to McCall), while Taylor's defenders asserted that Munroe had either acted within the guidelines of his previous orders or that he had taken his action, if unauthorized, on his own.[37]

In the capital itself, the New Mexico news set off frenzied activity on all sides. The cabinet met, according to one report, and the majority of its members favored ordering Colonel Munroe to use force to protect New Mexico from Texas. However, a minority—probably Secretary of War Crawford and Attorney General Johnson—put up such stiff opposition that the subject was temporarily postponed. Members of Congress began caucusing. Angry Southerners, sometimes irrespective of party, engaged in closed discussions almost nightly beginning on the 26th. At a meeting on the evening of June 27, Southern extremists secretly gathered, and some swore armed resistance if any bill adverse to slavery in the territories or to the Texas claim to New Mexico should pass Congress. The caucus even appointed a committee to confer with Southern state authorities on the matter. South Carolina, Mississippi, and Florida radicals dominated the proceedings, but some attendees dissented from taking radical steps.

On Friday evening, June 28, some forty Free-Soilers and administration Whigs, in favor of California admission unattached, held an open caucus. With nearly the whole Southern bloc reportedly now determined simply to push through the appropriations bills and then vote to adjourn the session with no settlement of the sectional questions, the Free-Soilers also wanted to block the appropriations unless California was admitted. Some prominent Whigs pleaded with the California caucus to allow the appropriations to pass, simply in order to keep the government functioning and not provide the secessionists with anything they might use for their purposes. But Northern extremists controlled the caucus and voted to sink the appropriations unless the California bill passed. One speaker at the meeting declared his intention to see California admitted if they were forced to drag Speaker Cobb physically from his chair and substitute one of their own as speaker. Even California's friends seemed driven to desperation by the New Mexico news.[38]

Certainly the Southern Whigs were the most desperate bloc of all. Southern Democrats had already branded most of them as "submissionists" for their willingness as part of a compromise bloc to admit one new free state. But if the Southern Whigs in Congress supported the addition of a second free state, with no offsetting compensation for the South, it would mean ruin for them in the next elections. The news of New Mexico's constitution destroyed what loyalty had lingered among most Southern Whigs for their Southern Whig president.

While Southern Democrats conducted another of their nightly meetings on Saturday, June 29, the Southern Whigs that same evening conducted a closed caucus attended by all but a few of their number. Even most of the moderates seemed ready to abandon any fealty to the administration and to push only the appropriations bills to passage before adjournment. They resolved, after a long discussion, to make a last-ditch appeal to President Taylor to induce him to change his policies, and, if he refused, to inform him that nearly all Southern Whigs would go into open opposition to the administration and act with the Democrats. The Southern Whig caucus selected three of its members to make separate visits to the president: Rep. Charles Conrad of Louisiana, a personal friend of Taylor's from his home state; Rep. Humphrey Marshall of Kentucky, who had served under Taylor in the Mexican War; and Rep. Robert Toombs of Georgia, who had been one of Taylor's most active partisans in 1848.[39]

The three would engage in their mission during a period of intense political paranoia. Rumors were flying about Washington that Texas was preparing to send thousands of volunteers into New Mexico, aided by thousands more Mississippians. Since the advent of news that New Mexico was even holding a convention, the Texas delegation in Washington had been ferociously promising military action. Other Southerners had begun chiming in with promises to aid the Texans. These boasts fed the rumor mill, along with the memory of Governor Bell's military proposals at the previous Texas legislative session, recent doses of vitriol in Texas newspapers, and a letter from Indian Agent Calhoun in New Mexico stating that he expected Major Neighbors to return from Texas in July with an armed force. The rumors quickly became reduced to numbers. In one story, Governor Bell or Senator Houston was supposed to lead 2,500 Texans into New Mexico in the early fall. In another, 3,000 Texans were already marching toward Santa Fe. Hugh Smith was one of those in Washington who believed the rumor. Some papers speculated that this force would invade New Mexico by way of Indian Territory rather than attempt to cross the desert wastes. The Washington correspondent of the *New York Commercial Advertiser* suggested that the Texan invaders planned to divide up New Mexico's land among the Texan volunteers. And if federal troops shed Texan blood, a telegraphic dispatch to Washington said, Mississippi governor John A. Quitman pledged to send 10,000 volunteers from his state to assist the Texans. This dispatch was another fraud, however, for no such promise had been made by Quitman.[40]

The rumors and actual potential for violent confrontation between Texans and federal troops fueled another editorial war of speculation in the public press. Not many Southern papers appeared to take a definite stand on the issue, but most that did argued that chances for collision in New Mexico were real and that Southern states would aid Texas if bloodshed occurred. Rep. William McWillie of Mississippi addressed a letter to this effect to the *Vicksburg Sentinel.* The Northern papers were much more prone to speculate on whether a collision would happen and what it would mean if it did. Correspondent Francis Grund stressed that the boundary question was the "tangible" issue likely to provoke a fight and that Anglo-Saxons historically had loved to fight over land. A Northern Democratic paper, the *Brooklyn Eagle,* speculated that the Taylor administration actually desired to foment conflict in order to divert attention from their other woes. Several Northern Whig papers agreed on the seriousness of the threat. Some of them definitely expressed confidence that the Union would defeat Texas if a conflict did break out; the *Toledo Blade* declared that the government would derive a large revenue from the "hemp tax" on rope used to hang Texan traitors. Many Northern Whig and Free-Soil presses also expressed incredulity that Texas would attempt to invade New Mexico and thereby commit treason. Some ridiculed the Texas "bluster" as a simple ploy to extort money from the government while others portrayed the endeavor as beyond the logistical and financial resources of Texas. A few Southern Whig editorialists also denied that Texas would really attempt to capture New Mexico.[41]

To avoid the appearance that Taylor was doing nothing to counteract the reported martial actions of Texas, the administration provided information to reporters on the recent transfer of six hundred new U.S. soldiers ostensibly to protect New Mexico's settlers from Indians. Clearly Taylor wanted those soldiers in New Mexico to repel a Texas invasion, but those forces were as yet under no such orders. Taylor learned that, in fact, the orders still in effect were ones sent by Crawford on March 26, 1849, telling the department commander that, if Texas attempted to extend its jurisdiction, he was to arrange his force so as not to come into conflict with the Texans. At a cabinet meeting, probably on July 2 or 3, Taylor demanded that the orders be changed. As Interior Secretary Thomas Ewing remembered his words to Secretary Crawford, Taylor said, "Revoke the [March 26, 1849] order at once, and direct the commandant to defend the country and people against all who may attack or assert dominion over them, whether Navajoes or Texans, until Congress or the Supreme Court shall order otherwise." Crawford, who had already discussed this issue with Toombs and Stephens and had been advised by them not to alter the orders then operative, frankly refused to change the orders and may have offered to resign. He believed that the move contemplated by Taylor would lead to civil war. Taylor apparently had anticipated this reaction by Crawford and coolly declared to the cabinet that the orders would go under his own signature, thus leaving no doubt that the policy change directly reflected the president's own desires. It was decided by Taylor and his cabinet majority to issue the new orders on July 6 and soon thereafter, reportedly on July 8, to communicate the new orders and their purpose in a message to Congress. Secretary of State Clayton had charge of drafting the message, and at least a rough draft of it was completed. Though some reports described this planned message as an elaborate policy statement, correspondent James Harvey, a close associate of Clayton's, later reported that the message was to have been a short and direct statement of the need for federal forces to defend New Mexico from threatened action by Texas. Some newspaper reports stated that the administration actually dispatched an agent to New Mexico with the new orders, and one even claimed that the secretary of war was supposed to have presented a plan of operations by July 10; these were simply two more of the many unsubstantiated rumors that titillated Washington imaginations in this intensely stressful, exciting period.[42]

The storm kindled by the news from New Mexico struck fear into even some of Taylor's strong supporters. When three senators friendly to the administration related their concerns to him, they discovered just how determined the old general was. As one to whom a senator described the scene reported it to a newspaper, President Taylor

> seemed anxious, and held his face a long time buried between his hands. Finally, dashing aside his chair, he rose, strode around the room twice or thrice, and, pausing before them with his foot firmly planted, said, in his peculiarly mild but firm voice, "Gentlemen, I was placed here to support the Constitution, I have sworn to do it; I can do it; and I will do it." Then throwing himself on the chair, he rose again, and in a louder, clearer tone exclaimed, "I will do it."

Taylor's tone reflected not only his earnestness and conviction that his course was right but also his confidence that his military forces could successfully deal with whatever challenge they faced from the Texan volunteers he disdained. Simultaneously, Sam Houston was defending the valor of Texans in the Mexican War during a two-day speech on June 29 and July 3. He also defiantly argued that the three thousand Texans already reported (incorrectly) on the march would valiantly defend the rights of Texas against the Santa Fe "rebellion." The administration's *Washington Republic* responded with one of its typical multicolumn defenses of Taylor's fairness to the Texans in the war plus a litany of Texan atrocities.[43]

On June 27 the Senate adopted a resolution by Foote and Rusk requesting the president to provide the Senate with information about Colonel Munroe's actions and about any government at Santa Fe in opposition to the jurisdiction of Texas. On July 1 President Taylor sent a message in response with a report from Secretary Crawford stating basically that there was no new information to add to what had already been provided to the Senate. On June 27 Lewis Cass offered a resolution for the Committee on Military Affairs to consider proposing a law to prohibit officers such as Munroe from exercising civil authority unless conferred by an act of Congress. After some debate, this resolution was tabled on June 29.[44]

On June 27 Foote pleaded for the compromise bill squarely on the ground that it was necessary to prevent bloodshed and civil war. Thousands, he promised, would aid Texas if federal forces shed a drop of Texas blood. Sen. James Cooper of Pennsylvania renewed the discussion on the boundary issue in his speech on June 29 and July 1. The only staunch supporter of the bill among the Northern Whig bloc, Cooper advocated it as the only reasonable alternative to a Texan invasion of New Mexico, which would probably succeed in spreading slavery over a people who hated both the institution and Texas. On July 2 Seward argued that the president's policy of New Mexico statehood was the way to prevent the extension of slavery by Texas into the already-free soil there. Seward declared that those Southerners who had labeled New Mexico as unfit for slavery would quickly change that attitude once gold or other valuable minerals were discovered. Many Southern Democrats stalked out of the chamber in contempt as the New Yorker spoke. Thurlow Weed and the Northern Whigs rejoiced at Seward's unequivocal support for President Taylor's policies, while Southern papers described Seward as the very incarnation of Satan himself.[45]

Seward's speech marked the end of his attempt to manipulate Senator Rusk of Texas out of the pro-Omnibus camp. When Seward had returned from his short sojourn in New York, probably on June 27, he had again requested a separate boundary-debt bill from Rusk. Rusk drew one with a boundary at 34° north latitude in exchange for twelve million dollars. Seward winced, insisting that he and his friends could support a bill for no more than ten million dollars, which would relinquish "New Mexico proper as she stood previously under the organization of Mexico." Seward promised to have it introduced into the House of Representatives. Rusk had a Senate clerk draw up a bill, and he gave it to Seward. What boundary it contained is not known, but Seward never had it introduced. Once Seward decided to align himself with Taylor's New Mexico statehood policy, his previous intrigues with Rusk held no further relevance for Seward. Thomas J. Rusk did not forget.[46]

While Taylor undoubtedly drew moral support from the defenses of his policies by Seward and others, he must have been equally anguished by what Vice President Millard Fillmore told him on one of those first days of July. Many had tried to guess which way Fillmore would vote if the Senate vote on the Omnibus ended in a tie. His bloc within the Whigs of New York had steadily supported President Taylor's policies, but Fillmore himself gradually leaned toward support of the compromise bill as the only possible peaceful resolution of the crisis. Conversely, New Mexico statehood may have seemed to him certain to provoke civil war. Whatever his motivation, Fillmore ultimately told Taylor that, if as vice president he had to cast a vote and felt a duty to vote for the bill, he wanted the president to understand that his vote would be cast in the nation's interest and not out of hostility to Taylor or his administration. Fillmore put it to the president as tactfully and diplomatically as he could.[47]

Much more alarming and exasperating for Taylor, however, were his encounters with the three Southern Whigs delegated by their caucus to entreat with him. It could not have pleased him that these men of his own party were threatening to openly oppose his administration. He was intellectually incapable of converting them to his position and policies, and he was too stubbornly wedded to his own plan ever to inch toward their view. Taylor could restate his policies to these Southern Whigs, stand up against their demands, and bear with their opposition, but his inability to exert influence on them and retain their adherence to his administration must have caused Taylor deep sadness. He had dealt quite successfully with enemies on the battlefield throughout a long military career; with these Southern leaders from his own party in a virtual state of mutiny, he did not quite know what to do except to resist them as he would anyone deemed an adversary.

The first to visit Taylor was his old Louisiana friend Charles Conrad, probably on Monday, July 1. He found the president "obstinately fixed in his purpose" and "so prejudiced" that he still ascribed all opposition to his program to the disappointment of presidential ambitions suffered by Clay, Webster, and Cass in 1848. When Conrad informed him of the Southern Whig determination to oppose him if he insisted on the admission of both California and New Mexico, the old general demanded that California be admitted immediately and promised to recommend New Mexico's admission as soon as its constitution arrived. As for the disaffection of Southern Whigs, Taylor stated that he realized that in order to achieve both goals he would be compelled to sacrifice one wing of the party. He could not be expected, he said, to give up eighty-four Northern Whigs to satisfy only twenty-nine from the South. The next Southern Whig visitor, probably on July 2, was Taylor's war comrade, Humphrey Marshall of Kentucky. The president responded to Marshall's pleas with an almost-verbatim repetition of his statement to Conrad.[48]

Robert Toombs of Georgia was the last of these Southern Whig emissaries to visit Taylor, doing so on Wednesday, July 3. When Toombs raised the Texas–New Mexico issue, the president informed him not only that he intended to press New Mexico statehood but also that the cabinet had discussed the matter already, that they had decided to order the U.S. troops in New Mexico to maintain federal possession of the territory against any Texan aggression, and that a brief message to Congress defining this policy was then being prepared. Toombs had already been informed of this by Crawford, but, having heard it now from the president's own lips, Toombs heatedly warned Taylor that he and every other Southern Whig would openly oppose the administration as soon as the message appeared. Besides, Toombs assured the president, the entire South would come to the aid of Texas if U.S. forces in New Mexico attempted to repel the Texans. The indomitable old general replied calmly that he owed nothing special to either sectional wing of the Whig party but that he was the president of the entire country and intended to act as such. Taylor then denied the validity of the Texas claim to New Mexico—"It was the damndest pretext of a title"—and said Texas had no more right to New Mexico than the filibuster Narciso Lopez and his "pirates" had to Cuba. Taylor promised to protect New Mexico against any hostile invaders, even if the only inhabitants of the place were Comanche Indians, until Congress decided on the proper disposition of the area. He finished with the declaration that he was a soldier, knew his duty, and would do it—whatever the responsibilities or consequences involved. Toombs apparently told a friend soon thereafter, in regard to Taylor's promise of military force to protect New Mexico, that "The worst of it is, he will do it."[49]

It is germane here to consider the state of President Taylor's health on July 3, given various reports later that Zachary Taylor was already ill on the day Toombs visited. According to several persons who saw Taylor on July 3 and during the days prior to that, his physical health and spirits were excellent. A female friend reported to Alexander Stephens on June 26 that Taylor looked better than she had ever seen him. Several persons who saw the president on July 3, including

Toombs, reported him to be in fine health. The visiting Swedish novelist Frederika Bremer described Taylor at a White House reception on July 3 as initially depressed but subsequently his cheerful self. Certainly reports of Taylor's apparent executive stress may have been misinterpreted by some newspapermen as symptomatic of suffering from the intestinal disorders so prevalent in Washington during the summer.[50]

If Taylor believed that Southern Whig pressure on him was over with the Toombs interview, he was mistaken. Alexander Stephens was another Southern Whig distraught over recent events. He too had heard Crawford talk about the cabinet's decision on the military in New Mexico and, on the morning of July 3, had been further alarmed by the *National Intelligencer*'s reprint of a Washington correspondent's report from the *New York Journal of Commerce*. That report related the rumor of 2,500 Texans preparing to march on Santa Fe, and the *Intelligencer* added a comment of concern over "the safety of Santa Fe and the detachment of the army whose duty it will be to defend it." The paper's assumption that there existed such a "duty" angered Stephens. Before Toombs left that day for his interview with Taylor, Stephens told his fellow Georgian that he intended to write a letter in response. Stephens apparently worked on his letter and had it copied in a neater hand by a clerk while Toombs was absent. Following Toombs's return with a report of no change in the president's stance, Stephens had his letter delivered to the *Intelligencer* office. It appeared in the next morning's edition, July 4.[51]

Beginning his letter with a brief reference to the newspaper's earlier statement about the "duty" of U.S. forces in New Mexico, Stephens then proceeded to his main point:

> But I wish to say to you, lest you may be mistaken in the opinions of others, that the first Federal gun that shall be fired against the people of Texas, without the authority of law, will be the signal for the freemen from the Delaware to the Rio Grande to rally to the rescue. Whatever difference of opinion may exist in the public mind touching the proper boundary of Texas, nothing can be clearer than that it is not a question to be decided by the army. Be not deceived, and deceive not others. "Inter arma leges silent." When the "Rubicon" is passed, the days of this Republic will be numbered. You may consider the "gallant State of Texas" too weak for a contest with the army of the United States. But you should recollect that the cause of Texas, in such a conflict, will be the cause of the entire South. And, whether you consider Santa Fe in danger or not,

you may yet live to see that fifteen States of this Union, with seven millions of people, "who, knowing their rights, dare maintain them," cannot be easily conquered! "Sapientibus verbum sat."[52]

There was nothing novel about Stephens's ideas. Numerous other voices had discussed the possibility of conflict and bloodshed on the Texas–New Mexico boundary. Henry Foote's bloodcurdling imagery of June 13 was particularly noteworthy. But it was Stephens's powerfully worded letter that quickly became the most prominent statement of the theme, and it was reprinted by other presses throughout the nation. Coming from Stephens, an acknowledged exponent of Southern Whig views in Congress, the contents of the letter could not easily be ignored. Most Southern newspapers reprinted the Stephens letter with little comment, since it suited their own editorial opinions anyway. The Northern and antislavery papers that chose to comment mostly ridiculed the letter as perverted blusterings and treasonous sentiments designed simply to bully the North into submission to Southern demands and the Texan indemnity.[53]

Whatever impact the letter may have had on Zachary Taylor will remain unknown. The president was too busy on July 4 to have bothered very much about the Stephens letter. The heat in Washington that day was terrible, as it had been for many days past. Daytime temperatures were running over ninety degrees (ninety-two degrees on July 4, one source recorded) with little relief at night. The humidity was crushing. The heat sapped the energies of the politicians and caused many to lose "flesh," as they said. Senator Felch of Michigan wrote to his wife that the heat was "melting all fat men, and dissolving all greasy women." On July 4 itself, one Washington correspondent noted that numerous people fainted and that several horses dropped dead in the streets from sunstroke.[54]

Despite the heat, Independence Day celebrations took place as scheduled in the capital. The principal Washington festivities occurred that afternoon at the uncompleted Washington Monument. Despite the miserable heat, Taylor appeared healthy to observers, as he and other dignitaries sat under an awning listening to an oration by Sen. Henry Foote. During the speech, Taylor dozed off intermittently but paid close attention as Foote approached the conclusion of his address. When the Mississippi senator had finished, Taylor shook his hand heartily and praised his effort. The president then attended other ceremonies nearby; these, unfortunately, were not under the shade of the awning. He then returned to the White House, not apparently suffering undue physical duress but nonetheless tired, hungry, and thirsty. The accounts of his menu vary, but raw vegetables and fruits, milk, and ice water apparently were consumed by the famished president. That night he developed an intestinal disorder, some form of gastroenteritis, which was very common in Washington then and originated in milk and water all too prone to contamination.[55]

Taylor was ill the next day, July 5, but it was not considered to be serious. Even though he remained in bed that morning and could not meet with Gen. David E. Twiggs, up from Florida to brief the president on Indian affairs there, Taylor felt well enough by that afternoon to conduct some business. He signed documents relative to the Clayton-Bulwer Treaty with Great Britain and also wrote a few letters, much of the time resting on a sofa.[56]

Sometime that afternoon, probably around 3 p.m. after the House of Representatives adjourned, President Taylor endured another badgering visitation, this time from Stephens and Toombs together. Conrad, Marshall, and Toombs had exhausted rational argument, and warnings of party and national disruption so far had had little effect on the stubborn old general. But there was a last element of leverage Stephens and Toombs could try in this desperate situation—the Galphin Claim then being debated by the House. Many Democrats were anxious to censure Taylor himself over the scandal. Perhaps, Stephens and Toombs thought, a threat of Southern Whig votes in favor of the congressional censure could jolt Taylor from his position on Texas–New Mexico. Such a public condemnation would impugn Taylor's integrity, signify the final break of Southern Whig leaders with him, and possibly lay the groundwork for an attempt to impeach him. Some Southern Whigs had apparently already discussed this drastic step in response to Taylor's New Mexico policy. Stephens and Toombs may have hoped that, having failed to appeal to Taylor's reason, they could appeal to his fears for his own reputation. Of course for the Georgians to vote for such a censure, because Taylor had earlier supported their friend Crawford, would force Stephens and Toombs to repudiate their earlier defense of the secretary of war. But, given their desperation, Stephens and Toombs were willing to perform such political pirouettes.

The two Georgia Whigs first informed the president that the slavery and New Mexico policies of his administration were those of the radical Free-Soilers and Seward, and they reiterated that Southern Whigs would be forced into "general opposition" to the administration on that account. The Georgians then shifted to the Galphin matter, bluntly informing Taylor of their intention to vote for censure of the president himself; if Crawford's conduct was censurable, so then was that of Taylor, who had approved of Crawford's action.

President Taylor did not respond to his visitors on the Galphin issue. As to the slavery question, the president stated that the cabinet, not he, had determined the policy. This refusal of the president to assume responsibility for policies obnoxious to the South angered Toombs, who retorted that he considered the president, as "ostensible head" of the administration, responsible for those policies, that the cabinet was answerable to no other power than the president, and that the president, in failing to use his authority to correct the evil course of his cabinet, was making those policies his own. Taylor answered by expressing sorrow but also proclaiming that the policy was fixed and could not now be altered and that he would not swerve from his course. According to one newspaper report some days later, Taylor added a warning in reference to disunion threats: "Gentlemen, . . . if ever the flag of disunion is raised within the borders of these United States while I occupy the Chair, I will plant the stars and stripes alongside of it, and with my own hand strike it down, if not a soul comes to my aid south of Mason and Dixon's line." With nothing more to be said, Stephens and Toombs took their departure from the ailing but determined executive.[57]

The two Georgians were extremely frustrated and outraged at their inability to shake Taylor from a position they realized could be catastrophic for Southern Whigs—and probably for the Union. Stephens and Toombs, following the Taylor interview, sought out Navy Secretary William B. Preston, a Virginian whom Stephens considered a cabinet traitor to Southern interests and whom some other Southerners believed to be Taylor's guiding hand on New Mexico policy. The two finally waylaid Preston on the steps of the Treasury building and warned Preston that they planned now to impeach Zachary Taylor. Incredulously, Preston inquired, "Who will impeach him?" Stephens replied, "I will if nobody else does."[58]

As had become common with President Taylor, during the July 5 interview he patriotically wrapped himself in the mantle of the Union and adamantly clung to his policies. However, the constant barrage of argument and threats and the thought of congressional censure tortured his mind. On the night of July 5–6, Zachary Taylor felt so burdened by his troubles that he could not sleep. On Saturday, July 6, his condition steadily worsened, and a physician was finally called in to attend him that afternoon. The House of Representatives that day only added to his miseries. During the debate over a resolution on the Galphin scandal, Rep. Jacob Thompson, anti-compromise Mississippi Democrat, proposed an amendment to censure the president's conduct in the affair. As Stephens and Toombs had promised Taylor they would, they now voted with the majority for the move to censure Taylor. The House would not have voted for this measure if the members had realized how dangerous the president's sickness was becoming. Some reports had indeed begun to circulate in the House chamber that day concerning the severity of the illness, but some members misinterpreted those reports as a *ruse de guerre* by the administration to possibly delay House action against the cabinet.[59]

As if anyone needed a reminder of the danger involved in the Texas–New Mexico boundary dispute, Texas's most radical congressman, Volney Howard, published in the *Southern Press* on July 6 a letter in defense of his state's position. Howard confined himself to arguing the merits of Texas's case until the end of the letter, when he abruptly changed to a more defiant tone and proclaimed that Texans would resist federal usurpation to the knife. Somewhat balancing Howard's viewpoint was the Senate address of Tennessee Whig John Bell, which he began on July 3 and concluded on the 6th. No one was certain how he would vote, but most observers felt that he would finally vote in favor of the Omnibus bill. In his speech, Bell at times seemed to favor compromise and at times vigorously defended Taylor's policies, especially in relation to New Mexico. The Tennessean favored statehood for New Mexico as the best solution to the problem and characterized President Taylor's use of the military in New Mexico as a peace-keeping gesture designed to maintain the status quo until the issue could be settled. Underwood of Kentucky joined Bell in arguing this point. After Bell's speech, no one was yet certain how Bell would vote.[60]

By Sunday all in Washington knew that the president was indeed seriously ill. But his condition did not yet appear grave, and no one really expected him to die. Stephens and Toombs even seemed to relish their newly assumed renegade status and personally boasted of their complete desertion of the Taylor administration. In conversations on the morning of July 7, the two Georgians openly declared that they intended to bring down the entire administration with Secretary Crawford rather than allow him to be victimized as a scapegoat. They still did not realize how little time this particular administration had left.[61]

Also on Sunday, a copy of the New Mexico constitution arrived in Washington, probably via mail from St. Louis. Although it was an unofficial copy, it was the first tangible evidence of the New Mexico proceedings received in the nation's capital. The cabinet immediately assembled for a meeting on Sunday evening at Secretary of State Clayton's residence to consider the new information. The cabinet majority firmly supported the federal defense of New Mexico "at all hazards" and the fledgling state's admission into the Union with the boundaries proposed in its constitution.[62]

Despite its determination, this cabinet would never have the chance to further pursue its goals. President Zachary Taylor was dying. His body could not withstand the intestinal disease nor the calomel, bleeding, and other medical nostrums applied by his doctors. By Monday, July 8, even Taylor himself accepted the likelihood of his death. He reportedly told one attendant that day that he had tried to do his duty honestly, but "my motives have been misconstrued, and my feelings most grossly outraged." The correspondent who relayed this felt that Taylor was referring primarily to the encounter between the president and the Georgians on July 5. The House of Representatives that Monday did a last favor for the dying president; the House majority voted down the Galphin resolution, thus also expunging its attached amendment censuring President Taylor. Taylor lingered on through the 8th and into the 9th. Finally, however, at 10:35 P.M. that Tuesday, July 9, 1850, he died.[63]

Zachary Taylor had courageously and consistently defended the policies he believed right—even to the end. Many had disagreed with him and concluded that his policy on New Mexico would lead to bloodshed, disunion, and civil war. Some of them had endeavored to convince and then force Taylor to change his policy. He would not, and the stresses that he endured because of his own convictions may have contributed to his death. Others would now have to cope with Texas–New Mexico and the other sectional questions that threatened to tear the nation apart.

❧

Chapter Seven

The Fillmore Administration's Baptism
Texas–New Mexico Destroys the Omnibus

AS CHURCH BELLS BEGAN TOLLING THROUGHOUT THE CITY TO SIGNAL THE president's passing, Toombs and Stephens, sitting in their hotel parlor, must have reflected on whether their recent badgering of Taylor on the Texas–New Mexico issue might have added to the old general's health problems. They may also have reflected on whether reports of their visits to Taylor would adversely affect their own public reputations. However, when such reports appeared in the press a few days later, Stephens was able to deflect criticism of his friend and himself by publishing a denial of any "deathbed" visit.[1]

When a messenger delivered the mournful tidings to Vice President Fillmore at his rooms in the Willard Hotel, Fillmore bowed his head and declared, "This is my first misfortune!" Since 6 A.M. the day before, various individuals had been hounding him with advice on how he should conduct his presidency after Taylor died.[2] Now he was to be president of the United States—Millard Fillmore, son of a poverty-stricken New York tenant farmer. His handsome good looks, impeccable dress, kindliness, and dignified bearing masked the tremendous struggles he had endured in order to raise himself up through the legal profession and New York Whig politics to national prominence. But he had not sought the presidency and did not relish the thought of its responsibilities.

After receiving official notification from the cabinet of the president's death, Fillmore spent a sleepless night at his lodgings, mulling over the severe problems that his administration would face. At noon the next day, July 10, Millard

Fillmore, attended by the cabinet and a joint committee of the two houses, arrived at the House of Representatives chamber to take the oath as president. Despite his attempt to maintain a calm demeanor, some observers thought he looked pale, unhappy, and ill at ease. Conducted to the speaker's chair, Fillmore read the oath from a printed copy he had taken from his pocket while resting his other hand on a Bible held by the octogenarian judge of the District of Columbia Circuit Court, William Cranch. The ceremony completed, President Fillmore retired from the chamber.[3]

The new president was intelligent though not brilliant, a conscientious and loyal Whig, and a devoted family man whose personal life was often described as abstemious. He was one of the most widely experienced Whig leaders in the country, was greatly respected and liked by his fellow politicians, with the exception of the Seward faction, and had listened attentively as president of the Senate to the entire debate over the sectional issues in that chamber. Millard Fillmore always impressed people as an imperturbable sort, a man who kept his emotions strictly under control even in the midst of crisis. Given the intense public anxiety in July 1850 over the fate of the Union, Fillmore's dignified calmness fortuitously became a factor in relieving some of the public tension.

Fillmore's reputation for caution, moderation, and deliberateness made it unlikely that he would endanger the Union by hasty, extreme, or careless acts. Whigs believed they finally had a president who would adhere to traditional party policies; Fillmore was the only professional Whig politician ever to serve as a Whig president. Many Taylor Whigs of the North entertained the notion that President Fillmore would follow Taylor's policies, especially in regard to protection of New Mexico from any Texas invasion. Seward and his friends demurred, believing that Fillmore leaned too strongly toward Clay, Webster, and the compromise and that Fillmore's caution was simply timidity. Northern pro-compromise men, both Whig and Democrat, gained renewed faith that Fillmore's administration would augur well for their cause, although some of the partisan Democratic papers could not bring themselves to praise even such a Whig as Fillmore. Free-soil elements hoped that Fillmore, with his antislavery background, would stand firm against Southern demands, but most of them feared that the new president might surrender New Mexico to Texas. Democratic fire-eaters in the South generally labeled Fillmore an abolitionist enemy, a charge that Southern Whigs answered by defending his moderation and his opposition to the Seward-Weed faction in New York. Even a few of the more extreme Southern presses adopted a wait-and-see attitude in recognition

of the possibility that the Northerner Fillmore might adopt policies more favorable to Southern interests than the Southerner Taylor had done.[4]

No one, of course, knew exactly what Fillmore would do, despite a general
feeling that he would lean more toward Clay's program of settlement. Despite
numerous urgings that he decisively and clearly state his views, Fillmore refused
to be drawn into the debate. Some criticized his lack of an early, definitive policy
statement as timidity and indecision, but Fillmore's silence was wise. A bold policy
statement from him at that time could have contributed little to settlement. The
situation was too fluid, and Fillmore had not yet decided on any particular avenue of compromise, except that he generally favored whatever bill or combination of bills seemed conducive to lasting sectional harmony. He wished to give
Congress every chance to work out a plan of its own choosing, with the assurance
that he would not veto anything reasonable. Besides, Fillmore's general silence
on the issues somewhat stifled the attacks of his Northern and Southern detrac-
tors; if the president did not state a definite policy, his enemies could not directly
attack it. His refusal to adopt such a policy also allowed many Whig papers of the
North, formerly aligned with Taylor's policies, to maintain for some weeks that
Fillmore was not abandoning Taylor's program.

Actually, Fillmore's actions on becoming the chief executive should have
left no doubt in anyone's mind that his sympathies were firmly with the compromisers. He consulted with many, even Seward, but Henry Clay and Daniel
Webster quickly became Fillmore's closest advisers. He met with Clay and
Webster for lengthy discussions on July 11 and again on July 12. The first major
item of business was the construction of a new cabinet.[5]

There was no possibility that Millard Fillmore would keep the late president's
cabinet, so dominated by Seward men who had hostilely proscribed Fillmore's
influence from Taylor's administration. Fillmore accepted all their tendered
resignations. He initially leaned toward Robert Winthrop for secretary of state,
rather than remove Daniel Webster's pro-compromise vote from the Senate.
But Winthrop supported the choice of Webster over himself, and Webster urged
the Massachusetts governor to appoint Winthrop to Webster's old Senate seat.
So Fillmore selected Daniel Webster for the prime cabinet post in his new administration. The Massachusetts statesman was at the time extremely fearful of
civil war erupting and believed he could best bring his influence in favor of a
peaceful settlement to bear as Fillmore's chief minister. A conservative Whig
cabinet was formed—thoroughly "doughface" in the eyes of Seward men—
during the next several weeks.[6]

The incendiary Texas–New Mexico issue allowed the new president and his advisers no respite. Fillmore knew that Taylor's cabinet had been preparing new, unambiguous orders for the army units in New Mexico and that Taylor had intended to accompany these orders with a public message. But Fillmore believed these steps would needlessly provoke Texas and so decided to withhold them. He was also well aware that an unofficial copy of New Mexico's proposed antislavery state constitution had arrived in Washington and that Northern free-soil advocates would eagerly support it, even though that constitution left intact the long-standing institution of peonage.[7]

Texans had been aware of the New Mexico statehood movement since Robert Neighbors's return in early June to Austin. They had reacted quickly to protest the federal military role in the statehood move, and a special courier with several missives from Governor Bell arrived in Washington on the evening of July 12. The items that he carried were all dated between June 13 and 15. One Washington correspondent reporting the arrival of the documents stated his belief that the nation now faced its greatest peril since the American Revolution.[8]

Governor Bell's communications concerned the Texas congressional delegation and the president. By far the longest of these was the letter to the delegation explaining what had transpired at Santa Fe and vehemently expressing Texan determination to protect its honor and enforce its jurisdiction against the "confident, supercilious air of power" assumed by the federal government in New Mexico. While the governor implied that his duty might necessitate the use of military force in New Mexico, he neither desired nor intended any conflict with the federal government and expressed his continuing hope that the president would finally order the military authorities at Santa Fe to relinquish civil jurisdiction or at least to observe a strict noninterference with Texan officials.[9]

Three of Bell's letters involved the president, and of course the governor had assumed that Taylor would still hold the office when the communications reached Washington. One was delivered by Rep. Volney Howard to Millard Fillmore on July 13. It delineated Colonel Munroe's interference with Major Neighbors and included a copy of Munroe's proclamation to assemble a statehood convention. Bell politely asked whether Munroe's actions had been ordered by the federal government or met with the president's approval. In a note transmitting Bell's letter, Representative Howard declared that Governor Bell wished to know if the federal authorities would use force to oppose Texas's attempts to enforce its jurisdiction in the disputed territory. Howard himself had received one of Bell's letters in which he had confided to Howard that "immediate military action" by Texas was required in New Mexico but that the governor had not yet decided whether to await the legislature's assistance in organizing the expedition. Bell urged Howard to press the president for a quick answer and enclosed a short protest note, involving no military threat by Texas, that Howard was to present to the president if he endorsed Munroe's acts.[10]

Fillmore refused to give a quick answer to Bell's letter, any more than he responded to other urgent demands for action from Sam Houston or influential Texas bondholder Gen. Leslie Combs of Kentucky. To Fillmore and his advisers, it was most important for Congress to act to resolve the crisis with as little direct intervention from the executive branch as possible. This did not mean that Fillmore was inactive, for within his particular realm of executive powers he was moving decisively and quietly to shift enough U.S. military forces to New Mexico to handle any confrontation that might develop there. Fillmore had always been a diligent worker, and he carried these habits over to his new office, toiling from 6 A.M. to 6 P.M. at the White House each day, even after his move to a cottage in the more healthful Georgetown in late July. Fillmore also continued to maintain his cordial relations with members of Congress. The president was not at all averse to meeting and talking with congressmen privately, and he was certainly not reluctant to discuss his general political views on the crisis in conversations with compromise supporters, always expressing his earnest desire for a permanent and peaceful settlement of the issues.[11]

The members of Congress were aware of the developments relative to Texas and New Mexico, and North Carolina Whig David Outlaw wrote that "intrigues without number" were afoot during the days following Taylor's death. The compromisers, encouraged now that they had a president who would not oppose an overall congressional settlement, worked to revive the moribund Omnibus bill. Various Washington correspondents reported a "Union caucus" on July 12, at which some Southern quasi-radicals and the Texans agreed with the compromisers to support a 34° north latitude boundary between Texas and New Mexico. While some of these same writers soon denied that such a caucus had occurred, apparently a few leaders had indeed met together in Clay's rooms at the National Hotel. The attendees were not named, but Stephen A. Douglas apparently suggested, and the others there accepted, the 34° north latitude line in order to attract some Southerners who had been allied to the extremists up to that time. That line would secure Texas the great bulk of disputed territory but place Santa Fe well within the area allotted for New Mexico. Actually this meeting on July 12, which may have struck some as unseemly on the eve of Taylor's funeral, was one of a half dozen or so informal strategy sessions that occurred between compromisers and quasi-radical Southerners during the July 12–15 period.[12]

The compromise advocates, probably at one of the meetings on the 12th or 13th, judging from the newspaper reports, also partially acceded to the principal Southern demand for a division of California at the line of 35° north latitude, if the new state of California so consented. Sen. Henry Foote of Mississippi was delegated to propose this and the Texas–New Mexico boundary amendments, and his name became publicly associated with them. However, several correspondents asserted that Senator Douglas, in consultation with Lewis Cass, was the originator of the California division plan. Neither Douglas nor Cass, of course, believed that slavery could take root in California under any circumstances. The principal Southern targets of the amendments to be offered by Foote, aside from Houston and Rusk, were King and Clemens of Alabama, Berrien of Georgia, Sebastian of Arkansas, and Morton of Florida. The compromise bloc finalized their Foote amendments strategy at a meeting on Tuesday, July 16.[13]

The friends of compromise had to exercise some caution too, lest they concede so much to Southerners that they cast adrift the Northern men who had supported compromise thus far. The situation in the Senate was delicate, to say the least. Nearly all commentators believed the prospects for the Omnibus bill to be at best doubtful, and most believed it would fail. Would the change in administration have enough impact on the Congress to help the Omnibus or another plan of settlement squeeze through? How much influence would President Fillmore and his advisers employ behind the scenes to get votes for the bill? Could the bill be so shaped that it would gain support from erstwhile Taylor Whigs and wavering Southerners without the changes costing more votes than they gained? And would Texas refrain from taking drastic actions that might remove the political questions entirely from the legislative arena and resign them to the arbitration of the sword? No one really knew the answers to these questions as Congress resumed its deliberations on Monday, July 15, amidst widespread press speculation on threats of military conflict over Texas–New Mexico.[14]

The Senate on the 15th voted 27 to 25 in favor of Berrien's amendment, adopted previously in Committee of the Whole, to prevent territorial legislatures from "establishing or prohibiting African slavery" rather than simply preventing legislation "in respect to" it, as it had been earlier worded. Six Northern men joined nearly the whole Southern bloc to approve the amendment. Senator Benton upstaged the compromisers and their plans by moving to substitute his earlier proposal for a western boundary of Texas at 102° west longitude for that of the Committee of Thirteen. Benton's purpose was to delay the progress of the bill and the compromisers' own amendment plans. The old frontier brawler, who had been rather silent since his June 10 speech, made the most of this opportunity in his verbal castigation of the bill and its progenitors. His performance impressed the visiting Swedish novelist Frederika Bremer as that of a bloodthirsty duelist. The Missourian asserted that the committee bill cut New Mexico in half, gave half of it to Texas, and proposed to pay Texas for the other half. After defending the late president's record in New Mexico and urging the use of federal military force against any Texan invasion, Benton closed and the Senate adjourned for the day.[15]

The battle resumed on Tuesday, July 16, with replies to Benton by Senators Rusk and Clay. Rusk painstakingly reviewed all the documentary evidence in support of the Texas claim and previous tacit recognition of it by federal authorities. He concluded that Texas would agree to any fair settlement but would never tamely submit to deprivation of its territory at sword's point. Clay attacked Benton's view that everything west of 102° north latitude, some three hundred miles on the Rio Grande below El Paso, had been part of New Mexico. The El Paso region had never been included in the jurisdiction of New Mexico under the Spanish or Mexican regimes. Clay particularly took exception to Benton's language in describing the Texas indemnity as a mere ploy to buy the votes of Texas, claiming that Benton had thus grievously insulted the integrity and motives of the Committee of Thirteen. Benton, always relishing the chance for another fight with his old adversary, denied that he had impugned the committee's integrity, but only their bill. Here, he declared, he had struck the "nerve" that Clay wished to avoid discussing—that the admission of California and the settlement of all other issues depended on how much money Texas was to be paid to push the log-rolling Omnibus through.[16]

After a bit more skirmishing, Foote of Mississippi finished the Omnibus proceedings for that day by finally giving notice of his amendments to set the Texas–New Mexico boundary at 34° north latitude and to divide California. His California amendment would urge the people of that state, after its admission, to consent to the establishment of a new territory of "Colorado" in its southern part. The northern boundary of this new territory would extend inland from the coast (near present-day Santa Maria) along 35° north latitude to the Sierra Nevadas, then north to 37° north latitude, and then east along this line until it intersected the Colorado River.[17]

When the bill's consideration was resumed on July 17, the Senate galleries were packed to hear Daniel Webster's parting address in the Senate, before he assumed his new duties as secretary of state. Beginning his speech calmly and heavily, Webster gradually brought the power and intensity of his voice and the beauty of his phrases to bear until the galleries were moved to numerous interruptions of thunderous ovations. Webster emphasized the North's and South's need for each other, nature's barrier against any extension of slave labor into the new territories, the North's gain of everything it wanted in the proposed compromise by surrender of only the needless Wilmot Proviso, the combined action of Northern and Southern extremists to kill the compromise, and the overwhelming need to compromise in order to save the Union. He warned that Congress should certainly not adjourn without settling the boundary dispute, on "the very eve of probable hostilities" and the probability of "collision, contest, and . . . bloodshed." Most newspaper commentators lavished praise on the speech and interpreted it as tangible evidence that Clay's compromise was the new administration's program, whether in the Omnibus form or in the separate bills that Douglas, near the beginning of his speech on July 17, promised Webster he would promote if the single bill failed.[18]

Subsequent to the Webster speech and some brief remarks by Clay and Hale, the Senate voted by a roll call of 36 to 18 to reject Benton's amendment. Only Wales of Delaware and Benton himself from the slave states voted in conjunction with sixteen Northerners for the proposition. Foote of Mississippi then introduced the two amendments that he had given notice of the previous day. Henry Clay briefly supported Foote's amendments, but he also expressed a preference for the bill as it had been framed. Foote characterized his amendments as intended to attract Southern votes, but Jefferson Davis of Mississippi and Andrew Butler of South Carolina seemed less than impressed. Davis saw no value in the bill for the South, if, as Webster had stated, the North gained all it wanted. Butler, in short remarks, revealed his skepticism over Foote's amendment to "exhort" the Californians to divide their state. The compromisers could at least claim to have resoundingly defeated Benton's boundary amendment on the 17th, but Benton could feel satisfied that his move had disrupted the compromise bloc's plans for two days.[19]

Joining Daniel Webster on July 17 in pro-compromise eloquence was Speaker of the House Howell Cobb, a Georgia Democrat. Publicly silent on the issues until then, he had listened as too many of his Southern friends in Congress constantly talked of disunion as if it were inevitable. Therefore Cobb addressed a long letter to his constituents, vigorously supporting Clay's compromise as the only workable settlement. Cobb stressed the importance of achieving a settlement and soon, for, like Webster, Cobb saw the most immediate danger as stemming from the boundary dispute. The likely contest between Texas and New Mexico over the boundary, he wrote, "presents a more urgent argument for its speedy adjudication than any political considerations which I can offer."[20]

Cobb was concerned not only by disunion talk by Southerners but also by the lingering issue of Hugh Smith's recognition as a delegate from New Mexico. Since early April, when the Committee on Elections had ruled it "inexpedient" to admit Smith to a seat, the subject had languished without further action in the Committee of the Whole House on the State of the Union. The House resumed consideration of Smith's credentials on July 15 and debated the issue for parts of four days.

During the debate, nearly all Southerners, whether in favor of or opposed to compromise, condemned Smith's admission as being totally without precedent, given that no territory had been established by Congress yet, and as implicitly deciding the boundary dispute against Texas, since Smith's constituency lived almost entirely east of the Rio Grande. Only a few Southern Whigs—Houston of Delaware, Bowie of Maryland, and Conrad of Louisiana—argued that Smith should be allowed to present his case and that his being recognized as a delegate by the House would not prejudice the boundary question. Both Texas representatives, Kaufman and Howard, strenuously denounced Smith's election as having no legal basis and the movement for his recognition as delegate as an insidious denial of Texas's boundary claims. During the debate, radical Democrat William Ashe of North Carolina reiterated the theme that the eruption of conflict on the Texas–New Mexico boundary would dissolve the Union. Joining the Southern opposition to Smith in the debate were several pro-compromise Northern Democrats—Gorman and Brown of Indiana, Strong of Pennsylvania, and Richardson of Illinois.

The great majority of those speaking on Smith's behalf were Free-Soilers and Northern Whigs. Many of these saw Smith's seating as an essential part in their overall design to save New Mexico from the Texans, whether as a territory or a state. Their view was that Smith deserved to be heard as a delegate from New Mexico in order to provide a counterweight to Kaufman and Howard of Texas and to present information on the New Mexico side of the case. If such recognition of Smith, prior to official territorial organization, appeared unprecedented in light of previous House practice, they said, then the House should set a new precedent. To do otherwise, they held, was to recognize implicitly the Texan claim to all of New Mexico east of the Rio Grande. On the other hand, Smith's advocates declared that his seating would not decide the boundary issue in New Mexico's favor. Two Northern Democratic supporters of compromise—Fitch of Indiana and Bissell of Illinois—added their voices in support of Smith, as did the three Southern Whigs mentioned previously.[21]

When discussions began on the 15th, many people believed that, since Congress had delayed providing a civil government for New Mexico, the House would probably admit Smith to voice that region's concerns. But as the debate developed and Southern opposition to Smith stiffened, his more lukewarm Northern supporters began deserting him. Once the debate officially closed on the 18th, the House's notorious five-minute rule—involving continuously renewed amendments with accompanying five-minute speeches—was utilized to extend the debate even further. Finally on the 18th, the House voted by a teller vote in Committee of the Whole to endorse the Committee on Elections decision that Smith should be denied a seat as delegate from New Mexico. The vote was 92 to 86, with a number of Northern men such as Robert Winthrop conveniently leaving the chamber just before the vote was taken. Encouraged by this victory, the opponents of seating Smith talked out the remainder of that day's session. On July 19 they felt sure enough of their majority that Gorman, a Democrat from Indiana, moved to table the whole subject. This was done on a roll call of 105 to 94. Winthrop, apparently feeling that his vote would not then affect the outcome, voted against the motion. The voting on this and several other roll calls on the 18th and 19th quite closely reflected the divisions that had appeared during the debate.[22]

On July 19, having rejected one applicant for a delegate seat, the House also refused to seat Almon Babbitt as a delegate from Utah. Hugh Smith, upset over his rejection, blamed Speaker Cobb for orchestrating the tactics and voting in opposition to him. Free-Soilers were outraged; Rep. Charles Durkee of Wisconsin wrote that New Mexico had been denied the right to a hearing in its own defense, which even criminals were granted. Compromise supporters, however, felt quite the opposite—that without Smith's defeat the efforts for a general settlement then progressing through the Senate would have been severely impaired if not entirely blocked. As the *Philadelphia Pennsylvanian*'s Washington correspondent wrote, Smith's seating would have united the Southerners against compromise and probably would have sparked the Texans to launch an expedition into New Mexico as quickly as possible. A telegraphic report from New Orleans, published in the *National Intelligencer* on July 18, that several public rallies in Texas had passed belligerent resolutions and that a special session of the Texas State Legislature had been called for August may have influenced some of the moderates in the House to vote against Smith.[23]

The Senate debates on July 18 and 19 had little to do with the Texas–New Mexico issue. Southern extremists made clear that a congressionally mandated division of California figured uppermost on their agenda. The Senate finally voted on the 18th—after Rusk and Benton put in final short addresses on opposite sides of the 34° north latitude Texas–New Mexico proposal—to reject the first of Foote's amendments. The vote was 34 to 20 against it, with the North entirely opposed to it. Clay, personally preferring the committee's line, also voted in opposition. The Senate then turned to Foote's California plan, which Southerners opposed because it recommended a division of the state, rather than required it. On July 19 Foote withdrew his own amendment and the Senate voted down two other plans by Southerners for California's division. Foote desperately concocted a new version of his amendment, definitely establishing a new territory of Colorado below 35°30' on the West Coast, although no one believed it had a chance to pass.[24]

It had proven impossible to devise a California provision at once agreeable to both Northern compromisers and Southerners. The amendments had failed, and King and Berrien were now expected to oppose the bill. After the action on the 19th, commentators all felt the Omnibus was lost, and Northern advocates of the bill angrily blamed Southern intransigence on the California issue for the impasse. Clearly, any amendment satisfactory to most Southerners would have lost more Northern votes for the Omnibus than the Southerners it attracted to the bill.[25]

What ensued on Saturday, July 20, could have only further disheartened the compromisers. While the Senate rested from the Omnibus bill debate for a day, it did not rest from the boundary dispute. Upon Cass's motion, the Senate took up his resolution of June 27 in reference to the exercise of unwarranted civil powers by the military authorities in New Mexico. James A. Pearce of Maryland, a usually quiet and scholarly Southern Whig whom the compromise bloc had assumed would finally be counted among those voting for the Omnibus, revealed in a well-prepared speech just how antagonistic he was toward the Texas claim to New Mexico. Buttressing his arguments with detailed references to documents and history, Pearce denied that either the federal government or the people of New Mexico had ever recognized or acknowledged the Texas claim of 1836. He condemned the threatened violence by Texas and warned that, even though the U.S. military would not fire the first shot, Texas's action would amount to levying war on the United States. Senator Rusk of Texas answered with a brisk, heated reply promising Texas's resistance, even if it be treason, to federal military usurpation of Texas's rights in New Mexico. The Senate then postponed the subject. After some further discussion of it on July 25, Cass's resolution was quietly tabled on the 29th.[26]

Though his compromise bill seemed doomed, and he himself was physically enervated from the long struggle, Henry Clay did not give up the fight. In his frustration he had grown noticeably more irritable in the summer's heat. He had curtly informed a group of Boston tariff lobbyists that they would do better to influence the fanatics in the Massachusetts congressional delegation to support the compromise. "Save your Country, and then talk about your tariff," he had recently told the lobbyists. Despondent though he was, Clay spoke in the Senate on Monday, July 22, for almost four straight hours. As he commenced, Clay appeared feeble and weak, his long fingers pallid and trembling. His complexion, however, gained color and his voice more vigor as he warmed to his topic. In making a point on which he felt a particularly strong conviction, Clay would move his head quickly to and fro, necessitating the constant use of his hands to brush the locks of his white hair back from his forehead.[27]

The speech as a whole was not great. It rambled from topic to topic in a loosely organized fashion. Clay reiterated the advantages of compromise for each section, the ban of nature against any further slavery expansion to the West, and the danger of civil war. At several points in the address, he spoke about the urgency of settling the boundary dispute. Two wars could erupt there, Clay said—one between New Mexicans and Texans, the other between North and South. His bill, he asserted, would give Texas all the area suitable for slave labor; if Texas were granted all the area it claimed, within a few decades the region would so fill up with nonslaveholders that their numbers might abolish slavery in all of Texas. Given the small numbers of Anglo-Americans in New Mexico, Clay believed its population more suited to territorial status than immediate statehood. At times his appeal for compromise and the Union struck his listeners as eloquent, bringing tears to the eyes of many, even his nemesis Benton. Sometimes, however, it came across as ineffective and pathetic. At one point he singled out the Delaware and Rhode Island senators as ones who should now support his bill.

The speech did contain momentary flashes of rhetorical brilliance, especially when Clay assailed the Northern and Southern extremists allied against him. Even while Clay spoke that day, Hale of New Hampshire and Clemens of Alabama were circulating around the Senate floor tallying lists of prospective opponents of the bill. When Clay accused the Southern radicals of conspiring with antislavery men to defeat his bill, Sen. James Mason of Virginia interjected that Southern men often consulted on "the dignity, honor, and safety of the southern States." Clay answered that the compromise Democrats and Whigs consulted on "the dignity, honor, and safety of the Union, and the Constitution of our country." The ovation from the galleries reverberated loudly throughout the chamber. Clay did not reserve his sharp phrases for Southern "ultras." He likewise denounced the antislavery radicals, declaring, "They live by agitation. It is their meat, their bread, the air which they breathe." When all was over and the Senate adjourned, even some of Clay's enemies admitted their admiration for the old man's stamina and patriotism. It had been a dramatic, sometimes inspiring, performance, but the Omnibus still clung to life only by the barest thread.[28]

Senate action and debate on July 23 was entirely consumed with Foote's latest California amendment and by disagreement between Foote and his Southern Democratic colleagues concerning the fine points of Southern doctrine on slavery's status in the Mexican cession. The most significant action involving the Omnibus bill, however, took place that day outside the Senate chamber. Supporters of the bill held a caucus that morning along with some of the doubtful friends of the bill. Their earlier plans having gone awry, the compromisers wished to concoct yet another scheme to sway some Northern and Southern men to vote for the Omnibus. Foote's California amendment, hopeless as it seemed, would be retained as part of the package to appeal to such senators as King, Berrien, Clemens, Sebastian, and Morton. The biggest change would consist of an entirely new formula for resolving the Texas–New Mexico issue. Who in particular devised the plan—Clay, Foote, William Dawson of Georgia, or someone else—is not clear, but the idea behind it had been suggested during debate back on June 20 by Sen. David Atchison of Missouri. The suggestion was to amend the Omnibus bill by having the president appoint three commissioners to consult with commissioners to be appointed by Texas and to have this mixed commission decide on a suitable Texas–New Mexico boundary and on an amount of monetary compensation that Texas should receive. The commission would make its report to the president, who would transmit the report and his recommendations to Congress. It would then be up to Congress and the Texas Legislature to ratify or reject the commission's findings.[29] Such commissions had determined the Georgia boundary in 1802 and had settled a disputed boundary between Missouri and Iowa in 1844.

Whoever originated the idea, the caucus selected Sen. James Bradbury, a Maine Democrat, to introduce the amendment in the Senate. Bradbury's conversion demonstrated just how chameleon-like politicians could become during the crisis. Until then he had been firmly opposed to the bill and had assured

Senator Benton that he could rely on him. The Maine Legislature had voted for instructions directing Bradbury to vote against the bill. But Bradbury was also friends with Henry Foote and the *Union's* Thomas Ritchie, and their influence may have played a strong role in Bradbury's decision to support an amendment that, if adopted, would ensure his vote for the bill. Bradbury may have been thinking for himself too. Reports of impending violence in New Mexico leading to Southern disunion may have seriously alarmed him about the need for a settlement. Certainly he was disenchanted with the land-for-money provision then in the Omnibus. Bradbury agreed with Benton's assertion of July 15 that the proposition appeared to involve the Senate in an unseemly auctioneering scheme. The compromise promoters fondly hoped that the commission amendment would attract other Northern and border-state politicians besides Bradbury—Pearce (W-Md.), Underwood (W-Ky.), Spruance and Wales (W-Del.), Clarke and Greene (W-R.I.), Shields (D-Ill.), Felch (D-Mich.), and Norris (D-N.H.). Pearce and Underwood in particular had expressed dislike for the indemnity clause, and their objections had been one reason that Senator Clay had, so far, left the clause blank as to amount. Bradbury's amendment would remove that problem.[30]

Unfortunately, the commission plan presented difficulties of its own. The most obvious one was that it would postpone settlement of what nearly everyone at the time considered the most volatile issue then facing Congress—the boundary dispute. It was doubtful that Texas would ever submit to such a commission, and the boundary dispute might erupt in violence and bloodshed before the commission could conclude its work. Many believed that Congress was dodging its responsibility in this explosive crisis by handing the resolution of the issue over to a separate commission. Congress would possibly face the very same controversies in a later session, when the commission made its report. Undoubtedly the advocates of compromise weighed some of these considerations in their July 23 caucus, but on balance they decided that the merits of diverting the Texas–New Mexico boundary dispute to a mixed commission would outweigh its detriments, help pass the Omnibus bill, and allow the Congress to finally act on the dispute in a future session in a calmer national atmosphere. A second caucus on the morning of July 24 finalized the new plan. Win or lose, the stratagem would allow the compromise bloc to regain the initiative.[31]

When Free-Soiler Salmon Chase learned of the planned maneuver on Wednesday morning, July 24, he aptly characterized it by writing that the Omnibus drivers were "reducing the size of the vehicle and taking off a wheel to fit

it through." Newspaper reporters, who in recent days had been writing epitaphs on the Omnibus bill, suddenly encountered a renewed confidence among
members of the compromise bloc. Clay looked happy for a change, while Benton
sat gloomily. According to the *New York Tribune*'s Stephen P. Andrews, Foote
excitedly bounced around the Senate chamber whispering confidentially to this
member and that. As the Omnibus bill was taken up, Foote arose and temporarily withdrew his own California amendment in order to allow Bradbury to
introduce the boundary commission proposal. Immediately after the Maine
Democrat had done so, Rusk of Texas moved to amend the new scheme to
confirm the 1836 boundary claim of his state. The Senate quickly rejected Rusk's
move 34 to 18, with only Southern senators in its favor.[32]

Hale of New Hampshire next proposed to amend Bradbury's plan to leave
the "rights and possession" of Texas and the United States as they were at that
time while the commission performed its duty. Rusk moved a substitute for
Hale's proposition: to leave the "rights and claims" of Texas and the United
States as they had been on March 15, 1849, before the Taylor administration had
promoted New Mexican statehood through executive action. Rusk then delivered an impassioned address worthy of any South Carolina fire-eater, vowing
that Texas would stand by its honor, even to the point of bloodshed and violence. A bit later, Hale modified his wording to allow both Texas and the United
States to retain the "rights" each possessed at the time of the exchange of
ratifications of the Guadalupe Hidalgo Treaty.[33]

If some promoters of the compromise thought the road for the commission
amendment would be an easy one, they were sadly mistaken. This became especially evident when Benton, following Rusk's speech, described the Bradbury
amendment as a colossal retrogression, an avoidance of settlement for what the
compromise advocates had claimed to be a major issue, and a maneuver that
would weight the commission's decisions heavily in Texas's favor. Bradbury
responded with a defense of the plan's reasonableness and the precedents for it.
He seemed most effective when attacking Benton's own proposal to give New
Mexico more land than it claimed by its recent state constitution. Benton's
arguments provided the foundation for newspaper commentaries opposing the
Bradbury amendment. Horace Greeley objected to any commission on which
New Mexico itself would have no direct representatives. Correspondent James
Harvey, writing as "Independent" in the *Philadelphia North American,* labeled
the Bradbury scheme a "miserable and catch-penny nostrum," "quackery," and
a "poor and contemptible evasion." Other papers adopted Bradbury's view that

the amendment would get the issue out of the contentious Congress, pave the way for settlement of the remaining issues, and probably prevent a violent incident that could lead to national disruption.[34]

It was obvious from Rusk's remarks on July 24 that the Texans instinctively distrusted the commission amendment. The surprising extremism of the usually moderate Rusk's address may have reflected the intelligences that the Texans had received the day before via courier from Austin—news of excitement and public meetings, Governor Bell's call for a special session of the legislature for mid-August, and the recruitment of volunteer military companies. The courier also delivered to Rusk a letter from his friend and supporter Jerome Robertson, one of the leaders of the Southern extremist faction in the Texas Senate. Robertson wrote that Texas would submit to no compromise until after the federal government unconditionally acknowledged the right of Texas to the disputed territory. Rusk, as part of his effort to convince the North of Texas's serious intent, saw to it that Robertson's letter was published in the newspapers. Certainly the Fillmore administration was alarmed by the new information from Texas, as it became one of the major topics discussed at the cabinet meeting on July 24.[35]

Some Northern newspapers took the news as foreboding, even though they also mostly promised that the federals would crush any Texas invasion. The United States must put the "graceless, unlicked cub" Texas in its place, declared the *Newark Advertiser* in an editorial typical of this view. Several Northern papers, however, continued to ridicule the Texan activities as an impossible bluff that could never be carried out due to cost and distance. The vast preparations around the "great city of Austin" were worthy of "Don Quixote and Hudibras," chuckled the *Middlebury* (Vt.) *Register*. "Oh dear! Oh dear! what a terrible time we shall have of it," mocked the *Toledo Blade*. The *Chillicothe* (Ohio) *Scioto Gazette* and the *Portsmouth* (N.H.) *Journal* both likened Texas to a puppy whose howling scared no one.[36] Many at the North simply could not convince themselves that Texas's threats were serious; no matter what strident pronouncements issued forth from the Lone Star, they seemed sheer bombast and "gasconade" to Yankee disbelievers.

As soon as the Bradbury plan was brought forward, rumors abounded in Washington that the proposal was attracting some votes for the Omnibus bill and possibly enough to pass both amendment and bill. This situation put the Northern and Southern opponents of the bill in a predicament as to how they would proceed to block the maneuver in the Senate. The strategy that emerged from their consultations was to delay the final voting on amendment and bill until the arrival of the two new senators from Massachusetts and Ohio to replace Daniel Webster and Thomas Corwin, who had resigned to join President Fillmore's cabinet as secretaries of state and treasury. All suspected that the governors of those states would select Robert Winthrop of Massachusetts and Thomas Ewing of Ohio, a former member of Taylor's cabinet, to fill the vacancies. Both men were expected to oppose the Omnibus bill, although antislavery men distrusted Webster's friend Winthrop. With those two prospective votes against the bill, the measure's enemies believed they could offset any votes gained by the Bradbury amendment for the Omnibus. To accomplish the necessary delay, the bill's opponents planned to continue introducing amendments and debating them as long as possible.[37]

The anti-bill strategy became very evident when debate resumed on July 25. Hale's amendment from the previous day was voted down 30 to 23, with the Southern "ultras" joining the compromise bloc against it. Benton then took charge of the delaying tactics, introducing several amendments to the Bradbury plan. His leadership of the coalition opposing the Omnibus led the Washington correspondent of the *Louisville Courier* to remark that the extremists all sneezed when he took snuff.[38] The first of Benton's offerings was innocuous enough and was quickly disposed of by Bradbury, who changed some words of his amendment to accommodate it. Benton then offered an amendment to force the proposed commissioners to exclude every part of New Mexico from the region to be incorporated within Texas's boundaries. This, of course, opened up a long discussion over what was New Mexico, or whether there even was an entity called New Mexico yet. Benton's amendment ultimately went down to defeat 38 to 16, his support coming primarily from Northern antislavery allies.

The Missourian then offered an amendment designed to make the commissioners determine the "true and legitimate" boundary of Texas. He soon withdrew this amendment in favor of a similar one by Southern extremist James Mason of Virginia. The debate dragged on, with Free-Soil Democrat Hannibal Hamlin of Maine defending Mason's proposition. The compromise forces had hoped to sit out the delaying tactics of the Omnibus opponents and reach a final vote that day, but the enemies of the bill proved too resourceful. Mason's amendment was finally defeated 28 to 25. After Rusk introduced an amendment to confirm all rights possessed by Texas as of the ratification of the Guadalupe Hidalgo Treaty, or at any time since that date, the bill's opponents mustered enough strength to pass an adjournment motion.[39]

If the concert of action on the part of Northern and Southern radicals escaped anyone's notice during the debates on July 25, their voting together on five roll calls that day provided incontrovertible evidence of their collaboration. (See Appendix B, votes C–G.) During the proceedings, this coalition voted together in favor of four motions to adjourn, including the last one, and in favor of the Mason amendment.[40] The emergence of this voting pattern on the 25th, for the first time since June 13 and 14, indicated the pattern that would follow on many Senate roll calls in subsequent days. Northern antislavery and Southern proslavery forces might take opposite views on Texas's rights east of the Rio Grande, but they could vote in unison on procedural motions of delay and on some amendments to the bill. The boundary issue, with its complexities and indefiniteness, constituted the only medium through which these mutual enemies could combine their efforts against an overall settlement. (See Appendix E, section 1.)

The July 26 Senate session, when the Omnibus was taken up, began with consideration of Rusk's amendment. New Jersey Whig senator William L. Dayton, supported by Hale and Seward, quickly interpreted the amendment to mean the implied recognition of Texas's entire claim east of the Rio Grande by President Polk's administration. Dayton and the others emphasized that New Mexico also had rights that should be respected. Rusk and Houston both vigorously defended the amendment and Texas's position, Rusk in a defiant manner, Houston in a more conciliatory one. Even several Southern radicals disavowed Rusk's proposal; Mason of Virginia felt that the Texans were only trying to increase the amount of territory that they wished to sell anyway. Rusk's amendment was defeated 35 to 12, with only ten Southerners joining the Texans in its favor.[41]

After further discussion, the stage was set for the day's main event. Senator William Seward of New York discerned that now was an opportune moment for him to assume the congressional leadership of the New Mexico statehood cause. Several days earlier he had asked his mentor, Thurlow Weed, if he should press the statehood issue, but Weed hadn't had a chance to answer yet. Seward also consulted several senators and was firmly convinced that his confreres fully assented to his plans, but they may have thought the New Yorker only meant to urge New Mexico's statehood in a speech that would form part of the stalling tactics while they awaited the new senators from Ohio and Massachusetts. Whatever their understanding of what Seward meant to do, his Senate friends were duly shocked on July 26 when Seward abruptly proposed an alteration of Bradbury's amendment that would authorize the president to proclaim New Mexico a state if its constitution had been popularly ratified in that region.[42]

After introducing his proposal, Seward spoke at some length in his usual droning, monotonous style, and what he said enraged many of his listeners. He rejected plans of concession and compromise as only securing temporary adjustments while simultaneously ignoring ultimate institutional reform. He declared that statehood had been approved by New Mexicans themselves and would place New Mexico on an equal footing with Texas in any boundary settlement procedure conducted under the auspices of a commission or the U.S. Supreme Court. Otherwise, he said, the greater part of New Mexico would probably be swallowed up, perhaps forcibly, by Texas before the commission suggested by Bradbury could ever report. Seward stated that he hoped his amendment would prevail if the Bradbury amendment and the bill were destined to pass Congress; he also voiced his intention to vote against both the Bradbury amendment and the bill, whether his New Mexico amendment was agreed to or not.[43]

Seward's speech exacted a venomous, and reportedly bibulous, retribution from Whig senator Thomas Pratt of Maryland, who ordinarily remained aloof from Senate debates. Pratt bitterly denounced Seward's proposition as a prime example of the New Yorker's theory of a "higher law" that might violate two provisions of that Constitution: first, New Mexico's constitution, no official copy of which had yet been received in Washington, might not have established a government republican in form, as required by the U.S. Constitution; and second, the new state might have expressly violated the section of the Constitution forbidding the formation of a state within the boundaries of another (since Texas claimed the whole region east of the Rio Grande) without the other's permission. Pratt held that Seward's belief in the "higher law" doctrine constituted a direct violation of his Senate oath to uphold the U.S. Constitution and that this was sufficient ground on which to expel him from the chamber.[44]

Dayton of New Jersey, embarrassed by Seward's move, attempted to extricate him from the mess by suggesting he withdraw his amendment, which would require unanimous consent. Henry Clay, anxious to watch Seward writhe in his own predicament, immediately objected to a withdrawal. Seward tried to demonstrate that New Mexico's government was indeed republican in form by reading sections from an unofficial copy of its constitution. However, Seward's usual coadjutors gave him little support, and Dayton, Hale, Baldwin, and Chase all disavowed his amendment. They objected to Seward's grafting of this plan onto a bill that he and they staunchly opposed. They believed his amendment would transfer to the executive branch Congress's authority to admit new states. And they were unwilling to act on New Mexico's statehood, even as a separate measure, before an official copy of its constitution was before them. They, especially Hale, at least defended Seward's character against the personal attacks of Pratt.[45]

At the end of this long debate, Seward's amendment ignominiously failed 42 to 1, his vote being the only one in its favor. Seward felt betrayed by his free-soil comrades, singling out Dayton's "cowardice" in a letter to Weed. Dayton complained that he had not been adequately consulted, but Seward's judgment on his supposed allies was that "Clay frowned and they fled." That was probably an unfair assessment on Seward's part; more likely it was Seward who had imprecisely and unclearly communicated to his colleagues just how and when he would employ his tactic. Weed added his chastisement in a letter to Seward a few days later, arguing that he had been wrong to try to amend an already "obnoxious" combination bill as the Omnibus was. The only consolation Seward may have derived from the fiasco was that his amendment had used up the greater part of another Senate day.[46]

Two other roll calls took place during the debate over his proposal on the 26th. Both were on motions to adjourn and both fitted the pattern of compromise advocates versus compromise opponents. The first of these motions, by Davis of Mississippi, failed 27 to 23; the second, by Berrien of Georgia, made immediately after the vote on Seward's move for New Mexico statehood, passed 30 to 20. (See Appendix B, votes H and I).[47]

The proceedings on the Bradbury amendment thus far had revealed the clear hostility of Rusk and Houston toward the measure without significant changes in the commission plan. Both Texans were reportedly prepared to vote in opposition to the amendment as it was then constituted; it simply included too many uncertainties to suit Texas. Would the validity of the Texan claim east of the Rio Grande be respected while the commission did its work? If so, what would be the status accorded the Taylor-sponsored statehood movement in New Mexico with its boundary claims infringing on those of Texas? Would the administration choose for its commissioners men who were hostile, friendly, or impartial to the Texan claim? Would Texas receive any monetary compensation for lands claimed by her but which the commission might assign to New Mexico?

The Texans were seriously worried about the vagueness of the Bradbury amendment on these matters and desired to be reassured by the Fillmore administration in regard to its attitude on the New Mexico situation. The administration had not yet defined a policy on the boundary dispute, although it was generally reported to be in favor of a comprehensive settlement. What was President Fillmore's view on the New Mexico statehood movement? Would he, as the Texans fondly hoped, rescind Taylor's orders to the U.S. military in Santa Fe to assist that movement? If Texas again attempted to assert its claimed authority in New

Mexico east of the Rio Grande, how would Fillmore react? Would he order his military forces to stand neutral, or would he interpose them against the Texan authorities, as Taylor would have done? The Texas delegation could not have been but alarmed over reports of U.S. reinforcements being then in transit to New Mexican posts. Were these movements really intended to provide more protection for the people there against Indians? Or possibly against Texans?

With all these questions on their minds, the Texas delegation went to see President Fillmore and Secretary of State Webster on Saturday, July 27. William Dawson (W-Ga.), who had been working hard to promote Clay's compromise, apparently had a hand in setting up the meeting and accompanied the Texas delegation to the White House. Reports of what transpired were very sketchy, but the Texans were apparently quite demanding. When they insisted that Fillmore state his policy on Texas–New Mexico, Fillmore refused to comply. He would not do so, he informed his visitors, until the cabinet had a chance to consider the matter, and at that point the new cabinet was not fully organized. There is no evidence that the Texans directly requested Fillmore to rescind Taylor's orders to Munroe. The military situation in both New Mexico and Texas was probably discussed, and it may have been this meeting at which Sam Houston was reported to have belligerently informed the president that he would resign his Senate seat and go home to lead the Texas troops if any conflict broke out. Fillmore appears to have given the Texans no indication that he would back off from the existing military arrangements in New Mexico, the reinforcement of those garrisons, or the previous administration's orders. The Texans, however, did find Fillmore and Webster more accommodating in reference to Bradbury's commission plan. Whether they debated what changes would be necessary in it to secure the votes of Houston and Rusk is not clear, but Fillmore and Webster did reassure the Texans that any commissioners appointed by the president would not be persons already prejudiced against the Texas claim. The Texas senators left the conference apparently more well-disposed toward the Bradbury amendment if some changes were made in it.[48]

Everyone in Washington sensed that the next week would decide the fate of Bradbury's amendment and the bill itself. One Northern Whig senator, whose views were shared by others, told Daniel Webster he would do anything to help the bill except vote for it, in order to be consistent with his previous stand. The enemies of the bill figured to pick up two additional votes for their side, as the Senate commissions for Ewing of Ohio and Winthrop of Massachusetts were imminently anticipated. Some members of the pro-compromise bloc pessimistically expected the bill's defeat, while many of their opponents believed that the bill would pass in some shape, possibly after further amendment. Benton and the Southern extremists were reported by Francis Grund to have many more amendments prepared and ready to introduce if it appeared necessary to delay the proceedings further. The morale of the compromisers was at least bolstered by the continued arrival in Washington of petitions—especially from New York City businessmen—supporting the Omnibus.[49]

While the allied radicals of North and South sometimes chided the Whigs and Democrats who consulted and caucused in favor of the Omnibus, the coalition against the bill appeared exotic and positively unholy to the compromisers. Seward, Benton, Hale, and Jefferson Davis were usually cited by reporters as the managers of the coalition. Francis Grund found it very amusing to watch Benton and Davis walking arm in arm to the Senate refreshment room, conferring as they went. At the end of each day's session, the radicals held regular caucuses at which they planned their strategy for the following day. The Southerners exacted an agreement from some of the Northern men in the House that they would not press Doty's California statehood bill while the Southerners in the Senate were cooperating in the fight to kill the Omnibus.[50]

Monday, July 29, arrived "hot as Egypt" in the words of *New York Herald* reporter George Wallis. A mob of people, anticipating that events were soon to reach a climax, crowded into the Senate gallery to watch their heroes and villains sweat through another session. Thomas Ewing took his seat as the new Whig senator from Ohio; Winthrop still awaited his own commission from Governor Briggs in Massachusetts. Promptly at noon the Omnibus was taken up, with Bradbury's pending amendment. William Dayton of New Jersey opened the battle by moving an amendment to Bradbury's that would leave it to the Supreme Court to settle the boundary dispute. The debate over Dayton's dilatory maneuver consumed several hours. Turney of Tennessee was the only Southerner besides Benton to join the Northern extremists in voting for the Dayton amendment as it went down to defeat 39 to 18.[51]

Benton immediately moved that no one appointed to the Bradbury commission should have already formed or expressed an opinion on the boundary issue. As S. P. Andrews of the *New York Tribune* pointed out, this was something of a practical joke by Benton put forward to emphasize the absolute impossibility of finding suitable commissioners who did not already possess preconceived ideas on this issue. Without debate, the Senate rejected Benton's offering on a roll call of 33 to 12. Mississippi's Davis and Virginia's Mason joined Benton and most of the Northern antislavery men in voting for it, but most of the Southern extremists who voted joined the large majority against it.[52]

The Bradbury amendment itself finally came to a vote. When the roll was completed, the tally stood at 28 to 28, thus defeating the amendment. Democrat Isaac Walker of Wisconsin, who reportedly liked the proposal but wished to abide by his state's instructions not to support the Omnibus, remained silent. Stephen Douglas, who had been counted on to cast his vote for Bradbury's proposal, missed the roll call under a most peculiar circumstance. Just before the vote was taken, Douglas's mother-in-law suddenly fainted in the stifling heat of the closely packed gallery. A lady called Douglas out of the chamber, probably to help his mother-in-law out to a carriage. He did not return until just after the roll call ended. On seeing that Douglas was absent, Sen. John Clarke (W-R.I.) unexpectedly voted for the amendment, knowing that it could not pass even with his vote. Clarke had been under much pressure from the compromise bloc and the administration; his vote was probably meant to signal his goodwill toward the compromise without offending the anti-compromise forces too badly. Supposed swing votes—Pearce, Underwood, King, Berrien, Felch, Norris, Shields, and the Delaware senators—cast their lot with the compromise bloc for the amendment against the anti-compromise coalition and the two Texas senators.[53] (See Appendix B, vote J.)

A short time after the defeat, Bradbury altered some of the wording in his amendment and introduced the same basic commissioner plan once more. Rusk quickly moved to amend it to declare null and void the orders by Colonel Munroe in reference to establishment of a New Mexico government. The Texans clearly would not assent to the commissioner plan if there existed any chance that, during the delay of settlement inherent in the scheme, the legitimacy of New Mexico's claim adverse to that of Texas might be recognized by the federal government east of the Rio Grande. Therefore the Texans demanded that the federal government recognize no civil government anywhere east of the Rio Grande, other than that of Texas, while the commission decided on a boundary. Rusk's amendment generated little enthusiasm and was crushed 42 to 12. This amendment had been the Texans' price for agreeing to Bradbury's amendment, and the defeat of Rusk's move led commentators to feel that the Texas votes were totally lost for the commissioner plan.[54]

After Underwood of Kentucky submitted and then withdrew another Supreme Court solution, Mason of Virginia moved to strike out that portion of Bradbury's amendment that would allow the proposed commissioners to agree on a convenient boundary, beginning at the intersection of the Red River and 100° west longitude, if they could not decide where the "true" boundary lay. No debate took place, but Mason's amendment was vague enough in content for the radical extremes to once again unite in voting and so was interpreted by reporters as a second test vote of the day. The roll call resulted in another tie at 29 to 29. Houston and Rusk voted for Mason's move, along with the anti-compromise bloc and both Rhode Island senators. Berrien, King, Pearce, Underwood, Felch, Norris, Shields, and the Delaware senators cast their votes with the compromisers to defeat the measure. Henry Foote held back his vote on the Mason amendment until the very last in order to vote against it, achieve a tie, and thus kill it. His deciding vote extricated the compromise bloc from a defeat, at least temporarily.[55] (See Appendix B, vote K.)

After the Senate then handily turned back an anti-Texas amendment by Hale of New Hampshire, Southern radical Hopkins Turney of Tennessee tried his hand at the amending process. He moved that if the commissioners could not decide on the "true line," then no monetary inducement was to be used to convince either party to accept some other line. Foote immediately branded it an invitation to civil war to withdraw the possibility of pecuniary consideration. Turney and Jefferson Davis both argued that, without Turney's proviso, the Bradbury plan was just another transparent, obnoxious plan to purchase some of Texas to transform it into free soil. Since neither the proslavery nor antislavery extremists approved the principle of such a purchase, Turney's amendment again represented fertile ground on which these traditional enemies could unite. But this time the vote stood 31 to 20 against the proposal, rather than being tied or nearly so. (See Appendix B, vote L.) A few senators had apparently left the chamber by this time, and three antislavery men—Ewing (W-Ohio), Smith (W-Conn.), and Hamlin (D-Maine)—threw their votes in with the pro-compromise forces against the Turney amendment. These three may have capitulated just to hasten the end of that day's session, for the Senate adjourned immediately after this roll call at about 4 P.M. As Eliab Kingman wrote, under the pseudonym "Ion," in the *Baltimore Sun,* the senators were "wearied, disgusted, and fagged out" by the time they adjourned.[56]

The advocates of the Omnibus were beset with gloom at the finish of the July 29 session. Even with most of their targeted senators now voting on their side, the compromisers had succeeded in achieving no better than a tie on the day's two most crucial votes. When Winthrop took his seat on the 30th, he was expected to tip the balance against the Omnibus. The compromise bloc needed to gain at least two more votes for the bill, and so they set about devising a scheme to mollify the Texas senators. At a pro-compromise caucus on the evening of July 29, Dawson of Georgia suggested a plan that Clay and most other compromisers adjudged to be fair and that the Texans accepted.[57]

Tuesday, July 30, was another hot, muggy day with a temperature over ninety degrees. Robert Winthrop was present as the new senator from Massachusetts, feeling, as he wrote, like a pawn placed on the chessboard when there was only a single move left. Everyone in the galleries and on the floor realized how crucial Winthrop's vote would be, and their scrutiny only added to the new senator's discomfort.[58]

After the Omnibus was once again taken up at noon, Dawson rose to offer his amendment to Bradbury's. The Georgia Whig proposed that until the boundary line had been finally agreed on by the United States and Texas, no territorial government for New Mexico and no state government would be established east of the Rio Grande. Benton at once attacked the amendment as virtually conceding everything on the eastern side of the river to Texas and as negating the constitutional right of Congress to determine when to admit new states. Clay defended Dawson's move but added that he himself might propose some time limit within which the commission should make its report. Douglas, who favored Bradbury's formula, dissented from Dawson's suggested proviso, arguing that, as it stood, the amendment would not prevent Texas from extending its jurisdiction over the region and would be an invitation to Texas never to agree to a boundary including less than the state's fullest claim. South Carolina's Butler still thought it ultimately amounted to another version of the land-for-money scheme, although Clay readily denied that. Clay believed that Texas would forbear sending its troops into the disputed region and thus precipitating a clash with U.S. forces while the commission performed its task. New Jersey Whig Jacob Miller felt it ridiculous to provide a territorial government west of the Rio Grande, where few people lived in New Mexico, while continuing the existing military regime on the eastern side until the boundary was settled. Dawson defended his amendment as protective of the rights of both the U.S. and Texas east of the Rio Grande and, only temporarily, would suspend the operation of New Mexico's territorial government there. And so went the debate.[59]

Three roll calls in rapid succession followed. Isaac Walker, a Wisconsin Democrat disdainful of the Texans, desirous of some compromise, and really anxious to avoid a direct vote if he could manage it, moved to table the bill. His motion failed 32 to 25, as the pro-compromise bloc mustered a few more Southerners than usual to defeat the anti-compromise coalition. (See Appendix B, vote M.) The question now recurred on the Dawson amendment, which passed 30 to 28. The great majority of Southerners rallied behind it; only Benton, Pearce, Underwood, Spruance, and Wales opposed it from the South. Four pro-compromise Northern Democrats—Jones and Dodge of Iowa, Sturgeon of

Pennsylvania, and Dickinson of New York—supported Dawson's amendment, as did two Northern Whigs, the consistently moderate James Cooper of Pennsylvania and, quite surprisingly, the antislavery Samuel Phelps of Vermont. Phelps thought he was rendering the Bradbury amendment more obnoxious and less passable by voting to tack Dawson's proviso onto it. Only time would tell, but for the moment he was taking quite a chance. The rest of the Northern bloc, including several Democrats whom the compromisers hoped would finally vote for the Bradbury amendment and the bill—Bradbury of Maine, Bright and Whitcomb of Indiana, Douglas and Shields of Illinois, Norris of New Hampshire, Felch of Michigan, and Walker of Wisconsin—voted against the Dawson proviso. Democrat Lewis Cass of Michigan dodged this roll call. Dawson's amendment was thus attached to Bradbury's commissioner plan, a victory for the Southerners, especially the Texans.[60]

The altered Bradbury amendment now came up for a vote. It passed also by a vote of 30 to 28, but this time the vote fitted the pro-compromise versus anti-compromise pattern. (See Appendix B, vote N.) Several of those who had just cast votes against Dawson's amendment now voted for the Bradbury-Dawson combination. The most interesting of these was James Shields of Illinois. He first cast his vote against the Bradbury amendment, but then, after Henry Foote talked with him, Shields changed his vote and saved the amendment. Walker voted for it, as did Cass. Among Southern Whigs, Pearce absented himself, while Underwood, Spruance, and Wales—disliking the Dawson proviso—voted against it. Their votes were offset by three Southerners who were attracted by the Dawson proviso but who had, up to that point, generally cooperated with the anti-compromise bloc—Democrats Robert Hunter of Virginia, Jere Clemens of Alabama, and William Sebastian of Arkansas. Houston and Rusk of Texas, of course, now advocated the Bradbury amendment and Omnibus bill. Phelps of Vermont, who voted against the Bradbury amendment, must have been having second thoughts about his previous vote, now that the Bradbury plan had been approved with the Dawson proviso as part of the Omnibus.[61]

Those Northern Democrats, such as Shields, who had opposed Dawson's plan but voted for the Bradbury-Dawson combination, may have been enticed by the promise of yet another amendment. On principle, the Northern Democrats much preferred Cass's strict congressional nonintervention to the recently passed formula that the South liked. Northern Democrats wished the territorial legislatures to be left entirely free to decide the slavery question themselves, whether Southerners liked this interpretation of nonintervention or not. Clay and Douglas consulted at some point in the proceedings, and Douglas persuaded Moses Norris of New Hampshire to offer an amendment, immediately following the Bradbury roll call, to strike out the words "establishing or prohibiting African slavery" from section 10 of the bill. This proposal shifted the debate for the remainder of that day's session from the Texas–New Mexico boundary dispute itself to the old question of congressional power over slavery in the territories. While Clay, Foote, Cass, and Thomas Pratt of Maryland defended the amendment as true nonintervention and essential to securing enough votes to pass the bill, most Southern speakers for and against the compromise attacked Norris's suggested change as an opening for territorial legislatures to abolish slavery and thus abridge the constitutional rights claimed by Southerners in reference to slave property during the territorial stage. The Senate adjourned before a roll call was taken on the Norris amendment. The compromisers, having succeeded in passing the Bradbury amendment, now felt confident of victory on the morrow for the Omnibus itself. They seemed oblivious to the possibility that changes they had made and the Norris amendment still pending might ultimately lose more votes for the bill than the ones gained by the amendments. As Roger Baldwin (W-Conn.) penned to his wife that day, "what fastens one screw unlooses another."[62]

After another evening of caucusing, the Senate met on Wednesday, July 31, for what most people believed would be the decisive day in regard to the Omnibus. Benton and Hale huddled for a final strategy session that morning. Henry Clay exuded confidence and radiated a more buoyant spirit than he had during the entire session. Clay informed Rep. Thomas Clingman (W-N.C.) that he now supported the Norris amendment, which would, he believed, secure enough Northern Democratic votes to pass the bill. When Clingman reminded Clay of his previous anticipations and subsequent disappointments that session, Clay impetuously waved his hand and gave Clingman a haughty look, saying as he did, "The administration was the only obstacle to the passage of my measures and I shall now carry them without difficulty." Clingman then walked across the chamber to where Senator Hunter of Virginia and Senator Soulé of Louisiana stood together. Hunter's vote had been crucial in passing the Bradbury-Dawson amendment on the 30th. When Clingman reported what Clay had declared, Hunter said, "Then you think we had better let it be destroyed." Clingman decidedly agreed. Southern radical disdain for the Norris amendment was perfervid. Clay did not realize how badly he had overestimated his control over Southern votes.[63]

Probably no one who witnessed Wednesday's session ever forgot it. The very endurance and stamina of the Senate members took on heroic proportions. The contest lasted for some nine hours "without intermission, and without food, and in a room as hot as an oven," as Senator Felch described it to his wife. On completion of the usual morning preliminaries, the Senate again resumed consideration of the Omnibus. Jefferson Davis of Mississippi began the proceedings with a lengthy, very clear explication of the reasons for Southern dislike of the Norris amendment. He charged that those who favored the amendment's version of nonintervention were the same ones who supported the U.S. Army's use against Texan enforcement of its claims in New Mexico. Mason of Virginia later added his endorsement of Davis's views. Roger Baldwin, Connecticut anti-slavery Whig, briefly supported the Norris amendment as a protection for the decision already made by the people of New Mexico to prohibit slavery. Thomas Ewing of Ohio, also an antislavery Whig, balked at giving a legislature representing a small frontier population such powers as implied by the amendment; he favored more restrictions, not fewer, and opposed Norris's plan. When the roll call was taken, the Norris amendment was added to the bill by a 32 to 20 margin. The pattern displayed quite a mixture of the various blocs. Most Northern free-soil men voted with the Southern Whigs and Northern Democrats for the amendment. All the Southern Democrats who voted, including Benton, opposed the Norris formula. Southern Whigs Morton of Florida (who ordinarily voted with the "ultra" Southern Democrats), Berrien of Georgia, and Pearce of Maryland, Northern Democrats Walker of Wisconsin and Whitcomb of Indiana, and Northern Whig Ewing of Ohio also cast negative votes.[64]

It can be argued that the passage of the Norris amendment sealed the doom of the bill by turning Southerners such as Atchison, Berrien, Downs, and Hunter—all of whom had voted for the Bradbury-Dawson amendment—irrevocably against the Omnibus. Clay and his friends, however, still entertained hopes for the bill's passage until Sen. James A. Pearce gave them a shock. Pearce, who detested the Texan claim to New Mexico and Dawson's amendment and who felt ignored and taken for granted by Clay's bloc, suddenly moved to strike out all of the Texas–New Mexico sections of the bill, with a view to then reinserting all of them except Dawson's proviso. Pearce minced no words; he stated that Dawson's plan rendered the bill "cranky, lop-eared, crippled, deformed, and curtailed of its fair proportions." An astounded Henry Clay defended the fairness of Dawson's arrangement and virtually accused Pearce of making a nitpicking gesture that would hazard the peace and safety of the Union. Foote said Pearce's amendment would defeat the bill, but Pearce held firmly to his stand. Daniel Dickinson of New York went over to Pearce and suggested that changes in a few words and the addition of a few lines might accomplish Pearce's object of protecting New Mexico without the radical surgery proposed by the Marylander. Bradbury was busily preparing the suggested changes. Pearce did ask the president pro tem (King of Alabama) if he could move to strike out only Dawson's amendment, but the chair decided that he could not move to strike out a section voted into the bill unless as a part of a larger portion requested to be stricken. So Pearce stayed with his original motion and added as a substitute for Dawson's proviso that New Mexico's territorial government would not take effect until March 4, 1851.[65]

A single telegraph dispatch sent out by a correspondent to several newspapers declared that Pearce, who was a long-time friend and associate of President Fillmore's, was "closeted" with the president some time on the day before and that the president, also disliking the Dawson amendment, delegated Pearce to somehow rid the bill of this feature. Some historians have related this report as fact while others have expressed doubts about its accuracy. There are good reasons to doubt the president's involvement. For one thing, it was not Fillmore's style to take a direct hand in a matter he genuinely wanted Congress to decide on its own. For another, there is no evidence that the president considered the Dawson proviso an unworkable detriment to the bill. Dawson was also well-acquainted with Fillmore and had escorted the Texans to the White House only a few days before; it seems unlikely that President Fillmore would subsequently attempt to engineer the elimination of his Georgia friend's formula after it had been voted into the bill. Even if Fillmore had wanted to get rid of the Dawson amendment, it was unlikely that he would have chosen Pearce, never known for parliamentary brilliance, to undertake such a delicate operation. In addition there are some contemporary pieces of evidence that cast doubt on the assertion of a role by Millard Fillmore in Pearce's move. A telegraphic dispatch to the *New York Commercial Advertiser* speculated that the reported Pearce-Fillmore meeting may have been only a rumor. Francis Grund, writing as "W" in the *New York Sun*, bluntly reported that Pearce's move was not sponsored by the administration and that the president and his cabinet were "chagrined" at Pearce for undertaking it. Pearce himself, in his only surviving letter on the subject, mentions no meeting with the president prior to his move on the 31st. Given Pearce's well-documented, conscientious belief that the Texas claim to New Mexico was totally invalid, it appears that the Maryland senator acted on his own without any encouragement from President Fillmore.[66]

Pearce's proposal opened the floodgates. After Rusk and Dawson defended the Georgian's proviso and the wavering Shields of Illinois expressed second thoughts about his previous vote for the Bradbury amendment, Senator Pearce allowed himself to be drawn into a parliamentary trap laid for him by Southern extremists Mason of Virginia and Yulee of Florida. Since there exists no reason to believe that Pearce was trying to destroy the bill rather than improve it by his amendment, his next move must be ascribed to sheer naivete or lack of political acumen. Mason, Yulee, and the other Southern extremists wanted to kill the bill entirely. Therefore, they did not want to vote for Pearce's motion as it was; they wished Pearce to split his motion into separate ones to strike and to reinsert, which would enable the Southern extremists to vote for the first and against the second. Mason, and then Yulee, suggested to Pearce that he split his motion, and Pearce, apparently oblivious to their real purpose, agreed to limit his first move to striking out the Texas–New Mexico sections.[67]

At the moment Pearce split his motion, the Northern and Southern enemies of the bill instinctively realized that the day was theirs. Benton rushed in for the kill with his most caustic attack yet on the Omnibus. The Missourian likened the measure, with its denial of civil government for the population east of the Rio Grande, to a group of strolling players who attempted to put on Shakespeare's *Hamlet* with the role of Hamlet left out because the ghost was sick. In this case, he said, the ghost of the Omnibus was sick. Gleefully he supported Pearce's move. In a more serious vein, Benton argued that the Dawson amendment, requiring Texas's approval of the commission's findings, surrendered New Mexico to Texas because Texas would never agree to anything less than her full claim.[68]

Following brief addresses by Dawson and Houston, voting then commenced. Including the earlier roll call on the Norris amendment, twenty-three roll-call votes were taken in the Senate on July 31. On nine of these, and on seven of the first nine following the Norris amendment vote, the pattern displayed a well-defined pro-compromise versus anti-compromise division. It was the same pattern that had exhibited itself on fourteen roll calls so far in the session. Over the entire series of twenty-five roll calls that followed this pattern, the cohesion of the pro-compromise bloc measured .836, while the cohesion of their opponents measured .841—very high levels of cohesion in both cases. The likeness between them, however, measured only .160, a level indicating almost no agreement in voting between the two blocs. (See Appendix B, sections 3 and 4.) Most striking of the likeness indices were the very high levels of agreement between the Southern "ultras" and the various Northern antislavery blocs over this series of roll calls. At no time during the antebellum sectional crisis did such an amazing voting alignment manifest itself, outside of these roll calls on the Texas–New Mexico boundary dispute in 1850. (See Appendix E.)

The first roll call after the one on Norris's amendment on July 31 was on Pearce's motion to strike out the Texas–New Mexico portion of the Omnibus. It passed 33 to 22. Of those who usually cast votes against the compromise, only Jere Clemens (D-Ala.) and William Sebastian (D-Ark.) broke rank to oppose Pearce's amendment. However, several of the pro-compromise bloc either voted for Pearce's motion or abstained from voting, thus providing the margin for its success. Southern Whigs Berrien (Ga.), Pearce (Md.), Underwood (Ky.), and Wales (Del.) and Illinois Democrats Douglas and Shields voted for the motion; Southern Whig Bell (Tenn.) and Northern Democrats Bradbury (Maine) and Felch (Mich.) did not vote. (See Appendix B, vote O.) Pearce then moved to reinsert everything except Dawson's amendment, with Pearce's March 4, 1851, proposal on New Mexican government as a substitute for Dawson's. Amid further discussion, Hale moved to indefinitely postpone the whole bill; the compromise bloc mustered nearly all the swing votes to beat back this move by the anti-Omnibus coalition by a vote of 32 to 27. (See Appendix B, vote P.)

Just before this, Douglas had offered an amendment as a substitute for Pearce's replacement in lieu of the Dawson proviso. Where Pearce proposed having the New Mexico territorial government not take effect before March 4, 1851, Douglas suggested that the boundary commissioners report by December 15, 1850, that the New Mexico territorial government not take effect unless the boundary had been settled or unless Congress took further action and that in the meantime the rights of both Texas and the United States would remain unimpaired. This time the Southern Whig swing votes joined the anti-bill forces in voting down the Douglas amendment 33 to 24. (See Appendix B, vote Q.) Next, Turney of Tennessee attempted to postpone the measure indefinitely; the pro-compromise forces barely defeated this effort by the bill's enemies on a 30 to 29 vote, as Houston and Rusk voted for the motion after having opposed Hale's. (See Appendix B, vote R.) Underwood moved to strike out Pearce's March 4, 1851, stipulation entirely, and his amendment failed 32 to 25; both the pro- and anti-bill groups seemed unsure of the effect of this proposal, and the voting pattern on it was very mixed. David Yulee of Florida then moved to strike out the boundary commission sections from Pearce's amendment to reinsert. It passed 29 to 28, a major victory for the Northern and Southern extremists. Houston and Rusk, realizing that the Dawson proviso was now hopeless, voted with the majority against the pro-compromise bloc, and their votes proved crucial in striking out the whole painstakingly constructed, though awkward, boundary settlement. (See Appendix B, vote S.)[69]

With the Omnibus then in its death throes, Salmon Chase moved for its indefinite postponement. By this time many House members had come over to watch the startling course of events in the Senate. Chase's motion failed 29 to 28 as Houston split from Rusk to join the then-desperate pro-compromise bloc in defeating it. (See Appendix B, vote T.) Sebastian of Arkansas moved to adjourn but only 14 agreed with him against a majority of 42. Pearce's amendment to reinsert, now reduced merely to the portion establishing New Mexico Territory, then came to a vote, and it was rejected 28 to 25. Houston and Rusk both voted with the anti-bill coalition against it, while the Southern Whig swing votes supported the amendment in what had become a lost cause. Henry Clay himself did not bother to vote on this roll call, possibly out of deep disdain for what Pearce had started that day. (See Appendix B, vote U.) Following some humorous repartee between Foote and Rusk in reference to the reasonableness of Texas, Davis of Mississippi moved an amendment to attach the area west of the Rio Grande, which had been considered part of New Mexico, to Utah Territory. On a mixed vote, the Senate rejected this by 34 to 22. Dawson moved to adjourn, but most senators were not ready for that yet; the motion failed 39 to 16. Walker of Wisconsin then attempted to strike out everything else except the California statehood provisions. Southerners and Northern Democrats squelched that move 33 to 22.[70]

Still the battle continued. Phelps of Vermont moved for an indefinite postponement, but the pro-compromise bloc, this time with the support of Houston and Rusk, defeated it 30 to 28. (See Appendix B, vote V.) The next roll call occurred on David Atchison's move to strike out the California sections; it failed 29 to 29 on a mixed vote. A bit later, however, Winthrop of Massachusetts succeeded in getting the Senate to reconsider this vote. Before the climactic vote could be taken, however, Clemens of Alabama moved to postpone the bill until the next December. The pro-compromise bloc rallied their forces one last time to defeat this motion by a vote of 30 to 25. (See Appendix B, vote W.) But what had become inevitable could no longer be staved off. The California provisions were stricken from the bill 34 to 25 on a mixed vote. Further debate and roll calls followed, but the once-mighty Omnibus had been stripped of everything but the Utah provisions. In a last gesture, the Senate voted 32 to 18 to engross for a third reading what had now been reduced to a bill to establish Utah Territory.[71]

The Senate scene during the final stages of the death of the Omnibus was one of stark contrasts. The Northern and Southern enemies of the bill, who had begun the day expecting defeat, were suddenly overjoyed. However, Clay's countenance prior to his departure "expressed a cold and dignified resignation," wrote

S. P. Andrews for Greeley's *Tribune;* in an often-quoted account, a correspondent of the *New York Express* stated that the Kentucky compromiser looked "as melancholy as Caius Marius over the ruins of Carthage." Cass looked anxious and unhappy. Foote was in absolute despair. Dawson mourned. Some of those who had fought for the bill seemed unconcerned, as if anticipating that this was not the end of the struggle. Douglas "looked thoughtful and wise." Sam Houston, in "calm serenity," sat and whittled "an elaborately wrought wooden spoon." Tennessee's John Bell, who had wavered constantly between Clay's and Taylor's plans, was said to look "half sorry, but two-thirds glad" by the *Express* reporter.

Among the victorious free-soil and proslavery men, however, unbounded ecstasy ruled. Enemies of the bill, North and South, heartily embraced. Their faces were all smiles. Correspondent Andrews wrote that Thomas Hart Benton reminded him of what Satan might look like watching over a quarrel between church members as the situation approached fisticuffs. The reporter for the *Express* said that Benton's few remaining hairs "actually bristled with electrical delight" as he savored the rout of Clay and the bill. Benton himself wrote in a letter that they were "all in the clouds triumphing over Clay, Webster, Cass, Foote, the omnibus, and the devil!" John P. Hale smiled and laughed "from his waistbands to the extremities—all over." Seward danced about "like a little top," while Dayton of New Jersey "shook his thick sides with sporadic spasms." Isaac Walker of Wisconsin, whose position had been most uncomfortable while the Omnibus survived, for once appeared to be actually happy now that that ordeal was over. Southerners shared the joy of the antislavery revelers. Soulé, the flamboyant Frenchman from Louisiana, shook the hands of Chase, the stodgy Ohio Free-Soiler. The countenances of Jefferson Davis and Andrew Butler veritably lit up with gleaming smiles. The spectacles of Butler's colleague Robert Barnwell seemed to twinkle in reflection of his joy. Clemens of Alabama beamed satisfaction, while Yulee of Florida "looked solemn in solitary glory."[72]

A sense of reality would have convinced the celebrants that the contest was not necessarily over, but for the moment they wished to enjoy themselves. The Northern and Southern radicals had united together on one issue—the Texas–New Mexico boundary dispute—and had steadfastly maintained their alliance until they had stricken those sections from the Omnibus. Thus imbalanced, the whole edifice of the bill then came tumbling down. As the *New York Evening Post's* correspondent described the "execution" of the bill, "The limbs were first peeled off from its venerable trunk and its heart was taken out with remorseless determination, and the thing was pronounced dead."[73] Of course, even some of those who had stuck by the conglomerate had not believed it the best route to an overall settlement. Those who deemed the Omnibus unworkable but who favored a plan of separate bills, like Douglas, might well have declared, as the drama closed on July 31, that the Omnibus might be dead but that the compromise still lived.

Chapter Eight

ॐ

Carrot and Stick
The Pearce Bill & Executive Firmness

BEATEN AND DEPRESSED, HENRY CLAY LEFT THE SENATE CHAMBER ABOUT AN hour before adjournment, after casting his vote in the losing cause to retain California statehood in the Omnibus. President Fillmore had earlier departed from his office at the White House, and had been driven to his cottage residence in Georgetown. No one apparently bothered to go inform him that evening regarding the day's momentous proceedings. Early the next morning, August 1, Whig congressman Orsamus Matteson, a member of the Weed-Seward faction in New York, found Fillmore in a barbershop and told him the news. The president maintained his unflappable demeanor; "What a pity," he exclaimed unemotionally. If he felt anger or sadness or the weight of new responsibilities that might face him due to the sudden turn of events, he chose not to share these feelings with the likes of Matteson.[1]

If Fillmore appeared outwardly unconcerned, many reporters and other commentators trivialized the seriousness of the situation. Understandably, most of these in some way compared the bill's demise to the wrecking of a vehicular omnibus, dumping out all the passengers save one. The *Pittsburgh Dispatch* declared that the Omnibus had been "razeed into a buggy." Matteson delightedly informed Thurlow Weed how all the passengers had been tipped out of the overturned Omnibus and Utah placed in a "cab." Lizzie Blair Lee penned the cutest of the epitaphs on the Omnibus defeat: "The Mormons alone got thru' living—the Christians all jumped out."[2]

There was nothing trivial about the destruction of the Omnibus in the opinions expressed by Northern and Southern radicals. Gleefully, triumphantly, they proclaimed their victory. The *Richmond Examiner* decreed that the Omnibus was as "dead as the gallows-bird" and was pleased that the California statehood "snake" hidden therein was now "out of the grass." Northern commentators among the anti-Omnibus forces now indeed became adamant about pushing for the immediate passage of a separate California bill, with other issues to be settled after that. A few demanded the imposition of the Wilmot Proviso and some writers wanted Congress to adopt the earlier Taylor plan in unadulterated fashion. Many Northern writers simply ridiculed the Texan threat to subjugate Santa Fe as impossible to carry out; other writers in the free states shouted defiance against the threat, promising to defend New Mexico even if Texas attacked and the South seceded. Horace Greeley, who had favored the Omnibus as fair to and protective of New Mexico, now sounded the cry to "haul California into the Union and give security, peace, order and freedom to New Mexico." Southerners pleased by the defeat of the Omnibus were now anxious for the South to unite on the Missouri Compromise platform as a defense against the North. They talked of resisting California's admission and sending volunteers to help Texas battle the federal usurpers in New Mexico if a collision occurred there. Southern extremists promised and Northern leaders expected that Southerners in Congress would block passage of the military appropriation bills in order to hamstring any attempt by the Fillmore administration to use the army in New Mexico against the Texans. Many writers suspected that an independent Southern nation was the ultimate goal of Southern radicals.[3]

While "ultras" rejoiced at the prospect of no compromise, most Omnibus supporters envisioned great danger, if not imminent catastrophe, for the Union. To them the Omnibus, despite its defects and unwieldiness, had represented the best program for an overall settlement of the issues. The bill's dismemberment left a void, which moderates feared the extremists of both sections would attempt to fill with schemes that would plunge the nation into anarchy, disunion, and civil war. The *Jackson* (Miss.) *Southron* warned its readers what various horrors these eventualities could bring to the Southern homeland. A sense of disorder and confusion pervaded the ranks of compromise advocates during the first few days of August. Some despaired of any settlement. Some asked Henry Clay to offer a new Omnibus, but Clay refused. Others talked of a forthcoming Omnibus plan in the House of Representatives, but it never materialized. Still others expressed confidence that some plan of peaceful arrangement would finally be achieved. All entertained doubts, but the most hopeful ones placed their faith in the passage of separate bills encompassing each part of the old Omnibus.[4]

The main question for moderates was whether Congress could pass even separate bills before disaster struck, probably in the form of a bloody clash over the Texas–New Mexico boundary. This issue above all others preoccupied the thoughts of politicians and newspapermen, for no other issue offered an opportunity for immediate bloodletting. Moderates saw the effort to settle only the California issue as an attempt to throw a "firebrand into the magazine" of the Texas–New Mexico conflict. One excited correspondent of the *New York Express* predicted that Senator Winthrop would soon propose to increase the army to 100,000 and that Senator Seward would introduce a bill for a loan of a hundred million dollars to support the war effort. In early August several other correspondents claimed to have uncovered an elaborate Southern conspiracy to secede from the Union and establish a new confederation with Mexico. It was a hoax, and even the more credulous reporters lost interest in it after a few weeks. Despite such exaggerations, moderates believed that real danger to the Union existed if no solution to the boundary dispute was found. They begged all parties to maintain peace.[5]

An ugly tendency to cast blame on each other for defeat of the Omnibus developed among the moderates on the day following the debacle. An exasperated Alexander Stephens privately vented his wrath on the whole Senate compromise bloc of "fools" for making "a complete fry" of the bill. More serious was the position assumed by Henry Clay in the Senate on August 1. Despite his age, his exhaustion, and the humid ninety-degree heat, Clay, before leaving town to lick his wounds, set himself to publicly humiliate those he believed had wronged him.[6]

In the morning on August 1, Southern extremists held a caucus and resolved to vigorously support Texas. On that day, Senator Douglas, who had never shown much confidence or faith in the Omnibus plan, began driving for a compromise based on the passage of separate bills. He got the remnant of the Omnibus changed in title to a Utah bill before its passage and called up the separate bill for California admission. After Foote of Mississippi again offered an amendment to divide California and after Dawson of Georgia reminded the Senate of Georgia's convention plans in the event of California's admission, Clay took the floor. In a short but electrifying address, he first drew down the wrath of the galleries on the heads of Southern extremists and their thinly veiled threats of secession. The ensuing ovation became thunderous as it reverberated through the chamber. But Clay also bitterly attacked Senator Pearce of Maryland, directly blaming his surprise move on July 31 for defeating the Omnibus. Clay's withering eloquence left his fellow Southern Whig and former friend a totally alienated scapegoat. Pearce began to receive numerous pieces of anonymous "hate" mail from disheartened Omnibus supporters. A bit later in the debate, both Senators Mason of Virginia and Butler of South Carolina responded to Clay, but Clay's Unionist eloquence again brought roars of approval from the galleries. Henry Foote of Mississippi then derided the Southern "ultras" with his own wit and sarcasm.[7]

The House, late on the afternoon of August 1, was in the midst of discussing adjournment when the Senate's secretary arrived with the Utah bill and announced its passage. Immediate, spontaneous, boisterous laughter erupted throughout the chamber among members of every party and section. As the remains of the once prodigious Omnibus were carried down the main aisle, anti-Omnibus Democrat "Long John" Wentworth of Illinois added to the overall merriment by exclaiming: "Give way, gentlemen!—the Omnibus is coming!—make way!" At least August 1 ended with one small piece of the compromise passed by one of the houses.[8]

On Friday, August 2, while the Senate continued its discussion of the California bill and Henry Clay made final preparations to leave town, Texas bond agent James Hamilton sent a telegraphic dispatch to Texas informing Governor Bell of the Omnibus's defeat and Hamilton's guess that Congress would enact a separate bill to establish a Texas–New Mexico boundary commission. But it was on that Friday evening that the Texas issue quickly resumed center stage in public attention. Col. George T. Howard, Bell's personal representative, arrived in Washington after a journey of two weeks or so from Austin. He immediately boasted to newspaper reporters that Texas had a force of 1,500 men ready to march on Santa Fe, that Senator Rusk would be requested to return home to assume command of them, and that Texas now awaited only the response of the federal government and action of the Texas Legislature before setting the expedition off for New Mexico. Howard apparently delivered these same inflated troop estimates to administration officials. Many people accepted Howard's assertions as established fact, and some rumors spread that the Texan forces were already on the march. More skeptical commentators labeled Howard's claim of 1,500 in readiness as a bluff and expressed the belief that any Texan expedition would face nearly insurmountable economic and logistic difficulties in trying to invade New Mexico. Exaggeration or not, the reports again reminded everyone of the threat of violence over the boundary dispute.[9]

Before departing from Washington on August 3 for his much-needed respite in Rhode Island, Henry Clay delivered another warning to Southern radicals. On that Saturday afternoon, Clay was exchanging pleasantries with the crowd of friends and well-wishers at the door of the National Hotel. A Southern "ultra" congressman standing nearby intimated that Congress might adjourn without passing the army and navy funding bills. This was an obvious reference to Southern threats to prevent interference with any Texan expedition by blocking passage of the military appropriations. "Ah sir," exclaimed Clay, "do your duty while you are here, and then, if you want to fight, go home and fight like a man. We will meet you. But don't, I beg of you, play the Capuchin here." At that point the carriage arrived to take Senator Clay to the railroad station to catch his northbound train.[10]

More momentous events than Clay's leave-taking occurred that Saturday. Sen. James A. Pearce of Maryland was very anxious to shake off the yoke of being known as the principal destroyer of the Omnibus, especially since he had been in fact pro-compromise. He had supported the Omnibus until the Bradbury-Dawson plan had left the boundary undefined, something Pearce felt Clay himself had opposed in President Taylor's scheme. Pearce wanted a boundary settlement and believed it incumbent on himself to construct a bill to provide for it. The Maryland senator began work on his proposal on Friday, originally hoping, as did Foote of Mississippi, that the Senate would pass a measure combining the Texas and New Mexico provisions. That idea lasted only until Pearce began consulting Senator Rusk, who adamantly opposed any combination of the boundary-debt and New Mexico territorial government issues. The Texan at this stage wanted no measure for New Mexico territorial government in the area claimed by Texas grafted onto a bill to settle the boundary itself. Rusk argued that such a combination would lose six or more senators who would be willing to support a bill solely covering the boundary and debt. Pearce initially consulted Rusk and Houston on Friday night and then gauged the views of many other senators from all sectional and party blocs over the weekend.[11]

On Saturday Pearce collaborated with Senator Douglas in devising what became commonly known as the Pearce bill. The major proposals for compromise up to that time had involved a diagonal line from the vicinity of El Paso to some point on the longitudinal parallel of 100° west longitude. Pearce and Douglas based their scheme on a very different plan, one reminiscent of Douglas's suggestions in early June. The boundary they proposed would be a function strictly of latitudinal and longitudinal lines. Pearce initially favored a line beginning at the intersection of the Missouri Compromise latitude (36°30' north latitude) with 100° west longitude, then extending westward to the line of 102° west longitude favored by Benton as a western limit for Texas and then south to 33° north latitude and, finally, west along that parallel to the Rio Grande. This last portion of such a boundary would place Doña Ana and other settlements below the Jornada del Muerto firmly within Texas. Pearce used the 102° line to attract Northern support, knowing that many Northern senators opposed any westward extension of Texas beyond that limit; 33° north latitude was a compromise between the 34° north latitude favored by Douglas and the friends of Texas and the 32° proposed by the Committee of Thirteen.[12]

As Pearce and Douglas broached their proposal to various senators, objections quickly materialized. The Texans disliked the 102° west longitude line because that would leave the state with a thin, odd-looking panhandle on the North. Northern senators apparently objected to the inclusion within Texas of traditionally New Mexican settlements north of El Paso. Pearce worked feverishly over the weekend to resolve the differences in a way acceptable to most. He finally managed this by shifting the western line to 103° west longitude and the southern line to 32° north latitude. The former would give Texas a wider panhandle; to satisfy Northern objections, it was pointed out that the extra land given to Texas consisted primarily of a desolate waste known as the Staked Plains, an area hardly conducive to any endeavor that might extend slavery further west. The 32° north latitude line would satisfy Northerners that Texas could neither exercise its sway over, nor possibly introduce slavery among, the people north of El Paso. The Texans did not like the southern limit of New Mexico brought as far south as 32° north latitude. But Rusk and Houston, probably influenced by reports of U.S. reinforcements sent to New Mexico and Colonel Howard's report of recruiting in Texas, reluctantly concluded that Pearce's bill constituted the best offer Texas was likely to get. Their reluctance so discouraged Pearce as to the bill's prospects that only an hour or so before he introduced it on Monday, August 5, he nearly decided not to introduce it at all. Finally, however, he resigned himself to the fact that this bill was the only plan practicable enough to have a chance for passage. Thus Pearce offered this boundary proposal on Monday, together with provisions to pay Texas ten million dollars to satisfy its creditors.[13]

Credit for the bill belonged mainly to Senator Pearce. Douglas had indeed helped to assemble it, and rumors implied that Fillmore, his cabinet, and especially Webster had played a large, if not decisive, role in authoring the bill. It was Pearce, though, who consulted with other leaders constantly that weekend, who restructured the boundary to meet various objections, who secured the absolutely essential assent of Rusk and Houston, and who worked to persuade Northern Whigs such as Winthrop of the bill's fairness. There is no evidence of substantial input by either the president or his cabinet into the bill; they supported his efforts, even though Fillmore's ideas differed somewhat from Pearce's proposal. When Pearce discussed matters with Webster on Sunday, they agreed to coordinate Pearce's bill with the administration's own political offensive; after his bill was introduced on Monday, August 5, two important documents from the president and secretary of state would follow on Tuesday, August 6.[14]

Fillmore and the administration continued their official silence on the issues during the first few days of August. On August 1 Rep. Volney Howard, fed up with the president's apparent dodging, communicated to him Governor Bell's formal protest against the federal attempt to deny Texas's right to a portion of its territory. In his cover letter, Howard declared that he must inform his governor before the Texas Legislature's special session that Fillmore's administration refused to disavow Col. John Munroe's acts in New Mexico.[15]

Actually the administration had not been as inactive as Howard assumed. Webster, convinced that the boundary issue was "the great point of difficulty" and that it "*must* be settled," as he wrote to George Ticknor Curtis, had been given Bell's letter of June 14 by President Fillmore a few days after the Texas courier delivered it. Fillmore entrusted the preparation of a respectful answer to Webster, who, as secretary of state, was at that time responsible for domestic affairs outside the jurisdiction of other departments. Secretary Webster began working on a draft for this response. Many political leaders urged that the president or secretary of state should assert leadership in solving the crisis.[16]

Webster completed a draft of the letter to Governor Bell by July 30 and presented it to Fillmore for his perusal. In a note to the president of that date, Webster confessed that he had included as much "soft" language as possible to soothe Texan irritation over the Santa Fe proceedings. Webster also expressed to Fillmore his doubts that President Taylor had intended Colonel McCall to actually direct the New Mexico statehood move as he did, but Webster believed the administration must avoid any words that appeared to reprimand McCall. Webster at the same time gave a copy of his draft to Senators Rusk and Houston for their consideration. The two senators read it over but decided that the letter, moderate in tone but nonetheless firmly in disagreement with Texas's position, would exacerbate rather than alleviate the tensions. Rusk and Houston, in reply to Webster on August 1, continued to emphasize the illegality of what Munroe and McCall had done and the wrongful approbation of their actions tacitly provided by the federal authorities in Washington.[17]

At some point during his work on the letter, and possibly on August 1, Webster conceived the idea that the vacuum left by the defeat of the Omnibus should be filled not simply by a letter of policy statement but also by a special message from President Fillmore. Certainly on August 1, Webster held an urgent conference with the president, Treasury Secretary Thomas Corwin, and Attorney General N. K. Hall on the pressing questions. It may very well have been that meeting where Webster proposed to Fillmore that an appropriate occasion for a presidential message had arisen. The president readily agreed and instructed the secretary of state to prepare a draft of the message in addition to the letter. Webster enlisted the aid of Rep. George Ashmun of Massachusetts and Edward Curtis, Washington lawyer and former New York congressman, in writing the message. Fillmore and other cabinet members held numerous consultation meetings over the next several days to consider and, if necessary, revise the documents. The documents were a team effort, even though Webster mainly wrote the original drafts. Webster insisted that the president revise them to his liking and take nothing simply out of courtesy to the secretary of state. A few late nights were spent refining the wording. George Ashmun ranged all over the city in the burning heat of Sunday, August 4, to consult with numerous senators and representatives. Amidst the flurry of activity, several correspondents learned what was afoot and began tipping off their newspapers and the public.[18]

On Monday, August 5, the day on which Pearce introduced his boundary-debt bill in the Senate, administration officials maintained their frenzied pace, and another special cabinet meeting was held. By this time all of Washington knew what was in the offing, and some of the more radical Southern senators held their caucus that evening to consider how they should react. Secretary Webster left his clerk up late that night to prepare the necessary copies of the documents. Webster was back on duty at five o'clock Tuesday morning, re-reading the papers to make certain that all was right. Webster apparently decided at this late stage of the proceedings that the letter to Bell should go from Webster himself, by the president's direction, rather than directly from the president. Fillmore agreed. The final draft of the letter was delivered to the president by messenger for a last examination. Twenty minutes or so later Webster personally carried the message to Fillmore's office. At nine o'clock on the morning of August 6 a final reading of the documents to Fillmore commenced. Before 11 A.M. the president signed his name to the message and sent the documents off to Congress. Throughout the proceedings of the previous days, Webster had become very favorably impressed with Fillmore's qualities as a leader; in a letter to his friend Franklin Haven, Webster wrote, "He is a man of business, a man of intelligence, & wide awake."[19]

President Fillmore's private secretary, Robert G. Campbell, delivered the chief executive's message and Webster's letter, along with the letter that Bell had originally written to Taylor, to the Senate and House. The Senate had been discussing several matters related to Texas–New Mexico before the message arrived there. Chief among these was Senator Pearce's move to take up his boundary-debt bill and thus give it precedence over other pending measures and scheduled business, only fifteen minutes before consideration of the California bill was due to be resumed. After a brief debate, the Senate agreed to a motion by Foote to make Pearce's bill the special order for 11:30 A.M. the next morning. The Senate then took up the California bill until the message interrupted those deliberations. The House meanwhile had been engaged with the Post Office appropriation bill, but the representatives knew that the message and other documents were on the way. An air of excited anticipation prevailed. David Kaufman of Texas, usually seated several rows back from the speaker's chair, that day took a chair nearly in front of the speaker. When Campbell appeared, it was Kaufman who moved that the documents be read to the House by the clerk. Every seat seemed occupied. The usual murmur of the chamber was replaced by an "utter stillness." Kaufman sat with an intense countenance as the reading of the message progressed. After the clerk finished with that document, cries went up for "The letter, now—the letter!" The clerk read that document to the chamber also.[20]

What the members of the two houses heard in the president's message was a clear statement of the executive's constitutional responsibilities to protect New Mexico if the Texans attempted to extend their jurisdiction over it by force and a plea encouraging the Congress to legislatively settle the boundary dispute before violence occurred. In the first part of the message and again later on, the president declared that, until Congress or other competent authority should define the boundary, the chief executive was forced to define New Mexico as extending over all the territory, some of it east of the Rio Grande, which had been possessed and governed by New Mexican authorities prior to the U.S. conquest in 1846.

The president outlined in detail his authority under the Constitution and laws of the United States to employ the nation's military forces to suppress any opposition to the execution of the laws within the country when that resistance to law proved too powerful for the normal enforcement apparatus to handle.

Any Texans attempting to carry Texan authority into New Mexico in obstruction of the legal authority of the United States would be regarded as mere "trespassers" and "intruders." Citing Article 6 of the Constitution, which defined the Constitution, federal laws, and U.S. treaties as the "supreme law of the land," President Fillmore quoted at length several sections of the Treaty of Guadalupe Hidalgo guaranteeing federal protection for the rights and property of Mexican people remaining within the conquered territory. Federal authority, according to the message, would be maintained in force over these people until superseded by other legal provisions, and the president would dutifully employ U.S. military force to quell any attempt to challenge that authority.

Fillmore specifically denied that the executive could settle the question of boundary; that was the prerogative of Congress to do, with the assent of Texas. He also asserted that Congress alone could legally establish a government in the territory of New Mexico. The president expressed hope that he would not be forced to exercise his military authority under the Constitution, for, as he stated it, "consequences might . . . follow of which no human sagacity can foresee either the evils or the end." He devoted the last part of the message to a plea for Congress to quickly pass legislation to settle the boundary. "All consideration of justice, general expediency, and domestic tranquillity call for this." Congress should legislatively define the boundary, rather than leave it to the courts or a commission to determine, for settlement via those alternatives might be so slow that collisions and bloodshed could result before the settlement was completed. The president believed that a fair and liberal indemnity should be awarded to Texas in exchange for a surrender of its claims. It was obvious to everyone that Fillmore strongly favored the bill just introduced the previous day by Pearce, but he was careful to mention that he would acquiesce in any other mode of settlement that Congress might prefer. He concluded the message by emphasizing the importance of the settlement of the boundary issue to the nation's peace and to the solution of all other issues in the crisis.[21]

Quite in contrast to the clarity and directness of the president's message stood the labored argument and "soft words" of Webster's letter, dated August 5, to Governor Bell. This document focused on the previous administration's instructions to Colonel McCall, the degree to which the Fillmore administration condoned Colonel Munroe's proclamation and the New Mexico constitution, and the nature of U.S. authority in New Mexico. In a delicate juggling act, the secretary of state attempted to convince the Texas governor that the U.S. government's role in New Mexico was not and had not been prejudicial to Texan rights; simultaneously he defended the legitimacy of the actions of Colonels McCall and

Munroe. As Webster pointed out, the Taylor administration's orders to McCall defined neither boundary nor territory, and therefore, as far as President Fillmore understood them, those orders had not been intended to invade any right of Texas. As for Colonel Munroe's proclamation assembling a statehood convention, Webster argued that this act did not constitute any maneuver by an agent of the federal executive to settle the boundary dispute. Munroe's action was taken simply to assist the people in framing a constitution and then exercising the same right to petition Congress that was open to all citizens. That New Mexico constitution, however, remained invalid until sanctioned by Congress and by itself could not adversely affect the rights of any parties involved. Therefore the Fillmore administration approved Munroe's proclamation and chose to interpret it as in no way derogatory to the claims of Texas. Only at the close of the letter did Webster allude to the "delicacy" of the crisis and the "possible dangers" inherent therein, but he expressed confidence that patriotism and moderation by all parties would see the Union through these rough times.[22]

Fillmore's message and Webster's letter were not the only documents issued by the administration on August 6, although these others were not made public. On that day Gen. Winfield Scott, the acting secretary of war, dispatched special orders to Gen. George Brooke and Col. John Munroe as the respective commanders of the Eighth and Ninth military departments. These instructions were to govern their conduct in the event of a Texan military expedition to New Mexico, and their issuance demonstrated both the multifaceted approach of the Fillmore administration to the crisis and the seriousness with which they viewed the potential for a Texan thrust toward Santa Fe. Scott, who told some Northern members of Congress of his personal preference for a return to Taylor's policy, also had informed them that he stood ready to issue orders as the president directed.[23]

The president's message quickly became the center of attention for a public anxious for the chief executive to provide strong leadership in the crisis. Reaction to the message was overwhelmingly favorable, and everyone seemed shocked by such boldness from the normally circumspect and conservative Millard Fillmore. Some of his Northern political enemies and the newspapers reflecting their viewpoint suddenly found themselves praising and supporting the message, although they voiced dissent against the president's recommendation to indemnify Texas for territorial claims the state might concede. Only a few Northern radicals such as Salmon Chase of Ohio might find no redeeming qualities in what he considered a two-faced message. Pro-compromise politicians were utterly delighted and addressed adulatory letters to President Fillmore; among these writers was Henry Clay, still at Newport. Virtually the entire

Southern Whig and pro-compromise Northern Whig and Democratic press celebrated the message for its straightforwardness and combination of firmness with moderation. Only a handful of Northern Democratic journals attacked the message, finding in its doctrines a Federalist-Whig desire to coerce the states into submission to the central government. A few pro-compromise presses in the South characterized the message in similar terms and expressed the fear that the administration's firmness toward Texas was too extreme and too dangerous. Naturally enough, the bitterest opponents of the president's message and its doctrines were Southern Democratic "ultras" and their newspapers. To them the message appeared to mean one thing—a declaration of war against Texas if that state and other Southern states attempted to enforce Texas's rights in New Mexico by force of arms.[24]

The likelihood or unlikelihood of military action depended largely on whether Congress quickly enacted the Pearce bill. Fillmore and his advisers worked on various senators in order to secure their votes for the bill. Primarily they targeted their Northern Whig brethren, who naturally desired to align themselves with a Whig administration if possible. Most of them personally liked Fillmore and greatly admired his August 6 message. These same senators had opposed the Omnibus, especially while Taylor still lived, but now became amenable to compromise if they could vote for it without sacrificing basic principles or contradicting previous stands. Compounding the dilemma for Northern Whig senators was the fact that one of their leading newspaper editors, Horace Greeley, unexpectedly came out in opposition to the Pearce bill after having favored the Omnibus. Greeley disliked the new measure because it would give Texas over 30,000 more square miles than the earlier bill had done and would allow the Texas panhandle to jut as far north as 36°30' north latitude.[25] But these senators also could not ignore the growing public opinion in support of Pearce's arrangement, and the favor shown to it by the great majority of Northern newspapers. The election by Boston's voters of moderate Whig Samuel Eliot to fill a vacant U.S. House seat undoubtedly helped influence the voting of Senators Winthrop and John Davis regarding Pearce's bill. Letters from political friends added their impact.

The bill itself possessed attractive features. It established a specific boundary and paid the pesky Texas bondholders. The line specified in the bill appeared to include in New Mexico, and free soil, all the populated areas and cultivable lands traditionally considered significant parts of that territory, thus allowing Congress to feel that it was fulfilling its treaty obligations to the people of New Mexico. A very important feature was that Pearce's boundary-debt proposal was now legislatively unconnected with any other issue, thereby negating the log-rolling feature that most Northern Whigs had found so distasteful in the Omnibus. As a separate measure, Northern Whigs could interpret the Pearce bill as the fulfillment of President Taylor's program to settle each issue on its own merits.

Finally, and perhaps decisively, there was the peace factor. In much of the press, the very question of peace or war appeared to hinge on the fate of Pearce's measure. Colonel Howard's report of Texan troop readiness and the arrival of former Texas governors J. P. Henderson and George Wood (for his second visit during the crisis) in Washington on August 7, with whatever alarming announcements they may have fed to politicians, probably helped several Northern Whig senators decide to vote for the Pearce bill. By supporting the bill, the Northern Whigs could claim that they were helping to save the Union and sectional peace against the disunionist schemes of their traditional enemies, the Southern Democrats.[26]

Despite all the factors that might have converted some Northern Whigs to the bill, their votes could not be taken for granted by the administration. These Whigs had denied the legitimacy of Texan claims to New Mexican territory east of the Rio Grande. If they supported Pearce's bill, they were conceding some of the disputed region to Texas. Worse still, the bill gave Texas more land than the Omnibus had done. Most Northern senators, Whigs, Free Soilers, and Democrats, remained under instructions from their state legislatures to oppose any surrender of free soil to slavery, even in the abstract. Northerners daring to vote for the bill opened themselves to the charge by Free-Soilers and Seward Whigs that they had become "doughfaces."

Southerners faced similar dilemmas. Having steadfastly defended the 1836 limits established by Texas, Southern "ultras" refused to deviate even though the Texan senators might be coaxed into accepting Pearce's formula. Any Southerners who favored the bill ran the risk of being labeled "submissionist" by their extremist colleagues, especially following President Fillmore's message with its threat of military force. On the other hand, Pearce's bill had secured the assent of Houston and Rusk, did give Texas more territory than the Omnibus, and did pay Texas handsomely for the claims it conceded. Southern senators other than the most radical desired a peaceful solution of the crisis; Pearce's bill might accomplish that goal, with no significant sacrifice of Southern principle or "honor."

Certainly the passage of the Pearce bill in the Senate could not be taken as a foregone conclusion, despite the hopes by many that it would succeed. The largest obstacle initially was the precedence of the California bill. For several days proponents had been anxiously attempting to bring the California

statehood measure to its final vote against equally determined Southerners trying to delay the consummation of what some of them considered their most
dreaded political fear—loss of slave-state equilibrium in the U.S. Senate. Southern delaying tactics ultimately helped the Pearce bill, even though Southern
extremists disliked it too. Southern "ultras" were sustained in their efforts to
delay or block California statehood by the more moderate Southerners, except
for Benton of Missouri, Underwood of Kentucky, and the two Delaware senators. On August 6, following the president's message, the pro-California men
decided that they would sit out their Southern opponents and bring the bill to
its final vote, even if the session extended far into the evening. Southerners had
other plans, as they forced repeated roll-call votes on an amendment and procedures and also monopolized debate. As David Yulee of Florida bored everyone with a lengthy address late in the afternoon, some two dozen senators left
the chamber to go eat and to prepare otherwise for what they expected would
be a long night. Assessing the situation correctly, a few more Southerners slipped
out to nearby rooms, and Pierre Soulé of Louisiana pointed out that the quorum necessary to conduct business had vanished. A few of the wayward reap-
peared at the sergeant-at-arms's behest, and Yulee droned on for a few minutes
longer until two Southerners again departed. With no prospect that the game
of the "vanishing quorum" would end soon, an exasperated Stephen A. Douglas moved successfully for adjournment at 5 P.M.[27]

On Wednesday, August 7, consideration of the boundary-debt bill commenced
with James A. Pearce's speech in its favor. He defended his proposed boundary at
length, even though he confessed his original preference for Benton's line. The
limits in the new bill, he felt, would satisfy a wider group than any other suggested plan, and he pointed to the similarity of his proposed line near El Paso to
that claimed by the New Mexico convention. Pearce spoke on the justice of paying Texas's debt and compensating that state for land claims ceded. What became
the most controversial part of his proposal was the final section on the debt,
which provided that the U.S. government would withhold half of the ten million
dollars from Texas until the creditors holding bonds, for which customs duties
had originally been pledged for payment, filed full releases with the U.S. Treasury. Even though Pearce labored to emphasize that Texas must be entrusted to
pay its creditors, the obvious intent of the "reserve clause" was to guard against
any ploy by Texas to partially repudiate or "scale down" its payment of creditors.
Southerners, and especially Texans, were incensed later on that five million dollars of the money was to be held in escrow to ensure that Texas dealt fairly with its
bondholders, but little protest was offered against the "reserve clause" when Pearce

first introduced his bill. Only briefly in his speech did he conjure up the threat of boundary violence as a reason to enact his legislation.[28]

Joseph Underwood of Kentucky, linked with Pearce in defeating the Omnibus, began a speech in opposition to Pearce's bill until Douglas interrupted to remind him that the hour had arrived to resume discussion on the California bill. Underwood agreed to continue the next day, and the Senate then approved Douglas's motion to postpone the Texas bill until 11:30 A.M. on August 8. With the California measure again before the Senate, Yulee of Florida continued his speech of the previous day for several hours. Everyone soon realized that a Southern filibuster was under way and that the two Georgia senators planned to extend it whenever Yulee quit. Many Northern supporters of California discerned that the only way to split the moderate Southern men off from the radicals was to grant precedence to the Texas bill until it was disposed of. It was obvious that most Southern moderates would not tolerate the California bill until the Pearce bill had succeeded. David Atchison of Missouri moved to postpone consideration of the California bill until noon the next day, a half hour behind the Texas bill, with the implication that the Texas bill would actually be kept under consideration to the exclusion of the California statehood measure. Just how frustrated Northern men had become was evident from the fact that Free-Soiler John P. Hale of New Hampshire and antislavery Democrat Hannibal Hamlin of Maine joined with the South and a few Northern Democrats to vote for and pass Atchison's motion by a 27 to 24 vote. The Senate then adjourned.[29]

Thursday, August 8, in the Senate opened with the major portion of Joseph Underwood's speech. Although exceedingly anxious to close the session and get home to his family, Underwood was a man of scrupulous conscience, and he sincerely believed that every part of the Texas bill was unjustified. For three solid hours, he detailed the wrongfulness of the Texan boundary claim and denied that the U.S. government had either a legal or a moral obligation to pay the Texas debt. Underwood reserved his most vicious attack for the Texans, accusing them of treason in the very act of raising troops. He interpreted the Texas–New Mexico issue as merely a "pretext" through which the extremist Southerners hoped to achieve disunion and civil war.[30]

With the Senate functioning in its capacity as Committee of the Whole, Thomas Ewing of Ohio assumed leadership of the Northern anti-bill forces by introducing several amendments. The first and most important would substitute for Pearce's line a boundary almost identical to that of the Omnibus bill. Two other amendments by Ewing would establish an Indian reserve and would refer to the area ceded by Texas as its "claims" rather than "territory." After the

Senate agreed to a few minor alterations by Senator Pearce to his "reserve" clause, Ewing moved to postpone consideration of the Texas bill in order to take up the California bill again. The Senate voted 31 to 19 against Ewing's motion, with nearly all his support among the Northern bloc.[31]

The debate on Ewing's amendments, especially the first, now resumed in earnest. Ewing himself argued that his line would protect more people properly considered New Mexicans than would Pearce's. He cited a piece of evidence that probably had to have been furnished to him by General Scott—the attempt by Maj. Enoch Steen to assert a Texas headright claim in Doña Ana. Ewing contended that the 1848 treaty guaranteed protection of liberty and property to all citizens in the conquered area and that any Mexican citizens, no matter how few, included within the limits of Texas would be subject to just such claims as Steen had tried to enforce at Doña Ana. This interesting line of debate died down after Senator Rusk pointed out that a U.S. officer, not a Texan, had been involved in making the Doña Ana claim.[32]

Toward the end of that discussion, Sen. John P. Hale, New Hampshire's Free-Soiler, delivered a shock to the anti-bill bloc. In a short address he expressed himself in doubt as to how he would vote and indicated that he might vote differently from those with whom he had theretofore acted. Hale's quandary may have reflected the intense public pressure in favor of the Pearce bill. Hale's Northern allies, probably Seward of New York chief amongst them, quickly dedicated themselves to the prevention of any last-minute conversion by Hale to the bill's support. James Cooper (W-Pa.) and George Badger (W-N.C.) also confessed their doubts, Cooper preferring the Ewing line and Badger questioning the validity of Texas's title, but both declared their intention to support the bill as an alternative to disruption of the Union. After Pearce himself then reiterated the themes of the bill's fairness and necessity, the Senate rejected Ewing's boundary amendment by a vote of 28 to 21. Underwood and the Delaware senators were the only Southerners to join the Free-Soilers and Northern Whigs who supported Ewing's amendment. Several Northern Democrats voted against the Ewing amendment despite their states' instructions to oppose slavery extension. Ewing's other two amendments were dropped after the failure of the main one.[33]

Following Senate rejection of an amendment by William Dayton (W-N.J.) to have Texas cede to the United States its vacant public lands in exchange for the ten million dollars, several minor changes were adopted without opposition. One of these substituted words referring to Texas's claim to territory rather than simply its territory, a move embodying the third Ewing amendment. Just before the Senate adjourned for the day, Sen. Robert Winthrop of Massachusetts reintroduced Benton's old proposal of the 102° west longitude line as the western boundary of Texas. His brief remarks indicated not only a strong cognizance on his part of the importance of the Pearce bill to a peaceful settlement but also betrayed the desire of Winthrop and other Northern Whigs to amend the line into a more palatable one from their standpoint. He also offered his amendment in order to delay the bill a bit longer because the votes of several Northern Whigs, including his colleague John Davis, who had begun leaning toward the bill, were still doubtful. The Senate soon heeded a Davis move to adjourn, leaving many still in doubt as to the final outcome.[34]

That evening Senator Winthrop consulted with several senators, who informed him that Benton's line was simply impracticable. Benton himself told Winthrop that he was prepared to abandon that part of his line anchored on the Rio Grande, and New Mexico's "delegate," Hugh Smith, counseled Winthrop that the southern boundary set by the New Mexico constitution was not that different from the southern line in Pearce's bill. Smith found Pearce's bill quite acceptable, since it included in New Mexico the same inhabited territory and the same population that had adopted the recent constitution. On the contrary, Smith deemed any insistence on the Benton line a nuisance, since he felt it would require New Mexico to hold another convention. After receiving such advice, Winthrop opened the session on Friday, August 9, by withdrawing his amendment. In his accompanying address he declared his preference for a different line than Pearce's and his hostility toward paying Texas what he felt was an exorbitant amount for its cession, but Winthrop did declare his support for the president's message and his conviction that the Pearce bill was the practicable means of securing peace and the continuance of the Union.[35]

Underwood of Kentucky immediately moved to substitute the earlier Omnibus bill line for Pearce's. The Senate defeated Underwood's move by the close vote of 25 to 24 on a general South-versus-North division. Northern Democrats Cass, Dickinson, Dodge of Iowa, and Sturgeon joined the Southerners against it, while Southern Whigs Spruance, Underwood, and Wales voted with the Northerners in its favor. There next ensued a protracted debate over a Southern "ultra" amendment to affirm the 1836 Texas boundary claim before it was defeated on a roll call of 37 to 14.[36]

The bill was then reported out of the Committee of the Whole, and the amendments adopted therein were brought before the Senate proper. The first of these was the amendment that had inserted "claim to" before "territory" in the second section of the bill. Considered innocuous by everyone when it was added the previous day, some Southerners now interpreted this amendment to implicitly deny the Texas title east of the Rio Grande. John Berrien, Georgia Whig, suggested wording of "title and claim" but his proposal was rejected and the previous day's amendment was affirmed. On both votes, only Daniel Dickinson, a Democratic "doughface" from New York, voted with the Southern minority. The next amendment considered was Pearce's altered "reserve" clause to withhold five million dollars of the Texan indemnity until certain conditions were met. Despite Pearce's disavowals of any distrust of Texas, some Southerners and a few Northern Democrats argued that Texas would interpret the section in just that fashion. The Senate confirmed the "reserve" clause by a large majority of 35 to 12.[37]

Kentuckian Joseph Underwood then resurrected his plan to change the boundary line to that of the Omnibus bill. Senator Rusk of Texas declared that his constituents would barely be willing to approve Pearce's line, which Rusk vowed to support even if, as he expected, it might cost him his Senate seat. But Rusk clearly opposed Underwood's amendment, and the Senate rejected it 28 to 23, a greater margin than on the day before thanks to the switch of the two Indiana Democrats, Bright and Whitcomb, to the opposition. Subsequent to this failure to reduce Texas's limits, John Davis of Massachusetts proposed reducing the money proffered to Texas to six million dollars. Cooper of Pennsylvania replied that the bill could not pass with an amount less than ten million dollars and said that the extra four million dollars was well worth it to prevent the collision and bloodshed likely to occur if the measure failed. Davis's amendment went down to defeat 26 to 20. Northern Whigs provided most of Davis's support. Thomas Ewing of Ohio then renewed his boundary amendment of the previous day, which without debate was rejected 26 to 24. The pattern on this roll call was similar to the earlier one, except that Bright and Whitcomb of Indiana voted in favor of it this time, after having opposed it the day before. The shifting of these two senators appeared to reflect their uneasiness over supporting compromise while laboring under state instructions that virtually prohibited such a course.[38]

After a final Southern-sponsored amendment was rejected and Bradbury of Maine reluctantly declared for the bill to expedite the settlement, the Senate came to its two climactic votes on the Pearce bill. The first of these was on whether to engross the bill for its third and final reading. The vote was close, but the Senate granted the bill its third reading by a 27 to 24 margin. (See Appendix B, vote X.) Here, for the first time in the Senate voting on the Pearce bill, the coalition of Northern and Southern extremists, which had joined to kill the Omnibus earlier, reared up once more but fell short of its goal this time. Bright and Whitcomb of Indiana held back from voting until they saw that their votes would not be needed for the engrossment, and then both men voted against it.[39]

The Fillmore administration's efforts were evident in the votes of Northern Whigs Greene and Clarke of Rhode Island, Winthrop and Davis of Massachusetts, Phelps of Vermont, Smith of Connecticut, and Cooper of Pennsylvania for the engrossment. Robert Winthrop emphasized that they had done this for peace and because they felt the bill saved New Mexico for free soil. John Davis's vote was somewhat of a surprise even to Winthrop, for Davis did not reveal to anyone how he would vote until the roll was called. Administration pressure probably also contributed to the absence of New Jersey's Whig senators, Dayton and Miller. They had gone home, pairing off as other absentees were reported to have done (Dayton had paired with Willie Mangum of North Carolina); Dayton and Miller had both been staunchly hostile to compromise until then.[40]

Among Southern votes for the bill was one surprise, that of Jere Clemens of Alabama. This often-fiery Democrat later wrote to his constituents that he had finally decided to support the bill in order to leave the option of accepting or rejecting it in Texas's hands. He agreed that the Texas title to the land in question was somewhat dubious. Clemens also argued that New Mexico east of the Rio Grande might now be saved for slavery under popular sovereignty, since the Mexican law prohibiting the institution would now be superseded by federal statute. Whatever Clemens's rationale for his vote, Southern radicals ascribed his submission to the Pearce bill to a lack of moral firmness possibly rooted in Clemens's bouts of heavy drinking. Two votes, which had always been rated as doubtful, were in the end cast in favor of the Pearce bill by Alabama Democrat William R. King and Georgia Whig John M. Berrien. King's essentially moderate attitude got the best of his fear that his Alabama enemies would smear him as a "submissionist." Berrien ultimately decided, as Clemens had, that Texas should decide on the proposition. He believed the measure to be conciliatory, economically very advantageous to Texas and therefore to the South, and also destructive of abolitionist plans to impose the Wilmot Proviso in New Mexico. One Southerner who had strongly advocated the Omnibus but who now opposed the Pearce bill was David Atchison of Missouri. For him the Omnibus had represented an overall settlement for peace and Union, but once that bill was broken up Atchison decided to vote on each separate measure according to his convictions. He believed in the validity of the 1836 Texas claim and therefore considered any compromise on this particular issue to be a surrender of slave territory to free soil. His Missouri colleague, Thomas Hart Benton, continued to occupy his peculiar ground as a Southern free-soil advocate; Benton denounced the Pearce bill as a humiliating attempt to purchase peace from Texas.[41]

The stage was now set for the vote on the bill's passage. In case the bill failed, the compromisers had in reserve plans to revive Ewing's idea for transforming some of the disputed region into an Indian Territory. But such was not needed. The margin of victory was safer this time as the bill passed on a roll call of 30 to 20. (See Appendix B, vote Y.) James Bradbury of Maine, angered over the way in which several of his Northern Democratic associates had held back their votes on the previous roll call, played the same game himself this time and waited until his colleagues had voted for the bill's passage before he cast his vote likewise. Bright and Whitcomb of Indiana were now counted among the bill's supporters, as was Spruance of Delaware. Maine's Free-Soil Democrat, Hannibal Hamlin, who had voted against engrossment, was absent when the passage vote was taken. There had been some speculation in previous days that Hamlin might actually support the bill, but Hamlin was too committed to free soil to vote for a bill that even vaguely smacked of slavery extension. He wrote that he would not be "factious" about the issue, and that may provide a clue to his absence on the final vote. Hale of New Hampshire, who had wavered the day before, opposed the Pearce bill on both its engrossment and passage.[42]

Senate passage of the Pearce bill, only a few days after its introduction, provided the first solid victory for the pro-compromise bloc. It confounded the extremists of both North and South. The "ultra" *Richmond Examiner* characterized the Southerners who had supported the bill as traitorous "whelps" at the den of corruption, dismembering Texas for money. Free-Soiler George W. Julian wrote a letter to his hometown newspaper in Indiana on August 14 condemning the measure as an insult to the North and proclaiming that "the broken doses are worse than the whole pill." Rant and rave as they might, the radicals were forced to concede that the forces of compromise, at least for the time being, possessed the initiative.[43] Troublesome times were by no means over, but the phoenix of compromise had begun to rise from the ashes of the Omnibus.

Chapter Nine

⁂

The U.S. Military Response
to the Boundary Dispute

Whatever differences of approach were taken by the Taylor and Fillmore administrations toward solving the crisis of 1850, both agreed on the absolute necessity for the federal government to bolster the strength of the U.S. Army forces stationed in New Mexico so that they could effectively repel any attempted invasion by Texas. The reinforcement program begun under President Taylor, the general, was continued and even enhanced under President Fillmore, the career politician. Both administrations utilized to the utmost the authority conveniently handed to the executive by Congress in an act to increase the army to protect the frontiers.

Frontier officers had begged for years for more troops, particularly the mounted variety, to help them control Indian raiders on horseback. Texas politicians and the New Mexico convention eagerly endorsed these demands, and Secretary of War Crawford recommended an increase in frontier forces. Congress took the matter up in February 1850, and the military affairs committees of both houses introduced bills to give the president authority to increase the numbers of privates in companies serving in frontier areas. The Senate took up and passed the legislation on May 1 without debate, amendments, or roll calls. The House Committee on Military Affairs adopted the Senate's version but proposed an amendment that called for the use of mounted infantry in frontier areas, a sort of compromise between foot soldiers of limited usefulness and more expensive, highly trained light cavalry or dragoons. On May 24 the House overwhelmingly passed the bill by a roll-call vote of 107 to 59; on June 11 the

Senate concurred in a voice vote of 24 to 18. President Taylor signed the bill into law on June 17, the same day he sent his message to the Senate reaffirming his commitment to maintenance of U.S. control over New Mexico until the boundary was determined "by some competent authority."[1]

Throughout the entire consideration of the army increase bill in Congress, no one in either house ever suggested or seemed cognizant of the possible relevance of the measure to the boundary dispute—that is, the fact that the president, by increasing the numbers of men in frontier units under the guise of defending settlers from Indians, could build up the U.S. forces in New Mexico to withstand any threatened onslaught from Texas. However, President Taylor was well aware of this power, and there was no accident that his most forceful statement to Congress on the New Mexico issue was made on the day he signed the bill. Just after he signed it, Taylor calmly reassured some Northern congressmen that Texas would not get New Mexico because he would send more troops to the region under the new act. One young officer who had become acquainted with Taylor in the Mexican War, 1st Lt. Alfred Pleasanton, was in Washington when he received his orders to rejoin his dragoon regiment in New Mexico. He visited with Taylor that day, and the old general described exactly what he intended to accomplish through the troop buildup in New Mexico. President Taylor said, as Pleasanton remembered the words,

> These southern men in Congress are trying to bring on civil war. They are now organizing a military force in Texas for the purpose of taking possession of New Mexico and annexing it to Texas, and I have ordered the troops in New Mexico to be reinforced, and directed that no armed force from Texas be permitted to go into that territory. Tell Colonel Munroe that he has my entire confidence, and if he has not force enough out there to support him (and then his features assumed the firmest and most determined expression), I will be with you myself; but I will be there before those people shall go into that country or have a foot of that territory. The whole business is infamous, and must be put down.[2]

Naturally enough, as the administration ordered hundreds of reinforcements to New Mexico and Southern "ultras" in Congress suddenly realized that they had aided and abetted the move by their own support of the army increase bill, some Southerners in Washington began protesting that these additional forces were intended to be used against Texas. The Northern Democratic *Brooklyn Eagle* joined the Southern chorus, viciously attacking administration militarism and intimating that the administration purposefully aimed to provoke a fight with Texas to produce bloodshed. Writers favorable to the administration responded with claims that the increase of force in New Mexico was a function strictly of frontier defense under the new law and had nothing to do with threats from Texas. Now that the statute was on the books, Southern radicals and anyone else who disliked it were powerless to prevent its enforcement.[3]

Planning for the reinforcement of the New Mexico garrison was well under way by the Taylor administration before the army bill ever passed. An interesting feature of the plan was that it would rely on raw recruits for the soldiers to be added to the units in the Ninth Military Department. Most of these untrained men would be hurried from several depots back east through St. Louis and Fort Leavenworth and then across the Santa Fe Trail to their destination. And after this rather hazardous journey, these novice troops might find themselves thrown into battle against Texan forces in a struggle for control of New Mexico. But the Taylor administration was anxious to transfer troops to New Mexico, and the army increase bill provided the opportunity to do this in a way that partially disguised the object of the move.

Secretary Crawford and General-in-Chief Scott also laid contingency plans for the transfer of regular units from other departments. Earlier in the year three companies in New Mexico had been slated for transfer to other departments; not only did the administration scrap that, but it also notified General Twiggs in Florida that Bvt. Col. Joseph Plympton's 7th U.S. Infantry Regiment might be pulled from his command and dispatched to an unspecified frontier assignment. This regiment ordinarily had been stationed in the Sixth Military Department at Jefferson Barracks near St. Louis. Since Twiggs had previously informed the administration that the Seminole Indian threat had diminished in his sector, Taylor's advisers looked to prepare the 7th Regiment for a theater where hostilities seemed more likely. Accordingly, the regiment embarked on steamers at Tampa Bay and sailed to New Orleans. Colonel Plympton, his staff, and five companies—over 250 men—arrived at New Orleans on June 17 on the steamer *Fashion*, which then returned to bring over the other five companies. Plympton's group left New Orleans on the 18th on the steamer *Concordia*, which reached St. Louis on June 25. The remainder of the 7th Regiment arrived at St. Louis on July 6 on the *Cora No. 2*. At Jefferson Barracks they awaited their orders for reassignment.[4]

The first order of business for the administration was the group of recruits. To implement the act of Congress, the Adjutant General's Office issued General Order No. 20 on June 22 to allow frontier units from the Great Plains to the

Pacific Coast to raise their total of privates to seventy-four, whereas under earlier regulations infantry and artillery units had been limited to forty-two and dragoons to fifty soldiers of the lowest rank. Up to half the men in infantry companies operating in Texas and New Mexico and at new posts on the Canadian and Arkansas rivers were authorized to be mounted.[5]

During the initial stage of the reinforcement of the Ninth Military Department, army headquarters ordered 612 recruits to be sent there, and newspapers reported the figure as 600. But there were not that many recruits immediately available, and the actual number sent was 580. By far the larger portion of them, 447, were to travel overland via the Santa Fe Trail; a smaller group of 133 were picked to go by ship from New York to Texas and act as an escort from San Antonio to El Paso for the American segment of the joint U.S.-Mexican boundary commission, led by John R. Bartlett. On reaching El Paso, these troops would be distributed among the companies of the 3d Infantry operating from that post. This latter group would be doubly disguised—both as Indian fighters and as Bartlett's escort to El Paso—but they would be just as capable of fighting Texans if need be.

Of the new soldiers destined for the overland migration, over half were slated to fill the ranks in the seven companies of the 1st and 2d Dragoon regiments, while the rest were intended for artillery and infantry companies. The recruits for this force were to be drawn from three depots—274 from New York Harbor, 50 from Carlisle Barracks, Pennsylvania, and 123 from Newport Barracks, Kentucky (across the Ohio River from Cincinnati). The largest contingent of recruits was conducted from Governor's Island and nearby Fort Wood, New York, on July 12 by 2d Lt. Samuel D. Sturgis, 1st Dragoons, and 2d Lt. George H. Paige, 2d Infantry. The detachment sailed upriver on the Hudson to Albany. By the time they reached that city, many of the soldiers had become drunk from liquor they had found on the vessel; some were so incapacitated that they had to be hauled in carts to the railroad depot in Albany. More liquor was discovered and consumed there before the train westward finally pulled out of the station. Arriving at Buffalo on July 15, the soldiers embarked on a lake steamer for Detroit, which they reached the next day. A train across Michigan to New Buffalo, a steamboat to Chicago, a slow canal boat to La Salle, and another steamboat down the Illinois River to the Mississippi and St. Louis completed the journey of the detachment to Jefferson Barracks. When they arrived there in the early morning hours of July 22, they were put into a stable to sleep on straw or on the bare floor. By this time eight to ten men had cholera and the detachment's strength was down to 170 from its original 274. A number had died; many had deserted.[6]

Several officers on their way back to companies in New Mexico or to other Western posts were ordered to escort the recruits from Carlisle and Newport. Lt. Pleasanton, 2d Dragoons, was one of these, as were Bvt. Capts. Abraham Buford and Lorimer Graham, 1st Dragoons; 1st Lt. Henry Schroeder, 3d Infantry; and Asst. Surgeon Rodney Glisan. Buford had overall command.[7]

This group's point of origin, Carlisle Barracks, was the principal depot for training recruits for the dragoon regiments. On July 11, Buford and the other officers led 50 enlisted men from the post, to the cheers of a crowd of well-wishers. Later that day, after eating in Harrisburg, they entrained for Huntingdon. From there a canal boat trip to Hollidaysburg and another train excursion brought them to Pittsburgh on Saturday, July 13. Despite previous orders to the U.S. quartermaster at Pittsburgh to have steamboat transportation arranged for that day, it was not available until Monday, when the officers and their recruits boarded the *Asia*. Great fear seized all the men at this point on the journey, for the dreaded Asiatic cholera epidemic, which had devastated the nation the previous year, was prevalent once again in the towns downriver and had just revisited Pittsburgh itself. Fortunately, the disease struck only one man during the trip on the Ohio, and he recovered. The *Asia* arrived at Newport Barracks on July 18 and the troops disembarked. At Newport, 123 recruits were added to the group, and Capt. N. C. Macrae of that depot placed these soldiers under the immediate command of Lieutenant Schroeder. From there to Louisville all the officers and recruits together were packed aboard a small steamer that was old, dirty, and very uncomfortable. However, the U.S. quartermaster at Louisville provided the much better ship *Fashion* for the remainder of their voyage down the Ohio and then up the Mississippi to Jefferson Barracks. Just before reaching that destination, one of the recruits died from the cholera, their first fatality. They arrived at Jefferson on July 22.[8]

Jefferson Barracks was the principal depot for training all arms of the service for frontier duty stations. Captain Buford's troops had to camp on the outskirts of the overcrowded facility. Gen. Newman S. Clarke, commander of the Sixth Military Department headquartered there, had orders to move the nearly 400 recruits out to Fort Leavenworth and get them on the trail to Santa Fe as soon as possible. The principal reason for haste was the desire to have the new soldiers in New Mexico before winter storms hit the Santa Fe Trail. Thus it became imperative, given the army's past experiences, that the recruits and their wagon train depart Fort Leavenworth no later than August 15. Clarke also wanted to keep the men moving before the cholera scourge ravaged the detachment. In fact he modified Dr. Glisan's orders so that Glisan could stay with the group for the

journey to Fort Leavenworth. The general also divided the recruits into two seg-
ments and assigned Dr. Elisha P. Langworthy to provide medical services to Paige's
detachment while Glisan attended to Buford's and Schroeder's.[9]

On the evening of July 22 Paige's men boarded the steamboat *St. Paul* for the
four-day trip up the muddy Missouri to Fort Leavenworth; two days later the
Buford-Schroeder contingent set out on the *Anna*. The recruits would have
gladly faced either Texans or Indians instead of the disaster that befell them
beginning on the first day aboard the two steamers. Cholera broke out and
spread rapidly through the huddled ranks of enlisted men. At the onset, the
symptoms were diarrhea, vomiting, and painful cramps; consequent dehydra-
tion gave the victim a bluish, pinched face, drawn and puckered skin, and dark-
ened, cold extremities. One could die within hours or linger for days before
succumbing; one could also contract a mild case and recover after a few days.
The panicky recruits on the *Anna* begged to be put ashore to march overland to
Fort Leavenworth, but Dr. Glisan absolutely refused to endorse their request
because he realized that such a trek in the July heat would kill anyone who had
the disease, and that meant most of the recruits. The officers in charge, none of
whom became ill during the voyage, directed the *Anna*'s captain to push toward Fort Leavenworth as speedily as possible and to make the minimum number of stops for wood. When the captain was forced to stop for fuel, every officer
had to stand guard with pistol in one hand and sword in the other to prevent a
general desertion by those recruits who were ambulatory. Nine of Paige's recruits died before the *St. Paul* arrived at the fort; no one on the *Anna* died until
the night of the 27th, after the ship docked at Fort Leavenworth, when several
soldiers passed away. The cholera was already raging at the fort when the recruit detachments landed; it had just claimed the life of the post commander,
Bvt. Brig. Gen. Richard Mason. During the next two weeks, while the recruits
encamped and their supplies and wagon train were assembled, cholera deaths
mounted to four or five a day, and the desertions soared. Gangs of three to
eight recruits at a time would escape.[10]

What awaited the Santa Fe–bound troops amounted to a rather prodigious
and hurried logistics operation. Quartermaster General Thomas S. Jesup and
Bvt. Brig. Gen. George Talcott, chief of ordnance, organized and coordinated
these efforts to get horses, mules, wagons, arms, clothing, and other supplies to
Fort Leavenworth on a schedule that would permit the long, arduous march to
Santa Fe to begin by at least August 15. These arrangements had been under
way since late June. Jesup handled much of this through General Clarke and
quartermasters at St. Louis and Fort Leavenworth. Horses on which to mount

the dragoon recruits, horses to be sent to New Mexico for mounted infantry, all the serviceable mules at Fort Leavenworth, the best wagons available at St. Louis—all these were to go with the recruits. Among the several hundred thousand pounds of stores ordered for the expedition was a large supply of clothing from the quartermaster's depot in Philadelphia. General Jesup directed that Bvt. Maj. Daniel H. Rucker personally accompany this clothing allotment to Fort Leavenworth "as speedily as possible." Rather than ship it across Pennsylvania to the Ohio River, where the department had already encountered transportation difficulties, Major Rucker was ordered to take the shipment via New York, Buffalo, the Great Lakes, Chicago, and down the Illinois River to the Mississippi. To purchase all the necessary items stretched the credit of the quartermaster's department to the limit, since Congress had not yet passed the regular appropriation bill for the army.[11]

Ordnance Chief Talcott originally planned to arm the recruits with Colt pistols and musketoons, the latter being much shorter weapons than muskets. The weapons were sent from Springfield Arsenal in Massachusetts. When these did not arrive in time at the St. Louis Arsenal, Maj. William H. Bell, at that installation, sent to Fort Leavenworth for the recruit detachment carbines (a little shorter than the musketoon), percussion pistols (fired by the use of a cap), and the hundred Colt pistols he had on hand. Talcott ordered Bell by telegraph to see that 1,500 rifles, 500 muskets, and the proper ammunition went to Santa Fe with the wagon train. These had been requested earlier by the military storekeeper at Santa Fe, and an express rider from Santa Fe delivered an order to the St. Louis Arsenal for another 2,000 stand of arms just after the Santa Fe train had left Fort Leavenworth. These weapons were intended for use by New Mexican volunteers if the Texans invaded. Major Kendrick at Santa Fe had previously ordered six new prairie carriages for the artillery pieces in the Ninth Department. These items, built at the arsenal in Watervliet, New York, were transported, along with 192 rounds of artillery ammunition, by way of Buffalo, Detroit, and Chicago to St. Louis. A steamboat then rushed this materiel nonstop to Fort Leavenworth. The arms and ammunition withdrawn from the St. Louis Arsenal were soon replenished by deliveries from arsenals at New York, Pittsburgh, and Baton Rouge.[12]

By August 10 all was in readiness. The recruits were again divided into separate detachments. On the 10th, Lieutenant Paige led one of these contingents on the trail to Santa Fe, accompanied by a supply train of sixteen mule-drawn wagons. Two days later on August 12, Lieutenant Schroeder followed with a large number of infantry recruits. Captain Buford did not start out from Fort

Leavenworth until August 25, heading up dragoon regulars and recruits. This last movement was done in conjunction with troops going out to build the "New Post on the Arkansas" (later Fort Atkinson). The soldiers were undoubtedly pleased to be leaving the pestilential Fort Leavenworth behind. Cholera no longer troubled the command as it ventured down the trail, and the remainder of the trip went smoothly. Judging from figures given when the various detachments arrived in New Mexico in September and October, only 249 of the original 447 recruits reached the Ninth Military Department. This means that cholera and desertion had exacted a very heavy toll of 45 percent on the troops who came overland to save Santa Fe from the Texas threat.[13]

The recruit detachment that escorted John R. Bartlett's boundary survey commission enjoyed a less traumatic travel experience. This large party of over one hundred members was scheduled to ship out from New York in early August for Texas, march from the Gulf Coast through San Antonio to El Paso, and there meet up with its Mexican counterpart under General Condé to determine the boundary line between the two nations. Since the frontier military companies that garrisoned El Paso qualified to receive augmentation under the recent act, the Taylor administration most conveniently decided that recruits for those units should escort the Bartlett commission. At the end of June, Bvt. Lt. Col. Lewis S. Craig, who had been on recruiting duty, and Bvt. Maj. Oliver B. Shepherd, both from the 3d Infantry, were chosen to lead 192 recruits to reinforce the companies of that regiment at El Paso. It soon became clear that that many recruits were not available, given the sudden demand for so many of them. Therefore Colonel Craig was selected to command whatever recruits could be gotten together by the time the expedition sailed, while Major Shepherd would follow later with a second detachment. Second Lt. Duff C. Green and Bvt. 2d Lts. Frederick M. Follett and Joseph E. Maxwell of the 3d Infantry were ordered to assist Craig. Another Bvt. 2d Lt., John W. Alley of the 3d Infantry, was designated to join the later contingent. The recruits in the first group numbered 81; those in the second group, which left New York in September, amounted to 52.[14]

The great majority of expedition personnel, including Craig's escort force, left from New York port on August 3 aboard the steamship *Galveston*. Bartlett and a few others followed ten days later on the *Georgia*. While Bartlett would be required to change ships at Havana and New Orleans, the *Galveston* carried the bulk of the commission straight through to Texas. The steamer docked at the wharf at La Salle on August 20 and at Indianola on the 22d. After Bartlett arrived on August 30, the whole group moved inland on September 6 to Victoria and San Antonio, reaching the latter on September 27. The War Department

had already arranged for all surplus wagons and stores in Florida to be transferred to Texas. Some of this materiel was undoubtedly intended for the use of
Bartlett's escort. The escort troops probably received their arms in San Antonio
at the Eighth Military Department headquarters.

From there, the commission split into two parts. Bartlett and a small advance party took the more northerly route to El Paso to more quickly rendezvous with the Mexican commissioner and his party. Colonel Craig's 3d Infantry recruits and the remainder of Bartlett's commission, hindered by the
slow-moving mule train and the even slower oxen-pulled wagons, journeyed
on the southern route taken earlier that year by Neighbors. They left San Antonio on October 17. The pace of this part of the expedition was slow enough that
Lieutenant Alley and his recruits, who did not start out until September, were
able to catch up to the main party. Little information is now available about the
march of Craig's soldiers to El Paso with the mule train. Altogether he ended
up with 133 recruits, a sizable number, but they were so raw and untrained that
the commission did not venture to send out separate survey parties on the way
to San Elizario because they did not trust the competence of these soldiers to
protect such groups. Therefore, the surveyors did no more than measure distances during the journey. Of the recruits, 25 deserted at various times, so that
Craig reached El Paso on December 12, 1850, with 108 recruits left to distribute
to the 3d Infantry units.[15] The desertion losses amounted to just less than 20
percent. Overall the reinforcements dispatched by the Taylor administration to
the Ninth Military Department via Fort Leavenworth and San Antonio lost
almost 40 percent of their total number due to desertion and disease. Of the
612 recruits that in June the War Department originally planned to send, only
357 actually made it to Santa Fe and El Paso several months later.

Millard Fillmore ascended to the presidency after these previous maneuvers to enlarge the U.S. military force in the Ninth Military Department had
been set in motion. The crisis had deepened and the likelihood of a Texan
invasion of New Mexico had become more palpable by that time. President
Fillmore valued the efficacy of preparedness as fully as Taylor had. Secretary of
War Crawford resigned on July 10, but Fillmore accepted it to take effect only
after July 22. A few days later, on July 24, because he had not yet appointed a
civilian replacement for the War Department, the president chose General-in-
Chief Winfield Scott to serve as secretary of war ad interim. Scott served in
that capacity for a little more than three weeks, until Charles M. Conrad of
Louisiana took the oath on August 16 as secretary and resigned his seat in the
House of Representatives.[16]

Indicative of just how urgent and threatening Fillmore and Scott considered
the Texas–New Mexico situation to have become is a report prepared by General Scott for the president on July 24, the very day Scott began his temporary
duties as secretary of war. In it Scott described routes and distances to Santa Fe,
the numbers of troops in and on their way to New Mexico, and the other units
available to be dispatched if needed:

Memoranda for the President

Land routes	*Miles*
From Independence, on the Missouri, to Santa Fe	913
From Fort Smith, on the Arkansas, to Santa Fe	819
From Lavaca, coast of Texas, to San Antonio,	153
miles, thence to El Paso, 650 miles &	
thence to Santa Fe 350	1153
There is no other known practicable route,	
from the Eastern States, by land to Santa Fe	
According to the latest returns there is,	
now in New Mexico, a nominal regular force,	
including Cavalry, Artillery & Infantry, of	1055
In route, for New Mexico—	
From Ft. Leavenworth, on the Mo. (recruits)	148
Other recruits to go *via* Ft. Leavenworth	420
Recruits *via* Texas	<u>192</u>
	1817
Deduct for casualties in New Mexico &	
in route thither (say) 20 pr. centum	<u>363</u>
	1454
And we may have, in N. Mexico, by the end	
of September the number of men last stated	
From this to find the *effective* strength,	
another deduction of 5 pr centum for the	
sick, must be made, viz.	<u>72</u>
	1382

The following reinforcements may be sent.—
Three companies of the 1st Dragoons, now on

the borders of the Missouri (say)   150
The 7th Infantry, now at Jefferson Barracks,
near St. Louis (say)   <u>480</u>
                                                                     2012

It may be too late in the season before we shall have another considerable detachment of recruits for New Mexico, and will be very difficult to find other troops to send thither.

Respectfully submitted to the President,
Winfield Scott
War Department
July 24, 1850[17]

Scott's "Memoranda" did not present a very accurate count of the recruits actually on the way to Santa Fe. Scott's figures were those that had been devised somewhat earlier in the Taylor administration to reflect the numbers projected to be transferred to New Mexico. The 148 recruits shown at Fort Leavenworth were apparently soldiers dispatched to New Mexico during the spring, before the army increase act ever passed Congress.[18] The estimates of recruits shown "in route" through Fort Leavenworth and Texas are the same ones given in various orders in late June. The document conjectured that the recruits would all be in New Mexico by late September, an overly optimistic estimate that reflected the Taylor administration's planning a month or more earlier. President Fillmore very likely requested General Scott to provide him with a quick enumeration of the actual and potential troop strength of U.S. forces in the Ninth Military Department. Scott provided the figures that he could lay his hands on at the time; they were not very realistic, but they were on hand.

Whatever the inaccuracies of the "Memoranda," the document revealed to President Fillmore that some units remained that could be ordered to New Mexico. Fillmore wanted those soldiers where the threat was. General Scott saw to it that these wishes were carried out at the beginning of August, just after the defeat of the Omnibus. Besides protecting New Mexico, President Fillmore believed that putting more of the army in motion toward New Mexico might help to influence Congress to act. Free-soilers and Southern radicals candidly expressed in letters their belief that Millard Fillmore would prove a timid soul, in contrast to Zachary Taylor, in dealing with Texas. Within a few weeks after assuming office, President Fillmore proved otherwise. Orders went out to the 7th Infantry Regiment and to companies F and K of the 1st Dragoons to proceed with all possible haste to Santa Fe. No attempt could be made to disguise the intent of these shifts of regular army units to Santa Fe; they were to stop a potential Texan invasion of New Mexico. Southern extremists in Florida were particularly incensed when they learned the destination of the 7th Infantry, which only a few months earlier had been protecting white Floridians from Indians. They portrayed the move as if the Fillmore administration were leaving Florida to the Seminoles while using the 7th Infantry to give New Mexico to "Mexicans and Mongrels." After Louisianian Charles Conrad became secretary of war in mid-August, the *New Orleans Courier* assailed him for assisting in the administration's designs to move every available soldier to New Mexico.[19]

On August 2 General Clarke at St. Louis was instructed to have the nearly 500 men of the 7th Infantry proceed "without unnecessary delay" to Fort Leavenworth in preparation for "distant service." On the same day, orders also went out to Bvt. Col. Edwin V. Sumner, commanding officer of the 1st Dragoons, to have Companies F and K of his regiment, then on duty to guard the Santa Fe Trail, ready for "distant service." It is a measure of the significance the Fillmore administration attached to the possibility of violent conflict over Texas–New Mexico that they decided to dispatch these regular army forces despite the lateness of the season for such expeditions. An early onset of winter storms on the trail could wreak havoc on these units before they even reached New Mexico.[20]

The 7th Infantry had been at Jefferson Barracks for less than a month before being ordered to Fort Leavenworth. In mid-August the steamers *St. Ange* and *Kansas* each transported about 250 men of the regiment to Fort Leavenworth. The army contracted for other steamers to take the horses, mules, and materiel. On instructions from General Scott, Quartermaster General Jesup ordered that 200 horses (and he specified that they be good ones) were to be sent by steamboat to the 7th Infantry, so that a sizable portion of these soldiers could become mounted infantry, as provided for in the June 17 act. The St. Louis Arsenal dispatched percussion muskets and ammunition, 200 musketoons, 210 sabers, and 15,000 musketoon cartridges to the men waiting at Fort Leavenworth. By telegraph to General Clarke on August 7, the day after Scott issued his instructions to Colonel Munroe and General Brooke on how they should operate if Texas invaded New Mexico, Adjutant General Jones in Washington issued Scott's order for Plympton's 7th Infantry to hasten to Santa Fe. Clarke's adjutant, Lt. Winfield S. Hancock, received this message on August 8 and immediately dispatched it to the commander at Fort Leavenworth. At that stage the 7th Regiment was still at Jefferson Barracks and would not be ready to march out of Fort Leavenworth for another month. Finally, in mid-September, Plympton's men and their hundred-wagon supply train began the journey toward Santa Fe.[21]

The situation for Companies F and K of the 1st Dragoons, already operating on the plains, was a lot less complicated. Company F, commanded by Bvt. 1st Lt. Orren Chapman, had been engaged in the vicinity of Camp Mackay, near the Santa Fe Trail's crossing of the Arkansas, and the Big Timbers area along that river in early September. On returning from the Big Timbers to Camp Mackay on September 23, the company received its special orders from Sixth Military Department headquarters to proceed to Santa Fe. On the same day Company K, under Bvt. 2d Lt. Nathan G. Evans, returned to Camp Mackay from an escort to Las Vegas, New Mexico, to receive the same orders as Company F. Two days later, September 25, these two companies headed west. They overtook the various recruit detachments on the trail and reached Las Vegas on October 16. Chapman brought in 47 men of Company F, while Evans led in 26 men of Company K.[22]

As previously mentioned, General Scott, in coordination with President Fillmore's message and Secretary Webster's letter to Governor Bell, issued special instructions to Colonel Munroe and General Brooke on August 6. After informing Munroe of the various reinforcements being sent to New Mexico and warning him that Texas would probably send a force into his department if Congress did not settle the boundary dispute, Scott wrote:

> In such event, your position, as the immediate commander of the U. States' forces in New Mexico, will be one of much delicacy and difficulty, and hence demanding adequate instructions from the highest in authority. . . . Accordingly, you are hereby instructed, in the case of any military invasion of New Mexico from Texas, or by armed men from any other State or states for the purpose of overturning the order of civil government that may exist in New Mexico at the time, or of subjugating New Mexico to Texas, to interpose as far as practicable, the troops under your command against any such act of violence.
>
> The invaders will probably announce their approach and purposes by proclamation. It may be expedient for you to meet them by a like public declaration, in terms at once moderate and firm, intimating the general character of these instructions from the President, and your purpose to execute them. You will also profit by all opportunities to remonstrate and

use such means of persuasion as may be in your power with the principal invaders to avoid, if possible, a resort to repulsive violence; but when necessary, and without losing any material advantage by delay, you will take all preliminary steps for defence and in the last resort resist with vigor.

Acts of violence on the part of the invaders may commence by the arrest of the existing civil functionaries of New Mexico, and imprisoning them; or by setting up substitutes for those functionaries, and imprisoning opposers and remonstrants; or the invaders may endeavor to coerce the inhabitants into submission by taking or destroying their property. Any such act will present a clear case for the direct and active employment of the forces under your command.

How far, prior to the commission of such acts of violence, the intention to commit them, avowed by proclamation or otherwise, on the part of the invaders, may warrant you to resist the advance of the invaders, must depend on the terms of the avowal, the exposed condition of the frontier settlements towards Texas, and other circumstances which may be better estimated in your position than by the Executive at this distance. His expectation is, that you will take all preliminary measures within your power to protect the people of New Mexico against violence and to repel force by force when clearly necessary to that end.

In order to warn Colonel Munroe more quickly of the Texan danger, General Scott sent a telegraphic dispatch to General Clarke in St. Louis on August 7 with orders to transmit it to Munroe by special messenger as quickly as possible. The dispatch related the claim by Colonel Howard of Texas that 1,500 Texans were prepared to march on New Mexico and ordered Colonel Munroe to take "all proper measures" to protect the New Mexico population as guaranteed under the 1848 treaty. Further letter orders would follow, the dispatch said.[23]

Scott forwarded a copy of Munroe's instructions to General Brooke at San Antonio, along with Brooke's own set of instructions from Scott. The general in chief informed Brooke of Howard's claim and then said to him:

From your position, you will earlier learn the views and movements of the Texan Government, on this subject than can be known here.

Should it therefore come to your knowledge, and you will take measures to obtain the earliest intelligence, that any considerable body of Texans, say two thousand men or more, are about to march, or have marched, against New Mexico, you will rapidly withdraw all the disposable forces now under your command, and, with them precede or follow the invaders, so as to be in the best positions, within New Mexico, to execute the views and instructions of the President of the United States as contained in the copy of the letter to Col. Munroe herewith. By disposable forces, I mean all your troops that can be spared from the holding of important posts, on the frontiers of Texas, having within them sick men and valuable public stores, which you may be obliged to leave behind.

It is not intended that you shall attack the invading forces of Texas in march towards New Mexico; but that you shall, if practicable, cause your troops to precede them, or at least closely follow the invaders, and on arriving within New Mexico, as defined for the occasion only, in the accompanying letter to Col. Munroe, you will govern yourself by that letter. Of course, if attacked in the march, by the Texans, short of New Mexico, your troops will repel force by force.

As soon as you shall be in easy communicating distance of Col. Munroe, you will assume the command of the 9th Military Department in addition to the 8th; give all orders needful to the service, and consider yourself assigned to duty according to your brevet rank of Major General.

It is not foreseen that it will be necessary to embody the whole or the greater part of the disposable forces of the 8th Department, before marching into New Mexico. They may march by detachments, at the same time, or as soon as each may find practicable, and by such routes as you may deem best; but the commanders of each separate detachment will be furnished with the views of the Executive as they are herewith communicated to you.[24]

Such was the federal military response to the emergency developing over the Texas–New Mexico issue. The U.S. forces in the Ninth Military Department, along with those under General Brooke in Texas, plus whatever volunteers could be organized among the New Mexican population itself, would be the ones called on to repel any Texan invasion. The question was whether Texas chose to challenge these guardians of New Mexico or to back off from its bravado and await congressional action.

Chapter Ten

❧

Texan Rage, Summer 1850

The arrival of Texas commissioner Robert Neighbors at Austin on June 3, follow-ing the collapse of his abortive Santa Fe efforts, inaugurated a period of intense excitement and anger in Texas. Neighbors immediately learned that some of his earlier communications, particularly a long letter of April 14, had not yet been received by Governor Bell. Therefore in his official report to Bell on June 4, he re-vealed for the first time the important influence that the Taylor administration had exerted on the statehood movement in New Mexico through its instruc-tions to Colonel McCall. Texans had feared since Kearny's conquest that federal officials were engaged in attempting to cheat the Lone Star out of its claim, and Neighbors's information confirmed their worst suspicions.

Unfortunately and unrealistically, Neighbors's report also led Bell into con-tinuing to entertain the myth that Texas could still succeed in organizing Santa Fe County if only the federal opposition were removed. Neighbors rejected the idea that New Mexican statehood was "a spontaneous movement" of the local population and implied that the only indigenous opposition to Texas jurisdic-tion stemmed from those who had received large land grants under Mexican auspices just prior to the U.S. conquest. Neighbors's attitude may have reflected the hopeful talk of the few Texas boosters like Palmer Pillans in Santa Fe, but he never specified what means the Texans could employ to change the hearts of the New Mexican populace, to disabuse them of their long-standing "preju-dice" against Texas. Certainly Neighbors's mention of the impossibility of or-ganizing Santa Fe County without a Texan military force on hand to support it appeared to contradict his expectations of popular acquiescence.[1]

Word of Neighbors's report circulated through Austin even before it was published in the *State Gazette* on June 8. On that day a public meeting to protest federal policy in New Mexico was organized at the Capitol. The meeting appointed a committee to draft resolutions and present them when the group reassembled on June 11 in the Senate chamber. Following some speeches, the meeting adopted resolutions defending the historical basis for the Texan title to the Santa Fe area, condemning the U.S. military's role there, requesting Governor Bell to demand an immediate renunciation by the federal government of its civil jurisdiction in Santa Fe County, declaring that the rebellion in that county must be forcibly put down, pledging full support for any effort that Governor Bell might make for that purpose, and recommending that all other counties in the state conduct similar public meetings to express popular opinion on the issue. W. D. Miller, the meeting's secretary, dispatched a copy of the proceedings to Senator Rusk in Washington so that he might use them to show other leaders the strength of feeling on the subject.[2]

At this juncture Governor Bell could have easily ridden the whirlwind of anger by invoking his executive authority to organize a military force of volunteers and march them to New Mexico. Given his friendship with the radically proslavery faction in Texas politics, some felt that the governor, on disunionist advice, might precipitate a bloody conflict. Moderates considered him a weak leader, acting as a mere "cats-paw of Carolina nullifiers."[3] No one then or now would rank Peter H. Bell as a great statesman. But neither did he act like a hotheaded fool during the "dog days" of August and September 1850. Maybe from weakness, maybe from prudence, the governor vacillated. He appeared willing to await further developments before taking direct or forcible action.

Bell's correspondence immediately subsequent to the Austin rally for Texan rights was that of a cautious, deliberate man. His initial concern seems not to have been so much with how to extend Texan jurisdiction to Santa Fe but more realistically how to retain and secure the Texan hold on the El Paso area that Neighbors had organized. Pursuant to this consideration, Bell sent a letter on June 12 to Judge Baird at Santa Fe. In the letter the governor stated his intention to defend Texas honor and rights by all legitimate means, but he urged Baird, for the time being, to remove himself to El Paso, where Baird's establishment of a district court might do some practical good and would give the people of the region greater confidence in the solicitude of the Texas government toward them.[4] Bell's communications of June 13–15 were also directed to the members of the Texas congressional delegation in Washington and to President Taylor.

If Bell needed convincing that Texans supported a firm policy on the Santa Fe question, indignation meetings in various counties during late June and the first week in July supplied it, as did the uniform condemnation of federal policy in the Texan press. Resolutions approved at these enthusiastic gatherings were usually similar to those passed at the Austin meeting earlier in June. These public assemblies occurred at: San Antonio and Seguin, June 22; Marshall and La Grange, June 29; Matagorda, July 1; Leon County, July 4; San Jacinto battlefield, July 5; and again at La Grange, July 6. The two most prominent and widely publicized of these were the gatherings at Marshall, in the Texas county (Harrison) with the densest slave population in the state, and on the San Jacinto battleground, the sacred shrine of Texas's martial past. The principal focus of the Marshall meeting was endorsement of the resolutions passed at the Nashville Convention against Northern encroachment on Southern rights in general. And to the citizens of Harrison County, federal administrative action at Santa Fe to deny Texas title to that region constituted a particular case study of Northern aggression. The invited guest speaker at Marshall was J. P. Henderson, former governor and the Lone Star's sole delegate at the Nashville Convention. Henderson delivered his main address at the public meeting at the courthouse in Marshall on the afternoon of June 29. He emphasized the relationship of Texas to the rest of the South, the need for Southern unity if Northern aggression were ever to be stopped, and the need for Texas to demonstrate solidarity with the other slaveholding states by resisting the federal government on the Santa Fe issue. The meeting passed resolutions endorsing Texas rights and the Nashville Convention resolutions.[5]

Citizens from Galveston, Liberty, and Harris counties were the main participants on July 5 in the large meeting at the San Jacinto battlefield just east of Houston. The grove where the crowd met conjured up visions of fallen heroes and memories of Houston's triumph over Santa Anna in 1836; the analogy to Texas's plight in 1850 could not have been clearer in the minds of the enthusiastic but solemn people who attended the meeting. Ironically the person called on by its organizers to chair the session was Dr. Ashbel Smith, physician, former surgeon general of Texas, famous diplomat in the Texas Republic, and a person of well-known moderate views in reference to Santa Fe. As recently as May, Dr. Smith had written a letter to the *New York Journal of Commerce* proclaiming that Texans "with great unanimity" would be willing to surrender their claim to Santa Fe in exchange for an indemnity. Even Smith, however, was swept up in the fierce tide of anger that followed the release of Neighbors's report, and he too insisted that Texas must assert its rights by force, although he disavowed any intent to dissolve the Union. He knew Colonel Munroe very well, he said, as an officer who always obeyed orders and who therefore had obviously been acting under federal orders when he thwarted Neighbors and called for the New Mexico statehood convention. Even after stating these sentiments, Smith said he desired a compromise by which Texas could barter Santa Fe for money to pay its debt. Other speakers at the San Jacinto meeting called for the use of force to defend the state's honor and denounced the movement for New Mexico statehood. The meeting approved resolutions to sustain the governor in whatever measures were necessary to maintain the Texas title.[6]

A few days prior to the San Jacinto assembly, Governor Bell had finally decided to take the steps preparatory to sending a military expedition to Santa Fe, steps that the citizens gathered at San Jacinto endorsed. On July 1 the governor wrote a letter, copies of which were sent to six militia officers: Col. Thomas M. Likens of Henderson and Capt. J. M. Smith of Shelbyville in east Texas; Capts. H. E. McCulloch of Seguin and Jacob Roberts from the area near Lockhart in southwest Texas; Capt. S. P. Ross of Waco Village in northwest Texas; and Capt. Eli Chandler from the area near Wheelock in central Texas. In most cases Bell seems to have chosen his commanders based on his knowledge of their abilities gained during his own career as a frontier militia officer. As for Likens and Smith, they came from the most staunchly proslavery and pro-Southern area of the state. Bell informed each officer that he had that same day issued a proclamation to convene the state legislature in special session on August 12 to take action in reference to "a contemplated military movement" to Santa Fe. In anticipation that the legislature would approve the sending of the expedition, the governor commissioned each of the six, if he accepted, to quickly enroll a company of one hundred men from his own and surrounding counties to be prepared to march no later than September 1. Each soldier enrolled would be required to furnish his own horse or mule, rifle, two pistols, and horse equipage. Governor Bell also informed the commanders that he would ask the legislature for authority to raise no fewer than one thousand additional troops for the expedition. These first six hundred were to be only the initial contingent. About two weeks after the issuance of the recruiting circular, Bell dispatched Colonel Howard to Washington as his personal emissary to inform the president of his plans.[7]

Likens, Smith, and McCulloch acknowledged receipt of their commissions in mid-July. Roberts did so in early August, Chandler in mid-August. There is no record that Ross answered Bell's summons. Newspapers in August reported several others commissioned to recruit companies, but it is unclear whether Governor Bell ever officially sanctioned these activities. Once it became publicly known that Bell had issued commissions, numerous individuals in Texas and elsewhere in the South wrote letters applying for commissions to recruit or offering their services to the planned expedition. A student at Princeton in New Jersey wrote that some students there were prepared to leave school and go fight for Texas. Samuel Colt, the Hartford arms manufacturer, offered to provide Texas with one thousand government-size pistols.[8]

Colonel Likens and Captain Smith tackled their assignments with great eagerness. Likens, once his mission became publicly known in Henderson, began receiving many applications from men anxious to join the expedition. Likens waited until July 27 to officially sign the men up in Marshall in order to coordinate this ceremony with the big public meeting planned for that day in the town. So much enthusiasm was generated by Likens's advertisements in Marshall and elsewhere in Rusk and Harrison counties that Likens grandiosely estimated that five thousand soldiers would be ready to march within twenty days. Likens enrolled his company, the "Bell Guards," to full strength on the 27th and paraded them on the public square in Henderson on August 3 to show off for the local citizens. Likens wrote to Bell of his readiness to march his unit to Austin whenever the governor so ordered. Meanwhile J. M. Smith organized his company from Shelby and San Augustine counties on July 31 at Shelbyville. Smith had already boasted to Bell that the "bhoys" of his county were itching to shoulder arms in order to scare the "traitorous greasers" at Santa Fe, and 146 enrolled for his unit. Both Likens and Smith provided J. P. Henderson, on his way back east, with information on their recruiting efforts, and Henderson saw to it that newspapers in Eastern cities printed the material. Henderson fully expected hostilities soon; he wrote that he was going to Philadelphia to extricate his summer-vacationing wife and daughters from the enemy's country before the war began.[9]

Those who signed up in the "Bell Guards" and other such units may have seriously cared about the issues involved, but contemporary letters describe their primary motivations as a desire to fight someone. Many who had already seen service against the Indians or Mexicans and who enjoyed hunting, camp life, and battle viewed the proposed Santa Fe expedition as a relief from monotony. As one of Senator Rusk's correspondents put it, these veterans "deprecate the quiet, and peaceable life"; they reveled in the thought of putting their Bowie knives and other weapons to use again. They also believed that they could conquer New Mexico, even if U.S. forces then present resisted the takeover, if Texas would send enough of these wild and woolly sorts to do the job. Felix Huston, former major general of the Texas militia during the Republic, wrote two articles in the *Natchez Free Trader* claiming that the 1841 expedition failed because Texas did not send a proper military force and that Texas could win this time if its troops reached New Mexico in the spring before the United States could send its reinforcements.[10]

As recruiting continued, so did public demonstrations in support of a Texan military solution to the jurisdiction problem in New Mexico. When news of Bell's proclamation for a special session reached San Augustine on the eastern edge of the state, the town's citizenry greeted the news with the firing of cannon and the ringing of church bells. Numerous counties conducted public meetings during late July and early August, nearly all of them passing resolutions in favor of military action in New Mexico.[11]

The meetings and resolutions suggested a unanimity of opinion on the issue that did not exist. For one thing, any group of citizens, no matter how small, could hold such an assembly, pass resolutions, and send them to the newspapers to represent the opinion of an entire county. One of the only meetings for which the number in attendance was reported was held by fire-eaters in Houston on August 8; it was attended by only twenty-six people, who claimed to represent the opinion of Harris County, the most populous county in the state. More moderate Texans often chose simply not to interfere with the radical meetings nor hold counterdemonstrations, even if theirs was the majority opinion. Some gatherings of a decidedly moderate persuasion did take place, especially after the middle of August while the legislature was in session. These meetings, which passed moderate sets of resolutions, always defended the Texan title and jurisdiction east of the Rio Grande, but they also favored the exhaustion of all peaceable means prior to military action and supported measures in Congress for federal purchase of the Texan claim. Such a "water-bucket" meeting, as the extremists dubbed it, was held at Houston on August 29 with some two hundred people reported in attendance. By the time the legislature began its special session, the enthusiasm of the radicals had been pretty well exhausted. The last vestige of this during the legislative session occurred when a group of Washington County "ultras" in Brenham got together to burn effigies of President Fillmore and Senator Pearce.[12] The moderate voices that began to assert themselves after mid-August desired to resolve the issues in ways that would not risk ignition of a civil war.

The public rallies for one position or another on the issue reflected the tremendous popular interest in what course the Texas Legislature would pursue and were designed to influence that course. Whether Texas would send an expedition or take steps less military in nature was a question of intense interest outside of Texas also. Southern extremists, who had forsaken any hope of being able to protect slavery while locked in the Union with an antagonistic North, had gradually come to realize that the Santa Fe issue constituted the single best chance in the 1850 crisis for them to accomplish their goal of disunion, regardless of whether civil war attended the disruption. As William Gilmore Simms of South Carolina wrote on July 11 to fellow secessionist Nathaniel Beverly Tucker of Virginia, the "new element" of Texas jurisdiction "will probably furnish a more conspicuous & fruitful issue than any other cause of quarrel. It is one which can be made intelligible to the people—which mere cunning partisans cannot torture into the equivocal or the innocent. In that is our hope; and the insolence of the [U.S.] military men may probably precipitate the events . . . by which we could bring on the one great conflict." Tucker fully agreed with his friend and on July 17 wrote to James Hammond of South Carolina that he hoped reports of aid pledges to Texas by Governor Quitman of Mississippi were not unfounded. Tucker also expressed his hope that President Fillmore would not rescind Taylor's orders for U.S. forces to defend New Mexico. "God grant it," Tucker wrote, for disunionist hope for a collision depended on a firm federal stand against Texas. Quitman, of course, was generally promising the aid of his own state and the rest of the South to Texas in a conflict, as he wrote to J. P. Henderson on August 18. To Quitman the issue was whether Texas would allow a free-soil entity to be planted on its borders and thus provide "a magazine of combustibles" to destroy slavery.[13]

Secessionists saw a greater danger to the slavery system if the South remained in the Union than if the South attempted disunion and embroiled the nation in civil war. Others believed that such a war would destroy the peculiar institution. One of Rep. Horace Mann's correspondents, William Kennick, hoped that any war begun by a Texan invasion of the territories would soon be "carried into Africa" and end with the total abolition of slavery in the South. On the same day, Missouri free-soiler Francis Preston Blair addressed similar sentiments to former president Martin Van Buren, telling him that disunion would lay the South itself "naked to all dangers, which they now only pretend to fear from the union."[14]

Given the national considerations at stake, the opening of the special session of the Texas Legislature on August 12 took on added significance. Austin was crowded, and the weather was oppressively hot, typical of August "dog days" in Texas. Among the nonlegislators who came to town for the session was the celebrated Robert Neighbors, whose status was now that of an expert adviser on the

New Mexican situation. His opinions exerted much influence on the lawmakers, and he stressed the absolute necessity of a Texan military presence in Santa Fe County. Neighbors was also there to lobby for reimbursement from the legislature for the expenses of his journey. Almost all the members of both houses were present when the session began, eschewing their usual tardiness in attending on the first day of a session. One notable absentee was Lt. Gov. John A. Greer, ex-officio president of the Senate, who was in Tennessee at the time and who did not receive the announcement of the special session until it was too late for him to attend. Another was Sen. Elisha Pease of Brazoria County, who resigned his seat to keep a wedding date with his intended in Connecticut.[15]

The Texas Legislature and Governor Bell were operating with a lack of information, given the great distance of Austin from Washington, as to just what progress Congress was making in passing a compromise proposal. The earliest news they received from Washington took at least two weeks to reach Austin. News would travel, not always accurately, via telegraph to New Orleans, where it was then printed in the daily press. Steamers would transport copies of these papers to Galveston; papers there would reprint the news reports from back East, and the overland mails would carry these papers via Houston to Austin. Any official communications from Washington, by mail or special courier, would take a week or so longer.

Only after the Austin legislators began their session did they receive their first news reports of the failure of the Omnibus bill. Absence of any concrete proposals from Washington, or even the likelihood that any would be forthcoming, added to the determination of some legislators to take action into their own hands, regardless of consequences or of what Congress might do. The local *State Gazette* fed the lawmakers a steady diet of extremist editorials and reports of aid-pledging meetings in other Southern states. Not all the members favored "ultra" measures, however, even though on the surface all maintained an attitude of steadfast defiance against federal policy and what they considered the state of insurrection in Santa Fe County. Even some more radical leaders, such as Rep. Guy M. Bryan of Brazoria, remained disposed to await, for a week or so at least, word of congressional action in Washington, hoping that Congress would make an honorable peace offer to Texas that would defuse the powder keg before Texan troops were authorized to take that fateful plunge into New Mexico. Moderates among the members, especially some "grave old senators," desired a peaceful solution to the crisis, but even they realized that, unless Congress soon offered Texas a fair proposal, no viable alternative to a Texan military advance would exist.[16]

On August 13, the second day of the session, the senators and representatives gathered together in the House chamber to hear the reading of Governor Bell's message. While expressing his devotion to the Union, the governor declared that Texas could never submit to federal usurpation and interference in the internal affairs of the state. Moderation in the face of such a threat would be shameful, and Bell proclaimed that Texas must assert its rights "at all hazards and to the last extremity" by adopting measures for the forceful occupation of Santa Fe. If these efforts brought on a conflict with federal troops, Texas would at least not have submitted to insult.

Bell requested the legislators to authorize a minimum of two regiments of mounted volunteers, who, since Texas possessed only six hundred stand of arms, would be required to furnish their own weapons, horses, and equipment and would have to wait to be reimbursed for their services in the future from the sale of the state's public lands. To offset some of the expenses of the expedition, Bell suggested converting the school fund of $34,443 to the purpose and utilizing any other money lying idle in the state treasury. He condemned the Omnibus bill in Congress as a device to sever a third of Texas's territory in an "unholy scheme" by antislavery fanatics to strike at the "vital interests" of Texas and the other slave states. Reiterating a view held by nearly all the legislators, Bell declared that Texas would only treat a proposal for sale of its northwestern frontier with respect if said proposal first acknowledged the Texan title to the area and confirmed the guarantees regarding slavery in that region according to the Texas annexation resolutions of 1845. But the governor now saw no possibility that the federal government would offer such a proposal and warned the legislature not to delay action based on "delusive hope." He called on the lawmakers to nobly assert and firmly maintain the rights of the state. During the reading of the message, members of both houses frequently interrupted with loud applause.[17]

The general approval that greeted Bell's message in the legislature and across the state masked strongly diverse opinions on the proper course for Texas to follow. Many Texans, legislators and citizens at large, were still convinced that the federal government would soon offer them a fair deal and that, therefore, the Lone Star should wait a while longer before putting its troops on the march. Certainly everyone in the legislature desired a say in what measures would be adopted, and this was reflected in a rather comical way during the first few days following Bell's message. A wide variety of proposals and motions were offered, and both houses quickly decided that a joint select committee should be appointed to consider the whole lot and reduce them to a few simple bills. But each house kept adding new members to the select committee, and on

August 16 the joint committee itself voted to invite all members of both houses to participate in its deliberations. The entire legislature thus became the "select" committee.[18]

Even before the joint committee was formed, on August 14 Rep. James W. Scott of Houston had introduced a resolution in the House to request Governor Bell to inform that body what steps he had already initiated relative to recruiting and equipping of troops for the expedition. The resolution also requested that the governor submit to the House any correspondence between Texas governors and federal authorities in relation to Santa Fe and any correspondence between the Texas executive and the governors of other states. Scott stated that he wanted to know officially whether Texas could depend for men, money, or arms on the other states. The whole resolution was tabled the next day, August 15, primarily because members felt that Texas should act for itself within its own limits and not look beyond them until collision with the United States seemed imminent. There apparently had been no such correspondence up to that time anyway.[19]

Once the first group, numbering thirty-four, had been appointed to the joint select committee, they held their first meeting on the evening of August 15 in the House chamber. The details of their discussion are not now extant, but the committee unanimously approved a resolution "That Texas will maintain the integrity of her Territory at all hazards and to the last extremity." The committee then adjourned until the next morning, when they planned to discuss the proper means for carrying out the resolution's goal. Even this small demonstration of united endeavor by the committee provoked a jubilant firing of cannons from the Capitol grounds that evening.[20]

On the morning of Friday, August 16, Sens. Jerome B. Robertson of Washington County and David C. Van Derlip of Bexar County introduced troop bills in the Senate. Both men were counted among the "ultra" faction in the legislature. Robertson's proposal provided that five thousand men, in five regiments, be raised to suppress the rebellion in Santa Fe. Two of these were to be enrolled and sent out immediately, while the other three were to be held in reserve. Governor Bell himself was to command the expedition. Van Derlip's bill called for the governor to enroll volunteers but did not specify any particular number; the governor was to enlist as many as he deemed necessary, and, if too few volunteered, he was to make up the deficit from the state militia. Both of the bills were referred to the joint committee.[21]

Friday the 16th was a very busy day for the committee. The principal subject of discussion was the number of troops to be raised. The select committee, then up to thirty-six members, passed another resolution unanimously, reasserting that Santa Fe County belonged to Texas. A calm, dignified, but lengthy debate then developed over the military force to be sent. The members unanimously approved a resolution declaring that such a force must be raised to subject Santa Fe County to Texan jurisdiction. But on the questions of how the troops were to be raised, what numbers were necessary, and how to equip and supply them, "almost as many conflicting opinions and clashing resolutions" were introduced as there were members on the committee. A consensus finally emerged that 3,000 volunteers would most effectively accomplish Texas's goals. Many legislators preferred to set a firm number rather than give Governor Bell an open-ended authority to enlist whatever forces he desired. The members decided that 1,700 men would be required to subdue the U.S. military forces stationed in New Mexico; and another 1,300 would be needed to subdue any insurgency from the local population. Rep. James C. Wilson of Wharton framed the 3,000-volunteers proposal into a resolution, to which the joint committee assented. They then delegated the responsibility to a subcommittee to frame an appropriate bill and report on it the following Monday. To acknowledge the joint committee's progress so far, a seven-gun salute was fired by the cannon on Capitol Hill that evening.[22]

The joint committee then turned on August 16 to the much more complex issue of how to finance the expedition. This subject was destined to occupy the joint committee for another week. Most of the lawmakers agreed with the governor that the school fund should be utilized in the cause, but that fund fell far short of being able to sustain an expedition to New Mexico. Senator Van Derlip suggested that a subcommittee of five be appointed to devise methods for raising the needed money. During the debate on Van Derlip's proposal, Rep. Guy M. Bryan of Brazoria, a hard-headed realist despite his "ultra" convictions, tried to awaken his colleagues to what would be required of them and of the Texas people. Bryan boldly pointed out that additional new taxes would be absolutely necessary to provide "the sinews of war," even though he felt confident that the people of Texas would gladly support the extra levy. Bryan also endorsed Van Derlip's motion for a subcommittee, for he believed that this smaller group would be able to efficiently assess the financial needs and the resources available and be able to work up tangible measures thereon. The subcommittee was approved and appointed. Over the next several days numerous propositions were offered and their sponsors given a chance to defend them. In the end, however, no alternative to increased taxes appeared, and the joint select committee approved, with only two dissenting votes, a direct tax designed to raise $77,000. That money, coupled with the school fund and various other revenues, would provide a total of \$135,000 to \$137,000 to fund an expedition. Some talked of raising taxes still further in order to pay the volunteers, but the majority decided to defer the payment to the future, with the volunteers probably to be reimbursed for their services by land grants from the public domain.[23]

Complicating the deliberations of the joint committee was intermittent arrival of news from Washington. Texans anticipated that the regular mail on Monday, August 19, would bring President Fillmore's reply to Governor Bell's letter. Instead, they received news of the failure of the Omnibus, Fillmore's message of August 6, and the U.S. Senate's passage of the Pearce bill. The next issue of the *State Gazette* angrily denounced both the message and the new bill, claiming that the president had now assumed even more aggressively anti-Texas ground than Taylor had. The news apparently hardened the joint committee's determination, for on August 22 they adopted their subcommittee's formulation for a 3,000-volunteer bill.[24]

One piece of information that did not arrive in that Monday's mail, however, was a record of how Senators Rusk and Houston had voted on the measure, even though telegraph accounts indicated Rusk's general support of the proposal. Members of the Texas Legislature were very anxious to know the vote, since it could affect their own decision-making on Santa Fe and because it could influence the reelection of Senator Rusk, which had been postponed since the previous session. Texas leaders at Austin reacted to the Pearce bill in a decidedly negative fashion. This reaction was not so much governed by the acreage involved, although, as one writer put it, the amount of land to be ceded was enough to make Texas "wince." What made Texans wince even more was the fact that the southern limit of part of the New Mexico boundary came all the way down to 32°. The *State Gazette* in Austin condemned the bill on that ground more than any other, for, the paper argued, this line brought free soil and a haven for fugitive slaves close enough to endanger security in Texas's slaveholding, cotton-growing regions. Governor Bell was reported to be so angry about the bill that he exclaimed that he would not sell a piece of Texas's territory as large as a handkerchief for a million dollars. Rusk, of course, had voted for the bill, and, even though many Texas legislators suspected he might have voted for it, they had no certain information on that yet. Rusk had already stated in the U.S. Senate that he believed that his vote would cost him reelection. Luckily for Rusk, he was enormously popular in Texas, and even most of the more radical members of the legislature supported him. It is doubtful, even had the lawmakers known how Rusk had voted, that enough would have opposed him to deny him reelection.[25]

Rusk's warmest supporters were nonetheless concerned and wished no obstacles to block his reelection. Sen. David Gage of Rusk County introduced a motion on August 16 to schedule the legislature to elect a U.S. senator, proposing that the election be held on Tuesday, August 20, at 11 A.M. The motion carried without division in the Senate. However, when the House took up the resolution, Benjamin C. Franklin of Galveston succeeded in carrying a motion, without division, to postpone further consideration of the resolution until Monday the 19th. Rusk's enemies in the House obviously hoped that Monday's mail would bring news that Rusk had voted for compromise, which Texas radicals could then use to build up opposition to his reelection.[26]

When Monday's mail did not specify how the Texas senators had voted on the Pearce bill, Rep. Hamilton Bee of Laredo, a former South Carolinian and among the staunchest "ultras" in the Texas House, moved to delay the election for U.S. senator until August 26 to allow time for the next mail to arrive. Bee's motion carried on a roll call of 25 to 19, despite lavish praise of Rusk's record and speeches by his strongest supporters. During debate on Bee's motion, B. C. Franklin bluntly stated that, since the Pearce bill conflicted with the positions adopted by the joint select committee, he did not believe the Texas Legislature should reelect Rusk if later information showed that he had voted for the bill. The legislature, he said, needed to be consistent, and he saw no need for hurrying the election. Guy M. Bryan endorsed Franklin's position on the need for delay, but he frankly defended Rusk's course in defense of Texas during that session of Congress and said that he would vote for Rusk if the election were held at that time. After a move by radical Darwin M. Stapp of Victoria to table the resolution altogether was defeated 22 to 21, the House voted, on a motion of moderate David Dickson of Anderson, to adopt the resolution by a vote of 27 to 17. The next day, August 20, the Senate readily concurred in the House decision to delay the election for U.S. senator until the 26th at 11 A.M.[27]

The news of Rusk's vote was received at Austin on Friday, August 23. Again, the information was part of a telegraph dispatch to New Orleans. Given the frequency of telegraphy errors, many in Austin were not sure whether to credit this account or not. Still, most of the legislators, friend and foe alike, must have surmised by that time that Rusk had voted for the Pearce bill. Rusk's enemies redoubled their efforts to block his reelection. Joseph Bates, one of the Whig leaders in the state and eager to sow internecine strife among the Democrats, came to the capital to lobby against Rusk. Bates chided the lawmakers for the seeming contradiction of reelecting Rusk, who now appeared in accord with the views of Fillmore and Webster, and simultaneously fashioning measures directly opposed to federal administration policy. Louis Wigfall of Marshall, leader of the state's most radically pro-Southern faction, was reported to be orchestrating some of the opposition to Rusk from his stronghold in Harrison County. Governor Bell himself was so determined to defeat Rusk that he personally lobbied senators and representatives, even on the morning they were to conduct the election, to postpone it until the next session. Bell pleaded the impropriety of the election, given other pressing matters at the special session, and swore that, if need be, he would appoint Rusk temporarily as senator until the legislative election occurred. Senator Rusk's friends saw through Bell's ploy; Bell might appoint someone, but it would not be Rusk. Not all the lobbying was against Rusk; James Hamilton, the bond agent, wrote from Washington to encourage Hamilton Bee, to no avail, to support Rusk as a former South Carolinian.[28]

On Monday, August 26, a final effort was made to put off the U.S. Senate election. In the House, B. C. Franklin moved to rescind the resolution scheduling the election that morning. Elisha Lott of Tyler promptly moved to table Franklin's move, and debate erupted. James Wilson, a self-described "ultra among ultras," stated that he wished to know for certain how Rusk had voted and how the people of Texas would react to that vote before the legislature chose a senator. He believed his constituents in the Wharton-Matagorda area would oppose anyone who had voted in Congress to encourage abolition by "bringing the limit of Texan and Southern sway down to our doors." Franklin himself declared that a reelection of Rusk constituted a virtual endorsement of placing a new free state on Texas's western border. The House majority, however, disregarded such pleas and tabled Franklin's motion by a roll call of 25 to 19. Promptly at 11 A.M., the members of the Senate arrived in the House chamber for the election. Rep. Adolphus Sterne, Rusk's fellow townsman from Nacogdoches, and Sen. Isaac Parker both nominated Thomas Jefferson Rusk for U.S. senator. Representative Franklin nominated "Blank." In the election that followed, 38 representatives and 18 senators cast votes for the incumbent; 4 representatives—Franklin, Wilson, Jeremiah Clough of Marshall, and Edward H. Winfield of Brownsville—and 1 senator—H. Clay Davis of the lower Rio Grande counties—voted for "Blank"; 2 representatives—Bee and R. E. Clements of Brownsville—and 1 senator—David Y. Portis of Austin County—voted for Louis Wigfall (Bee wrote back to Hamilton and told him that he had voted for a former South Carolinian more devoted to Southern interests than Rusk); 1 representative—James G. Sheppard of Washington County—voted for W. D. Miller. Several of those voting against Rusk announced that they did so because of his vote for the Pearce bill. Texas moderates interpreted Rusk's easy reelection victory as a clear indication that the legislature also would favor acceptance of Pearce's bargain.[29]

Actually, the final tally on Rusk's election gave a false impression of the degree of Texan moderation. Many of those favoring Rusk did so for personal reasons, despite his vote for the Pearce bill. More indicative of the true nature of divisions in the legislature were the five House roll-call votes during the ten days before Rusk's reelection. Two strongly cohesive and mutually antagonistic blocs developed on the five roll calls relative to delaying or not delaying the election. The Index of Cohesion for the "moderate" side opposed to any delay of the U.S. Senate election was .910 on the five roll calls; that of the "radical" group trying to delay the election was .726. The Index of Likeness between them was a very low .182. Representatives from the far southwestern frontier counties along with members from some more eastern counties, such as Harrison and Washington, formed the "radical" bloc; representatives from the Red River counties and most of east Texas tended to compose the "moderate" bloc. (See Appendix C, Section 3.)

Certainly one matter about which the legislature achieved consensus was the reimbursement of Maj. Robert Neighbors for outstanding expenses incurred on his mission to Santa Fe. Governor Bell sent a message to the legislature, dated August 18, including among its variety of subjects an enthusiastic endorsement of the reimbursement. The Senate unanimously adopted a resolution on August 21 expressing its sincere gratitude for the "able and dignified manner" in which Neighbors had conducted himself. After the House passed an appropriation of $770 for Neighbors, the Senate took up the bill on August 24. Sen. Isaac Brashear of Harris County moved to raise the appropriation to $1,256.50, which the Senate adopted. The House concurred in the amendment on August 26 by a 32 to 8 vote.[30]

Also on the 26th, the joint select committee finally produced its series of bills in reference to Santa Fe. The lawmakers were by that time aware that any Texan expedition would be resisted by the New Mexicans and U.S. forces. They were also aware that the Fillmore administration's firmness was forcing many Texans to face the reality that a real war might erupt if the legislature agreed to follow Bell's recommended policies. Desire for a peaceful settlement was growing in Texas—conditional on the terms of it being honorable to Texas. But even under these influences, the legislators could not yet retreat from their extremist path.[31]

The joint committee's bills were six in number. The centerpiece was the measure calling for the enlistment of three thousand mounted volunteers to put down the insurrection in New Mexico east of the Rio Grande. Section 6 provided that the governor was authorized to enroll more troops if the original number proved insufficient. Section 7 declared that the expedition should be marched immediately to the site of rebellion and that Governor Bell was authorized to command them in person. However, the same section stated that the march could be delayed if the governor felt that circumstances required it. This bill became popularly known as the "war" bill. Four of the other bills in the package related to expedition financing, while another provided punishment for treason and insurrectionary activities against Texas. While all six bills were introduced in both chambers of the legislature on the 26th, Sen. Jerome Robertson of Washington that day also introduced a separate bill as a counterproposal to the anticipated Pearce bill. Robertson's bill would offer to sell the region above 34° to the United States for ten million dollars, as opposed to the 32° line in the Pearce bill. Robertson's bill was read twice and referred to the Judiciary Committee in the Senate. James Gillett of Lamar County introduced a similar proposition in the House the next day.[32]

Despite the final introduction of the bills and the continued attempt of the *Gazette* to maintain Texan belligerency, the strength of the movement for an immediate military solution to the Santa Fe question had already begun to wane. The Fillmore administration's unexpected firmness forced many Texans to adopt a greater caution, and the Pearce bill made many Texans hopeful of a generous, peaceful settlement of the issues. The timing for an immediate expedition was all wrong; Texans would be marching into a winter campaign over a desolate terrain almost entirely devoid of forage if they left at that season. Besides, Texas could not finance the expedition without desperate budget maneuvers and painful taxes. When it became known that the treasurer did not really have enough funds on hand even to pay for the special session, some wags suggested that they might utilize the school fund for the purpose. Under the circumstances, the earlier "patriotic valor . . . oozed out at their [the members'] finger ends and pocket nerves," as one radical observer phrased it.[33]

A definite trend toward moderation became obvious on August 27. Moves were made in both the Senate and House to have Governor Bell submit any proposition from the U.S. Congress to a popular vote in Texas. Sen. Albert Latimer from the Red River area proposed during the "war" bill debate that if the popular vote rejected the U.S. offer, the Texan expedition was to march but not before January 1. Sen. David Portis of Austin County spoke against any compromise, demanded that Texas send the expedition, and stated that he did not believe President Fillmore would execute his threat to use the sword. Despite such talk, the bill itself was tabled on motion of Senator Wallace of east Texas. Latimer then renewed a resolution, introduced originally by Sen. John McRae of southeast Texas on August 23, to instruct the Judiciary Committee to report a popular vote measure. The Senate adopted this resolution without a division and then tabled the various expedition finance bills. Over in the House, an unlikely source—Rep. E. H. Winfield, a member from far southwest Texas who voted consistently on the radical side—introduced a popular vote resolution, the preamble to which confessed that the object for which the session had been called had ceased to exist. His resolution not only provided for a popular vote but also that the legislature should adjourn on the 28th. After the "war" bill was taken up, moderate representative Joshua Johnson of Titus County moved to table it until July 4, 1851—a virtual abandonment of the expedition idea. James Gillett vigorously attacked the move. Following the defeat of an adjournment motion, Guy M. Bryan resumed the radical condemnation of Johnson's motion. He called the resolution a test of whether the legislature would do anything at all. Bryan proclaimed the Pearce bill provisions to be only a mere newspaper rumor and warned against "indecent haste" in accepting a vaguely promised deal. He termed it disgraceful and dishonorable for Texas to haul down the flag without even being summoned to surrender by its enemies. The rest of the day was spent on motions to adjourn and in defeating by a 37 to 8 vote a move by David Dickson of Grimes and Montgomery counties to postpone the "war" bill until the following July 3.[34]

During the remaining days of the session, August 28–September 6, a number of roll calls were conducted on various lesser subjects related to the expedition. In the Senate, during discussions on a bill to organize a frontier defense force against marauding Indians, moderates attempted to insert a provision to prevent the use of these troops against Santa Fe. On the day before the session ended, Senator McRae and a few other moderates pushed forward a resolution expressing faith in the justice of the measures then before Congress and stating that Texas should not be preparing for an emergency that might never happen. Even some moderates opposed such a statement just prior to adjournment, and the move failed. Meanwhile in the House, radicals attempted to pass the direct tax bill, but after a few roll calls moderates were able to stop the bill from reaching its third reading. Related matters such as proposals to sell a smaller piece of territory to the United States than that embodied in the Pearce bill were sometimes taken up, discussed, and then shunted aside.[35]

But by and large the latter part of the session became a function of two bills—the "war" bill and a bill to require a popular referendum on any proposition offered by the United States. The "war" bill was predominantly a House measure, while the popular vote bill was primarily a Senate proposition. On August 28 maneuvering on the "war" bill resumed in the House. After a move by James W. Scott of Houston to temporarily table the bill failed by a roll call of 35 to 11, Guy M. Bryan of Brazoria offered an amendment to substantially alter the meaning of section 7 of the bill. While retaining authorization for Governor Bell to personally command the troops, Bryan's proposed substitute for the section would prohibit the military force from marching until Congress had taken final action on the boundary issue, as long as that action occurred prior to March 1, 1851. The amendment was a recognition of the impossibility of a winter campaign and of the likelihood that Congress would propose a settlement to Texas. Rep. Franklin of Galveston attempted to leave the discretion for immediately starting the expedition in the hands of the governor, but the House quickly rejected this move without a division. A move by Representative Fields of Anahuac to entirely eliminate the governor from command was also disposed of. Bryan's amendment may have appeared to water down the bill, but House moderates still did not like its stipulation of a particular date after which the expedition would definitely march if the U.S. made no acceptable proposition to Texas. Representative Scott of Houston moved to strike that proviso from Bryan's amendment, but the House left the March 1 ultimatum intact by a 33 to 10 vote. The House then passed Bryan's amendment by a vote of 34 to 10.[36]

The struggle continued on Thursday the 29th. Rep. Hardin Runnels of Bowie County, an extremist, offered an amendment to the "war" bill that would provide for a popular vote on any U.S. offer and, if it was rejected, would make a Texan counteroffer to sell the region above 35° to the United States for ten million dollars. After Runnels's amendment was tabled, moderate David Dickson, a physician from Anderson, offered a substitute that would change section 7 of the bill to prevent any expedition until no chance of amicable settlement was possible or until the federal government recognized a New Mexican state or territorial government on Texas land. He also proposed a popular vote on any federal offer. The House tabled Dickson's and Runnels's amendments and a similar proposition by William Cochran of Dallas County by identical 25 to 21 votes. A short time later all three amendments were taken up and referred to a select committee, with instructions to report a bill the next day. That committee produced two bills, one calling for a popular vote on any federal proposition and one to sell a portion of Texas to the United States. Neither of these bills advanced to passage. Once the original version of his amendment had been sidelined to the select committee, Dickson offered virtually the same proposal, worded a bit differently, later on the 29th only to see it defeated 26 to 19. The House voted without division to change the size of the authorized force from 3,000 to 2,000 on the motion of Rep. Darwin Stapp of Victoria. After the failure of another tabling motion, the House adjourned.[37]

Only a few shreds of the debate on August 29 still exist, but those few give some indication of how bitterly contested the House struggle was. During debate over Dickson's amendment, moderates cloaked themselves in love for the Union and implied that their opponents' course would lead to disunion. Representative Wilson of Wharton responded by denouncing the charge and vehemently denouncing Dickson's amendment as a total abstinence from action by Texas, which would humiliate the state in the eyes of its friends and allow the federal government to continue to steal its rights.[38]

On Friday, August 30, the "war" bill was engrossed on a 32 to 14 vote and passed to its third reading. On Saturday, after two more tabling motions were denied on roll-call votes, the "war" bill, calling for 2,000 troops but delaying any advance until at least the next March, passed the House by a vote of 29 to 15. The bill was a compromise that pleased neither the most moderate, who really opposed any expedition, nor the most radical, who abhorred any delay in occupying Santa Fe County. Even the moderate *Houston Telegraph* said Bryan's amendment had transformed the "war" bill into a "peace" bill, while the radical *Matagorda Colorado Tribune* claimed that the amendment changed the bill into a "man of straw." An "ultra" correspondent from New Orleans wrote in the Matagorda paper that the Bryan amendment "is the sober second thought, which, like desertion, is the better part of valor."[39]

In House voting on the twelve roll calls on the "war" bill, the radical faction proved considerably larger and more consistent. (See Appendix C, Section 4.) That faction's cohesion index stood at .806, a figure indicative of little defection across the set of roll calls. The more moderate and smaller faction, however, displayed ambivalent attitudes toward the "war" bill, especially on the four earliest roll calls, with many of their members casting votes with the radicals. Few at that stage, it seemed, wished to go boldly on record as opposed to the forcible occupation of Santa Fe. Covering all twelve roll calls, the cohesion index for the moderates was a low .496; but on the last eight roll calls, this faction achieved a cohesion of .752. The degree of likeness between the two factions on all twelve roll calls was .349; on the last eight it fell to .245, as the moderates intensified their efforts to delay the expedition.

The House bill went to the Senate, which had also been wrangling over its own "war" bill for several days. The Senate debate had primarily concerned the same subject as the Bryan amendment of the House bill—that is, the date before which the expedition was not to march. Eight roll calls had already been conducted in the Senate on the bill by the time the House version arrived on the 31st. The Senate radical bloc was neither as dominant in size, relative to the moderates, nor as cohesive as the moderate bloc. Two senators who had voted with the extremists during the previous session early in the year—John H. Moffett and Benjamin Rush Wallace of east Texas—now voted steadily on the moderate side on the "war" bill, and Wallace assumed a leadership role among that bloc in originating motions and amendments. One report stated that the arrival of President Fillmore's message heavily influenced Wallace's transformation from "ultra" to moderate. After several closely contested roll calls, the Senate had engrossed its bill by 11 to 9 on August 30, after having adopted a Wallace amendment to make February 15, 1851, the date before which no expedition could occur.[40]

Once the House version came to the Senate, radicals in that chamber adopted it as the only troop bill with a chance of passage through both houses. At this stage two more senators who had been voting with the radical bloc on the first eight roll calls—Albert Latimer from the Red River area and Wilds K. Cooke, who represented several central Texas counties—defected to the moderate bloc. Four more roll calls were taken on the bill in the Senate. The principal one took place on Monday, September 2, on the final passage of the House version. It resulted in a 10 to 10 tie, defeating the bill, with Lieutenant Governor Greer not present to cast a tie-breaking vote. Wallace's vote near the end of the roll was the one that clinched the bill's defeat. The Senate defeat of the "war" bill was easily accounted for; a number of members stated, according to a correspondent, that "they were not willing to rush into a conflict, while there was so fair a prospect of a peaceable and friendly proposition being made by Congress for an arrangement of all disputes." A radical commentator for the *Matagorda Tribune* felt that the senators had simply been charmed by the promise of federal money. On September 3, the day following the "war" bill's defeat, an errant telegraphic dispatch, which had appeared in some Southern papers and which claimed that the Pearce bill had actually passed the U.S. House, reached Austin by mail. After that bit of "news," the legislature showed little further interest in the "war" bill, and an attempt by Senator Robertson of Washington to revive it on September 4 garnered almost no support.[41]

Appendix C, Section 5, shows the alignment of senators on the twelve "war" bill roll calls. The index of cohesion for the moderate bloc measured .690, that of the radical bloc .530. The likeness between them was .390. Many defections were evident, especially by those whose voting only tenuously associated them with the extremist side on this issue.

As the enthusiasm for a military expedition became more qualified and conditional, the legislature's interest in having a popular vote on any propositions offered by the federal government increased accordingly. This seemed the only alternative if the lawmakers were not going to adopt a policy of their own. Proposals for the conduct of a popular referendum had been introduced in both houses and discussed simultaneously with the "war" bill. In the Senate, radical Jerome Robertson and moderate Jesse Grimes both devised bills for the purpose. The two measures differed in one principal regard: Robertson's bill would make the decision at the ballot box binding on the legislature, while Grimes's would not. Radicals wished to make the result of the popular vote binding on the legislature, in case the vote went in the extremists' favor. It was a desperate gamble but about all that the radicals had left to rely on if they were to ever get their cherished military expedition on the march. Both of the Senate's popular vote bills were referred to the Judiciary Committee on August 29. Later that day the committee reported a bill following the Grimes formula. After Robertson failed to get it altered to his liking and after Van Derlip failed to get it tabled until the following day, Robertson offered his original bill as a substitute. The Senate overwhelmingly rejected it 17 to 3 and then adopted the committee's moderate wording. A "binding" amendment, similar to Robertson's, by Senator Van Derlip of Bexar County, was defeated on August 30 by a vote of 12 to 7. The popular vote bill was then quickly engrossed, read a third time, and passed 14 to 5. Robertson, Portis, and a few other radicals formed the minority on the roll calls.[42]

The Senate's popular vote bill was reported in the House on August 31. That chamber had been considering its own bill. On the previous day the representatives had rejected a "binding" amendment by James Gillett of Lamar County and had engrossed the bill by a vote of 42 to 3, with only three radicals—Franklin of Galveston, Wilson of Wharton, and Crump of San Antonio—in the negative. On the 31st the House readily allowed the Senate version to supersede its own. The House approved, by a 24 to 14 vote, an amendment by Gillett to request rather than require Governor Bell to submit any U.S. propositions to a popular vote. While the most moderate members did not want to allow the governor any leeway on the matter, the House majority supported Gillett's wording. The bill then passed 37 to 3, with Franklin and Wilson this time joined by Jeremiah Clough of Marshall in the minority. On Monday, September 2, the

Senate adamantly refused to concur in the House amendment. After the failure of a tabling motion by Franklin, supported only by ten other members, the House voted without a division to recede from Gillett's amendment. The bill went to Governor Bell.[43]

Apparently word of the governor's displeasure with provisions in the bill and his intent to veto it was leaked to his friends in the two houses on September 3. Thus developed a very embarrassing situation for Bell's coterie of supporters and also for those moderates who felt a veto at this juncture would make the whole legislative process in Texas look ridiculous. Large majorities in both chambers had given their votes for the bill. In the House on September 3, moderate representative J. W. Scott of Houston moved that that body request the Senate to have the governor return the bill to the House. Most of the moderate faction, however, were quite anxious to have Bell deliver a veto, and they supported a move by P. Burrell Smith of Clarksville to table Scott's motion. But Smith's move failed 26 to 11, and Scott's move then passed without a division. In the Senate, moderates held the upper hand, and they refused to accede to the House's demand, defeating it 13 to 4. Only Robertson, Van Derlip, and two senators from the southwest frontier counties—H. Clay Davis and Henry L. Kinney—voted for the House proposal.[44]

Governor Bell did indeed veto the popular vote bill on September 4. He objected to the legislative branch ordering the executive to submit any U.S. proposition to a popular referendum, even if that proposition should be insulting or degrading to Texas in its terms. He assured the legislature that he would certainly submit any reasonable settlement to the electorate without any command of the legislature to do so. Bell undoubtedly believed that he was protecting the executive prerogative from legislative encroachment. His second reason for the veto was more technically based but also related to executive privilege. The state constitution empowered the governor alone to summon an extraordinary session of the legislature. Section 4 of the popular vote bill would require Bell to convene the legislature in special session after the plebiscite on any federal proposal in order to act on the recommendations of the electorate. Bell argued that the legislature had no right under the Texas Constitution to order the executive to do this.[45]

The Senate lost no time in trying to override the veto. On the 4th, the Judiciary Committee quickly considered the matter, and the majority—Wallace, Moffett, Latimer, and three others—curtly reported Bell's objections as "plausible" but neither "valid" nor "insuperable." The lone dissenter on the committee, David Van Derlip, filed a more extensive minority report, defending Governor Bell's second ground for the veto. The Senate majority stood unconvinced by Bell and Van Derlip, and voted 14 to 5 to override the veto. H. Clay Davis, Henry L. Kinney, Jerome Robertson, and David Van Derlip were joined by A. M. Truit of Nacogdoches and Shelby counties in the minority. The House received both the veto and the Senate override that day and referred them to its own Judiciary Committee, chaired by radical leader Benjamin C. Franklin. On September 5, Franklin, reporting on behalf of the committee, declared that the committee felt it within the legislature's competence to require the governor to submit a U.S. proposal to a popular vote but that the committee also concluded that section 4 of the bill did infringe on the executive's sole authority to convoke an extraordinary session. The House refused by a 27 to 13 vote to override the veto. The thirteen who voted to override consisted almost entirely of the moderate faction who had opposed the "war" bill. Bell was therefore left free to solicit a popular vote on his own authority, if he so chose. Nonetheless both chambers of the legislature adopted resolutions, before the session adjourned on September 6, stating that a popular referendum should be conducted if the federal government submitted an offer to Texas.[46]

When the legislature did adjourn on September 6, it was with the stipulation that it would reconvene on the third Monday in November. The adjournment resolution itself constituted a slap at Bell's prerogative; it did not specify that the governor would have to call the members back into session, only that they would reassemble. The special session of the Texas Legislature came to an end, having accomplished nothing in particular except in their choosing not to start a war immediately. They would wait on Congress to act, if it did, and then most likely sit down in November to judge the results of a popular vote on what Congress proposed. As of September 6, however, the Texas lawmakers still did not know what the U.S. House of Representatives was doing with the Pearce bill. General Brooke, who had come up to Austin for the last week of the session to spy on the legislature for General Scott, as well as consult with the lawmakers on frontier defense, still considered war certain if no settlement was forthcoming.[47]

≈≈

Chapter Eleven

The U.S. House and Texas–New Mexico, August–September 1850

WHILE U.S. MILITARY FORCES AND MATERIEL WERE HASTENED TOWARD SANTA Fe and Texas politicians in Austin pondered their unhappy options, the Fillmore administration and other supporters of compromise in Washington welcomed the Pearce bill's victory in the Senate. Much yet remained to be done—the Senate had to pass the other bills of the package, and the friends of compromise in the House had to forge a working majority from among the unruly elements of that body described by one editor as "the charmed cauldron of Macbeth's witches."[1]

The Senate passed the remaining compromise bills by comfortable margins and without much controversy, although the deliberations were attended by occasional outbursts by Southerners against California admission and by Northerners against the fugitive slave law. The Senate debated the California statehood bill on August 10, 12, and 13, passing it on the 13th by 33 to 18. The Senate considered the New Mexico Territory bill on August 14 and passed it on the 15th by 27 to 10. As in the already-passed measure for Utah, the New Mexico bill contained no express restriction on the territorial legislature in reference to slavery and provided that the territory would be later admitted to statehood with or without slavery according to its constitution at the time of admission. Salmon Chase, the Ohio Free-Soiler, offered the Wilmot Proviso as an amendment to the bill, but it failed by the fairly close vote of 25 to 20, with five Southern Democratic radicals absent. This led to speculation that Southern "ultras" plotted to use absenteeism in order to allow the Proviso to be attached to the territories, thus giving disunionists a platform on which to campaign for secession in their home states. The last two measures of the settlement, the fugitive slave bill and the District slave trade bill, passed the Senate on August 23 by 27 to 12 and on September 16 by 33 to 19, respectively. The majorities on each of the bills varied, but there emerged on none of them the strange alliance of Northern and Southern extremists voting together, as they had done on the boundary issue.[2]

The Senate, however, was not the center of national attention after it passed the Pearce bill; the focus of public suspense now shifted to the House and whether it would pass the Texas bill intact, amend it, or not enact it at all. Initially Washington was seized with euphoric optimism and a strong sense of confidence that the House would quickly approve the Pearce bill, in order to transmit the settlement to the Texas Legislature while it was still in session. A *Baltimore Clipper* correspondent listed 140 House members in favor of the bill. One overly enthusiastic telegrapher even misinterpreted a correspondent's prediction that the bill would pass by a margin of fifty in the House and sent out a dispatch reporting that the House had passed the bill on August 15 by that majority. Even some opponents of the Texas bill despaired of being able to prevent the quick passage of the measure on which the success of all the others hinged. As soon became apparent, though, neither proslavery nor antislavery radicals intended to withdraw from their fight to kill the boundary settlement and, with it, any compromise.[3]

Ardent proslavery men considered opposition to California's admission as their top priority, but the potential for violence and bloodshed over the Texas–New Mexico boundary had transformed that issue into a peculiarly convenient rallying point for the disunion that many Southern extremists believed California statehood would necessitate. The radicals' problem was lack of any Southern unity; Southern Whigs, except for Thomas Clingman of North Carolina, gravitated heavily toward compromise, while Southern Democrats were severely divided into radical and moderate camps. Southern speeches in the House on President Fillmore's message ran the whole gamut of Southern opinion in reference to the issues. Albert Gallatin Brown, Mississippi Democrat, worked himself into such a frenzied state of "chivalrous defiance" during his attack on the message that "his face glowed like a furnace" and it seemed that his eyes would pop out of his head in the August heat. The Georgia Whigs, Stephens and Toombs, both assaulted the message, even though they quietly worked for compromise. On the other hand, Christopher Williams, Tennessee Whig, vigorously defended the president's message in an address in which Williams sarcastically proclaimed that, if Congress gave Texas all the land it claimed instead of the ten million dollars, it would be the worst calamity that could befall Texas.[4]

In an attempt to see if some common program could be agreed on by the Southerners in the House, a caucus of slave-state members was held on three successive nights, August 8–10, at the Capitol. At the first meeting, on Thursday, August 8, the night before the Texas bill passed the Senate, forty-five Southerners discussed their situation and appointed a committee of fifteen members under the chairmanship of Robert Toombs of Georgia to draft resolutions. Several moderates openly dissented from the whole proceeding. The caucus reassembled on Friday evening but limited itself to discussion. On Saturday night forty-two Southerners were present to receive the committee's report. The resolutions favored recognition of Southern rights to slave property in the territories, division of the territories and California at 36°30' north latitude, and no agreement to a Texas–New Mexico boundary settlement until the territorial slavery issue was settled. Heated debate erupted and lasted until midnight. At the end fewer than thirty remained, and the caucus approved the resolutions by the close vote of 15 to 12, hardly the unity Southern extremists had looked for. They had hoped that the caucus would show at least forty-six members ready to assume the "ultra" position, since any attempt to block California by constantly calling the yeas and nays would require that number, a fifth of the House, to succeed. As it was, the caucus never even achieved that number in attendance from among the ninety House members from slave states.[5]

Northern opponents of compromise also caucused on August 10 to discuss ways to defeat the Texas bill. They realized that the bill's supporters would attempt to press the measure in the House during the next week, and on Monday, August 12, the pro-bill forces in the House prepared to do just that. The *Republic* and *National Intelligencer,* Whig and administration organs in Washington, were solidly behind the bill by that time. That morning administration friends, such as Hugh White of New York's delegation, circulated among the House members urging them to approve the Pearce bill arrangement before Texas could carry out its threats to invade New Mexico and assuring Whig members that the bill met with the president's approval. Detesting any move by those he termed "doughfaces" to do the bidding of the "Slave Power," Free-Soil leader Joshua Giddings took the floor for an hour to rally the anti-bill elements, speaking eloquently in an impromptu address against paying Texas any money for territory that rightfully belonged to New Mexico. And as for Texas threats, he said, even the women of his home county were not scared by such bluster. The Free-Soilers and Taylor Whigs were very proud of Giddings's effort, and the bill's supporters, now that their Northern opponents were in a state of high excitement, decided to drop their attempt to force the bill to a quick vote in the House. That night they met informally and reavowed their determination to get the bill considered and passed, even if they had to struggle through other business, such as appropriations bills, first. The Southern radicals also met informally that evening. They were as anxious as Giddings and his antislavery friends to hinder and delay the Texas bill.[6]

Every group seemed undecided at this stage on what moves to make and tactics to employ. At stake were the votes of House members, an untrustworthy "great mob," as one correspondent described them. The acoustics in the House chamber aggravated the apparent unruliness of the more than two hundred members. Any noise in the great hall echoed and reverberated to such an extent that very few could hear the proceedings, much less make themselves heard above the din. Therefore congressmen often left their seats and congregated in a mass in front of the speaker's desk until that officer ordered them back to their seats, only to have the same chaotic scene soon repeated. Most of the members were inexperienced, many lacked party discipline, and during dull moments in the House, some degenerated into the juvenile practice of flicking the little waferlike seals of dried paste (used in franking letters) at their enemies across the hall. At least these wafers would not inflict serious injury on their victims. Real danger lay in the possibility that some member might, in some heated moment, fire a pistol at one of his political opponents; several reports indicated that House members were packing sidearms just in case a severe disruption occurred.[7]

Certainly the great majority of members were eager to finish the business of this seemingly interminable session and get home. Sheer exhaustion from wrangling in the summer heat enervated the most hearty, and numerous members lost considerable weight. Speaker Cobb, once corpulent, lost some forty pounds and trimmed down to 175. Homesickness was rife among the members, especially since many of them had recently seen their families depart from Washington for what they hoped would be healthier climes. The capital had been a very sickly place that summer, and much worse was anticipated daily. Asiatic cholera was approaching from the Ohio Valley, renewing memories of the terrible epidemic of the previous year; cholera deaths were already being reported at Martinsburg and Harpers Ferry, and Washington appeared to be the next stop.[8]

The November elections made the House contest over the Texas bill and other aspects of the settlement doubly difficult. Some Northern members, under state legislature mandates to attach the Wilmot Proviso to any settlement, were reluctant to approve any territorial bills without that feature just before the elections. On the other hand, a representative's insistence on the Proviso might ruin any chance for an overall settlement and incur the wrath of those electors who wanted the issues quieted in some way. Southern moderates feared an electoral backlash and defeat by radicals because of their support for compromise; Southern radicals feared defeat too, because they sensed that the Southern populace generally favored the compromise bills rather than the risks involved in disunion. Since most members up for reelection could not get home to campaign, they took up a good deal of time delivering speeches and then dispatching printed copies thereof to their constituents—stump speaking by proxy, or buncombe, as it was commonly known. Such speeches were often delivered to a nearly empty hall and served no practical purpose in resolving the national crisis.[9]

Not only did members distribute printed copies of their speeches to home districts, but they in turn received letters and newspapers from home by which they could gauge the tenor of the public response to the Texas bill and the rest of the compromise. The anti-compromise presses of North and South hated the Pearce bill. Free-Soil, Northern Whig, and antislavery Northern Democratic papers portrayed the bill in terms of a ten-million-dollar swindle, fueled by Texas bondholders and designed to transform more free soil than even under the Omnibus bill into slave territory. These same papers ridiculed Southern and Texan threats as not in accord with majority sentiment in the South; but in the event that Texas did rashly invade New Mexico, they were confident that U.S. forces would easily defeat them. To free-soil elements, the bill represented abject servility to Texas and "Slave Power" extortion. The Wilmot Proviso remained the Northern radicals' goal in New Mexico, if full statehood proved unattainable. The pro-Benton *St. Louis Union* also campaigned for New Mexico statehood, even though it simultaneously acknowledged some legitimacy for the Texas claim. The presses of the anti-bill Democrats paid special attention to partisan considerations. They distrusted any measure that might help their Whig enemies and feared that the Fillmore administration might abandon any territorial settlement once the Texas bill was passed.[10]

Southern opposition to the Pearce bill was monopolized by radical Democratic newspapers. They also characterized the payment of the Texas debt as corruption money, but for the purpose of robbing Texas of a just, federally recognized land claim in order to establish a new free state in New Mexico. The money "bribe" would help no one but stockjobbing creditors. Southern radical presses seemed especially horrified at the participation of Southerners themselves in the nefarious scheme. J. F. H. Claiborne of Louisiana likened the bill to the Trojan Horse, a snake hidden in a flower vase, and a poisoned cup. Extremist Southern papers said that Fillmore, "His Accidency the Second," presented the South only the humiliating choices of submission to the Texas bill or coercion by U.S. military force. Given that choice, they hoped that Texas would assert its rights east of the Rio Grande by force, and they promised the aid of other Southern states to Texas if the U.S. military contested the Texan advance. In August and early September, the *Southern Press* in Washington regularly printed resolutions of public meetings in the South guaranteeing such aid. Only one Southern radical paper, the *St. Louis Times,* favored the Pearce bill—and only because it felt the bill's passage would prevent Fillmore from invading Texas itself for free-soil designs.[11]

Newspaper opinion in favor of the Texas bill was expressed in both North and South, by both Whigs and Democrats. Many Northern Whig papers now accepted the Pearce bill as the only feasible basis for a settlement of the most serious threat to the Union. Some of this support was grudgingly given, because the bill, on its merits, displeased many Northern Whigs; they wanted a boundary line more favorable to New Mexico, disliked the lack of the Wilmot Proviso in New Mexico, and were annoyed and exasperated by Texan threats. Many other factors, however, swayed Northern Whigs to promote the bill. The prospects of Southern disunion or a bloody collision on the Texas–New Mexico boundary appalled many Northern Whigs. The ten million dollars, even if the Texas claim were dubious, was far cheaper as a price for peace than the cost of war would be. In addition, they believed that the boundary line in the Pearce bill was acceptable, in the absence of a better one, for it secured to New Mexico the inhabited and inhabitable areas while surrendering to Texas principally the barren wastes of the Staked Plains. Since slave labor increasingly appeared impossible in any of this Southwest region, some Northern Whigs were beginning to drop their once-absolute commitment to the Wilmot Proviso. They rationalized the Texas bill into a simple matter of bargain and sale, involving no sacrifice of principles. Most Northern Whig partisans were well aware of President Fillmore's desire for a settlement and his tacit approval of Pearce's bill and did not wish to take a position directly hostile to that of a Whig administration. Many Northern Whigs were also well aware that California's admission as a free state at the session depended on the success of the Pearce bill, as did the faint hopes for a higher tariff still lingering in Northern Whig hearts.[12]

Northern Democratic journals favorable to the Texas bill tended to be less hesitant than the Whig press in the advocacy of it. While they shared in the general disdain for Southern and Texan bullying, Northern Democrats more readily acknowledged that Texas possessed legitimate foundations for its claims. They therefore recommended a generous settlement in land and money to Texas, simultaneously warning, however, that any precipitate Texan aggression would destroy whatever Northern goodwill existed toward the Lone Star. Most Northern Democrats had faith that bloodletting would be avoided and that most Texans and Southerners in general favored compromise, despite the attempts of a few radicals to use the Texas boundary issue to foment disunion and civil war. They appeared more confident than Northern Whigs that "natural limits" and the intensity of opposition by the local population would prohibit slavery expansion. Thus Northern Democratic papers condemned the Wilmot Proviso as an unnecessary device originated by abolitionist fanatics. One trait that these Northern Democrats displayed in common with the Northern Democrats opposed to the bill was a wary, distrustful attitude toward the Whig administration and the partisan advantages that the Whig Party might derive from the bill.[13]

Certainly the most cohesive bloc of newspapers in favor of the Texas bill and compromise were the Southern Whig presses. Southern Whigs were more convinced than any other group that the Pearce bill constituted the sine qua non for peace and continuance of the Union. Collision, bloodshed, and war were the only alternatives. They believed that Southern extremist Democrats were bent on disunion and that they, not the radicals, accurately reflected the greater portion of Southern popular opinion on the compromise. Like their Northern Whig counterparts, they seriously doubted the validity of Texas's claim to everything east of the Rio Grande. The Pearce bill offered a chance for Texas to unload a burden of barren land conquered by U.S. troops in exchange for a handsome sum of money that would substantially assist Texan economic development. Just as Northern Whig proponents of the bill interpreted it as no sacrifice of Northern free-soil principles, so did Southern Whigs view it as no sacrifice of Southern principles. Under the nonintervention or popular sovereignty principle, the territory given up by Texas to New Mexico would not be converted from slave soil to free soil because Southerners would, at least theoretically, not be barred from taking their slave property into New Mexico. Southern Whigs considered the decision of many Northerners to stop demanding the Proviso a major concession of principle. Of course Southern Whigs, in common with other Southerners, registered their objections to President Fillmore's message and threat of force against Texas, and they clearly expressed their unity with the rest of their section in opposition to further aggression on Southern rights. However, the Southern Whig critique of President Fillmore was mild in contrast to their outrage against reports of arming, recruiting, and expedition-planning in Texas.[14]

Southern Democrats who favored the Pearce bill, many from the upper South, used some of the same arguments employed by Southern Whigs—the importance of the bill to peace, the uselessness of the lands conceded by Texas, the economic benefits of the ten million dollars for the Lone Star. Pro-bill journals of the Southern Democrats considered the bill defective, dissenting particularly from the five-million-dollar reserve clause, but, as long as the arrangement had the endorsement of important Texas leaders in Washington, many Southern Democrats extended their approval. This support was less enthusiastic and wholehearted than that of Southern Whigs for the bill. These Democrats blamed the Whigs under Taylor for causing the problems in the first place and attacked Fillmore's message and the dispatch of U.S. military reinforcements to Santa Fe. But none of these reservations was enough to divert them from supporting the Pearce bill, for they seriously considered the activities and plotting by Southern disunionists not only an imminent danger to the Union but also a greater threat to the South itself than any outside enemy posed.[15]

The coalitions in Washington that mirrored the views of sections and parties consisted of incongruous elements. The Free-Soilers and antislavery Whigs and Democrats against the bill were opposed to the states rights Democrats of the South within their bloc except on the matter of the Texas bill. But on that one bill, the key to every other part of the compromise, the radicals of North and South achieved a remarkably stable coalition. Both groups clearly understood that their union with the opposite extreme was strictly an ad hoc association to combat the Texas bill and thus destroy compromise. By contrast the partisan and sectional groups composing the pro-bill forces demonstrated considerable difficulty in uniting on a plan of action. Just as many Northern Democrats did not trust the Whigs to pass the territorial bills without the Wilmot Proviso, once the Texas bill passed, Southerners entertained the same concern about Northern men in general. Fear that the Whigs might try to add the Proviso or drop the territorial bills altogether to avoid voting on it led many Northern Democrats and Southerners to demand that either the territory bills assume priority over the Texas bill or that a new Omnibus be assembled to combine the territory and Texas bills. Southerners definitely wanted Proviso-less territories established before permitting the admission of California. Southerners believed that if California statehood was agreed to first, as Northern Whigs desired, then that bloc would feel less inhibited about tacking the Proviso onto the territorial bills.[16]

These considerations induced some of the pro-compromise leaders to devise a new Omnibus as their principal strategy. The object was to maximize the potential vote and allay some of the distrust, although the originators of the scheme knew it might cost some support of Northerners opposed to any further combination of bills. The idea for a new Omnibus was clearly the brainchild of a few Democratic leaders, Sen. Stephen Douglas of Illinois and Rep. Linn Boyd of Kentucky, chairmen of the respective territorial committees, with the cooperation of Speaker Howell Cobb. The Fillmore administration was reported to be initially unenthusiastic about the plan. Details of the scheme may have been worked out at the informal caucus of compromise men on the evening of August 12, for it was within the next few days that reporters began discussing it in their columns. A few weeks later Douglas claimed that he had drafted the proposal for Boyd. Boyd would, at an opportune time, move to engraft the Utah and New Mexico territories bills onto the Texas bill.

The territories amendments would be near-copies of the Senate bills, except for the deletion of sections appropriating money for a library and public buildings. The absence of these minor provisions would obviate the difficulty presented by House rules that required any bills involving appropriations to first be referred to the Committee of the Whole House on the State of the Union. The compromisers desired above all to prevent such reference, for no parliamentary devices existed to force the bill out of the Committee of the Whole, and the bill's enemies could smother it in debate until the session ended. The Utah bill had passed the Senate with a $25,000 appropriation for public buildings, thus necessitating House reference of that bill to the Committee of the Whole. Some speculated that the Texas bill itself would also be sent to the Committee of the Whole, since it involved a provision that ten million dollars would be appropriated. However, Speaker Cobb could be expected to rule that the Texas bill did not necessarily have to be referred to the Committee of the Whole, since the bill's appropriation was only contingent on the decision of Texas to accept or reject the offer. If Boyd's move for a "little Omnibus" was successful, then the compromisers would move the previous question, a House parliamentary device to stop further delay and bring the combined bills to a direct vote.[17]

Just as the compromisers were busily piecing together their new package, their hope that Texas would prove receptive to such a proposal was embarrassed by an item of "news" from a Texan who arrived in Washington from San Antonio on the evening of August 14. He fed to journalists the startling report that eight thousand Texan volunteers were under arms and ready to march on Santa Fe, with another thousand prepared to enlist. This gross exaggeration represented quite an increase over the fifteen hundred such volunteers reported by Colonel Howard of Texas about ten days earlier. Peacemakers were shocked by the disclosure, and Southern "terrorists" were described as gleeful.

Northern presses reacted with disbelief and sarcasm, querying why these eight thousand mighty warriors were so eager to volunteer for a New Mexico campaign but unwilling to offer their services to fight the rampaging Indians that the Texans were constantly demanding federal troops to quell. The apparent contradiction became a favorite theme of the Northern press. Southern newspapers displayed no particular interest in the reports of Texan volunteers. As to the impact of Texan military preparations on the fate of the Texas bill, a few reporters claimed that these reports might bestir Congress to pass the bill to avoid the threatened violence. Most newspaper reaction, however, argued that threats only hurt the bill's chances by convincing the North that the perverse Texans were blackmailing the Union.[18]

Whether the accounts of expedition-planning in Texas were true, as Southern radicals hoped, or tall Texan tales, as Northern extremists believed, the blocs that comprised the anti-compromise coalition had to devise one or more viable strategies that might effectively kill the Texas bill. Two of these potential strategies were ones that Southern radicals would have to attempt to implement without the aid of their Northern antislavery allies. Having one-fifth of the House members constantly calling for the yeas and nays was one such means of blocking a bill. Newspapers and Southern congressmen had discussed this possibility often, and some Southerners still advocated it to defeat the Texas and California bills or the military appropriation bills. This method had successfully stopped Doty's California bill in the House on February 18. However, given the poor attendance at and divided opinions within the recent Southern caucus, successful utilization of the one-fifth rule by Southern members alone in the House appeared increasingly unlikely. [19]

A similar strategy often favored by Southerners to delay bills was to use, or abuse, as some said, the five-minute rule on amendments. Under Rule 34, members were allowed only five minutes to explain and argue amendments, which they offered after debate on the bill had been officially closed. A minority at that stage could delay a bill with a continuous cycle of amendments and five-minute speeches. However, the efficacy of this rule for obstruction was negated by the House on August 13 and 14. The House Rules Committee, led by Democrat George Washington Jones of Tennessee, devised an amendment to the five-minute rule, which Jones introduced on August 13. The committee proposed to change the rule by permitting no more than ten minutes' debate on each amendment, five minutes for and five minutes against, and by forbidding the amendment to be withdrawn without unanimous consent of the House. Southern "ultras" Jacob Thompson of Mississippi and Samuel Inge of Alabama vehemently protested the alteration as an abridgement of a key defense mechanism of the minority and a virtual denial of the right to debate measures. All this was to no avail, however, as the pro-compromise bloc joined the Northern antislavery factions to adopt the rule change by a vote of 113 to 46 on August 14. Southern extremists were angered at the connivance of Southerners on the Rules Committee—Jones himself, Stephens of Georgia, and Kaufman of Texas.[20]

Northern men opposing the Texas bill had disliked constant calling of the yeas and nays or resorting to the renewal of amendments under the five-minute rule. Antislavery men did not want to appear too obviously accessories to strictly obstructionist methods ordinarily associated with proslavery Southerners. For a while Northern men in the anti–Texas bill bloc toyed with two ideas in which they might secure the acquiescence of their Southern radical confreres. One of these, concocted by an Ohio member, was rather bizarre and was the opposite of the scheme that Seward had attempted to involve Rusk in a few weeks earlier. The plan was for antislavery men to join Southerners in amending the Texas bill so that it granted Texas all the territory it claimed east of the Rio Grande but gave Texas no money. Such an amendment, if passed, would make the bill unacceptable to Northern moderates who opposed forcing New Mexico into Texas's clutches, and the North would then vote almost unanimously to defeat the bill—exactly what Northern and Southern "ultras" desired. In concept the scheme may have initially looked intriguing to the bill's enemies; but the antislavery men in reality could never vote for an amendment to divest New Mexico of all its settled and valuable lands, even simply to defeat the bill, without contradicting their oft-stated principles.[21]

Even more outlandish was a Northern ploy to induce their Southern radical friends to support passively the addition of the Wilmot Proviso to New Mexico Territory. Northern antislavery men dearly wanted to lock the Proviso onto New Mexico, and virtually all Southerners attested that such an eventuality would be so insulting to them that Southern men would withdraw from Congress and encourage their states to secede. Some Northern free-soilers believed that Southern extremists who desired disunion were not unwilling to see the Proviso pass Congress and would even assist its passage by making certain that they were absent when the vote on the Wilmot Proviso occurred in the House. However, few Southerners could support this tactic. Only five extremist Southern senators had not voted on the Proviso during Senate deliberations on the New Mexico bill, perhaps a test of the absenteeism idea. Most Southerners had so steadfastly resisted the Proviso that it was inconceivable to them to stop fighting it now. Failing to vote against the Proviso might prove a very quick path toward political oblivion.[22]

Actually, the Northern and Southern opponents of compromise and the Texas bill could never agree on a strategy in which the mutually exclusive views of each bloc on slavery came to the fore. Only one device emerged that promised a coordinated opposition by the Northern and Southern "ultras" with a good chance of success. This was the procedural move to commit the bill to the Committee of the Whole, from which it would never surface again. Compromise men feared this plan more than any other opposition scheme, for they knew that this one could indeed gather enough support to kill the bill and the overall settlement and thereby lead to disunion and war.[23]

Northern antislavery men were also attempting to sow division between the Northern and Southern wings of the pro-compromise bloc by promoting the rumor that once the Pearce bill had been approved, President Fillmore would revert to Taylor's nonaction policy on the territories or refuse to sign the New Mexico bill without the Proviso. Fillmore's lack of clear policy statements had left him open to such an implication. He certainly now favored the Pearce bill and popular sovereignty in New Mexico and had carefully avoided lending any color of executive approval to Hugh Smith's claim to be a "delegate" from New Mexico.[24]

To counter the Washington rumor, Fillmore's friends in Congress, the pro-compromise press, and various cabinet members worked to reassure congressmen that the president indeed favored the entire compromise. On August 14 and 15, respectively, Reps. George Ashmun of Massachusetts and William Duer of New York, both of whom were ranked among the president's close advisers, delivered speeches in Congress defending his message on Texas–New Mexico and also defending the Senate bill. Pro-compromise journalists and editors denied that the chief executive favored either the Wilmot Proviso or nonaction. When doubts persisted after the Democratic *Washington Union* also raised the Proviso fear, Secretary of State Webster, Secretary of the Navy William Graham, and Attorney General John J. Crittenden personally told numerous congressmen that the president and administration wanted all the bills passed. Doubts and suspicions remained, but these efforts helped convince some compromise men that Fillmore, at least, was not a Seward man and was a firm supporter of a complete settlement.[25]

One nemesis that the compromise men did not have to contend with for two weeks was Seward. For several days following the passage of the Pearce bill in the Senate, he tirelessly worked with House members to organize the North-South coalition against the bill. Seward was fanatically determined to defeat the Texas bill. Then, quite suddenly on August 14, he took a hasty two-week departure from Washington for New York and Newport. He left so hurriedly that he did not even have a chance to forewarn Thurlow Weed of his coming. Exhaustion was given out by Seward's friends as the reason for his journey; but even if exhausted, Seward would have never left Washington as the contest over the Texas bill neared its climax in the House.[26] What really accounted for Seward's trip was that one of his intrigues had caught up with him.

Seward had reneged on his promise to Senator Rusk to have a ten-million-dollar appropriation to satisfy the Texas creditors introduced in the House after Rusk had drawn it up. Instead, Seward had voted against Pearce's ten-million-dollar bill and was struggling assiduously against the bill among House members. When Rusk learned of Seward's Janus-faced behavior, he challenged him with the facts of his duplicity and threatened to publicly expose it. Seward offered Rusk only a lame, legalistic excuse for opposing the Pearce bill in the Senate and claimed that reports of his activities against the bill in the House were exaggerations for which he blamed President Fillmore and his friends. Seward even argued to Rusk that he had been promoting the Pearce bill in the House! Rusk believed none of this, but, since Seward said he was going North for health reasons, Rusk refrained from publicly denouncing him. Several reporters learned the details, however, and published versions of it in their newspapers. Besides that, a few Northern Whigs later cited Seward's willingness to pay ten million dollars to Texas as a rationale to support their votes for the Pearce bill.[27]

Another key personage also vanished from Washington in mid-August—Georgia Whig Alexander Stephens. He would be absent in Georgia for the duration of the struggle over the Texas, California, and territories bills. Stephens's departure on the morning of August 19 was somewhat enigmatic but nonetheless explainable. He was disappointed by the defeat of the Omnibus, and his position had become increasingly difficult. He sincerely favored a workable compromise, but had written and spoken of the Texas issue in memorable phrases that made many of his fellow politicians and the public at large classify him as a fire-eater. Given the seeming contradiction between his rhetoric and his actual support of compromise, it was quite understandable for Stephens to decide to escape from Washington. His friend Toombs remained at the capital; the radical sentiments of his speeches had not become so notorious that they prevented Toombs from actively working and voting for the compromise bills. Stephens may have also wished to return to Georgia just then to offer a counterpoint to the radical Southern rally soon to be held at Macon. Two actions by Stephens before he left Washington well indicated his desire for the settlement to pass. First, he did not leave until after the House had amended the five-minute rule to prevent its use as a technique of extremist Southern obstruction. Stephens was a member of the Rules Committee, which recommended the amendment. Second, Stephens made certain that the absence of his votes for the compromise would be offset by the absence of a Northern member known to be adamantly opposed to the bills; Stephens paired with Chauncey Cleveland of Connecticut, a fervently antislavery Democrat.[28]

On that same Monday on which Stephens began his homeward journey came the first serious moves in the House to set a definite time to take up consideration of the Senate bills. First, William J. Brown, an Indiana Democrat, offered a resolution to make the Senate bills a special order for the next day and from then until disposed of, the order of the bills being New Mexico, Texas boundary, California, and finally Utah. Brown had been discussing the resolution with radical Southern Whig Thomas Clingman of North Carolina immediately prior to his presentation of it, and it reflected Southern desire to ensure that New Mexico Territory was organized without the Wilmot Proviso before any other subject of the compromise was considered. Since objection was made to his resolution, Brown therefore moved a suspension of House rules so that the resolution might be taken up immediately instead of having to "lie over" until a later time. This failed to secure even a majority, much less the two-thirds vote required for suspension. Southern Whigs and many of the Southern Democrats constituted the bulk of those favoring the proposition. The most extreme Southern Democrats, who opposed the Senate bills no matter what their order, joined the great majority of Northern men in opposing Brown's move.

This was immediately followed by Rep. George Ashmun's (W-Mass.) motion to suspend the rules in order to immediately consider his resolution to make the Senate bills the special order of the House beginning the next day. His resolution provided that the Senate bills would be considered in the order in which they stood on the speaker's table—Utah, Texas boundary, California, and then New Mexico. Since the Utah bill would have to be referred to the Committee of the Whole, Ashmun's resolution would give the Texas boundary bill priority of consideration in the House, in accordance with the desires of the administration and pro-compromise members. But confusion and distrust still prevailed. Northern anti-compromise forces wanted California statehood to have precedence. Many Northern Democrats still chafed at Whig leadership. Southerners, both moderates and radicals, feared that the order of bills under

Ashmun's resolution would leave New Mexico open to the Wilmot Proviso or nonaction once the others passed. Southerners remained wary of President Fillmore and felt that Ashmun spoke for the administration. When the vote, again requiring two-thirds for approval, was taken, it ended in a 94 to 94 tie and thus the motion failed. The pattern on this roll call was significant, for this was the first of what would become many House roll calls on which the Northern and Southern extremists voted together, in this case against Ashmun's move; the pattern otherwise was not so clear. (See Appendix D, vote A.)[29]

Unnoticed by reporters at the time on the Ashmun resolution roll call was the vote by Rep. Volney Howard of Texas in favor of the motion. Howard had been the first Southern Democrat in the House to condemn Fillmore's message, and among the Texas congressional delegation Howard was assumed to be the only one opposed to the Pearce bill. On August 9 he had dispatched a telegram to Governor Bell attacking the bill and relaying news that the president was reinforcing the New Mexico garrison up to a total strength of 2,200. Howard declared that Texas should send at least 3,000 in its expeditionary force and expressed to Bell his belief that aid to Texas from other slaveholding states would be forthcoming. But the dispatch also revealed a certain degree of vacillation and wavering on Howard's part, for, even though he then promised to oppose the bill, he admitted to Bell that the Pearce bill did offer Texas more than the Omnibus had done. His vote for Ashmun's motion revealed his gradual transition to a position in support of the Senate bill's settlement of the boundary and debt difficulties. Howard kept quiet about his change of heart, but he voted consistently in favor of compromise on subsequent Pearce bill roll calls. Only near the end of the voting did his colleagues appear to recognize his conversion to the compromise plan.[30]

Other Texans in Washington were also sending communications back to the Lone Star. Col. George T. Howard returned home on August 21, after a three-week sojourn at the capital, bearing letters from Senator Rusk and former Texas governor Wood. Rusk was well aware of Texas's volatility on the Santa Fe issue and was anxious to encourage the leadership within the state to pursue a course of "prudence" and "wisdom," even as they firmly defended the rights of Texas. Rusk praised Fillmore and expressed confidence that the administration sincerely desired to make Texas a "liberal and honorable" settlement. These were Rusk's sentiments in two similar letters, both dated August 21, one addressed to Governor Bell and the other to Texas state representative Guy M. Bryan of Brazoria, the noted extremist leader in the Texas House. Rusk added to his letter to Bell an admonition against any "intemperance"—that is, an invasion of New Mexico—that might embarrass Texas's friends and encourage its enemies. Former governor Wood wrote to his former secretary, Washington D. Miller, in a letter detailing the pros and cons of the Pearce bill, with a definite bias in favor of the bill. The gist of his argument was that the Senate bill paid the Texas debt and retained for the state a vast, undeveloped domain of great economic potential. If Texas chose the military alternative, Wood believed that Texas would be able to conquer New Mexico but at the costs of gaining an alien, resentful, and rebellious population, of being forced to incur perpetual military expenditures to keep the New Mexicans subjugated, and of receiving no federal relief from the state's debt burdens.[31]

While these Texans were promoting peaceful resolution of the crisis, the Fillmore administration assessed how best to influence House votes for the "peace" bills in Congress. The Ashmun resolution vote on August 19 at least served notice that a sizable bloc was eager to get to the matter of the Senate bills. The administration may have derived some comfort from other signs too. The trouble-making Seward was absent. The popular desire for a peaceful settlement of the crisis was growing stronger. Boston had recently elected pro-compromise Whig Samuel Eliot to Winthrop's former seat in the House by a sizable margin, and Eliot was expected to exercise a persuasive influence for the bill among wavering Northern members.[32]

The failure of two radical conventions, one Northern and one Southern, to generate any national interest, aside from torrents of abuse and ridicule, undoubtedly pleased the administration and compromisers in general. The less widely publicized of the two was a convention of fugitive slaves and abolitionists, organized by Gerrit Smith, that met at Cazenovia, New York, on August 21 to 22 to register their protest against the proposed fugitive slave law. None of this meeting's resolutions touched on the territorial issues or bills. The Cazenovia Convention stimulated some very negative editorials and appalled Southerners but attracted little other attention; at least it had not been planned as a, massive public gathering. A "mass meeting," however, was exactly how the promoters of the Macon Convention of August 22 had advertised this gathering of Southern "ultras." Meeting organizers predicted fifty thousand attendees, but only a few hundred delegates showed up. Disunionists Robert Barnwell Rhett of South Carolina and William Yancey of Alabama, along with lesser fire-eaters, were present to stir their followers, and Rhett recommended temporary secession as a Southern remedy. The convention endorsed resolutions similar to those of the Nashville Convention. All but the most committed radicals labeled the whole affair an unmitigated fiasco. Some editorialists lumped Cazenovia and Macon together as insignificant demonstrations by opposite extremes of the lunatic fringe.[33]

To compound the embarrassment endured by Georgia "ultras" in the Macon failure, Alexander Stephens a week later attracted crowds as large or larger than those at the radical convention for his speeches at Warrenton on August 29 and at Crawfordville on September 3. In these addresses, while he reiterated his oft-stated position that the South would and should aid Texas if a conflict between that state and the U.S. erupted over the boundary, Stephens placed himself squarely in favor of the Pearce bill and compromise in general. He offered an important counterweight for peaceful resolution against the proponents of dissolution in Georgia at a pivotal stage in the crisis.[34]

Ongoing public concern over the Texas–New Mexico situation and its potential to spark Southern secession also strengthened the Fillmore administration's faith that it could help engineer House passage of the Pearce bill. Congressional compromisers and the president's advisers wished to use public fear of the imminence of bloodshed or disunion as a tool to pass the bill before the fatal step was actually taken. News of Governor Bell's message to the Texas Legislature recommending the raising of volunteers for a Santa Fe expedition and that legislature's consideration of using the Texas school fund to help finance it brought reactions of horror from some and more editorials of sarcastic ridicule or stubborn defiance among Northerners. Francis Grund, in several of his newspaper columns, speculated that the disunionist Rhett had dispatched his agents to Texas and other states and that Rhett's agents from South Carolina were then in Austin perpetrating their evil designs. In reality no South Carolina agents came to Austin, but, in the paranoia of the times, many people undoubtedly believed such press reports.[35]

Newspaper accounts of the dispatch of federal troops to New Mexico and of requisitions on federal arsenals for weaponry and ammunition for these forces constantly reminded people of the danger of real conflict. Reports of turmoil within New Mexico itself heightened feelings of uncertainty and instability. The demand by Lieutenant Governor Alvarez that Colonel Munroe relinquish his civil authority to the new "state" government impressed many people as the height of arrogance and presumption on Alvarez's part. Northern public support for the statehood movement in New Mexico diminished appreciably, encouraging the pro-compromise men to feel that their plan of territorial government would meet with success as the only proper government to grant the New Mexicans.[36]

The negative side to all this, as the Fillmore administration understood, was that Texas bluster and Southern fire-eating might swing angered House members against the Pearce bill. In that event Northerners might renew their interest in granting statehood to New Mexico. It therefore became imperative to the administration for the Texas and New Mexico bills to pass Congress before New Mexico's "senator-elect," Richard Weightman, arrived in Washington with an official copy of the proposed state constitution. The Fillmore administration anticipated that Weightman would probably be in Washington during the first week in September. Weightman had left Santa Fe in mid-July and had reached St. Louis on August 23. He telegraphed a letter to President Fillmore from St. Louis on August 26, primarily to complain at length about the refusal of Colonel Munroe to recognize the Alvarez government. Weightman also sent a copy of the letter to Manuel Alvarez and expressed his uncertainty about New Mexico's chances for admission as a state. He was nevertheless satisfied with the stance of both Taylor and Fillmore in relation to the Texan threat to conquer New Mexico, which Weightman believed impossible. He told Alvarez that he was confident that President Fillmore would quickly repudiate Colonel Munroe's actions.[37]

Secretary of State Daniel Webster held a meeting of the cabinet members at his home on August 24 to evaluate the situation. The cabinet had worked together harmoniously on the compromise, and admired the president's qualities as a leader. Fillmore and Webster seemed to have a perfect understanding of their respective roles in promoting the settlement. Fillmore needed to appear the aloof executive, as far above the congressional fray as possible, advising Congress as he had done on August 6 but leaving its members to work out the details without undue executive influence. Webster, the "premier," became the president's chief strategist and liaison in dealing with Congress, a task he performed very energetically.[38]

At the meeting on the 24th, the cabinet concluded that all of the compromise bills would pass comfortably, after the civil and diplomatic appropriation bill then being discussed in the House was passed. That constituted an unrealistically positive assessment in regard to the Texas–New Mexico issue. Newspaper correspondents who analyzed the potential House vote achieved no consensus in their reports. Some predicted a close vote one way or the other, while some believed the Texas bill or a "little Omnibus" would succeed or fail by a wide margin. Uncertainty continued as probably the most prevalent attitude, but, during the days when the House was occupied with the civil and diplomatic appropriation bill, several newspapers reported that the Texas bill was daily losing support because of Texas's apparent belligerency. This trend was enhanced on August 25 with the publication in Washington of a telegraphic dispatch from New Orleans describing the very negative reaction of people in Galveston when news of Senate passage of the Pearce bill reached the Texas port.[39] This, combined with the news of Weightman's progress toward Washington, must have sounded new notes of alarm within administration and pro-compromise circles.

No matter what the chances, the administration pushed as hard as possible for the compromise and utilized every available tool to influence House members, with Webster coordinating the whole effort. Daniel Webster was suffering the aches and pains associated with aging, but the undiminished intellectual force of his arguments, accentuated by his massive head, piercing gaze, and legendary "Black Dan" scowl, could be very persuasive—and intimidating—in the Capitol lobbies. He worked closely with George Ashmun of Massachusetts, the administration leader in the House. William Graham and John Crittenden employed their influence with members. General Scott tried to convince some anti-slavery Whigs to support the Pearce bill as a matter of loyalty to a Whig administration. Compromise men telegraphed House absentees of similar persuasion to hasten back to Washington. Letters advocating the bill were sent out from Washington to numerous presses, and Webster himself contributed an editorial entitled "The Important Week" to the August 26 issue of the *National Intelligencer*.[40]

To supplement rational argument, federal patronage was brought into play. Southerners were pleased when the president responded to their entreaties and offered the Interior Department to Charles Jenkins of Georgia. When he declined, another Southerner, Alexander H. H. Stuart of Virginia, accepted the position. New Hampshire representative James Wilson had announced that he was soon resigning his seat in order to emigrate to California. The announcement struck most in Washington as a thinly veiled "wanted" advertisement for a federal appointment in California, and it was understood that he received such a promise from the administration. Not surprisingly, this Whig elected on strongly free-soil principles transformed into a consistently pro-compromise member of the House, whose votes excited derisive laughter among his former antislavery associates. Another representative was said to have secured the promise of a federal appointment for his son. Rep. William Duer of New York warned other House members that they could expect no control over appointments, especially post offices, in their districts unless they supported the administration's position on the compromise. Fillmore withdrew some of Taylor's postal appointments that had not yet been confirmed by the Senate, and requests by congressmen for even minor post offices were put on hold. These actions reportedly helped in converting some New York Whig members to the Pearce bill.[41]

The Texas bondholder lobby also worked vigorously for the bill. Their activities are somewhat shadowy, although Northern and Southern "ultras" believed that bondholders plied congressmen with Texas scrip at bargain prices with the assurance that the value would rise dramatically if the Pearce bill passed. Allegations abounded in the letters and newspapers of the time, but no substantiation has ever been produced to support the charge that House votes were actually bought through Texas bonds. The bondholders possessed an obvious interest in promoting the settlement in Congress, for the bond values would certainly rise if the bill was successful. At the beginning of 1850, the value was $.05–.06 on the dollar; on August 12 the value stood at $.75 on the dollar. The market value rose and fell daily based on the predicted fortunes of the bill. Values were falling toward the end of August as many lost faith that House votes could be found to pass it. It is possible that some congressmen were "purchased" with Texas bonds, but other factors—the fate of the Union and administration pressure—appear to have had a much more decisive impact. Undoubtedly some congressmen owned Texas bonds, but, even in the cases of those who did, their personal financial considerations may not have been the primary motivating factor in determining which way they would vote on the Pearce bill. It can be argued that the bond issue actually lost votes for the bill on balance because of the anger of Texas's friends in the South over the five-million-dollar reserve clause.[42]

Once the civil and diplomatic appropriation passed on August 27, the stage was set for the beginning of the titanic House struggle over the Texas bill. Both Henry Clay and William Seward returned to Washington at the end of August to advise their partisans in the House. A sense of excitement permeated the hall on Wednesday, August 28. Unfortunately for the members, the weather, having become milder in recent days, suddenly reverted back to its usual summertime oppressiveness. At least the news from Texas had improved; a newly arrived Texan in Washington now reported that an overwhelming majority of the Texas population favored the Pearce bill settlement. A similar report from a Galveston paper arrived a few days later. Pro-compromise forces could now derive some hope that their bill, if passed by Congress, would receive a favorable reception in the Lone Star state.[43]

After some preliminaries on the 28th, the Senate bills came up in the regular order of business, Utah having priority among them. George Ashmun appeared to be managing the pro-compromise forces amidst the general bedlam. Territories committee chairman Linn Boyd moved immediately that the bill, with its appropriation, be referred to the Committee of the Whole, and his motion passed without a division. Charles Sweetser, anti-compromise Ohio Democrat, moved to resolve the House into Committee of the Whole to consider the Utah bill, but only a minority, nearly all Southerners, supported him on a roll-call vote. This cleared the way for the consideration of the Texas bill after a few minor bills were quickly dispatched. Following the first reading of the Pearce bill (S. 307), fire-eater Samuel Inge (D-Ala.), apparently without consulting anyone, invoked the obscure, rarely used House Rule 116, which stipulated that the House could reject an entire bill directly subsequent to its first reading. Douglas's friend John McClernand (D-Ill.) attacked Inge's "test" of the bill, and the House seconded McClernand's move of the previous question to shut off debate on Inge's motion. The shock value of Inge's motion wore off as the House voted down the move 168 to 34, with only some antislavery radicals and Southern "ultras" joining in support of Inge. (See Appendix D, vote B.) The bill was then read a second time. Many members then competed for the floor in what one observer termed an "indescribably tumultuous scene." Speaker Cobb, undoubtedly by prearrangement, chose to recognize only Linn Boyd among the competitors. Boyd proposed, as expected, the "little Omnibus," moving to add the Senate's New Mexico and Utah territories bills to the boundary-debt measure. Richard Meade (D-Va.), another leader of the Southern extremists, objected that the amendment violated House Rule 55, which prohibited the addition of subject matter different from the original bill and forbade incorporation of bills then pending before the House.

Speaker Cobb ruled the amendment in order on the grounds that any subject relative to the Mexican cession was germane to the bill and that Boyd's amendment differed from the pending Senate bills because Boyd had dropped sections relating to public buildings in the territories. Anti-compromise Robert Schenck (W-Ohio) appealed the chair's decision, but the House sustained Cobb by a 122 to 84 vote; Schenck and other antislavery Northerners provided nearly the entire minority vote and were rather despondent about their prospects at this point. Linn Boyd continued to hold the floor while the House clerk proceeded with the reading of his lengthy amendment, and he refused to yield as various members attempted to interpose in order to add their amendments. Ultimately, when he believed that a consensus in favor of adjournment existed, Boyd gave way for that motion, which carried easily. The day's session ended favorably for the compromise, but many of those who had voted not to kill the measure still opposed many of its features. Many expected that California would soon be added to the bill and the whole former Omnibus driven through the House.[44]

On Thursday, August 29, action on the Texas bill opened with Southern Democratic radicals attempting a delay by raising points of order. Armistead

Burt of South Carolina tried to move a commitment of the bill to the Committee of the Whole, but Speaker Cobb ruled it out of order since Boyd was still entitled to the floor. Burt appealed, and Ashmun moved to table it, which the House did by a roll call of 154 to 54. The antislavery-proslavery coalition formed the minority. (See Appendix D, vote C.) Linn Boyd, who ordinarily did not speak at length, then vigorously and impressively defended the popular sovereignty or nonintervention principle as the only workable solution to the territorial slavery question, a solution that he said the South could constitutionally live with. To appease those who objected to inclusion of so much in a single bill, Boyd then withdrew the Utah provisions of his amendment.

Now that Boyd had finished, Thomas Clingman, the only Southern Whig in the anti-compromise bloc, offered an amendment to divide California into two territories at approximately the Missouri Compromise line, with the southern part designated as Colorado. Over objection that the amendment was not germane to the bill, Cobb ruled that it was on the same ground that he had ruled the Boyd amendment germane. Charles Allen, Massachusetts Free-Soiler, appealed this ruling but the House tabled the appeal by 129 to 67, with only the antislavery men and a few other Northerners voting on Allen's side. Clingman then presented the House with a rousing defense of the prospects for slave labor in the agriculture of his suggested territory of Colorado. Ashmun stated his willingness to accept either separate bills or an Omnibus and, to expedite action, moved the previous question. Ashmun, however, made no attempt to add California statehood to the Boyd package; many had anticipated that he would, but Ashmun and his friends had encountered a general hostility to the idea among House members they broached the subject to in discussions the night before. Anyway, the House refused to second the call for the previous question. A majority of the members still wanted an opportunity to make speeches or otherwise debate the issue, especially Northerners who disliked the Texas–New Mexico boundary limits in the Pearce bill. Some representatives who desired compromise simply revolted against being dragooned into quickly supporting a new Omnibus at this point.

After the failure of Ashmun's move, pro-compromise Democrat John McClernand of Illinois moved to commit the bill to the Committee of the Whole and moved the previous question. McClernand, continually advised by Senator Douglas, may have taken this action simply to force the enemies of the bill to show their hand. Free-Soiler Joseph Root of Ohio immediately moved to amend McClernand's motion by adding instructions that the Wilmot Proviso be grafted onto the bill. Root declared that his purpose in this was to "smoke out the doughfaces" among Northerners. The House adjourned just before 4 P.M., with the various motions and amendments still pending and the antislavery men more hopeful than on the previous day.[45]

Unfortunately for the compromisers desirous of a speedy settlement, several days of little progress were to follow. Advocates of settlement perceived that every day's delay only strengthened the ability of the opposition, especially with the calculating Seward now constantly advising them, to devise stratagems that would possibly kill the compromise. Dilatoriness in the House also led Texas bond interests to lose confidence, and the value of Texas bonds began to fall rapidly during the first days of September. The arrival of another Texan in Washington predicting that a Texan expedition would leave for New Mexico on October 1 did nothing to enhance House friendliness toward Texas or the bill. Delay, emotions, and uncertainty frayed members' nerves nearly to the breaking point.[46]

The main problem was that a number of House members wished no final action until they had edified their constituents with set speeches on the momentous issues. Much time on August 29 itself, on Friday, August 30, and on Monday, September 2, was consumed by these rhetorical displays, to the utter frustration of those who saw peace and Union imperiled. David Outlaw (W-N.C.) likened it to Nero's fiddling while Rome burned.[47] On Saturday, August 31, and Monday, September 2, the House became occupied with entirely extraneous matters.

Procedural moves of importance took place on September 2 and 3. On September 2 the House voted without a division for a motion by Linn Boyd to make the Pearce bill the special order for the next day and each subsequent day at noon until the fate of the bill was decided. Compromise advocates interpreted this as a good sign. Then, on September 3, radical Southern-rights defender John R. J. Daniel (D-N.C.) moved to substitute for Root's Proviso instructions to the Committee of the Whole an opposite set that would force the committee to nullify any laws prohibiting slavery in any territory. Following Daniel's and other speeches, Tennessee Whig Christopher Williams won the competition for the floor. Ironically, Boyd himself, with a vested interest in the bill and his amendment, was acting as speaker pro tem while Cobb took a much-needed break from duties he described as "extremely onerous." John McClernand asked Williams's indulgence to allow him to make an "explanation." The "explanation" proved to be McClernand's decision to withdraw his move to commit the bill to the Committee of the Whole, thus negating both Root's and Daniel's proposed instructions. Boyd naturally ruled McClernand's withdrawal to be in order. Williams then moved the previous question to cut off further amendments to the bill outside those already offered. Northern men, who had anticipated a clear-cut vote on the Proviso for electioneering purposes, and Southerners anxious to record their votes for Daniel's amendment were equally furious at McClernand's ploy. An irate Joshua Giddings (FS-Ohio) demanded that Williams also relinquish the floor to allow him by way of "explanation" to renew the motion to commit, but Williams refused. However, the House then refused to second the call for the previous question by a 92 to 76 teller vote.

The enemies of the bill were then handed a golden opportunity by one of the compromisers in a move that betrayed the laxity of discipline among the various elements favoring the settlement. Robert M. McLane (D-Md.), a strong supporter of the Pearce bill even though he also defended Texas's claim to the entire length of the Rio Grande, moved to commit the bill and amendments to the Committee of the Whole and demanded the previous question thereon. McLane intended it as a test vote and said he intended to vote against his own motion. But he was also playing both sides of the issue—if the House defeated his motion, the Pearce bill as it was would benefit; if the House approved his motion, the bill could possibly be amended in the Committee of the Whole to grant Texas the more favorable boundary that McLane desired. Compromisers shuddered at this move by one who professed to advocate their position, for most supporters of settlement considered commitment a virtual death sentence for the bill. Compromisers also shuddered because Governor Bell's belligerent message to his legislature was published in Washington that day. With McLane's motion pending, the House adjourned at about 4 P.M.[48]

The following three days, September 4–6, were the most intensely exciting of the entire congressional session. Many senators and cabinet members were present and spectators packed the galleries. Parliamentary tactics and the ability to marshal a majority of votes would now determine the fate of the Pearce bill, the other measures, and possibly the Union itself. At least the weather abruptly turned pleasantly cooler and made the working conditions in the chamber more comfortable. A further factor, which may have eased some congressmen's fears that Texans had abandoned moderation, was the *National Intelligencer's* reprinting on September 4 of a *Houston Democratic Telegraph* editorial of August 21 that condemned threats of violence by both the federal government and Texas and strongly urged Congress to pass the Pearce bill, a measure it described as "entirely acceptable" to Texas. Of twenty-eight roll calls taken in the House during these three days, twenty-three of them displayed the unity of Northern and Southern radicals against the settlement. These roll calls show a number of representatives, who had been voting in previous days, now casting no votes. David Wilmot, the

Pennsylvania Free-Soiler, paired with William Hamilton, a pro-compromise Maryland Democrat. Elbridge G. Spaulding, anti-compromise New York Whig, paired with Alexander Evans, a Maryland Whig supporting the compromise. Others, some of whom undoubtedly paired but left no record with whom the pair was, included: George Ashmun (W-Mass.); William H. Bissell (D-Ill.); Rufus Goodenow (W-Maine); Moses Hampton (W-Pa.); Andrew Hay (W-N.J.); Elijah Risley (W-N.Y.); and Amos Wood (D-Ohio).[49]

During September 4–6 the pro- and anti-compromise blocs remained rather well defined and cohesive and consistently antagonistic to each other in the voting. Appendix D presents the roll-call voting data on these and the few earlier roll calls of the same type and also the indexes of cohesion and likeness for the pro- and anti-compromise blocs as a whole and for subgroups thereof. As the indexes demonstrate, the voting did not follow either party or sectional lines. The only party bloc with a high degree of cohesion, as a whole, was the Free-Soil group. Within sections, the major parties split fairly evenly on both sides of the compromise. The only exception was the Southern Whig bloc, all but one of whom vigorously supported the Pearce bill. Even the one dissenter from that bloc, Thomas Clingman of North Carolina, cast more votes during these three days on the pro-compromise side than on the anti-compromise side. Southern Whigs who favored the Pearce bill achieved a higher degree of cohesion than even the Free-Soilers, whom they voted against almost entirely. No members of these two blocs cast more than a few votes alien to the bloc pattern.

The greatest confusion and inconsistency appeared among the Northern Whigs, whether pro- or anti-compromise. This situation reflected the intense anxiety under which Northern Whigs voted. Most of them had earlier assumed strong ground for the Wilmot Proviso and against slavery. Against these stands, however, were the influence of a new Whig administration for compromise, public pressure for a peaceful settlement, and the threat of bloodshed and civil war if no such settlement passed the House. Of Northern Whigs in the pro-compromise bloc, several cast anti-compromise votes during the earlier stages of the struggle but then began casting their votes in favor of the Pearce bill. Northern Whigs of the anti-compromise bloc who cast numerous pro-compromise votes appeared to do it in a more random fashion. The most remarkable voting pattern of all members in this group was that of James Meacham of Vermont, who cast the great majority of his votes on the pro-compromise side but at the end of the contest voted to defeat the Texas–New Mexico bill. Meacham was possibly an extreme case of those Northern Whigs who would do anything to support the compromise bill except vote for its passage.

Northern and Southern Democratic factions voted in fairly consistent patterns, whether pro- or anti-compromise. Few members of these Democratic groups defected from their respective bloc voting pattern more than a few times. The statistics that stand out most concerning the Democrats are the high degree of likeness achieved by the radical Southern Democrats with the antislavery Free-Soil, Northern Whig, and Northern Democratic factions opposed to compromise. Not only did these opposing groups of extremists vote together on roll calls, but on teller votes Northern and Southern "ultras" would sometimes parade through the tellers arm in arm to display the unity of their coalition.[50]

The Pearce bill proceedings on September 4 opened with haggling by Root against McLane's right to the floor, before the House finally seconded McLane's move for the previous question by 99 to 90 on a teller vote. Confusion and noise then ensued, and the speaker refused to conduct further business until better order prevailed. Antislavery Ohio Democrat Joseph Cable moved to table the bill and amendments; the House rejected this by a roll-call vote of 169 to 30, with only a few Southern extremists joining the Free-Soilers and some Northern Whigs for the move. (See Appendix D, vote D.) After more disorder, the House voted 133 to 68 to put the main question—McLane's motion; antislavery Northerners constituted the minority.

As the roll was then called on McLane's move to commit, it became obvious to the bewildered compromise forces that the motion would pass by a margin of 12 to 15 votes. Numerous moderates were unconvinced either that a "little Omnibus" was essential or that the Committee of the Whole would become the bill's graveyard. They resented keeping in step to the particular drumbeat of Boyd and Cobb. These moderates believed everyone should have a chance to have their amendments voted on and felt that under the new version of the five-minute rule they could stop debate on amendments after a short time. The danger in this, as the more zealous defenders of the bill pointed out, was that one or more amendments might pass in the Committee of the Whole that would effectively destroy the bill's chances. Therefore, the bill's friends frantically exhorted members to change votes before the final result was announced. These exertions were able to reduce the announced majority in favor of McLane's motion to 101 to 99. The "ultras" beamed with delight. The noise level rose again and various members badgered Cobb with procedural questions, but the speaker masterfully remained in control of the situation. Cobb, obviously by prearrangement, kept his gaze fixed on Hiram Walden, a pro-compromise Democrat from New York, for some minutes until Walden indicated his willingness to make a motion, and then Cobb obliged him with recognition. Walden moved to reconsider the previous vote. Root moved to table Walden's motion. Confusion reigned in the hall and the roll call, when taken on Root's motion, stood at 103 to 102. An unusual silence intervened before Speaker Cobb saved the bill by voting "No." The vote was thus tied, and Root's move failed. Walden's motion to reconsider then passed on a roll call of 104 to 98, as three pro-compromise members entered the chamber in time to support the move. The vote recurred on McLane's motion to commit—in an atmosphere of "breathless anxiety," according to one correspondent—but it failed by a vote of 103 to 101. All four of the roll calls relative to McLane's motion matched the compromise bloc squarely against the anti-compromise bloc, with a few members changing from one side to the other. Among the notable shifts toward the pro-compromise side on these roll calls were: Walter Underhill and Hiram Walden (W-N.Y.); John C. Mason and Richard H. Stanton (D-Ky.); and Hugh Haralson (D-Ga.). One congressman, Robert W. Johnson (D-Ark.), altered from the pro-compromise to the anti-compromise position. (See Appendix D, votes E, F, G, and H.)

The House followed the contest over McLane's motion by dispatching Clingman's California amendment by a 130 to 69 roll call against it. Only Southerners favored it. The same fate was then accorded a move to table the bill by William Ashe, a North Carolina radical; his motion failed by 141 to 61, with the extremist coalition in the minority. The House floor buzzed with so many private conversations that Cobb momentarily halted the proceedings. Linn Boyd's amendment to add New Mexico Territory to the Texas bill now came up and was rejected 106 to 98, as enough waverers joined the "ultra" phalanx to defeat the measure. Southern radicals, whose glum faces only shortly before reflected feelings of impending defeat, suddenly took cheer. Without the Boyd amendment, everybody now realized that the bill was dead. After another flurry of procedural wrangling and motions, Boyd moved an adjournment that the House refused 128 to 71. Numerous moderates helped the Northern and Southern radicals form the majority against Boyd's move. Some Northerners were still angry at McClernand's move the previous day that denied them a direct vote on the Wilmot Proviso. The last roll call of the day occurred on whether to engross the Pearce bill itself for a third reading. Many moderates such as Boyd himself deserted the bill and helped the extremists to defeat it 126 to 80. (See Appendix D, votes I, J, K, and L.) Great competition to be recognized by Speaker Cobb ensued, and Cobb recognized Boyd, much to the consternation of antislavery men who thought it amazing that amid all the confusion the speaker should see only Linn Boyd. Boyd moved to reconsider the previous vote and refused to yield the floor except for a motion to adjourn, which was soon forthcoming and to which the members readily agreed just after 4 P.M.[51]

The Pearce bill clung very precariously to life. Many of its adherents remained undaunted, ready to renew the battle the next day. Thomas L. Harris (D-Ill.) predicted that the bill would come forth like Lazarus from the tomb. Banker and Texas bond dealer W. W. Corcoran was still confident. Others became panicky and willing to settle for less than they had demanded previously; Howard of Texas even intimated that Texas would be willing to settle for the original Omnibus boundary line, if no better could be gotten, to make the bill more attractive to Northerners. A correspondent of the *Richmond Republican* (probably Francis Grund) even seemed to despair of any hope for the bill: "The dark deed is done! The fiend of Disunion is let loose!! . . . Satan with his imps is let loose among the majority of this House." Southern "ultras," on the other hand, cheerfully anticipated the final defeat of the bill. When a *Washington Union* reporter enquired of them if they had no fear of collision and bloodshed, several replied "Not at all" and declared that Texas would now be able to take possession of all the land it claimed by marching its regiments to Santa Fe.[52]

After an evening of discussions and meetings, the House reassembled on September 5 in an atmosphere charged with high emotion and taut suspense. The galleries were once again choked with spectators. Secretary Webster personally lobbied members to support the bill. Numerous senators were present, with Seward actively rallying the Northern opposition. Linn Boyd retained the floor, moved the previous question on his motion to reconsider the vote on the third reading, and refused to yield the floor. Inge of Alabama moved to table the move to reconsider. Excited members left their seats and crowded toward the front so that they could hear what was transpiring. Speaker Cobb finally halted the proceedings until members resumed their seats. Inge's tabling motion failed 135 to 71, as the extremist coalition was handily beaten on the roll call. The House then seconded Boyd's demand for the previous question and next voted 131 to 75 to reconsider the vote on the third reading.

Speaker Cobb again chose to recognize Boyd and give him the floor. A friend of Webster's, Joseph Grinnell (W-Mass.), immediately moved, with Boyd's leave, for the House to reconsider the vote on Boyd's "little Omnibus" amendment and demanded the previous question. A strongly anti-compromise Ohio Whig, Lewis D. Campbell, retaliated with a move to table Grinnell's motion, but a House roll call defeated Campbell's motion 108 to 96. The House seconded Grinnell's previous question move and then voted 106 to 99 to reconsider the vote on Boyd's amendment. Boyd held the floor again and refused to yield despite entreaties from Richard Meade of Virginia and other radicals. Cobb interrupted to order members back to their seats again. Boyd pointedly stated that he did not want to throw the bill open to amendments, which would, he felt, destroy it. Boyd attempted to prevent amendments by again calling for the previous question, but the House refused to second this move on a teller vote of 99 to 88.

With Boyd's amendment now open to alteration, Whig Robert Toombs of Georgia proposed an addition that would protect "life, liberty, and property" of U.S. citizens in New Mexico Territory and would provide that the U.S. Constitution and British Common Law, as it existed in the American colonies prior to July 4, 1776, be the exclusive laws of that territory in relation to slavery. After another pause in order to get members out of the aisles and back to their seats, Illinois Democrat "Long John" Wentworth moved to commit the bill to the Committee of the Whole with instructions to impose the Wilmot Proviso on all the Mexican cession east of California. Wentworth also proposed an instruction to move the Texas–New Mexico boundary eastward to the line of 102° west longitude. In order to secure Southern support for his motion, Wentworth also added instructions for the Committee of the Whole that were suggested to him by Southern members. One of these, by Volney Howard of Texas, would eliminate the five-million-dollar reserve clause that Texans disliked. Another, by Winfield Featherston of Mississippi, would confirm the boundary decreed by Texas in 1836. This mass of incongruous propositions led to a lengthy, confusing period of haggling over rules and procedure. Featherston then offered his Texas boundary instruction as a substitute for all the others and demanded the previous question. The House seconded this on a teller vote of 102 to 40 but then on a roll call voted down Featherston's proposal 128 to 72; Southerners provided the only votes in favor of the 1836 Texas-claimed boundary. The question then recurred on Wentworth's motion to commit with instructions, which would be virtually fatal to the bill if successful; the very act of commitment was more important to Wentworth than the instructions in this case. Speaker Cobb had earlier ruled that each of the separate instructions after the first could be voted on separately from the motion to commit with the first instruction (i.e., the Proviso). Southern radicals naturally believed that they might be able to load their demands onto the proposition without having to vote for the Proviso even if the Proviso instruction was finally included as part of the package sent to the Committee of the Whole. Southern extremists were as anxious to refer the Pearce bill and amendments to the Committee of the Whole as Wentworth was.

At this point Howell Cobb delivered the parliamentary master stroke of the session. Once Featherston's motion had been disposed of, Speaker Cobb changed his ruling on the divisibility of the motion to commit and instructions. House Rule 53 stated that a proposition could be divided only if it embraced subjects so substantively distinct from one another that each could stand independently. Cobb had already said that the motion to commit and the first instruction were not divisible since they depended on each other. Now, in an explanation of some length, Cobb reversed his decision of only a half hour before, that the other instructions might be voted on separately; his argument was that if the motion to commit with the first instruction was voted down, then the other instructions would necessarily also fall. Therefore the instructions subsequent to the first one could not stand independently, as specified in House Rule 53, and were not divisible from the motion to commit with the first instruction. Wentworth and the Southern radicals were simply dumbfounded by Cobb's interpretation, for it removed any chance that the Southerners would abet Wentworth's motion to commit; Southerners could not vote for their own propositions without also explicitly voting for the Proviso, which they would never do. According to one observer, a look of rage came over "Long John's" perspiring face. Inge of Alabama appealed Cobb's decision, but this move simply pitted the pro-compromise coalition against the radical coalition on a roll call of 101 to 86, upholding the speaker's decision. Numerous members laughed aloud at Wentworth's embarrassment. Cobb only added to Wentworth's stunned humiliation by patronizingly supporting his desperate requests to be allowed to withdraw his motion entirely. But that required unanimous consent, and those who relished Wentworth's predicament objected to his request. After more squabbling, Wentworth's motion was eliminated on a roll call of 119 to 80, with Northerners alone aligned with Wentworth. Cobb had saved the bill a second time.

The question now recurred on Toombs's amendment. Speaker Cobb ruled that this amendment was divisible, and the House without division adopted the first, very general, part of it. The second part, specifically concerning slavery in the territories, was then rejected on a roll call by 132 to 65, with Southerners alone favoring the amendment. With Toombs's small addition, Boyd's amendment once again came before the House, and this time the House manufactured a "little Omnibus" of the Texas and New Mexico bills by a roll call of 107 to 99. Several Southern members changed votes at the last instant to provide the margin of victory. The compromise forces won a majority over the extremes hostile to the bill, but the triumph proved short-lived. After rejecting moves by Inge to table the bill and adjourn, the roll call on the third reading of the bill proceeded amidst great uproar and confusion. Whigs John L. Taylor of Ohio and William Nelson of New York, plus two other New York Whigs, changed their votes against the third reading to votes in favor of it after the call of the roll ended. Three pro-compromise men, Edward Cabell (W-Fla.) and David Disney and Emery Potter (D-Ohio), held back their votes for the bill until Speaker Cobb began to announce the result. Many members demonstrated contempt for the last-minute changes and additions by hissing and laughing loudly. Compromisers hoped that enough New York and Pennsylvania men would change votes to save the bill, but it was not to be. The third reading was defeated 107 to 99. Volney Howard of Texas, who had voted to reject it because he still disdained the reserve clause, now concluded that the bill as it was was the only bill that could possibly pass and moved to reconsider the vote. Inge of Alabama moved to table Howard's motion, but Cobb ignored Inge's motion.

Speaker Cobb ruled that Howard's motion was not in order because the third reading had already been reconsidered once and, by House tradition, could not be reconsidered a second time. Howard appealed Cobb's decision. The House then adjourned just before 5 P.M. with the bill hanging by an even weaker thread than at adjournment the day before. A despairing David Outlaw (W-N.C.) wrote to his wife that "Faction rules the hour—passion has taken the place of reason."[53]

But all was not lost. Some believed that Cobb would reverse his ruling the next day and telegraphed that assumption to various cities. However, that would have placed the speaker in an extremely awkward position, since he had already reversed a ruling the previous day. Cobb simply did not want the onus of saving the compromise on his shoulders again, and therefore the compromisers assiduously went to work that evening to persuade members to vote for Howard's appeal the next day. Their basic argument was that the new bill was indeed a different one from the unadorned Pearce bill that had been lost on its third reading on September 4. This was now a Texas–New Mexico bill and entitled, on its own merits, to a reconsideration of its third-reading vote. Secretary of the Treasury Thomas Corwin met that evening with members from Ohio and other Western states to lobby for the bill. Whatever the arguments or inducements offered, the pro-bill group was convinced by 9 P.M. on September 5 that they had received enough pledges of vote changes to ensure victory for the compromise on September 6. Henry Clay remained uncertain on the morning of the 6th, although a reporter noticed a certain buoyancy in his gait as he strode toward the Capitol that day. Another correspondent observed the "cool and confident bearing" of the pro-compromise leaders on the floor of the House.[54]

Seward, Chase, Cass, Foote, and many other senators besides Clay were present on September 6, seated among the delegations of representatives. Antislavery men suspected that they were in for a bad day, and, as Joshua Giddings later termed it, they sat "sternly silent amid the moral pestilence which appeared to surround them."[55] Speaker Cobb chose to adhere to his ruling, but he also declared that the question of whether a second reconsideration was valid on the third reading of a bill amended since the first reconsideration was really a new question before the House. Cobb thus relinquished the decision to the vote of the House members themselves. Howard of Texas, who had originally intended to move an amendment to strike the five-million-dollar reserve clause, had, after discussions with friends of the bill, decided to forgo amendments. Instead he briefly defended his appeal and demanded the previous question thereon. William Duer, pro-compromise leader in New York's Whig delegation, tried to dissuade Howard from demanding the previous question, possibly so that the bill might be further amended. When Howard refused to budge, Duer moved to table Howard's appeal, which failed on a roll call of 122 to 79. Duer voted with the Northern and Southern extremist minority on the first vote of the day. A teller vote then seconded Howard's call for the previous question 102 to 57. The House next voted to overturn Cobb's ruling by a 124 to 82 roll call in favor of Howard's appeal. Howard retained the floor and moved the previous question on his motion to reconsider the third-reading vote. Once again the compromisers produced a decisive majority of 122 to 84 over the "ultra" coalition, and the third reading was granted a second chance. A hundred members or so clamored to get the floor, shouting "Mr. Speaker!" But Cobb was not about to let anything go awry at this stage in the proceedings, and he awarded the floor to Howard of Texas once more. Howard now moved to blanket the third reading itself with the previous question.

A frustrated antislavery Democrat from Ohio, Jonathan Morris, interrupted to urge the speaker to enforce the rule against unauthorized persons on the floor of the House. He specifically wished any Texas bondholders present to be relegated to the crowded galleries. Cobb replied that the rule would be enforced but then paid no further attention to Morris's request and went on with the business at hand. A teller vote of 103 to 91 seconded Howard's demand for the previous question. The next roll call took place on whether the main question—the third reading—should be taken then or left until the next day. The House voted 115 to 91 to take the vote that would decide the Texas–New Mexico bill's fate.

Noise in the House became deafening as the moment of climax approached. Repeated raps of the speaker's gavel and cries for "Order!" finally quelled the tumult. The roll call on the third reading then progressed amid "death-like stillness" on the floor and in the galleries above, according to the *Baltimore Patriot*'s correspondent. But excitement could not be long contained, and the din gradually resumed toward the end of the roll call. Nine representatives who cast votes for the third reading this time had voted against it the day before. Four were Northerners—Underhill and Schermerhorn (W-N.Y.), G. G. King (W-R.I.), and Whittlesey (D-Ohio). The other five were Southern Democrats—Howard of Texas, R. H. Stanton and Mason of Kentucky, and F. P. Stanton and Thomas of Tennessee. These five delayed voting until the roll had been called through, the other four waiting to see how Howard voted before they committed themselves. Brief applause from the galleries greeted Howard's "aye" vote. Some nervous representatives scurried to and fro, while most gathered in a great herd near the speaker's desk. Almost none remained in their seats. Some members changed their votes after the roll was finished, and others were reportedly prepared to do so if necessary to rescue the bill. Once all the votes and changes were in, the speaker struggled to make himself heard above the general hubbub in order to announce the final result. After the noise subsided a bit, Cobb began to announce the result when he was interrupted by a member begging to be allowed to change his vote to "aye." The speaker acceded to the request, despite objection by Burt of South Carolina. Howell Cobb's voice choked with emotion as he announced at 2:05 P.M. that the bill had been passed to a third reading by a margin of 108 to 98. The breathless anticipation of the previous minutes now released itself in a pandemonium of cheers, a loud "allegro whistle" that startled the House reporter, clapping hands, stomping feet, and even dancing. A disgruntled Southern radical, Ashe of North Carolina, moved to clear the galleries but, seeing how unchivalrous the ladies considered this gesture, did not press his demand. After some degree of quiet was restored, James Thompson (D-Pa.) moved the previous question on the bill's passage. After the third reading of the bill, the House seconded Thompson's move by a teller vote of 103 to 51. As a last-ditch measure of obstructionism, Armistead Burt of South Carolina moved to table the bill. At about 2:45 P.M., after this was unceremoniously rejected on a roll call of 108 to 97, the Texas–New Mexico bill finally passed the House of Representatives by the same vote.[56]

Senator Clay relieved his emotions in tears as the final roll calls were announced and well-wishers clasped his hand. Later, in the rotunda outside the chamber, he and Senator Cass embraced in the joy and relief of victory. Cass declared this the happiest hour of his life. Foote was in ecstasy. The cynical William Seward said with a grin that he supposed the country was now safe. The pro-compromise representative to whom he addressed the remark answered, "Yes, in spite of you." Seward departed the hall. Salmon Chase's countenance looked deathly, as did those of Preston King (FS-N.Y.), Armistead Burt (D-S.C.), and Abraham Venable (D-N.C.). Horace Mann wept, but for the opposite reason from Clay. Mann penned a letter to his wife during what he termed the "heart-sickening" events; commenting on those Northerners who had changed their votes from the day before, Mann wrote, "Dough, if not infinite in quantity, is infinitely soft. The north is again disgracefully beaten,—most disgracefully." Quite contrary were the feelings of Rep. Thomas Harris of Illinois, who dispatched a message of elation to Senator Douglas: "All's bright, and everybody but the Abolitionists or disunionists glad. . . . Glory to God in the highest." Several reporters noticed that some of the Southern radicals and their Northern antislavery allies clasped hands and arms or embraced each other, among them Franklin Bowden of Alabama and Charles Allen of Massachusetts. The gesture was not only a recognition of their defeat on the bill but also that their unique interrelationship in the fight against the bill could henceforth no longer exist.[57] In fact, never again in the antebellum sectional crisis did Northern and Southern extremists forge such a voting coalition. (See Appendix E.)

Chapter Twelve

༖

Completion of Victory

THOSE FAMILIAR WITH LIFE IN THE NATION'S CAPITAL IN 1850 COULD NOT RE-member anything quite approximating the relief engendered by the House pas-sage of the Texas–New Mexico bill and the passage of the California and Utah bills the next day, September 7. Beginning at 3 P.M. on the 6th and lasting for several days thereafter, the wildest and most unrestrained joy burst forth, ex-cept among a few free-soilers and disunionists. Characterizing the memorable proceedings were cannonades, limelights, fireworks, and drunken revelry; a huge, joyous crowd serenading the congressional compromise advocates as the U.S. Marine Band provided musical accompaniment; and general cheerfulness, even among many who had opposed compromise to the end.[1]

Amid the celebrations, the House of Representatives passed the California and Utah bills on September 7 with little fanfare. A few Southern die-hards at-tempted to block their passage, but these moves elicited derision even from fel-low Southern radicals. As the *Pittsburgh Gazette*'s correspondent related it, the California bill passed "in solemn and majestic silence," and "no excitement, no exultation" broke out when Speaker Cobb announced the result. Both Northern and Southern extremists grudgingly admitted their overall defeat, whether they ascribed it to venality, Texas bond bribery, patronage, or betrayal of principles.[2]

Monday's session in the U.S. Senate gave the coup de grace to the opponents of the Texas–New Mexico settlement. Daniel Webster's visit to the Capitol that morning, amidst congratulations from numerous members of both houses, reinforced the confident mood of the compromise forces. President Fillmore sent in a short message officially communicating the proposed New Mexico state constitution and accompanying documents brought to Washington by "senator-elect" Richard Weightman, who probably had arrived on Friday while the Texas–New Mexico bill was being considered by the House or just after its passage by that body. The president's message tactfully stated that, since both houses of Congress had passed a bill establishing a territorial government in New Mexico, he felt it inexpedient to make any recommendation in reference to state government there.[3] Besides adding a minor amendment regarding New Mexico Territory, the only substantial move by the House had been to conjoin the Senate's New Mexico and Texas boundary-debt bills. Ohio Free-Soiler Salmon Chase's brief attempt to delay Senate concurrence in the House's maneuver was quickly brushed aside.

The vote to concur in the "little Omnibus" was 31 to 10 in favor: 14 of the yeas were Northern, 17 Southern. Truman Smith of Connecticut, who had voted with the anti-compromise bloc until he had voted for the Pearce bill, voted to concur, as did Jackson Morton of Florida, the only Southern Whig who had voted against the Pearce bill. Arkansas Democrat William Sebastian, whose voting pattern on the issue had been variable so far, joined the majority now. David Atchison of Missouri and Joseph Underwood of Kentucky, opponents of the original Pearce bill, now voted to concur. The 10 nay votes were supplied by Northern proponents of the Wilmot Proviso plus the consistent Southern maverick, Thomas Hart Benton of Missouri. The Massachusetts senators, Winthrop and Davis, who earlier had broken with the antislavery bloc in casting their votes for the Pearce bill, now returned to the fold with a vote against the House version; and seven Southern extremists—Barnwell, Butler, Hunter, Mason, Turney, Soulé, and Yulee—sat without responding when their names were called. Two Northern senators, who favored the bill but also desired not to record their votes on this measure, Cooper of Pennsylvania and Greene of Rhode Island, also remained silent. President Fillmore signed the California, Utah, and Texas–New Mexico bills that day, fulfilling the joyful anticipations of the weekend celebrants. The District slave trade and the fugitive slave bills passed both houses in the next several days and were also signed into law by the president, who approved the latter one a bit hesitantly.[4]

The joy and celebration engendered by the passage of the compromise bills was not limited to the nation's capital. News of House action on the Texas–New Mexico measure reached New York by telegraph by 4 P.M. on September 6. Soon the whole city and the ships in the harbor were decorated with flags. From Baltimore north to Boston the popularity of the settlement was evident to all observers. Southerners also celebrated. The citizens of Raleigh, as observed by Alexander Stephens, welcomed the news of the Texas–New Mexico bill's success as if they had just been delivered from certain war. Music blared and guns fired salutes to honor the compromise in Petersburg and Winchester, Virginia, and in Nashville, Natchez, and New Orleans. The ecstasy and jubilation at New Orleans were so overwhelming that one commentator was inspired to write that a newly arrived stranger might have concluded that "some great natural catastrophe had been miraculously escaped." The majority of newspapers—Democrat and Whig, North and South—expressed their relief from fear of disunion and civil war, their pride in the perpetuation of the Union, and their renewed confidence in the nation's future.[5]

Despite all the rejoicing, the Fillmore administration realized that the work was not quite finished with the passage of the bills. Texas still had to accept the bargain. The administration demonstrated a marked sense of urgency in communicating news of the Texas–New Mexico bill's passage to Governor Bell of Texas. On Monday, September 9, after President Fillmore signed the bill, Secretary of State Webster and Attorney General Crittenden sent a telegraphic dispatch to Samuel L. Peters, Collector of Customs at New Orleans. Senators Houston and Rusk also signed the dispatch. It transmitted news of the act and ordered Peters to get the information to Austin without delay. Peters selected Col. J. B. Walton of the surveyor's department at the customs house to carry the message to Texas. On September 11, the day the dispatch arrived, Walton left New Orleans on the steamer *Portland*. The trip to Galveston and then overland to Austin took seven days, with Walton arriving at the Texas capital on September 18. Governor Bell answered by telegraph through New Orleans that the legislature had adjourned on September 6 and would reconvene in November. He promised that as soon as the act itself reached Texas, he would bring it before the people and would call a special session of the legislature, if he deemed it necessary, to consider the matter. The governor promised to communicate the decision of the people of Texas to Washington as soon as it was manifest. The only recorded public celebration in Texas over the arrival of news of the bill occurred in the town of Indianola on Matagorda Bay, where nearly everyone in town lit up their houses one evening to mark the event.[6]

Sam Houston had originally intended to carry the new law itself to Texas, but he and Senator Rusk prevailed upon Capt. G. K. Lewis, a Texan lobbyist for frontier defense, to act as the courier to transmit the act and also various letters. One of these, from Rusk to Governor Bell, proclaimed the fairness of the measure to Texas in giving Texas more land than the Omnibus provisions had and losing no soil with a real potential for slave labor to the state. Lewis wasted no time, reaching Montgomery, Alabama, by September 14 and Austin, Texas, on September 27. His was not the only such mission. Henry Hardy, former principal of a school in the District, received the task of delivering a certified copy of the act to Santa Fe, and he departed Washington on the afternoon of Tuesday, September 10. The message he carried from Secretary Conrad not only apprised Colonel Munroe of the new act but also stated the belief that there was little doubt of Texas's acceptance and ordered Munroe in the meantime to maintain peace with New Mexican officials by interfering in their civil functions as little as possible. Hardy, escorted by a special detail of mounted troops, reached Fort Leavenworth around September 24 and arrived at Santa Fe on October 23. Meanwhile, former New Hampshire congressman James Wilson sailed for California to deliver the glorious news of that state's admission to the Union.[7]

The urgency in getting the word out, and especially in securing Texan acquiescence in the settlement, stemmed from continuing administration concern over potentially disruptive events either before Texas accepted or after Texas should reject the compromise. Free-soil elements were no longer of much concern in this scenario. George Julian of Indiana might boast of a preference for war as opposed to a sacrifice of antislavery principles. And his colleagues might charge that Texas bondholders had corrupted congressmen (for which charge no proof has ever been offered), but the free-soilers were basically powerless to foment immediate trouble unless they attempted to interfere directly with the new fugitive slave law.[8] The real difficulty lay in what the Southern fire-eaters might do.

Southern radicals were livid at the success of what they realized was the keystone of the compromise—the Texas–New Mexico bill. They adjudged its passage to be the result of bribes and the threat of federal bayonets against Texas. Southern "ultras" recognized that Texas still had to accept or reject the settlement, and their editorialists strongly recommended that Texas reject the ten-million-dollar "bribe." Some radicals still pinned their hopes for secession on a Texas rejection, a Texan military advance against Santa Fe, and a bloody conflict between those troops and U.S. forces in New Mexico. But even radical leaders themselves understood that Texas would probably now accept the settlement, especially since the entire Texas congressional delegation supported it.[9]

Whether or not Texas accepted, extremist elements elsewhere in the South felt that they needed a platform on which to galvanize united Southern resistance to what these fire-eaters considered a humiliating defeat for the South.

The *Columbia* (S.C.) *Telegraph* likened the compromise to the classical Trojan horse. The *Richmond Examiner* claimed that the compromise gave the South the same "peace" as that enjoyed by a gallows victim before being exhumed by a grave-robber for the purpose of dissecting the corpse. The "outposts" now captured, the South's enemies would next assault the "citadel" itself, argued the *Savannah News.* "The Doom of the South" was nigh, according to the *Tallahassee Floridian.* The fire-eaters firmly believed that their Northern enemies would exploit their victory by increasing their agitation of slavery issues. The abolitionists would come to plunder the prostrate South, divide up her garments, abolish slavery, and instigate the terrible conflagration of race war.[10]

Most Southerners relegated this catastrophic scenario to the political paranoia of extremist imaginations. Whigs seemed deliriously happy with the compromise, and many Democrats, even those who believed the South was still imperiled, seemed willing to acquiesce rather than risk disunion. Southern newspapers of various persuasions proposed a policy of economic nonintercourse with the North, if agitation continued, and recommended the development of the South's own manufacturing establishment and foreign commerce to achieve economic independence. But Southern extremists, while supportive of such measures, also demanded a more immediate Southern reaction to the compromise.[11]

Some fire-eaters desired immediate secession; others looked first to state conventions and the next session of the Nashville Convention to pave the way for ultimate disunion. Frenzied activity characterized disunion advocates in late September. Governor Quitman of Mississippi called for the state legislature to convene on November 18, and Governor Towns of Georgia called for a state convention to assemble December 10. The second session of the Nashville Convention was already scheduled to meet on November 11. Secessionists busily traded epistles with each other preaching the necessity of disunion, but no concert of action or plan seemed to emerge from these consultations. The closest that anyone came to assuming leadership in coordinating the effort was Whitemarsh Seabrook, governor of South Carolina. He corresponded with the governors of Georgia, Mississippi, Alabama, and Texas, urging them to sustain the movement. But Seabrook refused to have South Carolina take the first steps. The Palmetto State would follow suit once two or more others had acted, and he assured Governor Bell of aid in men and money if Texas should continue to resist federal enticements and threats. South Carolina, however, remembered 1832 too well and how in the nullification crisis no other Southern state had backed South Carolina in defying President Jackson. Therefore what orchestration there was in the movement came from the leader of a state that remained reticent about leading the advance.[12]

There actually existed only one glimmering chance of success for the disunionist cause in the fall of 1850. That chance, remote as many people believed it might be, was that Texas would reject the boundary-debt proposal and precipitate bloodshed in New Mexico. Only such a sanguinary incident could have succeeded in definitively rallying united Southern support for the Texan cause and for the secession of the Southern states, either individually or in concert. Only bloodshed on the Texas–New Mexico border could have possibly, at this stage, transformed a Southern populace generally willing to submit to the compromise into a populace ready to stand in solidarity with the Texans in resistance to the federal authorities in New Mexico. The *Southern Press* in Washington declared, following the passage of the Texas–New Mexico bill, that the issue now depended on the people of Georgia and Texas—that is, on what the Georgians decided in convention and on whether the Texans chose to accept the "bribe" or resist it.[13] The success of the conventions really depended on the attitude of Texas. If Texans appeared inclined to take the ten million dollars and surrender their claim to New Mexico, then the disheartened Southern conventions would be reduced to "sound and fury, signifying nothing" as Shakespeare's Macbeth had soliloquized. But if Texas chose to resist, then the embers of disunion could continue to glow in Georgia, Mississippi, at Nashville, and elsewhere in the South.

Secessionists could not afford to be overly optimistic. The strongly Unionist record of Texas and its congressional delegation was against them. Houston and Rusk had too often repudiated Calhounite doctrine in the past, and both men had fought in the recent session to achieve a viable settlement. The entire Texas delegation, even Volney Howard, were finally counted on the compromise side in voting on the Texas–New Mexico arrangement. Besides, the people of Texas had exhibited a resounding lack of interest in selecting delegates for the first session of the Nashville Convention.

Politicians of all persuasions were convinced that Texas would accept. Despite flickering hopes to the contrary, Southern disunionists assumed that such would be the case. Free-soilers believed that Texas would ratify the settlement and that all previous talk of resistance to it was mere bluff designed to extort the ten million dollars from Congress in the first place. Many antislavery Northern Whigs characterized the payment as half "hush-money" and half "blood-money." Compromise advocates, still glorying in their recent congressional victories, proclaimed that Texan acquiescence was certain; Texans would appreciate the generosity of the nation in offering the state ten million dollars in exchange for relinquishing what amounted to a paper claim over barren terrain. The compromisers were convinced that, even though they might delay and hedge a bit, the people of Texas would eventually take the money rather than fight. As the *Springfield* (Mass.) *Republican* characterized the situation, even "the most eager maidens play a little coy at first."[14]

The Texas congressional delegation still in Washington and letter writers from Texas gave the decided impression that Texans would overwhelmingly ratify the settlement. Houston and Rusk declared that the Texas Legislature would endorse the Texas–New Mexico bill, even if Governor Bell attempted to stand in its way. James Love of Galveston assured Attorney General Crittenden in a September 26 letter that Texan extremists would be able to command no more than one-tenth of Texas voters in efforts to defeat the bill. Richard Hunt, editor of the *Bonham Advertiser* in Fannin County on the Red River, declared in a letter to Rusk that the bill enjoyed nearly unanimous approval in that area. Adolphus Sterne from Nacogdoches informed Rusk that "the old Texians and all the Farmers" favored the bill and peace. J. W. Scott from Houston provided Rusk with an estimate that about four-fifths of the people in Harris County supported the measure.[15]

The Texans in Washington were wise enough to know that the opponents of the bill in the state would continue to struggle against it and, despite the positive and glowing reports of their friends at home, realized that the extremists might still create difficulties. But the Texas delegation had to remain in Washington to work through the appropriation bills and other matters remaining for action near session's end. Even one last vestige of the boundary dispute issue had to be quieted. Richard Weightman, former "senator-elect" from the "state" of New Mexico, understandably desired Congress to reimburse him for travel expenses, and he enlisted the aid of Sen. William Dawson of Georgia. On September 23 Dawson twice attempted to amend the civil and diplomatic appropriation bill to include two thousand dollars for Weightman's mileage. These motions gave rise to a short but sharp debate. Dawson and a few others argued that it was only fair to recompense Weightman for the travel, even though Congress had rejected New Mexico statehood. Strong opposition to the proposal was voiced by the Texas senators, Foote of Mississippi, and their confreres. They denounced the whole proceeding in New Mexico, which had led to Weightman's election, as illegitimate and believed that any appropriation for the "senator-elect" would constitute a tacit endorsement by Congress of the validity of New Mexico's presumptions. Rusk labeled the amendments a "firebrand" of

continued agitation and a congressional sanction of New Mexico's rejection of
the Texan boundary claim. The Dawson amendments were defeated by a single
vote on each roll call, 24 to 23 and 20 to 19, respectively. Both votes contained
similar alignments. Free-Soil and Northern Whig senators, joined by several
Northern Democrats and Southern Whigs, supported the amendments, while
nearly all Southern Democrats, most Northern Democrats, and several Southern Whigs opposed them. These roll calls disposed, by a very narrow margin,
of a potentially irksome matter.[16]

The Texans experienced various pressures exerted on them in Washington,
from both administration officials and Congress, to encourage Texan acceptance
of the settlement. Aside from engrossment in the boundary-debt controversy,
Texans in Washington had also been involved in lobbying for the passage of two
measures related to defense of the Texan frontier. Administration officials and
members of Congress communicated clearly to these Texans that the successful
completion of the two bills in the next session depended on prior agreement of
Texas to the compromise. During the busy final days of the session, when telegraphic news arrived in Washington that Governor Bell had vetoed the bill for a
popular referendum on the compromise, Congress dropped any further consideration of a bill to add two additional U.S. mounted regiments to those already
protecting the Texas frontier. Assuming that the veto was evidence of Bell's ill
disposition toward the compromise plan, the members adamantly refused to
assist frontier defense in Texas unless the state first ratified the boundary-debt
settlement offered by Congress. In addition, former Texas governor George Wood
encountered obstacles to his effort to secure payment for Texan volunteers called
by him to frontier duty at the federal government's behest while he was governor
in 1848–49. Even though Congress finally appropriated the money for this purpose, Wood was informed that supplemental legislation would be required to
gain release of the funds, and obviously that could come about only if, in the
meantime, Texas submitted to the compromise proposals.[17]

As September ended, the assorted Texas leaders left Washington for home,
the long session's work behind them. In addition to Wood and the congressional delegation, former governor J. P. Henderson, Texas Supreme Court chief
justice John Hemphill, U.S. District Judge John C. Watrous, and Clarksville
editor Charles de Morse traveled westward. Most, if not all, journeyed overland to the Ohio River and took passage on steamboats down that river and the
Mississippi. At several stops along the way, delegation members addressed patriotic speeches to crowds of well-wishers. By the last week in October, all were
safely back in the familiar surroundings of the Lone Star State.[18]

The campaign for acceptance or rejection of the compromise bill was well under way in Texas before the delegation arrived. Newspaper editors and their correspondents continued the debate that had been raging in Texas during previous months. *Austin State Gazette* articles in late August and early September fiercely condemned the bill, emphasizing how closely on the borders of slavery the measure permitted the evils of free soil to intrude. Texas would be "forever disfigured by the plague spot of abolitionism upon her vitals"; the enemy would be at the gates with the "incendiary torch" to seal the doom of Texas itself. Texan propagandist Jane Cazneau, writing as "Cora Montgomery," contributed an enthusiastic letter to the *Gazette* outlining the positive benefits to Texas and the South of an immediate Texan military expedition to Santa Fe. The *Marshall Republican* reiterated the abstract themes of defending Southern and Texan honor against the Northern threat but also promoted the practical use of slaves in New Mexico's potentially rich mines and the significance to Texas of maintaining control of an area that possessed the most feasible route for a railroad to the Pacific. In striking contrast to the rejectionist press stood moderate newspaper voices such as the *Houston Democratic Telegraph, Victoria Advocate, Galveston Civilian,* and *Clarksville Northern Standard.* Whatever reservations they might express about some provisions of the settlement, these papers promoted acceptance of the plan as crucial to peace, preservation of the Union, and payment of the Texas debt. Texas, declared the *Advocate,* lost nothing in the bargain except a barren wasteland and a "mongrel population" hostile to Texan interests.[19]

In mid-September Austin received a reminder of the Neighbors mission to New Mexico, when Maj. William S. Henry passed through the state capital on his way to his new recruiting assignment in New York. Aware that Henry had been court-martialed and fined for feeding government corn to Commissioner Neighbors's animals, the people of Austin expressed high praise for an officer they considered an innocent victim of tyrannical administration policies. During his brief stay, Henry provided Governor Bell with a statement of his services to Neighbors, a copy of some of the court-martial proceedings against him, and his receipt for the ten-dollar fine he had paid the U.S. government for the corn issued for Neighbors's animals at Doña Ana. In the statement Major Henry requested Bell to refer the matter to the legislature so that that body might express its gratitude to him by reimbursing the ten-dollar fine to him. Town leaders on September 16 offered Henry a testimonial dinner in his honor. He thanked them for their solicitude but declined their offer because of his departure for New York early on the 17th. Governor Bell referred Henry's statement and enclosed documents to the legislature, and on December 2, 1850, the members passed a joint resolution to reimburse Henry for the ten-dollar fine imposed on him at his court-martial. A bill to grant Henry a league of land, proposed in the Texas House at that session by Rep. Louis Wigfall of Harrison County, passed the House but was not acted on in the Senate. However, in February 1852, after Major Henry's death, the Texas Legislature did award a league of land to his widow and children.[20]

Henry's short sojourn at Austin was followed almost immediately by the arrival of Colonel Walton from New Orleans on September 18 with the initial report of the Texas–New Mexico bill's success. The subsequent issue of the *State Gazette,* that of September 28, presented arguments on both sides of the issue. While the editors continued their decidedly anti-bill offensive, they also printed a letter by George W. Smyth, commissioner of the Texas General Land Office, strongly in favor of the compromise plan. Smyth calculated that the federal government, with its ten-million-dollar offer, was paying Texas more than twice the price per acre than unlocated claims had previously been selling for and, moreover, for "barren, uninhabitable waste" unfit for agriculture or slavery. Acceptance of the proposal by Texas, he wrote, would pay their debt, rid them of a population hostile to their institutions and interests, prevent them from having to raise taxes to send Texan forces to New Mexico and maintain them there, and possibly prevent civil war between North and South.[21]

This issue appeared the day after special courier G. K. Lewis communicated official documentation of the passage of the compromise bill to Governor Bell at Austin. That same day, September 27, Bell issued a proclamation ordering a public referendum to be directed by the chief justice of each Texas county on the bill. The voters were to express their opinions on the arrangement by writing "accept" or "reject" on their ballots. Two copies of the election returns were to be forwarded to the respective houses of the Texas Legislature.[22]

Captain Lewis brought more with him from Washington than the bill. Rusk, Kaufman, and Howard had supplied him with letters and two thousand copies of a map to employ in support of the bill's ratification. The map, which subsequently became known as "Kaufman's Map," was an extraordinary piece of gimmickry. Rep. James McDowell of Virginia had originally had the map drawn to augment his House speech on September 3. His map, based on the Disturnell map used in the 1848 Treaty of Guadalupe Hidalgo, included numerous statistical calculations of distances and area. Anyone familiar with more recent and more accurate maps could easily perceive the gross distortions of the Texas boundary produced by the Disturnell map, most notably in reference to the West Texas–New Mexico region. This map minimized the area that was surren-

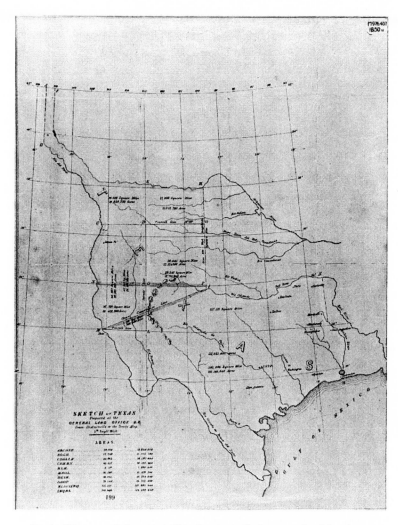

Sketch of Texas . . . 5th Sept. 1850. ("Kaufman's Map"). Courtesy of Dolph Briscoe
Center for American History, University of Texas at Austin.

dered by Texas to New Mexico in the compromise bill, and David Kaufman
understood how the map might prove a useful tool in convincing the Texan
populace to accept the bill. Kaufman, with McDowell's approval, had the U.S.
General Land Office make a copy of the map, which Kaufman then took to

lithographer C. B. Graham. Kaufman asked Graham to insert some of the principal Texas towns on the map and paid him to make a thousand copies, and Senator Rusk paid for another thousand. G. K. Lewis then brought them to Texas and saw that they were distributed.[23]

If he had desired a more accurate cartographic depiction, Kaufman certainly had better maps to choose from. The Jacob de Cordova–Robert Creuzbaur map, published in Houston in 1849, depicted the Texas–New Mexico region more accurately in an inset juxtaposed to a larger map of the settled areas of Texas. The Texas delegation in Congress had all attested to this map's accuracy. Better still was the delineation, in larger relief, of boundaries and geographic features in Sidney Morse's August 1850 version of an 1848 map by Adolphus Wislizenus.[24] Texans in Washington could not have been unaware of the Morse map, given its prominent display in several widely circulated New York newspapers in early August. The Disturnell map, however, suited Kaufman's propaganda purposes much better.

In Texas, Cordova and Creuzbaur were appalled at Kaufman's map. Cordova estimated that the area conceded to New Mexico by Texas in the bill was over 103 million acres, rather than the figure of 56.45 million in Kaufman's map. Robert Creuzbaur, chief draftsman of the Texas General Land Office, attacked numerous errors on the map. He not only emphasized the much greater acreage surrendered by Texas but also pointed out how much farther from the settled parts of Texas the Kaufman map made the "free soil" of New Mexico appear than it actually was. For instance, Creuzbaur stated that San Antonio was eighty-five miles closer to the New Mexico border than the Kaufman map indicated. Even Kaufman himself, after the campaign was over, confessed that the map contained errors, such as its placement of Marshall west of the Sabine River, rather than on the east side, and its failure to show the Trinity River at all. But Kaufman denied any intent to deceive; he blamed the errors on the U.S. General Land Office and declared that a more accurate map would not have changed the outcome of the Texas ratification elections. Kaufman believed that no more than a hundred votes had been directly influenced by his propaganda device. While his critics refrained from publicly charging Kaufman with willful misrepresentation, they blamed him for the map's errors and for "gross negligence" for relying on Disturnell's rather than on the Cordova-Creuzbaur map.[25]

Besides the Kaufman map, G. K. Lewis brought letters from Representatives Kaufman and Howard for publication in Texas newspapers. Volney Howard's letter, dated September 6, was first published in the *Galveston News* and then

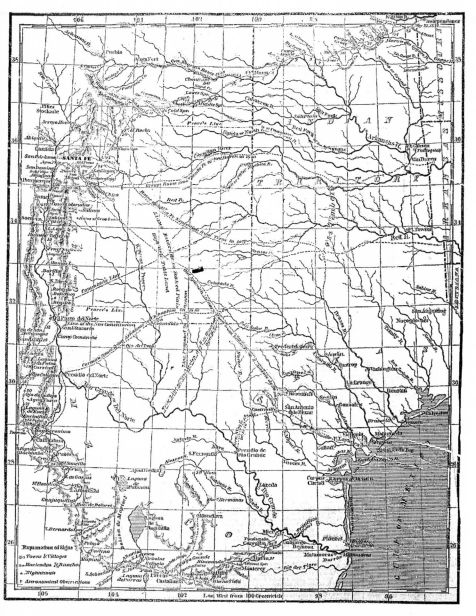

Morse's map of Texas–New Mexico, as printed in the *New York Courier and Enquirer* on August 14, 1850. *Courtesy of the Library of Congress.*

reprinted in the *Austin State Gazette* on October 5. Howard detailed his maneuvers to save the Texas–New Mexico bill on the day he wrote the letter, deserting his earlier steadfast condemnation of the bill. He declared that he changed
his position because he did not want the question of war to rest on his shoulders; the people of Texas, he believed, might prefer the bill rather than a contest
with the United States and should make the choice themselves. While men-
tioning Texas's freedom to choose, Howard stressed the advantages of the congressional bills, particularly his view that the New Mexico Territory provisions
did not discriminate against Southern slave property but would fully protect
its legality. Even though he disliked the five-million-dollar reserve clause in the
debt settlement, Howard expressed confidence that Congress would repeal this
restriction. If Texas chose to demand its entire land claim, whether or not this
led to conflict, there would be no money forthcoming from the federal government to help pay the debt.[26]

Kaufman, in his letter dated September 10 and published in the *State Gazette* on October 12, reiterated several themes in Howard's letter, but he also
stated his doubt that slaves would ever be taken to New Mexico, given its soil,
irrigation problems, and the hostility of Mexican-Americans to the institution.
Kaufman expressed dislike of the five-million-dollar reserve clause but did not
believe that it would prevent Texas from fully paying the debt. He pointed out
that many congressmen had believed that the United States was legally liable
for Texas's debts, for which import or tariff duties had been pledged, and these
congressmen therefore desired that creditors of Texas release the federal government from this liability before the five-million-dollar reserve was granted
to Texas.[27]

The Kaufman and Howard letters launched the subsequent newspaper campaign on the bill. Most newspapers in Texas ultimately supported acceptance
of the compromise settlement, but a sizable minority of the press continued its
heated denunciations of the measure. The *Houston Telegraph, Clarksville Standard,* and *Victoria Advocate* were joined by both San Antonio papers and two of
Galveston's three in vigorously proclaiming the benefits of acceptance. Several
papers once opposed to compromise—the *Marshall Patriot, San Augustine Red-
Land Herald,* and *Dallas Herald*—now joined the ranks of bill supporters. The
opposition included both Austin papers, the *Marshall Republican, Matagorda
Tribune, Washington Lone Star, Galveston News,* and *La Grange Monument.* Editorialists on both sides of the question rehashed all the familiar arguments.[28]

Besides the newspaper campaign, friends and foes of the bill conducted rallies and meetings in the various counties to stir up votes for their side. The

opposition, led by Louis Wigfall, John T. Mills, and J. P. Henderson, tirelessly fought to convince Texans to reject the proposition. Wigfall and associates attempted to steal a march on the pro-acceptance forces by staging a massive rally in Marshall on Monday, September 30. This was fertile ground for Southern extremism, since Harrison County was by far the largest slaveholding county in Texas.[29] The biggest crowd ever seen in Marshall up to that time thronged the streets by 10 A.M. Two-thirds of the county voters were reported present. As many as could assembled at the Baptist Church at 11 A.M. to hear speakers and adopt resolutions. But if the anti-bill leaders expected to simply stampede their resolutions to adoption without dissent, they overestimated their strength.

The first speaker, state senator James F. Taylor, surprised everyone with an address in favor of the bill. Taylor had so far sided with the anti-compromise bloc in the legislature, but now he courageously confessed that his views had changed because of the additional taxes required to raise and equip a Santa Fe expedition. He also declared that the compromise bill was a good bargain—ten million dollars for worthless land that would never support slavery. When he attacked Governor Bell as a man without family and an "ultra" who would sink himself and the state rather than give up an inch of ground, the audience cheered long and loudly in praise of Bell. The next speaker, state representative Jeremiah Clough, toed the radical line in claiming that only a small Texan force would be required to subdue New Mexico. Both Clough and Taylor then announced their resignations from the legislature, for which Taylor at least was roundly cheered. John T. Mills, a former South Carolina nullifier who had been invited by written petition to address the meeting, then castigated the bill to deafening applause. After Col. James A. Simpson offered a pro-acceptance resolution, the crowd demanded a speech from Wigfall, another former South Carolinian. He declined, however, until after the meeting overwhelmingly adopted a resolution condemning the bill. Wigfall then celebrated the victory by describing the abolitionist threat to Texas and the South and the potential use of slaves in New Mexican mines. Evening saw a continuation of speeches and band music through the town. The meeting resolutions condemned the bill, the whole compromise and both Texas senators, and endorsed the next session of the Nashville Convention. The "Anti-Everything" assemblage, as one observer characterized it, finally ended.[30]

The rejectionists remained on the offensive in early October. In a meeting at Gilmer in Upshur County, just west of Harrison County, on October 7, Wigfall debated the merits of the Texas–New Mexico bill with Judge Lemuel D. Evans. Some people there labored under the false impression that the compromise bill attached even the Red River counties of Texas to New Mexico. The Gilmer meeting recommended rejection and voted to award a proverbial brass collar to Charles de Morse, pro-compromise editor of the *Clarksville Standard,* the collar to be inscribed "Born a slave to Houston and Rusk." Radical resolutions passed on October 7 at Matagorda near the Gulf Coast supported rejection on the ground, among other reasons, that the proposed arrangement threatened the future of slavery in Texas and the South as a whole by surrendering slave soil. A few days later on October 12, state senator J. K. Holland led a "rejection" meeting at Carthage in his home county of Panola, bordering Harrison County on the south. But these initial radical enthusiasms began to run out of steam in mid-October. Opposition to the bill in the eastern counties began to subside, although Wigfall and friends continued speaking out in order to muster a strong "rejection" vote. Henderson, Mills, and Wigfall promoted their cause in several counties. Henderson and Mills argued in a rational, gentlemanly manner. Wigfall, however, sometimes injected vituperative comments; in a debate with Judge William Ochiltree, for instance, Wigfall compared Senator Rusk to Benedict Arnold.[31]

Gradually the pro-bill forces gained momentum. The *Bonham Advertiser's* editor reported all safe for the bill in Fannin County on the Red River, while a public rally of three hundred to four hundred in Clarksville on October 12 heartily endorsed "acceptance" despite dissent from John T. Mills and two others. A few "rejection" newspapers began shifting to "acceptance." Texas chief justice John Hemphill, a former South Carolinian, shocked many Texans by his advocacy of the settlement following his return from Washington. Rusk stumped for the bill at San Augustine in late October and at Washington-on-the-Brazos in November. Houston debated with J. P. Henderson at San Augustine on October 30. Representative Kaufman also debated Henderson there on November 2, before traveling to Milam County, northeast of Austin, and then to Washington-on-the-Brazos to campaign. By early November J. K. Holland, who still opposed the bill, was saying that its acceptance constituted no cause for disunion. So discouraged did the editors of the *Marshall Republican* become about their chances to defeat the bill that in early November they became nearly silent on the issue.[32]

The rising fortunes of the moderates and the despair of the radicals resulted primarily from the accumulation of votes heavily favoring adoption of the compromise plan. At the polls the bill's supporters were able to steal a march on the rejectionists. The first six counties whose official totals the *Austin State Gazette* listed on November 2 rolled up an impressive 1,136 to 190 vote in favor of acceptance. Bexar County provided a tremendous 449 to 32 majority for the bill; San

Antonio alone voted 417 to 22 in its favor. Travis County, even with both Austin papers unequivocally for rejection, favored the settlement 239 to 87. The vote of 222 to 24 in Huntsville accounted for the great majority of Walker County's 271 to 48 pro-acceptance margin. Three smaller counties—Burleson, McLennan, and Medina—also contributed large majorities for acceptance. These first official results received at Austin undoubtedly discouraged the rejectionists and convinced many Texans who seriously considered voting against the measure that the movement to accept the Texas–New Mexico bill could not be stopped. It is impossible to determine how many rejectionists, given these considerations, may have declined to vote at all in some of the subsequent county ballots, but certainly some were so influenced. The same consideration may have held true for pro-compromise voters, who decided not to vote because they did not feel their votes were necessary for the success of the compromise plan. Certainly Governor Bell was impressed by the initial election results, for on October 18 he responded to various letters offering military service to Texas by writing that, under the circumstances, those services would not be needed because an expedition had now become very improbable.[33]

Subsequent county vote records received at Austin did nothing to alter the trend. The great majority of Texans who voted favored acceptance of the bill. The *State Gazette* reported the vote on November 9 as 1,679 to 408 in favor and on November 16, just prior to the legislative session, as 2,536 to 793 for the compromise plan. By January 11, 1851, the totals stood at 9,439 to 3,418. As of that date, only 25 of the 92 officially listed Texas counties had communicated no vote totals to Austin. Certain areas of the state contributed vast numbers of ballots for acceptance. A twelve-county contiguous region along and just south of the Red River rolled up a 2,316 to 91 majority for the bill. Three counties in the southeast corner of Texas (Sabine, Jasper, and Newton) gave a 444 to 17 tally. A group of eight counties in South Texas counted 790 for and only 65 against. In addition to these three concentrations, several other counties in eastern Texas decisively voted to accept the bill. These included Walker and Nacogdoches counties, the respective homes of Senators Houston and Rusk, along with Anderson, Houston, and Burleson counties. Only two counties voted strongly for rejection—Harrison County on the Sabine River and Washington County on the Brazos River. These represented two of the three largest slaveholding counties in Texas. The Harrison County vote was 534 to 272, and the Washington County vote was 295 to 160. Even in these counties, however, substantial minorities voted for the compromise. Only four other counties gave majorities for rejection—Brazoria (with the second highest number of slaves),

Wharton, DeWitt, and Nueces, but the margins in these counties were much closer. A letter from Wharton County stated that a majority of that county would have favored "acceptance" if a poll had been opened at the town of Egypt and that, after the county election, opinion in the area had swung strongly in support of the settlement. In most of the other counties in Texas, vote totals favored the bill, but with substantial minorities for rejection.[34]

As the results favorable to acceptance poured into Austin, the Texas Legislature assembled there on November 18 for the special session called by the governor. Governor Bell welcomed the legislators back to Austin with a message indicative of his obvious relief at the course of events. He referred to the "improved auspices" for a peaceful settlement, a reference to the reception of a definite proposal from Congress and the Texan popular referendum heavily in its favor. Bell defended his proclamation for the plebiscite as a move to allow the people at large in democratic fashion to express their will to their elected representatives. The governor stated that the decisive vote left him little doubt that the legislature would now abide by the popular mandate and formally accept the settlement.[35]

On November 19, the legislature set up a special joint committee, consisting of five members from each house, to consider the several bills offered in reference to acceptance. The next day the joint committee presented its bill providing for a simple, unconditional acceptance. When the Senate voted on the measure on November 21, only minimal opposition developed. Three amendments, one by David Y. Portis and two by Jerome B. Robertson, were briskly swept aside by votes of 15 to 3, 17 to 2, and 14 to 3. On these and other roll calls, Portis and Robertson consistently voted together, joined only by H. L. Kinney on a few of them. Only Portis and Robertson voted against engrossment, and only Portis held out when the bill passed 18 to 1 that afternoon.[36]

The House meanwhile had taken up the joint committee's bill. The notorious Louis Wigfall, Jeremiah Clough's replacement from Marshall, and a small coterie of diehards pressed Wigfall amendments to change the debt settlement and to protect slavery in the area ceded to New Mexico until that territory became a state. The House majority perfunctorily rejected these without a division. When news arrived that the Senate had passed the bill, the House set its own aside and took up consideration of the Senate measure. Wigfall moved to amend the cession clause of the compromise bill by making it read "her [Texas's] territory" rather than "her claim to territory." Only four others—Guy M. Bryan of Brazoria County, R. E. Clements of the South Texas region, Zimri Hunt of

Austin and Colorado counties, and Wigfall's colleague, Joseph Taylor from Harrison County—joined Wigfall in support, and the amendment failed 39 to 5. After the House then amended the bill by a 23 to 21 vote to strike out notification of Washington by a special messenger, Wigfall made a second attempt to amend the Texas–New Mexico bill by substituting a statement that the ceded area was "owned by" rather than merely "claimed by" Texas. The House adjourned before a vote was taken on the amendment, but on the next day, November 22, it was rejected without a division. James G. Sheppard of Washington County moved an acceptance bill substitute that would say "her territory" in reference to the cession. Only Bryan, Hunt, Taylor, and Wigfall voted with Sheppard as the substitute lost 39 to 5. After a minor amendment on wording was added by a 36 to 8 vote, Wigfall moved to table the bill until the next day. The move was defeated 35 to 9. Later that afternoon a move to suspend the rule requiring bills be read on three separate days was approved 35 to 8. This opened the way for passage by a 40 to 5 vote, with Bryan, Hunt, Sheppard, Taylor, and Wigfall defiant to the end. All of the opponents except Hunt represented counties that had voted for rejection in the late election.[37]

Since the House had amended the Senate bill in two minor ways, the Senate now had to consider whether or not to accede to them. This the Senate refused to do in either case on November 23. A roll call was taken on the amendment eliminating a special messenger, but the Senate voted 10 to 9 to retain the section. When the House learned of Senate resistance to their amendments, they too stiffened their backs and refused to recede from them by a vote of 22 to 16. This vote was not indicative of opposition to the bill itself, for Taylor and Wigfall of Harrison County both voted to recede. Back to the Senate went the bill, but this time the upper house voted to concur in both House amendments by roll calls of 10 to 7 and 10 to 6. Governor Bell signed it on November 25 and mailed it to Washington. It arrived in December and President Fillmore officially proclaimed the settlement to be operative.[38]

The Texas Legislature, having accomplished its main task of the special session, showed no further interest in addressing sensitive issues. Senator Robertson introduced a resolution urging the Texan delegation in Washington to secure repeal of the five-million-dollar reserve provision of the compromise bill, but the Senate tabled it on November 29. Representative Wigfall expressed his basic fears for the South and slavery on November 28 when he offered a set of seven amendments that Texas should propose to the U.S. Constitution. Beginning with a long disquisition on Southern concern over continued Northern aggression, most of Wigfall's proposals were designed to prevent future interference with slavery or the interstate slave trade. The House gave Wigfall's radical measures no further consideration before the session finally adjourned on December 3.[39]

As the session drew to its close, the Texas capital received a last reminder of the Neighbors mission. Maj. Enoch Steen, on his way to Fort Leavenworth, passed through Austin at the end of November. The *State Gazette* lauded his assistance to Neighbors and decried the War Department's forcing Steen to return to Washington to explain his purchase of a Texas headright. Steen's interview with Adjutant General Jones occurred in February 1851. Jones deemed the veteran officer's explanation of his conduct satisfactory and returned him to his duties on the Western frontier. With the acceptance of the compromise bill by Texas, Steen's Texan land claims in Doña Ana had become as irrelevant as the former Texas claim to all of New Mexico east of the Rio Grande.[40]

❧

Conclusion

THE TEXAS–NEW MEXICO BOUNDARY ISSUE QUICKLY VANISHED FROM PUBLIC attention after Texas accepted the compromise bill. The various units of U.S. forces dispatched to New Mexico to thwart a potential Texan invasion arrived there during September and October. This proved quite serendipitous for the settlers in New Mexico, for most of these troops were retained in the Ninth Military Department to guard the frontier against hostile Indians. People had long been begging for more troops for that purpose, and thanks to the Texas threat they got them. The 7th Infantry Regiment, however, was ordered back to Jefferson Barracks in St. Louis, and its mounted companies were retained at Fort Leavenworth.[1]

New Mexico Territory, finally possessing congressionally defined boundaries, settled into its new status. James Calhoun, with Weightman's constant backing in Washington, received President Fillmore's appointment as territorial governor. Weightman himself became territorial delegate in Congress—not quite the U.S. Senate seat he had claimed but undoubtedly some consolation to his aspirations. Although Weightman confidently assured Manuel Alvarez that Alvarez would be appointed secretary for the new territory, the administration ultimately endowed an Anglo, William S. Allen, with that office. Former Texas agent Spruce M. Baird cast his lot with his adopted New Mexico. He officially resigned his Texas judgeship for the second time, on October 29, 1850, and immersed himself in New Mexican politics and ranching. Texas's former unofficial agent, Palmer Pillans, also entered politics in the new territory.[2]

315

Texans acknowledged the legitimacy of New Mexico Territory and accepted the boundaries between the two polities. The debt issue, however, included yet-unresolved questions and was not dismissed so easily. The federal government immediately paid Texas five million dollars for its ceded claims. The state used over one quarter of it to pay off the nonrevenue debt—that is, generally smaller claims due primarily to Texans and for which tariff revenues of the Texas Republic had not originally been pledged. Texas spent the bulk of the initial five million on schools, public buildings, and other improvements, financing nearly all such projects in the 1850s with federal money. Settlement of the revenue debt, however, dragged on for years. This constituted by far the largest portion of the debt due Texas's creditors and was owed to holders of Texas Republic bonds for which the republic's customs receipts had been pledged. Texans quibbled about federal control of the five-million-dollar reserve, of course, but they also disliked the fact that this revenue debt was held mainly by non-Texans and Eastern speculators. Texas balked at fully paying off creditors who had at times purchased Texas bonds very cheaply and who were not the original holders. Nearly all Texans wanted to "scale" the debt, a euphemism for partially repudiating it. Meanwhile, interest on the debt accrued and creditors petitioned Congress for relief. Ultimately, in 1855, Congress appropriated $7.75 million for a blanket settlement of all classes of remaining Texas creditors. This amounted to an award of only 76.9 cents on the dollar owed, but most creditors were satisfied with this arrangement, since the amount represented a considerable profit over what they had originally invested.[3]

With the threat of bloodshed on the Texas–New Mexico border gone and not even an enacted Wilmot Proviso to sustain them, Southern radicals discovered the Southern popular majority insurmountably apathetic to any attempts to foster disunion. Southern state conventions and the second session of the Nashville Convention in the fall of 1850 were lackluster affairs that generated little interest nationally. The moderate governor of Alabama, Henry Collier, refused even to call that state's legislature into special session. Governor Quitman of Mississippi managed to have his legislature pass an act to organize a convention, but Unionist opposition led by Senator Foote engineered the law so that the convention was not to meet until November 1851. The Georgia Convention, when held in December 1850, was clearly dominated by Unionists of the Stephens-Toombs-Cobb group, who approved a set of resolutions pledging Georgia's support for the compromise and the Union as long as the North did not further violate Southern rights. President Fillmore subtly helped to encourage Southern Unionism that fall by promising to use federal troops if necessary to enforce compliance with the new fugitive slave law in cities such as Boston. Fillmore also influenced the South Carolina fire-eaters to behave themselves by strengthening the Charleston forts and reinforcing federal garrisons in the Carolinas. The Nashville Convention's second session in November 1850 was a pitiable, poorly attended meeting that ended inconclusively after five days. No one from Texas came to this Nashville conclave. The Southern disunion movement thus proved abortive in late 1850.[4]

That might not have been the case had the compromise not passed or the Texas–New Mexico boundary dispute not been settled. What if the bill had failed? Some said that the boundary would then have been tacked onto the California bill and passed or that President Fillmore would have called an immediate special session of Congress if the regular one had ended without resolution of the crisis. But those speculations did not ensure a settlement any more than the previous months of deliberation had. No great feats of imagination are required to contemplate the probable consequences of a failure to settle the issues of 1850 in a manner acceptable to great majorities in both North and South. At the very least the subsequent Southern state conventions would have been more stridently disunionist. The Nashville Convention's second session would have assumed much greater importance if significant issues had remained unresolved. Texas, despite the logistical and financial difficulties involved, might have attempted to send a military force toward Santa Fe. A bloodletting could have occurred there, and, even though the Texans would have probably suffered defeat, the incident would probably have rallied the Southern states to aid Texas. Civil war between North and South would then have likely erupted. Many contemporaries and twentieth-century historians certainly envisioned this scenario as probable in the absence of a compromise agreement, especially on the boundary dispute. Looking at the crisis of 1850 from that perspective helps one to appreciate the sentiments of Daniel Webster, who wrote in October 1850 that "we have gone through the most important crisis that has occurred since the foundation of the Government." "Might-have-beens" and "what-ifs" are always dangerous for historians perhaps stretching too far, but some consideration of possible alternative outcomes can illuminate the significance of what did take place.[5]

Closely related to the question of what might have happened had there been no compromise is the question of which president—Zachary Taylor or Millard Fillmore—exhibited better leadership during the 1850 crisis. Historians and biographers have offered various opinions. K. Jack Bauer portrayed Taylor in a 1985 biography as a "mulish," inflexible man of limited intellectual capacity whose plans were at least as flawed as the plans he disliked. Similarly, Allan

Nevins believed that the stubborn Taylor, had he lived, would have embroiled the Union in some sort of bloody conflict over the boundary issue. Holman Hamilton presented the view that, even if Taylor's stern policy had driven some Southerners to drastic action, the South was not united enough in 1850 to have resisted the federal forces for long. Therefore Hamilton believed that Taylor's forcefulness in 1850 might have prevented the civil war that did break out a decade later. Robert Rayback favorably portrayed President Fillmore's tact and firmness in assisting the achievement of a compromise. David Potter credited Fillmore with settling the 1850 crisis "with such adroitness and seeming ease that history has scarcely recognized the magnitude of his achievement." More recently Elbert B. Smith has given both men high marks for their quite different approaches to the issues. He believes that the South in 1850 would not have ultimately taken up arms against Taylor, a slaveholder himself. Smith also emphasizes that Fillmore's attitude was not so different from Taylor's, as exemplified by Fillmore's firmly expressed warnings to Texas and his increase of U.S. troops to protect New Mexico. In another recent book, William L. Barney has credited President Fillmore with "the cautiously balanced touch of a seasoned politician," as he reinforced the federal garrison while smoothing the ruffled feathers of Texan pride.[6]

The viewpoint that I present in the preceding chapters is decidedly negative toward Zachary Taylor's handling of the issues and quite positive toward Fillmore. Much of the previous judgment about the respective abilities of these two presidents was colored by the Civil War a decade later. In that light, Taylor's position of determined refusal to bow to Southern demands becomes analogous to Lincoln's resistance to pressures for a pro-Southern compromise in early 1861. Fillmore, on the other hand, appears as simply another mediocre moderate in the Pierce-Buchanan mold, trying to stave off the inevitable bloody struggle over slavery. But if one does not judge the outcome of 1850 by later events, a different perspective emerges.

In 1850 a series of issues, especially the volatile boundary dispute, appeared to many contemporaries to seriously threaten the Union of North and South unless some compromise was reached. Assuming that both Taylor and Fillmore wished to avoid disruption of the Union and prevent civil war, which policy was better suited to achieve those goals? Taylor developed a simplistic plan based on the concept of circumventing the issue of slavery-in-the-territories by admitting California and New Mexico to full statehood without first subjecting them to territorial status. He would settle the other issues in a piecemeal fashion. But his plans were not viable in Congress, especially since the South would not accept the

California free state without a guarantee that no Wilmot Proviso would be imposed on the territories. Taylor's answer of New Mexico statehood to void the Proviso issue was unacceptable to the South, especially considering that the slave state of Texas claimed the entire region east of the Rio Grande. Taylor never displayed flexibility in this situation—it was not in his temperament to do so—and his relations with Congress deteriorated. With the president and Congress in deadlock with no resolution in sight, prolongation of the political struggle could only play into the hands of Southern extremists who desired secession, even at the price of civil war. Taylor's recalcitrance, therefore, was one factor that put the Union at risk in 1850. Whether or not he believed a dissolution could happen or bloodshed could occur, Zachary Taylor would brook no policy but his own, whatever consequences might result. He believed that his forces could dispose of any Texan threat, even if other Southern states aided the Lone Star, and he seemed almost to welcome the opportunity. But there were risks involved in such politics of confrontation. Violence, once begun, might run a course quite different from Taylor's expectations. He was willing to accept those risks, rather than adopt a more flexible policy that might succeed in Congress and achieve the president's basic goals without resorting to violence.[7]

Elbert Smith, a Taylor apologist, argues that Fillmore's program did not markedly differ from that of his predecessor. Taylor favored separate measures to settle each issue; the program passed under Fillmore involved several separate bills. Taylor adamantly refused to relinquish the inhabited portions of New Mexico to the Texans; Fillmore did likewise, although in a manner less directly challenging to the Texans.[8] Yet the Fillmore administration succeeded in getting Congress to enact a compromise, each part of which did not necessarily please or appease all the discordant factions but as a whole proved viable to great majorities in both the North and the South. Taylor did not possess a working relationship with Congress that would have permitted the passage of such a program, even if one assumes, as Smith does, that, if he had lived, Taylor would have approved the settlement finally achieved. Millard Fillmore favored compromise, proved flexible about what form Congress chose to give it, and fostered an atmosphere conducive to compromise. Fillmore's dignified bearing, his tactfulness, and his long experience in dealing with senators and representatives became invaluable assets in winning the close victory for compromise and continued sectional peace.

That peace did not last. Slavery was still an issue, although it was now rendered largely dormant on the national level for a while. The old national party system had grown weaker and the Whig union of free-soil Northerners and proslavery Southerners had become very tenuous. Daniel Webster in October 1850 foresaw a restructuring of the party system, especially if the Weed-Seward faction in New York continued to agitate for the Wilmot Proviso or repeal of the new fugitive slave law. Whig congressman J. Phillips Phoenix of New York was pleased with the compromise but pointed to the dangers posed by the constant demagoguery of Northern and Southern extremists. Phoenix was particularly alarmed, in talking with Southerners, to learn how the younger generation of white Southerners was growing up hostile to the Union because they were convinced that the North had become inimical to them. Some Southern Whigs simply gave up on their party. In Texas, the editor of the *Bonham Advertiser,* Richard Hunt, informed Senator Rusk that he was joining the Democrats because he believed the Northern wing of the Whig party had become abolitionized.[9] Hunt forgot that many Northern Whigs were the unsung heroes of the compromise in the U.S. Senate and House. While Clay, Webster, Douglas, and Fillmore were being praised then, and have been praised since, for their roles in engineering the settlement, no one seemed to recognize the contribution of those Northern Whigs in the Senate and House who had deserted their earlier hostility to the compromise and voted to help pass the crucial Texas–New Mexico bills. That turnabout on their part, however, did not suffice to eradicate the overall Southern public image of Northern Whigs as abolitionists.

The weakening of the Whig party and the Jacksonian party system did not in itself forebode disunion a decade later. The Whigs could possibly have rebounded as a national party if they had nominated the moderate Fillmore in 1852 rather than Winfield Scott, whose support by Seward and Weed chilled any Southern Whig ardor for the ticket and paved the way for the Democratic presidency of Franklin Pierce. There was nothing inevitable about Senator Douglas's Kansas-Nebraska Act of 1854, which reopened the sectional conflict at the national level and effected a major transformation of the party system. An alternative to Douglas's plan might have been devised, an alternative that would have settled that particular matter of territorial organization without resurrecting the slavery issue. Suggesting, however, that there existed possible alternatives to what did occur in 1852 and 1854, does not mean that something else might not have reopened the sectional contest later on. The point is that the Compromise of 1850 arrangement might have succeeded in maintaining the ties of Union indefinitely longer had politicians of the early 1850s not miscalculated so badly.

Some have questioned whether the settlement of 1850 even deserves the title of "compromise" and instead prefer to term it an "armistice."[10] But the word "armistice" connotes a halt to fighting in a war already begun and assumes the inevitability of renewed hostilities in 1861. But almost no one in 1850 considered a civil war inevitable after the compromise measures, particularly the Texas–New Mexico bill, passed. Despite the intense previous political struggle over slavery in the territories and talk of secession and war, no active hostilities had yet taken place, and few expected after the bills passed that they ever would. "Armistice," therefore, seems an inappropriate term for the settlement of 1850. Was it then a "compromise" as contemporaries and tradition have denominated the series of bills? Some might answer in the negative, pointing out that the bills were not enacted in a general spirit of concession but by varied coalitions on each bill. Radicals of both North and South felt unappeased and even humiliated by the arrangement, and their bitterness and frustration continued. Nevertheless "compromise" is the most appropriate term for what was accomplished in 1850. The bills taken together did involve mutual concession, and the great majority, North and South, welcomed the outcome. Southerners accepted California statehood; Northerners generally abided by the new fugitive slave law. The popular sovereignty formula in the territories did not reflect the initial desires of majorities from either North or South but became an agreement that eventually satisfied majorities of both sections at the time in regard to Utah and New Mexico. Certainly this represented "compromise" in the true sense.

And none of the bills in the 1850 settlement indicated "compromise" more fully than the Texas–New Mexico bill. It passed only after long and bitter struggle, but the final bill involved concession by both North and South. The boundary line of the compromise bill was not what either Texans or promoters of New Mexico had argued for, but it proved acceptable to all once it was passed in Congress. The success of the boundary bill itself evidenced a great deal of "compromise." Its passage in both the Senate and House was possible only because some senators and representatives showed themselves ultimately willing to vote for a bill that they had originally opposed. Granting all the influences and pressures under which they operated, many senators and representatives chose to rise above their stated platforms and campaign pledges in order to vote for a bill they hoped would preserve sectional peace. What they did is certainly best described by the appellation "compromise."

Once Kansas-Nebraska rekindled the embers in 1854, the fire of disunion spread, perhaps inexorably and inextinguishably. By 1860–61, after Bleeding Kansas, the Dred Scott decision, the Lecompton Constitution struggle, and John Brown's raid on Harpers Ferry had set the stage for the election of Illinois Republican Abraham Lincoln to the presidency, the Southern states chose secession and the establishment of their own Confederacy. No compromise—

and it would have required a miraculous one under those circumstances—was reached that would have restored the dismembered Union. War soon came.

Why was compromise between the sections possible in 1850 and not in 1860–61? One obvious difference concerns the types of issues. Northern and Southern radicals of 1850 liked to emphasize the relevance of particular issues, such as California statehood or the Wilmot Proviso, to the basic principles involved in the more general controversy over slavery itself and the right to maintain property in slaves in national territories of the West. But, in 1850, the developing crisis gradually became focused on what had initially appeared to be a rather mundane boundary and territorial dispute between Texas and New Mexico. By the summer of 1850 it became clear that the fate of the Union hinged more on the peaceful settlement of that boundary dispute than on the settlement of any other issue. However, as severe as the crisis over the boundary grew, that issue also provided an opportunity to quiet the whole struggle. Once the question of war or peace in 1850 became dependent on what was essentially a practical question of metes, bounds, and money, then a practical solution of that immediate problem provided the keystone for an overall resolution of several other issues. Much as "ultras" on both sides might preach that this issue also involved basic principles, the public at large and majorities in Congress ultimately chose to view it simply as a matter of bargain and sale. The solution was achieved, albeit not easily. By 1860–61, however, the sectional crisis over the future of slavery in the United States was no longer amenable to submersion in a settlement of such tangible issues as the Texas–New Mexico boundary dispute. Bitterly divisive emotions over slavery and slavery extension had accumulated to such an explosive point that no compromise such as that of 1850 proved possible. Simultaneously, as the issues had grown more uncompromisable after 1854, so did the influence of moderate elements in both North and South dwindle. In 1850, moderates had been able to press their compromise efforts to fruition and eke out a hard-won victory over the combined extremist blocs of both sections. By 1860 the extremes represented majority feeling in both the North and South; even had there been Unionist leaders of the national stature, wisdom and experience, and political ability of Clay and Webster in 1860–61, the nature of the issues would have rendered their efforts at compromise quite useless.[11]

Appendix A

Blocs in Texas Senate on New Mexico Jurisdiction Resolution, January 1850

Senator	Counties Represented
Moderate Bloc	
Isaac Brashear	Harris
David Gage	Panola, Rusk
Jesse Grimes	Grimes, Walker, Montgomery
Hardin Hart	Hopkins, Hunt, Fannin
Albert Latimer	Lamar, Red River
John McRae	Jasper, Newton, Saline, San Augustine, Angelina
Isaac Parker	Anderson, Houston, Cherokee
E. M. Pease	Brazoria, Galveston
Alexander Phillips	Calhoun, Dewitt, Gonzales, Jackson, Matagorda, Victoria
Matthias Ward	Bowie, Cass, Titus
Radical Bloc	
Edward Burleson	Bastrop, Caldwell, Fayette, Hays, Travis
W. K. Cooke	Brazos, Leon, Limestone, Navarro, Robertson
H. Clay Davis	Cameron, Starr, Webb
H. L. Kinney	Cameron, Goliad, Nueces, Refugio, San Patricio
J. H. Moffett	Jefferson, Liberty, Polk, Tyler
David Portis	Austin, Colorado, Fort Bend, Lavaca, Wharton
J. B. Robertson	Burleson, Milam, Williamson, Washington
J. F. Taylor	Harrison, Smith, Upshur

A. M. Truit   Nacogdoches, Shelby
D. C. Van Derlip   Comal, Bexar, Guadalupe
A. G. Walker   Collin, Dallas, Denton, Grayson, Henderson
B. Rush Wallace   counties east of Trinity River

Roll-Call Votes in U.S. Senate (Thirty-First Congress, First Session) That Define Pro- and Anti-Compromise Blocs

Section 1: Descriptive List of the Twenty-Five Roll Calls

Vote	Senate Journal Page	Date	Description	Yea-Nay
A	395	June 13	Underwood (W-Ky.) move to adjourn	30-23
B	398	June 14	Turney (D-Tenn.) move to strike out Tex.–N.M. sections from Omnibus	24-27
C	475	July 25	Clarke (W-R.I.) move to adjourn	25-31
D	475	July 25	Turney move to adjourn	26-26
E	476	July 25	Yulee (D-Fla.) move to adjourn	25-27
F	476	July 25	Mason (D-Va.) amendment to strike Bradbury (D-Maine) plan for boundary commission and substitute northern and western boundaries of Texas when admitted to Union	25*-28
G	476	July 25	Turney move to adjourn	28-25
H	480	July 26	Davis (D-Miss.) move to adjourn	23-27
I	481	July 26	Berrien (W-Ga.) move to adjourn	30-20
J	487	July 29	Bradbury amendment to have commissioners determine Tex.–N.M. boundary	28-28

Vote	Senate Journal Page	Date	Description	Yea-Nay
K	488	July 29	Mason amendment to modified Bradbury amendment to strike out portion allowing commissioners to determine "convenient" line if they cannot agree on true boundary	29-29
L	488	July 29	Turney amendment to modified Bradbury amendment to prohibit payment to commissioners to reconcile them to a boundary on which they could not agree earlier	20-31
M	491	July 30	Walker (D-Wisc.) move to table Omnibus	25-32
N	492	July 30	Modified Bradbury amendment for commissioners to determine boundary	30-28
O	501	July 31	Pearce (W-Md.) amendment to strike out Tex.–N.M. sections from Omnibus	33-22
P	507	July 31	Hale (FS-N.H.) move to postpone Omnibus indefinitely	27-32
Q	507	July 31	Douglas (D-Ill.) amendment to Pearce amendment (to reinsert Tex.–N.M. provisions except prohibition of government east of the Rio Grande while boundary settlement pending and to provide that no government take effect in N.M. until Mar. 4, 1851) to have commissioners report by Dec. 15, 1850, to prevent N.M. government until further action of Congress and to protect rights of both parties in disputed territory	24-33
R	508	July 31	Turney move to postpone Omnibus indefinitely	29-30
S	509	July 31	Yulee amendment to Pearce amendment to strike out section on boundary commission	29-28
T	509	July 31	Chase (FS-Ohio) move to postpone Omnibus indefinitely	28-29
U	510	July 31	Pearce amendment to reinsert N.M. provisions	25-28
V	512	July 31	Phelps (W-Vt.) move to postpone Omnibus indefinitely	28-30
W	513	July 31	Clemens (D-Ala.) move to postpone Omnibus until following December	25-30

Vote	Senate Journal Page	Date	Description	Yea-Nay
X	543	Aug. 9	Shall Pearce bill be engrossed and read third time?	27-24
Y	543	Aug. 9	Shall Pearce bill pass?	30-20

* The *Senate Journal* (p. 476) gives the total of "yea" votes on this roll call as 26; however, only 25 names are listed as having voted "yea."

Section 2: Roll-Call Votes of Pro- and Anti-Compromise Blocs

Vote		A B C D E F G H I J K L M N O P Q R S T U V W X Y	Frequency	
Pro-Compromise (1)=		N N N N N N N N N Y N N N Y N N Y N N N Y N N Y Y	1	0
Anti-Compromise (0)=		Y Y Y Y Y Y Y Y Y N Y Y Y N Y Y N Y Y N Y Y Y N N		

Pro-Compromise Bloc

Cooper, Jas.	Whig, Pa.	1 1 1 - - 1 - 1 1 1 1 1 1 1 - 1 1 1 - - - 1 1 1 1	18	0
Webster, D.*	Whig, Mass.	0 1 -	1	1
Bradbury, J.	Dem., Maine	- - 1 1 1 1 1 1 1 1 1 1 1 1 - 1 1 1 1 1 1 1 1 1 1	22	0
Bright, Jesse	Dem., Ind.	1 1 1 - 1 1 1 1 1 1 1 1 1 1 1 1 1 1 1 1 1 1 1 0 1	23	1
Cass, Lewis	Dem., Mich.	1 1 1 1 1 1 1 1 1 1 1 1 1 1 1 1 1 1 1 1 1 1 1 1 1	25	0
Dickson, D.	Dem., N.Y.	1 1 1 1 1 1 1 1 1 1 1 1 1 1 1 1 1 1 1 1 1 1 1 1 1	25	0
Dodge, A. C.	Dem., Iowa	1 1 1 1 1 1 1 1 1 1 1 1 1 1 1 1 1 1 1 1 1 1 1 1 1	25	0
Douglas, S. A.	Dem., Ill.	1 - 1 1 1 1 1 1 - 1 1 1 1 0 1 1 1 1 1 1 1 1 1 1 1	22	1
Felch, Alpheus	Dem., Mich.	- - 1 1 1 1 1 - 1 1 1 1 1 1 - 1 1 1 1 1 1 1 - 1 1	20	0
Jones, Geo. W.	Dem., Iowa	1 1 1 1 1 1 1 1 1 1 1 1 1 1 1 1 1 1 1 1 1 1 1 - -	23	0
Norris, Moses	Dem., N.H.	1 1 1 1 1 1 1 - - 1 1 1 1 1 1 1 1 1 1 1 1 1 1 1 1	23	0
Shields, Jas.	Dem., Ill.	0 1 1 1 1 1 1 1 1 1 1 1 - 1 0 1 0 1 1 1 - 1 1 1 1	20	3
Sturgeon, D.	Dem., Pa.	1 1 1 1 1 1 1 1 1 1 1 1 1 1 1 1 1 1 1 1 1 - 1 1 1 1	24	0
Whitcomb, J.	Dem., Ind.	1 1 1 1 1 1 1 1 1 1 1 1 1 1 1 1 1 1 1 1 1 1 1 0 1	24	1
Badger, Geo.	Whig, N.C.	1 1 1 1 1 1 - 1 1 1 1 1 1 1 1 1 1 1 1 1 1 1 1 1 1	24	0
Bell, John	Whig, Tenn.	0 1 0 - - - - - - 0 1 1 - 1 1 - 1 - 1 1 1 1 1 1 1	14	3
Berrien, J. M.	Whig, Ga.	0 1 0 0 0 1 0 1 0 1 1 1 1 0 1 0 1 1 1 1 1 1 1 1 1	18	7
Clay, Henry	Whig, Ky.	1 1 1 1 1 1 1 1 1 1 1 1 1 1 1 1 1 1 1 - 1 1 - - -	22	0
Dawson, W. C.	Whig, Ga.	1 1 1 1 1 1 1 0 1 1 1 1 1 1 1 1 1 1 1 1 1 1 1 1 1	24	1
Mangum, W. P.	Whig, N.C.	1 - 1 1 1 1 1 1 - 1 1 1 1 1 1 1 1 1 1 1 1 1 - - -	21	0
Pearce, Jas.	Whig, Md.	- 1 1 1 1 1 - - - 1 1 1 1 - 0 1 0 1 1 1 1 1 1 1 1	18	2
Pratt, Thos.	Whig, Md.	1 1 1 1 1 1 1 1 1 1 1 1 1 1 1 1 1 1 1 1 1 1 1 - -	23	0
Spruance, P.	Whig, Del.	- 0 1 1 - 1 1 1 0 1 1 1 1 0 1 1 0 1 1 1 1 0 1 0 1	17	6

Vote		A B C D E F G H I J K L M N O P Q R S T U V W X Y	Frequency	
Pro-Compromise (1)=		N N N N N N N N N Y N N N Y N N Y N N Y N N N Y N N Y Y	1	0
Anti-Compromise (0)=		Y Y Y Y Y Y Y Y Y N Y Y Y N Y Y N Y Y N Y Y Y N Y Y N N		
Underwood, J.	Whig, Ky.	0 1 1 1 1 1 0 1 0 1 1 1 1 0 0 1 0 1 1 1 1 1 1 0 0	17	8
Wales, John	Whig, Del.	0 0 1 1 1 1 1 1 0 1 1 1 1 0 0 1 0 1 1 1 1 0 1 1 1	18	7
Atchison, D.	Dem., Mo.	1 1 1 0 1 1 1 1 0 1 1 1 1 1 1 1 1 1 1 1 1 1 1 0 0	21	4
Downs, S. W.	Dem., La.	1 1 1 1 1 1 1 1 1 1 1 1 1 1 1 1 1 1 1 1 1 1 1 - -	23	0
Foote, Henry	Dem., Miss.	1 1 1 1 1 1 1 1 1 1 1 1 1 1 1 1 1 1 1 1 1 1 1 1 1	25	0
Houston, Sam	Dem., Tex.	1 1 1 1 1 1 1 - - 0 0 - 1 1 1 1 0 0 1 0 1 1 1 1	17	5
King, Wm. R.	Dem., Ala.	1 1 1 1 1 - 1 1 1 1 1 1 1 1 1 1 1 1 1 1 1 1 1 1	24	0
Rusk, Thos. J.	Dem., Tex.	1 1 1 1 1 1 1 1 0 0 - 1 1 1 1 1 0 0 0 0 1 0 1 1	17	7
	Total:		638	57

*Despite the fact that Webster cast one vote with and one vote against the compromise position on these roll calls, Webster's pro-compromise attitude makes it appropriate that he be classified with this bloc.

Anti-Compromise Bloc

Chase, S. P.	FS, Ohio	0 0 0 0 0 0 0 0 0 0 0 0 0 0 0 0 0 0 0 0 0 0 0 0 0	0	25
Hale, John	FS, N.H.	0 0 0 0 0 0 0 0 0 0 0 0 0 0 0 0 0 0 - - - 0 0 0 0	0	22
Baldwin, R. S.	Whig, Conn.	0 0 0 0 0 0 0 0 0 0 0 0 0 0 0 0 0 0 0 0 0 - 0 0	0	24
Clarke, J. H.	Whig, R.I.	0 0 0 0 0 0 0 0 1 0 0 0 0 0 0 0 0 0 0 0 0 0 0 1 1	3	22
Corwin, Thos.	Whig, Ohio	0 0 -	0	2
Davis, John	Whig, Mass.	0 0 0 0 0 0 0 0 0 0 0 0 0 0 0 0 0 0 0 0 0 0 0 1 1	2	23
Dayton, Wm. L.	Whig, N.J.	0 0 0 0 0 0 0 0 0 - 0 0 0 0 0 0 0 0 0 0 0 0 - -	0	22
Ewing, Thos.	Whig, Ohio	- - - - - - - - - 0 0 1 0 0 0 0 0 0 0 0 0 0 0 0	1	15
Greene, A. C.	Whig, R.I.	0 0 0 0 0 0 0 0 0 0 0 - 0 0 0 0 0 0 0 0 0 0 1 1	2	22
Miller, J. W.	Whig, N.J.	0 0 0 0 0 0 0 0 0 0 0 0 0 0 0 0 0 0 0 0 0 0 0 - -	0	23
Phelps, Saml.	Whig, Vt.	- - 0 0 0 - 0 - - 0 0 - 0 0 0 0 0 0 0 0 0 0 0 1 1	2	17
Seward, Wm. H.	Whig, N.Y.	0 0 0 0 0 0 0 0 0 0 0 0 0 0 0 0 0 0 0 0 0 0 0 0 0	0	25
Smith, Truman	Whig, Conn.	0 0 1 0 0 0 0 0 0 0 0 1 0 0 0 0 0 0 0 0 0 1 1 1	5	20
Upham, Wm.	Whig, Vt.	0 0 0 0 0 0 0 0 0 0 0 0 0 0 0 0 0 0 0 0 0 0 0 0 0	0	25
Winthrop, R.	Whig, Mass.	- - - - - - - - - - - - 0 0 0 0 0 0 0 0 0 0 1 1	2	11
Dodge, Henry	Dem., Wisc.	1 0 0 0 0 0 0 0 - 0 0 0 0 0 0 0 0 0 0 0 0 0 0 0	1	23
Hamlin, H.	Dem., Maine	0 0 0 0 0 0 0 0 0 0 0 1 0 0 0 0 0 0 0 0 0 0 0 -	1	23
Walker, I. P.	Dem., Wisc.	1 1 1 1 1 0 1 1 1 - 1 1 0 1 0 0 0 0 0 0 0 1 0 0 0	12	12
Morton, J.	Whig, Fla.	0 1 0 0 0 0 0 0 0 0 0 0 1 0 0 1 0 1 0 1 0 1 1 0 0	7	18
Barnwell, R.	Dem., S.C.	- - 0 0 0 0 0 0 0 0 0 0 0 0 0 0 0 0 0 0 0 0 0 0 0	0	23
Benton, Thos.	Dem., Mo.	0 0 0 0 0 0 0 0 0 0 0 0 0 0 0 0 0 0 0 0 0 0 0 0 0	0	25
Butler, A. P.	Dem., S.C.	0 0 0 0 0 0 0 0 0 0 0 0 0 0 0 0 0 0 0 0 0 0 0 0 0	0	25
Clemens, Jere.	Dem., Ala.	0 - - - - - 0 - - 0 0 0 1 1 1 0 0 0 1 0 1 0 0 1 1	7	11
Davis, Jeff.	Dem., Miss.	0 0 0 0 0 0 0 0 0 0 0 0 0 0 0 0 0 0 0 0 0 0 - 0 0	0	24

Vote		A B C D E F G H I J K L M N O P Q R S T U V W X Y	Frequency	
Pro-Compromise (1)=		N N N N N N N N N Y N N N Y N N Y N N N Y N N Y Y	1	0
Anti-Compromise (0)=		Y Y Y Y Y Y Y Y Y N Y Y Y N Y Y N Y Y Y N Y Y N N		
Hunter, Robt.	Dem., Va.	0 0 0 0 0 0 0 0 0 0 0 0 0 1 0 0 0 0 0 0 0 0 - 0 0	1	23
Mason, Jas. M.	Dem., Va.	0 0 0 0 0 0 0 0 0 0 0 0 0 0 0 0 0 0 0 0 0 0 0 0 0	0	25
Sebastian, Wm.	Dem., Ark.	0 - 1 - - 0 0 1 0 0 0 - 1 1 1 1 - 1 0 0 - - 0 - -	7	9
Soulé, Pierre	Dem., La.	0 0 0 0 0 0 0 0 0 0 0 0 - 0 0 0 0 0 0 0 0 0 0 0 0	0	24
Turney, H. L.	Dem., Tenn.	0 0 0 0 0 0 0 0 0 0 0 0 0 0 0 0 0 0 0 0 0 0 0 0 0	0	25
Yulee, D. L.	Dem., Fla.	0 0 0 0 0 0 0 0 0 0 0 0 0 0 0 0 0 0 0 0 0 0 0 0 0	0	25
		Total:	53	613

Section 3: Cohesion Indexes on Senate Roll Calls in Appendix B, Section 2

Pro-Comp.	0.836	Free-Soil	1.000	South	0.086
Anti-Comp.	0.841			Whig	0.622
		North	0.054	Pro-Comp.	0.728
Democrat	0.150	Whig	0.750	Anti-Comp.	0.440
Pro-Comp.	0.896	Pro-Comp.	0.900		
Anti-Comp.	0.822	Anti-Comp.	0.873	Democrat	0.285
				Pro-Comp.	0.776
Whig	0.082	Democrat	0.638	Anti-Comp.	0.882
Pro-Comp.	0.741	Pro-Comp.	0.957		
Anti-Comp.	0.836	Anti-Comp.	0.611		

Cohesion= Percent of majority less percent of minority within a bloc.

Section 4: Likeness Indexes on Senate Roll Calls in Appendix B, Section 2

	NWPC	SWPC	NDPC	SDPC	FS	NWAC	SWAC	NDAC
PC/AC*	0.160							
SWPC	0.912							
NDPC	0.974	0.886						
SDPC	0.936	0.976	0.910					
FS	0.048	0.136	0.022	0.112				
NWAC	0.111	0.199	0.085	0.175	0.937			
SWAC	0.328	0.416	0.302	0.392	0.720	0.783		
NDAC	0.242	0.330	0.216	0.306	0.806	0.869	0.914	
SDAC	0.107	0.195	0.081	0.171	0.941	0.996	0.779	0.865

Likeness=1.000 less (percent of ones in bloc A less percent of ones in bloc B).

*N=North; S=South; PC=pro-compromise; AC=anti-compromise; D=Democrat; W=Whig; FS=Free-Soil

Section 5: Number of Members in Blocs

Pro-Compromise	31	Free-Soil	2	South	29
Anti-Compromise	30			Whig	12
		North	32	Pro-Comp.	11
Democrat	32	Whig	15	Anti-Comp.	1
Pro-Comp.	18	Pro-Comp.	2		
Anti-Comp.	14	Anti-Comp.	13	Democrat	17
				Pro-Comp.	6
Whig	27	Democrat	15	Anti-Comp.	11
Pro-Comp.	13	Pro-Comp	12		
Anti-Comp.	14	Anti-Comp.	3		

❧

Texas Legislature, August–September 1850

Section 1: Members of Texas Senate Present for 3d Legislature, 2d Session

Member	Counties Represented
Brashear, I. W.	Harris
Burleson, Edward	Bastrop, Caldwell, Fayette, Hays, Travis
Campbell, Samuel R.	Collin, Dallas, Denton, Grayson, Henderson
Cooke, W. K.	Brazos, Leon, Limestone, Navarro, Robertson
Davis, H. Clay	Cameron, Starr, Webb
Gage, David	Panola, Rusk
Grimes, Jesse	Grimes, Montgomery, Walker
Hart, Hardin	Hopkins, Hunt, Fannin
Kinney, H. L.	Cameron, Goliad, Nueces, Refugio, San Patricio
Latimer, Albert H.	Lamar, Red River
McRae, John H.	Jasper, Newton, Sabine, San Augustine, Angelina
Moffett, J. H.	Jefferson, Liberty, Polk, Tyler
Parker, Isaac	Anderson, Houston, Cherokee
Phillips, Alexander H.	Calhoun, DeWitt, Gonzales, Jackson, Matagorda, Victoria
Portis, David Y.	Austin, Colorado, Fort Bend, LaVaca, Wharton
Robertson, Jerome B.	Burleson, Milam, Williamson, Washington
Taylor, J. F.	Harrison, Smith, Upshur
Truit, A. M.	Nacogdoches, Shelby
Van Derlip, David C.	Comal, Bexar, Guadalupe
Wallace, B. Rush	all counties east of the Trinity River
Ward, Matthias	Bowie, Cass, Titus

Section 2: Members of Texas House of Representatives
Present for 3d Legislature, 2d Session

Member	*Counties Represented*
Bee, Hamilton P.	Cameron, Goliad, Nueces, Refugio, San Patricio, Starr, Webb
Bogart, Sam	Collin, Grayson, Cooke
Bryan, Guy M.	Brazoria, Ft. Bend
Burney, George E.	Milam, Williamson
Charlton, N. B.	Jasper, Jefferson, Tyler
Clements, R. E.	Cameron, Nueces, Starr, Webb
Clough, Jeremiah M.	Harrison
Cochran, William M.	Dallas, Denton
Crump, William E.	Austin, Colorado
Crump, William G.	Bexar, Gillespie, Medina
Dickson, David C.	Grimes, Montgomery
Fields, William	Liberty, Polk
Franklin, B. C.	Galveston
Gillett, James S.	Lamar
Hardeman, Thomas M.	Caldwell, Hays, Travis
Hardeman, William N.	Nacogdoches
Holland, James K.	Rusk, Panola
Johnson, Joshua F.	Titus
Jowers, W. G. W.	Anderson, Houston
Keenan, C. G. (speaker)	Walker
Lewis, Henry M.	Bexar, Gillespie, Medina
Lloyd, Emery	Rusk
Lott, Elisha E.	Henderson, Smith
McKinney, Thomas F.	Galveston
Pace, Alfred E.	Fannin
Polk, John	San Augustine
Reynolds, J. M.	Harris, San Augustine
Runnels, Hardin R.	Bowie, Red River
Russell, William	Fayette
Scott, James W.	Harris
Selman, Benjamin	Cherokee
Shaw, James	Bastrop, Burleson
Shea, John	Harris
Sheppard, James G.	Washington
Smith, J. M.	Shelby
Smith, P. Burrell	Red River
Speights, Joshua H.	Newton, Sabine

Stapp, D. M.	DeWitt, Lavaca, Victoria
Sterne, Adolphus	Anderson, Angelina, Cherokee, Houston, Nacogdoches
Stewart, William H.	Comal, Gonzales, Guadalupe
Tarrant, Edward H.	Limestone, Navarro
Taylor, D. K.	Cass
Williams, William M.	Lamar, Fannin
Wilson, James C.	Calhoun, Jackson, Matagorda, Wharton
Winfield, E. H.	Cameron, Starr, Webb
Wren, Johnson	Hopkins, Hunt

Tables of Blocs—Texas Legislature, August–September 1850

The following tables divide the members of the Texas Senate and House of Representatives during the special session of August–September 1850 into blocs that are labeled "moderate," "radical," or "indeterminate" according to their roll-call voting on several key issues. The figures given for each member show the record of his voting on that particular issue. Figures to the left of the dash represent the number of times the member voted with the "moderate" position; figures to the right of the dash represent the number of times the member voted with the "radical" position.

Section 3: Texas House of Representatives—Issue: Election of U.S. Senator
(Five Roll Calls)

Moderate (pro-Rusk)		Radical (anti-Rusk)	
Bogart	4-1	Bee	0-5
Charlton	5-0	Bryan	1-4
Cochran	4-1	Clements	0-5
Crump, W. G.	5-0	Clough	0-5
Dickson	5-0	Crump, W. E.	1-2
Fields	5-0	Franklin	0-5
Hardeman, W. N.	5-0	Gillett	0-5
Holland	5-0	Hardeman, T. M.	1-4
Johnson	5-0	Lewis	0-1
Jowers	1-0	McKinney	0-4
Keenan	4-1	Pace	2-3
Lloyd	5-0	Reynolds	0-5
Lott	5-0	Russell	1-4
Polk	5-0	Shaw	2-3
Runnels	3-1	Shea	0-5
Scott	5-0	Sheppard	1-4

Selman	5-0	Smith, J. M.	2-3
Smith, P. B.	5-0	Stapp	1-4
Speights	5-0	Stewart	0-5
Sterne	5-0	Taylor	0-5
Tarrant	5-0	Wilson	1-4
Williams	4-1	Winfield	1-3
Wren	5-0		

Indeterminate

Burney   2-2

Section 4: Texas House of Representatives—Issue: "War Bill" (Twelve Roll Calls)

Moderate (anti-expedition)		Franklin	1-11
Bogart	8-3	Gillett	2-10
Charlton	12-0	Hardeman, T. M.	1-11
Dickson	9-3	Holland	0-12
Fields	10-2	Keenan	1-11
Hardeman, W. N.	8-4	Lewis	0-7
Johnson	9-3	Lloyd	1-11
Jowers	8-4	Lott	3-9
McKinney	12-0	Reynolds	0-12
Pace	9-3	Runnels	2-7
Polk	9-3	Russell	1-11
Scott	10-2	Shaw	5-7
Selman	7-5	Shea	0-12
Smith, P. B.	8-4	Sheppard	0-12
Speights	10-1	Smith, J. M.	0-12
Sterne	8-4	Stapp	1-11
Taylor	7-5	Stewart	0-10
Wren	7-5	Tarrant	0-12
		Williams	1-11
Radical (pro-expedition)		Wilson	0-12
Bee	3-8	Winfield	0-12
Bryan	1-11		
Clements	2-10		
Clough	2-10	*Indeterminate*	
Crump, W. E.	0-11	Cochran	6-6
Crump, W. G.	0-9		

Section 5: Texas Senate—Issue: "War" Bill (Twelve Roll Calls)

Moderate (pro-expedition)		Radical (anti-expedition)	
Campbell	10-2	Brashear	3-8
Grimes	10-2	Burleson	3-7
Hart	10-2	Cooke	5-7
McRae	8-3	Davis	1-10
Moffett	11-1	Gage	2-5
Parker	10-2	Kinney	0-10
Phillips	1-0	Latimer	5-7
Wallace	11-1	Portis	0-11
		Robertson	0-12
		Taylor	5-7
Indeterminate		Van Derlip	2-10
Truit	6-6	Ward	5-7

࿊

Roll-Call Votes in U.S. House of Representatives (Thirty-First Congress, First Session) That Define Pro- and Anti-Compromise Blocs

Section 1: Descriptive List of the Twenty-Six Roll Calls

Vote	HR Journal Page	Date	Description	Yea-Nay
A	1276–77	Aug. 19	Ashmun (W-Mass.) move to suspend rules to enable him to introduce resolution to make Utah Territory, Texas boundary, California statehood, and N.M. Territory bills, respectively, special order for next day and until disposed of	94-94 (required ⅔ to pass)
B	1321–22	Aug. 28	Inge (D-Ala.) move to reject Texas bill under 116th rule	34-168
C	1337–38	Aug. 29	Ashmun move to table appeal by Burt (D-S.C.) of speaker's decision that Burt's move to commit Texas bill to Committee of the Whole was out of order	154-54
D	1368–69	Sept. 4	Cable (D-Ohio) move to table bill and amendments	30-169
E	1370–72	Sept. 4	McLane (D-Md.) move to commit Texas bill and amendments to Committee of the Whole	101-99

Vote	*HR Journal Page*	*Date*	*Description*	*Yea-Nay*
F	1372–73	Sept. 4	Root (FS-Ohio) move to table move by Walden (D-N.Y.) to reconsider vote E	103-103 (speaker votes no)
G	1373–74	Sept. 4	Walden move to reconsider vote E	104-101
H	1374–75	Sept. 4	Reconsideration of vote E	101-103
I	1377–78	Sept. 4	Ashe (D-N.C.) move to table Texas bill and amendments	61-141
J	1384–85	Sept. 4	Boyd (D-Ky.) amendment to combine Texas and N.M. bills	98-106
K	1385–86	Sept. 4	Boyd move to adjourn	72-127
L	1386–87	Sept. 4	Shall Texas bill be read third time?	80-126
M	1388–89	Sept. 5	Inge move to table Boyd move to reconsider vote L	71-135
N	1389–91	Sept. 5	Boyd move to reconsider vote L	131-75
O	1391–92	Sept. 5	Campbell (W-Ohio) move to table Grinnell (W-Mass.) move to reconsider vote J	96-108
P	1392–93	Sept. 5	Grinnell move to reconsider vote J	105-99
Q	1395–96	Sept. 5	Inge appeal of speaker's decision that Inge cannot move to divide Wentworth (D-Ill.) move to commit bill to Committee of the Whole with instructions to ban slavery from N.M. Shall speaker's decision stand?	101-86
R	1400–1401	Sept. 5	Reconsideration of vote J	107-99
S	1402–3	Sept. 5	Shall Tex.–N.M. bill be read third time?	99-107
T	1404–6	Sept. 6	Duer (W-N.Y.) move to table appeal by Howard (D-Tex.) of speaker's decision that reconsideration of vote S not in order	79-122
U	1406–7	Sept. 6	Howard appeal—Shall speaker's decision stand?	82-124
V	1407–8	Sept. 6	Howard move to reconsider vote S	122-84
W	1408–9	Sept. 6	Shall main question of third reading be put?	115-91
X	1409–10	Sept. 6	Shall Tex.–N.M. bill be read third time?	108-98
Y	1411–12	Sept. 6	Burt move to table bill and amendments	97-108
Z	1412–13	Sept. 6	Shall Tex.–N.M. bill pass?	108-97

Section 2: Roll-Call Votes of Pro- and Anti-Compromise Blocs

Vote	A B C D E F G H I J K L M N O P Q R S T U V W X Y Z	Frequency	
Pro-Comp. (1) =	Y N Y N N N Y N N Y Y Y N Y N Y N Y Y Y Y N N Y Y Y N Y	1	0
Anti-Comp. (0)=	N Y N Y Y Y N Y Y N N N N Y N Y N N N N N Y Y N N N Y N		

Pro-Compromise*

Andrews, Geo.	Whig, N.Y.	- - - 1 1 1 - - 1 0 1 1 1 1 1 1 1 1 1 1 1 1 1 1 1	20	1
Ashmun, G.	Whig, Mass.	1 1 1 -	3	0
Bokee, D. A.	Whig, N.Y.	- 1 1 1 1 1 1 1 1 1 1 1 1 1 1 1 1 1 1 1 1 1 1 1 1 1	25	0
Briggs, Geo.	Whig, N.Y.	1 1 1 1 1 1 1 1 1 1 1 1 1 1 1 1 1 1 1 1 1 1 1 1 1 1	26	0
Brooks, Jas.	Whig, N.Y.	1 1 1 1 1 1 1 1 1 1 0 1 1 1 1 1 1 1 1 - 1 1 1 1 1 1	24	1
Butler, C.	Whig, Pa.	1 1 1 1 1 1 1 1 1 1 1 1 1 1 1 1 1 1 1 1 1 1 1 1 1 1	26	0
Casey, Jos.	Whig, Pa.	1 1 1 1 1 1 1 1 1 0 1 1 1 1 1 1 1 1 1 1 1 1 1 1 1 1	25	1
Chandler, J.	Whig, Pa.	1 1 1 1 0 0 0 0 1 - 0 1 1 1 1 1 1 1 1 1 1 1 1 1 1 1	20	5
Duer, Wm.	Whig, N.Y.	0 1 1 1 1 1 1 1 1 1 1 1 1 1 1 1 1 1 0 - 1 1 1 1 1 1	23	2
Duncan, J. H.	Whig, Mass.	0 1 1 1 0 0 0 0 1 0 0 0 1 1 1 1 1 1 1 1 1 1 1 1 1 1	19	7
Eliot, S. A.	Whig, Mass.	- 1 1 1 1 1 1 1 1 1 0 1 1 1 1 1 1 1 1 1 1 1 1 1 1 1	24	1
Gould, H. D.	Whig, N.Y.	0 1 1 1 0 0 0 0 1 0 0 1 1 1 0 0 0 0 0 0 1 1 1 0 - 1 -	11	13
Grinnell, Jos.	Whig, Mass.	1 1 1 1 1 1 1 1 1 0 0 1 1 1 1 1 1 1 1 1 1 1 1 1 1 1	24	2
Hampton, M.	Whig, Pa.	1 1 1 -	3	0
Hay, A. K.	Whig, N.J.	0 1 1 -	2	1
King, Geo. G.	Whig, R.I.	0 1 1 1 0 0 0 0 1 0 0 0 1 1 1 0 1 0 0 1 1 1 1 1 1 1	15	11
Levin, L. C.	Whig, Pa.	1 - - 1 1 1 1 1 1 1 0 1 1 1 1 1 1 1 1 1 1 1 1 1 1 1	23	1
McKissock, T.	Whig, N.Y.	0 1 1 1 0 0 0 0 1 0 1 1 1 1 1 1 1 0 1 1 1 1 1 1 1 1	19	7
Nelson, Wm.	Whig, N.Y.	0 1 1 1 1 1 1 1 1 0 1 0 1 1 0 0 0 1 1 1 1 1 1 1 1 1	20	6
Phoenix, J. P.	Whig, N.Y.	1 1 1 1 1 1 1 1 1 1 1 1 1 1 1 1 1 1 1 1 1 1 1 1 1 1	26	0
Pitman, C. W.	Whig, Pa.	1 1 1 1 1 1 1 1 1 1 1 1 1 1 1 1 1 1 1 1 1 1 1 1 1 1	26	0
Rose, R. L.	Whig, N.Y.	1 1 1 1 1 1 1 1 1 1 1 1 1 1 1 1 1 1 0 1 1 1 1 1 1	25	1
Schermerhorn	Whig, N.Y.	0 1 1 1 0 0 0 0 1 0 0 0 1 1 0 - 1 0 0 0 1 1 1 1 1 1	13	12
Taylor, J. L.	Whig, Ohio	0 1 1 1 0 0 1 0 1 0 - 1 1 1 1 0 1 1 1 1 1 1 1 1 1 1	19	6
Thurman, J. R.	Whig, N.Y.	- 1 1 1 1 1 1 1 1 0 1 1 1 1 1 0 1 1 1 1 1 1 1 1 1 1	23	2
Underhill, W.	Whig, N.Y.	1 1 1 1 0 0 1 1 1 0 0 1 1 1 0 1 1 0 1 1 1 1 1 1 1 1	20	6
White, H.	Whig, N.Y.	0 1 1 1 0 0 0 0 1 0 0 1 1 1 1 1 1 1 1 1 1 1 1 1 1 1	19	7
Wilson, Jas.	Whig, N.H.	1 1 1 1 1 1 1 1 1 0 1 1 1 1 1 1 1 1 1 1 1 1 1 - 1	24	1
Albertson, N.	Dem., Ind.	1 1 1 1 1 1 1 1 1 0 1 1 1 1 1 1 1 1 1 1 1 1 1 1 1	25	1
Bissell, Wm. H.	Dem., Ill.	- 1 1 -	2	0
Brown, Wm. J.	Dem., Ind.	1 1 1 1 1 1 1 1 1 1 1 1 1 1 1 - 1 1 1 1 1 1 1	25	0
Buel, A. W.	Dem., Mich.	- 1 1 1 1 1 1 1 1 1 1 1 1 1 1 1 - 1 1 1 0 1 1 1 1 1	23	1
Dimmick, M. M.	Dem., Pa.	1 1 1 1 1 1 1 1 1 1 1 1 1 1 1 1 1 1 1 1 1 1 1 1 1 1	26	0
Disney, D. T.	Dem., Ohio	1 1 0 1 0 0 0 0 1 0 0 1 1 1 1 1 1 1 1 0 0 0 0 1 1 1	15	11

Vote		A B C D E F G H I J K L M N O P Q R S T U V W X Y Z	Frequency	
Pro-Comp. (1)	=	Y N Y N N N Y N N Y Y Y N Y N Y Y Y Y N N Y Y Y N Y	1	0
Anti-Comp. (0)	=	N Y N Y Y Y N Y Y N N N Y N Y N N N N N Y Y N N N Y n		

		A B C D E F G H I J K L M N O P Q R S T U V W X Y Z		
Dunham, C. L.	Dem., Ind.	1 - 1 1 1 1 1 1 1 1 1 1 1 1 1 1 1 1 1 1 1 1 1 1 1	25	0
Fitch, G.	Dem., Ind.	1 1 1 1 0 0 0 0 - - 0 0 1 1 1 - 0 1 1 1 0 1 0 1 1 1	14	9
Fuller, T.J.D.	Dem., Maine	1 1 1 1 1 1 1 1 1 1 1 1 1 1 1 1 1 1 1 1 1 1 1 1 1 1	26	0
Gerry, E.	Dem., Maine	1 1 1 1 1 1 1 1 1 1 1 1 1 1 1 1 1 1 1 0 0 1 1 1 1 1	24	2
Gilmore, A.	Dem., Pa.	- 1 1 1 1 1 1 1 1 1 0 1 1 1 1 1 1 1 1 1 1 1 1 1 1 1	24	1
Gorman, W. A.	Dem., Ind.	1 1 1 1 1 1 1 1 - 1 1 1 1 1 1 1 1 1 1 1 1 1 1 1 1 1	25	0
Harris, Thos. L.	Dem., Ill.	1 - - 1 1 1 1 1 1 0 1 1 1 1 1 1 1 1 1 1 1 1 1 1 1 1	23	1
Hibbard, H.	Dem., N.H.	- 1 1 1 1 1 1 1 1 1 1 1 1 1 1 1 1 1 1 1 1 1 1 1 1 1	25	0
Hoagland, M.	Dem., Ohio	1 1 1 1 1 1 1 1 1 1 1 1 1 1 1 1 1 1 1 1 1 1 1 1 1 1	26	0
Leffler, S.	Dem., Iowa	1 1 1 1 1 1 1 1 1 1 1 1 1 1 1 1 1 1 1 1 1 1 1 1 1 1	26	0
Littlefield, N.	Dem., Maine	1 1 1 1 1 1 1 1 1 1 1 1 1 - 1 1 1 1 1 1 1 1 1 1 1 1	25	0
Mann, J.	Dem., Pa.	1 1 1 1 1 1 1 1 1 1 1 1 1 1 1 1 1 1 1 1 1 1 1 1 1 1	26	0
McClernand	Dem., Ill.	1 1 1 1 1 1 1 1 1 1 1 1 1 0 1 1 1 1 1 1 1 1 1 1	25	1
McDonald, J. E.	Dem., Ind.	1 1 1 1 1 1 1 1 1 1 0 1 1 1 0 1 1 1 1 1 1 1 1 1	24	2
McLanahan, Jas. X.	Dem., Pa.	1 1 1 - - - - - - - - - 1 1 1 1 1 1 1 1 1 1 1 1	17	0
Peaslee, Chas. H.	Dem., N.H.	1 1 1 1 1 1 1 1 0 1 1 1 0 0 1 1 1 1 1 1 1 1 1	23	3
Potter, E. D.	Dem., Ohio	1 1 1 - - - 1 1 1 - 0 0 1 1 1 1 - 1 1 - 1 1 1 1 1 1	18	2
Richardson, W.	Dem., Ill.	1 - 1 1 1 1 1 1 1 0 1 1 1 1 0 1 1 1 1 1 1 1 1	23	2
Robbins, J.	Dem., Pa.	1 1 1 1 1 1 1 1 1 1 1 1 1 1 1 1 1 1 1 1 1 1 1 1 1 1	26	0
Robinson, J.	Dem., Ind.	1 1 1 1 1 1 1 1 1 - 1 1 1 - 1 - 1 1 1 1 1 1 1 1	23	0
Ross, Thos.	Dem., Pa.	- 1 1 1 1 1 1 1 1 1 0 0 1 1 1 1 0 1 1 1 1 1 1 1 1	22	3
Strong, Wm.	Dem., Pa.	1 1 1 1 1 1 1 1 1 1 1 1 1 1 1 - 1 1 1 1 1 1 1 1	25	0
Thompson, Jas.	Dem., Pa.	1 1 1 1 1 1 1 1 0 1 1 1 0 0 1 0 1 1 1 1 1 1 1 1	22	4
Walden, H.	Dem., N.Y.	1 1 1 1 0 1 1 1 1 1 1 1 1 1 1 1 1 1 1 1 1 1 1 1 1	25	1
Whittlesey, W.	Dem., Ohio	1 1 1 1 1 1 1 1 0 0 0 1 1 0 0 0 0 0 1 1 1 0 1 1 1	17	9
Wildrick, I.	Dem., N.J.	1 1 1 1 1 1 1 1 1 0 1 1 1 1 1 1 1 1 1 1 1 1 1 1	25	1
Wood, A. E.	Dem., Ohio	1 1 1 -	3	0
Young, T. R.	Dem., Ill.	1 1 1 1 1 1 1 1 1 1 1 1 1 1 1 1 1 1 1 1 1 1 1 1 1 1	26	0
Alston, Wm.	Whig, Ala.	1 1 1 1 1 1 1 1 1 0 0 1 1 1 1 1 1 1 1 1 1 1 1 1	24	2
Anderson, J.	Whig, Tenn.	1 1 1 1 1 1 1 1 1 1 1 1 1 1 1 1 1 1 1 1 1 1 1 1 1 1	26	0
Bowie, R. I.	Whig, Md.	0 1 1 - - 1 1 1 1 1 1 1 1 1 1 1 1 1 1 1 1 1 1 1 1	23	1
Breck, Danl.	Whig, Ky.	1 1 1 1 1 1 1 1 1 1 1 1 1 1 1 1 1 1 1 1 1 1 1 1 1 1	26	0
Cabell, E. C.	Whig, Fla.	0 1 1 1 1 1 1 1 1 1 0 1 1 1 1 - 1 1 1 1 1 1 1 1	23	2
Caldwell, Jos.	Whig, N.C.	1 1 1 1 1 1 1 1 1 0 1 1 1 1 1 1 1 1 1 1 1 1 1 1	25	1
Deberry, E.	Whig, N.C.	1 1 1 1 1 1 1 1 1 0 1 1 1 1 1 1 1 1 1 1 1 1 1 1	25	1
Evans, A.	Whig, Md.	- 1 1 -	2	0
Gentry, M. P.	Whig, Tenn.	1 1 1 1 1 1 1 1 1 1 1 1 1 1 1 - 1 1 1 1 1 1 1 1	25	0

	Vote	A B C D E F G H I J K L M N O P Q R S T U V W X Y Z	Frequency	
	Pro-Comp. (1) =	Y N Y N N N Y N N Y Y Y N Y N Y Y Y Y N N Y Y Y N Y	1	0
	Anti-Comp. (0)=	N Y N Y Y Y N Y Y N N N Y N Y N N N N Y Y N N N Y N		

		A B C D E F G H I J K L M N O P Q R S T U V W X Y Z		
Haymond, T. S.	Whig, Va.	1 1 1 1 1 1 1 1 1 1 1 1 1 1 1 1 1 1 1 1 1 1 1 1 1 1	26	0
Hilliard, H.	Whig, Ala.	- 1 1 1 1 1 1 1 1 1 1 1 1 1 1 1 1 1 1 1 1 1 1 1 1 1	25	0
Houston, J. W.	Whig, Del.	- 1 1 1 1 1 1 1 1 1 1 1 1 1 1 1 1 1 1 1 1 1 1 1 1 1	25	0
Johnson, J. L.	Whig, Ky.	0 1 1 1 1 1 1 1 1 1 1 1 1 1 1 1 1 1 1 1 1 1 1 1 1 1	25	1
Kerr, J. B.	Whig, Md.	1 1 1 1 1 1 1 1 1 1 1 1 1 1 1 1 1 1 1 1 1 1 1 1 1 1	26	0
Marshall, H.	Whig, Ky.	1 1 1 1 1 1 1 1 1 1 0 1 1 1 1 1 1 1 1 1 1 1 1 1 1 1	25	1
McLean, F. E.	Whig, Ky.	1 1 1 1 1 1 1 1 1 1 0 1 1 1 1 1 1 1 1 1 1 1 1 1 1 1	25	1
Morehead, C.	Whig, Ky.	- 1 1 1 1 1 1 1 1 1 1 1 1 1 1 1 1 1 1 1 1 1 1 1 1 1	25	0
Morton, J.	Whig, Va.	0 1 1 1 1 1 1 1 1 1 1 1 1 1 1 1 1 1 1 1 1 1 1 1 1 1	25	1
Outlaw, D.	Whig, N.C.	1 1 1 1 1 1 1 1 1 1 1 1 1 1 1 1 1 1 1 1 1 1 1 1 1 1	26	0
Owen, A. F.	Whig, Ga.	- 1 1 1 1 1 1 1 - 0 1 1 1 1 - 1 1 - 1 1 1 1 1 1	21	1
Shepperd, A.	Whig, N.C.	1 1 1 1 1 1 1 1 1 1 1 1 1 1 1 1 1 1 1 1 1 1 1 1 1 1	26	0
Stanly, Edw.	Whig, N.C.	1 1 1 1 1 1 1 1 1 1 0 1 1 1 1 1 1 1 1 1 1 1 1 1 1 1	25	1
Thompson, J.	Whig, Ky.	1 1 1 - 1 1 1 1 1 1 1 1 1 1 1 1 1 1 1 1 1 1 1 1 1 1	25	0
Toombs, Robt.	Whig, Ga.	0 1 1 1 1 1 1 1 1 - 0 1 1 1 1 - 1 1 1 1 1 1 1 1 1	22	2
Watkins, A. G.	Whig, Tenn.	1 1 1 1 1 1 1 1 1 1 0 1 1 1 1 1 1 1 1 1 1 1 1 1 1 1	25	1
Williams, C.	Whig, Tenn.	- 1 1 1 1 1 1 1 1 1 1 1 1 1 1 1 1 1 1 1 1 1 1 1 1 1	25	0
Bay, Wm. V. N.	Dem., Mo.	1 1 1 1 1 1 1 1 1 0 1 1 1 1 1 1 1 0 0 1 1 1 1 1	23	3
Bayly, Thos.	Dem., Va.	0 1 - 1 1 1 1 1 1 0 0 1 1 1 1 1 1 0 0 1 1 1 1 1	20	5
Beale, Jas.	Dem., Va.	0 1 1 1 1 1 1 1 1 1 0 1 1 1 0 1 1 1 1 1 1 1 1 1	23	3
Bowlin, J. B.	Dem., Mo.	1 1 0 1 1 1 1 1 1 1 0 1 1 1 1 1 1 1 1 1 1 1 1 1	24	2
Boyd, L.	Dem., Ky.	1 1 1 1 1 1 1 1 1 1 0 1 1 1 1 - 1 1 1 1 1 1 1 1	24	1
Caldwell, G.	Dem., Ky.	0 1 1 - 1 1 1 1 1 1 0 1 1 1 1 1 1 1 1 1 1 1 1 1	23	2
Cobb, W.R.W.	Dem., Ala.	1 1 1 1 1 1 1 1 1 0 1 0 0 1 1 1 1 1 1 1 1 1 1 1	23	3
Edmundson, H.	Dem., Va.	0 1 0 1 0 0 0 0 1 1 0 0 1 1 1 1 0 1 1 1 0 1 1 1 1 1	16	10
Ewing, A.	Dem., Tenn.	0 1 1 1 1 1 1 1 1 1 1 1 1 1 1 1 1 1 1 1 1 1 1 1 1	25	1
Green, Jas. S.	Dem., Mo.	- 1 1 1 1 1 1 1 1 0 0 1 1 1 1 1 1 1 1 1 1 1 1 1	23	2
Hall, W. P.	Dem., Mo.	1 1 1 1 1 1 1 1 1 1 1 1 1 1 1 1 1 0 0 1 1 1 1 1	24	2
Hamilton, W.	Dem., Md.	1 1 1 -	3	0
Hammond, Edw.	Dem., Md.	0 0 1 1 1 1 1 1 1 0 1 1 1 1 1 1 1 1 1 1 1 1 1 1	23	3
Harris, I. G.	Dem., Tenn.	0 1 1 1 1 1 1 1 1 1 0 1 1 1 1 1 1 1 1 1 1 1 1 1	24	2
Howard, V. E.	Dem., Tex.	1 1 1 1 1 1 1 1 1 0 0 1 1 1 1 1 0 1 1 1 1 1 1 1	23	3
Johnson, A.	Dem., Tenn.	1 1 1 1 1 1 1 1 1 0 1 1 1 1 - 1 1 1 1 1 1 1 1 1	24	1
Jones, Geo. W.	Dem., Tenn.	1 1 1 1 1 1 1 1 1 1 1 1 1 1 1 1 1 1 1 1 1 1 1 1 1 1	26	0
Kaufman, D. S.	Dem., Tex.	- 1 1 1 1 1 1 1 1 0 1 1 1 1 1 - 1 1 1 1 1 1 1 1	23	1
Mason, J. C.	Dem., Ky.	1 1 0 1 1 0 1 1 1 1 - 0 1 1 1 1 1 0 1 1 1 1 1 1	21	4
McDowell, J.	Dem., Va.	0 1 1 1 1 1 1 1 - 1 1 1 1 1 1 1 1 1 1 1 1 1 1 1	24	1

Vote	A B C D E F G H I J K L M N O P Q R S T U V W X Y Z	Frequency	
Pro-Comp. (1) =	Y N Y N N N Y N N Y Y Y N Y N Y Y Y Y Y N N Y Y Y N Y	1	0
Anti-Comp. (0)=	N Y N Y Y Y N Y Y N N N Y N Y N N N N Y Y N N N N Y N		

Name	Party	A B C D E F G H I J K L M N O P Q R S T U V W X Y Z		
McLane, R. M.	Dem., Md.	- 1 1 1 1 1 1 1 1 1 1 1 1 1 1 1 1 1 1 1 1 1 1 1 1 1	25	0
McMullen, F.	Dem., Va.	- 1 1 1 1 1 1 1 1 1 1 1 1 1 1 1 1 1 1 1 1 1 1 1 1 1	25	0
Parker, R.	Dem., Va.	0 1 1 1 1 1 1 1 1 1 1 1 1 1 1 1 1 1 1 1 0 1 1 1 1 1	24	2
Savage, J. H.	Dem., Tenn.	0 1 0 1 1 1 1 1 1 1 0 1 1 1 1 0 1 1 1 1 1 1 1 1 1	22	4
Stanton, F. P.	Dem., Tenn.	- 1 0 1 1 1 1 0 1 0 0 0 0 0 0 0 1 0 0 0 0 1 1 1 1 1	13	12
Stanton, R. H.	Dem., Ky.	0 1 0 1 1 0 1 1 1 0 0 0 0 0 0 0 1 0 1 1 1 1 1 1 1	15	11
Thomas, J. H.	Dem., Tenn.	0 1 1 1 1 1 1 1 1 1 0 0 0 0 0 0 0 1 0 1 1 1 1 1 1 1	18	8
Wellborn, M.	Dem., Ga.	0 1 1 1 1 1 1 1 1 1 1 0 1 1 1 1 1 1 1 1 1 1 1 1 1	24	2
	Total:		2,522	252

Anti-Compromise Bloc*

Name	Party	A B C D E F G H I J K L M N O P Q R S T U V W X Y Z		
Allen, C.	FS, Mass.	- 1 0 0 0 0 0 0 0 0 0 0 0 0 0 0 0 0 0 0 0 0 0 0 0 0	1	24
Booth, W.	FS, Conn.	1 1 0 0 0 0 0 0 0 0 0 0 0 0 0 0 0 0 0 0 0 0 0 0 0 0	2	24
Durkee, Chas.	FS, Wisc.	0 0 0 0 0 0 0 0 0 0 0 0 0 0 0 0 0 0 0 0 0 0 0 0 0 0	0	26
Giddings, J.R.	FS, Ohio	0 0 0 0 0 0 0 0 0 0 0 0 0 0 0 0 0 0 0 0 0 0 0 0 0 0	0	26
Hunter, Wm. F.	FS, Ohio	0 0 1 1 0 0 0 0 0 0 0 0 0 0 0 1 0 0 0 0 0 - 0 0 0	3	22
Julian, Geo. W.	FS, Ind.	0 0 0 0 0 0 0 0 0 0 0 0 0 0 0 0 0 0 0 0 0 0 0 0 0 0	0	26
King. P.	FS, N.Y.	0 0 0 0 0 0 0 0 0 0 0 0 0 0 0 0 0 0 0 0 0 0 0 0 0 0	0	26
Mann, H.	FS, Mass.	0 1 0 1 0 0 0 0 0 0 0 1 0 0 0 - 0 0 0 0 0 0 0 0 0	3	22
Root, Jos. M.	FS, Ohio	0 0 0 0 0 0 0 0 0 0 0 0 0 0 0 0 0 0 0 0 0 0 0 0 0 0	0	26
Sprague, Wm.	FS, Mich.	0 1 1 1 0 0 0 0 1 0 0 0 1 0 0 0 0 0 0 1 0 0 0 0 0 0	6	20
Tuck, A.	FS, N.H.	- 1 1 1 0 0 0 0 1 0 0 0 0 0 0 0 0 0 0 0 0 0 0 0 0 0	4	21
Wilmot, D.	FS, Pa.	- 0 0 -	0	2
Alexander, H.P.	Whig, N.Y.	1 1 0 1 0 0 0 0 0 0 0 0 0 0 0 0 0 0 0 0 0 0 0 0 0 0	3	23
Baker, Edw. D.	Whig, Ill.	1 - 1 0 0 0 0 0 0 0 0 0 0 0 0 0 0 - 0 0 0 0 0 0	2	22
Bennett, H.	Whig, N.Y.	1 - 0 0 0 0 0 0 0 0 0 0 1 0 1 0 0 0 0 0 0 0 0 0	3	22
Burrows, L.	Whig, N.Y.	1 1 1 1 0 0 0 0 1 0 1 0 1 1 0 0 1 0 0 1 1 1 0 0 0	12	14
Butler, Thos. B.	Whig, Conn.	1 1 1 1 0 0 0 0 1 0 0 0 1 1 0 0 0 0 0 - 0 0 0 0 0 0	7	18
Calvin, S.	Whig, Pa.	0 1 1 1 0 0 0 0 1 0 0 0 1 1 0 0 0 0 0 0 1 0 0 0 0 0	8	18
Campbell, L. D.	Whig, Ohio	0 0 1 0 0 0 0 0 0 0 0 0 0 0 0 0 0 0 0 0 0 0 0 0 0 0	1	25
Clarke, Chas. E.	Whig, N.Y.	0 0 - 0 0 0 0 0 0 0 0 0 0 0 0 0 0 0 0 0 0 0 0 0 0 0	0	25
Conger, H. S.	Whig, N.Y.	- - - 1 0 0 0 0 1 0 0 0 1 1 0 0 1 0 0 0 0 0 1 0 0 0	6	17
Corwin, M. B.	Whig, Ohio	0 1 1 1 0 0 0 0 1 0 0 0 0 1 0 0 0 0 0 1 0 0 0 0 0 0	6	20
Crowell, J.	Whig, Ohio	0 1 1 1 0 0 0 0 0 0 0 0 0 0 0 0 0 0 0 0 0 0 0 0 0 0	3	23
Dickey, J. C.	Whig, Pa.	1 - 1 - - 0 0 0 0 0 0 0 0 0 0 0 0 0 0 0 0 0 0 0 0 0	2	21
Dixon, N. F.	Whig, R.I.	- 1 1 1 0 0 0 0 1 0 0 0 1 1 0 0 1 0 0 1 1 0 0 0 0 0	9	16

Vote		A B C D E F G H I J K L M N O P Q R S T U V W X Y Z	Frequency	
Pro-Comp. (1) =		Y N Y N N N Y N N Y Y Y N Y N Y Y Y Y N N Y Y Y N Y	1	0
Anti-Comp. (0)=		N Y N Y Y Y N Y Y N N N Y N Y N N N N Y Y N N N Y N		

		A B C D E F G H I J K L M N O P Q R S T U V W X Y Z		
Evans, N.	Whig, Ohio	0 1 1 1 0 0 0 0 0 0 0 1 1 0 0 0 0 1 1 0 0 0 0 0	7	19
Fowler, O.	Whig, Mass.	0 1 0 1 0 0 0 0 0 0 0 0 0 0 0 0 0 0 0 0 0 0 0 0	2	24
Freedley, J.	Whig, Pa.	- 1 1 1 - 0 0 0 1 0 0 0 1 1 0 0 0 0 0 0 1 0 1 - - -	8	13
Goodenow, R. K.	Whig, Maine	0 -	0	1
Gott, Danl.	Whig, N.Y.	0 1 0 1 0 0 0 0 0 0 0 0 0 0 0 0 0 0 0 0 0 0 0 0	2	24
Halloway, R.	Whig, N.Y.	0 1 0 1 0 0 0 1 0 0 0 1 1 0 0 - 0 0 0 0 - 0 0 0 0	5	19
Hebard, Wm.	Whig, Vt.	1 0 1 - 0 0 0 0 0 0 0 0 0 - 0 1 0 0 1 1 0 1 0 0 0	6	18
Henry, Wm.	Whig, Vt.	0 1 1 1 0 0 0 0 1 0 0 0 - - 0 0 0 0 0 0 0 0 0 0 0	4	20
Jackson, Wm. T.	Whig, N.Y.	1 1 1 1 0 0 0 0 0 0 0 0 0 0 0 0 0 0 0 1 1 1 0 0 0 0	7	19
King, Jas. G.	Whig, N.J.	0 1 1 1 0 0 0 0 1 0 0 1 1 1 0 0 1 0 0 1 1 - 0 0 0 0	10	15
King, J. A.	Whig, N.Y.	0 1 1 1 0 0 0 0 1 0 0 0 1 1 0 0 0 0 0 1 1 1 0 0 0 0	9	17
Matteson, O. B.	Whig, N.Y.	0 0 1 0 0 0 0 0 0 0 0 0 0 0 0 0 0 0 0 0 0 0 0 0	1	25
McGaughey,E.W.	Whig, Ind.	1 1 1 1 1 1 1 1 1 0 0 0 0 0 0 0 1 0 0 - - 0 1 0 0 0	12	12
Meacham, Jas.	Whig, Vt.	1 1 1 1 1 1 1 1 0 - 0 1 1 1 1 - 0 0 1 1 1 1 0 0 0	17	7
Moore, H. D.	Whig, Pa.	- 1 1 1 0 0 0 0 1 0 0 1 1 1 1 1 1 0 0 1 1 1 1 0 0 0	14	11
Newell, Wm. A.	Whig, N.J.	- 1 1 1 0 0 0 0 1 0 0 0 1 1 0 0 0 0 0 0 0 0 0 0 0	6	19
Ogle, A. J.	Whig, Pa.	1 1 1 1 0 0 0 0 1 0 0 1 1 1 0 0 1 0 0 1 1 1 0 0 0 0	12	14
Otis, J.	Whig, Maine	0 1 1 1 0 0 0 0 - 0 0 0 0 0 0 0 0 0 0 0 0 0 0 0 0 0	3	22
Putnam, H.	Whig, N.Y.	- 1 0 1 0 0 0 0 1 0 0 0 1 1 0 0 - 0 0 1 1 1 0 0 0 0	8	16
Reed, Robt. R.	Whig, Pa.	1 - - 1 0 0 0 0 1 0 1 0 1 1 1 1 0 0 0 1 0 0 0 0 0 0	9	15
Reynolds, G.	Whig, N.Y.	0 1 1 1 1 1 1 1 0 0 0 0 1 1 0 0 1 0 0 1 1 0 0 0 0 0	12	14
Risley, E.	Whig, N.Y.	0 -	0	1
Rockwell, J.	Whig, Mass.	0 1 1 1 0 0 0 0 0 0 0 0 1 0 0 0 0 0 0 0 0 0 0 0 0	4	22
Rumsey, D.	Whig, N.Y.	0 1 1 1 0 0 0 0 0 0 0 0 1 1 0 0 1 0 0 1 1 1 0 0 0 0	8	18
Sackett, Wm. A.	Whig, N.Y.	- 0 0 0 0 0 0 0 0 - 0 0 0 0 0 0 0 0 0 0 0 0 0 0 0	0	24
Schenck, R. C.	Whig, Ohio	0 1 1 1 0 0 0 1 0 0 1 1 1 0 0 0 0 1 0 1 0 1 0 0 0 0	9	17
Schoolcraft, J. L.	Whig, N.Y.	0 0 - 0 0 0 0 0 0 0 0 0 0 0 0 0 0 0 0 0 0 0 0 0 0	0	25
Silvester, P.H.	Whig, N.Y.	0 1 1 1 0 0 0 0 1 0 0 0 1 1 0 0 0 0 0 1 1 0 0 0 0 0	8	18
Spaulding, E.G.	Whig, N.Y.	0 0 0 -	0	3
Stevens, T.	Whig, Pa.	0 - 0 0 0 0 0 0 0 0 0 0 0 0 0 0 0 0 0 0 0 0 0 0	0	25
VanDyke, J.	Whig, N.J.	1 1 1 1 0 0 0 0 1 0 1 1 1 1 0 0 0 0 1 1 1 0 0 0 0	12	14
Vinton, S. F.	Whig, Ohio	0 1 1 1 0 0 0 0 1 0 0 1 1 1 0 0 1 0 0 1 1 1 0 0 0 0	11	15
Bingham, K. S.	Dem., Mich.	0 1 0 1 0 0 0 0 0 0 0 0 0 0 0 0 0 0 0 0 0 0 0 0 0	2	24
Cable, Jos.	Dem., Ohio	1 0 1 0 0 0 0 0 0 1 0 0 0 0 0 0 0 0 0 0 0 0 0 0 0	3	23
Cartter, D. K.	Dem., Ohio	1 1 1 1 - 1 - 1 1 0 1 0 1 0 1 0 0 0 0 1 1 0 1 0 0 0	12	12
Cole, O.	Dem., Wisc.	0 0 1 0 0 0 0 0 - 0 0 0 0 0 0 0 0 0 0 0 0 0 0 0 0	1	24
Doty, Jas. D.	Dem., Wisc.	0 0 0 0 0 0 0 0 0 0 0 0 0 0 0 0 0 0 0 0 0 0 0 0 0 0	0	26

Vote		A B C D E F G H I J K L M N O P Q R S T U V W X Y Z	Frequency	
Pro-Comp. (1) =		Y N Y N N N Y N N Y Y Y N Y N Y Y Y Y N N Y Y Y N Y	1	0
Anti-Comp. (0)=		N Y N Y Y Y N Y Y N N N Y N Y N N N N N Y Y N N N Y N		

Harlan, A. J.	Dem., Ind.	1 1 1 0 0 0 0 0 0 0 0 0 0 0 0 0 0 0 1 0 0 0 0 0	4	22
Howe, J. W.	Dem., Pa.	0 0 0 0 0 0 0 0 0 0 0 0 0 0 0 0 0 0 0 0 0 0 0 0 0 0	0	26
Morris, J. D.	Dem., Ohio	1 1 0 1 0 0 0 1 0 0 0 0 0 0 0 0 0 0 0 0 0 0 0 0	4	22
Olds, E. B.	Dem., Ohio	1 1 1 0 - 0 0 - 0 0 0 0 0 0 0 - 0 0 - 1 0 0 0 0 0	4	18
Peck, L. B.	Dem., Vt.	1 1 0 1 0 0 0 0 0 0 1 0 0 0 1 0 0 0 0 0 0 0 0 0	5	21
Sawtelle, C.	Dem., Maine	1 1 1 1 0 0 0 0 1 0 0 0 0 0 0 0 0 0 0 0 0 0 0 0	5	21
Stetson, C.	Dem., Maine	- 1 1 1 0 0 0 0 1 0 0 0 0 0 0 0 0 0 0 0 0 0 0 0 0	4	21
Sweetser, Chas.	Dem., Ohio	1 1 1 1 0 0 0 0 1 0 0 0 1 1 0 0 1 0 0 0 0 1 0 0 0 0	9	17
Waldo, L. P.	Dem., Conn.	1 1 1 1 0 0 0 0 1 0 0 0 0 0 0 0 0 0 0 0 0 0 0 0	5	21
Wentworth, J.	Dem., Ill.	1 1 1 1 0 1 0 0 1 0 0 0 1 0 0 - 0 0 0 1 1 1 0 0 0 0	10	15
Clingman, Thos. L.	Whig, N.C.	0 1 1 1 1 1 1 1 1 1 0 0 1 1 0 0 0 0 0 1 1 1 0 0 - 0	14	11
Ashe, Wm.	Dem., N.C.	0 1 0 1 0 0 0 0 1 0 0 0 0 1 1 - 0 0 0 0 0 0 0 0 -	5	19
Averett, Thos.	Dem., Va.	0 0 0 1 0 0 0 0 0 0 0 0 0 0 0 0 0 - - 0 0 0 0 0 0 0	1	23
Bowdon, F.	Dem., Ala.	0 - 0 0 0 0 0 0 0 0 0 - - - - - - - 0 0 0 0 0 0 0	0	18
Brown, A. G.	Dem., Miss.	0 0 0 - 0 0 0 0 0 0 0 0 0 0 0 1 0 0 0 0 0 0 0 0 0 0	1	24
Burt, A.	Dem., S.C.	0 0 0 0 0 0 0 0 0 0 0 0 0 0 0 0 0 0 0 0 0 0 0 0 0 0	0	26
Colcock, Wm.	Dem., S.C.	0 0 0 0 0 0 0 0 0 0 0 0 0 0 0 0 0 0 0 0 0 0 0 0 0 0	0	26
Daniel, J.R.J.	Dem., N.C.	0 - 0 - 0 0 0 0 1 0 0 0 0 0 0 0 0 0 0 0 0 0 1 0 0 0	2	22
Featherston, W. S.	Dem., Miss.	0 1 0 1 0 0 0 0 0 0 0 0 0 0 0 0 0 0 0 0 0 0 0 0 0 0	2	24
Haralson, H. A.	Dem., Ga.	0 1 1 1 0 1 1 1 1 1 1 0 0 0 1 1 1 1 0 0 0 0 0 0 0 0	13	13
Harris, S. W.	Dem., Ala.	0 0 0 1 0 0 0 0 0 0 0 0 0 0 0 0 0 0 0 0 0 0 0 0 0 0	1	25
Holladay, A. R.	Dem., Va.	0 - - 1 0 0 0 0 0 0 0 0 0 0 0 0 0 0 0 0 0 0 0 0 0 0	1	23
Holmes, I. E.	Dem., S.C.	0 - 0 0 - 0 0 0 0 0 0 0 0 0 0 0 0 0 0 0 - 0 0 0	0	23
Hubbard, D.	Dem., Ala.	0 0 0 1 0 0 0 0 0 0 0 0 0 0 0 0 0 0 0 0 0 0 0 0 0 0	1	25
Inge, S. W.	Dem., Ala.	0 0 0 0 0 0 0 0 0 0 0 0 0 0 0 0 0 0 0 0 0 0 0 0 0 0	0	26
Jackson, Jos. W.	Dem., Ga.	0 1 1 1 0 1 1 0 1 1 0 0 0 0 1 1 1 1 0 0 0 0 0 0 0 0	11	15
Johnson, Robt. W.	Dem., Ark.	0 0 0 1 1 1 0 0 0 0 0 0 0 0 0 0 0 0 0 0 0 0 0 0 0 0	3	23
LaSere, E.	Dem., La.	0 1 1 1 0 0 0 0 1 1 0 0 0 0 1 1 0 1 0 0 0 0 0 0 0 0	8	18
McQueen, J.	Dem., S.C.	0 0 0 0 0 0 0 0 0 0 0 0 0 0 0 0 0 0 0 0 0 0 0 0 0 0	0	26
McWillie, Wm.	Dem., Miss.	1 1 0 1 0 0 0 0 1 1 - 0 0 0 1 1 0 1 0 0 0 0 1 0 0 0	9	16
Meade, R. K.	Dem., Va.	0 0 0 1 0 0 0 0 0 0 0 0 0 0 0 0 - 0 0 0 0 0 0 0 0 0	1	24
Millson, J. S.	Dem., Va.	- 1 0 1 0 0 0 0 0 0 0 0 0 0 0 0 0 0 1 1 0 0 0 0 0	4	21
Morse, I. E.	Dem., La.	0 1 0 1 0 0 0 0 0 0 0 0 0 0 - 0 0 0 0 0 0 0 0 0 0	2	23
Orr, Jas. L.	Dem., S.C.	0 0 0 0 0 0 0 0 0 0 0 0 0 0 0 0 0 0 0 0 0 0 0 0 0 0	0	26
Phelps, J. S.	Dem., Mo.	0 1 1 1 0 0 0 0 1 0 0 0 0 0 0 0 0 0 0 0 0 0 0 0 0 0	4	22
Powell, P.	Dem., Va.	0 0 0 1 0 0 0 - 0 1 0 0 0 0 1 1 0 1 0 0 0 0 0 0 0 0	5	20
Seddon, Jas. A.	Dem., Va.	0 0 0 1 0 0 0 0 0 0 0 0 0 0 0 0 0 0 0 1 0 0 0 0 0	2	24

Vote		A B C D E F G H I J K L M N O P Q R S T U V W X Y Z	Frequency	
Pro-Comp. (1) =		Y N Y N N N Y N N Y Y Y N Y N Y Y Y Y N N Y Y Y N Y	1	0
Anti-Comp. (0)=		N Y N Y Y Y N Y Y N N N Y N Y N Y N N N N Y Y N N N Y N		

		A B C D E F G H I J K L M N O P Q R S T U V W X Y Z		
Thompson, Jacob	Dem., Miss.	0 1 1 1 1 1 1 1 0 0 0 0 0 0 0 0 0 0 0 1 1 0 1 0 0 0	10	16
Venable, A.W.	Dem., N.C.	0 1 0 1 0 0 0 0 0 0 0 0 0 0 0 0 0 0 0 0 0 0 0 0 0 0	2	24
Wallace, Danl.	Dem., S.C.	0 0 0 0 0 0 0 0 0 0 0 0 0 0 0 0 0 0 0 0 0 0 0 0 0 0	0	26
Woodward, J.A.	Dem., S.C.	0 0 0 0 0 0 0 0 0 0 0 0 0 0 0 0 0 0 0 0 0 0 0 0 0 0	0	26

	Total:		457	2,046

	Total both blocs:		2,979	2,298

*Included within each bloc are a few members who cast a majority of their votes against the bloc on this set of roll calls. The trend of their voting on the later roll calls of the set became the determining factor for which bloc to include them in.

Section 3: Cohesion Indexes on House Roll Calls in Appendix D, Section 2

Pro-Compromise	0.818	North	0.042
Anti-Compromise	0.634	Whig	0.040
		Pro-Comp.	0.706
		Anti-Comp.	0.493
Whig	0.228		
Pro-Comp.	0.827	Democrat	0.380
Anti-Comp.	0.479	Pro-Comp.	0.865
		Anti-Comp.	0.643
Democrat	0.147		
Pro-Comp.	0.810	South	0.258
Anti-Comp.	0.765	Whig	0.918
		Pro-Comp.	0.949
Free-Soil	0.866	Anti-Comp.	0.120
		Democrat	0.042
Cohesion= Percent of majority		Pro-Comp.	0.746
less percent of minority within		Anti-Comp.	0.766
a bloc.			

Section 4: Likeness Indexes on House Roll Calls in Appendix D, Section 2

	NWPC	SWPC	NDPC	SDPC	FS	NWAC	SWAC	NDAC
PC/AC*	0.273							
SWPC	0.879							
NDPC	0.921	0.958						
SDPC	0.980	0.990	0.941					
FS	0.213	0.092	0.134	0.193				
NWAC	0.400	0.279	0.321	0.380	0.813			
SWAC	0.707	0.586	0.628	0.687	0.506	0.693		
NDAC	0.325	0.204	0.246	0.305	0.888	0.925	0.618	
SDAC	0.263	0.142	0.184	0.243	0.950	0.863	0.444	0.938

Likeness= 1.000 less (percent of ones in bloc A less percent of ones in bloc B).
*N=North; S=South; PC=pro-compromise; AC=anti-compromise; D=Democrat; W=Whig;
FS=Free-Soil

Section 5: Number of Members in Blocs

Pro-Comp.	116	North	134	South	85
Anti-Comp.	103	Whig	73	Whig	27
		Pro-Comp.	28	Pro-Comp.	26
Whig	100	Anti-Comp.	45	Anti-Comp.	1
Pro-Comp.	54				
Anti-Comp.	46	Democrat	49	Democrat	58
		Pro-Comp.	34	Pro-Comp.	28
Free-Soil	12	Anti-Comp.	15	Anti-Comp.	30

Appendix E

✣

The Texas–New Mexico Boundary Dispute in Comparative Perspective

Section 1: U.S. Senate Likeness Indexes between Free-Soil/Northern Whig and Southern Democrat Blocs on Other Issues in the 1850 Crisis

	FS/S.Dem.	N.Whig/S.Dem.
Boundary dispute	0.642	0.767
Territorial slavery roll calls—Omnibus bill	0.126	0.157
California votes—Omnibus bill	0.099	0.211
California votes—statehood bill	0.155	0.105
Fugitive slave bill votes	0.068	0.209
D.C. slave trade bill votes	0.136	0.131

Section 2: U.S. Senate Likeness Indexes between Free-Soil/Northern Whig/Republican and Southern Democrat Blocs on Other Major Issues in the Sectional Crisis, 1846–61

	FS/S.Dem.	N.Whig/S.Dem.
Twenty-ninth Congress— Texas admission	—	0.000
Twenty-ninth Congress— Wilmot Proviso	—	0.000
Thirtieth Congress— territorial slavery	0.063	0.231
Thirtieth Congress— Clayton compromise	0.332	0.191
Thirty-first Congress— boundary dispute	0.642	0.767
Thirty-third Congress— territorial slavery— Kansas-Nebraska bill	0.049	0.109

	Rep./S.Dem.
Thirty-fourth Congress— Kansas	0.069
Thirty-fifth Congress— Kansas—Lecompton constitution	0.053
Thirty-sixth Congress— Crittenden compromise	0.162

The likeness indexes for the 1850 boundary dispute in Appendix E include all Northern Whigs and all Southern Democrats, whether they were members of the pro- or anti-compromise blocs. The statistics on the 1850 boundary dispute likeness indexes in Appendix E are derived from the data in Appendix B, Section 2, and are based on the absolute numbers of votes cast. The statistics for other issue categories in 1850 and the sectional issue categories for other Congresses are taken from Mark J. Stegmaier, "The U.S. Senate in the Sectional Crisis, 1846–1861: A Roll Call Voting Analysis" (Ph.D. diss., University of California, Santa Barbara, 1975), 51, 84–85, 133–34, 164, 232, 270, 294–95, and 363. The statistics other than those for the boundary dispute of 1850 are not based on the absolute numbers of votes cast in those issue categories; instead, these statistics represent averages of the indices for all of the individual roll calls included in that issue category.

The Popular Vote on the Compromise in Texas Reported in the *Austin State Gazette*, January 11, 1850

Counties	Acceptance	Rejection
Anderson	243	31
Angelina		
Austin	62	60
Bastrop	108	42
Bell	87	25
Bexar	449	32
Bowie	83	51
Brazoria	54	76
Brazos		
Burleson	103	7
Caldwell	74	46
Calhoun	70	24
Cameron		
Cass	225	158
Cherokee	492	226
Collin	208	6
Colorado	59	54
Comal	36	32
Cooke	15	
Dallas	266	15
Denton	70	
DeWitt	42	44
Ellis	55	20

Counties	Acceptance	Rejection
El Paso		
Falls		
Fannin	342	1
Fayette	161	127
Fort Bend	52	30
Freestone		
Galveston	137	61
Gillespie	52	44
Goliad	43	11
Gonzales	62	32
Grayson	99	3
Grimes	154	57
Guadalupe	55	16
Harris	244	80
Harrison	272	534
Hays	16	11
Henderson	33	12
Hopkins	226	11
Houston	128	18
Hunt	162	6
Jackson	60	3
Jasper	179	5
Jefferson	56	47
Kaufman	134	3
Kinney		
Lamar	227	16
LaVaca		
Leon	108	24
Liberty		
Limestone		
Matagorda	50	45
McLennan	28	10
Medina	46	6
Milam	80	52
Montgomery	112	73
Nacogdoches	381	19
Navarro	141	72
Newton	108	8
Nueces	34	54
Panola		

Counties	Acceptance	Rejection
Polk	85	62
Presidio		
Red River	237	17
Refugio		
Robertson	87	14
Rusk	527	265
Sabine	157	4
San Augustine		
San Patricio	27	1
Santa Fe		
Shelby	254	83
Smith		
Starr		
Tarrant		
Titus	330	14
Travis	230	91
Trinity		
Tyler		
Upshur		
Uvalde		
Van Zandt		
Victoria	135	10
Walker	271	48
Washington	160	295
Webb	30	2
Wharton	23	32
Williamson	103	40
Wood		
Worth		

The *Gazette* reported that these figures added up to a vote of 9,250 to 3,366 in favor of the bill. The *Gazette* apparently figured its total before recording some of the individual county returns listed. The actual overall total of the county-by-county figures was 9,439 to 3,418.

The twenty-five counties that did not send any voting record to Austin included eleven very remote or newly organized counties, among them Santa Fe and Worth counties, destined to be ceded to New Mexico by the Pearce bill. The other nine were El Paso, Falls, Freestone, Kinney, Presidio, Tarrant, Trinity, Uvalde, and Wood counties. A few of the official returns and a list of them are preserved in Election Returns Series, Secretary of State Records, Texas State Archives. Newspapers reported votes taken in several counties, the results of which were not reported in Austin. The *Houston Democratic Telegraph,*

November 23, 1850, reported the Brazos County majority for rejection, the Panola County majority for acceptance, and the vote in San Augustine County as 213 to 79 for acceptance. The *Clarksville Northern Standard*, November 9, 1850, reported a majority of 80 for the bill in Upshur County. The *Victoria Texian Advocate* on October 31, 1850, reported a nearly unanimous ballot for the bill in Refugio County and on November 14, 1850, reported a pro-acceptance vote in Lavaca County. Various newspapers reported figures that appeared to reflect incomplete returns. The *Clarksville Northern Standard, Houston Democratic Telegraph*, and *Victoria Texian Advocate* all published totals slightly less in most cases than the tallies in the *Austin State Gazette*. Votes reported for certain towns and precincts include: Houston (178 to 73 for the bill) and Richmond (46 to 25 for), cited in *Victoria Texian Advocate*, November 14, 1850; Galveston (137 to 61 for) and Victoria (145 to 10 for, with no balloting elsewhere in the county), cited in *Houston Democratic Telegraph*, October 30, 1850; Clarksville (191 to 12 for), cited in *Clarksville Northern Standard*, November 2, 1850; Washington (66 to 58 against), Independence (50 to 19 against), and Anderson (106 to 23 for), cited in *Austin State Gazette*, November 9, 1850; Mt. Pleasant (75 to 0 for), cited in *Clarksville Northern Standard*, November 9, 1850; Crockett (105 to 17 for), cited in *Washington Texas Ranger*, undated November or December 1850 issue in Texas State Archives; San Antonio (417 to 22 for), San Juan Precinct (28 to 4 for), and Castroville (all votes but 4 for), cited in *Matagorda Colorado Tribune*, November 8, 1850; Austin (183 to 83 for), Webber's Prairie Precinct (57 to 4 for), Columbus (45 to 24 against), Cummings Creek (35 to 0 for), Thomas Ware's (9 to 0 against), Bastrop (63 to 40 for), La Grange (82 to 74 against), Rutersville (22 to 0 for), Lower Cummings Creek Precinct (8 to 1 for), Round Top (30 to 6 for), and Ross's Prairie (majority of 3 for), cited in *La Grange Texas Monument*, November 6, 1850.

꿏

Notes

Introduction

1. See, for instance, the interpretation by Robert R. Russel emphasizing slavery in the territories and another by Roger L. Ransom emphasizing California and the fugitive slave law. Russel, "What Was the Compromise of 1850?" *Journal of Southern History* 22 (Aug. 1956): 292–309; Ransom, *Conflict and Compromise: The Political Economy of Slavery, Emancipation, and the American Civil War* (Cambridge: Cambridge Univ. Press, 1989), 109–20. An exception to this has been the recent work by Elbert B. Smith, which stresses the significance of the boundary issue. Smith, *The Presidencies of Zachary Taylor and Millard Fillmore* (Lawrence: Univ. Press of Kansas, 1988). The interpretation presented here disagrees with that of Smith, however, on a number of points.

2. Stuart A. Rice, "The Behavior of Legislative Groups: A Method of Measurement," *Political Science Quarterly* 40 (Mar. 1925): 62–64; and Lee F. Anderson, Meredith W. Watts, Jr., and Allen R. Wilcox, *Legislative Roll-Call Analysis* (Evanston: Northwestern Univ. Press, 1966), 32–35, 44–45. For pioneering uses of roll-call voting analysis by historians of the Jacksonian era, see Thomas B. Alexander, *Sectional Stress and Party Strength: A Study of Roll-Call Voting Patterns in the United States House of Representatives, 1836–1860* (Nashville: Vanderbilt Univ. Press, 1967); and Joel H. Silbey, *The Shrine of Party: Congressional Voting Behavior, 1841–1852* (Pittsburgh: Univ. of Pittsburgh Press, 1967). Both of these works used a different technique of analysis than the one employed in thepresent work, a technique known as Guttman-scaling, which is most handy for measuring gradations of adherence to a bloc by its individual members. Neither Alexander nor Silbey placed an emphasis on the boundary dispute's role in the 1850 congressional voting.

Chapter 1
The Boundary Dispute from Its Origins to the Mexican War

1. William C. Binkley, *The Expansionist Movement in Texas, 1836–1850* (Berkeley: Univ. of California Press, 1925), 1–11; J. J. Bowden, "The Texas–New Mexico Boundary Dispute along the Rio Grande," *Southwestern Historical Quarterly* 63 (Oct. 1959): 221–23; Isaac J. Cox, "The Louisiana-Texas Fron-

tier," *Quarterly of the Texas State Historical Association* 10 (July 1906): 1–75 and *Southwestern Historical Quarterly* 17 (July and Oct. 1913): 1–42, 140–87; idem, "The Southwest Boundary of Texas," *Quarterly of the Texas State Historical Association* 6 (Oct. 1902): 81–96; Glen M. Leonard, "Western Boundary-Making: Texas and the Mexican Cession, 1844–1850" (Ph.D. diss., University of Utah, 1970), 107–22; and Thomas M. Marshall, "The Southwestern Boundary of Texas, 1821–1840," *Quarterly of the Texas State Historical Association* 14 (Apr. 1911): 277–79.

2. Samuel F. Bemis, *John Quincy Adams and the Foundations of American Foreign Policy* (New York: Knopf, 1949), 305, 309–11, 321–25, 330–33, 350–52, 487; and Frederick Merk, *Manifest Destiny and Mission in American History: A Reinterpretation* (New York: Knopf, 1963), 19–20.

3. Binkley, *Expansionist Movement in Texas*, 11–12; Marshall, "Southwestern Boundary," 280; Paul Horgan, *Great River: The Rio Grande in North American History*, 2 vols. (New York: Rinehart and Co., 1954), 2:483; and John H. Williams, *Sam Houston: A Biography of the Father of Texas* (New York: Simon and Schuster, 1993), 105.

4. Bemis, *J. Q. Adams and Foreign Policy*, 530, 561–64; Mary W. M. Hargreaves, *The Presidency of John Quincy Adams* (Lawrence: Univ. Press of Kansas, 1985), 116–17; and William R. Manning, "Texas and the Boundary Issue, 1822–1829," *Southwestern Historical Quarterly* 17 (Jan. 1913): 218–44; John Niven, *Martin Van Buren: The Romantic Age in American Politics* (New York: Oxford Univ. Press, 1983), 280–81; Robert V. Remini, *Andrew Jackson and the Course of American Freedom, 1822–1832* (New York: Harper and Row, 1981), 202, 218–20, 289; and Remini, *Andrew Jackson and the Course of American Democracy, 1833–1845* (New York: Harper and Row, 1984), 352–56.

5. On Houston's 1833 letter, see Randolph B. Campbell, *Sam Houston and the American Southwest* (New York: HarperCollins, 1993), 43–44. The revolutionary council's decree is in "Provisional Government Letterbook, November 7, 1835–March 16, 1836," Letters, 12, Executive Record Books, Texas State Archives, Austin; and also in San Felipe de Austin *Telegraph and Texas Register*, Oct. 31, 1835. For Austin's views, see Henry S. Foote, *Texas and the Texans; or, Advance of the Anglo-Americans to the Southwest*, 2 vols. (Philadelphia: Thomas, Cowperthwait and Co., 1841), 2:196. Wharton's view is in "Provisional Government Letterbook," Letters, 185. Burnet's proclamation is in "Ad Interim Government Executive Record Book, March–October, 1836," 56, Executive Record Books. A handy recent summary of events leading to the Texas Revolution is given in Campbell, *Houston*, 39–58. For the Mexican side of these developments, see Gene M. Brack, *Mexico Views Manifest Destiny, 1821–1846: An Essay on the Origins of the Mexican War* (Albuquerque: Univ. of New Mexico Press, 1975), 57–73.

6. Hubert H. Bancroft, *The Works of Hubert Howe Bancroft*, Vol. 16: *History of the North Mexican States and Texas, 1801–1889*, (San Francisco: History Co., 1889), pt. 2:269–70; Campbell, *Houston*, 70, 72–73; and Amelia W. Williams and Eugene C. Barker, eds., *The Writings of Sam Houston*, 8 vols. (1938–43; reprint, Austin: Jenkins, 1970), 1:425.

7. Bemis, *John Quincy Adams and the Union* (New York: Knopf, 1956), 354; and Remini, *Jackson and American Democracy*, 355.

8. Bemis, *J. Q. Adams and Union*, 338, 355–58; Campbell, *Houston*, 76; James C. Curtis, *The Fox at Bay: Martin Van Buren and the Presidency, 1837–1841* (Lexington: Univ. Press of Kentucky, 1970), 152–53; Remini, *Jackson and American Democracy*, 357–60; Leonard L. Richards, *The Life and Times of Congressman John Quincy Adams* (New York: Oxford Univ. Press, 1986), 151–61; Justin H. Smith, *The Annexation of Texas* (New York: MacMillan Co., 1911), 52–63; and Major L. Wilson, *The Presidency of Martin Van Buren* (Lawrence: Univ. Press of Kansas, 1984), 18.

9. Binkley, *Expansionist Movement in Texas*, 22, 24–27; Brack, *The Texas Quest for New Mexico, 1836–1850* (Boston: American Press, 1984), 6–7; Curtis, *Fox at Bay*, 154–55; George P. Garrison, ed., *Diplomatic Correspondence of the Republic of Texas*, 3 vols. (Washington, D.C.: GPO, 1908, 1911), 1:127–35; Joseph M. Nance, *After San Jacinto: The Texas–Mexican Frontier, 1836–1841* (Austin: Univ. of Texas Press, 1963), 26, 29–32; Remini, *Jackson and American Democracy*, 363–64; and Wilson, *Presidency of Van Buren*, 148–49.

10. Senator Ellis's statement on the boundary bill was cited by Sen. Chester Ashley of Arkansas in the U.S. Senate in February 1845. *Congressional Globe*, 28th Cong., 2d sess., Appendix, 288 (hereafter cited as *Cong. Globe*, Cong.: sess.: pp.). For the bill in Texas documents, see 1st Cong., 1st sess., *Journals of the House of Representatives of the Republic of Texas*, 116–17; 1st Cong., 1st sess., *Journals of the Senate of the Republic of Texas*, 88, 91; and *Laws of the Republic of Texas* (1838), 133–34.

11. Campbell, *Houston*, 77–78; Marshall de Bruhl, *Sword of San Jacinto: A Life of Sam Houston* (New York: Random House, 1993), 231–34; Remini, *Jackson and American Democracy*, 364–68; and Williams, *Houston*, 173–74.

12. Bemis, *J. Q. Adams and Union*, 359–64; Binkley, *Expansionist Movement in Texas*, 29, 31–34; Curtis, *Fox at Bay*, 156–68; Nance, *After San Jacinto*, 35–38; Niven, *Van Buren*, 443–47, 567; Richards, *Congressman J. Q. Adams*, 161–62; Smith, *Annexation of Texas*, 63, 65, 67–75; and Wilson, *Presidency of Van Buren*, 149–53.

13. "Record of Executive Documents from December 10, 1838, to December 14, 1841: M. B. Lamar," 8, Executive Record Books; Binkley, *Expansionist Movement in Texas*, 35–42; Garrison, ed., *Diplomatic Correspondence* 1:422; William M. Gouge, *The Fiscal History of Texas . . .* (1852; reprint, New York: Augustus M. Kelley, 1968), 52–115; Marshall, "Southwestern Boundary," 288–92; Nance, *After San Jacinto*, 102, 181, 378, 428–29; Joseph W. Schmitz, *Texan Statecraft, 1836–1845* (San Antonio: Naylor, 1941), 89–92; Stanley Siegel, *Political History of the Texas Republic* (Austin: Univ. of Texas Press, 1956), 122–25, 136; and Patsy M. Spaw, ed., *The Texas Senate*, vol. 1 (College Station: Texas A&M Univ. Press, 1990), 77–78.

14. Horgan, *Great River* 2:551–59; Howard R. Lamar, *The Far Southwest, 1846–1912: A Territorial History* (New Haven: Yale Univ. Press, 1966), 28–51; and David J. Weber, *The Mexican Frontier, 1821–1846: The American Southwest under Mexico* (Albuquerque: Univ. of New Mexico Press, 1982), 33, 125–35, 180–82, 190–95, 210–11, 240–41, 261–65.

15. Binkley, *Expansionist Movement in Texas*, 43, 56–73; Brack, *Texas Quest*, 10–14; and Nance, *After San Jacinto*, 384, 396–97, 423, 453, 495, 500, 504.

16. "Executive Documents—Lamar," 132–34, 169–71, 231–43; Binkley, *Expansionist Movement in Texas*, 71, 73–76; and Garrison, ed., *Diplomatic Correspondence* 2:737–47.

17. Binkley, *Expansionist Movement in Texas*, 77–95; Brack, *Texas Quest*, 15–22; Thomas E. Chavez, *Manuel Alvarez, 1794–1856: A Southwestern Biography* (Niwot: Univ. Press of Colorado, 1990), 71–86; Herbert P. Gambrell, *Mirabeau Buonaparte Lamar: Troubadour and Crusader* (Dallas: Southwest Press, 1934), 252–72; Horgan, *Great River* 2:570–85; Noel M. Loomis, *The Texan–Santa Fe Pioneers* (Norman: Univ. of Oklahoma Press, 1958); D. W. Meinig, *Imperial Texas: An Interpretive Essay in Cultural Geography* (Austin: Univ. of Texas Press, 1969), 40; Nance, *After San Jacinto*, 433–34, 504–5, 518–19; Schmitz, *Texan Statecraft*, 170–72; and Siegel, *Political History*, 167–69.

18. "Executive Documents—Lamar," 283–88; "Executive Record Book: Sam Houston, December 13, 1841–December 9, 1844," 32–34, Executive Record Books; Binkley, *Expansionist Movement in Texas*, 91–93; Nance, *After San Jacinto*, 507–9, 518–19; idem, *Attack and Counter-Attack: The Texan-Mexican Frontier, 1842* (Austin: Univ. of Texas Press, 1964), 214; Siegel, *Political History*, 169–72; and Spaw, ed., *Texas Senate*, 103, 105–6.

19. "Executive Record Book: Houston, 1841–1844," 266–67; Clarksville, Tex., *Northern Standard*, June 22, July 27, Sept. 14, 21, 28, and Oct. 21, 1843; Binkley, *Expansionist Movement in Texas*, 106–18; Stephen B. Oates, *Visions of Glory: Texans on the Southwestern Frontier* (Norman: Univ. of Oklahoma Press, 1970), 4–24; Siegel, *Political History*, 218–19; and Otis E. Young, *The West of Philip St. George Cooke* (Glendale: Arthur H. Clark Co., 1955), 109–26. Despite the failure of the 1843 raids, many Texans remained confident that the trade of Santa Fe and Chihuahua would eventually be diverted from Missouri to Texas. San Augustine, Tex., *Red-Lander*, Oct. 7, 1843.

20. Adams's speech at Braintree, Massachusetts, Sept. 17, 1842, Clarksville *Standard*, Dec. 10, 1842.

21. Aside from Justin Smith's famous 1911 work, *The Annexation of Texas*, see William W. Freehling,

The Road to Disunion, Vol. 1: *Secessionists at Bay, 1776–1854* (New York: Oxford Univ. Press, 1990), 368–425; Frederick Merk, *Fruits of Propaganda in the Tyler Administration* (Cambridge: Harvard Univ. Press, 1971), 21, 23–26, 28–29, 97–104, 112–15, 118–20, 221–52; idem, *Slavery and the Annexation of Texas* (New York: Knopf, 1972), 3–32, 35–40, 56–57, 76, 78–79; Norma L. Peterson, *The Presidencies of William Henry Harrison and John Tyler* (Lawrence: Univ. Press of Kansas, 1989), 176–228; and David M. Pletcher, *The Diplomacy of Annexation: Texas, Oregon, and the Mexican War* (Columbia: Univ. of Missouri Press, 1973), 87–88, 116–49.

22. *Cong. Globe*, 28: 1: 702, App., 474–86, 549; Merk, *Slavery and Annexation*, 76, 78–79; and Elbert B. Smith, *Magnificent Missourian: The Life of Thomas Hart Benton* (Philadelphia: J. B. Lippincott Co., 1958), 86–87, 111–12, 115, 160, 188–97.

23. *Cong. Globe*, 28: 1: 699–703, 706–7, 719, 740, App., 568–76, 588–90, 607–11; Merk, *Slavery and Annexation*, 92–94; and Smith, *Magnificent Missourian*, 197–99.

24. James D. Richardson, comp., *A Compilation of the Messages and Papers of the Presidents, 1789–1897*, 10 vols. (Washington, D.C.: GPO, 1897), 4:341–45; Paul H. Bergeron, *The Presidency of James K. Polk* (Lawrence: Univ. Press of Kansas, 1987), 15–20; Binkley, *Expansionist Movement in Texas*, 118–22, 127; Merk, *Slavery and Annexation*, 99–100, 102, 109–10; Peterson, *Presidencies of Harrison and Tyler*, 233–51; and Pletcher, *Diplomacy of Annexation*, 150–78.

25. For the various proposals offered, see *Cong. Globe*, 28: 2: 16–17, 19, 26–27, 49, 65–66, 76, 81, 97, 99, 107, 113, 121, 127–30, 134–35, 140, 171, 173, 244–45, 278, 295. For references to New Mexico in the session, see ibid., 301, App., 213, 275, 336, 338, 369–70, 373, 388; and 28th Cong., 2d sess., *House Journal* (Serial 462), 220 (hereafter citations from U.S. congressional serial sets appear as Cong.: sess.: title and no. of docs. [ser. no.]: pp.). See also Robert M. Johannsen, *Stephen A. Douglas* (New York: Oxford Univ. Press, 1973), 153–57; Merk, *Slavery and Annexation*, 121–57; and Smith, *Magnificent Missourian*, 202–3.

26. *Cong. Globe*, 28: 2: 129–30, 191–94, 359, 362–63, 372, 385; Freehling, *Road to Disunion*, 440–49; Merk, *Slavery and Annexation*, 154–61; and Peterson, *Presidencies of Harrison and Tyler*, 255–58.

27. 29: 1: *House Docs.* 2 (Ser. 480): 71–73, 79, 88–92, 103; *Journals of the Convention, Assembled at the City of Austin on the Fourth of July, 1845, for the Purposes of Framing a Constitution for the State of Texas* (1845; reprint, Austin: Shoal Creek Publs., 1974), esp. 30, 42, 219–20, 247, 328; Bergeron, *Presidency of Polk*, 57–64; Merk, *Slavery and Annexation*, 167–74; Pletcher, *Diplomacy of Annexation*, 187–96, 201; and Spaw, ed., *Texas Senate*, 145, 158–60. For a good letter from a Texan opposing annexation, in part due to the undefined boundary, see Clarksville *Standard*, July 5, 1845. For a good report on boundary considerations at the constitutional convention, see the letter by James S. Gillett, dated July 14, in ibid., Aug. 9, 1845. The Texas legislature in April 1846 again considered a proposal to cede public lands to the United States in exchange for assumption of the state's debt. Austin *Texas Democrat*, Apr. 8, 1846.

28. Secretary of State James Buchanan to John Slidell, Nov. 10, 1845, 30: 1: *Senate Ex. Docs.* 52 (Ser. 509): 77–78. Buchanan had expressed his boundary reservation in a Senate speech on June 8, 1844. *Cong. Globe*, 28: 1: App., 726.

29. *Cong. Globe*, 29: 1: 39–40, 60–65, 88–92; and Richardson, comp., *Messages and Papers* 4: 386–92.

30. Richardson, comp., *Messages and Papers* 4:437–43. For the few references to the Santa Fe jurisdiction issue during the war bill debate and at other times during this session, see *Cong. Globe*, 29: 1: 558, 809, 814, 978, App., 641–42, 684, 686, 765, 804, 913–14, 918, 952, 1117.

31. Dwight L. Clarke, *Stephen Watts Kearny: Soldier of the West* (Norman: Univ. of Oklahoma Press, 1961), 105–13, 126–27; Thomas S. Edrington, "Military Influence on the Texas-New Mexico Boundary Settlement," *New Mexico Historical Review* 59 (Oct. 1984): 373–74; Lamar, *Far Southwest*, 56–59; and Smith, *Magnificent Missourian*, 213–14.

32. Edrington, "Military Influence," 374–75, gives an excellent account of Kearny's use of the Texas claim as his rationale. One Texas newspaper interpreted even Kearny's vague public procla-

mation as a maintenance of the Texas title to the Santa Fe region. Clarksville *Standard*, Oct. 24, 1846. See also Chavez, *Alvarez*, 100–101, 105, 107–8; Clarke, *Kearny*, 114, 121–37; Horgan, *Great River* 2:718–28; Robert W. Larson, *New Mexico's Quest for Statehood, 1846–1912* (Albuquerque: Univ. of New Mexico Press, 1968), 3–4; and Lamar, *Far Southwest*, 59–61.

33. Clarke, *Kearny*, 139–48; Horgan, *Great River* 2:728–36; Mary Loyola, *The American Occupation of New Mexico, 1821–1852* (Albuquerque: Univ. of New Mexico Press, 1939), 62–65; and Lamar, *Far Southwest*, 62–63.

34. Clarke, *Kearny*, 148–50; Larson, *New Mexico's Quest*, 4–5; Loyola, *American Occupation*, 65–66; Lamar, *Far Southwest*, 63–65; and Arie W. Poldervaart, *Black-Robed Justice: A History of the Administration of Justice in New Mexico from the American Occupation in 1846 until Statehood in 1912* (Santa Fe: Historical Society of New Mexico, 1948), 21.

Chapter 2
Santa Fe County, Texas, or New Mexico Territory, U.S.A.? 1846–1850

1. Richardson, comp., *Messages and Papers* 4:471–506, esp. 482–84 and 493–94.

2. *Cong. Globe*, 29: 2: 16, 50, App., 55–56, 104–5, 118–24, 251; Richardson, comp., *Messages and Papers* 4:506–7; 31: 1: *House Ex. Docs.* 17 (Ser. 573): 252–55; and Leonard, "Western Boundary-Making," 196–98.

3. 31: 1: *Sen. Ex. Docs.* 24 (Ser. 554): 2–3; Binkley, *Expansionist Movement in Texas*, 148–50; and Robert G. Winchester, *James Pinckney Henderson: Texas' First Governor* (San Antonio: Naylor, 1971), 92–93. Representative Kaufman of Texas assumed that Polk had disavowed not just a portion of the Kearny code but also the New Mexico government he had established. Kaufman's letter, dated January 29, is in Clarksville *Standard*, Mar. 20, 1847.

4. Freehling, *Road to Disunion*, 458–62; Michael F. Holt, *The Political Crisis of the 1850s* (New York: John Wiley and Sons, 1978), 49–58; Charles D. Hart, "The National Limits of Slavery Expansion: The Mexican Territories as a Test Case," *Mid-America* 52 (Apr. 1970): 119–31; Leonard, "Western Boundary-Making," 173–74, 195–97; and Chaplain W. Morrison, *Democratic Politics and Sectionalism: The Wilmot Proviso Controversy* (Chapel Hill: Univ. of North Carolina Press, 1967).

5. *Cong. Globe*, 29: 2: 241–45, 300, 353–55, App., 101, 229–30, 259–60, 321, 413, 469; *N. Y. Daily Tribune*, Jan. 25, Feb. 10, 1847; and Clarksville *Standard*, Mar. 27, May 13, 1847; and William R. Brock, *Parties and Political Conscience: American Dilemmas, 1840–1850* (Millwood, N.Y.: KTO Press, 1979), 237–39.

6. 30: 1: *Senate Reports* 91 (Ser. 512); and *N.Y. Tribune*, Mar. 19, Apr. 1, 24, 1847.

7. On the military situation in New Mexico in late 1846 and most of 1847, see General Order 49, Nov. 3, 1846, "General Orders and Circulars of the War Department and Headquarters of the Army, 1809–1860," M-1094, roll 5, Record Group 94—Records of the A.G.O., 1780s–1917, National Archives, Washington, D.C.; *N.Y. Tribune*, Mar. 3, 18, 19, Apr. 12, 19, May 6, 8, 21, 25, 27, 31, June 8, 11, 12, 22, 23, July 8, 27, 28, Aug. 11, 20, 21, 23, Sept. 13, 14, 15, 27, 28, Oct. 7, Nov. 3, 17, 23, 27, 1847; and Robert E. Shalhope, *Sterling Price: Portrait of a Southerner* (Columbia: Univ. of Missouri Press, 1971), 60–69.

8. Petition of Manuel Alvarez to be candidate for delegate to Congress, June 10, 1847, roll 1, Manuel Alvarez Papers, State Records Center and Archives, Santa Fe; *N. Y. Tribune*, July 27, Aug. 21, Oct. 7, 1847; *Santa Fe Republican*, Sept. 10, 24, 1847; F. Stanley (Fr. Stanley F. Crocchiola), *Ciudad Santa Fe: Territorial Days, 1846—1912* (Pampa, Tex.: Pampa Print Shop, 1965), 45; and idem, *Giant in Lilliput: The Story of Donaciano Vigil* (Pampa, Tex.: Pampa Print Shop, 1963), 141–42, 155–59.

9. *N. Y. Tribune*, Sept. 14, 1847; *Santa Fe Republican*, Sept. 10, 24, Oct. 30, Nov. 13, 20, 1847; Larson, *New Mexico's Quest*, 8–9; and Stanley, *Giant in Lilliput*, 151–52.

10. Santiago Ulibarri to Donaciano Vigil, Dec. 15, 1847,William G. Ritch Collection, Huntington Library, San Marino, California; Spruce M. Baird to Washington D. Miller, Sept. 23, 1849, Santa Fe Papers, Texas State Archives; Bancroft, *Works: History of Arizona and New Mexico*, 17:441–43; Chavez, *Alvarez*, 123–25; Lamar, *Far Southwest*, 71; Larson, *New Mexico's Quest*, 9–11; Shalhope, *Price*, 68–69; and Ralph E. Twitchell, *The History of the Military Occupation of the Territory of New Mexico from 1846 to 1851 by the Government of the United States* (1909; reprint, Chicago: Rio Grande Press, 1963), 149–52. A Durango, Mexico, newspaper account gives some details of the legislature that are not available elsewhere. It is reprinted in *N.Y. Tribune*, Mar. 29, 1848, and Washington, D.C., *Daily Union*, Mar. 28, 1848.

11. Clarksville *Standard*, Sept. 18, 25, Oct. 9, 16, 1847; and Winchester, *Henderson*, 93–94.

12. "Executive Record Book: George T. Wood, December 21, 1847–December 14, 1849," 1–2, 5–12, Executive Record Books; Clarksville *Standard*, Jan. 22, 29, 1848; and Victoria *Texian Advocate*, Jan. 20, 1848.

13. Sen. Bill No. 18 (Santa Fe militia), Joint Res. No. 11 (land cession), and "Journal of the Senate of the State of Texas," 2d Legis., 143, 277, 293, Records of the Legislature, Texas State Archives; 30: 1: *House Misc. Docs.* 27 (Ser. 523); Clarksville *Standard*, Jan. 15, 29, 1848; *N.Y. Tribune*, Mar. 20, 1848; D.C. *Union*, Mar. 17, 1848; and Spaw, ed., *Texas Senate*, 190, 192.

14. "Executive Record Book: Wood," 47–49 (Wood's message),and House State Affairs Committee Rpt., Feb. 25, 1848, and "Tex. Sen. Journal," 2d Legis., 310–11 (Sen. State Affairs Comm. Rpt.), Texas State Archives; Clarksville *Standard*, Mar. 18, 1848; and Victoria *Advocate*, Mar. 30, 1848.

15. "Executive Record Book: Wood," 55 (Baird appt.) and 61–62 (Wood to Polk, Mar. 23); and Sen. Bill No. 46 (11th Judicial Dist.) and No. 47 (Santa Fe County), House Federal Relations Comm. Rpt., Mar. 7, 1848, Joint Res. No. 53 (anti-Proviso) and No. 60 (instructs Cong. delegation, etc.), "Appendix to Tex. Sen. Journals," 2d Legis., 43–44, and James W. Webb to Special Comm. on the 11th Jud. Dist., Feb. 3, 1850, Comm. Rpt. No. 110, 3d Legis., Texas State Archives; 30: 1: *House Misc. Docs.* 91 (Ser. 523); Austin *Texas Democrat*, Mar. 18, 1848 (Sen. select comm. rpt.); Clarksville *Standard*, Apr. 22, 1848; *N.Y. Tribune*, Apr. 7, 1848; D.C. *Daily National Intelligencer*, Apr. 7, 20, 1848; D.C. *Union*, Apr. 22, 1848; and Walter P. Webb, ed., *The Handbook of Texas*, 2 vols. (Austin: Texas State Historical Assn., 1952), 2:873–74 (Webb). Wood's letter to Polk is also in Santa Fe Papers.

16. Richardson, comp., *Messages and Papers* 4:538–42; and Bergeron, *Presidency of Polk*, 204.

17. On congressional ignorance of geography, see *N.Y. Herald*, June 27, 1850; and Hart, "Natural Limits," 129. On Combs's petition, see 30: 1: *Sen. Misc. Docs.* 10 (Ser. 511) and *Sen. Rpts.* 91 (Ser. 512).

18. For Whig views in relation to New Mexico see *Cong. Globe*, 30: 1: 859–60, App., 98, 160, 212, 214–15, 264–65, 299, 310, 448, 451, 518; and *N.Y. Tribune*, Oct. 15, Nov. 18, Dec. 18, 31, 1847, Feb. 19, Mar. 22, 1848. For defenses of the Texan claim to Santa Fe by members of the Texas delegation and others, see *Cong. Globe*, 30: 1: 200, 859–60, App., 98, 102, 258–59, 361, 606; *N.Y. Tribune*, Jan. 31, 1848; Clarksville *Standard*, May 20, 27, 1848; and D.C. *Union*, Apr. 16, 1848.

19. D.C. *Natl. Intell.*, June 10, 14, 1848; Richardson, comp.; *Messages and Papers* 4:573–74, 587–93; and Leonard, "Western Boundary-Making," 202–3, 206–19.

20. *Cong. Globe*, 30: 1: 910–16, App., 933–35; Richardson, comp., *Messages and Papers* 4:587–93; D.C. *Natl. Intell.*, July 11, 12, 1848; and Leonard, "Western Boundary-Making," 245–47.

21. 30: 1: *Sen. Jour.* (Ser. 502): 465; *Cong. Globe*, 30: 1: 950, 994, 1002–5, 1078–80, App., 1158, 1185; *N.Y. Tribune*, July 14, 21, 27, 31, 1848; D.C. *Natl. Intell.*, Aug. 2, 1848; Morrison, *Democratic Politics and Sectionalism*, 164–66; and Thomas E. Schott, *Alexander H. Stephens of Georgia: A Biography* (Baton Rouge: Louisiana State Univ. Press, 1988), 87–90.

22. Kaufman letter, Apr. 24, 1848, in Clarksville *Standard*, May 27, 1848; *Cong. Globe*, 30: 1: 990–91, App., 783–88, 924–31, 944–46, 971–73, 1070; Richardson, comp., *Messages and Papers* 4:594–600; William J. Cooper, *The South and the Politics of Slavery, 1828–1856* (Baton Rouge: Louisiana State Univ. Press, 1978), 236–38; and Leonard, "Western Boundary-Making," 247–48.

23. Bancroft, *Works: History of Arizona and New Mexico* 17:443; Loomis M. Ganaway, *New Mexico and the Sectional Controversy, 1846–1861* (Albuquerque: Univ. of New Mexico Press, 1944), 20; and Smith, *Magnificent Missourian,* 244–45.

24. On Vigil's situation in early 1848, see Vigil to Manuel Armijo, May 21, 1848, Ritch Collection; Buchanan to Marcy, May 20, 1848, 30: 1: *House Ex. Docs.* 70 (Ser. 515): 16–17; Stanley, *Ciudad Santa Fe,* 31; and Stanley, *Giant in Lilliput,* 141–42, 155–59.

25. *N.Y. Tribune,* Apr. 13, 1848; *Santa Fe Republican,* Jan. 1, 15, 22, 29, Mar. 11, 1848; D.C. *Natl. Intell.,* May 9, 1848; and Larson, *New Mexico's Quest,* 11.

26. *Santa Fe Republican,* July 16, 1848; and Larson, *New Mexico's Quest,* 12.

27. *Santa Fe Republican,* July 24, Aug. 9, 31, 1848; and Edrington, "Military Influence," 378.

28. *Corpus Christi Star,* Oct. 24, 1848; *N.Y. Tribune,* Oct. 10, 1848; *Santa Fe Republican,* Aug. 1, 1848; Victoria *Advocate,* Oct. 12, 1848; D.C. *Natl. Intell.,* Oct. 10, 1848; Chavez, *Alvarez,* 127; and Larson, *New Mexico's Quest,* 13.

29. *N.Y. Tribune,* Oct. 2, Nov. 30, 1848; Ganaway, *New Mexico and Sectional Controversy,* 20; Larson, *New Mexico's Quest,* 14; Stanley, *Giant in Lilliput,* 161–62; and Morris F. Taylor, "Spruce McCoy Baird: From Texas Agent to New Mexico Official, 1848–1860," *New Mexico Historical Review* 53 (Jan. 1978): 41. The "gamblers" quote is from *Galveston Weekly News,* Mar. 16, 1849. On Angney's whereabouts, see Louise Barry, *The Beginning of the West: Annals of the Kansas Gateway to the American West, 1540–1854* (Topeka: Kansas State Historical Society, 1972), 780.

30. Baird to Miller, Sept. 23, 30, 1849, Santa Fe Papers; Binkley, *Expansionist Movement in Texas,* 166; and Larson, *New Mexico's Quest,* 14.

31. St. Louis *Daily Missouri Republican,* Nov. 23, 1848, quoting *Santa Fe Republican,* Oct. 18, 1848; Baird to Miller, Sept. 23, 1849, Santa Fe Papers; Binkley, *Expansionist Movement in Texas,* 165–66; Chavez, *Alvarez,* 127–28; Ganaway, *New Mexico and Sectional Controversy,* 39–41; Larson, *New Mexico's Quest,* 14–15; and Twitchell, *History of Military Occupation,* 154–58. The petition is in "Territorial Papers of the United States, 1789–1873," M-200, roll 14, RG 46—Records of the U.S. Senate, NA; and 30: 2: *Sen. Misc. Docs.* 5 (Ser. 533). Some indication of the developing factionalism is in Armijo to Alvarez, Sept. 24, and Theodore D. Wheaton to Alvarez, Nov. 6, 1848, Benjamin M. Read Collection, State Records Center and Archives, Santa Fe.

32. General Order 49, Aug. 31, 1848, M-1094, roll 5, RG 94; Washington to Marcy, Nov. 8, 1848, 31: 1: *Sen. Ex. Docs.* 1 (Ser. 549): 104; Secretary of War George Crawford to Commanding Officer, Santa Fe, Mar. 26, 1849, 31: 1: *House Ex. Docs.* 17 (Ser. 573): 272–73; St. Louis *Republican,* Nov. 23, 1848; and Kenneth F. Neighbours, "The Taylor-Neighbors Struggle over the Upper Rio Grande Region of Texas in 1850," *Southwestern Historical Quarterly* 61 (Apr. 1958): 436.

33. The only source of information on what happened to Webb is Webb's letter to the Special Committee on the 11th Judicial District, Feb. 3, 1850, Committee Reports No. 110, 3d Legis., Texas State Archives. On J. W. Webb himself, see Webb, ed., *Handbook of Texas* 2:873–74. Baird's travels are covered in Baird to Miller, Sept. 22, 1848, Santa Fe Papers; Taylor, "Baird," 40; and Clarence Wharton, "Spruce McCoy Baird," *New Mexico Historical Review* 27 (Oct. 1952): 302. Wharton's work presents some colorful details, but some of these appear to be based more on Wharton's conjecture than on historical sources. One work that erroneously indicates that Webb did go to Santa Fe is Seymour V. Connor and Jimmy M. Skaggs, *Broadcloth and Britches: The Santa Fe Trade* (College Station: Texas A&M Univ. Press, 1977), 139.

34. Baird to Miller, Nov. 10, 1848, and Sept. 23, 30, Nov. 6, 1849, and Baird to Wood, Mar. 30, 1849, Santa Fe Papers; *Galveston News,* Mar. 16, 1849; *N.Y. Tribune,* Feb. 20, Mar. 2, 12, 24, 1849; *Santa Fe Republican,* Aug. 24, 1848; D.C. *Natl. Intell.,* Feb. 21, Mar. 13, 1849; D.C. *Union,* Dec. 22, 1848; W. W. H. Davis, *El Gringo; or, New Mexico and Her People* (New York: Harper and Bros., 1857), 109; Binkley, *Expansionist Movement in Texas,* 159–64; Connor and Skaggs, *Broadcloth and Britches,* 139–41; and Wharton, "Baird," 303.

35. Baird to Miller, Sept. 30, 1849, Santa Fe Papers; *Galveston News*, Mar. 16, 1849; *N.Y. Tribune*, Mar. 2, 12, 1849; and Davis, *El Gringo*, 109.

36. Baird to Washington, Nov. 22, 1848, and Baird to Miller, Sept. 21, Nov. 6, 1849, Santa Fe Papers. In the November 6, 1849, letter Baird remembered Colonel Washington telling him initially that he favored the Texan claim; Baird's imagination may have invented this memory a year after it supposedly occurred.

37. Washington to Baird, Nov. 22, 23, 1848, ibid.; *N.Y. Tribune*, Mar. 12, 1849; Binkley, *Expansionist Movement in Texas*, 159–64; Edrington, "Military Influence," 379; Neighbours, "Taylor-Neighbors Struggle," 436–37; and Taylor, "Baird," 42–44.

38. Baird to Miller, Dec. 10, 1848, and Baird to Wood, Dec. 18, 1848, Mar. 30, 1849, Santa Fe Papers; and Stanley, *Giant in Lilliput*, 160.

39. Marcy to Commanding Officer, Santa Fe, Oct. 12, 1848, 31: 1: *House Ex. Docs.* 17 (Ser. 573): 261–62; K. Jack Bauer, *Zachary Taylor: Soldier, Planter, Statesman of the Old Southwest* (Baton Rouge: Louisiana State Univ. Press, 1985), 293; Binkley, *Expansionist Movement in Texas*, 166–67; Edrington, "Military Influence," 379; and Neighbours, "Taylor-Neighbors Struggle," 436.

40. Clarksville *Standard*, July 22, Sept. 16, 1848; *Civilian and Galveston Gazette*, Aug. 17, 1848; *N.Y. Tribune*, Nov. 3, 1848; D.C. *Natl. Intell.*, Nov. 1, 1848; D.C. *Union*, Apr. 8, 1849; Bauer, *Taylor*, 224, 226, 228, 249; and Joseph G. Rayback, *Free Soil: The Election of 1848* (Lexington: Univ. Press of Kentucky, 1970), 282, 286. Rayback's work is the most comprehensive treatment of all aspects of the election.

41. I found copies of Wood's October 6, 1848, letter to Polk in the following sources: Santa Fe Papers; "Executive Record-Book: Wood," 152–57; "Appendix to Tex. Sen. Journals," 2d Legis., 44–48, Texas State Archives; Austin *Texas Democrat*, Feb. 3, 1849. I have not located a copy among federal documents, but it is unlikely that the letter was never delivered.

42. *N.Y. Tribune*, Dec. 16, 1848; Richardson, comp., *Messages and Papers* 4:635, 638, 640–41, 643; and Bergeron, *Presidency of Polk*, 208. Extremist Texas opinion was expressed at this time in resolutions passed on December 30 at a public meeting in Marshall. These resolutions condemned the Wilmot Proviso, declared that Texas would determine her own borders by military force if necessary and at all hazards and against all parties. *Galveston News*, Jan. 19, 1849. Ibid., Dec. 15, 1848, contains a good editorial attack on the Wilmot Proviso.

43. *Cong. Globe*, 30: 2: 33–37, 48, 238, 309–18, 478–80, 608, App., 103–7, 247–49; Johannsen, *Douglas*, 241–46; and Leonard, "Western Boundary-Making," 254–59, 262–66, 268–71.

44. *Cong. Globe*, 30: 2: 33–37, 309–18; 30: 2: *Sen. Misc. Docs.* 5 (Ser. 533); John Niven, *John C. Calhoun and the Price of Union: A Biography* (Baton Rouge: Louisiana State Univ. Press, 1988), 322–23; and Smith, *Magnificent Missourian*, 245.

45. Pilsbury to Miller, Jan. 12, 1849, Washington D. Miller Papers, Texas State Archives; *Cong. Globe*, 30: 2: 146–47, 373–75; 30: 2: *House Jour.* (Ser. 536): 180; and *N.Y. Tribune*, Jan. 5, 1849.

46. *Cong. Globe*, 30: 2: 608, 610–12, App., 248–49; and *N.Y. Tribune*, Mar. 2, 3, Oct. 17, 1849.

47. A very detailed account of the confrontation between Rusk and Calhoun on January 13 is in a long letter in Clarksville *Standard*, Mar. 3, 1849.

48. Allan Nevins, ed., *Polk: The Diary of a President, 1845–1849* (London: Longmans, Green, 1952), 365–67.

49. Rusk's notes, Jan. 30, 1849, Thomas J. Rusk Papers, Barker Texas History Center, University of Texas, Austin; Clarksville *Standard*, Mar. 3, 10, 24, Apr. 14, 1849; *N.Y. Tribune*, Dec. 26, 1848, Jan. 17, 1849 (Greeley's letter); Brock, *Parties and Political Conscience*, 245–48; Campbell, "Texas and the Nashville Convention of 1850," *Southwestern Historical Quarterly* 76 (July 1972): 3; Margaret L. Coit, *John C. Calhoun: American Portrait* (Boston: Houghton Mifflin, 1950), 474–78; Cooper, *South and Politics of Slavery*, 269–71; Nevins, *Ordeal of the Union*, 2 vols. (New York: Charles Scribner's Sons, 1947), 1:221–25; Niven, *Calhoun*, 323–25; and Schott, *Stephens*, 97–100.

50. *Cong. Globe*, 30: 2: App., 256, 267, 288–89, 291, 306; Brock, *Parties and Political Conscience*,

252–55; Johannsen, *Douglas*, 246–48; Leonard, "Western Boundary-Making," 260–61, 266; and Nevins, *Ordeal of the Union* 1:225–27.

51. Bauer, *Taylor*, xxi, xxiii, 4, 43, 128, 238, 249–50, 254–55, 257, 327; Smith, *Presidencies of Taylor and Fillmore*, 26–28, 50; Holman Hamilton, *Zachary Taylor: Soldier in the White House* (Indianapolis: Bobbs-Merrill, 1951), 174, 240–41; Nevins, *Ordeal of the Union* 1:229–30, 259–60; *N.Y. Herald*, Mar. 3, 1850; Centreville *Indiana True Democrat*, Jan. 23, 1850; Clarksville *Standard*, Aug. 24, 1850; and Pittsburgh *Daily Morning Post*, Apr. 29, 1850. One of the most interesting accounts of Taylor in conversation comes from a letter written by a nonpolitician to a friend in Boston: "He has an impediment in speaking, and when he utters a long sentence he stops two or three times and twists his face until it is literally covered with wrinkles." The writer quoted Taylor discussing butter: "'Butter—is very good at the west, where the prairies—because the grass is eat off of them.'" *Portland Transcript*, June 1, 1850.

52. Annie H. Abel, ed., *The Official Correspondence of James S. Calhoun* (Washington, D.C.: GPO, 1915), xi–xiii, 17–18; Bauer, *Taylor*, 290–92; and Smith, *Presidencies of Taylor and Fillmore*, 94.

53. General Order 21, Apr. 3, 1849, M-1094, roll 6, RG 94; Crawford to Commanding Officer, Santa Fe, Mar. 26, 1849, 31: 1: *Sen. Ex. Docs.* 24 (Ser. 554): 4; Binkley, *Expansionist Movement in Texas*, 167–69; and Edrington, "Military Influence," 379–80.

54. Houston to Thomas M. Bagby, May 7, 1849, Williams and Barker, eds., *Writings of Houston* 5:92–93.

55. Baird to Washington and Washington to Baird, Mar. 21, Baird to Wood, Mar. 30, and Baird to Miller, Nov. 6, 1849, Santa Fe Papers; *N.Y. Tribune*, May 4, June 29, 1849; and D.C. *Natl. Intell.*, May 4, 1849.

56. J. L. Collins to J. M. Edgar, June 4, 1849, Ritch Collection; Baird to Washington and Washington to Baird, Apr. 5, and Baird's proclamation, June 18, 1849, Santa Fe Papers; *N.Y. Tribune*, May 28, 1849; D.C. *Natl. Intell.*, May 21, 26, 31, 1849; D.C. *Union*, May 27, 1849; and Edrington, "Military Influence," 380.

57. "Executive Record Book: Wood," 178–79, 183–89, 214–16, Executive Record Books. Miller to Baird, Apr. 14, and Wood to Taylor, June 30, 1849, are also in Santa Fe Papers.

58. Baird to Washington and Washington to Baird, July 3, 4, and Baird to Miller, Sept. 21, Nov. 6, 1849, Santa Fe Papers.

59. *N.Y. Tribune*, Sept. 4, 1849.

60. Ibid., June 1, Sept. 13, 21, 1849; *Santa Fe Republican*, Aug. 8, 1849; D.C. *Natl. Intell.*, June 14, 1849; and Abel, ed., *J. S. Calhoun Correspondence*, xiii, 17–18. The petition and Houghton's reply are in the Ritch Collection. See also Pillans to Rusk, Jan. 23, 1850, Rusk Papers; *N.Y. Tribune*, Sept. 25, 1849; and Chavez, *Alvarez*, 135.

61. Wayne R. Austerman, *Sharps Rifles and Spanish Mules: The San Antonio–El Paso Mail, 1851–1881* (College Station: Texas A&M Univ. Press, 1985), 5–7, 12–14; Kenneth F. Neighbours, *Robert Simpson Neighbors and the Texas Frontier, 1836–1859* (Waco: Texian Press, 1975), ch. 3; and Oates, *Visions of Glory*, 54–65.

62. George D. Phillips to Rusk, Apr. 2, John T. Mills to Rusk, Apr. 25, Rusk to Tod Robinson, Sept. 2, and Rusk to Rev. Mr. Harmon, Oct. 14, 1849, Rusk Papers; Houston to James Gadsden, Sept. 20, 1849, Williams and Barker, eds., *Writings of Houston* 5:95–106; Marshall *Texas Republican*, June 1, 29, July 6, 27, Aug. 3, 10, 16, 30, Sept. 6, 20, 27, Oct. 4, 11, 18, 25, Nov. 1, 8, 22, 1849; and San Augustine *Texas Union*, Aug. 18, Sept. 15, 29, 1849. The San Augustine paper staunchly defended the positions of Houston and Rusk.

63. Webb, ed., *Handbook of Texas* 1:141 (Bell), 2:853–54 (Howard).

64. F. Hatch to Miller, May 20, 1849, Miller Papers; *N.Y. Tribune*, Aug. 23, 1849; and Dudley G. Wooten, ed., *A Comprehensive History of Texas, 1685 to 1897*, 2 vols. (Dallas: William G. Scarff, 1898), 2:25–26.

65. Austin *Democrat*, July 14, 1849; *Corpus Christi Star*, June 16, 23, Aug. 4, 1849; *Galveston News*,

June 11, 18, July 13, 1849; and Marshall *Republican,* July 6, 27, 1849.

66. Hatch to Miller, June 17, and Wood to Miller, June 30, July 5, 15, Aug. 21, 1849, Miller Papers. The vote for Bell was 10,319 and for Wood 8,764. D.C. *Natl. Intell.,* Dec. 1, 1849.

67. *N.Y. Tribune,* Oct. 17, 25, 26, Nov. 1, 5, 6, 12, 20, 1849.

68. Baird to Miller, Oct. 9, 1849, Santa Fe Papers; and Davis, *El Gringo,* 109.

69. On the factions, see Pillans to Rusk, Jan. 23, 1850, Rusk Papers; Lamar, *Far Southwest,* 74–75; Larson, *New Mexico's Quest,* 29–30; and Twitchell, *History of Military Occupation,* 161–80.

70. *N.Y. Tribune,* Nov. 9, 1849, reprinting an account from *Santa Fe Republican,* Sept. 20, 1849; Austin *Texas State Gazette,* Oct. 20, Dec. 8, 1849; Binkley, *Expansionist Movement in Texas,* 168–70; and Twitchell, *History of Military Occupation,* 172–74, 392.

71. Juan Bernadet to Manuel Alvarez, Sept. 20, 1849, roll 1, Alvarez Papers; Baird to Miller, Oct. 9, 1849, and Baird's undated comments on the election, Santa Fe Papers; D.C. *Natl. Intell.,* Nov. 7, 1849; D.C. *Union,* Dec. 28, 1849, quoting Santa Fe letter from St. Louis *Republican;* Abel, ed., *J. S. Calhoun Correspondence,* 132–35; and Larson, *New Mexico's Quest,* 18.

72. The journal of the convention is in 31: 1: *House Ex. Docs.* 17 (Ser. 573): 93–104, and *House Misc. Docs.* 39 (581). See also Abel, ed., *J. S. Calhoun Correspondence,* 59; *N.Y. Tribune,* Oct. 1, 1849; D.C. *Natl. Intell.,* Oct. 2, Nov. 24, 1849; D.C. *Union,* Dec. 28, 1849; Bancroft, *Works: History of Arizona and New Mexico* 17:445–46; Chavez, *Alvarez,* 132–33; and Larson, *New Mexico's Quest,* 18–20.

73. Baird's letters and reports date from September 21 to November 6, 1849, Santa Fe Papers. Palmer Pillans soon expressed a similar view on the insurmountability of anti-Texas sentiment in New Mexico. Austin *State Gazette,* Dec. 29, 1849.

74. Baird to Bell, Dec. 4, 1849, Governors' Letters, Texas State Archives; Austin *State Gazette,* Jan. 5, 1850, quoting *Bonham* (Tex.) *Advertiser;* Houston *Democratic Telegraph and Texas Register,* Dec. 27, 1850; and Marshall *Republican,* Nov. 8, 1849, Jan. 24, 1850. On legislative action in re Baird, see *Tex. Sen. Journals,* 3d sess., 384; *Tex. HR Journals,* 3d sess., 393–94, 413–14; Houston *Telegraph,* Jan. 17, 1850; and W. F. Weeks, reporter, "Debates in the House of Representatives on the Santa Fe Question" (Austin, 1850), 6–7, 22, 26. A copy of these printed debates is in the Beinecke Library, Yale University, New Haven, Connecticut.

75. Austin *State Gazette,* Nov. 24, 1849, Jan. 5, 1850. The letters to Bell offering military service, dated from November 1849 to February 1850, are in the Santa Fe Papers.

76. Houston *Telegraph,* May 10 (military departments), Sept. 13 (Brooke), Oct. 18, 1849 (location of the capital). For another Texas editorial on the relevance of the capital location to the New Mexico issue, see *N.Y. Tribune,* Nov. 19, 1849, quoting Houston *Morning Star.* On the Santa Fe issue itself, see Houston *Telegraph,* Nov. 22, 29, Dec. 13, 1849, Jan. 10, 1850. For another plea for a nonmilitary solution and for sale of the disputed territory, see Austin *State Gazette,* Feb. 9, 1850. Division of the military departments was also of concern to the Texas Legislature and was mentioned in a special joint committee report on boundary problems on January 25, 1850. *Tex. Sen. Journals,* 3d sess., 551–53.

77. Austin *State Gazette,* Oct. 20, 1849. Wood's message of November 6, 1849, is in *Tex. HR Journals,* 3d sess., 12–23; and Austin *State Gazette,* Nov. 10, 1849.

78. For statistics on members of the Third Legislature, see Ralph A. Wooster, "Membership in Early Texas Legislatures, 1850–1860," *Southwestern Historical Quarterly* 69 (Oct. 1965): 163–73.

79. Weeks, reporter, "Debates . . . on the Santa Fe Question"; *Galveston News,* Dec. 17, 24, 1849; Matagorda *Colorado Tribune,* Dec. 24, 1849; D.C. *Natl. Intell.,* Jan. 3, 1850; and Lamar, *Far Southwest,* 75–76.

80. Binkley, "The Question of Texan Jurisdiction in New Mexico under the United States, 1848–1850," *Southwestern Historical Quarterly* 26 (July 1920): 23–24, discusses the acts and the new county boundaries. See also Spaw, ed., *Texas Senate,* 202. These four acts are printed in *Laws of 3rd Texas Legislature* (Austin, 1850), 21–22, 24–25, 26–27 (copy in Texas State Archives). The original acts are in Senate Bills nos. 25 and 31 and original bills nos. 39 and 77, Records of the Legislature, 3d

Legislature. The progress of these bills can be followed in *Tex. Sen. Journals,* 3d sess., 178, 181, 184–87, 195, 199, 202, 214, 317, 339, 374; and in *Tex. HR Journals,* 3d sess., 229, 238, 241–42, 244, 246, 254, 257, 333–34, 337, 379, 425.

81. *Tex. Sen. Journals,* 3d sess., 272–80; *Tex. HR Journals,* 3d sess., 319–27; and Austin *State Gazette,* Jan. 3, 1850.

82. *Tex. Sen. Journals,* 3d sess., 284–306; *Tex. HR Journals,* 3d sess., 338–61; Austin *State Gazette,* Dec. 29, 1849; Houston *Telegraph,* Jan. 3, 1850; Spaw, ed., *Texas Senate,* 202–3; and Binkley "Question of Texan Jurisdiction," 22–23.

83. On Neighbors's request for a salary advance, see Neighbors to Bell, Jan. 8, 1850, Governors' Letters; Joint Resolution No. 67, Records of the Legislature, 3d Legis.; and *Tex. Sen. Journals,* 3d sess., 482–83, 669–70. On the boundary resolution, see *Laws of 3rd Tex. Legis.,* 207–8; and *Tex. HR Journals,* 3d sess., 813, 815. On the slavery resolution see Joint Resolution No. 62, Records of the Legislature, 3d Legis.; W. F. Weeks, reporter, "Debates in the House of Representatives [during a portion of the session of 1849 and 1850]" (Austin, 1850), 60–78, 83–85 (copy in Texas State Archives); and Matagorda *Tribune,* Jan. 21, 1850. On the Nashville Convention resolution, see Joint Resolution No. 96, Records of the Legislature, 3d Legis.; *Tex. Sen. Journals,* 3d sess., 665–66, 670–71, 676, 678; *Tex. HR Journals,* 3d sess., 761–64, 781, 798–99; and Campbell, "Texas and the Nashville Convention," 6–7.

84. On one of the early resolutions for sale of land, see Joint Resolution No. 18, Records of the Legislature, 3d Legis.; *Tex. Sen. Journals,* 3d sess., 406–9, 440–41, 513, 542–43, 554; and *Tex. HR Journals,* 3d sess., 717.

85. For the joint committee report and action thereon, see *Tex. Sen. Journals,* 3d sess., 551–53, 578–79, 586, 587, 591; and *Tex. HR Journals,* 3d sess., 665–66, 805–7.

86. *Tex. Sen. Journals,* 3d sess., 578–79, 591. Several Senate roll calls on the Neighbors salary and Nashville Convention issues reveal no consistent voting patterns.

87. Original bills nos. 77 and 124, Records of the Legislature, 3d Legis.; and *Tex. Sen. Journals,* 3d sess., 644–45, 661, 681–82.

88. B. Rush Wallace to Rusk, Jan. 16, 1850, Rusk Papers.

Chapter 3
Neighbors, Munroe, and McCall: Three Men and the Fate of New Mexico

1. For Neighbors's earlier life and a photograph of him, see the fine biography by Kenneth F. Neighbours, *R. S. Neighbors and the Texas Frontier.*

2. Asst. Adj. Gen. W. G. Freeman to Munroe, May 26, June 20, 26, July 28, 1849, "Letters Sent by the Headquarters of the Army (Main Series), 1828–1903," M-857, roll 3, pp. 11, 26–28, 39–40, 69–70, RG 108—Records of the Headquarters of the Army, National Archives; Adj. Gen. Roger Jones to Munroe, May 26, 1849, 31: 1: *Sen. Ex. Docs.* 60 (Ser. 561): 2; Larson, *New Mexico's Quest,* 45; Edrington, "Military Influence," 382; and Francis B. Heitman, comp., *Historical Register and Dictionary of the United States Army, from its Organization, September 29, 1789 to March 2, 1903,* 2 vols. (Washington, D.C.: GPO, 1903), 1:736.

3. Adjutant general's report of November 30, 1849, printed in D.C. *Natl. Intell.,* Dec. 31, 1849; and *N.Y. Tribune,* Dec. 31, 1849, quoting a Santa Fe letter of October 28 to the St. Louis *Republican;* James S. Calhoun to Commissioner of Indian Affairs Orlando Brown, Nov. 2, 1849, Abel, ed., 69–70; Palmer J. Pillans to Thomas J. Rusk, Jan. 23, 1850, Rusk Papers; D.C. *Union,* Nov. 1, 1849, quoting a Fort Smith, Arkansas, letter of October 2 to the N.Y. *Sun;* and *N.Y. Tribune,* Sept. 25, 1849, quoting a long letter from Santa Fe to the *Daily Cincinnati Gazette.*

4. Weightman to Munroe, Dec. 1, 1849, Jan. 16, 1850, Munroe to Weightman, Jan. 16, 1850, and Weightman to Clayton, Jan. 17, 1850, "Letters Received by the Secretary of War, Registered Series,

1801–1860," M-221, roll 154, RG 107—Records of the Office of the Secretary of War, National Archives; Pillans to Rusk, Jan. 23, 1850, Rusk Papers; a letter by "J. M. D.," Philadelphia *Pennsylvanian*, July 2, 1850; *N.Y. Tribune*, Sept. 25, Dec. 24, 1849; and Twitchell, *Military Occupation*, 165–71.

5. Calhoun to Brown, Nov. 2, 1849, in Abel, ed., *J. S. Calhoun Correspondence*, 69–70; Austin *State Gazette*, May 4, 1850; *N.Y. Tribune*, Feb. 27, 1850; Santa Fe *New Mexican*, Nov. 24, 1849; Chavez, *Alvarez*, 133–34; and Lamar, *Far Southwest*, 75. The *N.Y. Herald*, on February 28, 1850, reprinted the address in its entirety from the December 8, 1849, *New Mexican*. The claim in the *New Mexican* that Frémont had extended the California boundary to the Sierra Madre mountains only fifty miles west of the Rio Grande is based on Charles Preuss's map published in 1848. Preuss also shows New Mexico lying on both sides of the Rio Grande. Donald Jackson and Mary Lee Spence, eds., *The Expeditions of John Charles Frémont*, 3 vols. and maps (Urbana: Univ. of Illinois Press, 1970–84), map 5; and Carl I. Wheat, *Mapping the American West*, 5 vols. (San Francisco: Institute of Historical Cartography, 1957–63), 3:map 559. On Texan activity in the El Paso–Doña Ana region, see Maj. J. Van Horne to Munroe, Sept. 23, 1849, 31: 1: *Sen. Ex. Docs.* 56 (Ser. 561): 3; F. S. Donnell, "When Texas Owned New Mexico to the Rio Grande," *New Mexico Historical Review* 8 (Apr. 1933): 68–71; and Neighbours, "Taylor-Neighbors Struggle," 443.

6. A nearly complete original copy of the "territory" broadside, in Spanish and entitled "A Nuestros Conciudadanos de N. M.," is item no. 237 in the Twitchell Collection, State Records Center and Archives, Santa Fe. A short excerpt from an English version of the address is in D.C. *Natl. Intell.*, March 1, 1850. See also Lamar, *Far Southwest*, 75, which identifies the group as nearly all officeholders under the military regime.

7. Kendrick's statement is in Austin *State Gazette*, July 20, 1850. On the charges against Weightman, see J. L. Collins, *Contestacion a Ciertos Representaciones Infamatorias de R. H. Weightman . . .* (Santa Fe: Gazette Office, 1852), Miscellaneous Record Collection—Political papers, 1852, New Mexico State Records Center and Archives, Santa Fe; and Larson, *New Mexico's Quest*, 47–48. On Pillans and his work for Texas, see Webb, ed., *Handbook of Texas* 2:378–79; Baird to Washington, July 4, 1849, Santa Fe Papers; Pillans to Bell, Apr. 14, 1850, Governors' Letters; and Pillans to Rusk, Jan. 23, 1850, Rusk Papers. As for Calhoun's probable communication with Rusk, there is a handwritten copy, dated March 17, 1850, of some anti-Texas resolutions adopted by a public meeting in Santa Fe. This copy, with the notation that it was examined by "JSC" (undoubtedly Calhoun), is in the Rusk Papers. On New Mexican fear of Texas, see Pillans to Rusk, Jan. 23, 1850; San Antonio *Western Texian*, quoted in D.C. *Natl. Intell.*, June 19, 1850; and Houston *Telegraph*, June 13, 1850.

8. On the early American settlements in the El Paso area, see W. H. Timmons, "American El Paso: The Formative Years, 1848–1854," *Southwestern Historical Quarterly* 87 (July 1983): 1–15. On the Van Horne expedition and the establishment of the military post, see ibid., 3, 7–8; Austerman, *Sharps Rifles and Spanish Mules*, 7–8; General Order 58, Nov. 7, 1848, M-1094, roll 6, RG 94; and D.C. *Natl. Intell.*, June 27, Nov. 24, 26, 1849.

9. Van Horne to Munroe, Sept. 23, 1849, 31: 1: *Sen. Ex. Docs.* 56 (Ser. 561): 3.

10. Munroe to Jones, Nov. 21, 1849, and Munroe to Van Horne, Dec. 28, 1849, 31: 1: *Sen. Ex. Docs.* 56 (Ser. 561): 2, 4–5; and Adj. Gen. Lafayette McLaws to Van Horne, Mar. 13, 1850, "Letters Sent by the 9th Military Department, the Department of New Mexico, and the District of New Mexico, 1849–1890," M-1072, roll 1-1849–56, 2:55–56, RG 393—Records of the U.S. Army Continental Commands, 1821–1890, National Archives.

11. General Order 58, Dec. 15, 1849, M-1094, roll 6, RG 94; Jones to Munroe, Feb. 15, Mar. 8, 1850, 31: 1: *Sen. Ex. Docs.* 56 (Ser. 561): 3–4, 5–7; Munroe to Jones, May 23, 1850, "Letters Received by the Office of the Adjutant General (Main Series), 1822–1860," M-567, roll 432, item M-411, RG 94; and Crawford to Jones, Mar. 8, 1850, "Letters Sent by the Secretary of War relating to Military Affairs, 1800–1889," M-6, roll 30, p. 86, RG 107.

12. James Webb to Neighbors, Jan. 8, 1850, *Appendix to Texas Senate Journals, 3d Legis., 2d Sess.*, 2–74; and Neighbors to Bell, Jan. 8, 1850, Governors' Letters.

13. Crawford to Bvt. Lt. Col. George A. McCall, Nov. 12, 19, 1849, 31: 1: *House Ex. Docs.* 17 (Ser. 573): 280–81; and George A. McCall, *Letters from the Frontiers . . .* (Philadelphia: J. B. Lippincott and Co., 1868), 485–86. McCall's copy of Crawford's November 19 letter is in New Mexico Miscellaneous Collection, Library of Congress. A printed copy of the same letter, in Spanish, is in *App. to Tex. Sen. Jours., 3d Legis., 2d Sess.,* 27.

14. On Aubry's trip to San Antonio and his meeting with Neighbors, see Houston *Telegraph,* Jan. 31, 1850; and D.C. *Union,* Feb. 20, 1850, quoting the San Antonio *Western Texian.* That Neighbors knew of McCall's presence in San Antonio, see Van Horne to McLaws, Feb. 23, 1850, "Register of Letters Received and Letters Received by Headquarters, 9th Military Department, 1848–1853," M-1102, roll 2-1850, RG 393. A notice that eight others accompanied Neighbors was printed in San Antonio *Western Texian,* Jan. 17, 1850. While copies of that issue no longer exist, the notice was reprinted in *Galveston News,* Feb. 4, 1850; and D.C. *Natl. Intell.,* Feb. 14, 1850.

15. On Cockburn, see: "Population Schedules of the Seventh Census of the United States, 1850," M-432, roll 915, p. 152, RG 29—Records of the Bureau of the Census, National Archives; Elizabeth L. Jennett, comp., *Biographical Directory of the Texan Conventions and Congress* (Austin: State of Texas, 1941), 34, 36, 38, 42; *Journals of the Convention, Assembled . . . for the Purpose of Framing a Constitution for the State of Texas,* 106 and 375; and *Members of the Texas Legislature, 1846–1980* (Austin: State of Texas, 1980), 3, 6; and Austin *State Gazette,* May 4, 1850.

16. On the two slaves, see Austin *State Gazette,* May 4, 1850. A short biographical sketch of Dr. Rowe is in Webb, ed., *Handbook of Texas* 2:510. On James's involvement, see Clarksville *Standard,* June 1, 1850, quoting San Antonio *Western Texian;* and Neighbors to Bell, Mar. 23, 1850, *App. to Tex. Sen. Jours., 3d Legis., 2d Sess.,* 5–6.

17. A notice that Neighbors took the Whiting-Smith route is in San Antonio *Western Texian,* Jan. 17, 1850, reprinted in *Galveston News,* Feb. 4, 1850. On the trip itself, see Neighbors to Bell, Mar. 23, 1850, *App. to Tex. Sen. Jours., 3d Legis., 2d Sess.,* 4–5; Austin *State Gazette,* Apr. 27, May 4, 1850; D.C. *Natl. Intell.,* July 28, 1849; and Ed Bartholomew, *800 Texas Ghost Towns* (Fort Davis, Tex.: Frontier Book Publishers, 1971), 41.

18. Austin *State Gazette,* May 4, 1850; and Edrington, "Military Influence," 384. Some deeds related to the saline deposits, involving Richard A. Howard, Benjamin B. Edwards, William G. Crump, Bartlett M. Browder, and Lenas Nash, are in "Transcribed Deed Records—El Paso County," Books A–C, pp. 38–42, 77–80, Special Collections, University of Texas Library, El Paso. On conflicts over the deposits and the "Salt War" of the 1870s, see David Montejano, *Anglos and Mexicans in the Making of Texas, 1836–1986* (Austin: Univ. of Texas Press, 1987), 33. On Hoppin, see J. Morgan Broaddus, Jr., *The Legal Heritage of El Paso* (El Paso: Texas Western College Press, 1963), 34, 61, 71; and Timmons, "American El Paso," 15–16, 18. On Hoppin's strong distaste for Mexican-American culture, see his letter in Mobile *Alabama Planter,* Sept. 9, 1850. On the Texan attitudes, Neighbors to Bell, Mar. 23, 1850, *App. to Tex. Sen. Jours., 3d Legis., 2d Sess.,* 3–4; and Baird to Bell, Feb. 27, 1850, ibid., 76, 78–79.

19. On his pledge, see Neighbors to Bell, Mar. 23, 1850, *App. to Tex. Sen. Jours., 3d Legis., 2d Sess.,* 4. Bell's Proclamation, Jan. 5, 1850, is in ibid., 69–72. Hoppin's letter to Bell, Jan. 3, 1850, is quoted at length in Timmons, "American El Paso," 15–16. On Van Horne's position and Neighbors's activities, see Van Horne to McLaws, Feb. 23, 1850, M-1102, roll 2, RG 393. A notice of White's resignation of jurisdiction is in St. Louis *Republican,* Apr. 24, 1850. On White himself, see Rex W. Strickland, *Six Who Came to El Paso: Pioneers of the 1840's* (El Paso: Texas Western College Press, 1963), 10–12.

20. On the El Paso County elections, see Neighbors to Bell, Mar. 23, 1850, *App. to Tex. Sen. Jours., 3d Legis., 2d Sess.,* 3–6; Neighbors's letter to a friend in San Antonio, Mar. 24, San Antonio *Western Texian,* reprinted in Clarksville *Standard,* June 1, 1850; John James's report, ibid.; Charles Hoppin's letter, Apr. 4, 1850, Mobile *Daily Register,* reprinted in *N.Y. Tribune,* June 18, and Cleveland *Daily True Democrat,* June 22, 1850; and the notice of Cockburn's return, Austin *State Gazette,* Apr. 27, 1850.

21. On the headright, see Austin *State Gazette,* Nov. 30, 1850; and the protest of Doña Ana citizens against the grant, which accompanies Munroe to Jones, May 20, 1850, M-567, roll 424, item M-312, RG

94. A copy of the headright itself no longer appears to exist, either in the Texas General Land Office records at Austin or in the deed records of early El Paso County. A few pages of the deed records are missing, and the headright may have been recorded on one of them. Neighbors's comments on Steen are in Neighbors to Bell, Mar. 23, 1850, *App. to Tex. Sen. Jours., 3d Legis., 2d Sess.,* 5.

22. Munroe to Jones, May 20, 1850, M-567, roll 432, item M-312, RG 94. Ruelas's role in the founding of Mesilla in 1850 is mentioned in Timmons, "American El Paso," 29, 32. Mesilla was on the Mexican side of the international boundary until 1853 when the U.S. acquired the Gadsden Purchase. A manuscript letter of McCall's, dated April 15, states that he arrived on March 21. A printed letter of his, dated March 12, says he arrived the evening before that; however the latter is a printing error in which the date was reversed, which means that he actually arrived on the evening of March 20. See McCall to Bliss, Apr. 15, 1850, New Mexico Miscellaneous Collection; and McCall, *Letters,* 490.

23. See Clarksville *Standard,* June 1, 1850, quoting John James's report in San Antonio *Western Texian* on the mineral wealth. On Steen's career, see Dan L. Thrapp, *Encyclopedia of Frontier Biography,* 3 vols. (Glendale, Calif.: Arthur H. Clark Co., 1988), 3:1363–1364.

24. Munroe's order of March 12 is in M-1072, roll 1, vol. 1:29, RG 393. Steen's copy is printed in *App. to Tex. Sen. Jours., 3d Legis., 2d Sess.,* 6.

25. Neighbors to Bell, Mar. 23, June 4, 1850, ibid., 4–5, 7; and Bell to Pres. Zachary Taylor, June 15, 1850, ibid., 50.

26. Henry's career is outlined in Heitman, *Historical Register* 1:524. His request to take his family to San Antonio is in Henry to McLaws, Jan. 26, 1850, M-1102, roll 2, RG 393. On the ore samples, see McLaws to Bvt. Maj. Enoch Steen, Apr. 13, 1850, M-1072, roll 1, vol. 2:64–65, RG 393. That Neighbors left Dona Aña on March 28 is in Houston *Telegraph,* May 23, 1850, quoting information from the Austin *South-Western American.* See also file GG232, "Court Martial Records, 1805–1939," RG 153—Records of the Office of the Judge Advocate General (Army), National Archives; and Henry to Governor Peter H. Bell, Sept. 15, 1850, Franklin Papers.

27. A good description of the Jornada is given by Colonel McCall in a July 15 report to the secretary of war. McCall, *Letters,* 506. For a general history of the area, see Brodie Crouch, *Jornada del Muerto: A Pageant of the Desert* (Spokane: Arthur H. Clark Co., 1989).

28. A Spanish copy of Houghton's proclamation is in Governors' Letters; an English translation is printed in *App. to Tex. Sen. Jours., 3d Legis., 2d Sess.,* 11–12. The Santa Fe resolutions, as copied on March 17, are in Rusk Papers. On the situation in Santa Fe at this time, see also Neighbors to Bell, June 4, 1850, ibid., 9; Calhoun to Brown, Mar. 16, 1850, in Abel, ed., *J. S. Calhoun Correspondence,* 163; Davis, *El Gringo,* 111; and a detailed report by William C. Skinner of the Houghton faction in the St. Louis *Republican,* Apr. 24, 1850, reprinted in D.C. *Natl. Intell.,* May 4, 1850.

29. See note 22 above on the issue of McCall's arrival date. On his actions when he arrived, see McCall, *Letters,* 490–92.

30. New Mexico Miscellaneous Collection. Historians who have used this collection include Ganaway, *New Mexico and Sectional Controversy,* 46–52; and Larson, *New Mexico's Quest,* 30–40. On the influence of Bliss in the Taylor administration, see Hamilton, *Taylor,* 173, 354; Bauer, *Taylor,* 248; and Smith, *Presidencies of Taylor and Fillmore,* 66–67. Sen. William Seward of New York, who was in New York at the time, did not arrive in Washington until November 28. William H. Seward to Thurlow Weed, Nov. 30, 1849, Thurlow Weed Papers, Rush Rhees Library, University of Rochester. It appears that the crafty Seward had no part in planning McCall's mission. One leading Free-Soil newspaper later detected the discrepancy between Colonel Munroe's strong actions and the more reserved official position assumed by President Taylor and concluded that Munroe had therefore been acting under orders not made public. Cleve. *True Democrat,* June 24, 1850.

31. On Crawford, see Hamilton, *Taylor,* 151, 152, 164, 172, 181–82, 380; Bauer, *Taylor,* 261–62, 311; and Smith, *Presidencies of Taylor and Fillmore,* 54, 56.

32. The best account of this is in McCall to Bliss, Apr. 15, 1850, New Mexico Miscellaneous Collection. On the *New Mexican,* see Weightman's later statement in *Cong. Globe,* 32: 1: App., 325. See also

Pillans to Bell and Neighbors to Bell, Apr. 14, 1850, Governors' Letters; Neighbors to Bell, June 4, 1850, *App. to Tex. Sen. Jours., 3d Legis., 2d Sess.*, 8–9; Davis, *El Gringo*, 111; *N.Y. Tribune*, July 3, 1850, quoting a Santa Fe letter from "A Southerner" in D.C. *Southern Press*; Poldervaart, *Black-Robed Justice*, 26; and Chavez, *Alvarez*, 137.

33. Neighbors to Bell, Apr. 14, 1850, Governors' Letters; and Neighbors to Bell, June 4, 1850, *App. to Tex. Sen. Jours., 3d Legis., 2d Sess.*, 8–9.

34. Neighbors to Bell, June 4, 1850, ibid., 8–9.

35. Ibid.; Pillans to Bell, Apr. 14, 1850, Governors' Letters; St. Louis *Republican*, June 4, 1850; Davis, *El Gringo*, 111; and Collins, *Contestacion*, 10 (p. 8 of trans.).

36. These documents are all printed in *App. to Tex. Sen. Jours., 3d Legis., 2d Sess.*, 24–32; and 31: 1: *Sen. Ex. Docs.* 56 (Ser. 561): 7–14.

37. References to these meetings, especially the riotous one, are sketchy. The most detailed account is in a letter by William C. Skinner in the St. Louis *Republican*, June 19, 1850. Colonel Washington, who left Santa Fe for Washington on April 16, said the riot took place not long before he left and gave a brief account of it to reporters. *N.Y. Commercial Advertiser*, June 4, 1850; Phila. *Pennsylvanian*, June 6, 1850. On Weightman's role, see Collins, *Contestacion*, 10 (p. 8 of trans.); and Larson, *New Mexico's Quest*, 48–49. See also Phila. *Pennsylvanian*, July 2, 1850; and D.C. *Natl. Intell.*, June 15, 1850.

38. The notice is printed in *App. to Tex. Sen. Jours., 3d Legis., 2d Sess.*, 32–33; and 31: 1: *Sen. Ex. Docs.* 56 (Ser. 561): 14. The signers of the meeting notice included Joab Houghton, T. S. J. Johnson, E. W. Prewitt, J. W. Folger, José M. Abreo, Domingo Fernandez, Ceran St. Vrain, Merrill Ashurst, Murray F. Tuley, Donaciano Vigil, and Francisco Ortiz y Delgado. While several of these men had been signatories to the Houghton faction's manifesto in late 1849, one of them, M. F. Tuley, had originally signed the November 1849 address of the original "state" party. See notes 5 and 6 above. Neighbors to Bell, June 4, 1850, *App. to Tex. Sen. Jours., 3d Legis., 2d Sess.*, 10.

39. Neighbors to Munroe, Apr. 15, and Munroe to Jones, Apr. 16, 1850, 31: 1: *Sen. Ex. Docs.* 56 (Ser. 561): 10–15.

40. Neighbors to Bell, Apr. 14, 1850, Governors' Letters. Pillans simultaneously recommended the quick dispatch of Texan military forces. Pillans to Bell, Apr. 14, 1850, ibid.

41. On the April 20 meeting, see Neighbors to Bell, June 4, 1850, *App. to Tex. Sen. Jours., 3d Legis., 2d Sess.*, 9. On the government employees and their role, see also Phila. *Pennsylvanian*, July 2, 1850; Jackson *Mississippian*, July 19, 1850; and New Orleans *Courier*, July 26, 1850. The distribution of delegates, as given in Munroe's April 23 proclamation, was: Taos, Rio Arriba, Santa Fe, and San Miguel, three each; Santa Anna and Bernalillo, two each; and Valencia, five. The resolutions of the April 20 meeting are printed in *N.Y. Tribune*, June 29, 1850. The proclamation is in *App. to Tex. Sen. Jours., 3d Legis., 2d Sess.*, 13–14. The claim about Weightman is in Collins, *Contestacion*, 12–13 (p. 10 of trans.); and Larson, *New Mexico's Quest*, 48. See also McCall to Bliss, undated comments, New Mexico Miscellaneous Collection.

42. Neighbors to Bell, June 4, 1850, *App. to Tex. Sen. Jours., 3d Legis., 2d Sess.*, 7; Henry to McLaws, Apr. 8, 1850, M-1102, roll 2, RG 393; file GG 232, "Court Martial Records, 1805–1939", RG 153; Henry to Bell, Sept. 15, 1850, Franklin Papers.

43. McLaws to Steen, Apr. 13, and Munroe to Steen, Apr. 15, 1850, M-1072, roll 1, vol. 2:48–49, 64–65, RG 393.

44. Steen to McLaws, Apr. 29, 1850, M-1102, roll 2, RG 393.

45. Munroe to Jones, May 20, 1850, M-1072, roll 1, vol. 2:78, RG 393.

46. Neighbors to Munroe, May 3, 1850, one of the documents enclosed with ibid.; and Neighbors to Bell, June 4, 1850, *App. to Tex. Sen. Jours., 3d Legis., 2d Sess.*, 7–10.

47. Baird to Bell, Feb. 20 and Apr. 18, 1850, Governors' Letters; Bell to Baird, Apr. 12, 1850, "Executive Record Book: Bell, 1849–1850," 112, Executive Record Books; and Austin *State Gazette*, May 4, 1850.

Chapter 4
The Momentous Thirty-First Congress Begins

1. On the Free-Soil–Northern Whig view of the Proviso, see Morrison, *Democratic Politics and Sectionalism*, 52–74; on the Southern view of the Proviso, see Freehling, *Road to Disunion*, 458–62; Holt, *Political Crisis of the 1850s*, 54–56; and Russel, "What Was the Compromise?" 304–6.

2. David M. Potter, *The Impending Crisis, 1848–1861* (New York: Harper and Row, 1976), 95; Thelma Jennings, *The Nashville Convention: Southern Movement for Unity, 1848–1851* (Memphis: Memphis State Univ. Press, 1980), 35–39; Hamilton, *Taylor*, 230–32; Nevins, *Ordeal of the Union* 1:247–48; Merrill D. Peterson, *The Great Triumvirate: Webster, Clay, and Calhoun* (New York: Oxford Univ. Press, 1987), 452; and *N.Y. Herald*, Feb. 5, 1850.

3. Freehling, *Road to Disunion*, 492; Schott, *Stephens*, 110; Robert J. Rayback, *Millard Fillmore: Biography of a President* (Buffalo: Buffalo Historical Society, 1959), 199–200; Bauer, *Taylor*, 271; Thomas Brown, *Politics and Statesmanship: Essays on the American Whig Party* (New York: Columbia Univ. Press, 1985), 210; Hamilton, *Taylor*, 225, 229–30; Holt, *Political Crisis of 1850s*, 71–72, 80; Peter B. Knupfer, *The Union as It Is: Constitutional Unionism and Sectional Compromise, 1787–1861* (Chapel Hill: Univ. of North Carolina Press, 1991), 178–79; and Nevins, *Ordeal of the Union* 1:240–44. One noted historian has referred to Taylor as "a kind of doughface in reverse." Don E. Fehrenbacher, *The Dred Scott Case: Its Significance in American Law and Politics* (New York: Oxford Univ. Press, 1978), 157.

4. Orsamus B. Matteson to Weed, Mar. 22, 1850, Weed Papers; *N.Y. Herald*, Dec. 6, 8, 16, 1849, Jan. 17, Mar. 4, 7, Apr. 25, 1850; Bauer, *Taylor*, 262; Brock, *Parties and Political Conscience*, 280; Hamilton, *Taylor*, 162–68, 233–35, 237–38, 323–24; Nevins, *Ordeal of the Union* 1:230–33; Remini, *Clay*, 717, 725, 727. The most positive view of Taylor's cabinet is in Smith, *Presidencies of Taylor and Fillmore*, 54–59.

5. *N.Y. Herald*, Jan. 31, Mar. 17, 18, 1850; Wilmington, N.C., *Weekly Commercial*, May 24, 1850; [T. N. Parmalee], "Recollections of an Old Stager," *Harper's New Monthly Magazine* 47 (Sept. 1873): 587–88; William O. Lynch, "Zachary Taylor as President," *Journal of Southern History* 4 (Aug. 1938): 284–85; Nevins, *Ordeal of the Union* 1:234–35; Rayback, *Fillmore*, 194–96, 199, 201–5; and Glyndon G. Van Deusen, *William Henry Seward* (New York: Oxford Univ. Press, 1967), 114. Even Taylor's most ardent defender admits that Taylor should have backed off from Seward somewhat. Smith, *Presidencies of Taylor and Fillmore*, 59–63.

6. On Taylor's attitude toward Clay and Webster, see *N.Y. Herald*, Apr. 29, 1850; Lucius Q. C. Elmer, *The Constitution and Government of the Province and State of New Jersey . . .* (Newark, N.J.: Martin R. Dennis and Co., 1872), 437–38; George R. Poage, *Henry Clay and the Whig Party* (Chapel Hill: Univ. of North Carolina Press, 1936), 229; Smith, *Presidencies of Taylor and Fillmore*, 121–22; and Nevins, *Ordeal of the Union* 1:233–34, 273–74. On Taylor's poor relations with Congress, see Bauer, *Taylor*, 265–66, 297; Potter, *Impending Crisis*, 95–96; and Nevins, *Ordeal of the Union* 1:259–60.

7. Bauer, *Taylor*, 323.

8. On apprehension of danger over Texas–New Mexico at the end of 1849 and beginning of 1850, see Austin *State Gazette*, Feb. 9, 1850; Baltimore *Sun*, Jan. 1, 11, 24, 1850; Boston *Pilot*, Jan. 12, 26, 1850; New Orleans *Daily Picayune*, Jan. 13, 1850; *N.Y. Herald*, Dec. 27, 30, 1849, Jan. 3, 4, 11, 29, 1850; *N.Y. Tribune*, Dec. 17, 28, 1849, Jan. 14, 15, 1850; Phila. *Public Ledger*, Jan. 3, 1850; Victoria *Advocate*, Feb. 8, 1850; D.C. *Natl. Intell.*, Jan. 3, 17, Feb. 8, 12, 14, 1850; and D.C. *Union*, Jan. 12, 18, 1850.

9. See the following for some explanation of Foote's political attitude in 1850: Roger S. Baldwin to Emily Baldwin, May 19, 1850, Baldwin Family Papers, Sterling Library, Yale University; William R. King to James Buchanan, Aug. 4, 1850, roll 16, Buchanan Papers, Historical Society of Pennsylvania, Philadelphia; and Cleo Hearon, *Mississippi and the Compromise of 1850* (Oxford: Mississippi Historical Society, 1913), 134.

10. On the matter of Rusk's reelection and its postponements, see J. P. Henderson to Rusk, Dec. 7, 1849, and Feb. 24, 1850, and Ben Rush Wallace to Rusk, Jan. 16, 1850, Rusk Papers; and Marshall

Republican, Dec. 20, 1849, Jan. 10, 1850. For examples of lobbying and early suggestions that Texas cede their land claim in satisfaction of the debt, see James Hamilton to Texas state representatives Franklin and Crump, Dec. 26, 1849, Franklin Papers; Isaac H. Register to Bell, Oct. 23, 1849, Governors' Letters; Clarksville *Standard,* Mar. 16, 1850, quoting *Boston Post* article by "Osceola," Texas bond lobbyist and Washington correspondent Francis Grund; and *N.Y. Herald,* Jan. 11, 1850.

11. The "pigmy" quote is taken from "Il Segretario" (Edward W. Johnson) in the *Louisville Daily Journal,* Aug. 19, 1850. For contemporary descriptions of these and other members of both houses in 1850, see John Forney's "Glances at Congress," Phila. *Pennsylvanian,* Apr. 30, May 2, 6, 13, 18, 22, 24, 29, 31, June 8, 17, 1850; Sara Jane Clarke's letters as "Grace Greenwood" in Philadelphia's *Saturday Evening Post,* June 22, 29, July 6, 13, 27, Aug. 3, 1850; *Detroit Daily Advertiser,* Sept. 9, 1850; Montgomery *Alabama Journal,* July 16, 1850; *Pittsburgh Daily Gazette,* June 5, 26, 1850; and numerous descriptions in Frederika Bremer, *Homes of the New World; Impressions of America,* 2 vols., trans. Mary Howitt (New York: Harper and Bros., 1854), vol. 1; and Oliver Dyer, *Great Senators of the United States Forty Years Ago, . . .* (New York: R. Bonner's Sons, 1889).

12. Frederick J. Blue, *The Free Soilers: Third Party Politics, 1848–1854* (Urbana: Univ. of Illinois Press, 1973), 191–97; Brock, *Parties and Political Conscience,* 281–84; Don E. Fehrenbacher, *Chicago Giant: A Biography of "Long John" Wentworth* (Madison: American History Research Center, 1957), 93–95; Hamilton, *Taylor,* 247–53; John T. Hubbell, "Three Georgia Unionists and the Compromise of 1850," *Georgia Historical Quarterly* 51 (Sept. 1967): 308–10; Nevins, *Ordeal of the Union* 1:251–54; William Y. Thompson, *Robert Toombs of Georgia* (Baton Rouge: Louisiana State Univ. Press, 1966), 56–59; and Charles M. Wiltse, *John C. Calhoun: Sectionalist, 1840–1850* (Indianapolis: Bobbs-Merrill Co., 1951), 449–52.

13. *Cong. Globe,* 31: 1: 44, 50–59; *N.Y. Herald,* Dec. 21, 22, 23, 1849; Smith, *Presidencies of Taylor and Fillmore,* 99–100; and Van Deusen, *Seward,* 119–20. A colorful description of Clemens is in Concord, N.H., *Independent Democrat,* July 11, 1850.

14. Richardson, comp., *Messages and Papers* 5:9–24; *N.Y. Herald,* Dec. 25, 26, 27, 1849; *N.Y. Tribune,* Dec. 25, 1849; Houston *Telegraph,* Jan. 10, 1850; Bauer, *Taylor,* 288–89; Hamilton, *Taylor,* 256–60; and Smith, *Presidencies of Taylor and Fillmore,* 101–2.

15. *Cong. Globe,* 31: 1: 87, 110–11, 155–56, 176–85.

16. Balt. *Sun,* Jan. 3, 1850; Houston *Telegraph,* Nov. 22, 1849, Jan. 10, 1850; *N.Y. Herald,* Dec. 31, 1849, Jan. 4, 7, 11, 1850; *N.Y. Tribune,* Dec. 26, 31, 1849; D.C. *Natl. Intell.,* Jan. 2, 3, 1850; D.C. *Union,* Dec. 28, 1849, Jan. 3, Feb. 5, 1850.

17. *Cong. Globe,* 31: 1: 74, 86–87, 94, 97–98, 119–23, 133–37, 150, 159, App., 91–97.

18. Ibid., 165–66; *N.Y. Herald,* Jan. 18, 1850; Phila. *Cummings' Telegraphic Evening Bulletin,* Jan. 17, 1850; Hamilton, *Taylor,* 274–75; and Leonard, "Western Boundary-Making," 340, 347–48, 350. Texan dislike of the Benton plan's consequence is in *N.Y. Herald,* Jan. 29, 1850; Victoria *Advocate,* Feb. 8, 1850.

19. *Cong. Globe,* 31: 1: 166–68; A. H. Stephens to L. Stephens, Jan. 17, 1850, Alexander H. Stephens Papers, Manhattanville College, Purchase, New York; *Cincinnati Gazette,* Dec. 3, 13, 1849; *N.Y. Herald,* Dec. 7, 1849, Jan. 4, 1850; William N. Chambers, *Old Bullion Benton, Senator from the New West: Thomas Hart Benton, 1782–1858* (Boston: Little, Brown, 1956), 356–57; Hamilton, *Taylor,* 275; and Leonard, "Western Boundary-Making," 352–53.

20. *Cong. Globe,* 31: 1: 168–71; Leonard, "Western Boundary-Making," 342; and Hamilton, *Taylor,* 275.

21. *Cong. Globe,* 31: 1: 198, 210–13, App., 58–74; and Hamilton, *Prologue to Conflict: The Crisis and Compromise of 1850* (Lexington: Univ. of Kentucky Press, 1964), 50–51. Northern opinion of Foote's plan is in *Cincinnati Gazette,* Jan. 22, 1850; and *N.Y. Tribune,* Jan. 30, 1850. On Texan opinion, see Kaufman to Bell, Jan. 17, 1850, and Charles C. Mills to Bell, Jan. 18, 1850, Governors' Letters; and Victoria *Advocate,* Feb. 8, 1850.

22. Richardson, comp., *Messages and Papers* 5:28–29.

23. Kaufman to Bell, Jan. 17, 21, 22, 23, 1850, Governors' Letters; and D.C. *Union,* Jan. 22, 1850.

24. Bauer, *Taylor,* 301; Maurice G. Baxter, *One and Inseparable: Daniel Webster and the Union* (Cambridge: Harvard Univ. Press, 1984), 409; George T. Curtis, *Life of Daniel Webster,* 2 vols. (New York: D. Appleton and Co., 1870), 2:397–98; Peterson, *Great Triumvirate,* 455; and Remini, *Clay,* 731–32.

25. On Clay's visits with Taylor and Clayton, see *N.Y. Herald,* Dec. 11, 22, 23, 1849. On Clay's relations with Taylor in general, see Nevins, *Ordeal of the Union* 1:233–34. On Clay's motivations for his plan, see Brown, *Politics and Statesmanship,* 150–51; Holt, *Political Crisis of 1850s,* 84; Knupfer, *Union as It Is,* 180; and Remini, *Clay,* 730–31. On Clay and the South, see *N.Y. Tribune,* Dec. 4, 1849, quoting Baltimore's *American and Commercial Daily Advertiser;* Freehling, *Road to Disunion,* 494; and Remini, *Clay,* 712, 716, 717–19, 724.

26. *Cong. Globe,* 31: 1: 244–47.

27. Ibid., 245. A map purporting to show Clay's line at 32° north latitude appeared in Hamilton, *Prologue to Conflict,* 57. More recently, William Freehling has posited the 32° north latitude as definitely what Clay proposed and has elaborated on the theme that Clay meant to bring emancipation to north Texas. This thesis constitutes an interesting piece of speculation but is without foundation in evidence, unless material can be cited to show that Clay seriously intended to emancipate north Texas or even that Clay definitely meant 32° north latitude to be the boundary. Freehling himself remarks that Clay's proposal for the District was sloppily worded. So was his boundary plan. Freehling, *Road to Disunion,* 366, 496–97. On congressional ignorance of southwestern geography in 1850, see *N.Y. Herald,* June 27, 1850.

28. *Cong. Globe,* 31: 1: 246–52, App., 173; and Hamilton, *Prologue to Conflict,* 54–55. For some Northern editorial attacks on Clay's plan, see *Cincinnati Gazette,* Jan. 31, 1850; and N.Y. *Independent,* Feb. 14, 1850. Southern and Texan objections in the press are in Houston *Telegraph,* Feb. 21, Mar. 14, 1850; Macon *Georgia Telegraph,* Feb. 12, 1850; *Mobile Register,* Feb. 5, 1850; Victoria *Advocate,* Feb. 22, 1850; and D.C. *Union,* Feb. 6, 7, 1850.

29. Richardson, comp., *Messages and Papers* 5:30–31; 31: 1: *Sen. Ex. Docs.* 24 (Ser. 554). On administration handling of Wood's letters to Polk and Taylor, see Crawford to Wood, Jan. 19, 1850, M-6, roll 30, RG 107; Kaufman to Crawford, Jan. 22, 1850, M-221, roll 153, RG 107; Kaufman to Bell, Jan. 17, 26, Feb. 11; Clayton to Kaufman, Jan. 22; Charles C. Mills to Bell, Jan. 18; and Rusk to Bell, Feb. 2, 1850, Governors' Letters.

30. *Cong. Globe,* 31: 1: 200–209, 257–61, 276–77, 279, 412, App., 74–78; *Ashtabula* (Ohio) *Sentinel,* Feb. 16, Mar. 2, 1850; Balt. *Sun,* Jan. 24, 1850; Centreville *Indiana True Democrat,* Feb. 13, 27, 1850; *Cincinnati Gazette,* Feb. 16, 1850; *N.Y. Herald,* Jan. 28, 1850; and D.C. *Union,* Feb. 19, 1850.

31. *Cong. Globe,* 31: 1: App., 115–27, esp. 119–21 on the boundary and debt issues.

32. For some negative reactions to Clay's speech, see Seward to Weed, Feb. 14, 1850, Weed Papers; Macon *Telegraph,* Feb. 19, 1850; Marshall *Republican,* Feb. 28, 1850; and Victoria *Advocate,* Mar. 8, 1850. For the positive impact of Clay's speech, see Balt. *Sun,* Feb. 8, 1850; Macon *Telegraph,* Feb. 26, 1850; *Mobile Register,* Feb. 14, 1850; *N.Y. Herald,* Feb. 8, 1850; Philip S. Foner, *Business and Slavery: The New York Merchants and the Irrepressible Conflict* (Chapel Hill: Univ. of North Carolina Press, 1941), 25–26; Holt, *Political Crisis of 1850s,* 84; Nevins, *Ordeal of the Union* 1:269–72; Peterson, *Great Triumvirate,* 458; and Remini, *Clay,* 734. On Ritchie's reconciliation with Clay, see Thomas Ritchie's letter in *Richmond Enquirer,* Sept. 10, 1852.

33. On the Texas bond situation, see *Cong. Globe,* 31: 1: 353; D.C. *Natl. Intell.,* Jan. 1, 1850; D.C. *Union,* Jan. 13, 1850; Hamilton, *Prologue to Conflict,* 66, 124–32; and Edmund T. Miller, *A Financial History of Texas* (Austin: Univ. of Texas Press, 1916), 118–20.

34. *Boston Pilot,* Feb. 23, 1850; Boston *Yankee Blade,* Mar. 2, 1850; *N.Y. Herald,* Jan. 16, Feb. 5, 1850; and D.C. *Natl. Intell.,* Feb. 8, 12, 14, 1850.

35. *Cong. Globe,* 31: 1: 323–24, App., 97–102, 202–11. On Houston's absence from Washington, see Donald Braider, *Solitary Star: A Biography of Sam Houston* (New York: G. P. Putnam's Sons, 1974),

260–61; Campbell, *Houston*, 123; de Bruhl, *Sword of San Jacinto*, 342–43; and Williams, *Houston*, 272–73.

36. On the events of February 18, see *Cong. Globe*, 31: 1: 375–86; Elbridge G. Spaulding to Weed, Feb. 18, 19, 1850, Weed Papers; *Boston Pilot*, Mar. 9, 1850; Boston *Yankee Blade*, Mar. 2, 1850; Centreville *True Democrat*, Mar. 6, 1850; New Orleans *Picayune*, Mar. 8, 1850; *N.Y. Herald*, Feb. 21, 1850; Phila. *Bulletin*, Feb. 20, 1850; and Victoria *Advocate*, Mar. 15, 1850.

37. The House speeches that discussed Texas–New Mexico in April are in *Cong. Globe*, 31: 1: App., 450–56. On continuing Southern interest in calling the yeas and nays to stop legislation, see Balt. *Sun*, Feb. 19, 1850; *Mobile Register*, Feb. 6, 1850; New Orleans *Picayune*, Feb. 24, 1850; *N.Y. Herald*, Apr. 11, 12, 1850; and Clingman's March 22 letter to D.C. *Republic*, in *Selections from the Speeches and Writings of Hon. Thomas L. Clingman of North Carolina* (Raleigh: John Nichols, 1877), 259–67. Howard's letter is in *Galveston News*, Mar. 11, 1850; and Austin *State Gazette*, Mar. 16, 1850.

38. *Cong. Globe*, 31: 1: 355–56, 365–69, 370–75, 395–406, 416–21.

39. Ibid., 365–68. Foote expressed his particular fear of the proviso in ibid., 366, 421 (on Feb. 25). See also A. H. Stephens to L. Stephens, Feb. 24, 1850, Stephens Papers, Manhattanville College; New Orleans *Picayune*, Mar. 1, 4, 1850; *N.Y. Herald*, Jan. 30, Feb. 2, 28, 1850; Victoria *Advocate*, Mar. 15, 1850; and D.C. *Union*, Feb. 16, 1850. Elbert B. Smith has advanced the thesis that the primary motivation of Foote (and Ritchie) in attempting to have a select committee established to combine California with other measures in a single bill was to exact as high a Southern price for California's admission as possible by securing to Texas as much of New Mexico's land east of the Rio Grande as possible. Smith, *The Death of Slavery: The United States, 1837–1865* (Chicago: Univ. of Chicago Press, 1967), 111; idem, *Francis Preston Blair* (New York: Free Press, 1980), 204; idem, *Magnificent Missourian*, 265; and idem, *Presidencies of Taylor and Fillmore*, 129–30. Foote did indeed later credit Thomas Ritchie with having originally suggested the establishment of a special committee to devise a compromise. Henry S. Foote, *Casket of Reminiscences* (Washington, D.C.: Chronicle Publishing Co., 1874), 25–26; and Ritchie's own letter on the subject, *Richmond Enquirer*, Sept. 10, 1852. Certainly Foote favored the Texan claim, as most Southerners did, and had visited Texas and written a two-volume work on the Republic a decade before; but he was not dogmatic about the Texan claim and during the 1850 crisis showed himself quite willing to accept various compromise boundary proposals, as later chapters of this work show. Contemporaries and historians have pointed out the fact that land included in Texas would extend slavery over that land while any land east of the Rio Grande that might be included in New Mexico would be free soil. See Marshall *Republican*, Dec. 20, 1849, Jan. 3, 10, 1850; *N.Y. Tribune*, Dec. 15, 17, 29, 1849; Victoria *Advocate*, Feb. 8, 1850; R. W. Johnson's letter, D.C. *Union*, Feb. 19, 1850; Freehling, *Road to Disunion*, 488; Robert E. May, *John A. Quitman: Old South Crusader* (Baton Rouge: Louisiana State Univ. Press, 1985), 229; and Smith, *Presidencies of Taylor and Fillmore*, 97, 138. Foote and other Southern leaders were as aware of this as anyone else, but this consideration did not keep Foote and some other Southern leaders from being willing to accept a compromise boundary. There is no specific evidence that the boundary, rather than the Wilmot Proviso, was central to Foote's motivation in proposing a select committee to combine measures. On Foote and Clay, see *Cong. Globe*, 31: 1: 368, 370–75, 395–406; Boston *Yankee Blade*, Mar. 2, 1850; and Remini, *Clay*, 739–40.

40. On Taylor's meeting with Southerners in mid-February, see Balt. *Sun*, Feb. 16, 20, 1850; *N.Y. Herald*, Feb. 28, Mar. 3, 1850; *N.Y. Tribune*, Feb. 25, 1850; St. Louis *Republican*, Mar. 11, Apr. 6, 7, 1850; Hamilton, *Prologue to Conflict*, 70; Nevins, *Ordeal of the Union* 1:308; and Mark J. Stegmaier, "Zachary Taylor Versus the South," *Civil War History* 33 (Sept. 1987): 224–25. Many historians, myself included, have mistakenly concluded that this meeting was the notorious one that New York Whig leader Thurlow Weed witnessed. Since the two correspondents for the Balt. *Sun*, Francis Grund ("X") and Eliab Kingman ("Ion"), reported Taylor's threat earlier in February, the date of Taylor's meeting with the unnamed Southerners was probably on February 13 or 14. Weed was still in New York at that time. Further research has now led me to conclude that the meeting that Weed recounted was in mid-April, as related later in this chapter. On the dinner for Mann and the Free-Soilers, see *N.Y. Herald*, Mar. 4, 1850; and Mary T. Mann, *Life of Horace Mann* (Boston: Walker, Fuller, and Co., 1865), 292–93.

The *Herald* mentioned among those attending Hale, Seward, Root, Doty, and Tuck and Wilson of New Hampshire. This account did not specifically refer to Mann but did say that other guests were also present. An item in the *Herald* account should be of interest to ethnocultural historians: President Taylor, in order not to offend the racial sensibilities of these antislavery men, did not have the dinner served by the black servants who ordinarily did so, but instead he hired Irish waiters from the Willard Hotel for the evening.

41. On the positive side of social relations among congressmen, see A. H. Stephens to L. Stephens, Feb. 11, 1850, Stephens Papers, Manhattanville College; Boston *Yankee Blade,* Mar. 2, 1850; Macon *Telegraph,* May 7, 1850; and *N.Y. Herald,* Feb. 27, 1850. On the Davis-Bissell difficulty, see ibid., Feb. 28, Mar. 3, 1850; and William C. Davis, *Jefferson Davis: The Man and His Hour* (New York: HarperCollins, 1991), 196. On the threat of violence breaking out in Congress, see Boston *Pilot,* Mar. 9, 1850; Boston *Yankee Blade,* Mar. 16, 1850; *N.Y. Herald,* Feb. 28, 1850; and Phila. *Public Ledger,* Jan. 18, 1850.

42. A. H. Stephens to L. Stephens, Mar. 29, Apr. 3, 1850, Stephens Papers, Manhattanville College; Bauer, *Taylor,* 303; Hamilton, *Prologue to Conflict,* 67; Holt, *Political Crisis of 1850s,* 80, 83, 85–86; Hubbell, "Three Georgia Unionists," 311–12; Johannsen, *Douglas,* 271–73; Nevins, *Ordeal of the Union* 1:303; Poage, *Clay and Whig Party,* 206–7; Rayback, *Fillmore,* 222–23; and Schott, *Stephens,* 113–14.

43. *N.Y. Herald,* Feb. 5, 25, 26, Mar. 3, 1850; Phila. *Bulletin,* Feb. 18, 1850; Irving H. Bartlett, *Daniel Webster* (New York: W. W. Norton, 1978), 245–46; Richard N. Current, *Daniel Webster and the Rise of National Conservatism* (Boston: Little, Brown, 1955), 161–62; Robert F. Dalzell, *Daniel Webster and the Trial of American Nationalism, 1843–1852* (Boston: Houghton Mifflin Co., 1973), 175, 192–95; Foner, *Business and Slavery,* 21–24; and Major L. Wilson, "Of Time and the Union: Webster and His Critics in the Crisis of 1850," *Civil War History* 14 (Dec. 1968): 300–301.

44. Balt. *Sun,* Feb. 26, Mar. 1, 1850; Phila. *Bulletin,* Feb. 27, Mar. 2, 1850; *N.Y. Herald,* Feb. 24, 25, 26, Mar. 3, 1850; and *Cong. Globe,* 31: 1: 436–39.

45. Phila. *Bulletin,* Mar. 2, 1850; *N.Y. Herald,* Mar. 3, 1850; and *Cong. Globe,* 31: 1: 436–39.

46. *Cong. Globe,* 31: 1: 439. Bell's plan, but not its connection with Webster, is discussed in Joseph H. Parks, *John Bell of Tennessee* (Baton Rouge: Louisiana State Univ. Press, 1950), 245–47.

47. On Texas's resistance to subdivision, see Austin *State Gazette,* April 13, 27, 1850; Balt. *Sun,* Apr. 26, 1850; Clarksville *Standard,* Apr. 13, 1850; Marshall *Republican,* May 23, 1850; Phila. *Public Ledger,* Apr. 27, 1850; D.C. *Natl. Intell.,* Apr. 26, 1850; and Victoria *Advocate,* Feb. 8, 1850.

48. The best sources of information for the Rio Grande Valley movement are Frank H. Dugan, "The 1850 Affair of the Brownsville Separatists," *Southwestern Historical Quarterly* 61 (Oct. 1957): 270–87; and Galen D. Greaser and Jésus F. de la Teja, "Quieting Title to Spanish and Mexican Land Grants in the Trans-Nueces: The Bourland and Miller Commission, 1850–1852," ibid. 95 (Apr. 1992): 445–64. See also *Cong. Globe,* 31: 1: 501–2; Henderson to Rusk, Feb. 24, 1850, Rusk Papers; Austin *State Gazette,* Feb. 23, Mar. 9, 1850; Houston *Telegraph,* Feb. 28, Apr. 11, 1850; Marshall *Republican,* Mar. 7, May 9, 1850; Matagorda *Tribune,* Apr. 8, 1850; San Antonio *Western Texian,* Feb. 28, 1850; Victoria *Advocate,* Feb. 22, Mar. 1, 1850; and Louis G. Wortham, *A History of Texas from Wilderness to Commonwealth,* 5 vols. (Ft. Worth: Wortham-Molyneaux Co., 1924), 4:224–26.

49. *Cong. Globe,* 31: 1: 154–55, 173, 233–37, 648–49, App., 416–17, 476.

50. For Webster's remarks on the subdivision of Texas, see ibid., App., 272. That part of his speech positively impressed Jeff Davis but not enough to convert Davis to compromise. W. C. Davis, *J. Davis,* 197. On the reaction in general to Webster's speech, see Baxter, *One and Inseparable,* 416–18; Hamilton, *Prologue to Conflict,* 79–81; Hamilton, *Taylor,* 311–14; Nevins, *Ordeal of the Union* 1:292–98; and Peterson, *Great Triumvirate,* 465–66. As to Seward's speech, the most positive modern analysis of it is in Brock, *Parties and Political Conscience,* 300–306. Seward's mentor, Thurlow Weed, was extremely disappointed in the extremist position Seward had assumed after Weed had assured President Taylor of Seward's loyalty to the administration's program. Weed to Seward, Mar. 14, 15, 17, 26, 1850, roll 36, William H. Seward Papers, Rush Rhees Library, University of Rochester, New York; and

Seward to Weed, Mar. 15, 31, 1850, Weed Papers. Horace Greeley praised the speech but criticized Seward for virtually ignoring the boundary issue in it. *N.Y. Tribune*, Mar. 19, 1850. Some nice details of Taylor's initial reaction to the speech are in [Parmalee], "Recollections of an Old Stager," 589–90. Seward may have helped put Taylor in a mood to forgive his speech by presenting him with a new silver currycomb for his famous horse, "Old Whitey," on the morning of March 6, the day before the speech. Balt. *Sun*, Mar. 7, 1850; Hamilton, *Taylor*, 322–23; and Smith, *Presidencies of Taylor and Fillmore*, 120. On the general reaction to Seward's speech, see Bauer, *Taylor*, 306; Hamilton, *Prologue to Conflict*, 85–86; Hamilton, *Taylor*, 321–23; Nevins, *Ordeal of the Union* 1:301–2; Smith, *Presidencies of Taylor and Fillmore*, 119–20; Van Deusen, *Seward*, 125–26; and Van Deusen, *Thurlow Weed: Wizard of the Lobby* (Boston: Little, Brown, 1947), 175.

51. *Cong. Globe*, 31: 1: 508–10, 517–21, 527–34.

52. Ibid., 592, 628–29; Hamilton, *Taylor*, 320–21; Johannsen, *Douglas*, 274–75; and Leonard, "Western Boundary-Making," 348–49. Howard's letter is in Houston *Telegraph*, May 2, 1850; and Victoria *Advocate*, May 17, 1850.

53. *Cong. Globe*, 31: 1: 602–4, 609–11; *Boston Pilot*, Apr. 6, 1850; and *N.Y. Herald*, Mar. 28, Apr. 3, 1850.

54. Victoria *Advocate*, Apr. 12, May 3, 17, 1850.

55. *N.Y. Herald*, Mar. 30, Apr. 1, 3, 4, 9, 10, 13, 1850; [Parmalee], "Recollections of an Old Stager," 586–87; Bauer, *Taylor*, 312–13; William P. Brandon, "The Galphin Claim," *Georgia Historical Quarterly* 15 (June 1931): 113–41; Hamilton, *Taylor*, 345–52, 355–56; Nevins, *Ordeal of the Union* 1:324–27; and Smith, *Presidencies of Taylor and Fillmore*, 123–28.

56. The piece of evidence that directly connects the two Georgians to a mid-April meeting with Taylor is a statement by correspondent Francis Grund ("Osceola") in the *Boston Statesman* (weekly edition of *Boston Post*), May 4, 1850. In this letter, dated April 24, Grund stated that Toombs and Stephens had seen Taylor during the week of April 7–13 and had urged him to change the cabinet. Weed had informed Seward that he would come to Washington as soon as the New York legislature's session ended, which was April 10. From this I have estimated that Weed came to Washington and met with Taylor on Friday, April 12, or Saturday, April 13, and that one of those was also the day when Toombs and Stephens had their row with the president. What may be oblique references to this meeting can be found in an April 15 letter by Alexander Stephens and a May 1 letter by George W. Julian. Weed to Fish, Apr. 17, 1850, roll 20, Hamilton Fish Papers, Library of Congress; Weed to Seward, Apr. 4, 1850, roll 37, Seward Papers; A. H. Stephens to L. Stephens, Apr. 15, 1850, Stephens Papers, Manhattanville College; *N.Y. Herald*, Apr. 11, 1850; and Centreville *Indiana True Democrat*, May 8, 1850. For my earlier version of the meeting, see Stegmaier, "Taylor Versus the South," 220–24.

57. *Cong. Globe*, 31: 1: 640–43. A few days later Webster's belief in the impossibility of slavery in New Mexico was confirmed by Hugh N. Smith. Smith to Webster, Apr. 9, 1850, Wiltse, ed. *Microfilm Edition of the Papers of Daniel Webster*, 41 rolls (Boston: Massachusetts Historical Society, 1971), roll 22; and Ganaway, *New Mexico and Sectional Controversy*, 27–28.

58. *Cong. Globe*, 31: 1: 656–65, 704–14, 751–62.

59. Ibid., 762–64, 1479–81.

60. Ibid., 770–75. It is quite possible, but unprovable, that Foote deliberately and successfully provoked Benton into threatening the Mississippian with physical assault. In their previous engagement, Benton had offered to "cudgel" Foote. Foote, aware of that and of Benton's volatile temper, may have wished to insult Benton into attempting a physical assault on Foote on the floor of the Senate in order to influence the thoroughly shocked members into taking final action on Foote's resolution. Foote used verbiage that personally referred to Benton in an insulting way. Foote could not have helped but realize that such a reference would very likely trigger a violent response by Benton. Given the arrangement of Senate seating, with Foote's and Benton's seats about twenty feet apart, just inside the railing at the rear of the chamber, Foote may have also realized that there was little chance

that Benton would be able to physically come in contact with him prior to being restrained by others. Foote, indeed, drew and cocked a fully loaded revolver; but rather than point it at Benton, Foote kept the gun's muzzle pointed down. Foote, of course, claimed that he intended to shoot no one but only carried the pistol for defense. I believe a case can be made that Foote pulled the loaded gun for its shock value. Rumors of firearms and potential for violence had been circulating for weeks. Foote suddenly gave a semblance of reality to those rumors. It seems strange that, in the ordinary course of Senate routine, Foote would even carry a pistol, despite his personal familiarity with dueling. Moreover, the pistol was fully loaded when Foote drew it, as if he was anticipating something that day—or planning to provoke an incident himself. If he plotted the incident, the gun would have to have been loaded and capable of being used for defense or Foote would look incredibly ridiculous in pulling an unloaded pistol on Benton. Foote never did point the gun at anyone but merely brandished the weapon. That in itself was dangerous enough, but Foote may have meant the gun for symbolic purposes more than anything else. Ibid., 762–64.

Chapter 5
New Mexico Seeks Statehood

1. On the relative strengths of the two factions, see McCall to Bliss, Apr. 15, 1850, New Mexico Miscellaneous Collection. On the influence of the prefects over the election process, see a June 20 letter by Charles Hoppin from Doña Ana, Mobile *Alabama Planter*, Sept. 9, 1850; letter by Pillans or Weightman from Santa Fe to Senator Mason of Virginia in Jackson *Mississippian*, July 19, 1850; and Lamar, *Far Southwest*, 77. The power and role of the army departments in the election and otherwise are detailed in the above letter to Senator Mason and in a letter by "JMD" in Phila. *Pennsylvanian*, July 2, 1850. All three of these letters, it must be noted, were written by biased opponents of the Houghton faction.

2. Calhoun's notice of May 2 to the tribe is in Ritch Collection.

3. 31: 1: *Sen. Ex. Docs.* 74 (Ser. 562): 16–17; and Larson, *New Mexico's Quest*, 31–32.

4. Munroe to Jones, May 13, 1850, M-567, roll 432, item M323, RG 94; McCall to Bliss, May 21, 24, 1850, New Mexico Miscellaneous Collection; and Larson, *New Mexico's Quest*, 32–33. One point on which McCall's letter is confusing is the timing of the sessions. I have concluded that the initial vote on Archuleta was on Saturday, May 18. Among historians who discuss the convention, Howard Lamar says the New Mexico constitution appeared to have been written months earlier, sent back East for examination by various senators, etc., and then returned to New Mexico for the convention. Lamar, *Far Southwest*, 77. I find no evidence for this assertion. For other accounts of the convention, see St. Louis *Republican*, June 25, 1850; Davis, *El Gringo*, 112; Bancroft, *Works: History of Arizona and New Mexico* 17:447; Binkley, *Expansionist Movement in Texas*, 189–90; Chavez, *Alvarez*, 138; Ganaway, *New Mexico and Sectional Controversy*, 49–50; and Loyola, *American Occupation*, 111–12.

5. McCall to Bliss, May 21, 24, 1850, New Mexico Miscellaneous Collection; 31: 1: *Sen. Ex. Docs.* 74 (Ser. 562): 2–17; ibid. 76 (Ser. 562): 9–11; and Larson, *New Mexico's Quest*, 33. Hoppin's views are in his June 20 letter. Mobile *Alabama Planter*, Sept. 9, 1850.

6. 31: 1: *Sen. Ex. Docs.* 74 (Ser. 562): 16–17; ibid. 76 (Ser. 562): 11; and Antonio José Otero et al. to Taylor, May 25, 1850, M-221, roll 154, RG 107. This set of documents is loosely organized in a generally alphabetical fashion. The memorial is in with other documents under "O," since Judge Otero's signature is first on the list.

7. 31: 1: *Sen. Ex. Docs.* 74 (Ser. 562): 2–3; Larson, *New Mexico's Quest*, 34; and Binkley, *Expansionist Movement in Texas*, 190.

8. 31: 1: *Sen. Ex. Docs.* 74 (Ser. 562): 3, 16; Mobile *Alabama Planter*, Sept. 9, 1850; Larson, *New Mexico's Quest*, 33–34; and Ganaway, *New Mexico and Sectional Controversy*, 50.

9. 31: 2: *Sen. Ex. Docs.* 1 (Ser. 587): pt. 2, 93–94; Bancroft, *Works: History of Arizona and New Mexico* 17:447–48; and Larson, *New Mexico's Quest*, 36. A copy of Munroe's May 28 proclamation, printed in Spanish, is item no. 205, Twitchell Collection.

10. McCall's undated list of candidates of "new" state party and McCall to Bliss, June 11, 1850, New Mexico Miscellaneous Collection; St. Louis *Republican*, June 25, July 8, 1850; Larson, *New Mexico's Quest*, 36; and Chavez, *Alvarez*, 138–39. Lamar, *Far Southwest*, presents an incorrect slate of candidates for the two parties (78–79).

11. McCall to Bliss, June 11,1850, New Mexico Miscellaneous Collection; St. Louis *Republican*, June 25, July 8, 1850; Larson, *New Mexico's Quest*, 36–37; and Chavez, *Alvarez*, 139.

12. McCall to Bliss, June 11, July 16, 1850, New Mexico Miscellaneous Collection; Ganaway, *New Mexico and Sectional Controversy*, 51; Larson, *New Mexico's Quest*, 37; and Chavez, *Alvarez*, 139.

13. Munroe's proclamation on June 6, in Spanish, is in Abel, ed., *J. S. Calhoun Correspondence*, 214. His joint proclamation with Calhoun of June 25 is in M-567, roll 432, item M429, RG 94; and 31: 2: *Sen. Ex. Docs.* 1 (Ser. 587): pt. 2, 101–2. On the Cochiti Pueblo matter, see McCall to Bliss, June 11, 1850, New Mexico Miscellaneous Collection; Calhoun to Brown, June 19, 1850, Abel, ed., *J. S. Calhoun Correspondence*, 213–14; and Larson, *New Mexico's Quest*, 37–38. On Weightman and the Tesuque Pueblo, see Calhoun to Brown, April 15, 1850, Abel, ed., *J. S. Calhoun Correspondence*, 187.

14. The comments on the violence of the election are in Calhoun to Brown, June 19, 1850, Abel, ed., *J. S. Calhoun Correspondence*, 213–14; and St. Louis *Republican*, Aug. 23, 1850. The Mexican-American enthusiasm for the campaign is mentioned in ibid., July 8, 1850, as reported by F.X. Aubry. The Houghton faction's tactics were detailed later by R. H. Weightman in *Cong. Globe*, 32: 1:324–25. Aragon's activities are in Aragon to Vigil, June 21, 1850, Ritch Collection. The "gachupín" comment about Alvarez is given in Weightman to Alvarez, Dec. 30, 1850, roll 1, Alvarez Papers; and Larson, *New Mexico's Quest*, 313 n.47. On intimidation tactics by the Houghton faction, see Theodore Wheaton to Angney, Alvarez, and Messervy, June 16, 1850, Ritch Collection; and Lamar, *Far Southwest*, 79.

15. Santiago Ulibarri to Vigil, June —, 1850, Ritch Collection; Weightman to Alvarez, Dec. 30, 1850, roll 1, Alvarez Papers; St. Louis *Republican*, July 8, Aug. 23, 1850; and Larson, *New Mexico's Quest*, 313 n. 47. I have derived the vote on the constitution from McCall to Bliss, July 16, 1850, New Mexico Miscellaneous Collection. 31: 1: *Sen. Ex. Docs.* 74 (Ser. 562): 2, gives the county-by-county breakdown of that vote. McCall, *Letters*, 522; Larson, *New Mexico's Quest*, 38; Lamar, *Far Southwest*, 80; and Chavez, *Alvarez*, 216 nn. 36, 37, give lower vote totals on the races for office than I have used. The figures I have used were apparently based on more complete returns and were reported as "official" in the St. Louis *Republican*, Aug. 23,1850. This listing was brought to St. Louis by R. H. Weightman on his way to Washington. Another report on the election, by R. T. McKinney, was published in ibid., Aug. 19, 1850. The *Cincinnati Gazette*, Aug. 29, 1850, copied statistics from the *Republican* and editorialized that New Mexico was daring to demand full statehood based on a voting population less than Hamilton County, Ohio (Cincinnati), alone.

16. The issue of Montoya's credentials was related in the St. Louis *Republican* on August 19 by Richard T. McKinney and on August 25 by Richard H. Weightman. Weightman's account gives a more detailed and accurate account of the matter. The same letter by Weightman details his enemy Houghton's attempt to imprison a representative. Although Weightman was extremely partisan and quite unscrupulous at times, I do not think he simply fabricated this item about the equally partisan and unscrupulous Houghton. The Montoya issue was used by one Southern radical paper to ridicule the establishment of the new state legislature in New Mexico. *Charleston Mercury*, Sept. 5, 1850.

17. McCall to Bliss, July 16,1850, and McCall's undated comments on New Mexico's government officials, New Mexico Miscellaneous Collection; Calhoun to Brown, July 15, 1850, Abel, ed., *J. S. Calhoun Correspondence*, 217–18; St. Louis *Republican*, June 25, July 8, Aug. 19, 23, 1850; 31: 1: *Sen. Ex. Docs.* 76 (Ser. 562): 5, 9; Larson, *New Mexico's Quest*, 39; Lamar, *Far Southwest*, 80; and Chavez, *Alvarez*, 146.

18. Alvarez's inaugural address is in M-200, roll 14, RG 46; 31: 1: *Sen. Ex. Docs.* 76 (Ser. 562): 5–7; and Stanley, *Giant in Lilliput*, 174–77.

19. Alvarez's July 8 message is in M-200, roll 14, RG 46; and 31: 1: *Sen. Ex. Docs.* 76 (Ser. 562): 7–9. The July 10 meeting is mentioned in Alvarez to Munroe, July 13, 1850, M-567, roll 432, item M447½, RG 94; and 31: 2: *Sen. Ex. Docs.* 1 (Ser. 587): pt. 2, 95–96. For the Riley opinion that Munroe sent Alvarez, see Jones to Munroe, Mar. 8, 1850, "Letters Sent by the Office of the Adjutant General (Main Series), 1800–1890," M-565, roll 17, 27:59–61; and Munroe to Alvarez, July 11, 1850, 31: 2: *Sen. Ex. Docs.* 1 (Ser. 587): pt. 2, 95. The Supreme Court case referred to by Riley was *American Insurance Company v. Cantor* (1828). See Theodore M. Grivas, *Military Governments in California, 1846–1850* (Glendale, Calif.: Arthur H. Clark Co., 1963), 23*n*. 37.

20. McCall to Bliss, July 16, 1850, New Mexico Miscellaneous Collection; Munroe to Alvarez, July 12, and Alvarez to Munroe, July 12, 13, 1850, M-567, roll 432, item M447½, RG 94; 31: 2: *Sen. Ex. Docs.* 1 (Ser. 587): pt. 2, 95–100, 103–5; Calhoun to Brown, July 15, 1850, Abel, ed., *J. S. Calhoun Correspondence*, 217–18; Bancroft, *Works: History of Arizona and New Mexico* 17:448–51; Twitchell, *History of Military Occupation*, 181–90; Chavez, *Alvarez*, 141–45; and Larson, *New Mexico's Quest*, 43–44.

21. McCall to Bliss, July 16, 1850, New Mexico Miscellaneous Collection; Munroe to Jones, July 16, 1850, M-567, roll 432, item M447, RG 94; and 31: 2: *Sen. Ex. Docs.* 1 (Ser. 587): pt. 2, 92; Larson, *New Mexico's Quest*, 42; and Chavez, *Alvarez*, 141.

22. McCall to Bliss, July 16, 1850, New Mexico Miscellaneous Collection; Munroe to Jones, July 16, 1850, M-567, roll 432, item M447, RG 94; and 31: 2: *Sen. Ex. Docs.* 1 (Ser. 587): pt. 2, 92. The original of Munroe's letter has a note on the outside that says "not to be copied," but it was published among the Senate documents anyway. See also Calhoun to Brown, July 15, 1850, Abel, ed., *J. S. Calhoun Correspondence*, 217–18; Twitchell, *History of Military Occupation*, 191–92; Chavez, *Alvarez*, 141; and Larson, *New Mexico's Quest*, 42–43.

23. The joint resolutions are in M-567, roll 432, item M536, RG 94; 31: 2: *Sen. Ex. Docs.* 1 (Ser. 587): pt. 2, 105–6; and Twitchell, *History of Military Occupation*, 191–92. The memorial to Congress is in 31: 1: *Sen. Ex. Docs.* 76 (Ser. 562): 3–5.

24. The unofficial list of acts and other moves made by the legislature is in: M-567, roll 432, item M447½, RG 94; and 31: 2: *Sen. Ex. Docs.* 1 (Ser. 587): pt. 2, 101. The existence of the joint resolution not listed was later mentioned by Acting Governor Alvarez in an August 8 proclamation. M-567, roll 432, item M536, RG 94; and 31: 2: *Sen. Ex. Docs.* 1 (Ser. 587): pt. 2, 107.

25. McCall to Bliss, July 16, 1850, and McCall's undated comments on New Mexico's government officials, New Mexico Miscellaneous Collection; 31: 2: *Sen. Ex. Docs.* 1 (Ser. 587): pt. 2, 101; and Larson, *New Mexico's Quest*, 42.

26. McCall to Bliss, July 16, 1850, New Mexico Miscellaneous Collection; Munroe to Jones, July 16, 31, 1850, M-567, roll 432, items M429 and M447, RG 94; and Summary of Contents, Santa Fe *New Mexican*, July 30, 1850, Miscellaneous, Read Collection. The original of this issue cannot now be located.

27. Calhoun to Brown, July 31, Aug. 13, 1850, Abel, ed., *J. S. Calhoun Correspondence*, 232, 252–53; and Weightman to Alvarez, July 19, 1850, roll 1, Alvarez Papers.

28. Baird's proclamation is in Abel, ed., *J. S. Calhoun Correspondence*, 233. Alvarez's proclamation is in ibid., 234; M-567, roll 432, item M429, RG 94; and 31: 2: *Sen. Ex. Docs.* 1 (Ser. 587): pt. 2, 102–5. The comment ridiculing Baird is in Summary of Contents, Santa Fe *New Mexican*, July 30, 1850, Miscellaneous, Read Collection.

29. Vigil's circular is in M-567, roll 432, item M429, RG 94; and 31: 2: *Sen. Ex. Docs.* 1 (Ser. 587): pt. 2, 102. Copies of Vigil's circular are in the Alvarez Papers and in the Read Collection. See also Summary of Contents, Santa Fe *New Mexican*, July 30, 1850, Miscellaneous, Read Collection, for that paper's anti-Alvarez propaganda.

30. M-567, roll 432, item M536, RG 94; 31: 2: *Sen. Ex. Docs.* 1 (Ser. 587): pt. 2, 107; Abel, ed., *J. S. Calhoun Correspondence*, 252–54; Francisco Tomás Cabesa de Baca to Alvarez, Aug. 4, 8, 1850, Read Collection; and Larson, *New Mexico's Quest*, 45.

31. On Major Henry's involvement in recruiting duty and orders to stay in the department, see McLaws to Henry, May 30; to Van Horne, June 12; to McCall, June 12; and to Henry, June 12, 1850, M-1072, roll 1, 2:88, 95, 97, 99–100, RG 393, NA. The charges against Henry are in the records of his court martial, file GG 232, "Court Martial Records," RG 153, NA.

32. The trial record is in file GG 232, "Court Martial Records," RG 153. See also a later statement by Henry for the Texas Legislature, Sept. 15, 1850, Franklin Papers. The order for Henry's release is in M-1072, roll 1, 2:143, RG 393.

33. Crawford's July 3 order for Steen's removal is in "Orders and Endorsements sent by the Secretary of War, 1846–1870," M-444, roll 1, vol. 2, RG 107. On other aspects of Steen's removal, see Thomas to Munroe, July 5, 1850, M-565, roll 17, p. 175, RG 94; Alexander to McLaws, Oct. 17, 1850, M-1102, roll 2, RG 393; and McLaws to Steen, Sept. 5, 1850, M-1072, roll 1, 2:162, RG 393.

34. Steen to Ogden and Hoppin deed, Sept. 10, 1850, p. 98, "Transcribed Deed Books—El Paso County," Books A–C, UTEP; C. M. Ogden's confirmation by Crawford as post sutler at Doña Ana, Apr. 23, 1850, M-444, roll 1, RG 107; and Buford to McLaws, Dec. 13, 1850, M-1102, roll 2, RG 393.

Chapter 6
Texas–New Mexico and the Omnibus Bill Debate, May 8–July 9, 1850

1. The telegraphic dispatch from St. Louis is in *D.C. Natl. Intell.* and *N.Y. Tribune,* May 4, 1850. The most detailed account of the proceedings of the Committee of Thirteen was given by correspondent James Harvey, writing as "Veritas" in the *Morning Courier and N.Y. Enquirer,* reprinted in *N.Y. Tribune,* Apr. 30, 1850. See also Webster to Franklin Haven, May 18, 1850, Wiltse, ed., *Microfilm Edition—Webster Papers,* roll 22.

2. Stephens to L. Stephens, Apr. 29, 1850, Stephens Papers, Manhattanville College; *Cincinnati Gazette,* May 3, 6, 1850; *N.Y. Tribune,* Apr. 30, 1850; Phila. *Bulletin,* Apr. 30, May 10, 1850; Phila. *Public Ledger,* May 4, 1850; St. Louis *Republican,* May 8, 1850, quoting Balt. *Sun; Cong. Globe,* 31: 1: 944, 1162, App., 791–92; and Hamilton, *Taylor,* 330–31.

3. R. S. Baldwin to R. S. Baldwin, Jr., May 9, 1850, Baldwin Family Papers; Lewis Cass to Robert McClelland, May 5, 1850, McClelland Papers, Burton Historical Collection, Detroit Public Library; Webster to Haven, May 18, 1850, Wiltse, ed., *Microfilm Ed.—Webster Papers,* roll 22; *Boston Daily Times,* May 6, 1850; *Cincinnati Gazette,* May 10, 1850; *N.Y. Evangelist and N.Y. Presbyterian,* May 23, 1850; and Baxter, *One and Inseparable,* 421.

4. Rusk to Berrien, May 6, 1850, Rusk Papers; *Cong. Globe,* 31: 1: 947, 950, 1164; *Cincinnati Gazette,* May 6, 1850; *N.Y. Tribune,* Apr. 30, 1850; and D.C. *Union,* May 2, 1850.

5. Hamilton, *Taylor,* 330; and Nevins, *Ordeal of the Union* 1:312–13. The work of the committee and their boundary provision do not bear out the contention of Elbert B. Smith that the committee's purpose was to give Texas as much of its claim as possible as the price for Southerners' acquiescence in California statehood. See Smith, *Death of Slavery,* 111; idem, *Magnificent Missourian,* 265–66; and idem, *Presidencies of Taylor and Fillmore,* 129–34. Webster's view of the intent of the Omnibus structure—to enhance the bill in the House—is in Webster to Haven, May 18, 1850, Wiltse, ed., *Microfilm Ed.—Webster Papers,* roll 22.

6. *Cong. Globe,* 31: 1: 944–48.

7. See ibid., 948–56, for mention of some of these themes on May 8.

8. For the reprint of Skinner's report, see D.C. *Natl. Intell.,* May 4, 1850. On Free-Soil distrust of Taylor on the New Mexico issue, see *Albany Daily State Register,* June 13, 1850, quoting N.Y. *Evening Post; Ashtabula Sentinel,* May 18, June 1, 8, 1850; Centreville *Indiana True Democrat,* June 26, 1850; Cleve. *True Democrat,* June 15, 17, 1850; and Phila. *Bulletin,* May 8, 1850. On Greeley's attitude, see James Wilson to Seward, May 26, and Greeley to Seward, May 27, 1850, roll 37, Seward Papers; Greeley

to Thaddeus Stevens, May 27, 1850, Stevens Papers, LC; and *N.Y. Tribune,* May 4, 18, 20, June 4, 18, 19, 1850. For alarm in May over Texas–New Mexico collision, in addition to ibid., see Balt. *Sun,* May 16, 22, 1850; and D.C. *Union,* May 2, 23, 1850. See also W. D. Miller to Rusk, May 21, 1850, Rusk Papers, in which Miller insisted that Texas militia would go into New Mexico if Neighbors were resisted there.

9. *Cong. Globe,* 31: 1: App., 567–73; Hamilton, *Taylor,* 332–33; and Remini, *Clay,* 747–48.

10. On the change of editors at the *Republic,* see Hamilton, *Taylor,* 333–34; and idem, *Prologue to Conflict,* 96–97. Whig editorials minimizing the differences between the two plans are in *Albany State Register,* June 6, 1850; *Burlington* (Iowa) *Hawkeye,* June 13, 20, 1850; Chillicothe, Ohio, *Daily Scioto Gazette,* June 10, 1850; *Frankfort Commonwealth,* June 4, 1850; *Knoxville Register,* July 13, 1850; Milledgeville, Ga., *Southern Recorder,* July 2, 1850; New Orleans *Daily Crescent,* June 6, 8, 1850; *Weekly Raleigh Register and North Carolina Gazette,* June 12, 1850; *Richmond Republican,* June 1, 3, 4, 1850; Trenton, N.J., *State Gazette,* June 24, 1850; *Vicksburg Weekly Whig,* June 19, 26, 1850; and Wilmington *Delaware State Journal,* June 21, 1850.

11. *Cong. Globe,* 31: 1: 1003–5. Douglas's motion to table failed 28–24, with Southerners and several Northern Democratic compromisers forming the majority. On Clemens's move, see ibid., 1019, App., 579–94.

12. Ibid., App., 612–16, 630–36; Seward to Weed, May 22, 1850, Weed Papers; Peterson, *Great Triumvirate,* 471; and Remini, *Clay,* 749–51.

13. R. S. Baldwin to E. Baldwin, May 22, 1850, Baldwin Family Papers; W. H. Seward to F. A. Seward, May 22, 26, 1850, Frederick W. Seward, *Seward at Washington as Senator and Secretary of State: A Memoir . . . , 1846–1861* (New York: Derby and Miller, 1891), 134–35; and D.C. *Republic,* May 27, June 3, 7, 17, 21, 22, 25, 1850.

14. 31: 1: *House Reports* 220 (Ser. 584); and *Cong. Globe,* 31: 1: 1038–41. Horace Greeley chastised Northern Whig congressmen for giving up Smith without a struggle and accused them of preparing to betray New Mexico to the "Philistines." Greeley to Stevens, May 27, 1850, Stevens Papers.

15. On Smith's letter, see *Cong. Globe,* 31: 1: 1408; Balt. *Sun,* May 25, 1850; *N.Y. Tribune,* May 22, 1850; D.C. *National Era,* May 30, 1850; and Larson, *New Mexico's Quest,* 23.

16. For references to the alliance of Northern and Southern radicals in May and early June, see John H. Clarke to William M. Meredith, June 1, 1850, Meredith Papers, Historical Society of Pennsylvania; David Outlaw to Emily Outlaw, May 12, 21, June 11, 1850, Outlaw Papers, Southern Historical Collection, University of North Carolina; Balt. *Sun,* June 12, 1850; *Boston Times,* May 15, 1850; Indianapolis *Indiana State Sentinel,* June 20, 1850; Macon *Georgia Journal and Messenger,* June 12, 1850; *N.Y. Morning Express,* June 10, 18, 1850; *N.Y. Herald,* June 19, 21, 1850; *N.Y. Journal of Commerce,* June 17, 1850; *N.Y. Tribune,* June 11, 1850; *Savannah Daily Republican,* June 8, 1850; and Wilmington, N.C., *Commercial,* May 24, 31, June 21, 1850. For a statement expressing some distrust of Southern men seemingly opposed to the bill, see John P. Hale's letter to Theodore Parker, May 15, 1850, mentioned in Richard H. Sewell, *John P. Hale and the Politics of Abolition* (Cambridge: Harvard Univ. Press, 1965), 132.

17. On pro-compromise public opinion and rallies in May and early June, see Thomas Metcalfe to John M. Clayton, June 18, 1850, Clayton Papers, LC; Balt. *Sun,* May 17, 1850; *Boston Times,* June 11, 18, 24, 1850; *Detroit Free Press,* June 20, 1850; *Lexington* (Ky.) *Observer and Reporter,* June 19, 1850; *N.Y. Herald,* June 16, 1850; *N.Y. Tribune,* June 11, 1850; Phila. *Public Ledger,* May 7, 1850; *Richmond Republican,* June 18, 1850; *St. Louis Intelligencer,* June 14, 1850; St. Louis *Republican,* June 4, 16, 19, 22, 1850; Savannah *Daily Morning News,* June 10, 1850; and Wilmington, N.C., *Commercial,* May 24, 1850. On Cooper's position, a fine analysis is given in Michael F. Holt, "Rethinking Nineteenth-Century American Political History," 19–23, paper presented at annual meeting of the Southern Historical Association, Nov. 14, 1991.

18. On Rusk's support of their friends' appointments, see Seward to Weed, Apr. 30, 1850, Weed Papers; and on Seward's blandishments to Rusk, see Rusk to James Brooks, Sept. 11, 1850, Rusk Papers.

19. *Albany State Register,* June 5, 1850; *Ashtabula Sentinel,* June 15, 1850; *Boston Times,* June 6, 1850; *Louisville Morning Courier,* June 12, 1850; *N.Y. Commercial Advertiser,* June 4, 1850; Phila. *Pennsylvanian,* June 6, 1850; and Savannah *News,* June 10, 1850. For details of Colonel Washington's journey, see St. Louis *Republican,* May 25, 28, 1850. The only written report by Washington is a twelve-page, rather bland description of the economic and human resources and Indian affairs in New Mexico. Washington to Crawford, July 8, 1850, M-221, roll 154, RG 107. See also McCall to Bliss, Apr. 15, 1850, New Mexico Miscellaneous Collection.

20. Henderson to Rusk, Apr. 14, 1850, Rusk Papers; Jennings, *Nashville Convention,* 75–76, 121–22; and Campbell, "Texas and Nashville Convention," 6–10. See also Marshall *Republican,* Apr. 18, May 2, June 20, 1850; and D.C. *Union,* May 14, 1850.

21. *Daily Nashville Union,* June 8, 1850; Jennings, *Nashville Convention,* 143–44; and Campbell, "Texas and Nashville Convention," 11.

22. *Nashville Union,* June 13, 1850; Jennings, *Nashville Convention,* 147–48; and Campbell, "Texas and Nashville Convention," 11.

23. James H. Hammond to William G. Simms, June 16, 1850, roll 9, Hammond Papers, LC; Henderson to Rusk, June 22, 1850, Rusk Papers; Marshall *Republican,* July 6, 1850; *Richmond Semi-Weekly Examiner,* July 2, 1850; Joseph Hodgson, *The Cradle of the Confederacy: or, the Times of Troup, Quitman and Yancey* (Mobile: Register Pub. Co., 1876), 279–80; and Nevins, *Ordeal of the Union* 1:317.

24. *Cong. Globe,* 31: 1: 1113–22, 1131–36; *Boston Times,* June 11, 1850; *Cincinnati Gazette,* July 3, 1850; Phila. *Bulletin,* June 7, 10, 1850; Phila. *North American and United States Gazette,* July 2, 1850; *St. Louis Intell.,* July 6, 1850; Fehrenbacher, *Dred Scott Case,* 168–70; and Hamilton, *Prologue to Conflict,* 98–99.

25. *Cong. Globe,* 31: 1: 1132–33, 1141–44, 1147.

26. Ibid., 1154–65.

27. Ibid., 1123, 1170, App., 700–701, 772–78, 936–40; and Leonard, "Western Boundary-Making," 338, 339, 353–54.

28. *Cong. Globe,* 31: 1: 1174–79, 1182–91, 1192–1201, 1212–20. See also Elbridge G. Spaulding to Weed, June 9, 1850, Weed Papers; *Pittsburgh Gazette,* June 17, 20, 1850; Schott, *Stephens,* 115–16; and Thompson, *Toombs,* 65–66.

29. *Cong. Globe,* 31: 1: App., 676–84 (Benton), 803–10 (Cass), and 810–18 (Dayton). Benton's speech has elicited the most commentary among these. Chambers, *Benton,* 364–65; Smith, *Magnificent Missourian,* 273–74; and Smith, *Presidencies of Taylor and Fillmore,* 149–51.

30. *Cong. Globe,* 31: 1: App., 789–93, 854–58; and Leonard, "Western Boundary-Making," 356–57.

31. *Cong. Globe,* 31: 1: App., 858–67; 31: 1: *Sen. Jour.* (Ser. 548): 395; *N.Y. Evangelist and Presbyterian,* June 20, 1850; Phila. *Bulletin,* June 14, 1850; *Pittsburgh Gazette,* June 18, 1850; Frederic Bancroft, *The Life of William H. Seward,* 2 vols. (New York: Harper and Bros., 1900), 1:274–75; Bauer, *Taylor,* 309; Chambers, *Benton,* 365–66; and Smith, *Magnificent Missourian,* 274–75.

32. *Cong. Globe,* 31: 1: 867–79; 31: 1: *Sen. Jour.* (Ser. 548): 396–98; Cass to McClelland, June 14, 1850, McClelland Papers; D. Outlaw to E. Outlaw, June 15, 1850, Outlaw Papers; *Cincinnati Gazette,* June 18, 1850; Cleve. *True Democrat,* June 21, 1850; *Detroit Free Press,* June 25, 1850; *Louisville Courier,* June 21, 1850; and *N.Y. Tribune,* June 17, 1850.

33. *Cong. Globe,* 31: 1: 1179.

34. Crawford to Taylor, June 15, 1850, "Letters Sent to the President by the Secretary of War, 1800–1863," M-127, roll 5, RG 107; Richardson, comp., *Messages and Papers* 5:48; *Ashtabula Sentinel,* June 29, 1850; Boston *Emancipator and Republican,* June 27, 1850; *Charleston Evening News,* July 2, 1850; Cleve. *True Democrat,* June 24, 1850; and *Mississippi Free Trader and Natchez Gazette,* July 6, 1850.

35. On Clay's condition and attitude in late June, see R. S. Baldwin to E. Baldwin, June 25, 1850, Baldwin Family Papers; John P. Hale to Lucy Hale, June 24, 1850, Hale Papers, New Hampshire Historical Society, Concord; June 21, 22 entries, John P. Kennedy Diary, Kennedy Papers, microfilm copy, Enoch Pratt Free Library, Balt.; and W. H. Seward to F. A. Seward, June 20, 1850, F. W. Seward, *Seward at Washington,* 140–41. For estimates of the Senate vote at this time, see Cass to McClelland,

June 29, 1850, McClelland Papers; Balt. *Sun*, June 28, 1850; *N.Y. Herald*, July 7, 1850; *N.Y. Journal of Commerce*, July 1, 3, 1850; *Pittsburgh Gazette*, July 10, 1850; and *Richmond Republican*, July 6, 1850. Clay's and Atchison's letters to Mangum are in Henry T. Shanks, ed., *The Papers of Willie Person Mangum*, 5 vols. (Raleigh: State Department of Archives and History, 1950–56), 5:178–79.

36. Nevins, *Ordeal of the Union* 1:324–27.

37. The June 18 Washington rumor is mentioned in H. Mann to M. Mann, June 18, 1850, M. Mann, *Life of Mann*, 303–4. For the news of Munroe's proclamation and correspondents' comments thereon, see Cleve. *True Democrat*, June 26, 1850; Jackson *Mississippian*, July 5, 1850; Milledgeville *Federal Union*, July 2, 1850; *N.Y. Tribune*, June 26, 1850; Phila. *Pennsylvanian*, June 25, 26, 1850; *Richmond Enquirer*, June 28, 1850; St. Louis *Republican*, June 20, 1850; and D.C. *Natl. Intell.*, June 21, 1850. For the news of the New Mexico constitution and correspondents' comments thereon, see *Boston Times*, July 2, 1850; *Cincinnati Gazette*, July 3, 1850; Cleve. *True Democrat*, July 1, 2, 1850; *N.Y. Express*, June 27, July 1, 1850; Phila. *Bulletin*, June 27, 1850; *Pittsburgh Gazette*, July 1, 1850; *St. Louis Intell.*, July 6, 10, 1850; Savannah *News*, July 1, 1850; and D.C. *Union*, June 27, 1850. Mann's "hydra" comment is in Mann to Sumner, June 27, 1850, Horace Mann Papers, Massachusetts Historical Society. Space does not permit a listing of the editorial comments, but most newspapers did express an opinion consistent with stands they had already taken on the issue. On the particular issue of whether President Taylor ordered Munroe's action, Taylor's defenders included some Southern Whig papers attempting to express their last vestiges of faith in the president. The papers that condemned Taylor for interference in New Mexico were all Democratic and mostly Southern.

38. On the initial Southern caucuses, see *Buffalo Commercial Advertiser*, July 5, 1850; *N.Y. Express*, June 27, July 3, 1850; *N.Y. Herald*, July 1, 1850; and Phila. *Bulletin*, July 1, 1850. On the California caucus, see *Buffalo Commercial Advertiser*, July 5, 1850; Phila. *Bulletin*, July 1, 1850; and Phila. *Pennsylvanian*, July 1, 2, 3, 1850.

39. On the Southern Whigs and their caucus, see John L. Schoolcraft to Weed, June 27, 1850, Weed Papers; D. Outlaw to E. Outlaw, June 25, 1850, Outlaw Papers; *N.Y. Herald*, July 1, 2, 1850, Aug. 17, 1876; *American Beacon and Norfolk and Portsmouth Daily Advertiser*, July 19, 1850, quoting *Richmond Times*; Phila. *Pennsylvanian*, July 3, 1850; and J. F. H. Claiborne, *Life and Correspondence of John A. Quitman*, 2 vols. (New York: Harper and Bros., 1860), 2:32.

40. On the Texas troop rumors in Washington, see Balt. *Republican and Daily Argus*, July 3, 1850; Balt. *Sun*, June 27, 1850; *N.Y. Commercial Advertiser*, June 28, July 5, 6, 8, 1850; D.C. *Natl. Intell.*, July 3, 1850; and D.C. *Union*, June 26, 1850. On Quitman's alleged promise of troops, which some reporters said amounted to 1,000 rather than 10,000 men, see Balt. *Sun*, July 8, 1850; Concord *New Hampshire Patriot and State Gazette*, July 11, 1850; Jackson *Mississippian*, July 19, 1850; *N.Y. Herald*, July 4, 1850; *N.Y. Tribune*, July 8, 1850; and Worcester, Mass., *Daily Spy*, July 4, 1850.

41. McWillie's letter is in *Vicksburg Sentinel*, July 18, 1850. Similar Southern views are in *Charleston News*, July 2, 1850; *Edgefield* (S.C.) *Advertiser*, July 3, 1850; Jackson *Mississippian*, July 12, 1850; New Orleans *Picayune*, July 4, 1850; Savannah *Georgian*, July 11, 1850; and D.C. *Southern Press*, July 3, 1850. Grund's articles are in *Boston Post*, July 2, 3, 1850; and Phila. *Public Ledger*, June 29, 1850. For other Northern Democratic views, see *Brooklyn Daily Eagle*, July 5, 1850; *Detroit Free Press*, July 1, 1850; *N.Y. Herald*, June 29, July 1, 4, 6, 1850; Portsmouth *N.H. Gazette and Republican Union*, July 9, 1850; and *Providence Daily Post*, July 8, 1850. For Northern Whig papers that took the threat seriously, see *Daily Toledo Blade*, June 27, 1850; *Boston Daily Advertiser*, July 6, 1850; *Hartford Daily Courant*, July 2, 6, 1850; *Lowell* (Mass.) *Daily Journal and Courier*, June 29, 1850; *N.Y. Express*, July 1, 1850; *N.Y. Tribune*, June 25, 1850; and *Providence Daily Journal*, July 9, 1850.

Northern Whig–Free-Soil papers ridiculing the Texas threat include *Albany Evening Journal*, July 2, 1850; *Bangor Daily Whig and Courier*, July 1, 10, 1850; *Boston Daily Mail*, July 6, 1850; *Buffalo Morning Express*, July 4, 1850; Chicago *Western Citizen*, July 16, 1850; Cincinnati *Daily Chronicle and Atlas*, July 6, 1850; *Cleveland Daily Plain Dealer*, July 11, 1850; Cleve. *True Democrat*, June 26, July 2, 1850; *Daily Dayton Journal*, July 2, 1850; Milwaukee *Wisconsin Free Democrat*, July 10, 1850; *Newark*

Daily Advertiser, July 6, 1850; and D.C. *National Era,* July 4, 1850. Southern Whig papers expressing disbelief in the Texas threat included *Louisville Journal,* July 2, 1850; New Orleans *Crescent,* July 2, 1850; and *Richmond Whig and Public Advertiser,* July 4, 1850.

42. For correspondents' reports of and comments on the troops sent, see *Ashtabula Sentinel,* July 13, 1850; Balt. *Sun,* June 28, 1850; *Boston Daily Journal,* July 5, 1850; *Cincinnati Gazette,* July 11, 1850; *N.Y. Courier and Enquirer,* July 3, 1850; *N.Y. Journal of Commerce,* July 8, 1850; *N.Y. Post,* July 3, 1850; and Phila. *Pennsylvania Inquirer and National Gazette,* July 2, 1850. Some editorials praising this action are in *Cincinnati Chronicle and Atlas,* July 13, 1850; *Cleveland Plain Dealer,* July 11, 1850; and Concord *N.H. Statesman,* July 5, 1850.

My estimate of the date of the cabinet meeting is based on the fact that earliest news reports of the meeting were written on July 4. *N.Y. Express,* July 6, 1850. On Crawford's conflict with Taylor at the meeting, see ibid.; *Charleston Courier,* July 23, 1850; Phila. *North American,* July 29, 1850; *N.Y. Herald,* Aug. 24, 1876; Claiborne, *Life of Quitman* 2:33; and Poage, *Clay and Whig Party,* 238. On the planned message, see also Matteson to Weed, July 13, 1850, Weed Papers; *Boston Journal,* July 11, 1850; *Charleston Courier,* July 16, 23, 1850; *N.Y. Commercial Advertiser,* July 13, 15, 1850; N.Y. *Evening Mirror,* July 15, 1850; *N.Y. Tribune,* July 13, 1850; Phila. *Bulletin,* July 9, 1850; *Pittsburgh Gazette,* July 16, 1850; Hamilton, *Taylor,* 382; and Nevins, *Ordeal of the Union* 1:332. One historian has mistakenly placed this event in July 1849. Bauer, *Taylor,* 293. While some papers said the new orders had already been sent, other papers corrected that, and no such orders were officially issued. The report of a plan of operations is in Jackson *Mississippian,* July 26, 1850. On the orders, in addition to works cited above, see D. Outlaw to E. Outlaw, July 7, 1850, Outlaw Papers; Cleve. *True Democrat,* July 15, 17, 1850; *N.Y. Commercial Advertiser,* July 6, 8, 1850; *N.Y. Express,* July 11, 15, 1850; Foote, *War of the Rebellion; or Scylla and Charybdis . . .* (New York: Harper and Bros., 1866), 155–56; and Henry Wilson, *History of the Rise and Fall of the Slave Power in America,* 3 vols. (Boston: Houghton Mifflin Co., 1872), 2:279.

43. Taylor's meeting with the senators is in *Norfolk American Beacon,* July 23, 1850, quoting article from *Salem* (Mass.) *Gazette.* On Taylor's attitude toward militia in general and Texans in particular, see D.C. *Republic,* July 6, 1850; Bauer, *Taylor,* 61, 87, 169–70, 184, 208–9; and Oates, *Visions of Glory,* 26–27, 29, 33–34. On Houston's speech, see *Cong. Globe,* 31: 1: App., 1711–16; and *N.Y. Herald,* July 1, 1850.

44. *Cong. Globe,* 31: 1: 1296–97, 1303, 1318–21, 1325–26; and Crawford to Taylor, July 1, 1850, M-127, roll 5, RG 107.

45. *Cong. Globe,* 31: 1: App., 984–1024; *Baltimore Patriot and Commercial Gazette,* July 3, 1850; and Brock, *Parties and Political Conscience,* 306–7. For comments praising Seward's speech, see Weed to F. A. Seward, July 4, and Weed to Schoolcraft, July 5, 1850, and numerous letters to W. H. Seward, roll 37, Seward Papers; *Buffalo Express,* July 9, 1850; Burlington, Vt., *Daily Free Press,* July 8, 9, 1850; and Utica *Oneida Morning Herald,* July 8, 1850. "Satanic" comments about Seward are in *Richmond Republican,* July 4, 1850; and Wilmington, N.C., *Commercial,* July 19, 1850.

46. Seward's dealings with Rusk are detailed by the latter in Rusk to James Brooks, Sept. 11, 1850, Rusk Papers.

47. Frank H. Severance, ed., *Millard Fillmore Papers,* 2 vols. (Buffalo: Buffalo Historical Society, 1907), 2:322–23; Matteson to Weed, July 13, 1850, Weed Papers; *Boston Times,* July 15, 1850; Concord *Patriot,* June 27, 1850; *Brownlow's Knoxville Whig and Independent Journal,* July 27, 1850; Phila. *Public Ledger,* July 12, 1850; Harry Carman and Reinhard H. Luthin, "The Seward-Fillmore Feud and the Crisis of 1850," *N.Y. History,* 24 (Apr. 1943): 175–76; Rayback, *Fillmore,* 237; and Sherry Penney, *Patrician in Politics: Daniel Dewey Barnard of New York* (Port Washington, NY: Kennikat Press, 1974), 106, 127. Fillmore wrote a letter to a friend in New York on July 4 discussing his view of the Texas–New Mexico issue, but the letter is no longer extant. D. O. Kellog to Fillmore, July 13, 1850, Lester W. Smith, ed., *Microfilm Edition of the Millard Fillmore Papers,* 68 rolls (Buffalo: Buffalo and Erie County Historical Society, 1975), roll 18.

48. I have determined the date, given the timing of the three interviews, the last of which was on

July 3. The Whig caucus had been on Saturday night, June 29, and Conrad probably would not have bothered Taylor the next day, a Sunday; therefore, Monday, July 1, seems the most likely date for Conrad's interview. *N.Y. Herald*, Aug. 17, 1876; and Claiborne, *Life of Quitman* 2:32–33.

49. Stegmaier, "Taylor Versus the South," 226–28. Toombs gave details of the interview to several individuals. See Matteson to Weed, July 13, 1850, Weed Papers; A. H. Stephens to L. Stephens, July 10, 1850, Stephens Papers, Manhattanville College; *N.Y. Herald*, July 6, 1850; *Boston Journal*, July 18, 1850; *N.Y. Courier and Enquirer*, July 17, 1850; and Phila. *North American*, July 17, 1850. The Toombs statement is in *N.Y. Herald*, Aug. 24, 1876.

50. Stegmaier, "Taylor Versus the South," 228. For personal testimony as to Taylor's physical condition at this period, see D. Outlaw to E. Outlaw, July 3, 1850, Outlaw Papers; A. H. Stephens to L. Stephens, June 26, July 10, 1850, Stephens Papers, Manhattanville College; *Albany Journal*, Sept. 14, 1850, quoting Bremer's account; Columbia *Daily Telegraph*, July 16, 1850; and *N.Y. Journal of Commerce*, July 13, 1850.

51. A. H. Stephens to L. Stephens, July 10, 1850. I believe the original of Stephens's letter to the *National Intelligencer* is in the Guy M. Bryan Papers at the Barker Texas History Center. It is a neatly handwritten copy such as Stephens would have had a clerk execute so that there would have been no problem for the newspaper staff in printing it correctly. This particular copy was used for a reprinting of the letter in M. L. Crimmins, ed., "A Letter of Alexander H. Stephens," *New Mexico Historical Review* 6 (July 1931): 249–52.

52. D.C. *Natl. Intell.*, July 4, 1850. One difference between the printed version and the manuscript in the Guy M. Bryan Papers is that the newspaper printed the words "opinions of others" rather than "opinion of others" in the handwritten document.

53. For some comments, see *Albany Atlas*, July 9, 1850; *Albany Journal*, July 6, 1850; *Buffalo Commercial Advertiser*, July 9, 1850; *Cincinnati Enquirer*, July 12, 1850; *N.Y. Commercial Advertiser*, July 9, 1850; *Pittsburgh Gazette*, July 8, 10, 1850; *Utica Daily Gazette*, July 9, 1850; and D.C. *National Era*, July 11, 1850.

54. On the heat and its effects, see R. S. Baldwin to E. Baldwin, June 23, July 8, 1850, Baldwin Family Papers; Alpheus Felch to Lucretia Felch, June 28, July 3, 1850, Felch Papers, Bentley Historical Library, University of Michigan, Ann Arbor; R. C. Winthrop to J. P. Kennedy, July 3, 1850, Kennedy Papers; and *Knoxville Whig*, July 20, 1850.

55. On President Taylor's activities and health on July 4, see Balt. *Republican and Argus*, July 5, 1850; *Chicago Daily Democrat*, July 18, 1850; *N.Y. Express*, July 11, 1850; N.Y. *Post*, July 12, 1850; *N.Y. Tribune*, July 6, 1850; Phila. *Bulletin*, July 11, 1850; Phila. *Public Ledger*, July 12, 1850; John Wentworth, *Congressional Reminiscences* (Chicago: Fergus Printing Co., 1882), 9–10; Bauer, *Taylor*, 314–15; Hamilton, *Taylor*, 388; Nevins, *Ordeal of the Union* 1:332–33; and Smith, *Presidencies of Taylor and Fillmore*, 155–56. On people becoming sick from drinking iced water, eating ice cream, etc., in 1850, see H. Mann to M. Mann, July 6 and 18, 1850, Mann Papers; Joshua Giddings to Lura Giddings, July 14, 1850, George W. Julian Papers, Indiana State Library, Indianapolis; and July 8, Aug. 7, 1850, entries, J. P. Kennedy Diary, Kennedy Papers.

56. *Boston Herald*, July 6, 1850; *Buffalo Courier*, July 15, 1850; *N.Y. Express*, July 12, 1850; *N.Y. Herald*, July 6, 1850; Bauer, *Taylor*, 315; and Hamilton, *Taylor*, 389.

57. The detailed account was by "Examiner," the Phila. *Pennsylvanian's* Washington correspondent in the July 16, 1850, issue. The Stephens quote is from Myrta L. Avary, ed., *Recollections of Alexander H. Stephens* (New York: Doubleday, Page and Co., 1910), 26. The quote from Taylor is from N.Y. *Mirror*, July 10, 1850. The *Mirror* did not credit a source for the quote. For a lengthy discussion of the evidence regarding the July 5 meeting, see Stegmaier, "Taylor Versus the South," 230–41.

58. Avary, ed., *Recollections of Stephens*, 26. On Stephens's and Southern attitudes toward Preston, see A. H. Stephens to L. Stephens, Apr. 15, 1850, Stephens Papers, Manhattanville College; and Augusta *Daily Constitutionalist*, July 11, 1850.

59. Taylor's sleeplessness on the night of July 5–6 is mentioned in a report in *Fredericksburg News*, July 16, 1850. On Stephens, Toombs, and the censure vote, see Hamilton, *Taylor*, 391; and Stegmaier, "Taylor Versus the South," 239.

60. For Howard's letter, see D.C. *Southern Press*, July 6, 1850. On Bell's speech, see *Cong. Globe*, 31: 1: App., 1094–102; R. S. Baldwin to E. Baldwin, July 3, 1850, Baldwin Family Papers; Willie P. Mangum to Charity A. Mangum, July 5, 1850, Mangum Papers, LC; D. Outlaw to E. Outlaw, July 5 and 6, 1850, Outlaw Papers; Seward to Weed, July 5, 1850, Weed Papers; Seward to F. A. Seward, July 5, 6, 7, 1850, F. W. Seward, *Seward at Washington*, 143; Phila. *Bulletin*, July 6, 1850; *Richmond Examiner*, July 9, 1850; *St. Louis Intell.*, July 16, 1850; and Parks, *Bell*, 253–58.

61. Balt. *Republican and Argus*, July 8, 1850; *Boston Daily Atlas*, July 9, 1850; Boston *Daily Evening Transcript*, July 9, 1850; *Cincinnati Enquirer*, July 13, 1850; *Hartford Courant*, July 9, 1850; *N.Y. Herald*, July 9, 1850; and *N.Y. Tribune*, July 8, 16, 1850.

62. On the arrival of the constitution and the cabinet meeting of July 7, see *Louisville Courier*, July 15, 1850; and D.C. *National Era*, July 18, 1850. On the arrival of copies of the New Mexico constitution at St. Louis, see St. Louis *Republican*, June 25, July 8, 1850; and Donald Chaput, *Francois X. Aubry: Trader, Trailmaker and Voyageur in the Southwest, 1846–1854* (Glendale: Arthur H. Clark Co., 1975), 90–91. The sections of the constitution on slavery and the boundaries were published in the D.C. *Natl. Intell.*, July 8, 1850.

63. Phila. *Bulletin*, July 11, 1850; *Cong. Globe*, 31: 1: 1343–47; and Hamilton, *Taylor*, 390–91.

Chapter 7
The Fillmore Administration's Baptism: Texas–New Mexico Destroys the Omnibus

1. Stephens to L. Stephens, July 10, 1850, Stephens Papers, Manhattanville College; and Stegmaier, "Zachary Taylor Versus the South," 240.

2. Burlington, Vt., *Free Press*, July 20, 1850; Phila. *Pennsylvanian*, July 13, 1850; and Bremer, *Homes of the New World* 1:449.

3. Stephens to L. Stephens, July 10, 1850, Stephens Papers, Manhattanville College; Boston *Transcript*, July 16, 1850; *Charleston Courier*, July 15, 1850; *N.Y. Tribune*, July 13, 1850; Bremer, *Homes of the New World* 1:449; and Rayback, *Fillmore*, 239–41.

4. For some positive views of Fillmore by Northern Whigs, see R. S. Baldwin to E. Baldwin, July 9, 12, 1850, Baldwin Family Papers; Winthrop to Everett, July 19, 1850, Frederick S. Allis, Jr., ed., *Microfilm Edition of the Edward Everett Papers*, 54 rolls (Boston: Massachusetts Historical Society, 1972), roll 13; Winthrop to John H. Clifford, July 14, 1850, Marjorie F. Gutheim, ed., *Microfilm Edition of the Winthrop Papers*, 53 rolls (Boston: Massachusetts Historical Society, 1976), roll 39; also quoted in Robert C. Winthrop, Jr., *A Memoir of Robert C. Winthrop* (Boston: Little, Brown, 1897), 128; Richard W. Thompson, *Recollections of Sixteen Presidents from Washington to Lincoln*, 2 vols. (Indianapolis: Bowen-Merrill Co., 1894), 2:313; *Boston Journal*, July 16, 1850; *Cincinnati Gazette*, July 19, 1850; *Cleveland Herald*, July 16, 1850; *Detroit Advertiser*, July 27, 1850; *Milwaukee Daily Sentinel and Gazette*, July 12, 17, 19, 1850; *N.Y. Commercial Advertiser*, July 15, 1850; *N.Y. Courier and Enquirer*, July 15, 16, 18, 1850; and *Providence Journal*, July 20, 26, 1850.

For some views of the Seward Whigs on Fillmore, see T. Ewing to P. Ewing, July 10, 1850, Thomas Ewing Papers, Ohio Historical Society, Columbus; Weed to Seward, July 10, and Roswell Colt to Seward, July 12, 1850, roll 38, Seward Papers; Seward to Weed, July 12, 14, 15, 16, Matteson to Weed, July 13, and Schoolcraft to Weed, July 16, 1850, Weed Papers; Seward to F. A. Seward, July 10, 11, 12, 14, 1850, F. W. Seward, *Seward at Washington*, 143–46; and *Albany Journal*, cited in *N.Y. Tribune*, July 13, 1850.

Some views of pro-compromise Northern Whigs on Fillmore are in Webster to Franklin Haven, July 11, 12, 16, 21, 1850, Wiltse, ed., *Microfilm Edition—Webster Papers*, roll 22; *Boston Advertiser*, July

17, 1850; *Buffalo Commercial Advertiser,* July 17, 1850; and *Rochester Daily American,* July 16, 1850.
Pro-compromise Northern Democratic opinion supporting Fillmore is in D. S. Dickinson to J.
A. Osborn, July 27, 1850, Daniel S. Dickinson Papers, New York Public Library; A. Felch to L. Felch,
July 21, 1850, Felch Papers; *Boston Times,* July 11, 15, 19, 1850; *Detroit Free Press,* July 20, 1850; N.Y.
Sunday Times and Noah's Weekly Messenger, July 14, 21, 1850; Phila. *Public Ledger,* July 12, 17, 1850; and
Providence Post, July 12, 1850.

Partisan Democratic papers that expressed negative attitudes on Fillmore as too Whiggish, too
anti-Southern, etc., included *Brooklyn Eagle,* July 12, 1850; *Hartford Daily Times,* July 10, 11, 1850;
Pitts. *Morning Chronicle,* July 11, 1850; and Trenton *Daily True American,* July 12, 1850.

Some Free-Soil opinions include S. P. Chase to Belle Chase, July 12, 13, 1850, roll 1, and Chase to
Eli Tappan, July 22, 1850, roll 8, Salmon P. Chase Papers, LC; Giddings to J. A. Giddings, July 22, 1850,
roll 3, Joshua Giddings Papers, Ohio Historical Society; H. Mann to M. Mann, July 10, 12, 13, 1850,
Mann Papers; *Albany Atlas,* July 11, 13, 20, 1850; Chicago *Western Citizen,* July 16, 23, 30, 1850; Cleve.
True Democrat, July 16, 17, 1850; Milwaukee *Wisconsin Free Democrat,* July 17, 24, 1850; *Syracuse Daily
Standard,* July 13, 19, 1850; and D.C. *National Era,* July 18, 1850.

Some Southern extremist criticism of Fillmore's accession is in Robert Barnwell to Hammond,
July 25, 1850, roll 9, Hammond Papers; Augusta *Constitutionalist,* July 14, 1850; *Memphis Tri-Weekly
Appeal,* July 13, 18, 1850; *Natchez Free Trader,* July 17, 20, 31, 1850; *Richmond Examiner,* July 16, 23,
1850; *Daily St. Louis Times,* July 18, 1850; and Tallahassee *Floridian and Journal,* Aug. 3, 1850.

Some Southern Whig support for Fillmore is in D. Outlaw to E. Outlaw, July 9, 10, 14, 1850,
Outlaw Papers; *Knoxville Whig,* July 27, 1850; *Louisville Courier,* July 17, 1850; *Memphis Daily Eagle,*
July 17, 1850; *Mobile Daily Advertiser,* July 16, 1850; *Nashville True Whig,* July 23, 1850; New Orleans
Picayune, July 17, 1850; *Richmond Republican,* July 11, 20, 1850; St. Louis *Republican,* July 11, 12, 14,
1850; *Savannah Republican,* July 17, 1850; and *Vicksburg Whig,* July 24, 1850.

Southern extremist presses initially open-minded about Fillmore include Jackson *Mississippian,*
July 19, 1850; Jacksonville *News,* Aug. 3, 1850; Mobile *Alabama Planter,* July 22, 1850; and *Vicksburg
Sentinel,* July 18, 1850. Texas radical J. P. Henderson expressed the same view in a letter to Mississippi's
governor. Henderson to Quitman, July 22, 1850, in Claiborne, *Life of Quitman* 1:41.

5. Clay to Thomas H. Clay, July 18, 1850, Clay Papers Project, University of Kentucky, Lexington;
Seward to Weed, July 21, 1850, Weed Papers; Winthrop to Clifford, July 14, 1850, Gutheim, ed., *Micro-
film Edition—Winthrop Papers,* roll 39; Seward to F. A. Seward, July 14, 15, 21, 1850, F. W. Seward,
Seward at Washington, 146–48; *Detroit Free Press,* July 20, 1850; Phila. *Pennsylvanian,* July 16, 1850;
Pittsburgh Gazette, July 16, 1850; and Poage, *Clay and Whig Party,* 242.

6. R. S. Baldwin to R. S. Baldwin, Jr., July 12, and to E. Baldwin, July 16, 20, 1850, Baldwin Family
Papers; numerous letters to Fillmore, July 10, 11, 19, 21, 1850, Smith, ed., *Microfilm Edition—Fillmore
Papers,* rolls 18, 19; July 10, 11, 20 entries, J. P. Kennedy Diary, Kennedy Papers; and Winthrop to
Kennedy, July 17, 1850, ibid.; H. Mann to M. Mann, July 19, 20, 21, 1850, Mann Papers; Stephens to L.
Stephens, July 16, 20, 1850, Stephens Papers, Manhattanville College; Webster to Haven, July 12, 16, 21,
1850, Wiltse, ed., *Microfilm Edition—Webster Papers,* roll 22; numerous letters to Weed, July 13, 14, 16,
17, 18, 20, 21, 1850, Weed Papers; letters from Winthrop to Nathan Appleton, July 26, John P. Kennedy,
July 17, and John Clifford, July 14, 17, 1850, Gutheim, ed., *Microfilm Edition—Winthrop Papers,* rolls
26, 39; and Henry W. Hilliard, *Politics and Pen Pictures at Home and Abroad* (New York: G. P. Putnam's
Sons, 1892), 231.

7. On Fillmore's withholding of Taylor's message, see a report by Washington correspondent "Le
Diable Boiteux" (probably Alexander Bullitt) in New Orleans *Picayune,* July 17, 1850. For Democratic
attacks on New Mexican peonage, see *Daily Albany Argus,* July 24, 26, 1850; Columbus *Daily Ohio
Statesman,* July 18, 1850; New Orleans *Daily Delta,* July 28, 1850; *N.Y. Herald,* July 18, 1850; and D.C.
Union, July 20, 1850. An interesting antipeonage letter by "Cora Montgomery" (Jane Cazneau) from
Eagle Pass, Texas, appeared in *N.Y. Tribune,* July 15, 1850.

8. The correspondent mentioned in the last sentence was "Junius" in the *Pittsburgh Gazette*, July 17, 1850. See also *N.Y. Commercial Advertiser*, July 13, 15, 1850.

9. Bell to Texas congressional delegation, June 13, 1850, *App. to Tex. Sen. Jours., 3d Legis., 2d Sess.*, 42–48. The letter was printed in *N.Y. Tribune*, Aug. 5, 1850. Editorial comments followed in *Hartford Courant*, Aug. 7, 1850; and Springfield, Mass., *Republican*, Aug. 14, 1850.

10. Bell to Howard, June 13, and to Taylor, June 14, 15, 1850, *App. to Tex. Sen. Jours., 3d Legis., 2d Sess.*, 48–50; and Howard to Fillmore, July 13, 1850, Smith, ed., *Microfilm Edition—Fillmore Papers*, roll 18. For some Northern editorials on Bell's letter to the president, reasserting the Northern determination to protect New Mexico, see *Buffalo Commercial Advertiser*, July 29, 1850; *N.Y. Times and Messenger*, Aug. 4, 1850; *N.Y. Tribune*, July 16, 1850; Phila. *North American*, July 19, 1850; and D.C. *National Era*, July 25, 1850.

11. Combs to Fillmore, July 10, 1850; and Houston to Fillmore, July 11, 1850, Smith, ed., *Microfilm Edition—Fillmore Papers*, roll 18. On Fillmore's working hours and Georgetown residence, see Mark J. Stegmaier, "The Case of the Coachman's Family: An Incident of President Fillmore's Administration," *Civil War History* 32 (Dec. 1986): 319–20. Fillmore's support of settlement in private conversations is mentioned in *Charleston Courier*, July 20, 1850; and *Knoxville Whig*, July 27, 1850.

12. The "intrigue" comment is in D. Outlaw to E. Outlaw, July 11, 1850, Outlaw Papers. Initial reports of the "Union caucus" are in *Alexandria Gazette*, July 16, 1850; *Boston Post*, July 17, 1850; *Charleston Courier*, July 16, 1850; *N.Y. Courier and Enquirer*, July 13, 1850; *N.Y. Express*, July 13, 1850; and *N.Y. Tribune*, July 13, 1850. Repudiations of the "caucus" report appeared in *Charleston Courier*, July 17, 1850; *N.Y. Express*, July 16, 1850; Phila. *Inquirer*, July 17, 1850; and *Pittsburgh Gazette*, July 19, 1850. Confirmation that a meeting took place is in *Boston Journal*, July 16, 1850; *Baltimore Patriot*, July 15, 1850; and Phila. *Bulletin*, July 15, 1850. The report of numerous meetings is in Phila. *Pennsylvanian*, July 17, 1850.

13. Balt. *Sun*, July 17, 18, 1850; *Boston Post*, July 17, 1850; New Orleans *Picayune*, July 20, 21, 1850; Phila. *Bulletin*, July 15, 17, 1850; Phila. *Pennsylvanian*, July 17, 1850; and Phila. *Public Ledger*, July 18, 1850. The Southern senators to be converted by the amendments are mentioned in *Boston Post*, July 17, 1850; *Charleston Courier*, July 27, 29, 1850; Concord *Patriot*, July 18, 1850; N.Y. *Post*, July 11, 1850; Phila. *Pennsylvanian*, July 24, 1850; and *Richmond Examiner*, July 16, 1850. The July 16 meeting is mentioned in *Charleston Courier*, July 20, 1850.

14. For varied attitudes on the threatened military conflict, see *N.Y. Tribune*, July 15, 16, 17, 19, 25, 26, 1850 (pro–New Mexico); D.C. *Southern Press*, July 13, 22, 26, 29, 31, 1850 (pro-Texas); and D.C. *Union*, July 12, 13, 17, 19, 24, 27, 29, 1850 (pro-compromise). For some letters to President Fillmore on the urgency of settling the Texas–New Mexico issue to avoid civil war, see D. F. Roysdon to Fillmore, July 22, and A. P. Granger to Fillmore, July 26, Smith, ed., *Microfilm Edition—Fillmore Papers*, roll 19.

15. 31: 1: *Sen. Jour.* (Ser. 548): 450; *Cong. Globe*, 31: 1: 1378–83; Francis P. Blair to Martin Van Buren, Aug. 1, 1850, roll 32, Van Buren Papers, LC; *Boston Statesman*, July 27, 1850; Phila. *Inquirer*, July 17, 1850; Phila. *Post*, July 27, 1850; Bremer, *Homes of the New World* 1:481–83; Hamilton, *Prologue to Conflict*, 108; Poage, *Clay and Whig Party*, 244; Smith, *Magnificent Missourian*, 275–76; and Leonard, "Western Boundary-Making," 350–51. The *Albany State Register*, July 20, 1850, in attacking Benton's line, pointed out that it gave New Mexico more territory than even the New Mexico constitution claimed.

16. *Cong. Globe*, 31: 1: 1391, App., 1258–66; *Boston Statesman*, July 27, 1850; N.Y. *Post*, July 17, 1850; Bremer, *Homes of the New World* 1:481–83; and Smith, *Magnificent Missourian*, 276.

17. *Cong. Globe*, 31: 1: 1391–92.

18. Ibid., App., 1266–70; Winthrop to Kennedy, July 17, 1850, Kennedy Papers; *Boston Atlas*, July 20, 1850; *Boston Times*, July 19, 20, 1850; *Cleveland Herald*, July 31, 1850; *N.Y. Courier and Enquirer*, July 20, 1850; N.Y. *Mirror*, July 30, 1850; N.Y. *Sun*, July 20, 1850; Phila. *Post*, July 27, 1850; *Pittsburgh Gazette*, July 22, 1850; *Rochester American*, July 25, 27, 1850; Springfield, Mass., *Republican*, July 26,

1850; Trenton *State Gazette,* July 27, 1850; and Bremer, *Homes of the New World* 1:477–80. Free-soil criticism of Webster's speech is in Seward to Weed, July 17, 1850, Weed Papers; Cleve. *True Democrat,* July 25, 30, 1850; and Worcester *Spy,* July 24, 1850, quoting the Cleve. *True Democrat.* The last cited source commented that Webster was attempting to poison the nation by using as an antidote an increase in the dose from which it was already dying.

19. 31: 1: *Sen. Jour.* (Ser. 548): 455; and *Cong. Globe,* 31: 1: App., 1270–73.

20. Thomas L. Harris to Charles H. Lanphier and George Walker, July 19, 1850, Charles Lanphier Papers, Illinois State Historical Society, Springfield; Cobb to William H. Hull, July 17, 1850, Ulrich B. Phillips, ed., *The Correspondence of Robert Toombs, Alexander H. Stephens, and Howell Cobb* (Washington, D.C.: American Historical Association, 1913), 205; N.Y. *Sun,* July 31, 1850; Hubbell, "Three Georgia Unionists," 316–17; and George F. Milton, *Eve of Conflict: Stephen A. Douglas and the Needless War* (Boston: Houghton Mifflin, 1934), 71. The letter was published in Augusta *Daily Chronicle and Sentinel,* Aug. 20, 21, 1850; and D.C. *Union,* Aug. 8, 1850.

21. For the House debate on Smith, see *Cong. Globe,* 31: 1: 1371–75, 1383–89, 1392–97, 1398–1409, App., 976–78, 981–84, 1132–37; Ashe's remark is in ibid., 1388.

22. Ibid., 1398–409, 1411–13; 31: 1: *House Jour.* (Ser. 566): 1143–46, 1149–52; Harris to Lanphier and Walker, July 19, 1850, Lanphier Papers; D. Outlaw to E. Outlaw, July 17, 1850, Outlaw Papers; Stephens to L. Stephens, July 18, 1850, Stephens Papers, Manhattanville College; *Ashtabula Sentinel,* July 27, 1850; Centreville *Indiana True Democrat,* July 31, 1850; *Chicago Democrat,* July 27, 1850; Chicago *Western Citizen,* July 30, 1850; Cleve. *True Democrat,* July 24, 1850; Milwaukee *Free Democrat,* July 31, 1850; N.Y. *Post,* July 26, 1850; and *Pittsburgh Gazette,* July 19, 22, 23, 1850.

23. *Cong. Globe,* 31: 1: App., 1413–16; N.Y. *Post,* July 26, 1850; Milwaukee *Free Democrat,* July 31, 1850; Phila. *Pennsylvanian,* July 20, 23, 1850; and D.C. *Natl. Intell.,* July 18, 1850. For some editorial opinion condemning the defeat of Smith, see Akron, *Free Democratic Standard,* Aug. 8, 1850; *Cincinnati Gazette,* July 29, 1850; *Hartford Courant,* July 24, 27, 1850; and *N.Y. Tribune,* July 22, 1850. For some editorials praising Smith's defeat, see *Hartford Times,* July 25, 1850; New Orleans *Crescent,* July 29, 1850; N.Y. *Times and Messenger,* July 21, 1850; and *Providence Post,* Aug. 28, 1850.

24. 31: 1: *Sen. Jour.* (Ser. 548): 462; and *Cong. Globe,* 31: 1: 1410–11, App., 1382–405. For a discussion of Foote's 35°30' north latitude proposal, see Freehling, *Road to Disunion,* 505–7.

25. Hamlin to "My Dear Sir," July 19, 1850, Hamlin Papers, Huntington Library; D. Outlaw to E. Outlaw, July 18, 1850, Outlaw Papers; Blair to Van Buren, July 20, 1850, roll 32, Van Buren Papers; *Baltimore Clipper,* July 22, 1850; Balt. *Sun,* July 19, 20, 1850; *Charleston Mercury,* July 26, 1850; Concord *Patriot,* July 25, 1850; Macon *Telegraph,* Aug. 6, 1850; New Orleans *Picayune,* July 25, 28, 1850; N.Y. *Journal of Commerce,* July 22, 24, 1850; N.Y. *Post,* July 20, 1850; Phila. *North American,* July 22, 1850; Pittsburgh *Gazette,* July 23, 25, 1850; and Springfield, Ill., *Daily Register,* July 30, 1850.

26. *Cong. Globe,* 31: 1: 1424, 1456, 1472, App., 1024–29; Balt. *Sun,* July 22, 1850; Cleve. *True Democrat,* July 26, 1850; N.Y. *Herald,* July 22, 1850; Phila. *North American,* July 23, 1850; and Bernard C. Steiner, "James Alfred Pearce," *Maryland Historical Magazine* 18 (Dec. 1923): 348–49.

27. On Clay's rebuke to the tariff lobbyists, see Wentworth, *Congressional Reminiscences,* 28–29. On Clay's irritability at this time, see ibid.; and Bremer, *Homes of the New World* 1:441–42. For physical descriptions of Clay during the speech, see ibid., 480–81, 497; and Boston *Yankee Blade,* Aug. 3, 1850.

28. *Cong. Globe,* 31: 1: App., 1405–15. The comment about Hale and Clemens is in *Albany State Register,* July 25, 1850. Some of the better descriptions of the speech by observers are in Boston *Yankee Blade,* Aug. 3, 1850; *Louisville Courier,* July 29, 1850; Phila. *Bulletin,* July 23, 1850; and Phila. *Post,* Aug. 3, 1850. Among those who disagreed with Clay but praised his July 22 performance were H. Mann to M. Mann, July 23, 1850, Mann Papers; Seward to F. A. Seward, July 22, 1850, F. W. Seward, *Seward at Washington,* 148; *Albany Atlas,* July 24, 31, 1850; Phila. *North American,* July 26, 1850; *Pittsburgh Gazette,* July 26, 1850; and *Utica Gazette,* Aug. 2, 1850. Southern radical presses saw no redeem-

ing value in Clay's speech. Columbia *Telegraph,* Aug. 2, 3, 6, 1850; Milledgeville *Federal Union,* Aug. 6, 1850; *Natchez Free Trader,* Aug. 7, 1850; and *Richmond Examiner,* July 26, 30, 1850. Pro-compromise editorialists and correspondents, too numerous to list here, lavishly praised Clay's address.

29. *N.Y. Journal of Commerce,* July 25, 1850; *N.Y. Commercial Advertiser,* July 25, 1850; *Cong. Globe,* 31: 1: 953, App., 1420, 1431; and William E. Parrish, *David Rice Atchison of Missouri: Border Politician* (Columbia: Univ. of Missouri Press, 1961), 102.

30. *Cong. Globe,* 31: 1: App., 1425; and Blair to Van Buren, Aug. 1, 1850, roll 32, Van Buren Papers. On the Bradbury amendment and some of the senators who were its targets, see R. S. Baldwin to E. Baldwin, July 26, 1850, Baldwin Family Papers; *Albany State Register,* July 23, 1850; *Ashtabula Sentinel,* Aug. 3, 1850; Balt. *Sun,* July 27, 1850; *Charleston Courier,* July 27, 29, 1850; *Chicago Democrat,* Aug. 1, 1850; Cleve. *True Democrat,* Aug. 2, 1850; New Orleans *Picayune,* Aug. 1, 9, 1850; *N.Y. Express,* July 20, 1850; *N.Y. Herald,* July 22, 24, 25, 26, 1850; N.Y. *Post,* July 25, 1850; and Phila. *Pennsylvanian,* July 21, 1850.

31. *Cong. Globe,* 31: 1: App., 1420. The meeting on July 24 is mentioned in Balt. *Sun,* July 24, 1850; and *Boston Journal,* July 26, 1850. The analogy of the bill to a cat is in N.Y. *Post,* July 25, 1850.

32. S. P. Chase to B. Chase, July 24, 1850, roll 1, Chase Papers (the letter is mistakenly filed out of order among 1849 letters); *N.Y. Tribune,* July 26, 1850. The changing prospects of the bill, almost on a daily basis sometimes, caused no end of frustration for reporters trying to speculate on the outcome of the struggle. A good article on this by a correspondent appeared in Balt. *Republican and Argus,* July 25, 1850.

33. *Cong. Globe,* 31: 1: App., 1420–22, 1426.

34. Ibid., 1422–29; and D. Outlaw to E. Outlaw, July 25, 1850, Outlaw Papers. Greeley's view is in *N.Y. Tribune,* July 26, 1850. For Harvey's caustic commentary, see Phila. *North American,* July 26, 1850. He also attacked the amendment in his columns in *Boston Journal,* July 26, 1850; *N.Y. Courier and Enquirer,* July 27, 1850; and *St. Louis Daily New Era,* Aug. 2, 1850. Some other critiques of the commission amendment are in *Boston Atlas,* July 27, 1850; Cleve. *True Democrat,* July 30, 1850; and N.Y. *Post,* July 29, 1850. Positive comments on the Bradbury plan are in Balt. *Sun,* July 25, 1850; *N.Y. Herald,* July 26, 1850; *N.Y. Journal of Commerce,* July 26, 1850; New Orleans *Daily True Delta,* July 30, 1850; and Phila. *Inquirer,* July 26, 1850. Daniel Webster believed the amendment would enhance the bill's chances. Webster to D. Fletcher Webster, July 24, 1850, Wiltse, ed., *Microfilm Edition—Webster Papers,* roll 22.

35. Jerome Robertson to Rusk, July 5, 1850, Rusk Papers; *N.Y. Commercial Advertiser,* July 24, 1850; *N.Y. Journal of Commerce,* July 26, 1850; N.Y. *Sun,* July 26, 1850; *N.Y. Tribune,* July 25, 1850; Phila. *Pennsylvanian,* July 25, 1850; *Pittsburgh Gazette,* July 27, 1850; D.C. *National Era,* Aug. 1, 1850; and D.C. *Union,* July 24, 1850. The papers publishing Robertson's letter did not give the name of the author.

36. *Newark Advertiser,* July 30, 1850; Cleve. *True Democrat,* July 30, 1850; *Hartford Courant,* July 29, 1850; *Pittsburgh Chronicle,* Aug. 1, 1850; *N.Y. Tribune,* July 25, 1850; and *Providence Journal,* July 26, 29, Aug. 1, 1850; *Middlebury* (Vt.) *Register,* July 30, 1850; *Toledo Blade,* July 30, 1850; Chillicothe *Scioto Gazette,* July 27, 1850; and *Portsmouth Journal of Literature and Politics,* Aug. 3, 1850. Other papers with similar views included *Cincinnati Gazette,* July 26, Aug. 1, 1850; and N.Y. *Times and Messenger,* July 28, 1850. The *Middlebury Register*'s mention of Don Quixote and Hudibras refers to the crazed knight of Miguel de Cervantes's early-seventeenth-century novel and to a similar Puritan character who, in Samuel Butler's late-seventeenth-century anti-Puritan poem, sets out to suppress popular amusements.

37. S. P. Chase to B. Chase, July 26, 1850, roll 1, Chase Papers; J. P. Hale to L. Hale, July 26, 1850, Hale Papers; D. Outlaw to E. Outlaw, July 25, 27, 1850, Outlaw Papers; Seward to F. A. Seward, July 25, 1850, F. W. Seward, *Seward at Washington,* 149; Cleve. *True Democrat,* July 31, 1850; Phila. *Bulletin,* July 27, 1850; Phila. *North American,* July 27, 1850; and *Pittsburgh Gazette,* July 30, 1850.

38. *Louisville Courier,* July 31, 1850.

39. *Cong. Globe*, 31: 1: 1456–57, App., 1154–58, 1429–36; R. S. Baldwin to E. Baldwin, July 26, 1850, Baldwin Family Papers; S. P. Chase to B. Chase, July 26, 1850, roll 1, Chase Papers; Seward to F. A. Seward, July 25, 1850, F. W. Seward, *Seward at Washington*, 149; *Norfolk American Beacon*, July 28, 1850; and Parrish, *Atchison*, 103.

40. 31: 1: *Sen. Jour.* (Ser. 548): 475–76.

41. Ibid., 479; and *Cong. Globe*, 31: 1: App., 1436–40.

42. Ibid., 1440–42; and Seward to Weed, July 21, 27, Aug. 3, 1850, Weed Papers.

43. *Cong. Globe*, 31: 1: App., 1442–44.

44. Ibid., 1444; and N.Y. *Post*, July 29, 1850.

45. *Cong. Globe*, 31: 1: App., 1444–47. The copy Seward read from was probably one of those brought to St. Louis in early July by F. X. Aubry.

46. 31: 1: *Sen. Jour.* (Ser. 548): 481; Seward to Weed, July 27 ("Clay frowned . . .") and Aug. 3 (Dayton's "cowardice"), 1850, Weed Papers; and Weed to Seward, July 31, 1850, roll 38, Seward Papers. Other accounts of the fight over Seward's amendment are in J. P. Hale to L. Hale, July 28, 1850, Hale Papers; Seward to F. A. Seward, July 26, 1850, F. W. Seward, *Seward at Washington*, 149; *Albany State Register*, July 30, 1850; *Charleston Courier*, Aug. 1, 1850; *Louisville Courier*, Aug. 2, 1850; *N.Y. Evangelist and Presbyterian*, Aug. 1, 1850; *N.Y. Express*, July 29, 1850; *N.Y. Journal of Commerce*, July 29, 1850; and N.Y. *Post*, July 29, 1850.

47. 31: 1: *Sen. Jour.* (Ser. 548): 480, 481.

48. For the Texans, their concerns at this time, and the few shreds of information about their meeting with the president and Webster, see S. P. Chase to B. Chase, July 29, 1850, roll 1, Chase Papers; Seward to Weed, July 27, 1850, Weed Papers; Blair to Van Buren, Aug. 1, 1850, roll 32, Van Buren Papers; *Boston Post*, July 31, 1850; *Boston Times*, July 31, 1850; Boston *Transcript*, Aug. 5, 1850; *Cleveland Plain Dealer*, Aug. 1, 1850; Marshall *Republican*, Aug. 24, 1850; New Orleans *Picayune*, Aug. 2, 1850; *N.Y. Express*, July 29, 1850; *N.Y. Herald*, July 29, 30, Aug. 4, 1850; *N.Y. Journal of Commerce*, July 31, 1850; N.Y. *Post*, July 27, 1850; Phila. *North American*, July 30, 1850; Phila. *Public Ledger*, July 29, 1850; *Richmond Enquirer*, Aug. 2, 1850; D.C. *Union*, July 27, 1850; and Poage, *Clay and Whig Party*, 255.

49. For opinions in regard to the bill's fate, see R. S. Baldwin to E. Baldwin, July 26, 1850, Baldwin Family Papers; S. P. Chase to B. Chase, July 27, 28, 1850, roll 1, Chase Papers; J. P. Hale to L. Hale, July 26, 1850, Hale Papers; H. Mann to M. Mann, July 29, 1850, Mann Papers; Seward to Weed, July 28, 1850, Weed Papers; Webster to George Ticknor, July 28, 1850, Curtis, *Webster* 2:463–64; Balt. *Republican and Argus*, July 27, 1850; *Charleston Mercury*, Aug. 1, 1850; *Chicago Democrat*, Aug. 1, 1850; *N.Y. Courier and Enquirer*, July 31, 1850; *N.Y. Express*, July 29, 1850; *N.Y. Tribune*, July 29, 1850; and Phila. *Pennsylvanian*, July 30, 1850. Planned amendments by Benton and others are mentioned in *Boston Post*, July 31, 1850. Northern Whig concerns over consistency are in Webster to Haven, July 26, 1850, Wiltse, ed., *Microfilm Edition—Webster Papers*, roll 22; and Balt. *Sun*, July 31, 1850. On the petition from New York City, see Foner, *Business and Slavery*, 29–32.

50. Webster to Ticknor, July 28, 1850, Curtis, *Webster* 2:463–64; D. Outlaw to E. Outlaw, July 25, 1850, Outlaw Papers; Balt. *Sun*, July 29, 1850; *Boston Post*, July 31, 1850; *Boston Times*, July 31, 1850; Concord *Patriot*, Aug. 8, 1850; N.Y. *Sun*, July 30, 1850; and Phila. *Public Ledger*, July 30, 31, 1850.

51. *Cong. Globe*, 31: 1: App., 1447–55; 31: 1: *Sen. Jour.* (Ser. 548): 485; Balt. *Sun*, July 30, 1850; *Charleston Courier*, Aug. 2, 1850; *N.Y. Herald*, July 31, 1850; *N.Y. Tribune*, Aug. 1, 1850; and Phila. *North American*, Aug. 1, 1850.

52. *Cong. Globe*, 31: 1: App., 1455; 31: 1: *Sen. Jour.* (Ser. 548): 486; and *N.Y. Tribune*, Aug. 1, 1850.

53. *Cong. Globe*, 31: 1: App., 1456; 31: 1: *Sen. Jour.* (Ser. 548): 487; *Baltimore Clipper*, July 30, 1850; Balt. *Sun*, July 30, 1850; *Chicago Western Citizen*, Aug. 13, 1850; *N.Y. Courier and Enquirer*, July 31, 1850; N.Y. *Post*, July 30, 1850; *N.Y. Tribune*, Aug. 1, 1850; *Norfolk American Beacon*, July 31, Aug. 1, 1850; Phila. *Bulletin*, July 30, 1850; Phila. *North American*, Aug. 1, 1850; *Richmond Enquirer*, Aug. 2, 1850; Parrish, *Atchison*, 103; and Poage, *Clay and Whig Party*, 255.

54. *Cong. Globe*, 31: 1: App., 1456; 31: 1: *Sen. Jour.* (Ser. 548): 487; *N.Y. Courier and Enquirer*, July 31, 1850; *N.Y. Herald*, July 29, 30, 1850; *N.Y. Journal of Commerce*, July 31, 1850; Phila. *North American*, Aug. 1, 1850; and Phila. *Public Ledger*, July 31, 1850.

55. *Cong. Globe*, 31: 1: App., 1456; 31: 1: *Sen. Jour.* (Ser. 548): 488; *N.Y. Herald*, July 31, 1850; and *N.Y. Tribune*, Aug. 1, 1850.

56. *Cong. Globe*, 31: 1: App., 1456–57; and 31: 1: *Sen. Jour.* (Ser. 548): 488; Balt. *Sun*, July 30, 1850; and *N.Y. Tribune*, Aug. 1, 1850.

57. H. Mann to M. Mann, July 30, 1850, Mann Papers; *Boston Journal*, Aug. 1, 1850; *N.Y. Courier and Enquirer*, Aug. 1, 1850; Phila. *North American*, Aug. 1, 1850; Johannsen, *Douglas*, 291–92; Poage, *Clay and Whig Party*, 255; and Rayback, *Fillmore*, 248–49.

58. Winthrop to Everett, Aug. 1, 1850, Allis, Jr., ed., *Microfilm Edition—Everett Papers*, roll 13; Laura D. Winthrop to R. C. Winthrop, Jr., July 31, 1850, Gutheim, ed., *Microfilm Edition—Winthrop Papers*, roll 26; Winthrop to Clifford, July 29, 1850, ibid., roll 39; and *N.Y. Herald*, Aug. 1, 1850.

59. *Cong. Globe*, 31: 1: App., 1458–63; *Baltimore Sun*, July 31, 1850; *N.Y. Journal of Commerce*, Aug. 1, 1850; *N.Y. Post*, July 31, 1850; Phila. *Bulletin*, July 31, 1850; Phila. *North American*, Aug. 1, 1850; Phila. *Inquirer*, Aug. 1, 1850; *Pittsburgh Gazette*, Aug. 3, 1850; Johannsen, *Douglas*, 291–92; and George D. Harmon, "Douglas and the Compromise of 1850," *Journal of the Illinois State Historical Society* 21 (Jan. 1929): 489–90.

60. *Cong. Globe*, 31: 1: 1481; 31: 1: *Sen. Jour.* (Ser. 548): 491; Blair to Van Buren, Aug. 1, 1850, roll 32, Van Buren Papers; Winthrop to Morey, July 30, 1850, Gutheim, ed., *Microfilm Edition—Winthrop Papers*, roll 26; Balt. *Republican and Argus*, July 31, 1850; *Boston Journal*, Aug. 1, 1850; *Charleston Courier*, Aug. 3, 1850; *N.Y. Courier and Enquirer*, Aug. 1, 1850; *N.Y. Express*, Aug. 1, 1850; *N.Y. Herald*, Aug. 1, 1850; *N.Y. Post*, July 31, 1850; Phila. *North American*, Aug. 1, 2, 1850; *Pittsburgh Gazette*, Aug. 3, 1850; Hamilton, *Prologue to Conflict*, 108–9; Harmon, "Douglas," 489–90; Johannsen, *Douglas*, 291–92; and Glyndon G. Van Deusen, *The Life of Henry Clay* (Boston: Little, Brown and Co., 1937), 411.

61. *Cong. Globe*, 31: 1: 1481; 31: 1: *Sen. Jour.* (Ser. 548): 492; Blair to Van Buren, Aug. 1, 1850, roll 32, Van Buren Papers; Balt. *Sun*, July 31, 1850; *Boston Journal*, Aug. 1, 1850; *Charleston Courier*, Aug. 3, 1850; *N.Y. Express*, July 30, 1850; *N.Y. Herald*, Aug. 1, 1850; *N.Y. Journal of Commerce*, Aug. 1, 1850; *N.Y. Post*, July 31, 1850; Phila. *Pennsylvanian*, Aug. 1, 1850; Phila. *Public Ledger*, Aug. 1, 1850; Hamilton, *Prologue to Conflict*, 108–9; Harmon, "Douglas," 489–90; Johannsen, *Douglas*, 291–92; Parrish, *Atchison*, 103; and Poage, *Clay and Whig Party*, 255.

62. *Cong. Globe*, 31: 1: App., 1463–70; R. S. Baldwin to E. Baldwin, July 30, 1850, Baldwin Family Papers; D. Outlaw to E. Outlaw, July 30, 1850, Outlaw Papers; *Baltimore Patriot*, July 31, 1850; Balt. *Sun*, July 31, 1850; *Boston Journal*, Aug. 1, 1850; *Charleston Courier*, Aug. 3, 1850; *N.Y. Commercial Advertiser*, July 31, 1850; *N.Y. Courier and Enquirer*, Aug. 1, 1850; *N.Y. Herald*, Aug. 1, 1850; *Norfolk American Beacon*, Aug. 2, 1850; Phila. *Bulletin*, July 31, 1850; Phila. *North American*, Aug. 1, 2, 1850; Phila. *Pennsylvanian*, Aug. 1, 3, 1850; Fehrenbacher, *Dred Scott Case*, 174; Johannsen, *Douglas*, 292; Poage, *Clay and Whig Party*, 255; and Frank H. Hodder, "The Authorship of the Compromise of 1850," *Mississippi Valley Historical Review* 22 (Mar. 1936): 532–33.

63. The Benton-Hale consultation is related in Phila. *Pennsylvanian*, Aug. 3, 1850. Clingman's talks with Clay, Hunter, and Soulé were related by Clingman later in a letter published in *N.Y. Herald*, Aug. 17, 1876, and reprinted in *Selections from Clingman Speeches*, 273. See also Remini, *Clay*, 753.

64. A. Felch to L. Felch, Aug. 1, 1850, Felch Papers; *Cong. Globe*, 31: 1: App., 1470–73; 31: 1: *Sen. Jour.* (Ser. 548): 495; *N.Y. Commercial Advertiser*, Aug. 1, 1850; and Smith, *Presidencies of Taylor and Fillmore*, 175–76.

65. Blair to Van Buren, Aug. 1, 1850, roll 32, Van Buren Papers; James A. Pearce to ——, Aug. 5, 1850, Pearce Papers, Maryland Historical Society, Baltimore; *Cong. Globe*, 31: 1: App., 1473–74; *Alexandria Gazette*, Aug. 2, 1850; Balt. *Sun*, Aug. 1, 2, 1850; *Boston Journal*, Aug. 3, 1850; *Boston Times*, Aug. 5, 1850; *Charleston Courier*, Aug. 8, 1850; Concord *Patriot*, Aug. 8, 1850; New Orleans *Picayune*, Aug.

9, 1850; *N.Y. Courier and Enquirer,* Aug. 2, 1850; *N.Y. Herald,* Aug. 2, 1850; *N.Y. Journal of Commerce,* Aug. 2, 1850; Phila. *North American,* Aug. 3, 1850; Phila. *Public Ledger,* Aug. 2, 1850; *Pittsburgh Gazette,* Aug. 5, 1850; Hamilton, *Prologue to Conflict,* 110–11; Poage, *Clay and Whig Party,* 256; Potter, *Impending Crisis,* 107–8; Smith, *Presidencies of Taylor and Fillmore,* 177; and Steiner, "Pearce," 349–50.

66. Pearce to ———, Aug. 5, 1850, Pearce Papers; *N.Y. Commercial Advertiser,* Aug. 1, 1850; *N.Y. Express,* Aug. 2, 1850; *N.Y. Herald,* Aug. 2, 1850; N.Y. *Post,* Aug. 1, 1850; N.Y. *Sun,* Aug. 6, 1850; Springfield *Illinois Daily Journal,* Aug. 3, 1850; Benson L. Grayson, *The Unknown President: The Administration of President Millard Fillmore* (Washington, D.C.: Univ. Press of America, 1981), 45; Hamilton, *Prologue to Conflict,* 113; Johannsen, *Douglas,* 293; Poage, *Clay and Whig Party,* 256; Rayback, *Fillmore,* 249; Smith, *Presidencies of Taylor and Fillmore,* 177; Steiner, "Pearce," 349–50; and Van Deusen, *Clay,* 411.

67. Blair to Van Buren, Aug. 1, 1850, roll 32, Van Buren Papers; *Cong. Globe,* 31: 1: App., 1474–76; *Alexandria Gazette,* Aug. 2, 1850; Balt. *Sun,* Aug. 2, 1850; *Boston Times,* Aug. 5, 1850; Hamilton, *Prologue to Conflict,* 110–11; Nevins, *Ordeal of the Union* 1:340; Parrish, *Atchison,* 103–4; Poage, *Clay and Whig Party,* 256; Rayback, *Fillmore,* 250; and Smith, *Presidencies of Taylor and Fillmore,* 177–78.

68. *Cong. Globe,* 31: 1: App., 1476–79; and Smith, *Magnificent Missourian,* 277.

69. *Cong. Globe,* 31: 1: App., 1479–81; 31: 1: *Sen. Jour.* (Ser. 548): 501–9; *Louisville Journal,* Nov. 18, 1851; New Orleans *Picayune,* Aug. 9, 1850; *N.Y. Express,* Aug. 5, 1850; *N.Y. Herald,* Aug. 2, 1850; Phila. *North American,* Aug. 3, 1850; Phila. *Pennsylvanian,* Aug. 3, 1850; Hamilton, *Prologue to Conflict,* 109–13; Johannsen, *Douglas,* 293; Parrish, *Atchison,* 104; Poage, *Clay and Whig Party,* 256–57; and Smith, *Presidencies of Taylor and Fillmore,* 178.

70. *Cong. Globe,* 31: 1: App., 1481–82; 31: 1: *Sen. Jour.* (Ser. 548): 509–11; Centreville *True Democrat,* Aug. 7, 1850; *N.Y. Herald,* Aug. 2, 1850; Hamilton, *Prologue to Conflict,* 111; Johannsen, *Douglas,* 293; and Smith, *Presidencies of Taylor and Fillmore,* 178–79.

71. *Cong. Globe,* 31: 1: App., 1482–85; 31: 1: *Sen. Jour.* (Ser. 548): 512–15; *N.Y. Herald,* Aug. 2, 1850; Hamilton, *Prologue to Conflict,* 111; Johannsen, *Douglas,* 293; Parrish, *Atchison,* 104–5; and Smith, *Presidencies of Taylor and Fillmore,* 179.

72. The two best accounts of the Senate scene as the Omnibus died are in *N.Y. Express,* Aug. 2, 1850, and *N.Y. Tribune,* Aug. 3, 1850. See also Concord *Statesman,* Aug. 9, 1850; and Phila. *Bulletin,* Aug. 2, 1850. Benton's comment is quoted in Smith, *Blair,* 205; and Smith, *Presidencies of Taylor and Fillmore,* 179. The *Express* account has been quoted in Nevins, *Ordeal of the Union* 1:340; Poage, *Clay and Whig Party,* 257–58; Potter, *Impending Crisis,* 108; and Sewell, *Hale,* 136.

73. N.Y. *Post,* Aug. 2, 1850.

Chapter 8
Carrot and Stick: The Pearce Bill and Executive Firmness

1. Clay's early departure is mentioned in *N.Y. Express,* Aug. 2, 1850. For the Matteson-Fillmore meeting the next morning, see Matteson to Weed, Aug. 1, 1850, Weed Papers; and Hamilton, *Prologue to Conflict,* 116.

2. *Pittsburgh Daily Dispatch,* Aug. 3, 1850; Matteson to Weed, Aug. 1, 1850, Weed Papers; and Smith, *Blair,* 205–6, quoting Lizzie Lee's letter.

3. *Richmond Examiner,* Aug. 2, 1850. For some praises of the fall of the Omnibus, see Augusta *Tri-Weekly Republic,* Aug. 3, 1850; Boston *Emancipator and Republican,* Aug. 8, 1850; *Charleston Mercury,* Aug. 2, 1850; Cleve. *True Democrat,* Aug. 3, 1850; Columbia *Tri-Weekly South Carolinian,* Aug. 3, 1850; Jackson *Mississippian,* Aug. 9, 1850; N.Y. *Post,* Aug. 1, 2, 1850; Norfolk *Daily Southern Argus,* Aug. 1, 1850; and D.C. *Southern Press,* Aug. 1, 1850. For the Northern radical view, see *Boston Mail,* Aug. 3, 1850; *Cincinnati Gazette,* Aug. 7, 1850; *Cleveland Plain Dealer,* Aug. 3, 1850; Columbus *Daily Ohio State Journal,* Aug. 2, 3, 1850; Concord *Independent Democrat,* Aug. 1, 8, 1850; *Detroit Free Press,* Aug. 5, 1850; Hartford *Republican,* Aug. 1, 1850; Milwaukee *Daily Wisconsin,* Aug. 5, 1850; *N.Y. Tribune,*

Aug. 2, 3, 5, 1850; *Newark Daily Mercury,* Aug. 3, 1850; Phila. *North American,* Aug. 3, 1850; *Pittsburgh Chronicle,* Aug. 3, 1850; *Providence Journal,* Aug. 1, 3, 5, 6, 1850; *Rochester Daily Advertiser,* Aug. 2, 5, 1850; and *Syracuse Standard,* Aug. 3, 1850.

On the Southern extremists, see Blair to Van Buren, Aug. 3, 1850, roll 32, Van Buren Papers; *Albany State Register,* Aug. 5, 8, 10, 1850; *Boston Times,* Aug. 7, 1850; Cleve. *True Democrat,* Aug. 9, 1850; *Louisville Journal,* Aug. 7, 1850; Macon *Telegraph,* Aug. 6, 1850; *Memphis Appeal,* Aug. 3, 1850; Nashville *Daily Centre-State American,* Aug. 6, 1850; N.Y. *Times and Messenger,* Aug. 4, 1850; Phila. *Bulletin,* Aug. 2, 1850; Phila. *Pennsylvanian,* Aug. 3, 1850; *Richmond Enquirer,* Aug. 9, 1850; *Savannah Georgian,* Aug. 2, 3, 1850; Trenton *True American,* Aug. 5, 1850; and D.C. *Southern Press,* Aug. 6, 1850.

4. W. R. King to Buchanan, Aug. 4, 1850, roll 16, Buchanan Papers; J. A. McClernand, July 31, and T. L. Harris, Aug. 5, 1850, to Lanphier and Walker, Lanphier Papers; Webster to Peter Harvey, Aug. 2, 1850, Wiltse, ed., *Microfilm Edition—Webster Papers,* roll 22; Kennedy to Winthrop, Aug. 2, 1850, Gutheim, ed., *Microfilm Edition—Winthrop Papers,* roll 26; Stephens to L. Stephens, Aug. 1, 1850, Stephens Papers, Manhattanville College; D. Outlaw to E. Outlaw, Aug. 1, 1850, Outlaw Papers; Phila. *Bulletin,* Aug. 2, 1850; Balt. *Sun,* Aug. 2, 1850; *Boston Times,* Aug. 7, 1850; N.Y. *Post,* Aug. 3, 1850; *N.Y. Tribune,* Aug. 3, 1850; New Orleans *Courier,* Aug. 2, 1850; New Orleans *Delta,* Aug. 3, 1850; New Orleans *Picayune,* Aug. 3, 1850; New Orleans *True Delta,* Aug. 4, 1850; Phila. *Bulletin,* Aug. 2, 1850; *Richmond Republican,* Aug. 5, 1850; St. Louis *Daily Reveille,* Aug. 4, 1850; Springfield, Ill., *Register,* Aug. 6, 1850; Springfield, Mass., *Republican,* Aug. 2, 1850; Trenton *True American,* Aug. 3, 1850; and Washington, N.C., *North State Whig,* Aug. 7, 1850; *Buffalo Commercial Advertiser,* Aug. 5, 6, 1850; Columbus, Ohio, *State Journal,* Aug. 2, 1850; Harrisburg *Pennsylvania Telegraph,* Aug. 7, 1850; Madison *Democrat,* Aug. 10, 1850; New Orleans *Picayune,* Aug. 7, 1850; N.Y. *Commercial Advertiser,* Aug. 1, 2, 1850; *Norfolk American Beacon,* Aug. 6, 1850; *Portland Daily Advertiser,* Aug. 3, 1850; *Providence Post,* Aug. 5, 1850; and D.C. *Union,* Aug. 1, 1850; Jackson, *Southron,* Aug. 16, 1850.

5. *Boston Times,* Aug. 7, 1850; Boston *Yankee Blade,* Aug. 17, 1850; *Buffalo Commercial Advertiser,* Aug. 5, 1850; Columbus *State Journal,* Aug. 3, 1850; *Detroit Advertiser,* Aug. 8, 1850; *Hartford Courant,* Aug. 6, 8, 1850; N.Y. *Express,* Aug. 2, 6, 1850; *N.Y. Journal of Commerce,* Aug. 3, 1850; *New Orleans Bee,* Aug. 5, 1850; *N.Y. Herald,* Aug. 4, 6, 1850; Phila. *Bulletin,* Aug. 2, 1850; and D.C. *Union,* Aug. 1, 4, 1850; Madison (Ind.) *Daily Courier,* Aug. 9, 1850; New Orleans *Crescent,* Aug. 3, 1850; New Orleans *True Delta,* Aug. 6, 1850; and Wilmington, N.C., *Commercial,* Aug. 9, 1850. Items in the Washington press showing the anger and determination of the Texans only added to the fears. D.C. *Union,* Aug. 2, 1850; D.C. *Southern Press,* Aug. 2, 1850. For a detailed account of the supposed plot, see Mark J. Stegmaier, "Treachery or Hoax? The Rumored Southern Conspiracy to Confederate With Mexico," *Civil War History* 35 (Mar. 1989): 28–38.

6. Stephens to L. Stephens, July 31, Aug. 2, 1850, Stephens Papers, Manhattanville College; Winthrop to Everett, Aug. 1, 1850, Allis, Jr., ed., *Microfilm Edition—Everett Papers,* roll 13.

7. *Cong. Globe,* 31: 1: 1503–4, App., 1485–96. The Southern extremist caucus is mentioned in Phila. *Bulletin,* Aug.2, 1850. On Clay and Pearce, see Winthrop to Kennedy, Aug. 4, 1850, Kennedy Papers; Pearce to ——, Aug. 5, 1850, Pearce Papers; and James H. Hammond to N. B. Tucker, Aug. 11, 1850, Tucker-Coleman Papers, College of William and Mary, Williamsburg, Virginia. For other comment on the Senate proceedings of August 1, see Winthrop to Everett, Aug. 1, 1850, Allis, Jr., ed., *Microfilm Edition—Everett Papers,* roll 13; Stephens to L. Stephens, Aug. 2, 1850, Stephens Papers, Manhattanville College; Blair to Van Buren, Aug. 3, 1850, roll 32, Van Buren Papers; Seward to F. A. Seward, Aug. 1, 2, F. W. Seward, *Seward at Washington,* 151; *Baltimore Clipper,* Aug. 2, 1850; *Baltimore Patriot,* Aug. 3, 1850; Chicago *Western Citizen,* Aug. 13, 1850; *Louisville Journal,* Aug. 9, 1850; N.Y. *Express,* Aug. 6, 1850; N.Y. *Sun,* Aug. 6, 1850; N.Y. *Tribune,* Aug. 3, 1850 (an excellent report by Horace Greeley); and Phila. *Inquirer,* Aug. 3, 1850.

8. *Cong. Globe,* 31: 1: 1502; Milwaukee *Free Democrat,* Aug. 21, 1850, quoting D.C. *Globe;* and Chicago *Western Citizen,* Aug. 13, 1850.

9. Hamilton's dispatch to Bell, Aug. 2, 1850, is in Governors' Letters. Some reports and comments

on Colonel Howard's arrival and statements are in Balt. *Republican and Argus,* Aug. 5, 1850; Concord *Patriot,* Aug. 8, 1850; *N.Y. Herald,* Aug. 4, 5, 6, 1850; *N.Y. Post,* Aug. 3, 5, 16, 1850; *N.Y. Tribune,* Aug. 5, 7, 1850; and Phila. *Pennsylvanian,* Aug. 6, 1850. Articles on the difficulties Texas would face in getting to New Mexico are in *Albany State Register,* Aug. 6, 1850; *Buffalo Express,* Aug. 6, 1850; *N.Y. Herald,* Aug. 5, 1850; *N.Y. Post,* Aug. 6, 1850; and *Pittsburgh Gazette,* Aug. 8, 1850.

10. *Albany State Register,* Aug. 10, 1850. The Washington correspondent of this paper is the only reporter who recorded this interesting exchange. Clay used the term "Capuchin" to mean someone attempting to impoverish the military. The Capuchins are a Roman Catholic religious order emphasizing the vow of poverty.

11. Pearce to ——, Aug. 5, 1850, Pearce Papers; *Baltimore Clipper,* Aug. 3, 5, 1850; Concord *Patriot,* Aug. 8, 1850; Phila. *Public Ledger,* Aug. 5, 1850; Balt. *Sun,* Aug. 3, 6, 13, 1850; *Charleston Courier,* Aug. 8, 1850; *N.Y. Tribune,* Aug. 6, 1850, quoting Phila. *North American;* New Orleans *Picayune,* Aug. 13, 1850; *St. Louis Intell.,* Aug. 12, 1850; and Winthrop to Clifford, Aug. 11, 1850, quoted in Winthrop, Jr., *Memoir of Winthrop,* 135–36.

12. Douglas to Lanphier and Walker, Aug. 3, 1850, Johannsen, ed., *The Letters of Stephen A. Douglas* (Urbana: Univ. of Illinois Press, 1961), 191–93; Hamilton, *Taylor,* 403; Smith, *Presidencies of Taylor and Fillmore,* 181; Poage, *Clay and Whig Party,* 258; and Hodder, "Authorship of the Compromise," 535–36. Some information about the early form of Douglas's and Pearce's bill is in Pearce's August 7 speech in *Cong. Globe,* 31: 1: 1541; Balt. *Sun,* Aug. 5, 1850; *Boston Times,* Aug. 7, 1850; *N.Y. Tribune,* Aug. 6, 1850; Phila. *North American,* Aug. 7, 1850; Phila. *Inquirer,* Aug. 5, 1850; and Phila. *Public Ledger,* Aug. 6, 1850.

13. Balt. *Sun,* Aug. 6, 1850; *Boston Journal,* Aug. 9, 1850; *Charleston Courier,* Aug. 8, 1850; *N.Y. Express,* Aug. 8, 1850; *N.Y. Tribune,* Aug. 6, 1850; Phila. *North American,* Aug. 7, 10, 1850; Phila. *Pennsylvanian,* Aug. 7, 1850; Leonard, "Southwestern Boundaries," 51; and Leonard, "Western Boundary-Making," 357–58.

14. Rumors emphasizing the role of others than Pearce are in *N.Y. Herald,* Aug. 8, 1850; and Phila. *Bulletin,* Aug. 6, 1850. Statements that the president and his cabinet were not heavily involved in devising the Pearce bill, except to approve it, are in *N.Y. Sun,* Aug. 6, 1850; *N.Y. Tribune,* Aug. 9, 1850; and Phila. *North American,* Aug. 12, 1850. On Pearce's activities, see also Webster to Haven, Aug. 10, 1850, Wiltse, ed., *Microfilm Edition—Webster Papers,* roll 22; and Winthrop to "Dear Sir," Aug. 6, 1850, Gutheim, ed., *Microfilm Edition—Winthrop Papers,* roll 26. A correspondent close to the administration reported that the president disagreed somewhat with the Pearce bill but did not specify what the disagreement was. *Buffalo Commercial Advertiser,* Aug. 17, 1850.

15. For Bell's protest and Howard's letter, see Bell to Taylor, June 15, 1850, *App. to Tex. Sen. Jours., 3d Legis., 2d Sess.,* 50; and Howard to Fillmore, Aug. 1, 1850, Smith, ed., *Microfilm Edition—Fillmore Papers,* roll 19.

16. Webster to Curtis, July 28, 1850, quoted in Curtis, *Webster* 2:464; and Webster to Haven, Aug. 10, 1850, Wiltse, ed., *Microfilm Edition—Webster Papers,* roll 22.

17. Webster to Fillmore, July 30, 1850, Wiltse, ed., *Microfilm Edition—Webster Papers,* roll 22; and Rusk and Houston to Webster, Aug. 1, 1850, "Miscellaneous Letters of the Department of State," M-179, roll 122, RG 59.

18. Webster to Haven, Aug. 10, and to Fillmore, Aug. 1, 3, 1850, Wiltse, ed., *Microfilm Edition—Webster Papers,* roll 22; Balt. *Sun,* Aug. 3, 1850; *N.Y. Express,* Aug. 2, 3, 5, 1850; *N.Y. Tribune,* Aug. 6, 1850, quoting Phila. *North American;* Phila. *Public Ledger,* Aug. 6, 1850; and Dalzell, *Webster,* 208.

19. Webster to Haven, Aug. 10, and to Fillmore, Aug. 6, 1850, Wiltse, ed., *Microfilm Edition—Webster Papers,* roll 22; *N.Y. Tribune,* Aug. 6, 1850; and Phila. *Pennsylvanian,* Aug. 8, 1850.

20. *Cong. Globe,* 31: 1: 1524–25, 1531–32; Balt. *Republican and Argus,* Aug. 7, 1850; and *N.Y. Tribune,* Aug. 8, 1850.

21. Richardson, comp., *Messages and Papers* 5:67–73.

22. Webster to Bell, Aug. 5, 1850, 31: 1: *Sen. Ex. Docs.* 67 (Ser. 562): 7–12.

23. Scott to Munroe and to Brooke, Aug. 6, 1850, M-565, roll 17, pp. 206–8, RG 94; N.Y. *Post*, Aug. 7, 1850.

24. Among Northerners often critical of Fillmore were several who praised his message. H. Mann to M. Mann, Aug. 7, 1850, Mann Papers; and Seth Hawley to Seward, Aug. 8, 1850, roll 38, Seward Papers. For Chase's view, see Chase to E. S. Hamlin, Aug. 14, 1850, roll 8, Chase Papers. For Clay's letter, see Clay to Fillmore, Aug. 10, 1850, Smith, ed., *Microfilm Edition—Fillmore Papers*, roll 19. Numerous other letters in praise of the message are on the same roll. As for editorials praising the message, there is not enough space to list them here. Free-soil papers that praised the message but dissented from any monetary remuneration of Texas included *Albany Atlas*, Aug. 9, 1850; Chicago *Western Citizen*, Aug. 20, 1850; and *Syracuse Standard*, Aug. 10, 1850. Northern Democratic papers critical of the message included *Boston Times*, Aug. 13, 1850; Columbus *Daily Ohio Statesman*, Aug. 9, 12, 1850; and Trenton *True American*, Aug. 7, 9, 1850. Southern journals that favored compromise but criticized the message included *Nashville Union*, Aug. 12, 1850; New Orleans *Courier*, Aug. 12, 15, 1850; *Richmond Enquirer*, Aug. 9, 13, 16, 1850; and *Wilmington* (N.C.) *Journal*, Aug. 16, 1850. The Southern radical press uniformly condemned the message Augusta *Republic*, Aug. 10, 13, 1850; *Charleston Mercury*, Aug. 10, 12, 1850; Jacksonville *News*, Aug. 17, 1850; *Memphis Appeal*, Aug. 15, 1850; Nashville *American*, Aug. 11, 13, 14, 16, 1850; *Natchez Free Trader*, Aug. 21, 1850; *Richmond Examiner*, Aug. 9, 1850; and D.C. *Southern Press*, Aug. 8, 12, 1850.

25. On Greeley's view and critiques of it, see Greeley to Schuyler Colfax, Aug. 10, 1850, Greeley Papers, N.Y. Public Library; Alexander Johnson to Seward, Aug. 20, 1850, roll 38, Seward Papers; *N.Y. Tribune*, Aug. 8, 1850; and Utica *Herald*, Aug. 15, 1850. The figure of 33,333 extra square miles conceded to Texas is given in Smith, *Presidencies of Taylor and Fillmore*, 181; and Poage, *Clay and Whig Party*, 258.

26. R. S. Baldwin to E. Baldwin, Aug. 10, 1850, Baldwin Family Papers; Winthrop to Kennedy, Aug. 10, 1850, Kennedy Papers; Cass to McClelland, Aug. 10, 1850, McClelland Papers; numerous Winthrop letters, Aug. 6–18, 1850, Gutheim, ed., *Microfilm Edition—Winthrop Papers*, rolls 26 and 39; *Albany State Register*, Aug. 13, 1850; *Baltimore Clipper*, Aug. 12, 1850; Balt. *Sun*, Aug. 9, 1850; *Buffalo Commercial Advertiser*, Aug. 15, 1850; *Louisville Courier*, Aug. 17, 1850; Macon *Telegraph*, Aug. 20, 1850; New Orleans *Delta*, Aug. 14, 1850; New Orleans *Picayune*, Aug. 18, 1850; *N.Y. Courier and Enquirer*, Aug. 7, 13, 1850; Phila. *North American*, Aug. 12, 1850; Phila. *Inquirer*, Aug. 10, 12, 1850; Grayson, *Unknown President*, 48; Holt, *Political Crisis of the 1850s*, 87; and Rayback, *Fillmore*, 251.

27. *Cong. Globe*, 31: 1: 1532–33, App., 1510–17. An excellent account by a Washington correspondent of the Southern tactics on the 6th is in *Boston Atlas*, Aug. 12, 1850.

28. *Cong. Globe*, 31: 1: 1540–42; and Steiner, "Pearce," 350.

29. *Cong. Globe*, 31: 1: 1542–45; D. Outlaw to E. Outlaw, Aug. 7, 1850, Outlaw Papers; *Boston Times*, Aug. 12, 1850; Cleve. *True Democrat*, Aug. 13, 1850; *N.Y. Evangelist and Presbyterian*, Aug. 15, 1850; N.Y. *Post*, Aug. 9, 1850; N.Y. *Sun*, Aug. 15, 1850; *N.Y. Tribune*, Aug. 12, 1850; Phila. *Bulletin*, Aug. 7, 1850; *Pittsburgh Gazette*, Aug. 10, 13, 1850; *Richmond Enquirer*, Aug. 9, 1850; Poage, *Clay and Whig Party*, 258; and Rayback, *Fillmore*, 252.

30. Joseph R. Underwood to Elizabeth Underwood, July 18, Aug. 12, 22, 1850, Underwood Papers, Western Kentucky University, Bowling Green; *Cong. Globe*, 31: 1: App., 1193–1204; New Orleans *Picayune*, Aug. 16, 1850; *N.Y. Tribune*, Aug. 12, 1850; and Phila. *North American*, Aug. 10, 1850; and William A. Keleher, *Turmoil in New Mexico, 1846–1868* (1952; reprint, Albuquerque: Univ. of New Mexico Press, 1982), 40–41.

31. *Cong. Globe*, 31: 1: App., 1562–64; and 31: 1: *Sen. Jour.* (Ser. 548): 536.

32. *Cong. Globe*, 31: 1: App., 1564–65.

33. Ibid., 1565–67; 31: 1: *Sen. Jour.* (Ser. 548): 537; Winthrop to Morey, Aug. 10, and to Clifford, Aug. 11, 1850, Gutheim, ed., *Microfilm Edition—Winthrop Papers*, rolls 26, 39; and *N.Y. Tribune*, Aug. 12, 1850.

34. *Cong. Globe*, 31: 1: App., 1567–69; Winthrop to Morey, Aug. 17, 1850, Gutheim, ed., *Microfilm*

Edition—Winthrop Papers, roll 26; and Cass to S. Beardsley, Aug. 8, 1850, Lewis Cass Papers, Clements Library, University of Michigan, Ann Arbor.

35. *Cong. Globe,* 31: 1: App., 1568–69; Winthrop to Morey, Aug. 9, 10, 17, 1850, Gutheim, ed., *Microfilm Edition—Winthrop Papers,* roll 26; and *N.Y. Tribune,* Aug. 12, 1850.

36. *Cong. Globe,* 31: 1: 1554, App., 1569–75.

37. Ibid., 1555, App., 1575–77.

38. Ibid., 1555, App., 1577–81; and *N.Y. Tribune,* Aug. 12, 1850.

39. *Cong. Globe,* 31: 1: 1555, App., 1581; and *N.Y. Express,* Aug. 12, 13, 1850.

40. R. S. Baldwin to E. Baldwin, Aug. 10, 1850, Baldwin Family Papers; Winthrop to Morey, Aug. 10, 1850, and to Clifford, Aug. 11, 1850, Gutheim, ed., *Microfilm Edition—Winthrop Papers,* rolls 26, 39; Truman Smith to Webster, Aug. 5, 1850, and Webster to Haven, Aug. 9, 10, 1850, Wiltse, ed., *Microfilm Edition—Webster Papers,* roll 22; and *Cong. Globe,* 31: 1: App., 1570.

41. Clemens letter, Aug. 20, 1850, in D.C. *Union,* Sept. 4, 1850; Robert Barnwell to Hammond, Aug. 14, 1850, roll 9, Hammond Papers; King to Buchanan, Aug. 26, 1850, roll 16, Buchanan Papers; Berrien letter, Aug. 17, 1850, in Macon *Telegraph,* Aug. 27, 1850; Atchison speech at Platte City, Missouri, Nov. 4, 1850, in Liberty, Mo., *Tribune,* Dec. 13, 1850; Benton speech, Aug. 9, 1850, in *Cong. Globe,* 31: 1: App., 1580–81; Atchison speech, Aug. 8, 1850, in ibid., 1562; and Parrish, *Atchison,* 105. Pratt (W-Md.) was absent due to his wife's illness. *Baltimore Clipper,* Aug. 13, 1850.

42. The vote is given in *Cong. Globe,* 31: 1: 1555. The Indian Territory amendment is mentioned by James Harvey in *N.Y. Courier and Enquirer,* Aug. 13, 1850; and Phila. *North American,* Aug. 10, 1850. For Bradbury's tactic, see *N.Y. Express,* Aug. 13, 1850. On Hamlin, see Hamlin to "My Very Dear Sir," Aug. 9, 1850, Miscellaneous—Hamlin Papers, New York Historical Society; Concord *Patriot,* Aug. 8, 1850; and H. Draper Hunt, *Hannibal Hamlin of Maine: Lincoln's First Vice-President* (Syracuse: Syracuse Univ. Press, 1969), 65.

43. *Richmond Examiner,* Aug. 13, 1850; Centreville *True Democrat,* Aug. 21, 1850. For some similar comments, see S. P. Chase to B. Chase, Aug. 9, 1850, roll 1, Chase Papers; Seward to F. A. Seward, Aug. 9, 1850, F. W. Seward, *Seward at Washington,* 153; and Boston *Emancipator and Republican,* Aug. 15, 1850.

Chapter 9
The U.S. Military Response to the Boundary Dispute

1. On Texan concern regarding the frontier troops, see Kaufman to Crawford, Jan. 25, 1850, M-221, roll 153, RG 107. For Secretary Crawford's views, see Crawford to Howard, Feb. 25, and to Kaufman, Mar. 1, and to James H. Quinn et al., July 2, 1850, M-6, roll 30, pp. 70–71, 76–77, 223–24 RG 107; Crawford's note in "Letters, Endorsements and Reports Sent to the Secretary of War, 1812–1889," 9:462, RG 156—Records of the Office of the Chief of Ordnance; and Crawford's report in 31: 1: *Sen. Ex. Docs.* 1 (Ser. 549): 90–91. The demand of the New Mexico convention is in Antonio José Otero et al. to Taylor, May 25, 1850, M-221, roll 154, RG 107. On the army increase bill of 1850, see *Cong. Globe,* 31: 1: 395, 421, 884, 983, 1010, 1012, 1024, 1045–54, 1059–61, 1081, 1139, 1179–81; and Richardson, comp., *Messages and Papers* 5:48.

2. *Pittsburgh Gazette,* June 24, 1850; Alfred Pleasanton to Weed, Sept. 22, 1876, printed in Thurlow Weed Barnes, *Memoir of Thurlow Weed* (Boston: Houghton, Mifflin and Co., 1884), 180–81. Pleasanton's orders to New Mexico are in Asst. Adj. Gen. Irwin McDowell to Pleasanton, July 1, 1850, M-857, roll 3, p. 339, RG 108.

3. *Brooklyn Eagle,* July 5, 1850; *Boston Journal,* July 5, 1850; *Cincinnati Gazette,* July 11, 1850; *N.Y. Courier and Enquirer,* July 3, 1850; Phila. *North American,* July 2, 1850; and *St. Louis Intell.,* July 11, 1850.

4. Freeman to Munroe, May 27, 1850, M-1102, roll 2, RG 393; Crawford to Bvt. Maj. Gen. David E. Twiggs, May 24, 1850, M-565, roll 17, p. 126, RG 94; *St. Louis Republican,* June 26, July 7, 1850; and

Barry, *Beginning of the West*, 960.

    5. Gen. Order 20, June 22, 1850, M-1094, roll 6, RG 94.

    6. Freeman to Bvt. Col. C. A. Waite (superintendent, Recruiting Service, New York), July 2, 1850, M-857, roll 3, p. 342, RG 108; Waite to 2d Lt. George H. Paige, July 8, 1850, M-1102, roll 2, RG 393; *Charleston News*, July 17, 1850, quoting *N.Y. Journal of Commerce*; and Clinton E. Brooks and Frank D. Reeve, eds., "James A. Bennett: A Dragoon in New Mexico, 1850–1856," *New Mexico Historical Review* 22 (Jan. 1947): 58–60.

    7. McDowell to 1st Lt. Henry B. Schroeder, June 28, and to Pleasanton, July 1, and Freeman to Bvt. Capt. Abraham Buford, July 2, to Bvt. Lt. Col. P. St. G. Cooke (cmdg. officer at Carlisle Barracks and superintendent of Dragoon Recruiting Service), July 2, and to Waite, July 9, 1850, M-857, roll 3, pp. 335, 339–41, 343–44, 348–49, RG 108; and Rodney Glisan, *Journal of Army Life* (San Francisco: A. L. Bancroft and Co., 1874), 11.

    8. Capt. N. C. Macrae to Schroeder, July 18, 1850, M-1102, roll 2, RG 393; Q. M. Gen. Thomas S. Jesup to Capt. E. Harding, July 10, 11, 23, and to Cooke, July 10, 1850, "Letters Sent by the Office of the Quartermaster General, Main Series, 1818–1870," M-745, roll 25, pp. 700–702, 714, RG 92—Records of the Office of the Quartermaster General; *Savannah News*, July 29, 1850; *Columbus* (Ga.) *Times*, Aug. 6, 1850; and Glisan, *Journal*, 11–13.

    9. Glisan, *Journal*, 14–15; and Freeman to Jesup, June 28, and to Clarke, July 2, 1850, M-857, roll 3, pp. 330, 342–43, RG 108.

    10. Schroeder to McLaws, Sept. 28, 1850, M-1102, roll 2, RG 393; 32: 1: *Sen. Ex. Docs.* 12 (Ser. 614): 18; Glisan, *Journal*, 17, 21–22; Brooks and Reeve, eds., "Bennett," 60–61; Barry, *Beginning of the West*, 955; Louis Pelzer, *Marches of the Dragoons in the Mississippi Valley: An Account of Marches and Activities of the First Regiment United States Dragoons in the Mississippi Valley Between the Years 1833 and 1850* (Iowa City: State Historical Society of Iowa, 1917), 170: and Charles E. Rosenberg, *The Cholera Years: The United States in 1832, 1849, and 1866* (Chicago: Univ. of Chicago Press, 1962), 2–3.

    11. On the efforts of the quartermaster's department to outfit the Santa Fe recruits, see letters in M-857, roll 3, pp. 330, 342–43, RG 108; and M-745, roll 25, pp. 691–92, 706–7, 717, and roll 26, pp. 61, 78, RG 92. A news report stated that on August 19, thirty-five tons of supplies costing $45,000 were shipped out of New York for Santa Fe and El Paso. Austin *State Gazette*, Sept. 21, 1850, quoting *N.Y. Courier and Enquirer*.

    12. On the ordnance arrangements, see letters in "Letters Received, 1812–1894," box 124, items B358, B362, B384, B385, B388; "Letters, Telegrams, and Endorsements Sent to Ordnance and Military Storekeepers, 1839–1889," 82:378–79, 386–87, 394–95, 398, 412, 443; "Miscellaneous Letters Sent, 1812–1889," 83:273, 278, 280, RG 156; and M-565, roll 17, p. 174, RG 94. On the arms requisition from Santa Fe, see St. Louis *Republican*, Aug. 18, 1850; and Barry, *Beginning of the West*, 960. A Texan in St. Louis who was familiar with the flow of arms through the arsenal, wrote a detailed letter about this to the Austin *American*. Reprinted in San Antonio *Western Texan*, Sept. 19, 1850; and Matagorda *Tribune*, Oct. 25, 1850.

    13. Bvt. Capt. Barnard Bee to Alexander, Oct. 23, 1850, M-1072, roll 1, 2:207–9, RG 393; Alexander to McLaws, Oct. 17, 1850, and Bvt. 1st Lt. Orren Chapman to McLaws, Oct. 12, 1850, M-1102, roll 2, RG 393; 32: 1: *Sen. Ex. Docs.* 1 (Ser. 611): 298; Brooks and Reeve, eds., "Bennett," 61–64; and Barry, *Beginning of the West*, 958–59, 961.

    14. For matter relating to the escort of Bartlett's expedition, see letters in M-6, roll 30, pp. 220–23, RG 107; and M-857, roll 3, pp. 335, 355, 358–64, 372–73, 379, RG 108. To figure the actual numbers of men in the escort, I used information found in Bvt. Lt. Col. Harvey Brown (cmdg. officer, Ft. Wood, N.Y.) to Jones, Aug. 5, 1850, M-567, roll 424, item B425, RG 94; Van Horne to McLaws, Nov. 14, and Dec. 1, 1850, M-1102, roll 2, RG 393; and John R. Bartlett, *Personal Narrative of Explorations and Incidents in Texas, New Mexico, California, Sonora, and Chihuahua . . .*, 2 vols. (New York: D. Appleton and Co., 1854), 1:6–7.

    15. Thomas to Twiggs, June 24, 1850, M-565, roll 17, p. 148, RG 94; 2d Lt. George C. Barber to

Jones, Sept. 16, and Brooke to Jones, Oct. 17, 1850, M-567, roll 424, items B581 and B639, RG94; letters from Jesup to quartermasters at Tampa Bay and New Orleans, M-745, roll 25, pp. 696–97, and roll 26, pp. 64–65, 102, RG 92; Van Horne to McLaws, Nov. 14, Dec. 2, 15, 1850, M-1102, roll 2, RG 393; Victoria *Advocate*, Aug. 30, Sept. 6, 1850; John Bull to John R. Bartlett, Feb. 10, 1853, 32: 2: *Sen. Ex. Docs.* 38 (Ser. 660): 2–4; Bartlett, *Personal Narrative* 1:6–9, 33, 47, 136, 149, 152; and Odie B. Faulk, *Too Far North . . . Too Far South* (Los Angeles: Westernlore Press, 1967), 44–50.

16. Crawford to President, July 10; Fillmore's appointment of Scott, July 24; and Conrad's oath as secretary of war, Aug. 16, 1850, are in "Letters Sent to the President by the Secretary of War, 1800–1863," M-127, roll 5, pp. 60–62, RG 107; and Fillmore to Crawford, July 20, 1850, M-221, roll 154, RG 107.

17. The "Memoranda" document is in Fillmore to Crawford, July 20, 1850, M-221, roll 154, RG 107. This roll is arranged alphabetically, but the letters and documents thereon are often filed without reference to order. For instance, the document here cited is filed with a letter on New Mexico by Col. John M. Washington and is filed under "W."

18. A contingent of recruits were sent to New Mexico in the spring. Macrae to Bvt. Lt. Col. C. S. Chandler, Apr. 5, 1850, M-1102, roll 2, RG 393; and Chandler to Jones, July 13, 1850, M-567, roll 426, item C516, RG 94.

19. Giddings to J. A. Giddings, July 22, 1850, roll 3, Giddings Papers; Barnwell to Hammond, July 25, 1850, roll 9, Hammond Papers; H. Mann to M. Mann, July 10, 12, 13, 1850, Mann Papers; Seward to Weed, Aug. 3, 1850, Weed Papers; and Thomas Ewing to Phil Ewing, July 10, 1850, Ewing Papers. Later, in speeches in 1854, Fillmore stated that army moves had had a salutary effect on Congress. Severance, ed., *Fillmore Papers* 1:432, 436. The "mongrels" quote is from Tallahassee *Floridian & Journal*, Aug. 31, 1850. For similar views, see ibid., Sept. 7, 1850; and Jacksonville *News*, Aug. 24, 1850. Florida Whigs had defended the removal of the 7th Infantry from Florida, pointing out that the 1200 remaining soldiers were quite adequate to protect the state from its Indians. Tallahassee *Florida Sentinel*, July 16, 1850. The comment on Conrad is in New Orleans *Courier*, Aug. 27, 28, 1850.

20. Jones to Clarke and to Bvt. Col. E. V. Sumner, Aug. 2, 1850, M-565, roll 17, pp. 208–9, RG 94. On the concern over sending these troops out to Santa Fe that late, see New Orleans *Commercial Bulletin*, Aug. 28, 1850; and Savannah *News*, Aug. 24, 1850, quoting the St. Louis *Republican*.

21. Jones to Clarke, Aug. 6, 17, and to Bvt. Col. Joseph Plympton, Aug. 12, 1850, M-565, roll 17, pp. 180, 186–87, 210, RG 94; Jesup to Capt. N. J. T. Dana (asst. quartermaster, St. Louis), Aug. 7, 1850, M-745, roll 26, p. 69, RG 92; Clarke to Jones, Aug. 11, 14, 22, 1850, M-567, roll 426, items C443, C460, C485, RG 94; Maj. William H. Bell (St. Louis Arsenal) to Bvt. Brig. Gen. George Talcott, Aug. 16, Sept. 7, 1850, "Letters Received, 1812–1894," box 124, items B399, B433, RG 156; 32: 1: *Sen. Ex. Docs.* 12 (Ser. 614): 16, 17; *N.Y. Express*, Aug. 21, 1850; *Washington* (Ark.) *Telegraph*, Sept. 4, 1850, quoting *St. Louis Intell.*; and Barry, *Beginning of the West*, 960.

22. Jones to Clarke, Aug. 14, and to Munroe, Dec. 14, 1850, M-565, roll 17, pp. 210, 272–73, RG 94; Clarke to Jones, Aug. 22, 1850, M-567, roll 426, item C485, RG 94; Alexander to McLaws, Oct. 17, and Bvt. 1st Lt. Orren Chapman to McLaws, Oct. 12, 1850, M-1102, roll 2, RG 393; and returns for 1st Dragoons and for Companies F and K, "Returns from Regular Army Cavalry Regiments," M-744, roll 16, RG 94.

23. Scott to Munroe, Aug. 6, 1850, M-565, roll 17, pp. 206–7, RG 94. The dispatch of August is quoted in Munroe to Jones, Aug. 31, 1850, M-567, roll 432, item M-538, RG 94.

24. Scott to Brooke, Aug. 6, 1850, M-565, roll 17, pp. 207–8, RG 94.

Chapter 10
Texan Rage, Summer 1850

1. Neighbors to Bell, June 4, 1850, *App. to Tex. Sen. Jours., 3d Legis., 2d Sess.*, 7–10. The earlier letter is Neighbors to Bell, Apr. 14, 1850, Governors' Letters. Neighbors was much more explicit in the

earlier letter in insisting on the absolute necessity of Texan military force as a prerequisite to the practicable extension of Texan civil jurisdiction to New Mexico. He suggested in that letter that Bell lead these troops. See also W. D. Miller to Rusk, June 10, 1850, Rusk Papers.

2. Austin *State Gazette*, June 8, 15, 1850; Clarksville *Standard*, July 13, 1850; Houston *Telegraph*, July 4, 1850; Miller to Rusk, June 15, 1850, Rusk Papers; and Neighbours, "Taylor-Neighbors Struggle," 456.

3. The quote is from Richard S. Hunt to Rusk, Sept. 17, 1850, Rusk Papers. See also *N.Y. Journal of Commerce*, Aug. 29, 1850, for a similar assessment by some in Washington who knew Bell.

4. Bell to Baird, June 12, 1850, *App. to Tex. Sen. Jours., 3rd Legis. 2d Sess.*, 81–83.

5. On the San Antonio meeting, see Austin *State Gazette*, July 6, 1850; and Nashville *American*, July 27, 1850. The Seguin meeting is covered in Austin *State Gazette*, July 6, 1850. The meeting at Marshall is covered in ibid., Aug. 3, 1850; Clarksville *Standard*, July 6, 1850; and Marshall *Republican*, July 6, 1850. The La Grange meetings are covered in La Grange *Texas Monument*, July 20, 1850; Austin *State Gazette*, July 13, 1850; Governors' Letters; and Neighbours, "Taylor-Neighbors Struggle," 456. The Matagorda meeting is covered in Austin *State Gazette*, Aug. 3, 1850; Matagorda *Tribune*, July 5, 1850; D.C. *Southern Press*, Sept. 4, 1850; and Governors' Letters. The Leon County meeting is covered in D.C. *Union*, Aug. 24, 1850; and Governors' Letters.

6. Smith's letter is reprinted in Marshall *Republican*, May 30, 1850. He also expressed his pro-compromise views in a letter to Sam Houston, July 20, Ashbel Smith Papers, Barker Texas History Center. It is unfortunately a faded letter-press copy and very difficult to read. For accounts of the San Jacinto meeting, see ibid; Houston *Telegraph*, July 18, 1850; Nashville *American*, July 27, 1850; and D.C. *Southern Press*, Sept. 10, 1850. On Dr. Smith himself, see Webb, ed., *Handbook of Texas* 2:620–21; and Elizabeth Silverthorne, *Ashbel Smith of Texas: Pioneer, Patriot, Statesman, 1805–1886* (College Station: Texas A&M University Press, 1982).

7. Bell's letter to the commanders, July 1, 1850, is in *App. to Tex. Sen. Jours., 3d Legis., 2d Sess.*, 53–54; and "Executive Record Book: Bell," 176–78, Executive Record Books. Bell specified in the letter that each company should have one captain, one first lieutenant, two second lieutenants, four sergeants, four corporals, two buglers, one farrier and blacksmith, and eighty-five privates. Bell's July 1, 1850, proclamation to call a special session of the legislature is in ibid., 175–76.

8. The acknowledgments of the commissions by the five officers are in Governors' Letters. News reports of others claiming commissions to recruit are in Austin *State Gazette*, Aug. 17, 1850; and Matagorda *Tribune*, Aug. 16, 1850. The collection of Santa Fe Papers at Texas State Library contains more than twenty letters from Texas and other Southern states offering services to Texas. The Princeton student's letter is in Austin *State Gazette*, Sept. 14, 1850. Colt's offer is in Samuel Colt to Rusk, July 26, 1850, Rusk Papers.

9. On the companies of Likens and Smith, see Likens to Bell, Aug. 3, and J. M. Smith to Bell, July 15, 1850, Governors' Letters; Austin *State Gazette*, Aug. 10, 24, 31, 1850; Houston *Telegraph*, Aug. 28, 1850; Marshall *Republican*, July 20, 1850; D.C. *Natl. Intell.*, Aug. 19, 1850; D.C. *Union*, Aug. 14, 16, 1850; and Neighbours, "Taylor-Neighbors Struggle," 457. For Henderson's attitude, see Henderson to Hammond, July 21, 1850, roll 9, Hammond Papers; and Henderson to Quitman, July 22, 1850, Claiborne, *Life of Quitman* 2:41.

10. John H. Moffett to Rusk, Aug. 28, 1850, Rusk Papers; Mobile *Alabama Planter*, Sept. 23, 1850; and *Natchez Free Trader*, Aug. 14, 17, 1850.

11. Clarksville *Standard*, July 27, 1850, quoting San Augustine *Red-Land Herald*. On the meetings at Goliad and Crockett on July 13, see Austin *State Gazette*, Aug. 3, 1850; at La Grange on Aug. 5, 13, see La Grange *Monument*, Aug. 7, 21, 1850; in Fort Bend County on July 20, see Houston *Telegraph*, Aug. 1, 1850; in Tyler County in later July, see D.C. *Union*, Aug. 24, 1850; at Carthage about July 20, and at Shelbyville on July 20, see Marshall *Republican*, July 27, 1850; at Mount Enterprise in later July, see Austin *State Gazette*, Aug. 10, 1850; at Marshall when Likens's troops were enrolled on July 27, see Marshall *Republican*, Aug. 3, 1850; at Gilmer on July 27, see ibid., Aug. 10, 1850; at Clarksville on July 27, see Clarksville *Standard*, Aug. 3, 1850; at Wharton on July 29, and Aug. 5, see Matagorda *Tribune*,

Aug. 16, 1850; at Cameron, Huntsville, and Caldwell on Aug. 5, see Austin *State Gazette*, Aug. 10, 24, 31, 1850; in Fayette County on Aug. 5, see *N.Y. Tribune*, Sept. 3, 1850; at Houston on Aug. 8, see Houston *Telegraph*, Aug. 14, Sept. 11, 25, 1850, and Marshall *Republican*, Sept. 28, 1850; and at Bastrop on Aug. 9, see Austin *State Gazette*, Aug. 24, 1850. These meetings all endorsed radical resolutions on the Santa Fe issue, except for the Clarksville meeting on August 3 and the Fayette County meeting on August 5, both of which adopted more moderate resolutions. Several other meetings apparently took place but there is no surviving information about them in the press. These were at Galveston, mentioned in Ashbel Smith to Houston, July 20, 1850, Smith Papers; at Nacogdoches, mentioned in W. C. Duffield to Rusk, July 28, 1850, Rusk Papers; and in Lamar County, probably at Paris, mentioned in William M. Williams to Rusk, Aug. 14, 1850, ibid.

12. Houston *Telegraph*, Sept. 11, 1850; Duffield to Rusk, July 28, 1850, Rusk Papers. The earliest recorded moderate meeting was at Upper Cummings Creek in Colorado County on August 5. La Grange *Monument*, Aug. 7, 14, 1850. On the meeting at Indianola in mid-August, see Victoria *Advocate*, Aug. 16, 1850; at San Antonio later in August, see *N.Y. Tribune*, Sept. 13, 1850, and Brooke to Scott, Aug. 25, 1850, M-567, roll 424, item B-612, RG 94; at Houston on August 29, see Houston *Telegraph*, Sept. 11, 25, 1850, and Marshall *Republican*, Sept. 28, 1850; and at San Augustine on Sept. 7, see Austin *State Gazette*, Sept. 28, 1850. On the Brinham meeting, see ibid., Aug. 31, 1850; and Matagorda *Tribune*, Sept. 20, 1850, quoting Washington, Tex., *Lone Star*.

13. Simms to Tucker, July 11, 1850, Tucker-Coleman Papers; also printed in Mary C. S. Oliphant, Alfred T. Odell, and T. C. Duncan Eaves, eds., *The Letters of William Gilmore Simms*, 5 vols. (Columbia: Univ. of South Carolina Press, 1952–56), 3:54; Tucker to Hammond, July 17, 1850, roll 9, Hammond Papers; and Claiborne, *Life of Quitman* 2:42.

14. William Kennick to Mann, Aug. 3, 1850, Mann Papers; and Blair to Van Buren, Aug. 3, 1850, roll 32, Van Buren Papers.

15. Austin letter, Aug. 16, in *N.Y. Herald*, Sept. 9, 1850; Austin *State Gazette*, Aug. 17, 1850; and Clarksville *Standard*, Sept. 7, 1850. Fuller attendance at the beginning of the session is mentioned in an Austin letter in Matagorda *Tribune*, Aug. 30, 1850. On Greer's situation, see J. A. Greer to Miller, Aug. 11, 1850, Miller Papers. Letter is printed in Austin *State Gazette*, Sept. 7, 1850. On Pease, see Spaw, ed., *Texas Senate*, 198.

16. On the situation as the session began, see Guy M. Bryan to James and Emily Bryan, Aug. 13, 1850, Bryan Papers; letters to Sen. Rusk from Thomas J. Jennings, Aug. 13, William M. Williams, Aug. 14, and John H. Moffett, Aug. 14, 1850, Rusk Papers; and an Austin letter in Matagorda *Tribune*, Aug. 30, 1850. The quote on senators is from an Austin letter in *N.Y. Herald*, Sept. 9, 1850. See also Austin *State Gazette*, Aug. 10, 1850, for its attitude.

17. *Tex. Sen. Jours.*, 3d Legis., 2d sess., 5–17; Austin *State Gazette*, Aug. 17, 1850; Clarksville *Standard*, Sept. 7, 1850; and Spaw, ed., *Texas Senate*, 203–4, 206. Reports from the state adjutant general and the state treasurer presented by the governor to the legislature are in *App. to Tex. Sen. Jours., 3d Legis., 2d Sess.*, 51–52, 54–68. Echoing Bell's adverse attitude toward the Omnibus, one radical paper in Texas termed the bill "that idol of the Abolitionists." Matagorda *Tribune*, Aug. 16, 1850.

18. *Tex. Sen. Jours.*, 3d Legis., 2d sess., 21–23; and Austin *State Gazette*, Aug. 17, 24, 1850. No copies of the printed House journals for this session still exist, so the researcher must rely on the House proceedings as reported in the *Gazette*. Luckily those accounts are almost exactly the same as what would have been printed in the official journals.

19. Austin *State Gazette*, Aug. 17, 1850; and *N.Y. Tribune*, Sept. 9, 1850, quoting the San Antonio *Western Texan*.

20. Austin letters in Clarksville *Standard*, Sept. 7, 1850, and Matagorda *Tribune*, Aug. 30, 1850; and *D.C. Natl. Intell.*, Sept. 4, 1850, quoting Austin *American*.

21. On the bills, see original bill no. 2 (Robertson's), Records of the Legislature, 3d Legis., 2d sess., Texas State Archives; *Tex. Sen. Jours.*, 3d Legis., 2d sess., 22; and Austin *State Gazette*, Aug. 17, 24, 1850.

22. Miller to Rusk, Aug. 16, 1850, Rusk Papers; Matagorda *Tribune,* Sept. 6, 1850; Clarksville *Standard,* Sept. 7, 1850; and *N.Y. Tribune,* Sept. 9, 1850.

23. Summary of Bryan's remarks, Aug. 17, 1850, Bryan Papers; Austin letter in Matagorda *Tribune,* Sept. 6, 1850; and *N.Y. Tribune,* Sept. 9, 1850. Most of the proposals considered in the joint committee are included in Joint Resolution No. 9, Records of the Legislature, 3d Legis., 2d sess., Texas State Archives.

24. Isaac Parker to Rusk, Aug. 20, 1850, Rusk Papers; and Austin *State Gazette,* Aug. 24, 1850.

25. On the arrival of news of Rusk's attitude on the Pearce bill, see Miller to Rusk, Aug. 23, 1850, Rusk Papers. The "wince" remark is from a New Orleans letter in Matagorda *Tribune,* Aug. 30, 1850. See Austin *State Gazette,* Aug. 24, 1850, for their initial attack on the Pearce bill. Bell's reaction is given in John H. Moffett to Rusk, Aug. 28, 1850, Rusk Papers. On support for Rusk, see Miller to J. K. Holland, Oct. 26, 1850, Miller Papers; letters to Rusk from R. D. Johnson, July 28, William M. Williams, Aug. 14, John H. Moffett, Aug. 14, W. D. Miller, Aug. 16, and Isaac Parker, Aug. 20, 1850, Rusk Papers. For an editorial attack on Rusk's and Houston's records as favoring free soil, see Marshall *Republican,* Sept. 7, 1850.

26. Parker to Rusk, Aug. 20, 1850, Rusk Papers; *Tex. Sen. Jours.,* 3d Legis., 2d sess., 22; and Austin *State Gazette,* Aug. 24, 1850.

27. *Tex. Sen. Jours.,* 3d Legis., 2d sess., 26; Austin *State Gazette,* Aug. 24, 1850; Matagorda *Tribune,* Sept. 13, 1850; and Marshall *Republican,* Sept. 7, 1850.

28. Miller to Holland, Oct. 26, 1850, Miller Papers; and letters to Rusk from John H. Moffett, Aug. 28, Adolphus Sterne, Sept. 18, and J. W. Scott, Sept. 20, 1850, Rusk Papers. Hamilton's letter to Bee is mentioned in Marshall *Republican,* Sept. 7, 1850.

29. On the moves prior to the election, see Austin *State Gazette,* Aug. 31, 1850. Wilson's statement about himself is in Matagorda *Tribune,* Sept. 20, and his remarks are in ibid., Sept. 13, 1850. Franklin's remarks are in Marshall *Republican,* Sept. 7, 1850. On the election itself, see Parker to Rusk, Aug. 26, 1850, Rusk Papers; *Tex. Sen. Jours.,* 3d Legis., 2d sess., 47; Austin *State Gazette,* Aug. 31, 1850; and Marshall *Republican,* Sept. 7, 1850. The Bee-Hamilton correspondence is mentioned in ibid. Among the Senate radicals, David Gage, Jerome Robertson, and H. L. Kinney were solidly pro-Rusk. Letters to Rusk from W. D. Miller, Aug. 16, and G. K. Lewis, Nov. 28, 1850, Rusk Papers. On the relation of the election to the proposed Pearce bill, see Austin letters to Galveston papers, quoted in *N.Y. Tribune,* Sept. 17, 1850; and *Charleston Mercury,* Sept. 14, 1850.

30. *Tex. Sen. Jours.,* 3d Legis., 2d sess., 30–31, 35, 57; and Austin *State Gazette,* Aug. 24, 31, 1850.

31. Besides knowing of Fillmore's firm-minded message by that time, the members of the legislature were also aware of reports of preparations in New Mexico and U.S. reinforcements on their way to Santa Fe. Austin *State Gazette,* Aug. 17, 1850; and *Charleston Mercury,* Sept. 12, 1850, quoting an Austin letter, dated August 27, to New Orleans *Picayune.* The San Augustine *Herald* had earlier commented defiantly in regard to the news that more U.S. troops were being transferred to Santa Fe: "Truly, the war is but at our doors, and our citizens should even now be under arms." Quoted in D.C. *Union,* Aug. 2, 1850. The editorials in the Houston *Telegraph,* Aug. 21, 28, 1850, give a good view of the moderates' dissent from Bell's plans, support for the Pearce bill, and concern over the possible outbreak of war.

32. *Tex. Sen. Jours.,* 3d Legis., 2d sess., 44–46, 48–53; and Austin *State Gazette,* Aug. 31, Sept. 7, 1850.

33. The winter campaign problem is discussed in an Austin letter to *Galveston News,* reprinted in *New Orleans Commercial Bulletin,* Sept. 12, 1850; and in an Austin letter to *Galveston News,* reprinted in *N.Y. Tribune,* Sept. 17, and in *Charleston Mercury,* Sept. 12, 1850. The comment about using the school fund to finance the session is in Houston *Telegraph,* Sept. 11, 1850. The quote about "patriotic valor" is in an Austin letter dated August 30 in the Matagorda *Tribune,* Sept. 13, 1850.

34. *Tex. Sen. Jours.,* 3d Legis., 2d sess., 54–57; Austin *State Gazette,* Sept. 7, Oct. 19, 1850; Austin *American,* Sept. 2, 1850; and Matagorda *Tribune,* Sept. 20, 1850.

35. *Tex. Sen. Jours.,* 3d Legis., 2d sess., 79–81, 115; and Austin *State Gazette,* Sept. 14, 1850.

36. Austin *State Gazette,* Sept. 7, 1850.

37. Ibid.

38. Wilson's speech is in Matagorda *Tribune,* Oct. 11, 1850.

39. Austin *State Gazette,* Sept. 14, 1850; Houston *Telegraph,* Sept. 11, 1850; and Matagorda *Tribune,* Sept. 13, 27, 1850.

40. *Tex. Sen. Jours.,* 3d Legis., 2d sess., 67–69, 71, 73–75. Moffett's view is given in Moffett to Rusk, Aug. 28, 1850, Rusk Papers. On Wallace's change, see Marshall *Republican,* Sept. 21, 1850.

41. *Tex. Sen. Jours.,* 3d Legis., 2d sess., 81, 85, 87–88, 106; and Spaw, ed., *Texas Senate,* 206–7. On Wallace's vote, see Marshall *Republican,* Sept. 21, 1850, quoting San Augustine *Herald.* The quote on members' reasoning for opposing the "war" bill is from an Austin letter to the *Galveston News,* reprinted in *New Orleans Commercial Bulletin,* Sept. 21, 1850. The radical comment is from an Austin letter in Matagorda *Tribune,* Sept. 13, 1850. The "news" of the Pearce bill passage is referred to in an Austin letter of September 3 printed in New Orleans *Delta,* Sept. 12, 1850; in La Grange *Monument,* Sept. 4, 1850; and in a statement by Rep. J. W. Scott in the House on September 6, printed in Austin *State Gazette,* Sept. 21, 1850. See chapter 11, note 3 for a fuller discussion of the mistaken dispatch.

42. *Tex. Sen. Jours.,* 3d Legis., 2d sess., 58, 61–62, 67–69, 72.

43. Ibid., 84, 87; and Austin *State Gazette,* Sept. 14, 1850.

44. *Tex. Sen. Jours.,* 3d Legis., 2d sess., 95; and Austin *State Gazette,* Sept. 14, 1850.

45. Bell's message is in *Tex. Sen. Jours.,* 3d Legis., 2d sess., 104–6; and Austin *State Gazette,* Sept. 7, 1850.

46. *Tex. Sen. Jours.,* 3d Legis., 2d sess., 106–10, 112–14, 118–19; Austin *State Gazette,* Sept. 21, 1850.

47. Austin *State Gazette,* Sept. 21, 1850; and Brooke to Scott, Aug. 25, Sept. 12, 1850, items B-612, B-573, respectively, M-567, roll 424, RG 94.

Chapter 11
The U.S. House and Texas–New Mexico, August–September 1850

1. *Nashville True Whig,* Aug. 31, 1850.

2. *Cong. Globe,* 31: 1: 1573, 1578–79, 1583–85, 1588–89, App., 1517–61. The votes are in 31: 1: *Sen. Jour.* (Ser. 548): 549–50, 553–54, 557, 559–61, 565–66, 573, 575–76, 580–81, 589, 597–98, 620–21, 626, 631–33, 637. The best secondary account on these Senate bills is Hamilton, *Prologue to Conflict,* 138–44. A few interesting reports by correspondents are in N.Y. *Sun,* Aug. 19, 1850; and Boston *Yankee Blade,* Aug. 24, 1850.

3. Expressions of optimism or confidence of quick passage are in H. Cobb to M. Cobb, Aug. 12, 1850, Cobb Papers; Webster to Samuel Lawrence, Aug. 10, 1850, Wiltse, ed., *Microfilm Edition—Webster Papers,* roll 22; *Ashtabula Sentinel,* Aug. 24, 1850; *Charleston Courier,* Aug. 15, 1850; *Boston Pilot,* Aug. 17, 1850; Cleve. *True Democrat,* Aug. 16, 1850; N.Y. *Journal of Commerce,* Aug. 12, 1850; N.Y. *Post,* Aug. 16, 1850; D.C. *Natl. Intell.,* Aug. 12, 1850; and D.C. *Republic,* Aug. 13, 14, 1850. The list of 140 House members supposedly in favor of the bill is in "Aristide's" column in *Baltimore Clipper,* Aug. 15, 1850. The dispatch predicting House passage by a margin of fifty is in N.Y. *Tribune,* Aug. 16, 1850. The false report that it was passed by fifty was printed in a number of papers. The error was traced to a telegrapher for the Balt. *American,* who retracted it. Montgomery *Journal,* Aug. 22, 29, 1850; and *Savannah Republican,* Aug. 19, 1850. For the influence of the telegraphic error on the Texas Legislature, see chapter 10; Austin *State Gazette,* Sept. 21, 1850; and Austin letter in New Orleans *Delta,* Sept. 12, 1850.

4. For Southern Whig speeches in the House between August 6 and 16 on the president's message, see *Cong. Globe,* 31: 1: 1577 (Toombs, Ga.), App., 1051–54 (Williams, Tenn.), 1076–80 (Houston,

Del.), 1080–84 (Stephens, Ga.), 1150–54 (Marshall, Ky.). Speaker Howell Cobb (D-Ga.) was very fearful that Toombs and Stephens would desert the compromise and join the extremists, leaving him alone to defend the Union. H. Cobb to M. Cobb, Aug. 8, 1850, Cobb Papers. Southern Democratic extremists attacked the president's message as a threat to the South as a whole. *Cong. Globe,* 31: 1: 1528 (Morse, La.), 1548–50 (Brown, Miss.), 1558 (Woodward, S.C.), 1585–87 (Ashe, N.C.), 1065–68 (Haralson, Ga.), 1112–16 (Seddon, Va.), 1141–46 (Venable, N.C.). Four other Southern Democrats attacked the message but later voted with the pro-compromise bloc. Ibid., 1528 (Howard, Tex.), 1589 (Bayly, Va.), App., 1032–34 (Savage, Tenn.), 1049–51 (Johnson, Tenn.). Distinctly pro-compromise sentiments were expressed by three Southern Democrats. Ibid., App., 1068–72 (Jones, Tenn.), 1109–12 (Ewing, Tenn.), 1116–20 (McLane, Md.). The Washington correspondent "Southron" gave good descriptions of several of these speeches in the Chicago *Western Citizen,* Aug. 20, 27, 1850.

5. Some of the better accounts of the Southern caucus given by correspondents are in Augusta *Chronicle and Sentinel,* Aug. 16, 1850; Balt. *Sun,* Aug. 12, 13, 1850; *Boston Herald,* Aug. 16, 1850; *Boston Times,* Aug. 14, 1850; *Buffalo Commercial Advertiser,* Aug. 13, 1850; Chicago *Western Citizen,* Aug. 27, 1850; *N.Y. Commercial Advertiser,* Aug. 12, 13, 1850; *N.Y. Courier and Enquirer,* Aug. 13, 1850; *N.Y. Express,* Aug. 10, 1850; *N.Y. Sun,* Aug. 14, 1850; *N.Y. Tribune,* Aug. 10, 13, 1850; Phila. *North American,* Aug. 13, 1850; Phila. *Inquirer,* Aug. 15, 1850; *Pittsburgh Gazette,* Aug. 15, 1850; St. Louis *New Era,* Aug. 21, 1850; and D.C. *Southern Press,* Aug. 12, 1850. See also Houston to Webster, Aug. 11, 1850, Andrew Jackson Houston Papers, Texas State Archives; and Cass to McClelland, Aug. 10, 1850, McClelland Papers.

6. *Cong. Globe,* 31: 1: App., 1124–28; Giddings to J. A. Giddings, Aug. 12, 22, 1850, roll 3, Giddings Papers; *Ashtabula Sentinel,* Aug. 24, 1850; and James B. Stewart, *Joshua R. Giddings and the Tactics of Radical Politics* (Cleveland: Case Western Reserve Univ. Press, 1970), 186–87. Mention of the Northern radical caucus of August 10 is in *N.Y. Express,* Aug. 13, 1850. The compromise and Southern radical caucuses of Aug. 12 are mentioned in *N.Y. Sun,* Aug. 16, 1850.

7. The "mob" comment is in Victoria *Advocate,* Sept. 26, 1850. For a good discussion of House acoustics by a correspondent, see *Boston Courier,* Sept. 10, 1850. On wafer-snapping in the House, see *Madison* (Ind.) *Courier,* Aug. 23, 1850; *Boston Atlas,* Aug. 27, 1850; *Boston Courier,* Sept. 10, 1850; *Vicksburg Whig,* Sept. 4, 1850; and Hamilton, *Prologue to Conflict,* 154. On firearms reports, see *N.Y. Tribune,* July 20, 25, 1850; and Chicago *Western Citizen,* Aug. 6, 1850.

8. On Cobb's situation, see H. Cobb to M. Cobb, Aug. 26, Sept. 8, 1850, Cobb Papers; and Phila. *Pennsylvanian,* Aug. 21, 1850. On general exhaustion and homesickness, see H. Cobb to M. Cobb, Aug. 15, 1850, Cobb Papers; J. R. Underwood to E. Underwood, Aug. 12, 22, 1850, Underwood Papers; Boston *Yankee Blade,* Aug. 24, Sept. 7, 1850; Norfolk *Southern Argus,* Aug. 21, 1850; Phila. *Bulletin,* Aug. 27, 1850; and Thompson, *Toombs,* 70. On the fear of cholera in 1850, see H. Cobb to M. Cobb, Aug. 10, 15, 1850, Cobb Papers; A. Felch to L. Felch, Aug. 12, 1850, Felch Papers; entries for Aug. 1, 7, 8, 11, 16, J. P. Kennedy Diary, Kennedy Papers; Boston *Yankee Blade,* Aug. 31, 1850; *Chicago Democrat,* Aug. 19, 1850; Columbus, Ohio, *Journal,* Aug. 3, 1850; and Iowa City *Iowa Republican,* July 24, 1850.

9. Contemporary comment on the influence of the coming elections on House members is in *Baltimore Clipper,* Aug. 21, 26, 1850; Balt. *Sun,* Aug. 20, 21, 1850; *Boston Post,* Sept. 4, 1850; *Louisville Courier,* Sept. 10, 1850; *N.Y. Express,* Aug. 31, 1850; N.Y. *Sun,* Aug. 30, 1850; Phila. *Inquirer,* Sept. 9, 1850; and Phila. *Pennsylvanian,* Aug. 23, 24, 1850. On buncombe speeches, see *Boston Pilot,* Sept. 7, 1850; and Boston *Yankee Blade,* Aug. 10, 1850.

10. For some representative Free-Soil editorials, see Chicago *Western Citizen,* Aug. 13, 27, 1850; Hartford *Republican,* Aug. 22, 1850; and Milwaukee *Free Democrat,* Aug. 21, 1850. Anti-bill Northern Whig views are in *Boston Atlas,* Aug. 19, 1850; *Lowell Journal and Courier,* Aug. 19, 1850; *N.Y. Tribune,* Aug. 12, 19, 1850; *Pittsburgh Dispatch,* Aug. 13, 1850; and *Portland Transcript,* Aug. 13, 1850. Some Northern Democratic editorials against the bill are in Milwaukee *Wisconsin,* Aug. 30, 1850; Portsmouth *Gazette,* Aug. 27, 1850; *Syracuse Standard,* Aug. 14, 1850; and N.Y. *Post,* Aug. 28, 1850. Senator

Benton's attitude is reflected in *St. Louis Union*, Aug. 15, 19, 20, 1850.

11. For Southern radical editorials, see Columbia *Telegraph*, Aug. 12, 27, 29, 1850; Nashville *American*, Aug. 16, 27, 1850; *Memphis Appeal*, Aug. 22, 1850; *Richmond Examiner*, Aug. 13, 1850; *Savannah Georgian*, Sept. 3, 11, 1850; *Vicksburg Sentinel*, Aug. 20, 22, 1850; and D.C. *Southern Press*, Aug. 10, 12, 17, 20, 1850. Claiborne's letter is in Jackson *Mississippian*, Aug. 30, 1850. For resolutions of Southern meetings promising aid to Texas, see D.C. *Southern Press*, Aug. 16–17, 19, 21–23, 26, 31, Sept. 3–7, 9–11, 1850. The unusual position taken by the *St. Louis Times* is in its editorial of August 20, 1850.

12. Some Northern Whig editorials in favor of a compromise or the Pearce bill are in *Boston Journal*, Aug. 12, 1850; Cincinnati *Chronicle and Atlas*, Aug. 14, 16, 1850; *Hartford Courant*, Aug. 15, 20, 1850; Milwaukee *Sentinel and Gazette*, Aug. 19, 24, 1850; Phila. *Bulletin*, Aug. 15, 1850; Pittsburgh *Gazette*, Aug. 12, 1850; *Providence Journal*, Aug. 26, 29, 1850; and *Utica Gazette*, Aug. 13, Sept. 4, 1850.

13. For Northern Democratic newspaper opinion in favor of the bill, see *Daily Cincinnati Commercial*, Aug. 12, 14, 1850; N.Y. *Times and Messenger*, Aug. 18, 25, Sept. 1, 1850; Phila. *Pennsylvanian*, Aug. 16, 19, 1850; Pitts. *Chronicle*, Aug. 13, 16, 19, 22, 1850; *Providence Post*, Aug. 22, 1850; and Trenton *True American*, Aug. 16, 1850.

14. Southern Whig editorials are in Helena, Ark., *Southern Shield*, Aug. 24, 1850; Jackson *Southron*, Aug. 30, 1850; Montgomery *Journal*, Aug. 22, 1850; Raleigh *N.C. Star*, Aug. 14, 1850; *Richmond Whig*, Aug. 13, 23, 1850; *Savannah Republican*, Aug. 21, 23, 29, 1850; *Vicksburg Whig*, Aug. 21, 28, Sept. 4, 11, 1850; and Wilmington, N.C., *Commercial*, Aug. 16, 1850.

15. For pro-bill attitudes in Southern Democratic papers, see Houston *Telegraph*, Aug. 21, 28, 1850; *Nashville Union*, Aug. 31, Sept. 5, 1850; New Orleans *Courier*, Aug. 17, 19, 21, 24, 27, 28, 1850; Raleigh *North Carolina Standard*, Aug. 14, 1850; *Richmond Enquirer*, Aug. 23, Sept. 6, 1850; and Victoria *Advocate*, Aug. 23, 30, 1850.

16. On distrust in the pro-compromise bloc, see T. L. Harris to Lanphier and Walker, Aug. 12, 1850, Lanphier Papers; *Baltimore Clipper*, Aug. 19, 21, 1850; Balt. *Sun*, Aug. 15, 17, 23, 1850; *Boston Post*, Aug. 19, 26, 1850; Macon *Telegraph*, Aug. 27, 1850; N.Y. *Journal of Commerce*, Aug. 31, 1850; Phila. *Pennsylvanian*, Aug. 22, 1850; *Pittsburgh Gazette*, Aug. 24, 1850; D.C. *Union*, Aug. 18, 1850; and *Wilmington* (N.C.) *Journal*, Aug. 23, 1850.

17. Discussion of the plan for a new Omnibus is in Douglas to Walker and Lanphier, Sept. 5, 1850, Johannsen, ed., *Letters of Douglas*, 194; D. Outlaw to E. Outlaw, Aug. 14, 1850, Outlaw Papers; Balt. *Sun*, Aug. 29, 1850; *Charleston Courier*, Aug. 22, 1850; New Orleans *Picayune*, Aug. 22, 1850; N.Y. *Commercial Advertiser*, Aug. 22, 1850; N.Y. *Journal of Commerce*, Aug. 21, 1850; and Phila. *Pennsylvanian*, Aug. 20, 1850. Use of the previous question device is in Phila. *Public Ledger*, Aug. 29, 1850; N.Y. *Sun*, Aug. 17, 1850; and D.C. *Southern Press*, Aug. 30, 1850.

18. On the report of eight thousand volunteers and reactions to it, see Balt. *Republican and Argus*, Aug. 15, 1850; *Cleveland Herald*, Aug. 19, 1850; N.Y. *Express*, Aug. 15, 19, 22, 1850; N.Y. *Herald*, Aug. 15, 17, 1850; *Providence Journal*, Aug. 19, 1850; and D.C. *Union*, Aug. 14, 16, 1850. For some commentary on Texas's need for help against the Indians while threatening to cross swords with the United States, see *Boston Herald*, Aug. 21, 1850; *Cincinnati Gazette*, Aug. 17, 23, 1850; *Dayton Journal*, Aug. 31, 1850; Franklin, Tenn., *Western Weekly Review*, Sept. 6, 1850; *Hartford Courant*, Aug. 30, 1850; Milwaukee *Free Democrat*, Aug. 28, 1850; D.C. *National Era*, Aug. 29, 1850; and *Wilmington* (Del.) *State Journal*, Aug. 23, 1850. Writers who believed the threats helped the bill expressed their views in Balt. *Sun*, Aug. 26, 1850; and Boston *Yankee Blade*, Aug. 31, 1850. The opposite view was expressed in Balt. *Sun*, Aug. 31, 1850; N.Y. *Journal of Commerce*, Aug. 23, 1850; Phila. *Inquirer*, Aug. 15, 28, 1850; and *Providence Journal*, Sept. 4, 1850.

19. On the tactic of calling the yeas and nays, see *Albany State Register*, Aug. 10, 1850; Columbia *South Carolinian*, Aug. 20, 1850; *Columbus* (Ga.) *Times*, Sept. 3, 1850; *Hartford Courant*, Aug. 24, 1850; *Louisville Courier*, Aug. 19, 1850; Macon *Telegraph*, Aug. 27, 1850, reprinting a disunion article by "Randolph of Roanoke" (Seth Barton) from D.C. *Southern Press*; N.Y. *Sun*, Aug. 17, 1850; and a letter

from a Virginia congressman (probably James Seddon of Richmond) in *Richmond Examiner,* Aug. 23, 1850.

20. Good descriptions of the operation of the five-minute rule are in *Albany State Register,* Aug. 10, 1850; *Hartford Courant,* Aug. 24, 1850; and *N.Y. Courier and Enquirer,* Aug. 15, 1850. On the move to change the rule, see *Cong. Globe,* 31: 1: 1566–68, 1575–76; H. Mann to M. Mann, Aug. 13, 1850, Mann Papers; *Buffalo Commercial Advertiser,* Aug. 17, 19, 1850; *N.Y. Courier and Enquirer,* Aug. 14, 15, 16, 1850; and *Pittsburgh Gazette,* Aug. 17, 1850.

21. The plan was discussed in *Baltimore Clipper,* Aug. 24, 1850; New Orleans *Picayune,* Sept. 4, 6, 1850; *N.Y. Tribune,* Aug. 26, 27, 1850; and Victoria *Advocate,* Sept. 26, 1850.

22. On the plan to attach the Proviso via Southern absenteeism, see *Detroit Free Press,* Aug. 16, 1850; *Louisville Courier,* Aug. 23, 1850; New Orleans *Picayune,* Sept. 10, 1850; N.Y. *Sun,* Aug. 19, 20, 1850; Phila. *Inquirer,* Aug. 19, 1850; and *Rochester American,* Aug. 23, 1850.

23. On the desire of anti-bill men to commit the bill to Committee of the Whole, see N.Y. *Post,* Aug. 17, 1850; Phila. *Public Ledger,* Aug. 29, 1850; N.Y. *Sun,* Aug. 20, 1850; *Boston Times,* Aug. 19, 1850; and New Orleans *Picayune,* Sept. 6, 1850.

24. For suggestions in the anti-bill press that President Fillmore was not committed to the Pearce bill or that he favored Taylor's nonaction, see *Buffalo Express,* Aug. 23, 24, 1850; *Columbus* (Ga.) *Times,* Sept. 3, 1850; and *N.Y. Tribune,* Aug. 26, 1850. Fillmore himself privately wrote that preservation of harmony, peace, and Union was the height of his ambition as president. Fillmore to Robert L. Carruthers, Aug. 20, 1850, Smith, ed., *Microfilm Edition—Fillmore Papers,* roll 20. That Fillmore did not inform Smith of the administration's new orders to Munroe is obvious from the fact that Smith left Washington in August without knowing whether new orders had been issued, even though he seemed certain that they had been. *N.Y. Commercial Advertiser,* Aug. 14, 15, 19, 1850.

25. For the Ashmun and Duer speeches, respectively, see *Cong. Globe,* 31: 1: App., 1120–24, 1169–73; for comment on their impact, see New Orleans *Picayune,* Aug. 27, 1850. For press defenses of the administration policy, see *Boston Post,* Aug. 21, 1850; *Buffalo Commercial Advertiser,* Aug. 24, 1850; Concord *Patriot,* Aug. 22, 1850; New Orleans *Courier,* Aug. 31, 1850; *N.Y. Courier and Enquirer,* Aug. 22, 1850; Phila. *Pennsylvanian,* Aug. 22, 1850; and *Richmond Republican,* Aug. 23, 1850. The D.C. *Union,* Aug. 18, 1850, expressed fear that the administration still favored the Proviso. Reports of cabinet members visiting with House members to refute the rumors are in ibid., Aug. 20, 1850; and New Orleans *Courier,* Aug. 31, 1850.

26. Webster to Harvey, Aug. 11, 1850, Wiltse, ed., *Microfilm Edition—Webster Papers,* roll 22; *Boston Times,* Aug. 14, 1850; New Orleans *Picayune,* Aug. 22, 1850; and D.C. *Union,* Aug. 13, 1850. On Seward's trip, see Weed to Seward, Aug. 21, 1850, roll 38, Seward Papers; Balt. *Sun,* Aug. 15, 1850; Concord *Patriot,* Sept. 5, 1850; and New Orleans *Picayune,* Aug. 28, Sept. 10, 1850.

27. For reports of Seward's intrigue and Rusk's threat to expose it, see James Brooks to Rusk and Rusk to Brooks, Sept. 11, 1850, Rusk Papers; "H" to Fillmore, Aug. 14, 1850, Smith, ed., *Microfilm Edition—Fillmore Papers,* roll 20; *Baltimore Clipper,* Aug. 17, 27, Sept. 3, 1850; New Orleans *Picayune,* Aug. 28, 1850; and *N.Y. Journal of Commerce,* Sept. 11, 1850. This is one of those items in Seward's career that his biographers have all overlooked.

28. Stephens to L. Stephens, Aug. 2, 1850, Stephens Papers, Manhattanville College; Winthrop to Nathan Appleton, Aug. 18, 1850, Gutheim, ed., *Microfilm Edition—Winthrop Papers,* roll 26; *Baltimore Clipper,* Aug. 19, 1850; *Louisville Courier,* Aug. 26, 1850; *N.Y. Courier and Enquirer,* Aug. 27, 1850; Phila. *Bulletin,* Aug. 21, 1850; and *Rochester American,* Aug. 23, 1850. Various of the newspapermen speculated that Stephens returned to Georgia to attend the Macon meeting, campaign for reelection, or attend courts. His pairing with Cleveland is mentioned in *Cong. Globe,* 31: 1: 1795.

29. On the Brown and Ashmun moves on August 19, see *Cong. Globe,* 31: 1: 1598–1600; *Boston Post,* Aug. 26, 1850; Concord *Patriot,* Aug. 29, 1850; Macon *Telegraph,* Aug. 27, 1850; *N.Y. Journal of Commerce,* Aug. 22, 23, 1850; *N.Y. Post,* Aug. 22, 1850; *N.Y. Sun,* Aug. 23, 1850; *N.Y. Tribune,* Aug. 21,

1850; Phila. *Pennsylvanian*, Aug. 22, 1850; and *Pittsburgh Gazette*, Aug. 24, 1850. An interesting reaction to the failure of the Ashmun resolution was provided by Free-Soiler George Julian in the Centreville *True Democrat*, Aug. 30, 1850: "Fillmore has drawn the sword, and so has Texas, and although I have no doubt they are both cowards, yet neither of them desires to back out. The President calls on his Whig friends to come to his rescue; but a portion of them only are willing to wear his collar. He invokes the aid of the democrats, but they dislike to fight under his whig banner. One by one they are deserting his standard, while his forces are becoming more and more dismayed."

30. Howard's brief remarks on the message are in *Cong. Globe*, 31: 1: 1528. For his dispatch to the Texas governor, see Howard to Bell, Aug. 9, 1850, Governors' Letters; and Neighbours, "Taylor-Neighbors Struggle," 459–60. Also in Governors' Letters is a telegraphic dispatch from James Hamilton to Bell, also dated August 9, informing him of the Senate's passage of the Pearce bill. For correspondents' views that Howard opposed the bill, see Jackson *Mississippian*, Sept. 6, 1850; Marshall *Republican*, Sept. 28, 1850; and Victoria *Advocate*, Aug. 30, 1850.

31. For Rusk's letters, see Rusk to Bell, Aug. 21, 1850, Governors' Letters; and Rusk to Bryan, Bryan Papers. Wood's letter, undated but marked wrongly as September 1850, is in Wood to Miller, Miller Papers.

32. On Eliot's election, see W. A. Graham to James Graham, Aug. 25, 1850, J. G. de Roulhac Hamilton, ed., *The Papers of William Alexander Graham*, 4 vols. (Raleigh: State Department of Archives and History, 1957–61), 3:370; *Ashtabula Sentinel*, Aug. 31, 1850; Balt. *Sun*, Aug. 21, 22, 1850; *Louisville Courier*, Aug. 26, 1850; New Orleans *Picayune*, Aug. 18, 30, Sept. 5, 1850; *N.Y. Journal of Commerce*, Aug. 24, 1850; and Nevins, *Ordeal of the Union* 1:342.

33. On the Cazenovia Convention itself, see *Albany State Register*, Aug. 24, 1850; *New Haven Daily Palladium*, Aug. 24, 1850; *Utica Gazette*, Aug. 23, 24, 29, 30, Sept. 2, 1850; and Ralph V. Harlow, *Gerrit Smith: Philanthropist and Reformer* (N.Y.: Henry Holt and Co., 1939), 289. Comment on it can be found in *Albany Atlas*, Aug. 24, 1850; Cincinnati *Chronicle and Atlas*, Aug. 29, 1850; *Cleveland Herald*, Aug. 26, 1850; Franklin, Tenn., *Western Review*, Sept. 27, 1850; *Milwaukee Sentinel and Gazette*, Aug. 21, 1850; *Newark Advertiser*, Aug. 24, 1850; *N.Y. Express*, Aug. 29, 1850; and Phila. *Pennsylvanian*, Sept. 6, 1850.

34. Accounts of the Macon Convention and enormously variant versions of attendance at it are in S. T. Chapman to Alexander H. Stephens, Aug. 31, 1850, roll 1, Stephens Papers, LC; Augusta *Constitutionalist*, Aug. 28, 1850; Columbia *Telegraph*, Aug. 30, 1850; Columbus (Ga.) *Times*, Sept. 3, 1850; Macon *Journal and Messenger*, Aug. 28, 1850; Milledgeville *Federal Union*, Aug. 27, 1850; Milledgeville *Southern Recorder*, Aug. 27, 1850; *New Orleans Commercial Bulletin*, Aug. 31, 1850; *Raleigh Register*, Sept. 4, 1850; and *Savannah Republican*, Aug. 24, Sept. 2, 1850. Mirabeau B. Lamar, former Texas president, refused to attend but opposed Texan acceptance of money in exchange for her honor. *Mobile Alabama Planter*, Sept. 2, 1850. For a few positive assessments of the Macon Convention in the Southern press, see Augusta *Republic*, Aug. 17, 27, 1850; Columbus (Ga.) *Times*, Sept. 3, 1850; *Edgefield* (S.C.) *Advertiser*, Sept. 4, 1850; and Nashville *American*, Aug. 31, 1850. Some negative editorial comment is in Athens *Southern Banner*, Aug. 29, 1850; *Buffalo Express*, Aug. 30, 1850; Macon *Journal and Messenger*, Sept. 4, 1850; *Daily Republican Banner and Nashville Whig*, Sept. 2, 1850; Pitts. *Chronicle*, Aug. 31, 1850; and *Rochester Advertiser*, Sept. 5, 1850.

For synopses of Stephens's two speeches, see Augusta *Chronicle & Sentinel*, Sept. 4, 1850; Augusta *Constitutionalist*, Sept. 5, 1850; and Milledgeville *Southern Recorder*, Sept. 10, 1850. For editorial comment on them, see Athens *Southern Herald*, Sept. 12, 1850; Augusta *Constitutionalist*, Sept. 13, 1850; Augusta *Republic*, Sept. 3, 1850; Columbus (Ga.) *Times*, Sept. 10, 1850; and Macon *Journal and Messenger*, Sept. 11, 1850. The speeches are described and analyzed very well in Schott, *Stephens*, 124–26.

35. For some Northern press reaction to Governor Bell's message, see *Boston Advertiser*, Aug. 27, 1850; *Boston Mail*, Aug. 27, 1850; *Buffalo Express*, Sept. 7, 1850; Cincinnati *Chronicle and Atlas*, Sept. 5, 1850; Cleve. *True Democrat*, Sept. 2, 1850; *N.Y. Commercial Advertiser*, Aug. 24, 1850; *N.Y. Express*,

Sept. 6, 1850; Pitts. *Chronicle,* Sept. 5, 1850; *Rochester American,* Sept. 5, 1850; and Springfield, Mass., *Republican,* Sept. 3, 1850. For Grund's claims of Rhett's agents at Austin, see *Boston Post,* Sept. 2, 1850; and Phila. *Public Ledger,* Aug. 28, 1850. Grund did not wholly concoct this rumor himself but elaborated on a recently published letter from a Texas legislator, dated August 1, who expected that Southern secessionists would be present at Austin in "large numbers." This letter, originally in the D.C. *Union,* was reprinted in the *Richmond Enquirer,* Aug. 23, 1850.

36. *Charleston News,* Aug. 30, 1850; *Detroit Advertiser,* Sept. 3, 1850; *New Orleans Commercial Bulletin,* Aug. 28, 1850; *N.Y. Commercial Advertiser,* Aug. 21, 1850; *N.Y. Express,* Aug. 21, 1850; *N.Y. Journal of Commerce,* Aug. 23, 1850; *Pittsburgh Gazette,* Aug. 24, 1850; *Salem Gazette,* Aug. 31, 1850; Savannah *News,* Aug. 24, 1850; and D.C. *Southern Press,* Aug. 30, 1850. For reports in reference to New Mexico, see *Louisville Courier,* Sept. 4, 1850; *Savannah Georgian,* Sept. 11, 1850; Springfield, Mass., *Republican,* Aug. 24, 1850; D.C. *Natl. Intell.,* Sept. 3, 1850; and D.C. *Union,* Aug. 31, Sept. 3, 1850.

37. Weightman to Alvarez, July 19, Aug. 26, 1850, and Munroe's Proclamation, July 23, 1850, roll 1, Alvarez Papers; Alvarez to Fillmore, July 15, 1850, and Weightman to Fillmore, Aug. 26, 1850, Smith, ed., *Microfilm Edition—Fillmore Papers,* rolls 18, 20; *Albany State Register,* Sept. 3, 1850; *Baltimore Clipper,* Aug. 28, 1850; St. Louis *Reveille,* Aug. 24, 25, 1850; and Barry, *Beginning of the West,* 959. On the cabinet's consideration of New Mexico statehood, see Hamilton, ed., *Graham Papers* 3:378–82.

38. W. A. Graham to J. Graham, Aug. 25, 1850, Hamilton, ed., *Graham Papers* 3:369–71; and Nevins, *Ordeal of the Union* 1:342.

39. For some correspondents' guesses as to the outcome, see *Baltimore Clipper,* Aug. 15, 1850; Balt. *Sun,* Aug. 14, 1850; *Boston Times,* Aug. 29, 1850; Milledgeville *Federal Union,* Aug. 20, 1850; *N.Y. Express,* Aug. 17, 1850; Phila. *Bulletin,* Aug. 26, 1850; Phila. *Pennsylvanian,* Aug. 20, 1850; *Pittsburgh Gazette,* Aug. 29, 1850; Springfield, Ill., *State Journal,* Aug. 24, 1850; *N.Y. Journal of Commerce,* Aug. 23, 1850; and *N.Y. Tribune,* Aug. 24, 1850. On the reaction in Galveston, see D.C. *Union,* Aug. 25, 1850;, and *N.Y. Herald,* Aug. 24, 1850.

40. For an interesting description of what it was like conversing with Webster, see George P. Fisher to J. M. Clayton, Aug. 19, 1850, Clayton Papers. On Webster's and the administration's influence, see H. Mann to M. Mann, Aug. 25, Mann to Samuel Downer, Aug. 25, and Mann to Charles Sumner, Aug. 26, 1850, Mann Papers; Webster to Fillmore, Aug. 23, Webster to Haven, Sept. 5, and Webster's editorial, Aug. 26, 1850, Wiltse, ed., *Microfilm Edition—Webster Papers,* roll 22; D. Outlaw to E. Outlaw, Aug. 23, 1850, Outlaw Papers; Balt. *Sun,* Aug. 23, 1850; Boston *Yankee Blade,* Sept. 7, 1850; Cleve. *True Democrat,* Aug. 26, 28, Sept. 2, 1850; Macon *Telegraph,* Aug. 27, 1850; *N.Y. Journal of Commerce,* Aug. 24, 29, 1850; *N.Y. Tribune,* Aug. 17, 1850; *Pittsburgh Gazette,* Aug. 29, 1850; Charles W. Elliott, *Winfield Scott: The Soldier and the Man* (New York: MacMillan Co., 1937), 603; Albert D. Kirwan, *John J. Crittenden: The Struggle for the Union* (Lexington: Univ. of Kentucky Press, 1962), 267; Poage, *Clay and Whig Party,* 261; and Nevins, *Ordeal of the Union* 1:342.

41. On use of patronage to pass the bill, see Schoolcraft to Weed, Aug. 22, and Matteson to Weed, Sept. 4, 1850, Weed Papers; Aug. 31, Sept. 3, 4, 10, 1850 entries, J. P. Kennedy Diary, Kennedy Papers; Augusta *Chronicle and Sentinel,* Sept. 15, 1850; Cleve. *True Democrat,* Sept. 10, 1850; and Holt, *Political Crisis of 1850s,* 87.

42. The only congressman whom I have found to have been specifically named as holding Texas bonds is Whig representative Hugh White of New York; someone informed Free-Soil representative Preston King of N.Y. that this was so. Schoolcraft to Weed, Aug. 12, 1850, Weed Papers. A prominent, unnamed Northern politician, noted for his earlier antislavery views, was reported to have purchased $100,000 worth of Texas bonds at $.20 on the dollar and to then be using his influence with other members of his delegation to garner their votes for the compromise. *Ashtabula Sentinel,* July 6, 1850, quoting a correspondent of the N.Y. *Post.* Some newspapers stated as a general fact that many congressmen held Texas bonds. Phila. *Bulletin,* July 25, 1850; and *Portland Transcript,* June 29, 1850. But even a careful recent study of the 1850s corruption has discovered no corroborative evidence to

substantiate free-soiler charges that the passage of the compromise was "purchased" with Texas bonds. Mark W. Summers, *The Plundering Generation: Corruption and the Crisis of the Union, 1849–1861* (New York: Oxford Univ. Press, 1987), 186–87, 219–23, 337–38. See also Hamilton, *Prologue to Conflict,* 124–30; and Smith, *Presidencies of Taylor and Fillmore,* 186–87. On shifting values of the Texas bonds, see H. Mann to M. Mann, Sept. 9, 1850, Mann Papers; *Charleston News,* Sept. 3, 1850; Cleve. *True Democrat,* Sept. 2, 13, 1850; and Concord *Statesman,* Aug. 16, 1850. On the reserve clause as a detriment to the bill, see N.Y. *Sun,* Aug. 29, 1850.

43. The return of Clay and Seward to Washington is mentioned in Balt. *Sun,* Sept. 2, 1850; Concord *Patriot,* Sept. 5, 1850; *Louisville Courier,* Sept. 4, 1850; and New Orleans *Picayune,* Sept. 10, 1850. The hot weather is mentioned in H. Cobb to M. Cobb, Aug. 28, 1850, Cobb Papers. The more positive reports from Texas are in *N.Y. Commercial Advertiser,* Aug. 26, 1850; and *N.Y. Herald,* Aug. 27, Sept. 1, 1850.

44. *Cong. Globe,* 31: 1: 1681–87, App., 1189–93; and 31: 1: *House Jour.* (Ser. 566): 1321–35. Among the better newspaper accounts of the proceedings on the 28th are *Ashtabula Sentinel,* Sept. 7, 1850; Balt. *Republican and Argus,* Aug. 29, 1850; *Boston Times,* Sept. 3, 1850; *Charleston Courier,* Sept. 2, 1850; Chicago *Western Citizen,* Sept. 10, 1850; Cleve. *True Democrat,* Sept. 5, 1850; N.Y. *Post,* Aug. 30, 1850; Phila. *Bulletin,* Aug. 29, 1850; Phila. *Inquirer,* Aug. 30, 1850; and *Pittsburgh Gazette,* Aug. 31, Sept. 2, 1850. See also H. Cobb to M. Cobb, Aug. 28, 1850, Cobb Papers; Mann to Samuel Downer, Aug. 28, 1850, Mann Papers; D. Outlaw to E. Outlaw, Aug. 28, 1850, Outlaw Papers; Hamilton, *Prologue to Conflict,* 156; and Poage, *Clay and Whig Party,* 262.

45. *Cong. Globe,* 31: 1: 1695–1704; and 31: 1: *House Jour.* (Ser. 566): 1336–40. Among the better newspaper accounts of the proceedings on the 29th are *Ashtabula Sentinel,* Sept. 7, 1850; *N.Y. Courier and Enquirer,* Aug. 31, 1850; N.Y. *Post,* Aug. 31, 1850; Phila. *Inquirer,* Aug. 31, 1850; and *Rochester American,* Sept. 3, 1850. See also G. W. Julian to A. E. Julian, Aug. 29, 1850, Julian Papers; D. Outlaw to E. Outlaw, Aug. 29, 1850, Outlaw Papers; Hamilton, *Prologue to Conflict,* 156; and Poage, *Clay and Whig Party,* 262.

46. Falling Texas bond values are mentioned in *Charleston News,* Sept. 3, 1850. The prospective Texan expedition was reported in *N.Y. Herald,* Sept. 3, 1850.

47. D. Outlaw to E. Outlaw, Aug. 31, 1850, Outlaw Papers.

48. *Cong. Globe,* 31: 1: 1727, 1735–38, App., 1315–18; 31: 1: *House Jour.* (Ser. 566): 1358, 1363–65; *Baltimore Clipper,* Sept. 4, 1850; Balt. *Republican and Argus,* Sept. 4, 1850; Balt. *Sun,* Sept. 4, 1850; *Buffalo Commercial Advertiser,* Sept. 7, 1850; *Charleston Courier,* Sept. 7, 1850; Cleve. *True Democrat,* Sept. 10, 1850; *Detroit Advertiser,* Sept. 10, 1850; Macon *Telegraph,* Sept. 10, 1850; New Orleans *Picayune,* Sept. 11, 1850; *N.Y. Commercial Advertiser,* Sept. 5, 1850; *N.Y. Herald,* Sept. 4, 1850; N.Y. *Post,* Sept. 5, 1850; Phila. *Inquirer,* Sept. 5, 1850; *Richmond Republican,* Sept. 6, 1850; Utica *Herald,* Sept. 7, 1850; and Robert M. McLane, *Reminiscences, 1827–1897* (1903), 94–95, 103–4.

49. H. Cobb to M. Cobb, Sept. 3, 1850, Cobb Papers; and D.C. *Natl. Intell.,* Sept. 4, 1850. The Hamilton-Wilmot pair is given in *Cong. Globe,* 31: 1: 1763; and Balt. *Sun,* Sept. 7, 1850. The Evans-Spaulding pair is also mentioned in ibid.

50. Northern and Southern ultras parading arm-in-arm through tellers is mentioned by a correspondent in *Detroit Advertiser,* Sept. 10, 1850. For some statistics and analysis on House voting, see Freehling, *Road to Disunion,* 508–9; and Hamilton, *Prologue to Conflict,* 161–65, 195–200.

51. *Cong. Globe,* 31: 1: 1746–50; and 31: 1: *House Jour.* (Ser. 566): 1368–87. Among the better newspaper accounts of proceedings on the 4th are *Buffalo Commercial Advertiser,* Sept. 9, 1850; *Detroit Advertiser,* Sept. 10, 1850; *N.Y. Commercial Advertiser,* Sept. 6, 1850; *N.Y. Journal of Commerce,* Sept. 6, 1850; *N.Y. Tribune,* Sept. 6, 1850; Phila. *North American,* Sept. 7, 1850; and Phila. *Public Ledger,* Sept. 6, 1850. See also Joshua R. Giddings, *History of the Rebellion: Its Authors and Causes* (New York: Follett, Foster and Co., 1864), 327–28; Fehrenbacher, *Chicago Giant,* 101–2; Hamilton, *Prologue to Conflict,* 157–58, 165–66; Milton, *The Eve of Conflict,* 76; and Poage, *Clay and Whig Party,* 262. Holman

Hamilton emphasized the pro-compromise votes cast by Wentworth (D-Ill.), Jackson (D-Ga.), and Thompson (D-Miss.) of the anti-compromise bloc on Root's move. Actually, a glance at the overall voting pattern of these three (Appendix B) shows that they were very inconsistent on roll calls. Hamilton also has the vote tally on Root's motion wrongly as 104–103. Cobb's vote only made the vote a tie at 103, thus defeating Root's move.

52. T. L. Harris to Lanphier, Sept. 4, 1850, Lanphier Papers; *Richmond Republican,* Sept. 7, 1850; and D.C. *Union,* Sept. 5, 1850.

53. *Cong. Globe,* 31: 1: 1751–58; and 31: 1: *House Jour.* (Ser. 566): 1388–1403. Among the better newspaper accounts of proceedings on the 5th are Austin *State Gazette,* Oct. 5, 1850; *Alexandria Gazette,* Sept. 7, 1850; *Ashtabula Sentinel,* Sept. 14, 1850; Balt. *Sun,* Sept. 6, 1850; Centreville *Indiana True Democrat,* Sept. 20, 1850; *Charleston Courier,* Sept. 9, 1850; Cleve. *True Democrat,* Sept. 13, 1850; *Detroit Advertiser,* Sept. 12, 1850; *Louisville Courier,* Sept. 12, 1850; *N.Y. Commercial Advertiser,* Sept. 6, 7, 1850; N.Y. *Post,* Sept. 6, 1850; Phila. *North American,* Sept. 6, 1850; Phila. *Inquirer,* Sept. 7, 1850; and Phila. *Public Ledger,* Sept. 6, 1850. See also Webster to Haven, Sept. 5, 1850, Wiltse, ed., *Microfilm Edition—Webster Papers,* roll 22; Giddings, *History of the Rebellion,* 327–31; Fehrenbacher, *Chicago Giant,* 101–2; Hamilton, *Prologue to Conflict,* 158; and Poage, *Clay and Whig Party,* 262. The David Outlaw quote is from his letter to Emily Outlaw, Sept. 5, 1850, Outlaw Papers.

54. Clay to Thomas H. Clay, Sept. 6, 1850, Clay Papers, LC; Boston *Yankee Blade,* Sept. 21, 1850; *Charleston Courier,* Sept. 11, 1850; *Charleston Mercury,* Sept. 11, 1850; Cleve. *True Democrat,* Sept. 11, 1850; *Louisville Courier,* Sept. 12, 1850; and New Orleans *Picayune,* Sept. 15, 1850.

55. Giddings, *History of the Rebellion,* 329.

56. *Cong. Globe,* 31: 1: 1762–65; and 31: 1: *House Jour.* (Ser. 566): 1404–13. Among the better newspaper accounts of proceedings on the 6th are Austin *State Gazette,* Oct. 5, 1850; *Ashtabula Sentinel,* Sept. 21, 1850; *Baltimore Clipper,* Sept. 7, 1850; *Baltimore Patriot,* Sept. 7, 1850; Balt. *Republican and Argus,* Sept. 7, 1850; Balt. *Sun,* Sept. 7, 1850; *Boston Courier,* Sept. 10, 1850; *Boston Post,* Sept. 12, 1850; Boston *Yankee Blade,* Sept. 21, 1850; *Charleston Courier,* Sept. 11, 1850; *Charleston Mercury,* Sept. 11, 1850; Chicago *Western Citizen,* Sept. 17, 1850; Cleve. *True Democrat,* Sept. 11, 1850; Concord *Patriot,* Sept. 12, 1850; *Detroit Advertiser,* Sept. 12, 1850; Indianapolis *State Sentinel,* Sept. 19, 1850; *Louisville Courier,* Sept. 12, 13, 14, 1850; Macon *Telegraph,* Sept. 17, 1850; New Orleans *Picayune,* Sept. 15, 17, 1850; *N.Y. Commercial Advertiser,* Sept. 7, 9, 1850; *N.Y. Courier and Enquirer,* Sept. 9, 1850; *N.Y. Express,* Sept. 7, 9, 1850; *N.Y. Journal of Commerce,* Sept. 9, 1850; N.Y. *Post,* Sept. 7, 1850; N.Y. *Sun,* Sept. 10, 1850; Phila. *Inquirer,* Sept. 9, 1850; *Richmond Republican,* Sept. 10, 1850; and *St. Louis New Era,* Sept. 17, 1850. See also Giddings, *History of the Rebellion,* 329–31; Fehrenbacher, *Chicago Giant,* 101; Hamilton, *Prologue to Conflict,* 158; Milton, *Eve of Conflict,* 76; and Poage, *Clay and Whig Party,* 262.

57. Mann's comments are in H. Mann to M. Mann, Sept. 6, 1850, Mann Papers. Harris's note is quoted in Milton, *Eve of Conflict,* 76. See also *Boston Post,* Sept. 12, 1850; Indianapolis *State Sentinel,* Sept. 19, 1850; *Louisville Courier,* Sept. 13, 1850; and N.Y. *Sun,* Sept. 10, 1850.

Chapter 12
Completion of Victory

1. Nevins, *Ordeal of the Union* 1:343; and Hamilton, *Prologue to Conflict,* 160.

2. *Cong. Globe,* 31: 1: 1769–76; and *Pittsburgh Gazette,* Sept. 12, 1850. On the attitudes of Southern radical members, see ibid.; Phila. *Bulletin,* Sept. 9, 1850; Phila. *Public Ledger,* Sept. 11, 1850; *Cong. Globe,* 31: 1: 1775; and Barnwell to Hammond, Sept. 9, 26, 1850, roll 9, Hammond Papers. For the attitudes of Free-Soil and Seward Whig members, see H. Mann to M. Mann, Sept. 8, 9, 14, 1850, Mann Papers; and the letters of Orsamus Matteson, Sept. 15, William A. Sackett, Sept. 20, and John L. Schoolcraft, Sept. 20, 1850 to Weed, Weed Papers. Thaddeus Stevens of Pennsylvania personally told

Thomas Clingman of North Carolina a few days later that, after frightening the North so effectively, the South had surrendered all points to the North. Because of this, Stevens said, the South could not scare the North again for the North would consider it a "sham." *Selections from Clingman Speeches,* 274.

3. It is not certain when Weightman arrived in Washington. I have concluded from the available evidence that he arrived on Friday, Sept. 6. See Weightman to Fillmore, Sept. 6, 1850, Smith, ed., *Microfilm Edition—Fillmore Papers,* roll 20; and Weightman to Alvarez, Sept. 14, 1850, roll 1, Alvarez Papers. The documents that Weightman brought with him are in "Communication of R. H. Weightman and accompanying memorial of the Legislature of New Mexico setting forth sundry grievances and calling upon Congress for their correction," Sept. 11, 1850, M200, roll 14, RG 46; and 31: 1: *Sen. Ex. Docs.* 76 (Ser. 562): 1–11. See also Richardson, comp., *Messages and Papers* 5:75. While the Senate had not yet at that point approved the House version of the Texas–New Mexico bill, there was no material difference in reference to New Mexico territory between the Senate and House versions.

4. *Cong. Globe,* 31: 1: 1783–84; Fillmore to Hamilton Fish, Sept. 9, 1850, Smith, ed., *Microfilm Edition—Fillmore Papers,* roll 20; Winthrop to Morey, Sept. 20, 1850, Gutheim, ed., *Microfilm Edition—Winthrop Papers,* roll 26; Winthrop to Kennedy, Sept. 1850, Kennedy Papers; *N.Y. Commercial Advertiser,* Sept. 10, 1850; *N.Y. Journal of Commerce,* Sept. 11, 1850; Phila. *Bulletin,* Sept. 10, 1850; and *Richmond Whig,* Sept. 13, 1850. *Commercial Advertiser* listed King of Alabama and Berrien of Georgia among the silent ones, but both were recorded as voting for the bill. Fillmore hesitated on signing the fugitive slave bill until he received Attorney General Crittenden's opinion supporting its constitutionality. Stanley W. Campbell, *The Slave Catchers: Enforcement of the Fugitive Slave Law, 1850–1860* (Chapel Hill: Univ. of North Carolina Press, 1968), 96–97; Rayback, *Fillmore,* 252; and Smith, *Presidencies of Taylor and Fillmore,* 200–201.

5. Hiram Ketchum to Fillmore, Sept. 7, and John S. Graham to Fillmore, Sept. 9, 1850, Smith, ed., *Microfilm Edition—Fillmore Papers,* roll 20; M. Mann to H. Mann, Sept. 9, 1850, Mann Papers; G. K. Lewis to Rusk, Sept. 14, 1850, Rusk Papers; Stephens to L. Stephens, Sept. 11, 1850, Stephens Papers, Manhattanville College; Webster to Harvey, Sept. 13, 1850, Wiltse, ed., *Microfilm Edition—Webster Papers,* roll 22; Concord *Patriot,* Sept. 19, 1850; Franklin, Tenn., *Western Review,* Sept. 27, 1850; Matagorda *Tribune,* Sept. 27, 1850; *Nash. Banner and Whig,* Sept. 19, 1850; *Natchez Courier,* Sept. 24, 1850; *N.Y. Express,* Sept. 9, 1850; Phila. *Pennsylvanian,* Sept. 11, 13, 1850; *Raleigh Register,* Sept. 18, 1850, quoting the Petersburg *Daily Intell.;* Raleigh *Standard,* Sept. 18, 1850; D.C. *Union,* Sept. 10, 1850; and Washington, N.C., *Whig,* Sept. 18, 25, 1850. Of some 170 newspapers that expressed opinions on the compromise after its passage and with which I am familiar, 103 (just over 60 percent) expressed a favorable opinion. The great majority of those were decidedly pleased with the outcome; some were happy that the strife was over but were concerned over whether the opposing section would abide by it.

6. Webster and Crittenden to New Orleans Collector of Customs, Sept. 9, 1850, Rusk to Bell, Sept. 7, 1850, and Samuel Peters to Bell, Sept. 11, 1850, Governors' Letters; Bell to Webster, Crittenden, Houston, and Rusk, Sept. 20, 1850? (misdated Sept. 10), Smith, ed., *Microfilm Edition—Fillmore Papers,* roll 20; Austin *State Gazette,* Sept. 21, 1850; Houston *Telegraph,* Sept. 18, 1850; New Orleans *Delta,* Sept. 13, 1850; *N.Y. Tribune,* Sept. 16, 1850; and Llerena B. Friend, *Sam Houston: The Great Designer* (Austin: Univ. of Texas Press, 1954), 211. The Indianola celebration is recorded in Victoria *Advocate,* Sept. 26, 1850.

7. Weightman to Alvarez, Sept. 14, 1850, roll 1, Alvarez Papers; Jones to Clarke, Sept. 10, 1850, Jones to Beall, Sept. 10, 1850, and Secretary of War Charles M. Conrad to Munroe, Sept. 10, 1850, M-565, roll 17, pp. 204, 210–11, RG 94; Munroe to Freeman, Oct. 31, 1850, M-1072, roll 1, 2:214–15, RG 393; Conrad to Henry Hardy, Sept. 10, 1850, M-6, roll 30, pp. 264–65, RG 107; Jesup to Capt. L. C. Easton, Sept. 10, 1850, M-745, roll 26, p. 114, RG 92; 32: 1: *Sen. Ex. Docs.* 1 (Ser. 611): 298; *Tex. HR Jours.,* 3d Legis., 3d sess., 8–9; *Baltimore Clipper,* Sept. 12, 1850; *Norfolk American Beacon,* Sept. 14, 1850; Phila. *Bulletin,* Sept. 12, 1850; Springfield, Ill., *Journal,* Sept. 25, 1850; and Victoria *Advocate,* Oct. 3, 17, 1850. On his

journey, Hardy had, besides his military escort, four teamsters, four horses, twelve mules, and two wagons. Barry, *Beginning of the West*, 968.

8. H. Wilson, *Rise and Fall of Slave Power* 3:302. That Texas bonds had been liberally distributed among congressmen and senators and administration officials was a theme chanted by the free-soil chorus. H. Mann to M. Mann, Sept. 9, 1850, Mann Papers; *Albany Atlas*, Sept. 11, 1850; Harrisburg *Telegraph*, Sept. 11, 1850; N.Y. *Post*, Sept. 9, 1850; and Utica *Herald*, Sept. 10, 1850. An abolitionist wrote a letter to D.C. *National Era* stating that the administration had passed the bill by "plying the timid with the lash and the mercenary with Texas scrip." Quoted in Lawrence R. Murphy, *Antislavery in the Southwest: William G. Kephart's Mission to New Mexico, 1850–1853* (El Paso: Univ. of Texas, 1978), 11.

9. For Southern opinion that bribery passed the Texas–New Mexico bill, see Milledgeville *Federal Union*, Sept. 10, 1850; Rep. Albert Gallatin Brown's letter in *Natchez Free Trader*, Sept. 14, 1850; and *Richmond Examiner*, Sept. 10, 1850. For other aspects of the Southern radical attitude in the aftermath of the Texas–New Mexico bill's passage, see Austin *State Gazette*, Oct. 5, 1850, quoting Charlotte *Hornet's Nest and True Southron;* Columbia *Telegraph*, Sept. 10, 16, 1850; *Columbus* (Ga.) *Times*, Sept. 17, 1850; Jackson *Mississippian*, Sept. 13, 1850; Norfolk *Southern Argus*, Sept. 9, 1850; and *Vicksburg Sentinel*, Sept. 14, 1850.

10. Columbia *Telegraph*, Sept. 16, 1850; *Richmond Examiner*, Sept. 13, 17, 1850; Savannah *News*, Sept. 24, 1850; and Tallahassee *Floridian and Journal*, Sept. 28, 1850. Other Southern papers expressing the belief that Northern agitation would continue included Columbia *South Carolinian*, Sept. 21, 1850; Jackson *Mississippian*, Sept. 13, 27, 1850; Little Rock *Arkansas Banner*, Oct. 8, 1850; *Memphis Appeal*, Sept. 24, 26, 1850; Mobile *Alabama Planter*, Oct. 7, 1850; and *Savannah Georgian*, Sept. 18, 1850.

11. Southern Democratic papers willing to acquiesce in a settlement they did not like included *Fredericksburg News*, Oct. 4, 1850; Little Rock *Arkansas State Gazette and Democrat*, Oct. 4, 1850; Mobile *Alabama Planter*, Oct. 7, 1850; Nashville *American*, Sept. 15, 19, 1850; and New Orleans *Delta*, Sept. 19, 1850. On economic independence proposals and nonintercourse with the North, see Athens *Southern Herald*, Sept. 19, 1850; *Edgefield* (S.C.) *Advertiser*, Sept. 4, 1850, quoting Columbus *Southern Sentinel;* Little Rock *Banner*, Oct. 8, 1850; *Memphis Appeal*, Sept. 10, 12, 1850; *Daily Memphis Enquirer*, Sept. 8, 1850; Milledgeville *Federal Union*, Oct. 8, 1850; Nashville *American*, Sept. 14, 1850; *Nashville Union*, Sept. 13, 14, 1850; and Raleigh *Star*, Oct. 2, 1850.

12. Barnwell to Hammond, Sept. 26, John J. Seibels to Hammond, Sept. 19, and Tucker to Hammond, Sept. 21, 1850, roll 9, Hammond Papers; Simms to Tucker, Sept. 11, 1850, Tucker-Coleman Papers; J. A. Quitman to Eliza Quitman, Sept. 21, 1850, John A. Quitman Papers, Southern Historical Collection, University of North Carolina, Chapel Hill; Whitemarsh Seabrook to J. A. Leland, Sept. 18, 21, and to Governor Henry W. Collier of Alabama, Sept. 20, Governor G. W. Towns of Georgia to Seabrook, Sept. 25, and Quitman to Seabrook, Sept. 29, 1850, Seabrook Papers, LC. Seabrook to Bell, Sept. 11, 1850, Peter H. Bell Papers, Barker Texas History Center; and Seabrook to Quitman, Sept. 20, 1850, J. F. H. Claiborne Papers, Mississippi Department of Archives and History, Jackson. For newspapers supporting the movement but no single method of procedure, see Augusta *Republic*, Sept. 24, 1850; Columbia *South Carolinian*, Sept. 12, 14, 1850; Columbia *Telegraph*, Sept. 11, 1850; *Edgefield* (S.C.) *Advertiser*, Sept. 18, 1850; Jackson *Mississippian*, Sept. 13, 27, Oct. 4, 1850; Macon *Telegraph*, Sept. 17, 1850; Milledgeville *Federal Union*, Sept. 17, 24, 1850; *Savannah Georgian*, Sept. 12, 1850; and *Vicksburg Sentinel*, Sept. 28, Oct. 1, 1850. On Governor Seabrook's conspiratorial efforts, see Freehling, *Road to Disunion*, 520–23.

13. D.C. *Southern Press*, Sept. 7, 1850.

14. James G. Blaine, *Twenty Years of Congress: From Lincoln to Garfield*, 2 vols. (Norwich, Conn.: Henry Bill Pub. Co., 1884),1:98; and Springfield, Mass., *Republican*, Sept. 9, 1850.

15. James Love to Crittenden, Sept. 26, 1850, roll 8, John J. Crittenden Papers, LC; letters to Rusk from Richard S. Hunt, Sept. 17, 1850, Adolphus Sterne, Sept. 18, 1850, and J. W. Scott, Sept. 20, 1850,

Rusk Papers; and *Norfolk American Beacon*, Sept. 27, 1850, quoting *Baltimore Clipper*.

16. *Cong. Globe*, 31: 1: 1933–35, 1948–49; and Larson, *New Mexico's Quest*, 60–61. Houston's remarks are also printed in Williams and Barker, eds., *Writings of Houston* 5:256–58.

17. On the two-regiment bill, see *Cong. Globe*, 31: 1: 1290, 1604; 31: 1: *Sen. Reports* 183 (Ser. 565); and Austin *State Gazette*, Sept. 21, 1850, quoting a G. K. Lewis letter, July 20, to the Brownsville *Rio Grande Sentinel*. On the loss of the bill at the end of the session, see the informative letters of Washington correspondents in Victoria *Advocate*, Sept. 26, Oct. 3, 17, 31, 1850; and Conrad to Wood, Oct. 1, 1850, M-6, roll 30, pp. 287–88, RG 107. On the impact of Governor Bell's veto in Washington, see James A. Hamilton to Rusk, Sept. 28, 1850, Rusk Papers. On the measures to pay the Texas volunteers, see *Cong. Globe*, 31: 1: 701, 1182, 1738, 2035–36, 2063. Senator Rusk's short speeches on 2035–36 were very informative concerning the background of the measure. Also informative is the printed report of the House Committee on Military Affairs, 31: 1: *House Reports* 352 (Ser. 584). Wood outlined his role in Wood to Bell, Nov. 25, 1850, Governors' Letters, also printed in Austin *State Gazette*, Dec. 7, 1850. See also Victoria *Advocate*, Oct. 31, 1850.

18. Clarksville *Standard*, Nov. 2, 9, 1850; and Victoria *Advocate*, Aug. 30, Oct. 31, 1850. For handy biographical sketches of Hemphill, Henderson, and Watrous, see Webb, ed., *Handbook of Texas* 1:795–96, 2:869–70. Representative Howard and Judge Hemphill arrived at Indianola on the steamer *Galveston* on October 24. Their date of arrival in Texas is the only one definitely mentioned in the newspapers. Presumably the others arrived at about the same time.

19. Austin *State Gazette*, Aug. 31, Sept. 14, 1850. For similar editorial opinions from other Texas newspapers, see ibid., Sept. 21, 1850; Marshall *Republican*, Sept. 14, 21, 1850. Cazneau's letter is in Austin *State Gazette*, Sept. 7, 1850. For the moderate view, see Victoria *Advocate*, Aug. 30, Sept. 26, 1850; Houston *Telegraph*, Sept. 18, 1850, with its own editorial and one reprinted from the *Galveston Civilian;* and Clarksville *Standard*, Sept. 21, 28, 1850.

20. Henry to Bell, Sept. 15, 1850, Franklin Papers; Joint Resolution No. 2, Records of the Legislature, 3d Legis., Texas State Archives; *Tex. Sen. Jours.*, 3d Legis., 3d sess., 19–20; *Tex. HR Jours.*, 3d Legis., 3d sess., 33, 55–56, 71–72, 78–79, and 108; *Laws of the Third Legis.*, vol. 3, pt. 4:849; Austin *State Gazette*, Sept. 21, 1850; Matagorda *Tribune*, Oct. 11, 1850; and Neighbours, "Taylor-Neighbors Struggle," 461.

21. Austin *State Gazette*, Sept. 28, 1850. See also George W. Smyth to Rusk, Nov. 31 (30?) 1850, Rusk Papers.

22. Ibid., Oct. 5, 1850; and "Executive Record Book: Bell," 252–60, Executive Record Books.

23. Kaufman described the origin of the map in a letter in Marshall *Republican*, Nov. 23, 1850. For McDowell's speech, see *Cong. Globe*, 31: 1: App., 1678–85.

24. The map was engraved by Sidney Morse, geographer, mapmaker, and also editor of the *N.Y. Observer*, a religious weekly. The map was based on one published two years earlier in the *Memoir* of Adolphus Wislizenus's travels during the Mexican War. Morse even reprinted the dates of Wislizenus's journey given on the map and simply added lines relative to the Compromise of 1850. For the original map, see Adolphus Wislizenus, *Memoir of a Tour to Northern Mexico, Connected With Col. Doniphan's Expedition, in 1846 and 1847* (Washington, D.C.: Tippin and Streeper, Printers, 1848). Morse's version appeared in *N.Y. Journal of Commerce*, Aug. 14, 1850; *N.Y. Courier and Enquirer*, Aug. 14, 1850; *N.Y. Post*, Aug. 17, 1850; *N.Y. Commercial Advertiser*, Aug. 20, 1850; and *N.Y. Observer*, Aug. 17, 24, 1850. The version presented here is from the *Courier and Enquirer* (courtesy of the Library of Congress).

25. For discussion of the "Kaufman map," see Austin *State Gazette*, Oct. 12, 1850; and Marshall *Republican*, Oct. 12, Nov. 2, 23, 1850.

26. Austin *State Gazette*, Oct. 5, 1850. After the fall 1850 campaign was over, Howard published a much lengthier defense of his conduct and the bills, emphasizing the Southern victory in defeating the Wilmot Proviso, the practical recognition of Southern rights in the New Mexico bill, the honorableness of the land cession for Texas, the tremendous economic burden of maintaining Texan con-

trol in New Mexico, the advantage of eliminating abolitionist New Mexicans from Texas, and the bright economic prospects for Texas's future. Ibid., Dec. 28, 1850.

27. Ibid., Oct. 12, 1850.

28. For a list of presses supporting and opposing the bill, see ibid., Nov. 9, 1850. For changes by some papers to a pro-bill position, see Marshall *Republican,* Sept. 21, Oct. 12, Nov. 16, 1850. Matagorda *Tribune,* Sept. 27, 1850, expressed strong dissatisfaction with the explanations given by the Texas delegation for their votes, given their previous extremist rhetoric: "This out-herods Mexican faithlessness in an eminent degree." One of the best editorials in support of the bill is in Victoria *Advocate,* Oct. 17, 1850. For other editorials and editorial letters supporting the bill, see ibid., Sept. 26, Oct. 3, 10, 1850; Clarksville *Standard,* Nov. 2, 1850; Houston *Telegraph,* Sept. 18, Oct. 23, 1850; and San Antonio *Western Texan,* Oct. 2, 1850. For the best anti-bill editorial, see Marshall *Republican,* Oct. 26, 1850. For other anti-bill editorials and editorial letters, see ibid., Oct. 5, 12, 19, 26 (reprinting editorials from Austin *American* and Rusk (Tex.) *Cherokee Sentinel*), 1850; La Grange *Texas Monument,* Oct. 2, 9, 16, 1850; Austin *State Gazette,* Oct. 5, 12 (the latter reprinting editorials from *Galveston News*), 1850; and Matagorda *Tribune,* Oct. 4, 11, 1850. The *State Gazette* revealed the "rejectionist" paranoia over abolitionism by inferring that the escape of six slaves there was the work of abolitionist emissaries from the North encouraged by the fact that the Pearce bill moved the boundary of New Mexico's free soil three hundred miles closer to the borders of Texas slavery. Cited in Matagorda *Tribune,* Oct. 11, 1850.

29. One contemporary listing indicated that in 1850 Harrison County possessed 6,213 slaves. The nearest county to it in slave population was Brazoria County on the Gulf Coast, with 3,507 slaves. No other Texas county in 1850 had over 3,000 slaves. *The Texas Almanac for 1857* (Galveston: Richardson and Co., 1856), 69–70. A recent study, based on county tax rolls, shows Harrison County with 4,839 slaves and Brazoria County with 3,161 slaves in 1850. R. B. Campbell, *An Empire for Slavery: The Peculiar Institution in Texas, 1821–1865* (Baton Rouge: Louisiana State Univ. Press, 1989), 264–65. For statistics on Harrison County itself, see R. B. Campbell, *A Southern Community in Crisis: Harrison County, Texas, 1850–1880* (Austin: Texas State Historical Association, 1983), 20, 119–20.

30. Holland to Miller, Oct. 3, 1850, Miller Papers; Marshall *Republican,* Oct. 5, 1850; and Campbell, *Southern Community,* 160–61.

31. Marshall *Republican,* Oct. 5, 12, 19, 26, Nov. 2, 1850; and Clarksville *Standard,* Oct. 19, 1850. The *Standard* referred to the people who awarded the brass collar as "Jackasses." See also Matagorda *Tribune,* Oct. 11, 1850; and Houston *Telegraph,* Oct. 23, 1850.

32. On these aspects of the campaign, see Clarksville *Standard,* Oct. 19, and Nov. 16, 1850, quoting San Augustine *Herald;* Houston *Telegraph,* Oct. 30, and Nov. 23, 1850, quoting San Augustine *Herald* and Marshall *Republican,* Nov. 9, 1850; Hunt to Rusk, Oct. 11, Kaufman to Rusk, Nov. 6, 1850, and Rusk to L. D. Evans, Nov. 14, 1850, Rusk Papers.

33. Austin *State Gazette,* Nov. 2, 1850. The vote from Huntsville is given in Victoria *Advocate,* Oct. 31, 1850. Mentions of voters who avoided the polls because they were convinced the bill would be overwhelmingly approved are in Marshall *Republican,* Nov. 2, 1850, quoting *Huntsville Item;* and Austin *State Gazette,* Nov. 9, 1850, quoting *Galveston News.* Statements that a third or less voted in Galveston and western Texas are in Houston *Telegraph,* Oct. 30, 1850; and Victoria *Advocate,* Oct. 31, 1850. San Antonio's vote is given in Matagorda *Tribune,* Nov. 8, 1850. Bell's letters of October 18, 1850, are in "Executive Record Book: Bell," 264–73, Executive Record Books.

34. Austin *State Gazette,* Nov. 9, 16, Jan. 11, 1851. The totals of January 11 are given in appendix F. The *State Gazette* also printed tables of the official vote on December 7 and 14, 1850. The letter regarding the Wharton County vote is in Matagorda *Tribune,* Oct. 25, 1850.

35. *Tex. HR Jours.,* 3d Legis., 3d sess., 8–15; *Tex. Sen. Jours.,* 3d Legis., 3d sess., 6–13; Rusk to Jesse Grimes, Nov. 14, 1850, Jesse Grimes Papers, Barker Texas History Center.

36. *Tex. Sen. Jours.,* 3d Legis., 3d sess., 18–20; and original bill no. 1 and committee report no. 4, Records of the Legislature, 3d Legis., Texas State Archives.

37. *Tex. HR Jours.,* 3d Legis., 3d sess., 20–23, 26–27, 29–31, 35–39. Representative Bryan, in a letter

to his sister, highly praised Wigfall's course and declared his intent to continue voting against the bill but disavowed any "factious opposition." Bryan to Eliza Perry, Nov. 21, 1850, Bryan Papers. Bryan spoke in the House on November 22, the day the bill passed that body, in opposition to "acceptance." He emphasized the theme that the settlement doomed slavery's future in Texas and the South as a whole by transforming slave soil into free soil. He stated his belief that the South should have demanded an absolute constitutional guarantee that the federal government would never interfere with slavery in the South. His speech is printed in Matagorda *Tribune,* Dec. 21, 1850.

38. *Tex. Sen. Jours.,* 3d Legis., 3d sess., 27–31, 34–35; *Tex. HR Jours.,* 3d Legis., 3d sess., 45–46, 51, 54; Webster to Bell, Dec. 17, 1850, Governors' Letters; and Larson, *New Mexico's Quest,* 55.

39. *Tex. Sen. Jours.,* 3d Legis., 3d sess., 46, 58; *Tex. HR Jours.,* 3d Legis., 3d sess., 87–90; *Laws of the Third Legis.,* vol. 3, pt. 4:4–5. Robertson's resolution is Joint Resolution No. 20, Records of the Legislature, 3d Legis., Texas State Archives. G. K. Lewis wrote that Wigfall, when he realized he could not defeat the measure, accepted it with as good grace as he could muster. Lewis to Rusk, Nov. 28, 1850, Rusk Papers. James Hamilton wrote from Austin that the legislature showed no desire to tamper with the Pearce bill, even the five-million-dollar reserve. Hamilton to Rusk, Dec. 17, 1850, Rusk Papers.

40. Austin *State Gazette,* Nov. 30, 1850; McLaws to Steen, Sept. 5, 1850, M-1072, roll 1, 2:162, RG 393; Jones to Steen, Dec. 13, 1850, and Feb. 22, 1851, M-565, roll 17, RG 94; and Thrapp, *Encyclopedia of Frontier Biography* 3:1363–64.

Conclusion

1. Information on these troop dispositions can be found on M-565, roll 17, RG 94; M-1072, roll 1, and M-1102, roll 2, RG 393; and Bvt. Lt. Col. H. L. Scott to Clarke, Sept. 21, 1850, M-857, roll 3, p. 380, RG 108. Besides the 7th Infantry's not being needed in New Mexico at that point, the steamboat carrying their supplies had sunk on the way from St. Louis to Fort Leavenworth. Conrad to Fillmore, Nov. 30, 1850, M-127, roll 5, p. 67, RG 107.

2. Weightman to Alvarez, Sept. 18, 1850, roll 1, Alvarez Papers; Baird to Bell, Oct. 29, 1850, Governors' Letters; Larson, *New Mexico's Quest,* 60, 63; Lamar, *Far Southwest,* 82; and Taylor, "Baird," 48–49.

3. These matters of the debt settlement are treated in much greater detail in Miller, *Financial History of Texas,* 117–32. Banker W. W. Corcoran's role is treated in detail in Henry Cohen, *Business and Politics in America from the Age of Jackson to the Civil War: The Career Biography of W. W. Corcoran* (Westport, Conn.: Greenwood Press, 1971), 129–43. For a view of the corruption involved in the process, see Summers, *Plundering Generation,* 186–87, 203–4. See also Hamilton, *Prologue to Conflict,* 179–80; T. R. Fehrenbach, *Lone Star: A History of Texas and the Texans* (New York: MacMillan Co., 1986), 276–78.

4. On the conventions, see Jennings, *Nashville Convention,* 192–97; May, *Quitman,* 243–48; Schott, *Stephens,* 126–30; Thompson, *Toombs,* 72–76; Rayback, *Fillmore,* 268–77; Smith, *Presidencies of Taylor and Fillmore,* 211–12, 217; Hubbell, "Three Georgia Unionists," 318–21; Campbell, "Texas and Nashville Convention," 13; Houston *Telegraph,* Nov. 23, 1850.

5. On the potential importance of the Nashville Convention's second session had no settlement been reached, see Hamilton, *Taylor,* 372–73; *Albany State Register,* June 14, 1850. Some who expressed fear of disruption during the crisis changed after the compromise passed and denied they had ever had such fears. See for example, *Cincinnati Evening Nonpareil,* July 23, Sept. 9, 1850. Among twentieth-century scholars who have judged that Taylor's death may have avoided a bloody confrontation with Texas that could have led to civil war, see Bauer, *Taylor,* 309–10; Brainerd Dyer, *Zachary Taylor* (Baton Rouge: Louisiana State Univ. Press, 1946), 391–92; Smith, *Death of Slavery,* 113; Smith, *Magnificent Missourian,* 275; Smith, *Presidencies of Taylor and Fillmore,* 98; Nevins, *Ordeal of the*

Union 1:334. One historian speculated that if Taylor had lived and bloodshed had taken place, Taylor might have won more easily than Lincoln did later. Hamilton, *Taylor,* 383, 407. See also Webster to Harvey, Oct. 2, 1850, in Allis, Jr., ed., *Microfilm Edition—Everett Papers,* roll 13.

6. Bauer, *Taylor,* 323–24, 327; Nevins, *Ordeal of the Union* 1:334; Hamilton, *Taylor,* 407; Rayback, *Fillmore,* 251–52; Potter, *Impending Crisis,* 110; Smith, *Presidencies of Taylor and Fillmore,* 189–93; William L. Barney, *Battleground for the Union: The Era of the Civil War and Reconstruction, 1848–1877* (Englewood Cliffs, N.J.: Prentice-Hall, 1990), 43.

7. A few days after the Texas–New Mexico bill passed theHouse, Webster wrote a similar analysis of Taylor's attitude and stated his belief that Taylor "had a little fancy . . . to see how easily any military movement by Texas could have been put down." Webster to Haven, Sept. 12, 1850, Wiltse, ed., *Micro-film Edition—Webster Papers,* roll 22; Nevins, *Ordeal of the Union* 1:346. Webster remained convinced that concessions to Texas had been necessary in 1850 to avert certain civil war, and in a Syracuse speech in May 1851 he attacked those who disagreed with that view for possessing a "bloodthirst." M. L. Wilson, "Of Time and the Union," 293.

8. Smith, *Presidencies of Taylor and Fillmore,* 189–93.

9. Webster to Harvey, Oct. 2, 1850, in Allis, ed., *Microfilm Edition—Everett Papers,* roll 13; J. Phillips Phoenix to Hamilton Fish, Sept. 26, 1850, Fish Papers; Hunt to Rusk, Dec. 17, 1850, Rusk Papers.

10. The term "armistice" is used in Bruce Collins, *The Origins of America's Civil War* (New York: Holmes and Meier, 1981), 86–87; Potter, *Impending Crisis,* 90, 113–20; Ransom, *Conflict and Compromise,* 109; Freehling, *Road to Disunion,* 509–10. An argument that the1850 settlement was aptly named "compromise" is in Knupfer, *Union as It Is,* 196–200.

11. For a somewhat similar comparison of the 1850 and 1860–61 situations, see Smith, *Presidencies of Taylor and Fillmore,* 193.

Essay on Sources

In discussing the most significant sources of information on the Texas-Mexico boundary dispute, I think it important to begin with the source that first revealed the dispute's significance to me—congressional roll-call votes in the *Journals* of the respective houses. The startling contrast between the pattern on these roll calls and the pattern on those relative to other issues in the 1850 crisis was what initially fired my determination to research this topic further. Historians dealing with congressional topics—whether they use sophisticated or unsophisticated methods of analysis—should never ignore the roll-call voting, for therein may reside some pleasant surprises. Studying roll calls alone, however, will prove rather lifeless unless the researcher is willing to complement that analysis with a study of the debates in the *Congressional Globe*. The speeches of senators and representatives are an absolutely essential source for researching the boundary dispute or any other political issue of that era. Granting all the rhetorical grandstanding involved in some addresses, the speeches of members of the Senate and House also include sincerely held viewpoints, inspiring uses of language, tremendous amounts of information, and sometimes great drama. Presidential messages are printed in the *Globe* and in the important compilation *Messages and Papers of the Presidents*.

The manuscript collections of writings by political leaders are very important to researchers of the sectional crisis. Among collections by Northerners, I found the following most helpful: the microfilm editions of the papers of Daniel Webster, the Winthrop family, and Edward Everett, published by the Massachusetts Historical Society, and the Horace Mann papers at the same institution; the William Seward and Thurlow Weed papers at the University of Rochester; the microfilm edition of the Millard Fillmore Papers by the Buffalo and Erie County Historical Society; the Baldwin Family Papers at Yale University; the Robert Winthrop letters in the John P. Kennedy Papers microfilm at the Enoch Pratt Library, Baltimore; the John P. Hale Papers at the New Hampshire Historical Society, Concord; the James Buchanan Papers at the Historical Society of Pennsylvania, Philadelphia; the Salmon P. Chase and Martin Van Buren papers at the Library of Congress; the Lewis Cass letters in the Robert McClelland Papers at the Detroit Public Library; the Alpheus Felch Papers at the University of Michigan, Ann Arbor; and the letters by Stephen Douglas and other political leaders in the Charles H. Lanphier Papers at the Illinois State Historical Society, Springfield.

I found fewer extensive collections of papers by Southern leaders. Those most informative for my study were: the Alexander H. Stephens Papers at Manhattanville College, Purchase, New York; the Howell Cobb Papers at the University of Georgia, Athens; the Thomas Jefferson Rusk Papers at the University of Texas, Austin; the David Outlaw Papers at the University of North Carolina, Chapel Hill; the James H. Hammond Papers at the Library of Congress; and the Tucker-Coleman Papers at William and Mary College, Williamsburg, Virginia.

For both information and viewpoints, the newspapers of the era provide an absolute wealth of research material. I am particularly indebted for coverage of the Washington political scene to the columns written by the pioneering Washington correspondents. Some of these reporters were members of Congress themselves, some held federal patronage jobs, and some were professional newspapermen. They are usually impossible to identify, as they employed pseudonyms, a customary practice of the time. But occasionally these reporters would drop each other's names, and a few others can also be identified. The two most prolific "scribblers" were Francis Grund and James Harvey, both of whom wrote for several papers. The Washington correspondents were not always accurate in their reports; they sometimes gullibly passed on mere rumors as fact, and they were often deliciously biased in their comments about political leaders. But the researcher who ignores their columns will miss one of the most important sources of information about American political life during the sectional crisis. As with any other source material, these columns must be used judiciously and cautiously, but they must be used by historians.

For the Texas political scene, I found the state government records at the Texas State Archives in Austin invaluable. The Santa Fe Papers and Washington D. Miller Papers at the same institution are also essential. Senator Rusk's papers in the Barker Texas History Center at the University of Texas, Austin, are extensive and most informative. Texas newspapers are an essential resource for any study of the state's politics, and Austin's *Texas State Gazette* has accounts of some legislative proceedings for which the actual journals are missing.

The political developments in early New Mexico are sometimes difficult to research because the material is widely scattered. The Governors' Letters and Santa Fe Papers in the Texas State Archives give good accounts of the New Mexico scene. The Manuel Alvarez Papers and the Benjamin Read and Twitchell collections at the State Records Center and Archives in Santa Fe are helpful. Additional manuscript materials are in the William G. Ritch Collection at the Huntington Library, San Marino, California. Many documents relative to New Mexican government were sent to Washington and were printed among the documents in the congressional serials set. Manuscript copies of these and other documents can be found on microfilm series in the National Archives. Many New Mexican documents and military correspondence are buried in the military records at the National Archives and are available on microfilm. Colonel McCall's letters in the New Mexico Miscellaneous Collection at the Library of Congress are both informative and opinionated. Copies of the *Santa Fe Republican* newspaper issues still exist for most of its run, but issues of the succeeding *New Mexican* are almost nonexistent. Much of the important material from the *New Mexican* in 1850, however, was reprinted or summarized in the *St. Louis Missouri Republican* and other St. Louis presses. The St. Louis papers also contain reports from travelers just arriving from Santa Fe.

The military situation relative to New Mexico and to the crisis of 1850 is extensively documented in the various series of letters in the military records of the National Archives. No study of military aspects of the boundary crisis is possible without these records. Most of the relevant documents are available on microfilm, but some still must be examined in hard copy at the National Archives itself.

Historians and biographers have used many of the source materials cited above, along with printed primary sources, in fashioning their previous accounts of the sectional crisis, the Texas–New Mexico issue, and the settlement of 1850. While in this bibliographic essay I have emphasized the primary sources that I found most useful, I must also express my indebtedness to a huge number of secondary sources. They are too numerous to list here, but if my own work has been able to contribute to a better understanding of this part of the sectional crisis, it is only because of the excellent foundation already provided by past and present historians and biographers.

Index

Texas, New Mexico, and the Compromise of 1850
was designed and composed on a Gateway 2000 PC
using PageMaker 5.0 for Windows
at The Kent State University Press;
imaged to film from PS files,
printed by sheet-fed offset on 50-pound Glatfelter
Supple Opaque Natural stock
(an acid-free recycled paper),
notch bound in signatures and cased into binder's boards
covered in Arrestox B-grade cloth,
and wrapped with dustjackets printed in three colors
on 100-pound enamel stock finished with film lamination
by Thomson-Shore, Inc.;
designed by Will Underwood;
and published by
THE KENT STATE UNIVERSITY PRESS
KENT, OHIO 44242